Apparel
Design, Textiles & Construction
10th Edition

Louise A. Liddell
Memphis, Tennessee

Carolee S. Samuels
Frankfort, Illinois

Publisher
The Goodheart-Willcox Company, Inc.
Tinley Park, Illinois
www.g-w.com

Copyright © 2012
by
The Goodheart-Willcox Company, Inc.

Previous editions copyright 2008, 2004, 2002, 1996, 1991, 1988, 1985, 1981, 1977
(Previously published as *Clothes & Your Appearance* by
Louise A. Liddell and Carolee S. Samuels.)

All rights reserved. No part of this work may be reproduced, stored in a retrieval system, or transmitted in any form or by any means, electronic, mechanical, photocopying, recording, or otherwise, without the prior written permission of The Goodheart-Willcox Company, Inc.

Manufactured in the United States of America.

ISBN 978-1-60525-593-4

1 2 3 4 5 6 7 8 9 10 – 12 – 17 16 15 14 13 12

The Goodheart-Willcox Company, Inc. Brand Disclaimer: Brand names, company names, and illustrations for products and services included in this text are provided for educational purposes only and do not represent or imply endorsement or recommendation by the author or the publisher.

The Goodheart-Willcox Company, Inc. Safety Notice: The reader is expressly advised to carefully read, understand, and apply all safety precautions and warnings described in this book or that might also be indicated in undertaking the activities and exercises described herein to minimize risk of personal injury or injury to others. Common sense and good judgment should also be exercised and applied to help avoid all potential hazards. The reader should always refer to the appropriate manufacturer's technical information, directions, and recommendations; then proceed with care to follow specific equipment operating instructions. The reader should understand these notices and cautions are not exhaustive.

The publisher makes no warranty or representation whatsoever, either expressed or implied, including but not limited to equipment, procedures, and applications described or referred to herein, their quality, performance, merchantability, or fitness for a particular purpose. The publisher assumes no responsibility for any changes, errors, or omissions in this book. The publisher specifically disclaims any liability whatsoever, including any direct, indirect, incidental, consequential, special, or exemplary damages resulting, in whole or in part, from the reader's use or reliance upon the information, instructions, procedures, warnings, cautions, applications or other matter contained in this book. The publisher assumes no responsibility for the activities of the reader.

Library of Congress Cataloging-in-Publication Data

Liddell, Louise A.
    Apparel–Design, Textiles & Construction/Louise A. Liddell, Carolee S. Samuels
       p. cm.
    Rev. ed. of: Clothes & Your Appearance/Louise A. Liddell, Carolee S. Samuels. c 2008.
    Includes index.
    ISBN 978-1-60525-593-4
       1. Clothing and dress. 2. Clothing trade–Career Guidance.
       1. Samuels, Carolee S. (Carolee Stucker) II. Title

TT507.L5 2012
646'.3-dc22   2006041068

Cover Image—©Jose Luis Pelaez, Inc., Photographer/CORBIS

Introduction

With a new look and a new title, this edition of *Apparel: Design, Textiles & Construction* is designed with you in mind. Chapter topics will lead you through many concepts and issues related to the role of apparel in your life and the lives of others. You will learn about the textile and apparel industry from the U.S. and global viewpoint, the latest trends in fashion and apparel, the impact of fashion design on the industry, and a focus on career opportunities in textiles and apparel. In addition, you will also learn how to make the best decisions regarding the selection and care of apparel and the basic techniques of apparel construction.

Throughout this text, you will learn how to identify and evaluate a wide array of design, textile, and apparel options to fill human needs. Hundreds of beautiful photos effectively illustrate design concepts, textile information, and clothing construction. The charts and illustrations help demonstrate and clarify important text information. An introduction to apparel construction includes the selection and use of equipment, fabric, and patterns.

Apparel: Design, Textiles & Construction reflects contemporary life. Topics include current trends and the latest information. Special features focus on interesting historical facts, cutting-edge trends, and the latest technology. At the end of each chapter, you will find a wealth of practical questions and activities to help you evaluate and apply what you have learned. *Workplace Links* activities help you apply chapter content to workplace situations. Because involvement with student and professional organizations is key to career success, the *FCCLA* activities at the end of each chapter reinforce teamwork, workplace skills, and community involvement.

About the Authors

Louise Liddell's career in family and consumer sciences includes 15 years of teaching high school in Tennessee. As Assistant Superintendent for a youth development center, she continued her work with teens. Louise's leadership roles in professional organizations include service at local, regional, state, and national levels. As president of the Tennessee Vocational Association, she received a Life Membership award in AVA for outstanding leadership. Louise is also the coauthor of the text *Building Life Skills*, as well as many magazine and newsletter articles. Louise has a bachelor's degree from the University of Georgia and a master's degree from Memphis State University.

Carolee Stucker Samuels served as Editorial Director for Family and Consumer Sciences and Career Education at Goodheart-Willcox Publisher, where she began as an Assistant Editor. Prior to her work as an editor, Carolee was a family and consumer sciences teacher in Illinois and Indiana for 14 years, teaching textiles and apparel to high school students as well as adults. She is active in numerous professional organizations and has held many offices. Carolee has a bachelor's degree from Iowa State University and a master's degree from the University of Illinois.

4   *Apparel*   Design, Textiles & Construction

Organized for Learning Success

Each chapter begins with a consistent plan of learning for success.

Chapter Objectives
The objectives summarize learning goals for each chapter and correlate to main chapter headings.

Key Terms
The presentation of important terms creates a framework for building an apparel vocabulary.

Reading with Purpose
These quick strategies help you engage with chapter content and enhance your reading skills.

Bold, Red Terms
To reinforce terms introduced at the beginning of the chapter, the bold, red terms emphasize the vocabulary.

Apparel Design, Textiles & Construction

Outcome-Oriented Learning Applications

Each chapter ends with multiple opportunities for self-assessment and application of chapter concepts.

Summary
Detailed chapter summaries deliver a quick overview and reinforcement of chapter concepts.

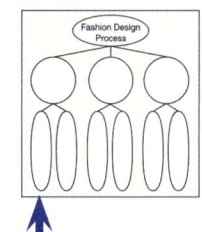

Review the Facts
Questions and statements that review basic concepts offer an opportunity to evaluate understanding chapter content.

Apparel Applications
These activities provide a practical application of information and skills discussed in the text.

Academic Connections
Practical activities in key academic skills in such areas as reading, writing, social studies, and math, help you link chapter content to all areas of life.

Graphic Organizer
The graphic organizer offers an alternative visual way to review one or more chapter concepts.

Think Critically
While using critical-thinking skills, these questions and activities allow unique interpretations of chapter content.

FCCLA
Individual and team activities link key chapter content to related FCCLA programs and activities.

Workplace Links
These activities help you extend chapter content beyond the classroom and into the apparel and textile workplace.

Apparel Design, Textiles & Construction

Informative Charts

Look for informative charts throughout the text that extend and clarify chapter concepts.

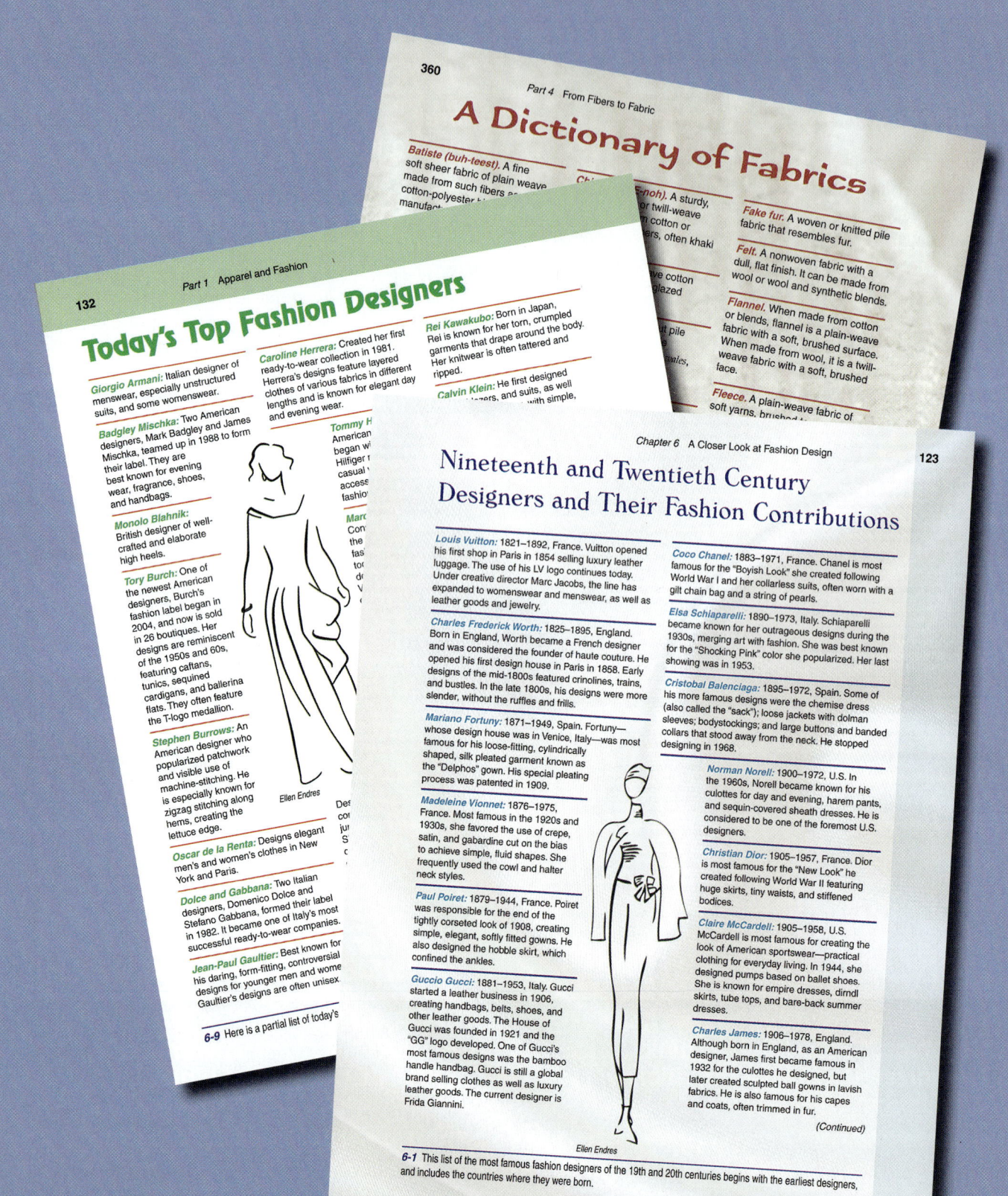

A Dictionary of Fabrics

Batiste (buh-teest). A fine soft sheer fabric of plain weave made from such fibers as cotton-polyester...

Chino (chee-noh). A sturdy, ...for twill-weave ...cotton or ...ers, often khaki...

...ve cotton ...glazed...

...d pile ...les,...

Fake fur. A woven or knitted pile fabric that resembles fur.

Felt. A nonwoven fabric with a dull, flat finish. It can be made from wool or wool and synthetic blends.

Flannel. When made from cotton or blends, flannel is a plain-weave fabric with a soft, brushed surface. When made from wool, it is a twill-weave fabric with a soft, brushed face.

Fleece. A plain-weave fabric of soft yarns, brushed...

Today's Top Fashion Designers

Giorgio Armani: Italian designer of menswear, especially unstructured suits, and some womenswear.

Badgley Mischka: Two American designers, Mark Badgley and James Mischka, teamed up in 1988 to form their label. They are best known for evening wear, fragrance, shoes, and handbags.

Monolo Blahnik: British designer of well-crafted and elaborate high heels.

Tory Burch: One of the newest American designers, Burch's fashion label began in 2004, and now is sold in 26 boutiques. Her designs are reminiscent of the 1950s and 60s, featuring caftans, tunics, sequined cardigans, and ballerina flats. They often feature the T-logo medallion.

Stephen Burrows: An American designer who popularized patchwork and visible use of machine-stitching. He is especially known for zigzag stitching along hems, creating the lettuce edge.

Oscar de la Renta: Designs elegant men's and women's clothes in New York and Paris.

Dolce and Gabbana: Two Italian designers, Domenico Dolce and Stefano Gabbana, formed their label in 1982. It became one of Italy's most successful ready-to-wear companies.

Jean-Paul Gaultier: Best known for his daring, form-fitting, controversial designs for younger men and women. Gaultier's designs are often unisex.

Caroline Herrera: Created her first ready-to-wear collection in 1981. Herrera's designs feature layered clothes of various fabrics in different lengths and is known for elegant day and evening wear.

Tommy H... American... began w... Hilfiger... casual... accesso... fashion...

Marc... Con... the... fas... de... V...

Des... co... ju... S... c...

Rei Kawakubo: Born in Japan, Rei is known for her torn, crumpled garments that drape around the body. Her knitwear is often tattered and ripped.

Calvin Klein: He first designed ...ers, and suits, as well ...with simple,...

Ellen Endres

6-9 Here is a partial list of today's...

Nineteenth and Twentieth Century Designers and Their Fashion Contributions

Louis Vuitton: 1821–1892, France. Vuitton opened his first shop in Paris in 1854 selling luxury leather luggage. The use of his LV logo continues today. Under creative director Marc Jacobs, the line has expanded to womenswear and menswear, as well as leather goods and jewelry.

Charles Frederick Worth: 1825–1895, England. Born in England, Worth became a French designer and was considered the founder of haute couture. He opened his first design house in Paris in 1858. Early designs of the mid-1800s featured crinolines, trains, and bustles. In the late 1800s, his designs were more slender, without the ruffles and frills.

Mariano Fortuny: 1871–1949, Spain. Fortuny—whose design house was in Venice, Italy—was most famous for his loose-fitting, cylindrically shaped, silk pleated garment known as the "Delphos" gown. His special pleating process was patented in 1909.

Madeleine Vionnet: 1876–1975, France. Most famous in the 1920s and 1930s, she favored the use of crepe, satin, and gabardine cut on the bias to achieve simple, fluid shapes. She frequently used the cowl and halter neck styles.

Paul Poiret: 1879–1944, France. Poiret was responsible for the end of the tightly corseted look of 1908, creating simple, elegant, softly fitted gowns. He also designed the hobble skirt, which confined the ankles.

Guccio Gucci: 1881–1953, Italy. Gucci started a leather business in 1906, creating handbags, belts, shoes, and other leather goods. The House of Gucci was founded in 1921 and the "GG" logo developed. One of Gucci's most famous designs was the bamboo handle handbag. Gucci is still a global brand selling clothes as well as luxury leather goods. The current designer is Frida Giannini.

Coco Chanel: 1883–1971, France. Chanel is most famous for the "Boyish Look" she created following World War I and her collarless suits, often worn with a gilt chain bag and a string of pearls.

Elsa Schiaparelli: 1890–1973, Italy. Schiaparelli became known for her outrageous designs during the 1930s, merging art with fashion. She was best known for the "Shocking Pink" color she popularized. Her last showing was in 1953.

Cristobal Balenciaga: 1895–1972, Spain. Some of his more famous designs were the chemise dress (also called the "sack"); loose jackets with dolman sleeves; bodystockings; and large buttons and banded collars that stood away from the neck. He stopped designing in 1968.

Norman Norell: 1900–1972, U.S. In the 1960s, Norell became known for his culottes for day and evening, harem pants, and sequin-covered sheath dresses. He is considered to be one of the foremost U.S. designers.

Christian Dior: 1905–1957, France. Dior is most famous for the "New Look" he created following World War II featuring huge skirts, tiny waists, and stiffened bodices.

Claire McCardell: 1905–1958, U.S. McCardell is most famous for creating the look of American sportswear—practical clothing for everyday living. In 1944, she designed pumps based on ballet shoes. She is known for empire dresses, dirndl skirts, tube tops, and bare-back summer dresses.

Charles James: 1906–1978, England. Although born in England, as an American designer, James first became famous in 1932 for the culottes he designed, but later created sculpted ball gowns in lavish fabrics. He is also famous for his capes and coats, often trimmed in fur.

(Continued)

Ellen Endres

6-1 This list of the most famous fashion designers of the 19th and 20th centuries begins with the earliest designers, and includes the countries where they were born.

Apparel Design, Textiles & Construction

Engaging Features

Highlights in History
Profiles historical topics that impacted today's textile and apparel industry.

Focus on Technology
Features focus on such topics related to textiles and apparel as nanotechnology, virtual reality and fashion, and online résumés.

Did You Know?
Features highlight assorted topics ranging from *green* fabric dyes and finishes to key components of a business plan.

Trends Making News
Features highlight a variety of industry trends that influence apparel and textiles.

Green Features
Look for this symbol on features with an environmental focus.

Apparel Design, Textiles & Construction

Acknowledgments

The authors and Goodheart-Willcox Publisher would like to thank the following professionals who provided valuable input:

Technical Reviewer

Karen M. Mueser
Adjunct Professor of Textiles
Dominican University
River Forest, Illinois

Reviewers

Terri Dance
Family and Consumer Sciences
    Teacher
Canfield High School
Canfield, Ohio

Nancy Doerr
Family and Consumer Sciences
    Teacher
Hazelwood East High School
St. Louis, Missouri

Sharon Mang
Family and Consumer Sciences
    Teacher
Greensburg High School
Greensburg, Indiana

Terry L. Miller
Family and Consumer Sciences
    Teacher
Blue Valley West High School
Overland Park, Kansas

Melodie Wheeler
Family and Consumer Sciences
    Teacher
Plainfield North High School
Plainfield, Illinois

Brief Contents

Part 1—Apparel and Fashion

Chapter 1
Understanding Clothing 22

Chapter 2
Understanding Fashion 40

Chapter 3
Textiles and Apparel
Through the Years 64

Chapter 4
The Textile and Apparel Industry 84

Chapter 5
The Worldwide Apparel Industry ... 102

Chapter 6
A Closer Look at Fashion Design 120

Part 2—Apparel Decisions

Chapter 7
Planning a Wardrobe 138

Chapter 8
Apparel Decisions and Choices 154

Chapter 9
Consumer Rights and
Responsibilities 170

Chapter 10
Choices as a Consumer 186

Chapter 11
Get Your Money's Worth 206

Chapter 12
Selecting Apparel for
Family Members 224

Chapter 13
Keeping Apparel Looking Its Best ... 238

Chapter 14
Laundry and Dry Cleaning 252

Chapter 15
Repair, Redesign, and Recycle 268

Part 3—Color and Design

Chapter 16
Color 284

Chapter 17
The Elements and Principles
of Design 302

Part 4—From Fibers to Fabrics

Chapter 18
The Natural Fibers 320

Chapter 19
The Manufactured Fibers 334

Chapter 20
From Yarn to Fabric 348

Chapter 21
Fabric Color and Finishes 364

Part 5—Sewing Techniques

Chapter 22
Figure Types and Pattern Sizes..... 378

Chapter 23
Selecting Patterns and Fabrics 392

Chapter 24
Sewing Equipment 408

Chapter 25
Getting Ready to Sew 426

Chapter 26
Basic Sewing Skills 442

Chapter 27
Advanced Sewing Skills 472

Chapter 28
Serging Skills 490

Part 6—Career Preparation

Chapter 29
Preparing for a Career 514

Chapter 30
A Job and a Career 526

Chapter 31
Entrepreneurship—Profiting
from Your Skills 554

Appendix A—
Metric Conversions for
Apparel Construction 568

Appendix B—Needlecrafts 571

Glossary 579

Index 592

Contents

PART 1

Apparel and Fashion 22

Chapter 1
Understanding Clothing 24
Clothing Meets Human Needs 25
Clothing Communicates 30
Influences on Clothing Choices 33
Highlights in History: From Humble T-Shirt to Fashion Statement 34

Chapter 2
Understanding Fashion 40
The Importance of Fashion 41
Fashion Terms 42
Highlights in History: Hemlines—
   The Highs and the Lows of the Last 100 Years 45
Fashion Cycles 46
Garment Features and Styles . . 48

Chapter 3
Textiles and Apparel Through the Years . . . 64
Influences on Fashion 65
The History of Textiles and Apparel 69
Highlights in History:
   The Discovery of Silk 72
Textiles and Apparel Today 81

Chapter 4
The Textile and Apparel Industry 84
Textile Production Segment 86
Apparel Production Segment 89

  The Retail Segment 94
  Vertical Integration of the Textile and Apparel Industries 99

Chapter 5
The Worldwide Apparel Industry 102
  U.S. Apparel Industries and World Economies 104
  Highlights in History: The Lowell System 108
  Ethical and Unethical Practices Within the Industry 113
  Technological Advances in the Apparel Industry 114

Chapter 6
A Closer Look at Fashion Design 120
  Ready-to-Wear versus Couture 122
  Nineteenth and Twentieth Century Designers and Their Fashion Contributions 123
  Knockoffs 125
  Licensing 125
  Fashion Categories and Price Points 126
  Where Do Fashion Designers Work? 127
  The Fashion Design Process 128
  Today's Fashion Designers 131
  Today's Top Fashion Designers 132
  Fashion Publications and Associations 134
  Highlights in History: Christian Dior: A Name Synonymous with Fashion 135

PART 2

Apparel Decisions 138

Chapter 7
Planning a Wardrobe 140
  Making a Wardrobe Plan 141
  Adding to Your Wardrobe 144
  Stretching Your Clothing Dollars 145
  Trends Making News: Teens as Trendsetters 148
  Selecting Appropriate Clothes 148

Chapter 8
Apparel Decisions and Choices 154
Decision Making 155
Factors Affecting Family Clothing Decisions 158
Trends Making News: Backpacks—A Real Pain in the Back 161
Meeting Family Clothing Needs 162

Chapter 9
Consumer Rights and Responsibilities 170
Labels and Hangtags 171
Federal Legislation to Help Consumers 172
Consumer Products Safety Act and Consumer Products Improvement Act 176
Did You Know? Flammability Standards for Children's Sleepwear 177
Consumer Protection Agencies and Organizations 178
Your Rights as a Consumer 179
Your Responsibilities as a Consumer 179
Trends Making News: Shoplifting—A Cost to Everyone 180

Chapter 10
Choices as a Consumer 186
Types of Stores 187
Nonstore Shopping 191
Trends Making News: .com Shopping—Buyer Beware 194
Shopping Strategies 195
Paying for What You Buy 199

Chapter 11
Get Your Money's Worth 206
Getting the Right Fit 207
Judging Garment Quality 208
Specific Points to Check for Quality and Fit 212
Consider Alterations 214
Making the Buying Decision 214
Buying Accessories 216
Highlights in History: A Sneaking Success 218

Chapter 12
Selecting Apparel for Family Members 224

Selecting Clothes for Children 225
Highlights in History: Pink and Blue for Children's Clothing 226
Clothes for Adults 231
Clothes for Older Adults . . 232
Selecting Clothes for People with Disabilities 233

Chapter 13
Keeping Apparel Looking Its Best ..238

Daily Clothing Care 239
Clothing Storage 242
Clothing Care Products . . 243
Clothing Care Equipment 247

Chapter 14
Laundry and Dry Cleaning 252

Understanding Care Labels 253
Preparing Clothes for Washing 256
Focus on Technology: What's New in Cleaning Clothes? 258
Washing Clothes 259
Drying Clothes 262
Pressing and Ironing 263
Dry Cleaning 264

Chapter 15
Repair, Redesign, and Recycle................... 268

Repairing Clothes 269
Altering Clothes 272
Redesigning Clothes 273
Recycling Clothes 275
Did You Know? Patchwork Is a Work of Art 278

PART 3

Color and Design 282

Chapter 16
Color. 284

Color and Its Meanings 286
Understanding Color Terms 286
The Color Wheel 288
Choosing Your Best Colors 292
Did You Know? Blue Rules as the Most Popular Color 298

Chapter 17
The Elements and Principles of Design 302

Figure Types 303
Elements of Design 305
Principles of Design 309
Achieving Harmony 313
Focus on Technology:
  Virtual Reality Puts You
  in the Fashion Picture 315

PART 4

From Fibers to Fabrics 318

Chapter 18
The Natural Fibers 320

Fiber Characteristics 321
Natural Fibers 322
Trends Making News: Recycled Jeans. 325

Apparel   Design, Textiles & Construction

Chapter 19
The Manufactured Fibers 334

- Manufacturing Fibers 336
- Fiber Modifications 336
- Characteristics of Manufactured Fibers 337
  - *Trends Making News: Tie-Dyeing— A Fun Way to Design Your Own Fabric* 345

Chapter 20
From Yarn to Fabric 348

- Yarns 349
- Woven Fabrics 351
  - *Focus on Technology: Microfiber Textiles* 352
- Knitted Fabrics 355
- Other Fabric Constructions 358
  - *A Dictionary of Fabrics* 360

Chapter 21
Fabric Color and Finishes 364

- Adding Color 365
- Finishes 368
  - *Focus on Technology: Nanotechnology in the Apparel Industry* 371
  - *Did You Know? Coloring and Finishing the Green Way* 373

PART 5

Sewing Techniques 376

Chapter 22
Figure Types and Pattern Sizes 378

- Determining Figure Type 379
- Determining Size 380
- Taking Body Measurements 381

Selecting a Pattern That Fits 386
Did You Know? You Can Learn to Sew with Kit Projects 387

Chapter 23
Selecting Patterns and Fabrics 392

Pattern Catalogs 393
Understanding the Pattern. 394
Choosing a Pattern 399
Did You Know? Patterns—New Kinds, New Places 400
Choosing a Fabric 401
Other Items to Sew 402

Chapter 24
Sewing Equipment. 408

Cutting Tools 409
Measuring Tools 410
Marking Tools 411
Needles 412
Pins 412
Pincushions 413
Thimbles. 413
Notions. 413
Highlights in History: Inventions We Can't Live Without. 415
Pressing Equipment. 418
The Sewing Machine 419

Chapter 25
Getting Ready to Sew 426

Preparing the Fabric 427
Preparing the Pattern 430
The Pattern Layout 433
Did You Know? Sewing for a Cause . . 435
Pinning the Pattern Pieces . . . 435
Cutting. 436
Transferring Pattern Markings 437

Chapter 26
Basic Sewing Skills ... 442

- Machine Stitching Techniques ... 443
- Darts ... 447
- Seams and Seam Finishes ... 447
- Facings ... 452
- Interfacing ... 453
- Zippers ... 455
- Hems ... 458
- *Trends Making News: Quilting—an Outlet for Creativity* ... 462
- Fasteners ... 464
- Pressing Techniques ... 467

Chapter 27
Advanced Sewing Skills ... 472

- Collars ... 473
- Sleeves ... 476
- Pockets ... 478
- Waistline Treatments ... 480
- Casings ... 482
- Sewing with Knits ... 484
- *Did You Know? Fleece—A Popular Choice for Cold-Weather Wear* ... 486
- Sewing with Pile Fabrics ... 486

Chapter 28
Serging Skills ... 490

- How the Serger Functions ... 492
- Serger Machine Parts ... 492
- Basic Serger Stitches ... 495
- Selecting Thread and Accessories ... 497
- Threading the Serger ... 498
- Operating the Serger ... 499
- Adjusting Thread Tension ... 500
- Adjusting Stitch Length and Width ... 502
- Using a Serger in Clothing Construction ... 502
- Serging Seams ... 504
- *Trends Making News: Sewing—Not Just for Grandma Anymore* ... 508
- Serger Care ... 509

PART 6
Career Preparation 512

Chapter 29
Preparing for a Career 514
- Leadership 515
- Effective Team Membership 516
- Student Organizations 520
- Conducting Meetings 522

Chapter 30
A Job and a Career 526
- Exploring the Career Clusters ... 528
- Making Career-Related Decisions 530
- A Job for You 530
- Focus on Technology: Posting Your Résumé Online 534
- Focus on Technology: Technology and the Interview Process Join Forces.... 545
- Succeeding on the Job 545
- Leaving a Job 550
- Managing Multiple Roles 551

Apparel Design, Textiles & Construction

Chapter 31
Entrepreneurship—Profiting from Your Skills....... 554

- The Pros and Cons of Entrepreneurship 556
- Characteristics of Successful Entrepreneurs 557
- Types of Small Businesses 558
- Entrepreneurial Opportunities 559
- Preparing for Entrepreneurship 561
  - *Did You Know? A Business Plan Is Key to Success. 562*
- Profiting from Your Skills 563

Appendix A:
Metric Conversions for Apparel Construction. 568

Appendix B:
Needlecrafts 571

Glossary 579

Index 592

Special Features

Trends Making News

Teens as Trendsetters. 148
Backpacks—A Real Pain
　in the Back 161
Shoplifting—A Cost to Everyone . . 180
.com Shopping—Buyer Beware . . . 194
Recycled Jeans 325
Tie-Dyeing: A Fun Way to
　Design Your Own Fabric 345
Quilting—an Outlet for Creativity . . 462
Sewing—Not Just for
　Grandma Anymore 508

Highlights in History

From Humble T-Shirt to
　Fashion Statement 34
Hemlines—The Highs and
　the Lows of the Last 100 Years . . 45
The Discovery of Silk 72
The Lowell System 108
Christian Dior: A Name
　Synonymous with Fashion 135
A Sneaking Success. 218
Pink and Blue for
　Children's Clothing 226
Inventions We Can't Live Without . . 415

Did You Know?

Flammability Standards for
　Children's Sleepwear 177
Patchwork Is a Work of Art 278
Blue Rules as the
　Most Popular Color 298
Coloring and Finishing
　the Green Way 373
You Can Learn to Sew
　with Kit Projects. 387
Patterns—New Kinds,
　New Places 400
Sewing for a Cause 435
Fleece—A Popular Choice
　for Cold-Weather Wear 486
A Business Plan Is Key to Success . . 562

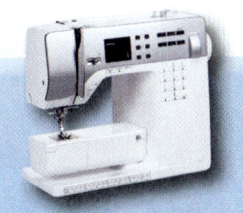

Apparel Design, Textiles & Construction

Focus on Technology

What's New in Cleaning Clothes?........ 258
Virtual Reality Puts You in the Fashion Picture......... 315
Microfiber Textiles............. 352
Nanotechnology in the Apparel Industry............ 371
Posting Your Résumé Online..... 534
Technology and the Interview Process Join Forces................ 545

Leadership, Clothing, and Human Needs............. 39
Improving Interpersonal Skills... 63
Textiles and Apparel History..... 83
Careers in the Textile and Apparel Industry.......... 101
Take the Lead—Providing Clothes for People in Need.. 119
Fashion Design.............. 137
Take the Lead—Providing Work Wardrobes.......... 153
Using the Planning Process.... 169
Investigating Consumer-Related Careers.......... 185
School Resale Shop.......... 205
Learning About Consumer Clout................... 223
Working with an Older Adult.... 237
Investigating Laundry and Appliance Careers......... 251
Sustainable Laundry Practices.. 267
Teamwork—Reclaiming Shoes.. 281
Leading the Way with Color.... 301
Using the Elements and Principles of Design........ 317
Informing Others About Eco-Friendly Natural Fibers.. 333
Informing Others—Technology and Fabrics..... 363
Informing Others About Textile Finishes................ 375
Leading the Way on Fashion Tours............. 391
Community Service—Clothes for Protection............. 407
Service Project Display........ 425
Volunteer Sewing............ 441
Fashion Construction—Child... 471
Fashion Construction—Teen or Adult............. 489
Take the Lead in Community Service........ 511
Using Communication Skills.... 525
Interview Competition......... 553

Safety
Short safety tips appear throughout the text where appropriate.

PART 1

Apparel and Fashion

Chapters

1. Understanding Clothing
2. Understanding Fashion
3. Textiles and Apparel Through the Years
4. The Textile and Apparel Industry
5. The Worldwide Apparel Industry
6. A Closer Look at Fashion Design

Chapter 1

Understanding Clothing

Chapter Objectives

After studying this chapter, you will be able to
- **analyze** how clothing helps satisfy human needs.
- **summarize** how clothes reflect personality, values, and self-concept.
- **assess** how clothes can create positive first impressions.
- **summarize** factors that influence clothing choices.

Key Terms

need
modesty
conformity
peer pressure
self-esteem

self-adornment
culture
status
prestige
self-actualization

individuality
personality
values
self-concept
media

Reading with Purpose

Read the review questions at the end of the chapter *before* you read the chapter. Keep the questions in mind while reading to help determine which information is most important.

Clothes are an important part of your life. You wear them every day, and they help you look your best. They can even help you feel good about yourself. They also tell other people a lot about who you are.

Your clothes can speak for you. They can express your personality, values, and self-concept. You can even use clothes to express your individuality. However, there are some very basic reasons why people wear clothes, too.

Clothing Meets Human Needs

All people share certain basic human needs. A **need** is something required for a person's continued survival. These needs cause people to behave as they do. Everyone has the same basic needs. It is how people meet these needs that varies from person to person.

Abraham Maslow, a noted American psychologist, suggests that humans are motivated to satisfy five basic types of needs. He arranged these needs in order of importance from the lowest to the highest, **1-1**. A person must satisfy the lower needs before meeting the higher needs. These needs are physical, safety and security, love and acceptance, esteem, and self-actualization. The physical needs are the most basic and a person must meet these needs first.

Clothing can help to satisfy physical, psychological, and social needs. Protection, comfort, and safety are physical needs. Self-adornment and identification are psychological needs. Status and prestige are social needs. Clothing can help meet all these needs.

1-1 According to Abraham Maslow, the lowest level needs, which are physical needs, must be satisfied before higher level needs can be met.
Goodheart-Willcox Publisher

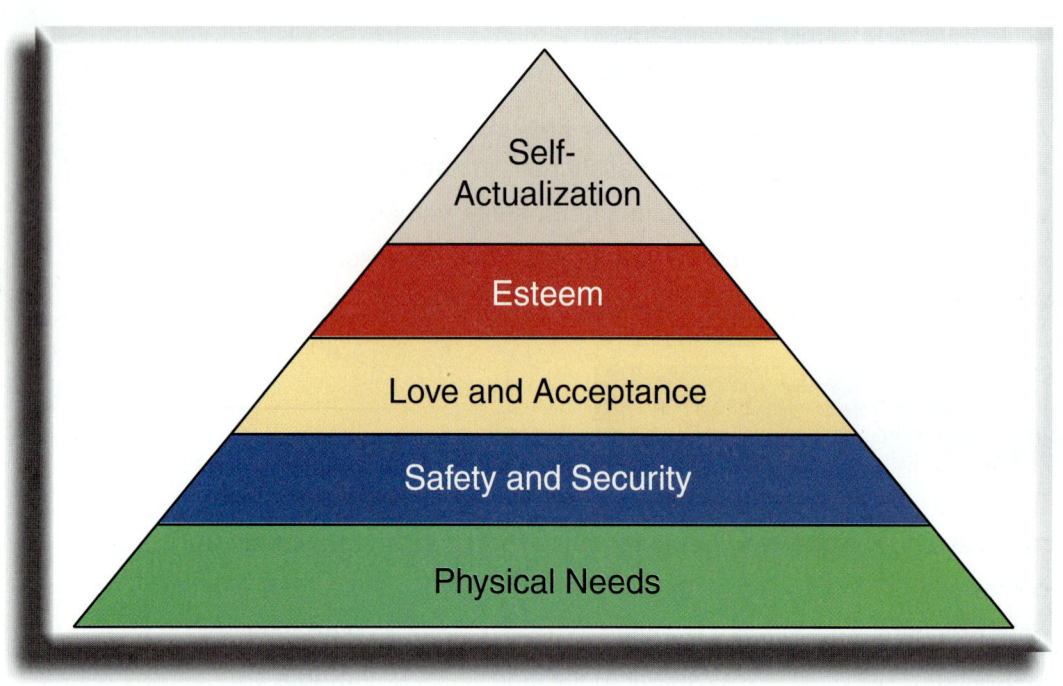

Physical Needs

Protection from weather is the most important physical role played by clothing. Whether you live in a cold climate or a hot climate, clothing helps to maintain the body temperature. Many Alaskan Natives wear clothing with fur linings. This clothing traps the warm air from their bodies in the clothing and creates a layer of warmth. People in some African countries wear long, white robes and headdresses. White reflects heat, and the long robes keep the sun from shining directly on the skin. The loosely fitted garments let air circulate around their bodies. This helps to keep them cooler and more comfortable.

Where you live often determines what types of clothing you need for protection and comfort. If you live in Minnesota, you will need more clothing for warmth than if you live in Florida. Hats and gloves help provide comfort by retaining body heat in cold weather. In contrast, a beach cover-up helps protect skin from overexposure to the sun. Rain gear keeps you and your clothes dry, *1-2*. When going on a long hike, wearing hiking boots helps protect feet from injury or blistering.

Safety and Security Needs

Clothing is sometimes worn to keep you safe from harm or injury. When boating, you wear a life vest. Football and hockey players wear safety headgear. Bicycle and motorcycle riders wear helmets. Race car drivers wear special helmets and safety clothing made of flame-resistant fibers and finishes. Cyclists and runners often wear reflective-fluorescent tapes on their clothing so they are more visible to motorists. For skateboarding, knee pads, elbow pads, wrist supports, and a helmet are a must.

Safety clothing is required in some occupations. Firefighters wear heavy boots and flame-resistant clothing. They also wear specially designed helmets. On many industrial construction sites, workers wear hard hats and safety shoes with steel reinforced toes. Road repair workers, traffic officers, and school-crossing guards wear brightly colored vests so drivers can easily see them. Wearing such clothing helps avoid accidents. Agricultural workers who handle chemicals wear special gloves. Medical workers wear gloves, gowns, and masks to protect themselves and their patients from exposure to disease-causing organisms, 1-3. These coverings are then discarded after one use.

Love and Acceptance Needs

The need for love and acceptance can influence how people choose to dress. People have a need to receive affection from others. They also want to feel like they belong to a group. This need guides them in their clothing choices.

Through the years, you learn from your family, friends, and teachers what is expected of you. These are standards that are pretty well set. They include behavior guidelines as to what society considers acceptable. These expectations also include standards of dress. Standards of dress can vary from one culture to another. They can also change over time.

Modesty

In most societies, modesty is important. **Modesty** means covering the body according to what is appropriate by the society in which you live. Modesty standards may vary by culture. Some Muslim women, for instance, must cover their bodies and faces completely. Only their eyes are unveiled.

Standards of modesty can change through the years. In the 1800s, society in this country dictated that a considerable degree of cover-up was important for social acceptance. Women wore long dresses and layers of clothing. Today, it is acceptable to show more of the legs. Think how swim suits have changed through the years. In earlier times, swimwear for both men and women nearly covered the entire body. In the 1960s, the bikini bathing suit became popular. Standards have changed in modern times, but a certain amount of coverage is still expected.

Modesty standards vary according to the situation. Clothing a woman wears to work in an office will be different from what she wears for a special evening event. Evening wear can show more skin. Clothes you wear to school also must conform to certain standards. No matter what clothes you choose to wear, school authorities require a certain level of modesty in your dress.

1-2 This child's rain gear keeps her dry while she enjoys playing outside on a rainy day. *Shutterstock*

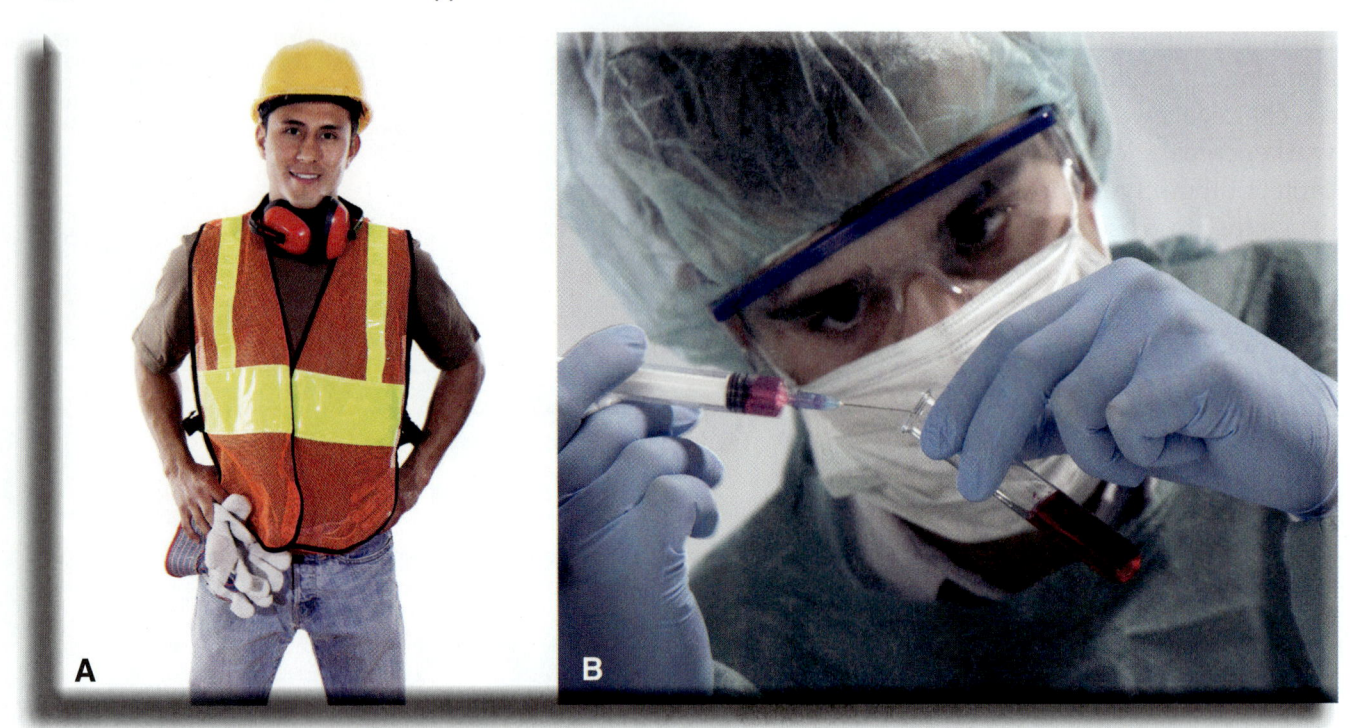

1-3 The hard hat, bright color, and reflective bands on this worker's clothing help keep him safe while on the job. (A) The protective clothing of this medical researcher is discarded after each use. (B) *A & B Shutterstock*

Conformity

Conformity means following or obeying some set standard or authority. People choose to conform in order to feel accepted. Peer pressure can lead to conformity. **Peer pressure** is the social pressure a person feels to adopt a type of behavior, dress, or attitude in order to have acceptance in a group. For instance, you probably prefer to wear the clothing styles that other teens are wearing. You want to *fit in* with what is in style this year. Jeans are popular choices for teens. When you wear them, you feel like you are a part of the group—that you are accepted.

Attraction

In your teen years, you are more aware of the opposite sex. Your desire to attract the attention of someone you would like to date may influence what you choose to wear. When you were younger, you probably didn't care as much about your clothing and appearance. You had other things on your mind. Now, you may spend a lot of your time planning what you are going to wear to school tomorrow or to the game Friday night. You may be trying to attract someone's interest.

Esteem

In addition to love and acceptance, Maslow stated that people have a need for *esteem*. This is a need for respect, admiration, recognition, and social approval by others. It is also a need for self-esteem—feeling good about yourself as a person. If you have **self-esteem,** you have a feeling of self-worth. You feel important. Clothes can play a role in fulfilling this need.

Self-Adornment

Throughout history, people have practiced **self-adornment**, or decoration of their bodies. They have followed certain practices to make themselves beautiful according to the customs of their *culture*. The beliefs and social customs of a particular group of people form their **culture**, 1-4. People have painted their bodies with clay and vegetable dyes. They have inserted jewelry in their ears, noses, and lips. They have used colorful stones, metal bands, feathers, and animal teeth to decorate their bodies. People in some parts of the world still carry on these practices.

Today, people still decorate their bodies, but a little differently. Many people use cosmetics and clothes for adornment. Accessories such as jewelry, scarves, and neckties also provide adornment. Some people use body piercing and tattoos as forms of self-adornment.

Status and Prestige

People wear clothing to express status, prestige, wealth or importance. **Status** refers to a person's position in relation to others. **Prestige** is widespread respect and admiration for someone based on his or her achievements. Some clothing symbols indicate achievements. For example, service stripes on military uniforms show years of service in the armed forces. Ribbons, pins, and badges show achievements in scouting. Letters on school letter jackets indicate performance in athletic or academic events.

Some people choose clothes to imply they are of a higher status than others. Designer clothes are a status symbol for some people. The names of famous fashion designers or their logos are often printed or woven into garments. Expensive jeans or athletic shoes often highlight the name brand in a highly visible place. Some people also consider expensive jewelry and fur coats to be status symbols. They may use these symbols to indicate their wealth or achievement in life.

Identification

You can often identify people by the clothing they wear. You can easily identify police officers and mail carriers by their uniforms. Flight attendants of an airline dress alike. Hotel staff or restaurant wait staff at a particular establishment may also dress alike. In this way, you can easily identify them. Their attractive uniforms help to create a good image for their companies. Different branches of the armed forces, such as the Air Force or Navy, have specially designed uniforms for their branches, 1-5. Uniform designs also show rank. A general's uniform is quite different from that of a private.

In sports, such as football, members of one team wear the same uniforms. This helps identify players and teams. Imagine how confusing it would be to

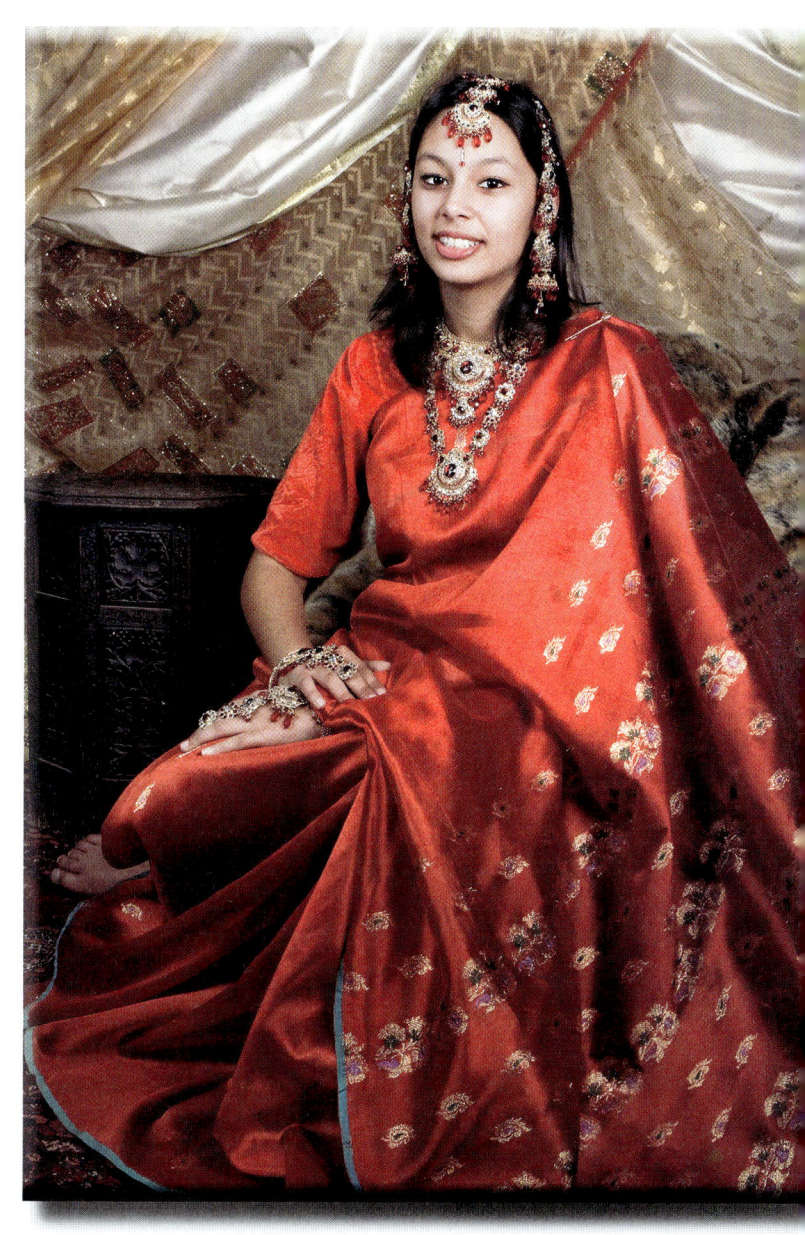

1-4 This young Indian woman wears the traditional sari with her wedding jewelry following the style of her culture. *Shutterstock*

1-5 Military uniforms are designed to identify the branch of the armed services, as well as the rank of the officer.
Shutterstock

watch a football game if both teams dressed alike. Think about the type of clothing referees wear. You can always identify them.

Some groups wear clothing and jewelry to indicate a certain religious membership. These people may wear jewelry such as crosses, stars, and other religious symbols. In certain religious events, special clothing—such as prayer shawls or special robes—is worn.

During certain ceremonies, people sometimes wear special clothes. At graduation, the graduates wear caps and gowns. At a wedding, a bride often wears white. At funerals, the mourners often wear black.

Self-Actualization

The highest level of need according to Abraham Maslow is self-actualization. **Self-actualization** needs relate to success in personal achievements, expressions of personal creativity, and self-fulfillment. To reach this level, you must at least partially fulfill the other levels of needs.

Individuality

At this level of need fulfillment, people may choose to express their individuality. **Individuality** is what sets one person apart from others. In contrast to conformity, individuality is the expression of a person's uniqueness. If everyone in a group dresses the same way, a person expressing individuality will choose something entirely different. He or she rejects peer pressure to conform, choosing instead to make a personal statement. People often use clothes as a form of self-expression.

Clothing Communicates

Just as no two people look exactly alike, neither do they think and feel the same. The thoughts and feelings that make you different from others are a part of your personality. Your clothes say a lot about you—your personality, your values, and your self-concept.

Personality

Your **personality** is everything about you that makes you unique, including your behavioral and emotional tendencies. Your habits and actions as well as your interests and skills are part of your personality.

The way you dress is one way you express your personality. If you are a carefree person, you may have less concern about what you wear than someone who always wants to look perfect. You may like to wear casual clothes most of the time. If acceptance by others is important to you, wearing the same type of clothes as your friends may make you feel more comfortable. In contrast, if you like to be unique, you might enjoy wearing styles of clothes that are not like those of your friends. This could be a way of communicating that you enjoy being original and different.

What type of personality do your clothes express? The clothes in your wardrobe should express your personality. When shopping for clothes, has a friend ever held up an item and said, "This looks like you"? If so, your friend was saying that the clothing matched your personality.

Your clothes should help you say, "I am trying to be me. This is how I feel about myself." You want to wear clothes that are in style, but you also want to choose the styles that express your personality. For example, some young women may express quiet and soft-spoken personality traits by choosing soft, flowing fabrics and small, delicate designs. Others may choose clothes with minimum design details, strong colors, and rough textures to express more forceful personalities.

Many young men like to wear casual outfits, *1-6*. They feel neat, but comfortable. As they create these outfits, they are expressing their personalities.

Young women can wear casual outfits based on jeans or slacks. They also have the option of showing their femininity by wearing skirts, dresses, or other types of pants. They can express the businesslike side of their personalities by wearing suits.

Values

Your **values** are the qualities, standards, principles, and ideals you consider important or desirable. They guide your actions and impact your decisions. They influence almost all aspects of your life in some way or another. Some of your values may relate to family, friends, education, wealth, and status.

Values form over a lifetime. Your family shapes many of your values. For instance, your family may place a high value on caring for one another, honesty, and perseverance. Because of your up-bringing, you are likely to share these same values. Family values generally pass from one generation to the next. Friends, school, community, and cultural traditions also impact your values.

1-6 Most young men feel more comfortable in casual outfits such as these. *Shutterstock*

How Values Influence Dress

Your values often influence the decisions you make about what you wear. For example, if you value status you might choose clothes with the logo of a popular designer. If this logo is a favorite among your friends, wearing clothes with this logo can give you status within the group.

If you value wealth, you may buy expensive clothes to show off your wealth. In contrast, if you value economy, you might prefer to buy clothes that are practical, durable, and easily laundered. You will likely look for classic styles that will not go out of fashion. You may place a higher value on education, choosing to save money for future educational expenses. If you value entertainment, you may choose to spend more money on movies and concerts and less on clothes.

Your values will change throughout your lifetime. What you value as a teen may change during your adult years. Now you may value clothes that are unique and trendy. In the future—as a young, working professional—you may value basic wardrobe pieces suitable for starting a career. As an older adult, you will probably place more value on clothing comfort.

Self-Concept

The mental picture you have of yourself—of who you are and what you are like—is your **self-concept**. Your view of yourself is usually personal and private. If you like what you see, you have a positive self-concept. If you do not like what you see, you have a negative self-concept.

A positive self-concept is the result of feeling good about yourself and feeling you are a worthwhile person. You enjoy life and like people. You feel you can achieve your goals. Having a positive self-concept generally means you have a good outlook on life, **1-7**.

Some people do not think highly of themselves. They have a negative self-concept. They often think about their shortcomings and failures instead of their good qualities. When given a compliment, they shrug it off thinking they are not worthy of affirmation. They may be unsure of themselves and uncomfortable with others. Often, they accept the ideas of others and seldom assess how they really feel. When they make a mistake, they dwell on their failure instead of learning from it.

1-7 These girls are dressed for fun, choosing clothes that express their personalities.
Shutterstock

Appearance and Self-Concept

The way you dress and your overall appearance can affect your self-concept. When wearing a new outfit, you may feel great all day. You know the color is one of your best and the style is very fashionable right now. When you know you look good, you feel better about yourself.

Sometimes the opposite happens. Suppose you got up late one morning and had to dress quickly. The clothes you grabbed did not go together well and had some stains on them. All day long you may have felt grumpy, embarrassed, and uncomfortable because of the way you were dressed.

Studies reveal that your feelings about yourself usually show in your appearance. Clothing reflects your mental attitude. Do you try to look nice most of the time, but dress sloppily on some days? On these days, your choice of clothing may reflect your unusual mood.

Some teens think that looking good is never important. They do not feel that clothes can express their innermost feelings. However, most teens with positive self-concepts show this by dressing well.

First Impressions

Along with your self-concept, you have a public image. This is the way you look to others. Within a few seconds after meeting you, people form their impression of you. They may guess your age, size, nationality, and whether they would like to know you better. A first impression is the way you feel about people when you first meet them.

The way people dress is one way they influence others' impressions of them. Clothing is the first thing you see. You notice clothing before you see faces or hear voices.

Someone once said that clothing is a silent language—it speaks for those who wear it! Therefore, clothing is important in making a first impression. What first impression do you want others to have of you? If you want others to desire to get to know you better, start with a good first impression. They will then make an effort to learn more about you.

Influences on Clothing Choices

As you know, clothes satisfy physical, psychological, and social needs. Clothes also communicate personality, values, and self-concept. What factors influence your clothing choices? Perhaps you need special clothes for dressy occasions, for certain sports, or for your hobbies. Maybe you need warm clothes for cold winters or extra swimsuits for days spent on the beach. These and other factors influence your clothing choices.

Activities

Your activities—where you go and what you do—also influence your clothing choices. Attending school may be your most frequent activity. Therefore, most of the clothes you choose will be for school wear. In most instances, you can wear these same outfits for such leisure activities as attending ball games, going shopping or to the movies, or just hanging out with friends.

If you work part-time, you may need special clothes for your job. A uniform or sturdy work pants and shirt may be a requirement. If you participate in sports, you may need clothing for these activities. Sports clothes need to be comfortable, protective, and durable.

Highlights in History

From Humble T-Shirt to Fashion Statement

From its humble beginnings, the T-shirt has morphed into a canvas for designers. It has gone from an affordable undergarment to a vehicle for advertising. Where and when did it all begin?

Though no one knows for certain, the U.S. Navy might deserve the credit. In 1913, a crew-necked, short-sleeved, white cotton undershirt was designed to be worn under the Navy's deep, V-necked collared shirt. Because of its shape, it was called a "T". It wasn't until the late 1930s that companies including *Hanes, Sears,* and *Fruit of the Loom* started to market the shirts. In 1938, Sears proclaimed that the undershirt could also be worn as an outer garment. During World War II, the short-sleeved T-shirts gained popularity among soldiers because of their greater absorption under the arms and comfort under backpacks. Soldiers often wore them as outer garments. When the soldiers returned from the war, the shirts came home with them.

The T-shirt gained popularity in the 1950s when Marlon Brando wore one in the movie classic *A Streetcar Named Desire* and James Dean in the movie *Rebel Without a Cause*. Walt Disney was one of the first people to see the marketing value of T-shirts when he began having letters and simple designs printed on the shirts for souvenirs. With the 1960s came the popularity of tie-dyeing among hippies, and T-shirts were easy to buy and dye. Improvements in printing and dyeing in the '70s allowed graphic images to be printed on shirts. Rock bands and performers sold T-shirts with their images on them. The era of message T-shirts had begun. Corporations also found a new way to advertise. Imagine a walking billboard!

Enter the era of the fashion statement. When Sharon Stone paired a black T-shirt with an Armani skirt for the Oscars in 1996, the garment had truly arrived. T-shirts today come in different weights, colors, and styles. Sometimes they are plain and sometimes they have embellishments. People layer them with other T-shirts or wear them under various garment styles. No matter how people wear them, they have become a staple of most everyone's wardrobe. The T-shirt has truly become a classic.

Shutterstock

The clothes you choose may be completely different than those of the person sitting beside you. Your friend may need hiking boots, but you might not need them if you never go hiking. Some people do not need dressy or fancy clothes. Casual clothes and jeans are acceptable for the parties and events they attend. Other people who go to many events at their places of worship and elsewhere need several dressy outfits.

Compare the people in **1-8**. They have planned different activities, so they have chosen different clothing. They are all suitably dressed for what they will be doing.

1-8 This couple is dressed for a special dance at school. (A) A day of hiking with the family calls for casual pants and sturdy shoes. (B) *A & B Shutterstock*

Climate

Different climates create different clothing needs. In some areas, temperatures remain fairly warm all year. In these places, people do not give much thought to seasonal clothing. They can wear most of their clothes year-round.

In other regions, people must have some clothing that is comfortable in warm weather and other clothes for cold weather. Because of seasonal clothing needs, people who live in these regions will probably spend more money for clothes than people in mild climates. For example, a winter coat is a major expense. Boots, hats, scarves, and gloves are additional expenses for people living in cold climates.

In many regions, medium-weight clothing is appropriate for the climate. People can add extra sweaters and lightweight jackets to medium-weight garments when days are cold. Several layers give more warmth than one heavy garment. The layers trap air between them which becomes warm from body heat. In some climates, a lightweight coat is all people need. One all-purpose coat with a heavy zip-out lining is a practical choice for those who live in a colder climate because they can wear it during fall, winter, and spring.

The layered look is great for allowing people to adjust to different temperatures. It is a popular, attractive, and practical fashion for both males and females. Depending on the weather, you can combine shirts, sweaters, and jackets in several different ways, depending on the weather.

What Is Most Flattering

When making clothing decisions, people usually want to choose garments that make them look their best. Have you ever noticed that an outfit you put on one day made you look taller? On another day, perhaps a friend said to you, "That color looks great on you." Have you ever wondered why? The colors, garment styles, and accessories you choose can make a difference in how you look to yourself and others.

Family and Friends

Family members and friends often influence your clothing choices. Your parents may have an opinion about what is appropriate for you to wear to school and when going out with friends. Parents often base these opinions on family values. It is generally in your best interest to listen to what they have to say. They will be honest about what looks best on you. As you get older, family values may continue to influence your clothing choices.

Your friends are often your peers. You may enjoy having their opinions about the clothes that you buy. However, peer pressure may create problems when buying clothes. Your friends may try to persuade you to buy a garment that is not a good choice for you. This could be a garment that will not go with anything else in your wardrobe. It could be an item that costs more than you should spend. When you shop for clothes, keep your best colors and styles and what you already own in mind. It is fine to listen to your friends' opinions, but the final decision is yours. See **1-9**.

Cost

The amount of money a person has to spend on clothes is often a key factor in making clothing choices. Your clothing budget affects the decisions you make about clothes. Few people have an unlimited amount of money to spend on clothes. If you plan your spending wisely, you can buy the clothes you need. You can save for the more costly items and items you do not need right away. Creating a spending plan helps you acquire the clothes that you need and want.

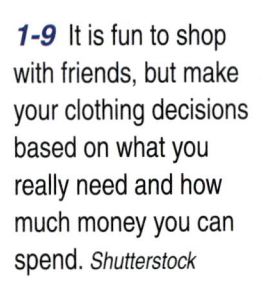

1-9 It is fun to shop with friends, but make your clothing decisions based on what you really need and how much money you can spend. *Shutterstock*

Media

The media plays a key role in influencing clothing choices. The **media** includes the various forms of mass communication, such as television, radio, magazines, newspapers, and the Internet. Articles written for the media inform you of the latest trends in fashion. Television shows and websites feature fashions celebrities are wearing. Advertisements show you what is currently available in stores and on sale.

All of these media outlets influence what you choose to buy and wear, **1-10**. They can be helpful and informative, but the main intent may be to get you to spend money. Ads often attempt to influence your choices by appealing to your emotional side. They promote the idea that buying a product will make you look more attractive or be more popular.

Most people want to wear clothes that are the current fashion. Perhaps you saw your favorite celebrity wearing a new style and you decided to buy a similar outfit. Before choosing to follow the latest fashion trend, think about it. Will it soon go out of style? Will this new fashion look good on you? Can you afford it?

1-10 Websites are designed to make it hard for you to resist buying the advertised items. *Shutterstock*

Summary

- Clothing helps satisfy human needs. These include the physical needs for protection and comfort. They also include the needs for safety and security, love and acceptance, esteem, and self-actualization.
- Influences on clothing choices include modesty, conformity, attraction, esteem, self-adornment, status, prestige, and identification.
- Clothing choices reflect your personality, values, and self-concept.
- People form first impressions within a few seconds of meeting you. If this first impression is a positive one, they will want to get to know you better. The way you dress can help create a positive first impression.
- Several other factors also influence your clothing choices. These include your activities, the climate of your region, what looks most flattering, your family and friends, your clothing budget, and the media.

Graphic Organizer

Draw a star diagram to identify the different types of needs that clothing meets. Then name a type of clothing that meets each need.

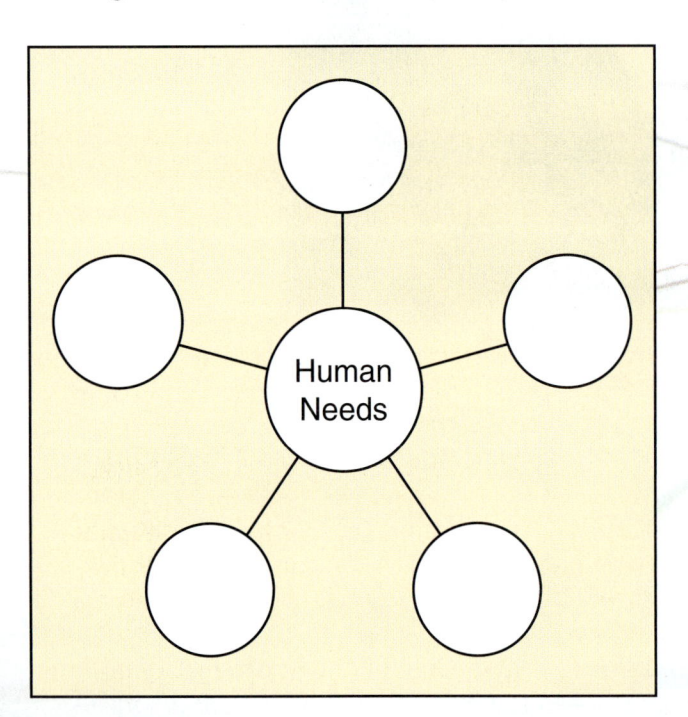

Review the Facts

1. Does everyone have the same basic needs? Explain your answer.
2. How do clothes help meet your physical needs? Explain your answer.
3. Which need is being met when you wear plastic goggles in chemistry lab?
4. Explain why modesty standards vary within a society.
5. Summarize how peer pressure can lead to conformity.
6. Give an example showing how clothing can express status or prestige.
7. Who or what influences a person's values? Give an example showing how values impact clothing choices.
8. People who only see their own weaknesses and faults are likely to have a ____ ____.
9. Describe how your appearance can affect your self-concept.
10. How does the climate in your region influence your clothing choices? Give two examples.
11. Which media outlet do you feel has the greatest influence on the clothes teens buy? Explain your answer.

Think Critically

12. **Identify evidence.** Discuss the popularity of certain brand names of clothes among teens. What evidence shows their pressure to buy expensive clothes to achieve status in your school?
13. **Compare and contrast.** Compare and contrast *conformity* with *individuality* in regard to the way a person chooses to dress. Is one better than the other? Why or why not?
14. **Draw conclusions.** Does wearing school uniforms increase learning? reduce violence? reduce stereotyping and prejudice? What conclusions can you draw?
15. **Analyze evidence.** Analyze factors that impact personality. Include evidence about both positive and negative influences.

Apparel Applications

16. **Online poster.** Create an interactive online poster (with a school-approved web-based application) showing examples of why people wear clothes. Use your creativity to write clever captions for images on your poster. Share your poster with friends and classmates.
17. **Clothing list.** Make a list of all the different groups to which you belong. Identify special clothing that you might wear to show that you are a member of each group.
18. **Identifying personality.** With a classmate, watch a current TV program. Select and write notes about the personality of a TV character, including both positive and negative traits. How does this person's appearance reflect his or her personality? Give an oral report to the class about your findings.
19. **Web-based video slideshow.** Collect digital photos that illustrate your personality through your clothing preferences. Use a school-approved web-based application to create a video slideshow. Add text and music to enhance your presentation to further reflect your personality. Share your slideshow with the class.
20. **First impressions.** Make a list of the things that impact your first impression of a person. Compare your list with those of your classmates. Make a master list naming the most mentioned items first.

Academic Connections

21. **Social studies.** Research native dress or costumes people wear in other countries. Select one item of dress typical of one particular country. Write a report to share with the class discussing how culture influences this style dress.
22. **Writing.** Write a journal entry describing the formation of your values. What influences have family and friends had on your values? How do your values impact your clothing choices?
23. **Writing.** Write a paragraph titled "As I See Me." Do not sign your paper. Give your paper to your instructor who will then give your description to another student to read. This student will try to identify who wrote the paragraph. Was the person who read your paragraph able to identify you? Do others see you as you see yourself? Why or why not?

Workplace Links

24. **Employer interview.** Conduct interviews with several employers regarding standards of dress in their businesses. Find out why they have these standards. Share your findings with the class.
25. **Portfolio builder.** The first thing to include in your career portfolio is a *letter of introduction*. In this letter, describe who you are and why you are interested in a specific apparel-related career. Identify your career goals. Save a copy of this letter on your computer or on a flash drive to update as needed.

Leadership, Clothing, and Human Needs

What do community service and your ideas about suitable clothing have in common? Both likely involve the things you value. Observe the people in your community. What clothing-related concerns do you see? Are there people walking around town without adequate clothing? Unemployed families and those living in homeless shelters may lack the type clothing necessary to protect them in various climates.

Join with a team of classmates to plan and implement an FCCLA *Community Service* project to help meet the clothing needs of a group in your community. For example, you might sponsor a coat drive to provide warm coats for local children in need.

Use the FCCLA *Planning Process* and related Community Service program documents to plan, implement, and evaluate your project. See your adviser for information as needed.

Chapter 2

Understanding Fashion

Chapter Objectives

After studying this chapter, you will be able to
- **summarize** the importance of fashion.
- **define** fashion-related terms.
- **explain** fashion cycles.
- **recognize** the most common garment features and styles.

Key Terms

fashion
apparel
style
fashion trend
trendsetter
classic
fad
avant-garde
retro
vintage
fashion cycle
set-in sleeve
kimono sleeve
raglan sleeve
waistband
dart

Reading with Purpose

Find an article on the Google News website related to the topic of this chapter. Print the article and read it before reading the chapter. As you read the chapter, highlight sections of the news article that relate to the text.

One of the most exciting aspects of clothing is fashion. A **fashion** is a particular style of apparel that is popular at a given time. **Apparel** includes all men's, women's, and children's clothing. Fashion influences apparel choices.

The Importance of Fashion

Fashion is important for several reasons. First, it reflects a time and a place. What is fashionable today is quite different from what was in fashion 100 years ago. (If you study fashion changes throughout history, you will learn how they relate to the economic, political, and social conditions of a time.) Fashion mirrors social issues and changes, as well as current events. Fashion often reflects social positions, too.

What is in fashion in the U.S. is often different from what is fashionable in other countries. Economic, political, and social conditions, as well as the climate of a country, form the basis of these differences.

The economic conditions of a time period are also evident in fashion. If economic conditions are poor, people have less money to spend on clothing. In such times, the latest fashions become less important. People have little interest in what is currently fashionable and will make do with what they have. These economic conditions affect the entire fashion industry.

The fashion industry employs many people, from designers and manufacturers to retailers and salespeople. It is one of the largest industries in the United States. If consumers spend less on apparel, there is less need for people to design, manufacture, and sell clothing. Jobs are cut which increases unemployment. When economic conditions improve, companies hire more people to work in the industry. This occurs locally as well as globally.

Fashion Terms

Many clothing terms may be familiar to you. Sometimes people use these terms interchangeably, but each has a specific meaning. Some terms important to the clothing industry are *style, fashion, classic,* and *fad*.

Style

A **style** refers to a particular design, shape, or type of garment or apparel item. Specific garment features help identify certain styles. These styles have common names that people use in the fashion industry.

There are different styles of pants, shirts, dresses, skirts, necklines, collars, and sleeves. For example, an A-line skirt is different than a pleated or gathered skirt. Each skirt has a distinct style. Sweater styles include the pullover and the cardigan (open front), 2-1. A parka is a style of coat. The pockets, hood, and length make it distinct from other coat styles. Jeans are a style of pants.

Fashion

A fashion is a style that is currently popular with consumers. Most people prefer to wear the clothing styles that are in fashion at the present time. What is fashionable this year may not be in fashion a few years from now. Fashions that were popular with previous generations often reappear. This is why you may have heard the saying, "Fashion repeats itself."

A **fashion trend** is the direction in which a particular change or fashion is moving. It is a comparison of what is in fashion this year with previous years. A fashion trend gains popularity and soon becomes accepted by more and more people. Typically, a fashion trend lasts three to seven years. There are fashion trends for different markets. For example, a fashion trend in the teen market might not be a trend in women's career wear.

2-1 The pullover is a popular sweater style.
Shutterstock

Trendsetters often wear the newest fashions and are not afraid to try new styles. A **trendsetter** is a person who takes the lead or sets an example. Trendsetters can be teens or adults, however, they are usually leaders in their respective social groups. Many people soon copy and wear their clothing styles.

As fashions change, the details of the basic styles change, too. For example, in men's suits, the width of lapels, the shape of pockets, and the location and number of buttons change over time. However, the basic style of the suit remains the same, **2-2**.

Fashion changes quickly today because of instant communication. The Internet allows consumers to see the latest styles as they appear in designer fashion shows in Europe and New York. Professional websites, as well as personal blogs and other social-networking sites, enable people to share their views about the latest trends in fashion. However, some people wear styles they like even if those styles are not in fashion. Personal satisfaction is more important to some people than what others think is fashionable.

This attitude did not always exist. For instance, when high heels first became fashionable, almost all women wore them regardless of their comfort. People simply accepted the current fashion. Today, though high heels are popular with many women, other heel heights are also in fashion. Women can select the heel style or height they like. People today are freer to choose the styles they prefer.

Classic

A **classic** is a style that stays in fashion for a long time. A tailored shirt and a simple pullover sweater are classics. A navy-blue blazer is a classic. The blazer buttons may change from metal to white or blue in different years. Lapels may become wider or narrower. However, the classic blazer stays in fashion. Blue, gray, black, or faded jeans may be the fashion from time to time. The legs of the jeans may be wide, tapered, or very narrow. However, jeans are a classic, **2-3**.

2-2 The details of the suit jacket, such as the width of the lapels, change with fashion.
Shutterstock

Many other clothes have become classics, including T-shirts, polo shirts, trench coats, business suits, and tuxedos. For example, at a particular time, a tuxedo may have wide or narrow lapels, and may be made of a variety of colors and fabrics. In any variation, the classic style is still easy to recognize.

Fabrics, designs, and colors also become classics. Linen, crepe, velvet, seersucker, suede, and corduroy rarely go completely out of fashion. Plaids, dots, checks, and stripes are classic design patterns. Black and gray are classic colors year after year.

Fad

A **fad** is something new in clothing that quickly becomes popular, but only for a short time. It appeals to many people for a short period of time, but fades quickly. Many times, fads are extremely unusual styles or accessories. They are often most popular with teens.

At one time, blue jeans and athletic shoes were fads. However, teens and adults like them so much that their popularity continues. Now, everyone considers them to be classics. However, faded jeans with holes in them may be popular one season and not the next. For guys, baggy pants that ride low on the hips are a current fad. Skinny jeans for women go in and out of style. Colored beads or plastic bracelets are sometimes fads, **2-4**.

Savvy consumers are careful not to spend too much of their clothing money for fad items. These items are fun to wear, and consumers might feel good wearing "the latest" fashions. However, fad items should be purchased only when they have extra money.

Avant-Garde

The term **avant-garde** refers to fashions that are innovative, extreme, and daring. These styles are popular with people who want to break away from mainstream styles. Pop stars and rock-group members who want to call attention to themselves often wear such fashions. People who wish to develop their own sense of style may also choose avant-garde fashions. They want to look different from everyone else. Because these fashions are so extreme, most people do not choose them.

Have you seen someone who is avant-garde in his or her appearance? An avant-garde look may be a wild outfit, an extreme hairdo, severe makeup, or multiple body piercings or tatoos. In most instances, avant-garde looks disappear in a few years as new ones appear. In some cases, the avant-garde fashion becomes acceptable by more people over time.

The next time you go clothes shopping, look for styles, fashions, classics, and fads. Save most of your money for styles that will last. Identify the latest fashion details within a basic style. Spend less on fads or avant-garde items that will be out of fashion next year. To build a long-lasting wardrobe, invest a greater portion of your clothing dollars in classics.

Retro and Vintage

Have you ever noticed that some new garments resemble ones that were popular when your parents were younger? If so, you may have seen retro styles. **Retro** refers to clothing that resembles styles from at least 20 years ago. Some

2-3 Denim jeans are classics that have been in fashion for a long time. *Shutterstock*

2-4 Colorful flip-flops may be a fad that will quickly be replaced by another fad.
Comstock, Inc.

Highlights in History

Hemlines—The Highs and the Lows of the Last 100 Years

For hundreds of years, the hemlines of women's skirts always touched the floor. It wasn't until the 1900s that hemline length began to creep upward, and then it wasn't a continual rise. There were highs and lows often related to economics, politics, art, world events, wars, revolutions, and technology. Let's take a closer look at some dates and changes in hemlines.

1908—Hemlines rise just slightly off the floor.
1918—Skirts rise above the ankle for the first time since anyone can remember, just before the Nineteenth Amendment gave women the vote in 1920.
1925—Hemlines rise above the kneecap.
1930—Following the stock market crash, hems plunge to eleven inches off the floor.
1939—Nylon stockings appear, creating the desire for more exposed leg and higher hems.
1941—Hems head north as wartime regulations restrict fabric yardages in dresses.
1943—The jitterbug craze creates the need for more legroom.
1947—Dior unveils his New Look of longer skirts at midcalf, which remained popular through the 1950s.
1961—Oleg Cassini designs Jacqueline Kennedy's inaugural skirt at midknee.
1964—London designer Mary Quant responds to the demands of the youth culture and their modern dances with the invention of the miniskirt, which remains popular throughout the 60s.
1970s—Maxiskirts, reaching midankle, appear on the scene during the Vietnam and Watergate years as the feminist movement takes place.
1980s—Hems are on the rise again as women decide it's OK to be sexy and liberated.
1990s—Some years are up and some are down as women embrace the freedom to choose.
2000s—Hemlines of all lengths are available to suit women's many moods and needs.

Will skirt hemlines ever again hit the floor? Who can predict what lies ahead?

current designers may include features from garments of the 50s, 60s, 70s, or 80s in their latest fashions, 2-5. Examples may include bell-bottom (wide flared) pants or crochet sweater vests from the 1960s. A designer might introduce a version of these in his or her latest collection. Ballet flats are another example of an old style regaining popularity.

Vintage refers to second-hand clothing with a sense of history. Previously worn clothing items from thrift shops or items passed down from older family members may be vintage if they represent specific events. Some shops even specialize in vintage clothing. Vintage items can be expensive if the garments were made by famous designers or were first worn during important historical events.

People with a sense of *nostalgia* (affection for the past) may choose to wear vintage clothes. They may wear them every day or only on special occasions. Others may choose to wear vintage as an expression of their individuality. Even celebrities may wear vintage clothes to stand apart from others. Vintage T-shirts are often popular with teens and adults.

Fashion Cycles

A **fashion cycle** is the periodic return of specific styles and general shapes. This means that fashions go through periods of popularity, followed by periods of being unacceptable, or "old-fashioned." Fashions are popular, disappear, and later return to popularity.

The following stages represent a fashion cycle, 2-6:

- *Introduction stage.* A fashion cycle often begins when a designer creates a new style. The designer introduces the style to the fashion industry in the form of high-priced garments. People who are fashion leaders buy these garments at the start of the cycle. These are people who like others to see them in the latest fashions and can afford to buy designer clothes. Celebrities often buy these garments because they want to stand out. They also have the money to buy new fashions and discard them when newer styles come along.

2-5 This retro outfit features a pill-box hat, pearls, gloves, and large buttons popular in the 60s. *Shutterstock*

The Fashion Cycle

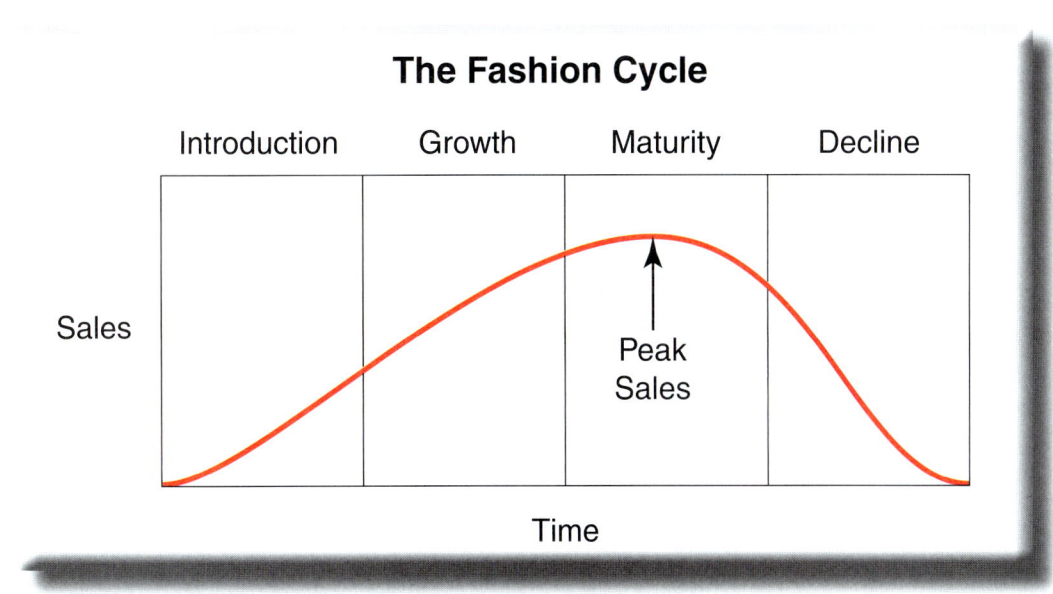

Stages: Introduction | Growth | Maturity | Decline

(Sales vs. Time curve; Peak Sales occurs during Maturity.)

2-6 Fashions go through four stages of popularity called the fashion cycle. Sales peak during the maturity stage. *Goodheart-Willcox Publisher*

- *Growth stage.* In the next stage of the fashion cycle, the fashion becomes affordable and gains popularity with the general public. Soon the fashion is visible everywhere as sales volume increases. All of the major retailers promote the style and carry various versions at different prices.
- *Maturity stage.* In the maturity stage, more people feel comfortable with the style and add it to their wardrobes. It is during this stage that the style is worn by the most people. Sales of the style peak at this stage. At the same time, the fashion leaders and trendsetters are looking at the next fashion style.
- *Decline stage.* Before long, the style's popularity declines. Because many people wear it, the style becomes less interesting. It is then likely to appear on sale racks as retail stores make room for newer styles. The fashion life cycle ends. Soon, the style disappears altogether.

The length of time a style remains at each stage varies. It can be a few months or it can be years. A fad will never pass out of the introduction stage because it has the shortest life cycle. A classic style, however, will never completely disappear. After many years, the classic style may reappear at the beginning of a new cycle. It might not be exactly the same. Designers may give the classic a different look with the addition of new and different details.

In the past, fashion cycles moved slowly. Every 100 years, only three basic dress silhouettes, or shapes, went through the fashion cycle. These silhouettes were the *bell, back fullness,* and *tubular,* 2-7. With each introduction, these silhouettes had new and different features. Each period of dress had features that set it apart from other time periods. The changes in men's fashion cycles were apparent through changes in the widths of lapels, neckties, and pant legs.

Today, fashions cycle at a faster rate because society is changing faster. It is not unusual for fashion cycles to occur every 20 to 30 years. As technology develops, clothing production improves. These changes mean that more styles are available at a quicker rate. The increase in worldwide communication makes it easier to see what other people around the world are wearing.

Fashion Cycle Silhouettes

1740s Bell
1780s Back fullness
1820s Tubular
1850s Bell
1880s Back fullness
1920s Tubular

2-7 The bell, back fullness, and tubular silhouettes have been repeated throughout the years.
Goodheart-Willcox Publisher

Garment Features and Styles

As you study fashion, you will want to refer to specific garment features and styles. Combinations of garment features create styles. Common garment features are necklines, collars, and sleeves. These combine with other garment features to create basic styles. Designers put their own twists on fashion as they combine garment features in unique ways.

Garment Features

Though there are many features to every garment, shirts, blouses, coats, and dresses have several types of features in common. They all have necklines or collars and have either sleeves or are sleeveless.

Necklines

Garments designed for the upper body will always have a neckline—the area surrounding the neck and shoulders. Necklines can be high, normal, or low. They can take various shapes such as round, square, V, or horseshoe. The edges can be scalloped or plain. Some necklines have specific names. The following are the most common necklines, 2-8.

- *Jewel.* A high, rounded neckline at the base of the neck.
- *Crew.* A high, flat neckline (made of stretchable fabric) that sits close to the neck.
- *Halter.* A high panel at the front of the neckline that is tied around the neck in the back. The back and shoulders are exposed.
- *Scoop.* A U-shaped or rounded neckline that is usually higher in the back and lower in the front.
- *Bateau or boat.* A shallow, boat-shaped neckline that runs from shoulder to shoulder. It is the same depth in the front and the back.
- *Sweetheart.* This low neckline curves into a point in the front that resembles a heart.
- *Henley.* A collarless neckline with a button opening. It was first worn in 1839 by the oldest rowing regatta in Europe held at Henley-on-Thames, England.
- *Cardigan.* A collarless opening in the front of a garment.
- *Cowl.* A piece of fabric attached to the neckline that can be used as a hood or draped in soft folds.

Necklines

Jewel	Low wide scoop	U scoop	Bateau/boat
Square	V-neck	Sweetheart	Crew
Henley	Cardigan	Keyhole	Slit
Strapless	One-shoulder	Halter	Cowl

2-8 Necklines can be high, normal, or low, and take various shapes. *Ellen Endres*

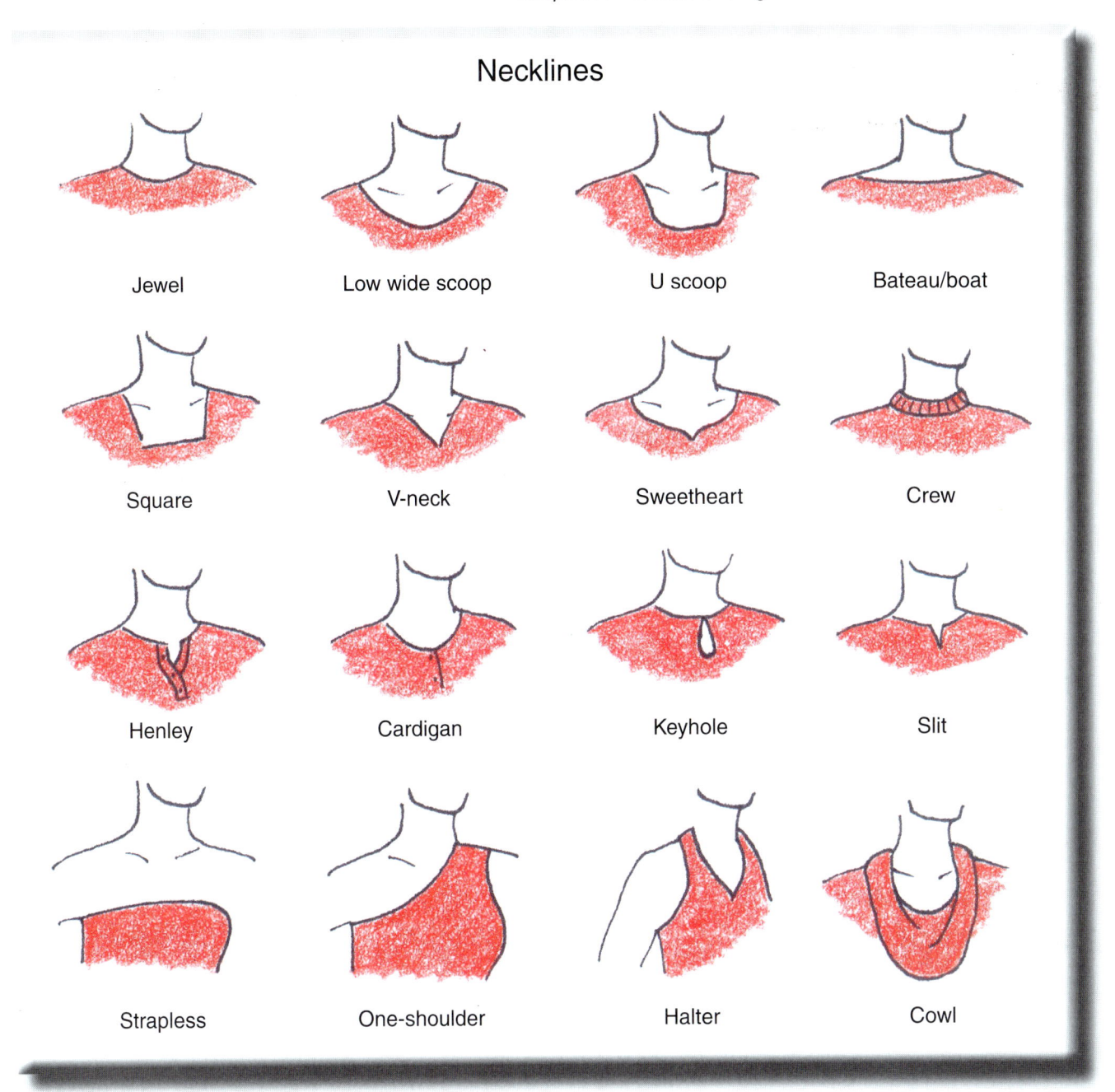

Collars

The necklines of shirts, dresses, coats, and jackets often have collars. A *collar* is a band of fabric attached to the neckline. It can stand upright or turn over. Collars come in many sizes and shapes. The edges may be long or short, pointed or round. Review the following classic collar styles in Figure 2-9.

- *Mandarin.* A stand-up collar that originated in China. It may also be called a Nehru collar.
- *Ruff.* A stand-up ruffle surrounding the neckline.
- *Turtle.* A high, close-fitting collar on a knitted sweater or pullover.
- *Ascot.* A long piece of fabric, attached at the neckline, worn around the neck and looped under the chin.
- *Jabot.* A decorative frill of lace, or other delicate fabric, attached at the base of the neck and flowing down the garment front.

Collars

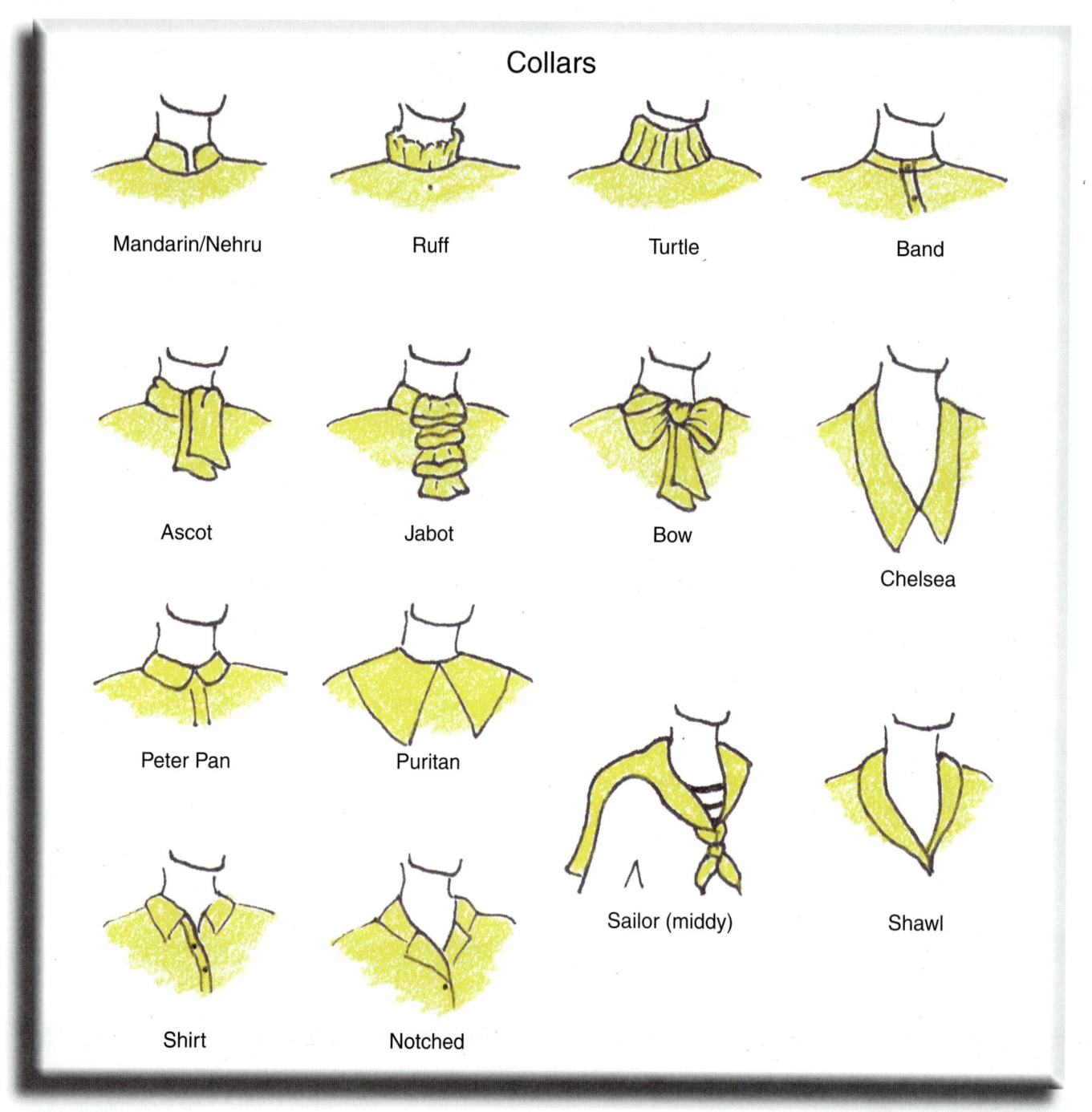

- Mandarin/Nehru
- Ruff
- Turtle
- Band
- Ascot
- Jabot
- Bow
- Chelsea
- Peter Pan
- Puritan
- Sailor (middy)
- Shawl
- Shirt
- Notched

2-9 There are many sizes and shapes of collars. These are the most common ones.
Ellen Endres

- *Chelsea.* A long, pointed collar that dips low in the front. It was named for the fashion-leading Chelsea area of London.
- *Peter pan.* A flat, round collar no more than two to three inches deep. It was named after Peter Pan, a character in J. M. Barrie's 1904 play by the same name.
- *Sailor.* A square of fabric that falls down the garment back. It narrows to a point in the front and is tied in a knot.
- *Shirt.* A collar attached to a band of fabric, that makes the collar stand up around the neck when buttoned. A variation is the *button-down collar* where the points of the collar button to the shirt body.
- *Notched.* A collar that forms a "notch" where it joins a lapel. A *lapel* is the front part of a shirt or jacket that turns back or folds over. A *convertible collar* is one that can be worn open at the neck or closed.

- *Shawl.* A collar that is an extension of the lapel, and not a separate piece. The garment front extends around the back of the neck in a continuous line.

Sleeves

Most garments have sleeves. There are many types of sleeves, but most fall into one of three categories: set-in, kimono, and raglan, **2-10**. They can be of any length, from barely covering the top of the shoulder to below the wrist.

- *Set-in.* A **set-in sleeve** is attached to the body of the garment with a seam that circles the armhole near the shoulder. The sleeve can be short, three-quarters length, or long. Variations of the set-in sleeve are shown in **2-11**. Notice they all have a seam at the top of the shoulder.

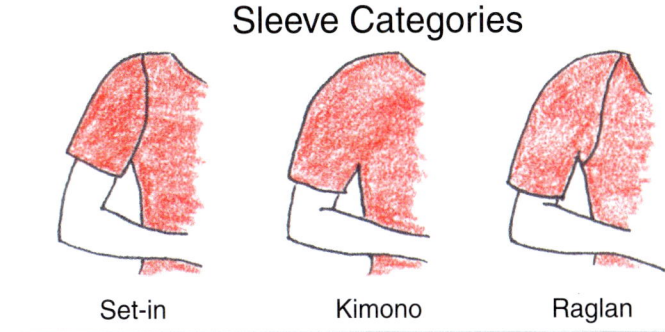

2-10 Sleeves fall into three basic categories: set-in, kimono, and raglan. *Ellen Endres*

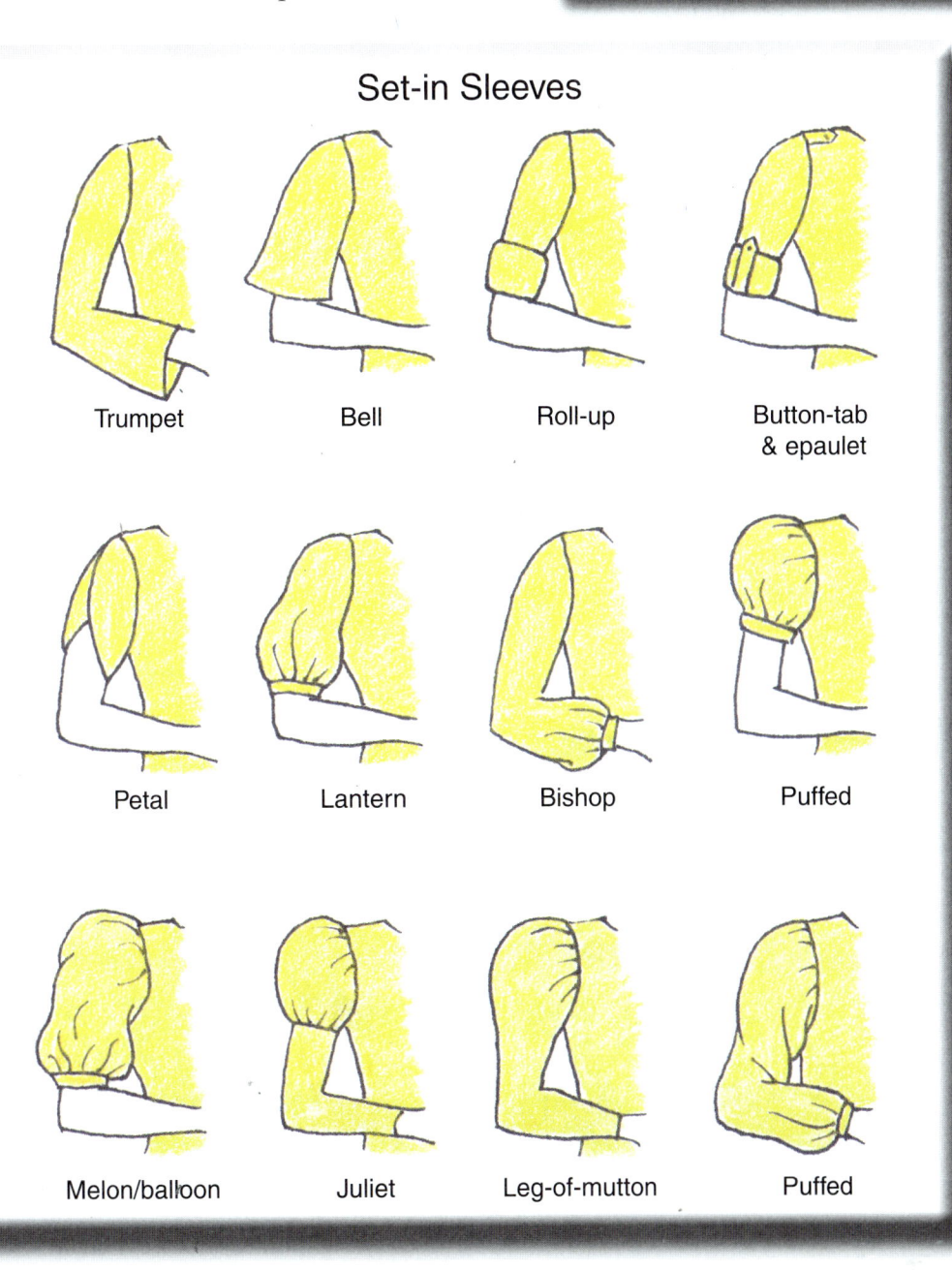

Sleeve Categories

Set-in | Kimono | Raglan

Set-in Sleeves

Trumpet | Bell | Roll-up | Button-tab & epaulet

Petal | Lantern | Bishop | Puffed

Melon/balloon | Juliet | Leg-of-mutton | Puffed

2-11 These are all variations of the set-in sleeve. They all have a seam at the top of the shoulder. *Ellen Endres*

- *Kimono.* A **kimono sleeve** is an extension of the garment front and back. It has no seam attaching the sleeve to the body of the garment. It forms by joining the front and back together from the neckline and underarm areas to the end of the sleeve. There are several variations of the kimono sleeve, **2-12**. The *dolman* sleeve is very wide at the underarm. The *batwing* sleeve has a deep, wide armhole that reaches from the waist to a narrowed wrist.
- *Raglan.* A **raglan sleeve** features diagonal seams in the front and back that extend from the neck to under the arms. Raglan sleeves can be any length.

Another type of sleeve is the *cap sleeve*. The cap sleeve is a small, triangular sleeve that sits on the shoulder. It can be an extension of the shoulder line or a short, set-in sleeve, **2-13**. It is popular for summer wear.

2-12 The kimono sleeve has four common variations.
Ellen Endres

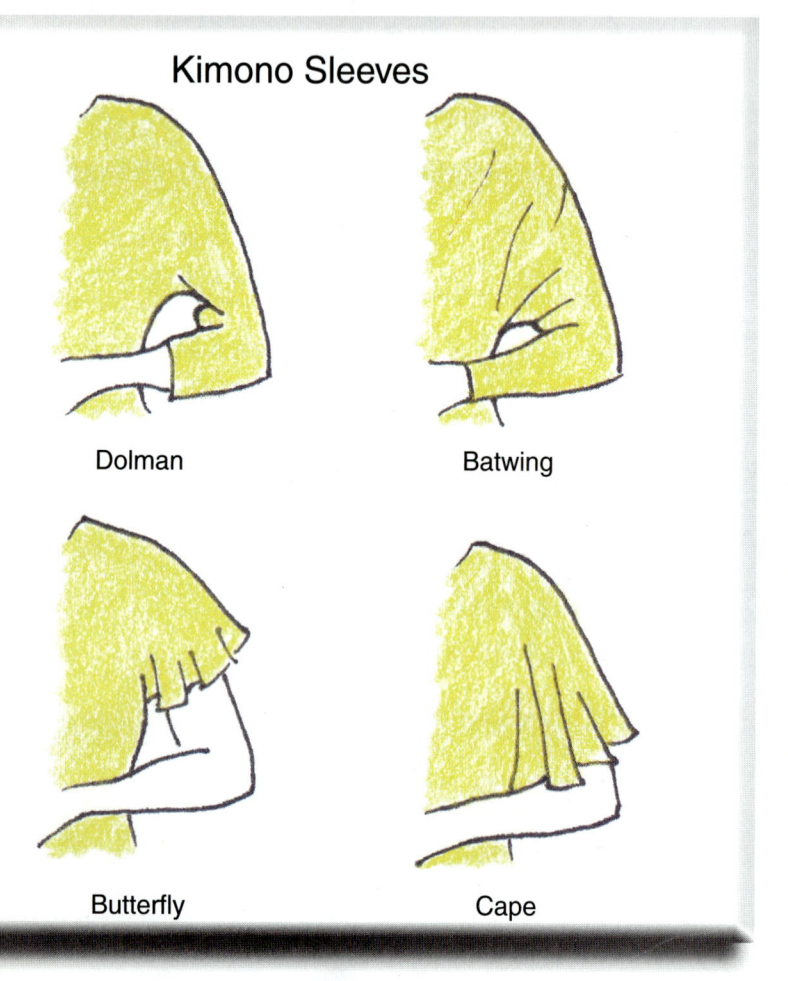

Kimono Sleeves

Dolman

Batwing

Butterfly

Cape

2-13 The cap sleeve may be set in or an extension of the shoulder line.
Ellen Endres

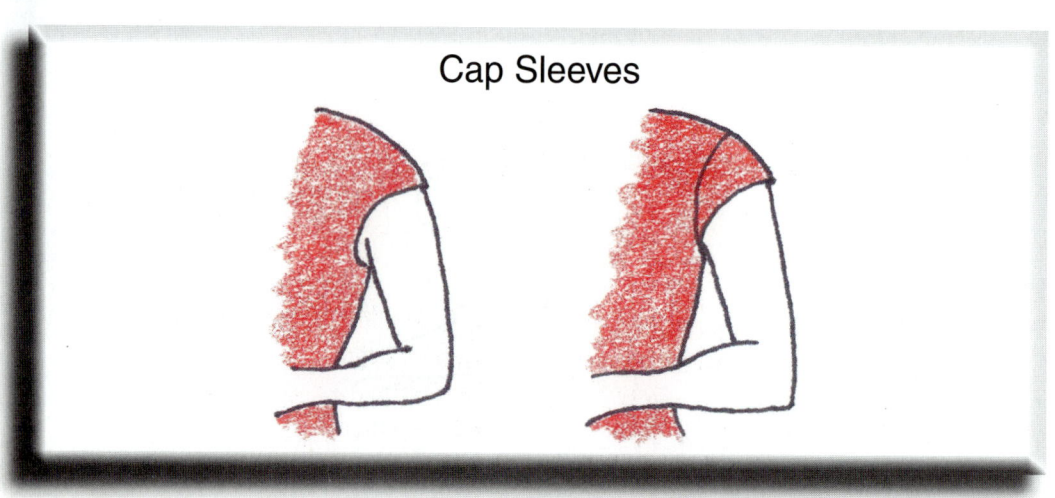

Cap Sleeves

Garment Styles

Designers use varying combinations of these garment features to create basic garment styles. Many of these styles have specific names that fashion designers and industry leaders commonly use. Knowing the names of these garment styles improves your fashion awareness and can be beneficial when working in the fashion field.

Blouses and Shirts

The blouse was originally designed as a loose, upper garment for women. It could have long or short sleeves and was traditionally tucked into a skirt. With the introduction of pants for women in the early 20th century, there came a need for a more tailored upper garment. Fitted shirts, similar to men's shirts, were then designed for women.

The following are a few of the most common types of blouses and shirts women wear today, **2-14**.

Blouses/Shirts

Tank top — Shell — Camisole — Peasant

Sport shirt — Western — Fitted — Bib front

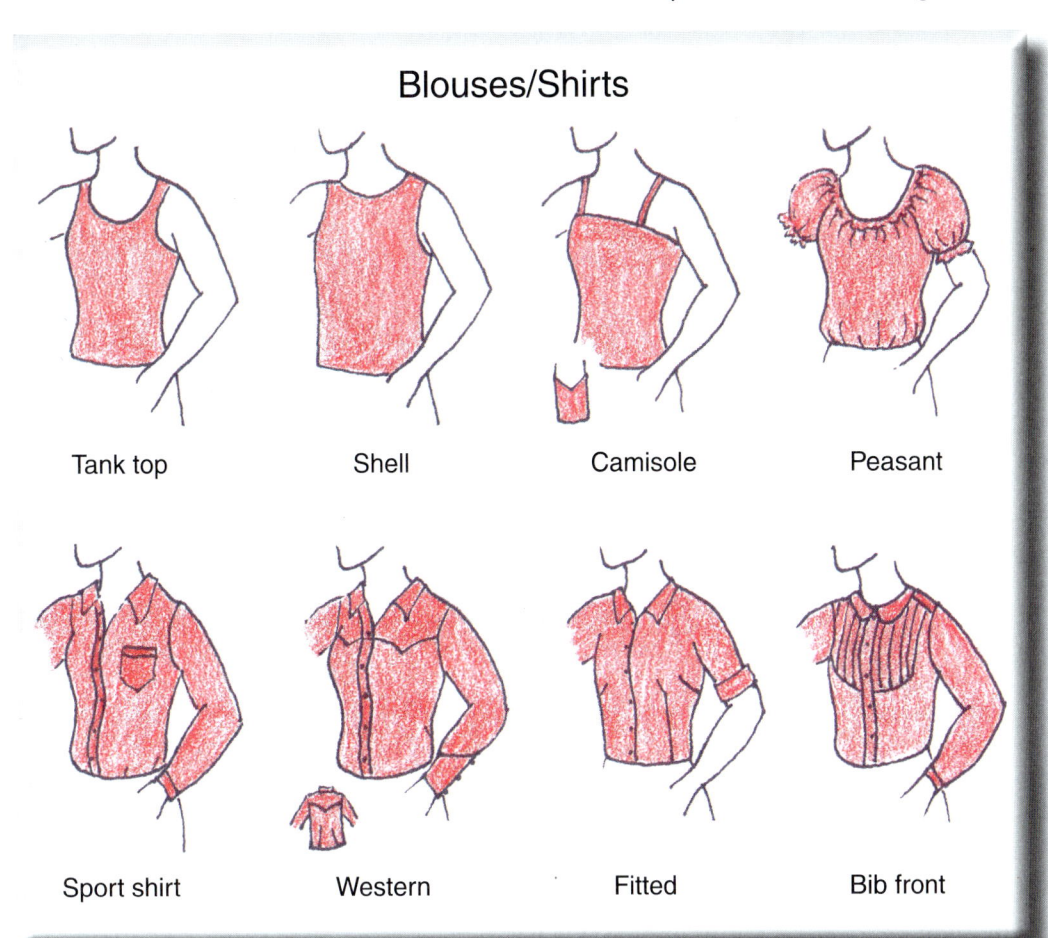

2-14 Blouses and shirts may be fitted or loose. These are the most common styles.
Ellen Endres

- *Tank top.* A short, close-fitting, sleeveless top usually made of knit fabric.
- *Shell.* A woman's sleeveless sweater or blouse, often worn under a jacket.
- *Camisole.* A blouse that covers the body from the bust to the waist with thin shoulder straps. It was introduced in the early 19th century as an item of underwear worn between the corset and dress. Women now wear camisoles alone or under jackets.
- *Sport shirt.* A more casual version of a man's dress shirt. Sport-shirt sizes are small, medium, large, and extra large. *Dress shirts* are sized by collar measurement and sleeve length and are designed to wear with ties.
- *Bib front.* This shirt features a stitched-pleat front that is bib-like in shape. It can be seen with various collars. Tuxedo shirts often have bib fronts.
- *Peasant.* A blouse that features full, puffed-sleeves created by elastic or drawstrings at the neck and sleeve edges.

Skirt Styles

There are many styles of skirts, **2-15**. Skirts can be full or slim, long or short, and feature darts, gathers, or pleats. Some have waistbands while others have none. A **waistband** is a strip of fabric attached at the waistline edge of the garment. The following are the most common skirt styles:

- *Straight.* This skirt is the slimmest and falls straight from the hipline. There is no added fullness at the hemline. It is also called a fitted or *pencil* skirt.
- *A-line.* This style flares slightly from the hipline to the hemline, forming an "A" shape.

Skirts

Straight	Straight trouser	A-line	6-gore

Notched-down knife pleat	Hip-stitched box pleat	Dirndl	Full gathered

Flare	Circular	Wrap	Sarong

2-15 Skirts vary in the amount of fullness they have. The straight skirt has the least amount of fullness. *Ellen Endres*

- **Gored.** Fitted at the waistline, *gored skirts* flare out at the hem. Seams form where the gores join together. The gore is the flared panel. There can be four, six, or even more gores in a skirt.
- **Pleated.** *Knife-pleated skirts* have regular sharp folds of fabric evenly spaced around the waist. *Box pleats* are made of two fabric folds turned inward toward each other. Pleats may or may not be stitched to the hip in either style.

- *Dirndl and full gathered.* A *dirndl skirt* has gathers at the waistline before falling straight to the hem. A *full-gathered skirt* is much fuller at the hemline.
- *Flared and circular. Flared skirts* are full at the hemline. *Circular skirts* actually form a circle when opened and laid flat. They are very full at the hemline.
- *Wrap and sarong.* A *wrap skirt* wraps around the body, overlapping at the front or back side. They fasten with buttons or ties. The *sarong* is a variation of the wrap skirt that is knotted at the side.

Pants Styles

Pants (also called slacks or trousers) have been worn by men since ancient times. Women in the U.S. did not commonly wear pants until the 1920s. During World War II, pants became more common as women replaced men in the factories. After the war, women went back to wearing dresses and skirts except for leisure wear. By the 1970s, however, drastic changes in social rules and attitudes began occurring. Today, women wear pants for almost any occasion.

Pants come in a variety of lengths, 2-16. They can be quite short or very long. They also vary in the degree of fullness through the leg area, ranging from a 13- to 22-inch leg opening. The waist may fall at the natural waistline or ride lower on the hips. The following are some common pants styles, 2-17:

- *Straight.* The legs are the same width from knee to hem with a 15-inch leg opening.
- *Tapered.* The legs are narrower at the hem than at the knee with a 13-inch leg opening.
- *Bell-bottom.* The legs are tight-fitting through the thigh but flare out at the knee, forming a bell shape.
- *Flared.* The legs are wider at the hem than at the knee. The flare can begin above the knee, closer to the waist. A typical leg opening is 22 inches.
- *Palazzo.* Palazzo pants are full at the waist and flare widely at the hem.
- *Jeans.* Denim jeans, now a classic, are available in many variations today. They are usually made of denim fabric with double stitching, and typically five pockets. Style variations include tightness of fit, leg style, fabric treatment, waist type, pocket type, and denim type.
- *Hip-hugger (low-rise).* The waistline of these jeans or pants sits on the upper hips, below the natural waistline. Hip-huggers first became popular in the 1960s. The term *low-rise* is commonly used today.

2-16 Pants can be quite short or very long as illustrated above.
Ellen Endres

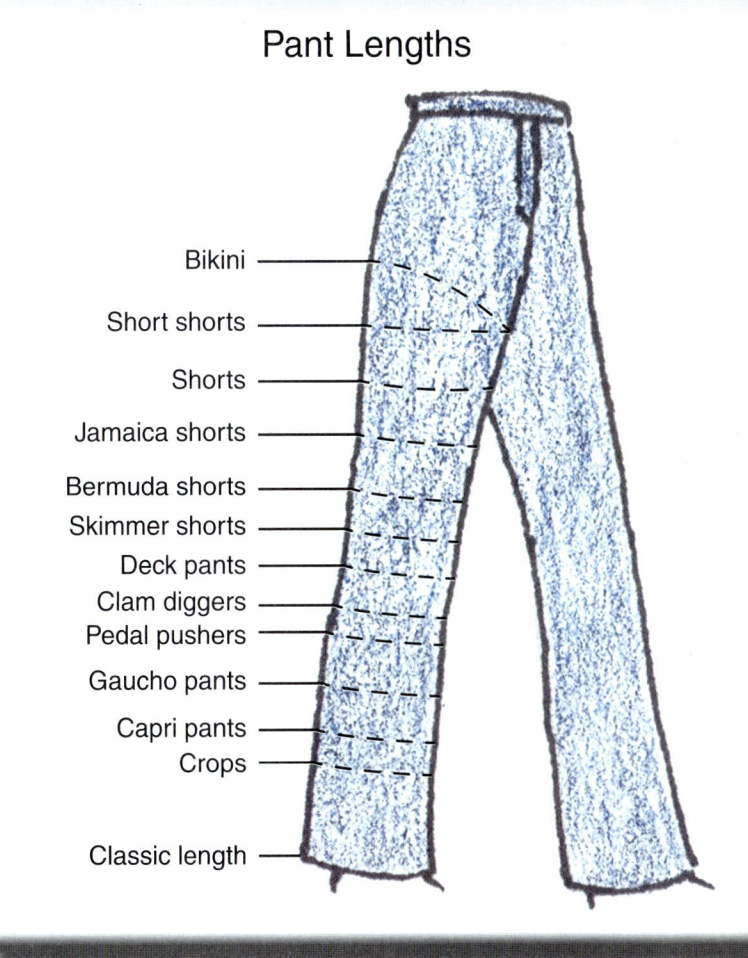

Pant Lengths

- Bikini
- Short shorts
- Shorts
- Jamaica shorts
- Bermuda shorts
- Skimmer shorts
- Deck pants
- Clam diggers
- Pedal pushers
- Gaucho pants
- Capri pants
- Crops
- Classic length

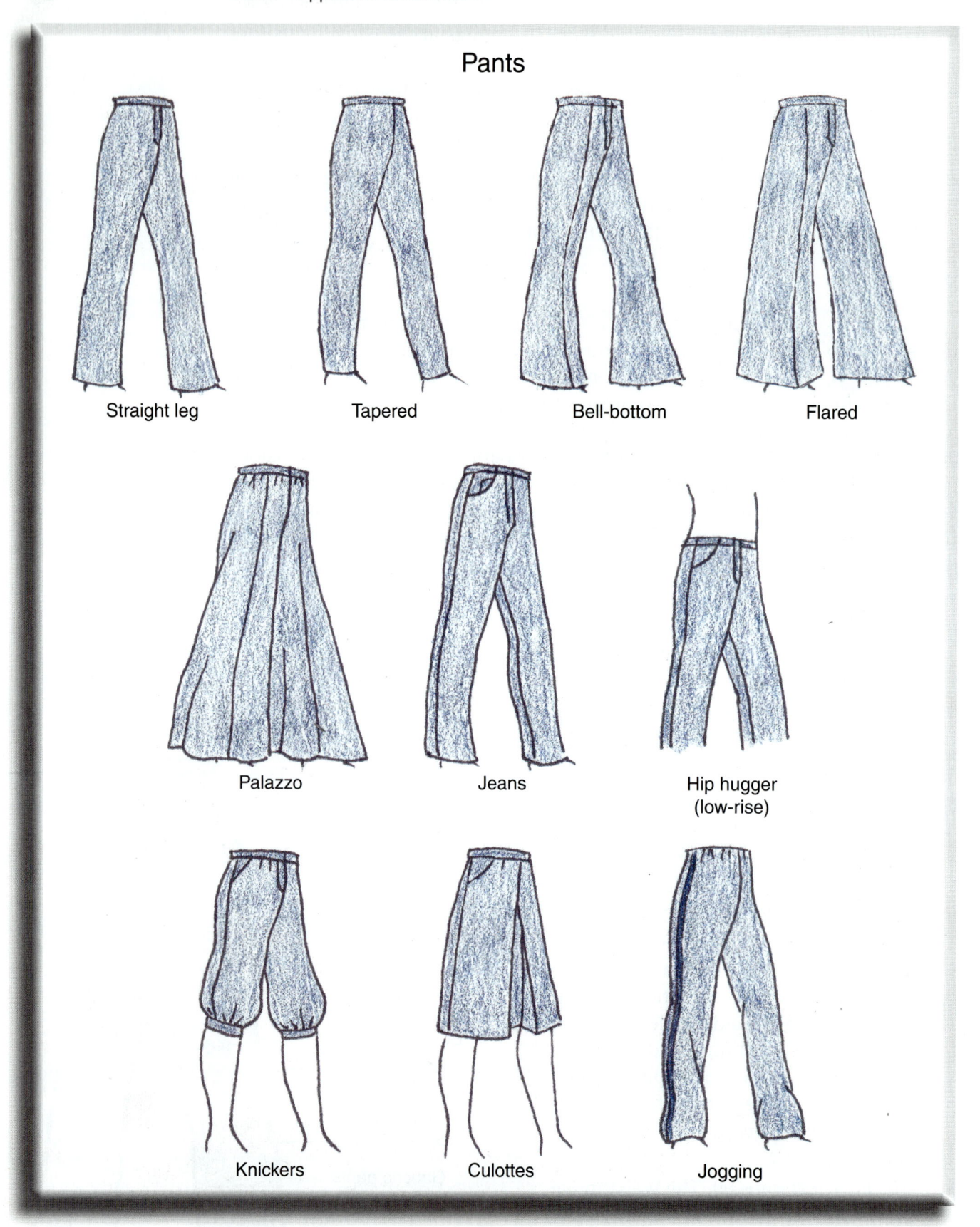

Pants

Straight leg — Tapered — Bell-bottom — Flared

Palazzo — Jeans — Hip hugger (low-rise)

Knickers — Culottes — Jogging

2-17 Pants styles vary in length and fullness, as well as in waist treatments. *Ellen Endres*

- *Knickers.* The legs gather into a band just below the knee.
- *Culottes.* Wide pants that give the appearance of a skirt.
- *Jogging.* Jogging pants, also called warm-ups or sweat pants, are usually made of knit fabrics. They are elasticized at the waist and ankle. Some may have drawstrings at the waist.

Dress Styles

There are several classic dress styles that remain in fashion year after year. Some are described below.

- **Sheath.** The *sheath style* has no waistline, but is fitted with darts. A **dart** is a stitched fold of fabric that provides shape and fullness to a garment, 2-18.
- **Shift.** The *shift* (also called a *chemise*) is less fitted at the waist and hangs loose. It also has no waistline seam.
- **A-line.** An "A" shape is created as the dress flares out from the shoulders and waist to a full hemline. This dress style has no waistline seam. The *tent* style is even fuller and hangs away from the body.
- **Princess.** The *princess* style features two seams that extend from the shoulder or armhole to the hemline. The seams give shape to the garment. There is no waistline seam.
- **Surplice.** This dress overlaps and fastens to one side of the front. This creates an *asymmetrical* design—one that is different on the left and right sides of the garment.

A number of these styles do not have waist seams. Others have seams that appear at, above, or below the natural waistline, 2-19. The *blouson dress* features fullness above the natural waistline. The *shirtwaist* dress looks much like a full-length tailored shirt and is usually belted at the waistline. The *empire* dress has a seam that falls above the waist. A *drop-waist* dress has a seam below the natural waistline.

2-18 This classic sheath dress is fitted with darts to create shape. *Shutterstock*

Dresses

Sheath	Shift	A-line	Princess
Tent	Surplice	Coat dress	Blouson
Shirtwaist	Empire float	Drop-waist	Strapless

2-19 These illustrations show the most common dress styles. *Ellen Endres*

Jacket and Coat Styles

Jackets and coats are necessary garments that provide warmth and protection from the weather. Coats are full length and jackets are short, **2-20**. As you look at the styles in these illustrations, you will notice that some are single-breasted and others are double-breasted. A *single-breasted* garment has a single row of buttons up the front. A *double-breasted* garment has two rows of buttons and the sides have a wider overlap. The following are common jacket styles, **2-21**:

- *Bolero.* An open, sleeveless or sleeved jacket that reaches almost to the waist.
- *Chanel.* A short, collarless jacket originally designed by Coco Chanel. It features braid trim and patch pockets.
- *Aviator/Bomber.* A short jacket tightly gathered at the waist and cuffs.
- *Pea jacket.* A heavy, double-breasted, hip-length jacket originally worn by sailors. It, too, was made popular by Coco Chanel.
- *Safari.* A belted, hip-length jacket featuring patch pockets with button flaps. It was originally worn in the African bush country in the late 19th century.
- *Cardigan.* A collarless jacket or sweater that opens down the front. It may or may not have buttons.

2-20 These coats and jackets represent a variety of styles to meet consumer needs.
Shutterstock

60 Part 1 Apparel and Fashion

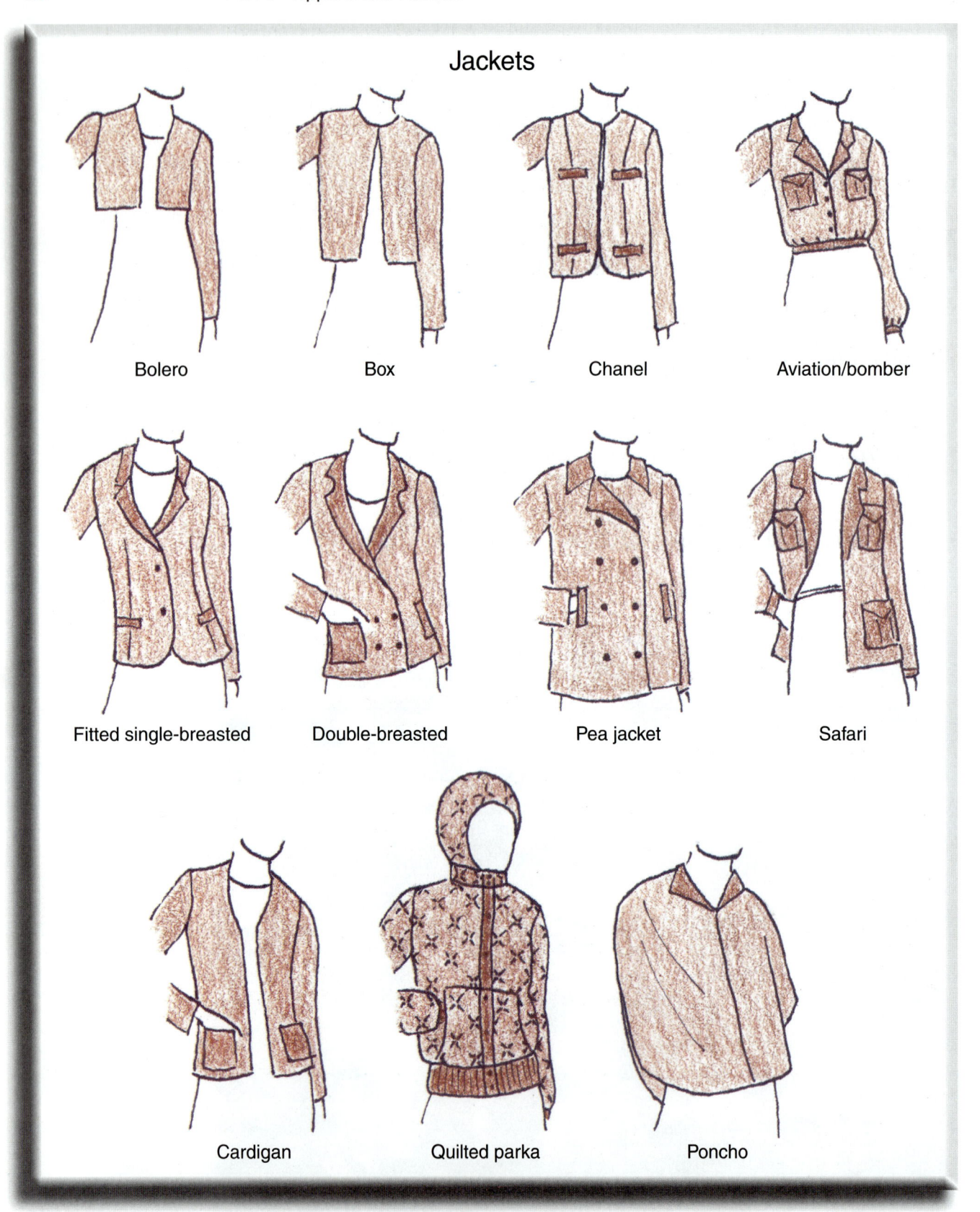

Jackets

Bolero Box Chanel Aviation/bomber

Fitted single-breasted Double-breasted Pea jacket Safari

Cardigan Quilted parka Poncho

2-21 Jackets vary in length, but they also may be single-breasted or double-breasted. *Ellen Endres*

Chapter 2   Understanding Fashion   61

Figure **2-22** shows several popular coat styles. A true classic is the trench coat. The trench coat is a loose, belted, double-breasted raincoat that features a double yoke across the shoulders. The shoulders also have decorative straps called *epaulets*. The basis for this style is a World War I soldier's coat. The *polo* style is a camel-colored wool coat with a full skirt at the back. The *chesterfield* coat was named after the Earl of Chesterfield in the 1830s. It features long lines and a black velvet collar.

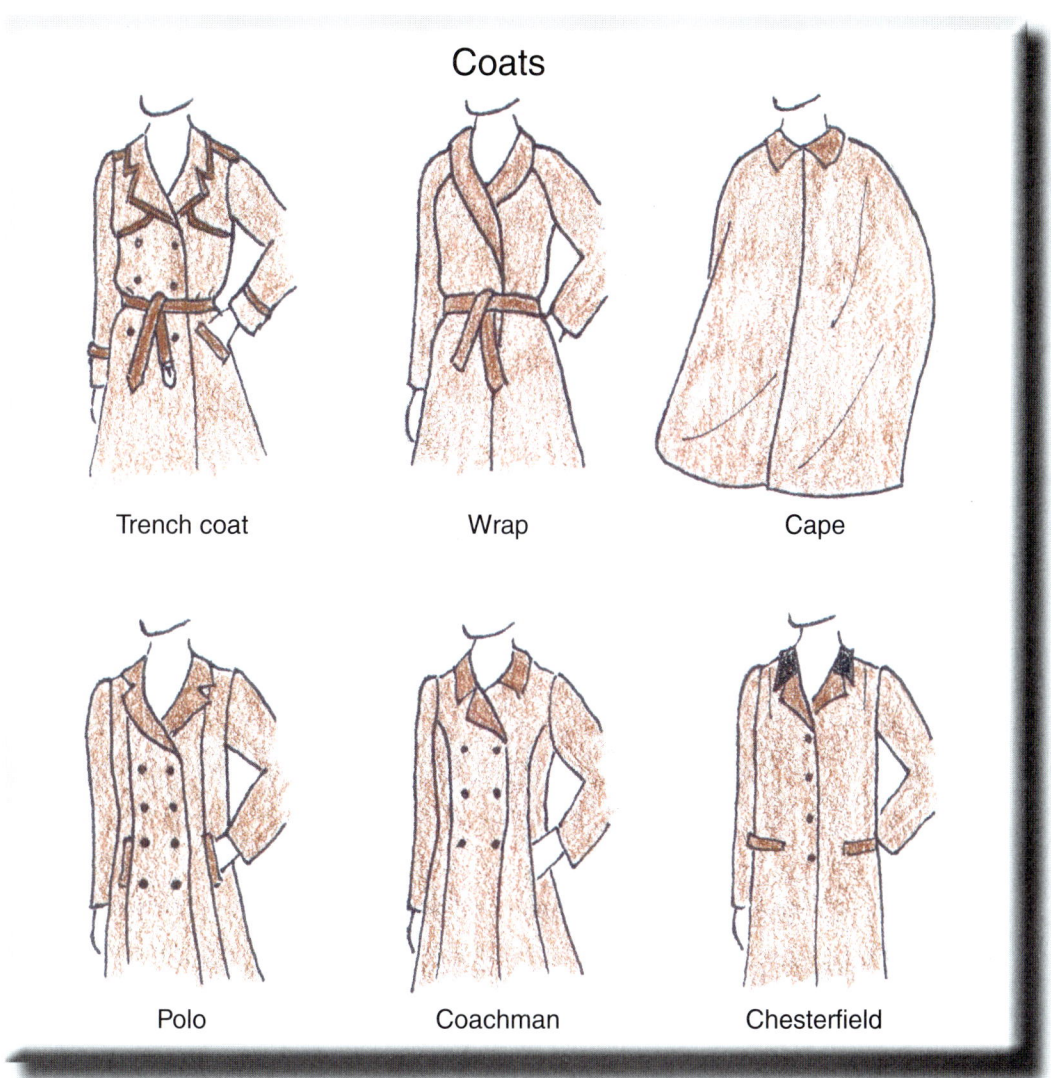

Coats

Trench coat   Wrap   Cape

Polo   Coachman   Chesterfield

2-22 The most classic coat style is the trench coat, but other styles remain popular as well.
Ellen Endres

Summary

- Fashions reflect a time and place. What is in fashion is influenced by the economic, political, and social conditions of the time.
- A fashion is a particular style of apparel that is popular at a given time.
- Fashions go through cycles of being popular, disappearing, and later returning to popularity.
- Fashion cycles have four stages. They occur at a faster rate today due to improved communication worldwide.
- A combination of garment features creates a style. Common garment features are necklines, collars, and sleeves. These combine with other garment features to create basic styles.

Graphic Organizer

Draw a star diagram like the one you see here and identify six key fashion terms.

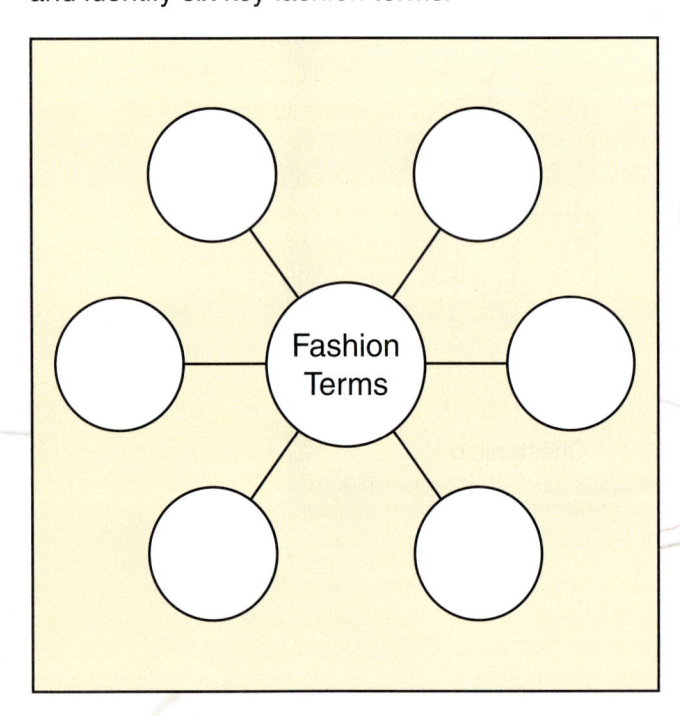

Review the Facts

1. Give an example showing how the economic conditions in a country can influence fashion.
2. Which of these is not a style? A) pleated skirt; B) black coat; C) bow tie; D) cardigan
3. Explain the difference between a classic and a fad. Give an example of each.
4. Why should you spend less on fads and avant-garde fashions when building a long-lasting wardrobe?
5. Compare and contrast retro and vintage apparel.
6. Describe the four stages of the fashion cycle.
7. Why do fashions cycle at a faster rate today than they did in the past?
8. What garment typically has a crew neckline?
9. How does a kimono sleeve differ from a raglan sleeve?
10. Explain the differences between a sport shirt and a dress shirt.
11. What is another name for a pencil skirt?
12. Which pants style was first designed by Levi Strauss?
13. Which dress style fits closer to the body, the sheath or the shift?
14. Name two features of the trench coat.

Think Critically

15. **Make inferences.** What are some of the current fashion trends for women? men? teens? Which do you think will remain "in fashion" the longest?
16. **Identify evidence.** What groups of students in your school appear to be trendsetters? What evidence can you give to support your views?
17. **Draw conclusions.** Why have well-worn jeans and T-shirts long been popular styles with teens? Draw conclusions about their popularity and predict whether you think this will change anytime soon.
18. **Analyze behaviors.** Why do you think many celebrities dress in avant-garde fashions? What behaviors support your rationale?
19. **Make predictions.** Create a list of current fads. As a class, predict which item will become a fashion and why.

Apparel Applications

20. **Digital bulletin board.** Use a school-approved online application to collect pictures from magazines and newspapers of styles, fashions, classics, and fads. Arrange the four groups of pictures on your digital bulletin board to share with the class.
21. **Fashion cycle blog.** Use online catalogs to locate pictures of fashions you feel fall into each of the four stages of the fashion cycle. Find one example per stage. Use a school-approved collaboration application to create a digital brochure. Post each photo to the brochure (crediting the source) and note the stage it represents. Below each image, write why you think it is in this stage.
22. **Fashion trends.** Review a fashion website that predicts the fashion trends for next season. List these trends. Which of these have been in fashion before and are coming back around? Share your findings in class.
23. **Vintage fashions.** Do you have a T-shirt or other apparel item that might be considered vintage? If so, what makes it vintage? Take a digital picture of your vintage item and write a caption describing why you consider it vintage. Post your picture and caption on a class bulletin board.
24. **Style inventory.** Do a style inventory of your own clothing. Try to identify the garment features and styles described in this chapter. Make a list of the "matches" you found. For example, a Henley shirt, a cardigan, a western shirt, jeans, etc. Are the items in your wardrobe fads, fashions, or a mix of both?

Academic Connections

25. **Social studies.** Review current fads and fashions in fashion magazines. Then use an Internet or print resource on the history of costume to identify which fashion details from the past that appear in current fashions. Use presentation software and digital images to share a summary of your findings with the class.
26. **Writing.** Conduct an oral history interview of three older adults. Ask each to list different fashions that he or she recalls cycled one or more times. Compare their responses. How did the cycles change? Write a summary of your findings.

Workplace Links

27. **Interview.** Tour a vintage clothing store in your area. Interview a salesperson. Ask what vintage items are most popular. Who is most likely to buy vintage clothes? for what reason? Report your findings to the class.
28. **Fashion article.** As a fashion writer for a local department store, your current assignment is to write an online press release about teen fashions for the coming season. Research upcoming fashions and write your press release using language to capture teen attention. Be sure to identify the hottest fashion trends for the season.

Improving Interpersonal Skills

Do you like to work with people? Perhaps a career in apparel sales is for you. Presume you work in a specialty apparel shop. Your goal is to learn how to serve your customers better. Use the FCCLA *Leaders at Work* project idea called *Just Your Style*. Follow the project guidelines. See your adviser for questions and further information.

Chapter 3

Textiles and Apparel Through the Years

Chapter Objectives

After studying this chapter, you will be able to
- **summarize** the cultural, social, religious, political, economic, and technological influences on clothing design.
- **describe** how textiles and apparel have evolved from prehistoric times to the present.
- **describe** developments during the industrial revolution that influenced apparel manufacturing.
- **summarize** the differences between natural and manufactured fibers.

Key Terms

societies	market economy	piecework
customs	free enterprise system	mass production
heritage	command economy	ready-to-wear (RTW)
economics	technology	manufactured fibers
bartering	natural fibers	synthetics

Reading with Purpose

As you read the chapter, write a "top ten" list of the most important concepts.

Have you ever wondered how and why clothing styles have changed so much through the centuries? Perhaps you have seen pictures in history books of cave dwellers wearing animal skins as clothing. Maybe you have seen illustrations of ancient Romans wearing togas or early Japanese wearing kimonos. These garments were unique to a particular place and time.

Many events throughout the history of the world have influenced the textiles used, the designs created, and the uses made of clothing. Some influences have been cultural, social, and political. Others relate to a country's economy. Technological advances have also played an important part.

Influences on Fashion

As you read about the history of textiles and apparel, you will notice a number of factors influencing the fashions worn at any particular time. Throughout this chapter, examples of how these factors influenced apparel are given. As you read about the changes in apparel over the years, you will see these influences at work.

Cultural Influences

For thousands of years, people in different societies have worn clothes unique to their culture, **3-1**. **Societies** are groups of people with broad, common interests who live and work together. The beliefs and social customs of a particular group of people form their *culture*. **Customs** are traditions one generation hands down to the next. These customs form a part of a person's cultural **heritage**—the background and traditions the person acquires from previous generations.

People have followed certain practices to make themselves beautiful according to the customs of their culture. For example, since the beginning of its civilization, one of the most popular garments in India for women is a wrapped dress called a *sari*. Indian people also still wear pants called a *dhoti*, hats called *turbans*, and a variety of scarves.

Social Influences

Throughout the centuries, social changes have brought about changes in fashion. What people wore reflected their lifestyles and values. In addition, clothing often displayed special status within groups. For example, early people lived in small, isolated groups. Members of tribes who were brave warriors or outstanding hunters wore special animal skins, such as tiger or lion, to show how important they were. A special status within a group was also apparent through the display of elaborate headdresses, tattoos, and ornate jewelry.

For many centuries, the nobility in Europe wore clothing that showed they were the highest class in their society. Clothing was elegant and extravagant with lots of lace, beads, and embroidery. The fine fabrics used were made of imported silks and linens, 3-2.

3-1 These Waja women from Nigeria, photographed in 1982, continue to use gourds to carry food. They also use decorated gourd bowls to protect their infants from the hot sun as they carry them on their backs. *Photographer: Marla C. Berns*

Religious Influences

In almost all societies, religion influences how people dress. For instance, religious customs require Muslim women to wear veils in public to hide their faces from strangers. Amish people believe in plain clothing to go with their simple lifestyles. In most cultures, people wear robes, masks, or other accessories for religious ceremonies. In some cultures, people think these clothes may help the religious leaders perform their jobs.

Political Influences

The governing process of a country and who is in political office often influences the clothing its citizens wear. For example, during the Middle Ages, there were different class divisions among the people in many countries.

Rulers—kings, queens, and other nobility—wanted their clothing to be superior to that of their subjects. Some countries passed *sumptuary laws*. These were laws that regulated what each class of people could wear.

Today, some Middle Eastern governments are trying to curb the influence of Western dress for their women. In Saudi Arabia, for example, women are required to wear flowing, black, head-to-toe robes whenever they leave their homes.

Economic Influences

Economics involves how a society chooses to produce, distribute, and consume its goods and services. Goods, such as apparel, come to you largely through the economic activities of producers. They make and sell goods and services to satisfy consumer needs and wants. The exchange of goods and services takes place within the framework of an economic system.

Thousands of years ago, however, these systems didn't exist. People made clothing from the natural resources that were available. Later, they learned to grow fibers that could be spun and woven into fabrics. Some people were more skilled at spinning and weaving than others. They found that they could barter their skills. **Bartering** is trading your skills or goods for another person's skills or goods. Bartering provided the society with better goods and services.

Today there are two basic types of economic systems. These are the market economy and the command economy. The type of economic system of a country influences fashion choices.

3-2 This silk gown decorated with silver thread and lace was worn between 1740 and 1760. *973.399.a-.c Photograph courtesy of the Royal Ontario Museum, © ROM*

Market Economy

A **market economy** is a system in which private individuals and businesses respond freely to the needs of the marketplace. Another name for a market economy is the **free enterprise system**. Manufacturers try to respond to the needs of their customers. Consumers are important in this system. What they choose to buy affects the profits of the manufacturers. Competition exists between manufacturers, creating many of choices for consumers. Due to competition, new clothing designs are available every season. Manufacturers advertise their new designs to get you to choose their clothes. A wide variety of types of retailers provide many options for consumers. In the U.S. and most European countries, the market economy system exists.

Within the market economies, a significant change has occurred in the last half century that has influenced fashion. More and more women are working outside the home. Families have two paychecks, which has resulted in increased buying power. More clothing is available because families have more money to buy new fashions. Women also buy more clothes as a requirement for their jobs. As people buy more clothes, there is more money in circulation, and the economy is better.

A more recent economic trend has been the increase of spending money among teens, 3-3. Teens have more spending money today than ever before. Manufacturers recognize this trend, and aim their advertising to this very important market segment. Most teens who work spend a large portion of their money on clothes.

Command Economy

In a **command economy**, the state or some other central authority controls economic activities. You will usually find this type of economy with socialist or communist forms of government. The central authority decides who will produce manufactured goods and how much they will produce. The government also sets the prices of goods and services. The needs and wants of consumers are not always a consideration. This often leads to limited choices for consumers. Because there is no competition, prices are fairly firm. Fashions change very slowly in this type of economy.

Technological Influences

Technology is the manner of accomplishing a task using current technical methods or knowledge. Technological influences on fashion have been significant. Methods of technology used in the production of clothing have changed dramatically from early times.

During the Stone Age, people made stone tools to kill animals for food and their furs. Later, with the invention of sewing needles made from bone, people were able to sew skins together and make better clothing. The simple invention of the eyed sewing needle is perhaps the single most important technological event to influence clothing production.

3-3 Teens today have more money to spend than in previous generations. *Shutterstock*

Spinning and weaving were later developments. All spinning and weaving was done by hand until the invention of foot- and water-powered machinery in the 1700s. This development was followed by the invention of the sewing machine in the 1800s.

Today, machinery and procedures undergo constant improvement and development. The development of manufactured fibers from chemicals is a major technological advance of the twentieth century. In the later part of the same century, the use of computers allowed great advancement in textile design and manufacturing. Because of computers, all aspects of fashion design and production proceed faster and with greater accuracy.

The History of Textiles and Apparel

From the Stone Age to the Space Age, the types and uses of textiles have changed tremendously as have the styles of apparel. These changes are the result of the influences on fashion previously described.

Early Wearing Apparel

Fiber fragments among the findings in archaeological excavations dating back thousands of years provide clues to the clothes of the time. Pictures found on cave walls show that people in the Stone Age used animal skins as clothing. These sources give evidence about some of the earliest uses of textiles and clothing.

Historians know that prehistoric people living in cold climates used animal skins to cover their bodies. As people learned to make and use tools from stones and sticks, they applied these tools and skills to making clothing. Softening animal skins by rubbing them with stones or beating them with sticks made the skins pliable for clothing. With the invention of bone needles and thread from animal tendons, people were able to sew sections of skin together. This resulted in forming more closely fitted garments, **3-4**.

Feathers, shells, and vegetation were common adornments for such clothing. Families were close, and young people learned customary dress from their elders.

Early people living in hot climates wore clothing as protection from the hot sun. These people made garments from trees and plants. They gathered bark from certain trees and soaked it in water. Pounding the bark into a thin sheet and treating it with oils produced a soft, strong fabric for use in making clothes. Soft grasses were also useful for garments and other items. Grasses were gathered and laced or woven together to form loose-fitting garments, hats, fishing nets, and baskets.

In ancient times, groups of people wandered from one place to another hunting food. Later, people began living together in village settlements. By living in one place, people had more time to develop skills. They learned how to grow plants and raise animals for food.

The raising of plants and animals led to the development of fabric making using natural fibers. **Natural fibers** are fibers taken from nature, such as cotton, flax, wool, and silk. People discovered the seed pods of cotton plants and the inner section of flax plants contained fibers. They discovered the hair of sheep

3-4 Early people used animal skins as garments. *Provided by Louise Liddell*

and the cocoons of silkworms were fibers, too. People also learned how to use these fibers to make cotton, linen, wool, and silk fabrics.

For hundreds of years, cotton, flax, wool, and silk were the only fibers in use. All fibers were spun into yarns by hand. The weaving of yarns to make fabrics was done by hand, too.

Ancient Civilizations

As civilization progressed, people began living together in villages. The villages grew into large communities or societies. With the formation of these societies, came establishment of governments. The governing rulers, nobles, priests, and warriors maintained absolute power over the great masses of people. In these types of societies, general styles of clothing survived for thousands of years. The following are some of the earliest civilizations and the clothing styles most commonly worn at that time.

Ancient Egypt

Located in eastern North Africa, pharaohs ruled from around 3150 BC until the area fell to the Roman Empire in 30 BC. Because of the warm climate in Egypt, the basic fabric was linen. Egyptians were highly acclaimed for their fine linen weaving as early as 3000 BC. Men wore white loincloths wrapped around the body and fastened in front. Women wore straight sheath dresses supported by shoulder straps. Such items as embroidery, beads, and feathers were common adornments on these white dresses. Both women and men wore broad bib-like collars made of beads. Both males and females shaved their heads and wore brightly colored wigs. Gold rings and bracelets were other adornments, 3-5.

3-5 The garments worn by men and women of ancient Egypt are depicted in this illustration. *Shutterstock*

Minoan Civilization

Northwest of Egypt, on the island of Crete, lived the Minoans between 1900 and 1400 BC. Though the men here also wore loincloths, the women wore dresses with long, bell-shaped skirts and tight bodices. The dresses were elaborate for the time, with flounces, pleats, tucks, and layers of skirts. They were brightly colored and trimmed with braid and embroidery.

Ancient Greece

The ancient Greek civilization thrived from about 1100 BC until it, too, fell to the Roman Empire around 150 BC. Greek garments were loose, free, and graceful. The most important article of clothing, for both men and women, was the *chiton*. This was a large, rectangular piece of dyed wool or linen draped over the left arm and fastened at the shoulder with a brooch. The right arm was left free, but the chiton was sometimes fastened at both shoulders. The chiton could be knee-length or longer. Geometrical designs often formed the decorative border of the cloth. Men and women also wore a long, woolen robe called the *himation* over the chiton. The himation was an oblong piece of fabric, 12 to 15 feet long, draped around the body, **3-6**.

Roman Empire

The Roman Empire existed from 800 BC to 500 AD Two items of clothing were common—the toga and the tunic. The *toga* was heavy with symbolic meaning. Only citizens with the right to vote could wear it. Colors and decorations indicated status. At one point, its size was 20 feet long by seven to ten feet deep. The shape was a segment of a circle. The draping of the toga was complex. At a later time, a *tunic* was worn under the toga. This garment was made of two pieces of fabric sewn across the shoulders and up the sides. It had short cap sleeves. Roman women wore garments similar to the Greeks.

The Middle Ages (400-1500)

Though clothing styles were still influenced by the wrapped garments of Rome, clothing gained more shape during the Middle Ages. In the earlier decades of the Middle Ages, men wore short, loose, sleeveless tunics belted at the waist with leather thongs. Women wore ankle-length gowns covered by an outer short tunic. The sleeves were loose and sometimes reaching the knees.

Farther north in Europe, men and women needed protection from the colder climate. Leather garments and furs provided the necessary warmth. Here men wore coats, cloaks, simple hats, long hose, and loose trousers. During the sixth century, the introduction of trousers marked a significant change in the way people dressed. Trousers were first worn by the barbarians and considered disgusting by most Europeans. Later, highly cultured men of rank and position adopted and wore the trouser garment style.

Another significant event occurred in the sixth century. For three thousand years, the Chinese had carefully guarded their secret of silk production. Silk is the strongest and most lustrous of all natural textile fibers and the most desired. In the year 551 AD, two Persian monks were able to secretly bring a quantity of silkworm eggs out of China and in to Constantinople (now Istanbul, Turkey). From these eggs, came the production of all subsequent generations of silkworms that stocked the Western world. The most beautiful silks, some woven with gold and silver threads, came from the factories of Constantinople. China no longer had a monopoly on silk.

During this time frame, the garments of royalty became more and more elaborate. Early on, the style was still a simple cloak with linings of furs, silks,

3-6 The white garment on the left is the Greek chiton. A himation is worn over the chiton or worn alone, as shown on the right. *North Wind Picture Archives*

and imported brocades. The basic dress remained rectangular until the late fourteenth and fifteenth centuries. At that time, society became more sophisticated and complex. Clothing gradually abandoned the simple lines and became quite elaborate. Buttons became popular as fasteners and for decoration.

In the fifteenth century, the male's usual garment was a loose, pleated tunic with either a fur lining or edging. Sleeves were long and baggy and buttoned at the wrists. Hose reached to the waistline. Men wore hooded cloaks over all garments. Women's gowns were long and had tight bodices. The skirts fell loosely to the ground in wide folds. Sleeves either buttoned at the wrist or extended far below the hands.

The 1600s

For centuries, kings and queens set fashions that members of their courts closely followed. They wore elegant, elaborate garments made of fine linens and colorful silks. Certain colors, such as purple, were for royal use only. The purple dye that came from mollusks, a type of shellfish, was rare, difficult to obtain, and therefore expensive.

Highlights in History

The Discovery of Silk

According to legend, a young Chinese Empress named Si Ling-Shi discovered silk. One day, as she sat in the garden drinking tea, she noticed a fat, white worm on a leaf of a mulberry tree. It moved its head back and forth while spraying a fine white thread from two tiny holes below its mouth. As she watched, she saw the worm wrap the thread around itself forming a cocoon. She caught it and dropped it into her cup of hot tea. When it softened, she saw the fiber floating in the tea. As she lifted it, the cocoon unwound into a long thread.

There are many versions of this story. No one knows which one is correct. From records, people know that for about 3000 years after the discovery of the silkworm, only the Chinese know how to make silk. They named the lustrous cloth *Si* for their Empress. Si is still the Chinese name for silk.

The Western world was mystified as to how silk was made. They speculated as to whether it came from a vegetable, animal, or mineral. Envoys were sent to China to discover this secret, but without success. Other countries had to buy the silken material and then unravel it to obtain the silk threads. The threads were then rewoven into lengths of silk, which were exchanged for more than their weight in gold. Very little silk could make its way to Rome and Europe. This increased its value, and the price could only be paid by the wealthiest people. Silk was in such demand and so costly that it was known throughout the world as the *cloth of kings*.

In the third century AD, Japan once again sent an envoy to China to either bribe or capture some of their silk-weavers and bring them to Japan to teach the process to the Japanese. This led to the beginning of the silk industry in Japan. Eventually, the silkworm eggs were smuggled to other countries of the world, and sericulture (silkworm cultivation) flourished.

The wealthy, powerful nations influenced clothing styles. In the 1600s, France became a European power. Soon it became the fashion leader of the world. Other countries copied the French designers' creations. Even today, France is still a fashion leader.

In colonial days in the United States, tailors and dressmakers made clothing mainly for wealthy people. Clothing took many hours to make and was expensive. Most families took care of their own needs for cloth and garments. They spun yarns and wove fabrics using spinning wheels and looms in their own homes. Family members cut these handwoven fabrics into pieces and sewed them into garments by hand.

Social life still centered around the family, but wealth increased. Dress became a way to distinguish between social classes. Farm families wore rough, homemade garments. Wealthy merchants and planters and their families wore expensive clothing made of imported fabrics.

The 1700s

A great change occurred in clothing styles after the French Revolution, which took place in the late 1700s. With the changeover of France from a monarchy to a democracy, people wanted to have a say in what kinds of fashions designs were available. Simpler fashions replaced the elegant fashions of the French nobility, 3-7.

The Industrial Revolution

In England in the late 1700s, the production of textiles began to change. This time period signaled the start of the Industrial Revolution. This was a movement marked by major economic changes due to the invention of many machines. The introduction of steam power and the development of the factory system also sparked this movement.

In 1769, Richard Arkwright invented a spinning frame. Driven by water power, it combined several hand-operated spinning devices into one large machine. Sixteen years later, in 1785, Edmund Cartwright invented a steam-powered loom. This brought the spinning and weaving steps together under one roof in a textile mill. Inside the mill, raw materials went from fiber to yarn to finished cloth. Samuel Slater built the first successful textile mill in the United States in 1789.

3-7 The elaborate dress of the French nobility is illustrated by this gentleman and lady of Louis XIV's court.
North Wind Picture Archives

In the years that followed, the invention of many other machines had great impact on the textile industry. The use of these machines allowed fewer people to produce more fabric than ever before. See Figure 3-8 for significant inventions of this period.

After beginning in England, the Industrial Revolution rapidly spread to other countries. Agriculture declined as offices and factories took over. Elegant knee breeches, brocaded vests, and fancy waistcoats for men gave way to black coats, long trousers, and high top hats. While men's attire became somber, women were wearing layers of petticoats and tight-fitting corsets, 3-9.

3-8 Machines invented during the Industrial Revolution had a great impact on the development of the textile industry.

Inventions in the Textile Industry

1733 John Kay—Flying shuttle
A tool used to weave the crosswise threads back and forth on a loom. Before this invention, the shuttle was moved by hand. On wide fabrics, two weavers operated the shuttle. With Kay's shuttle, the weaver pulled a stick and the shuttle automatically moved across the loom, hence the name the "flying" shuttle.

1769 Richard Arkwright—Water frame
This spinning machine was powered by water instead of by manpower. It was faster than hand spinning.

1770 James Hargreaves—Spinning jenny
Until this time, yarns were spun on a single rod called a spindle. The spinning jenny had eight spindles so a spinner could spin eight yarns at the same time.

1779 Samuel Crompton—Spinning mule
Features of the spinning jenny and water frame were combined into a huge machine. It could produce as much yarn as 200 spinners.

1785 Edmund Cartwright—Power loom
This loom was powered by steam instead of by operators using their hands.

1785 Thomas Bell—Cylinder printing
This invention allowed repetitious designs to be printed rapidly on cotton fabrics. Before this time, designs were block printed by hand.

1793 Eli Whitney—Cotton gin
A machine that separated the cotton fibers from the seeds. Before this time, this was done by hand using various crude tools.

1804 Joseph Marie Jacquard—Jacquard loom
This loom allowed the operator to weave different patterns in fabric automatically.

There was still a wide gap between the rich and the poor classes. Farmers and factory workers had very few clothes. A woman might have one dress for special occasions. The rest of the time she wore dark, cotton garments, **3-10**. A man had one suit for religious events and funerals.

The 1800s

Napoléon Bonaparte became Emperor of France in the early 1800s. His wife, Empress Josephine, made the Empire style world famous. Her dresses had low necklines and high waistlines, often with drawstrings. Many women worldwide quickly adopted this style, **3-11**.

Although fabric production evolved greatly, most garments were still made one at a time. Until the mid 1800s, many companies paid women to sew for them in their homes. These women received a certain payment amount for each garment or each step they finished. This was called **piecework**.

During the Civil War in the United States, **mass production** started to take over. Garment factories were built to produce many garments at the same time. Instead of one person sewing an entire garment, several people shared the job. Each person sewed only one part of the garment. A worker might sew only leg seams or collars. Then the item moved to someone else to complete another step. This continued until the garment was completed.

One of the inventions that greatly increased garment production was the band knife machine. Until the advent of this machine, workers cut out garment pieces by hand using shears or a short knife. This machine could cut around pattern pieces through many layers of fabric, cutting hundreds of garment pieces at the same time.

Mass production made it possible to finish garments faster. Each worker became more skilled and could work faster at his or her particular step. Mass production made more clothes available to more people at lower prices than ever before. Production increased and factories were operating around the clock making ready-made clothing.

3-9 In 1789, these garments were worn to George Washington's inaugural ball. The woman's dress shows the tight bodice common in the late 1700s. *Open Robe, 1789: Gift of Mrs. Henry Wheeler de Forest in memory of her husband. Court Suit, 1780s: Gift of E.Coster Wilmerding. Museum of the City of New York. 54.209ab; 50.256a-h*

3-10 These dresses were typical of those worn by women around 1900. *From the collection of American Textile History Museum, Lowell, Mass. Photographer: Anton Grassl 1100.19.3, 1100.63-A-B, 1996.24.3-A-B*

3-11 This gown illustrates the Empire style that was popular in the 1800s. *North Wind Picture Archives*

The Development of the Sewing Machine

As early as the mid 1700s, attempts to develop a machine to sew fabrics occurred. In 1830, Barthélemy Thimonnier—a Frenchman—patented a single-thread sewing machine. A number of these machines were made and used to make army uniforms. However, the machines were destroyed by a mob of tailors who feared becoming unemployed because of the machines.

The first really usable sewing machine did not come about until 1846. In this year, Elias Howe designed a two-thread sewing machine. With an eye-pointed needle and an underthread shuttle, this machine design allowed stitches to be *locked* into the fabric.

The first sewing machine that could sew continuously was developed by Isaac Singer in 1851. Howe's machine was powered by a hand crank. However, Singer's model used a foot treadle to make it run allowing the sewer to use both hands to guide the fabric. Use of electric motors to power sewing machines began in 1889.

Paper Patterns

During the time that all sewing was done at home, people exchanged patterns with each other. They were cut from muslin (a type of cotton fabric) or newsprint and were fitted to the body. Sewers made the pattern pieces larger or smaller as needed to fit family members.

Commercial paper patterns became available to home sewers during the middle of the nineteenth century. One tailor, Ebenezer Butterick, had many requests for patterns he was using. Butterick was the first to make patterns graded for different sizes. He decided to duplicate and sell them. He first created heavy cardboard templates, but soon realized he couldn't fold and ship the heavy patterns. Ebenezer tried lighter papers and discovered that tissue paper was ideal to work with and to package. In 1863, he started a company to send patterns to customers by mail order. The company is still in business today selling Butterick patterns.

In 1869, James McCall added another improvement to the graded-pattern business. He used drawings as guides to show the user how to layout and cut fabric from the tissue-paper patterns. In 1919, The McCall Pattern Company first sold printed patterns, 3-12.

1900 to 1950

In the early 1900s, technology led to widespread and rapid change. Electricity led to many laborsaving devices in the home. An increased interest in sports for women led to the creation of new styles that were less cumbersome and let women move more freely, 3–13. Women were beginning to venture into the work world as teachers, nurses, and clerks. With the invention of the typewriter, a new career opened for them. Ready-made, mass-produced clothing became available. The *shirtwaist*, a tailored white linen blouse, was the first ready-to-wear fashion item available to women. **Ready-to-wear (RTW)** is clothing made in factories in standard sizes and is completely ready for a person to wear.

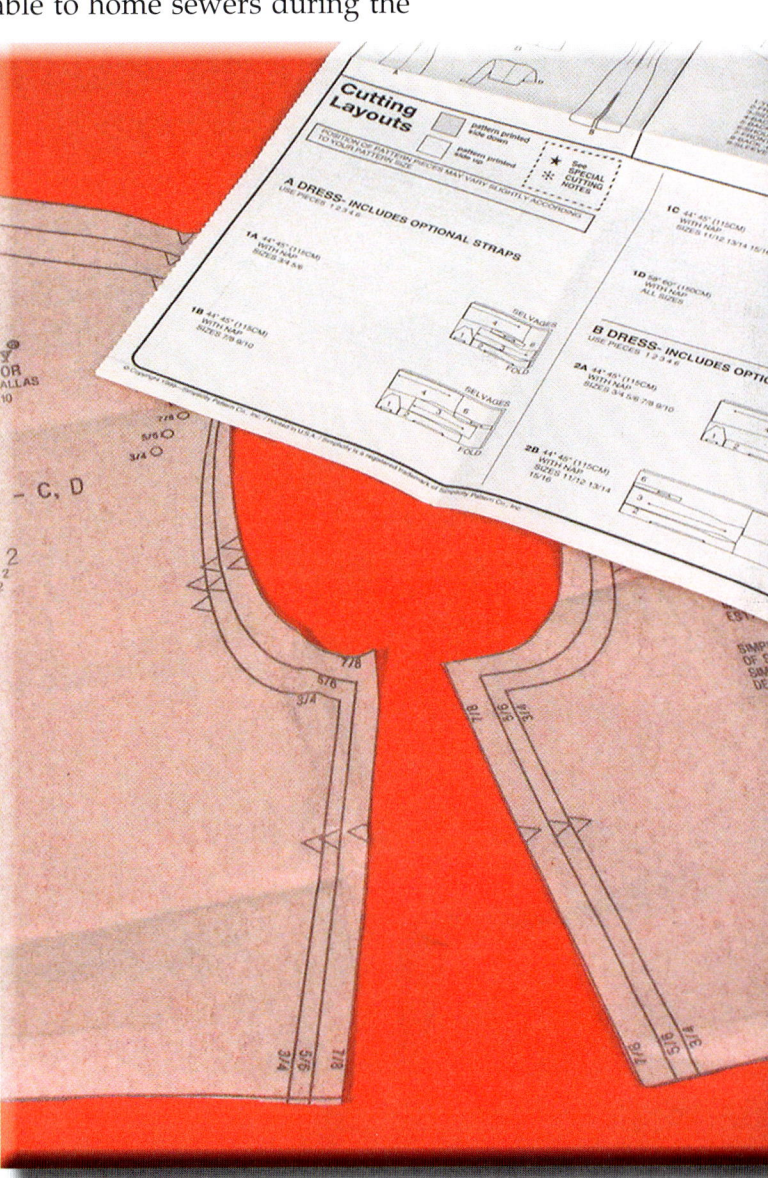

3-12 This is today's version of the paper patterns introduced in the 1860s.
McCalls Pattern Company

During World War I, women contributed to the war effort by working in offices, shops, and factories. Clothing needed to be less cumbersome and restrictive than in the past. Bustles, high necklines, and full sleeves disappeared. The result was a *boyish* look that included short-cropped hair and loose clothing, 3-14. Women factory workers wore bloomers. *Bloomers* were loose, full, trouser-like undergarments gathered in somewhere between the knee and ankle.

During World War II, civilian use of fabric was restricted since it was needed for military use. New fashions were limited to specific amounts of fabric. Women's clothing styles became shorter, sleeveless, and collarless. Zippers and trims were not allowed.

3-13 Can you imagine swimming in this swimsuit in 1910? It was not long before less bulky swimsuits became popular.
Marjorie Russell Clothing and Textile Center, Nevada State Museum, Carson City. Photographer: Scott Klette

3-14 This display of women's suits shows how styles changed from 1912 (center) to one worn in 1986 (left, back). *Valentine Museum*

The Development of Manufactured Fibers

Manufactured fibers are fibers not found in nature. Experimental production of manufactured fibers began around 1850. Rayon, originally sold as *artificial silk*, was the first manufactured fiber to be developed. Commercial production began in the United States in 1910.

Rayon is produced from cellulose, the fibrous substance in all plants. At first, *linters*—the small fibers left on cotton seeds after ginning—were the main source of cellulose. Later, wood from softwood trees became the cellulose source for rayon. Cellulose is also the fiber source for two other manufactured fibers: acetate and triacetate.

The other manufactured fibers—or **synthetics**—are made completely from chemicals. Four elements form the basis for these fibers. They are carbon (from petroleum or natural gas), hydrogen (from water), nitrogen (from air), and oxygen (from air).

In 1935, the DuPont Company became the first to make a synthetic fiber completely from chemicals. This fiber was nylon. Other synthetic fibers include polyester, olefin, acrylic, modacrylic, rubber, and spandex.

1950 to 2000

After World War II, the *New Look* became fashionable thanks to Christian Dior, a French designer. Dresses had longer, fuller skirts, **3-15**. During the 1950s, designers created fashions for the mature woman with a full, shapely figure.

The beginning of the 1960s saw another radical change in fashion. Because more than half of the population was under the age of 25, this group demanded its own look. Skinny, boyish figures were the inspiration for this design look. Along with the introduction of the miniskirt by Mary Quant in 1960, came changes in colors and accessories. Bright, bold colors and patterns with colorful stockings became popular, **3-16**.

During the Vietnam War in the late 1960s and early 1970s, many young people started the *hippie* movement to protest the war. Their clothing was very casual, emphasizing comfort and practicality. With less interest in dressing for status, jeans became the popular norm. Both men and women wore faded, tattered jeans along with tie-dyed clothing. *Unisex* dressing (similarity of dress worn by the sexes), which began in the 1950s, became more common. African-Americans became more interested in expressing their heritage. They adopted the Afro hairstyle and wore traditional African garments made of kente cloth. *Kente* is a colorful, intricately designed fabric of golds, yellows, reds, blacks, greens, and blues.

3-15 Christian Dior designed this afternoon ensemble in 1948. It illustrates the long, full skirts for which he was known. *Fine Arts Museums of San Francisco, Gift of Mrs. Eloise Heidland, 1982.18.4a-b; Hat gift of Mr. E. J. Larson, 1984.24.5.*

3-16 Italian designer Emilio Pucci was known for his vibrant colors and patterns. In 1965, he designed this special collection for Braniff Airlines hostesses.
Emilio Pucci, Braniff Airlines Hostess Uniforms, 1965-66, Texas Fashion Collection, University of North Texas. Photo by Michael Bodycomb.

In the early 1970s, President Richard Nixon went to China to resume relations with the Chinese government. Soon afterward, the mandarin collar and Asian designs became fashionable in clothing and jewelry. The interest in physical fitness led to more clothing items designed for physical activity, such as jogging suits and running shorts. Because of the development of activewear clothes, Spandex, an elastic fiber, was increasingly popular. It allowed for more give in garments used for movement.

The 1980s saw women entering the world of work in record numbers. They not only went to work, but many desired to climb the corporate ladder. To do so, they needed to be taken seriously. These women dressed in conservative business suits—often referred to as *power suits*—featuring tailored jackets with straight skirts covering the knees.

Television shows, such as *Dallas* and *Dynasty* were a strong influence on the styles of the 80s. Princess Diana became a fashion leader following her marriage to Prince Charles. Women's blouses, jackets, and dresses featured large shoulder pads, **3-17**. Big hairstyles and lots of glitz were popular. Hawaiian shirts and leather jackets were popular with men.

The 1990s began with the introduction of the *grunge look*. Both sexes wore flannel shirts and other outdoor clothing, creating an unkempt look. Acid-wash jeans became popular, as were spandex tights and leggings worn with short dresses, oversized sweaters, and long sweatshirts. Many wore sports team jerseys and jackets with basketball shorts. Preppy styles of polo shirts and jeans were made popular by the designer Tommy Hilfiger. The oversized baggy hip-hop look became popular among some teens.

Casual dress for the office became acceptable at many companies. Men could wear khaki slacks, button-down shirts, and polo shirts to work. Neckties were optional. Men and women alike began wearing classic blazers with blue jeans. The dressing down of the 90s was in sharp contrast to the glitz of the 80s.

Textiles and Apparel Today

Today, people in Western societies are freer to dress as they wish. There are general social standards regarding dress, but the rules are less rigid. The trend is toward more casual dress, even for office workers. There is a wide variety in types of clothing available due to mass production. More people have more wealth, allowing them to buy more clothes than in earlier generations.

Media influences how people dress, especially movies, music, and television. Celebrities of music and film are important promoters of the latest fashions. When a clothing style appears on television or the Internet, people become more aware of it. This is a global awareness. Fashion styles popular in one country can quickly become popular in other countries around the world. Retail stores in the U.S. often have branches in foreign countries. This allows consumers almost anywhere in the world to have access to the latest fashions.

During the last 30 years, almost 250 different fiber variations have been manufactured. Currently, synthetic fibers account for 94 percent of worldwide fiber production. North American companies make only 14 percent of the synthetic fibers, down by 9 percent over the last 20 years. Asian countries produce 65 percent of the world's supply of synthetic fibers.

3-17 This 1980s *power suit* by Yves Saint Laurent represented the growing presence of women in the workplace. © The Museum at FIT

Summary

- Many events throughout history have influenced the fabrics used, the designs created, and the uses made of clothing. Influences have been cultural, social, religious, economic, political, and technological.
- Early people used animal skins for clothing. The raising of plants and animals led to the development of fabrics using natural fibers. Natural fibers are fibers taken from nature, such as cotton, flax, wool, and silk.
- With the progression of civilization, people began living in villages. The villages grew into large communities or societies. These societies established governments where rulers, nobles, priests, and warriors maintained absolute power over the great masses of people.
- In ancient Egypt, Greece, and Rome, general styles of clothing survived for thousands of years.
- Trousers were introduced during the sixth century. This garment style marked a significant change in the way people dressed.
- The Industrial Revolution led to the production of textiles using spinning frames and steam-powered looms. Mass production greatly increased garment production, as did the invention of the sewing machine.
- Manufactured fibers are fibers not found in nature. They are a fairly recent development. Experimental production of manufactured fibers began around 1850. Rayon was the first manufactured fiber to be developed. It was produced in 1910.
- From the 1950s to 2000, such historical events as the Vietnam War, a reopening of diplomatic relations with China, and the marriage of Princess Diana and Prince Charles greatly influenced worldwide fashions. Television shows and celebrities in music and film also greatly influenced fashions.

Graphic Organizer

Create a KWHL chart to identify what you know, what you want to learn, how you want to learn it, and what you have learned about the history of fashion.

What I Know	Want to Know	How to Learn	What I Learned

Review the Facts

1. Give an example of a recent fashion trend that reflects a social influence.
2. Summarize a historical event and how it influenced fashion.
3. In which type of economic system does the consumer play an important role?
4. List two developments in technology that have led to more and improved fabrics and apparel.
5. How were animal skins prepared and sewn in prehistoric times?
6. Name four natural fibers.
7. Describe two articles of clothing that were worn during ancient times.
8. What event that occurred during the Middle Ages most affected the fashion and apparel of Europe?
9. Name four inventors and their inventions that affected the textile and apparel industry.
10. Contrast manufactured fibers with natural fibers.
11. Contrast the fashions worn by women during and immediately following World War II.

Think Critically

12. **Interpret facts.** Which historical event do you think had the greatest impact on apparel design? Write a summary expressing your interpretation of the facts. What data support your interpretations?
13. **Draw conclusions.** Clothing in earlier times often reflected a person's wealth and status. What conclusions can you draw about how the clothes of today reflect wealth and status? Make a list of your conclusions to share with the class.
14. **Compare and contrast.** How do the factors that influenced mass production during the Industrial Revolution compare and contrast to those that influence mass production today?
15. **Identify evidence.** Which do you think are the most significant fashion changes that occurred from the 1950s to 2000? Give evidence that supports your reasoning.

Apparel Applications

16. **Archaeological research.** Use Internet or print resources to research archaeological evidence of textile and garment use by prehistoric people. Use presentation software to prepare a visually enhanced report of your findings for the class.
17. **Fashion collage.** Collect pictures or drawings of fashions worn at various times in history. Create a fashion collage and note how each was influenced by political, economic, or technological events in history.
18. **Fashion time line.** As a class project, develop a time line showing major social, religious, political, and technological events of the 20th century. Include the fashions that were popular at those times.

19. **Historic-fashions tour.** Tour a museum that features exhibits of historic fashions. Prepare a report for the class.
20. **Cultural research.** Research your cultural heritage and the apparel worn by your ancestors. Use a school-approved social networking site to share what you have learned.

Academic Connections

21. **Social studies.** Conduct an oral history interview with an older adult who remembers World War II. Ask how the war effort influenced fashions and fabrics during that time. Share a summary of your interview with the class.
22. **Writing.** Choose a decade of the 20th century. Use Internet or print resources to research the fashions of that decade as well as the influences on those fashions. Write a report on your findings. Enhance your report with images if possible.

Workplace Links

23. **Sales presentation.** Presume you are an inventor from the Industrial Revolution. Give an oral "sales presentation" to the class. Use visual aids to explain how your invention works. Try to convince your audience why they should give your invention a try. Conduct Internet or library research to prepare for your presentation.
24. **Interpreting information.** Presume you work for a children's clothing manufacturer. The marketing team at your company needs some historical information on children's clothing in the 20th century for a new marketing campaign celebrating the company's 100th anniversary. Locate at least three reliable information sources. Write a report to the marketing team summarizing your key findings.

Textiles and Apparel History

Alone or with a team, prepare an FCCLA *Illustrated Talk* STAR Event on the topic of textile and apparel history. Identify cultural, social, religious, political, economic, and technological influences on clothing over time. What specific factors influenced clothing in your community or region? Follow the presentation requirements in the *STAR Events Manual*. See your adviser for information as needed.

Then give your presentation at several school or community events. Step up to the challenge and give your presentation at your FCCLA state competition.

Chapter 4

The Textile and Apparel Industry

Chapter Objectives

After studying this chapter, you will be able to
- **analyze** the three segments of today's textile and apparel industry.
- **summarize** the structure of the textile and apparel industry.
- **describe** occupations and careers in the textile production, apparel production, and the retail segments and the education and training they require.
- **summarize** the concept of vertical integration.

Key Terms

research
development
marketing
forecasting
merchandising plan
wholesale

retail
market week
fashion center
apparel mart
custom-made
retailers

fashion merchandising
fashion promotion
commission
vertical integration

Reading with Purpose

Make a list of everything you already know about the topic of this chapter. As you read the chapter, check off the items that the chapter covers. Write notes on concepts that are new to you.

One of the biggest business success stories of the last 200 years is the amazing growth of the textile and apparel industry. It became one of the largest industries in the United States. In recent years, however, foreign companies are competing for more of this market. Many U.S. textile mills have had decrease production or close altogether. More apparel manufacturing also occurs in foreign countries, affecting U.S. apparel producers.

The textile and apparel industry consists of three segments. These segments include

- *Textile production.* This first segment of the industry focuses on production of fabrics for apparel and other uses. It deals with fibers, yarns, dyes, finishes, and methods of fabric production.
- *Apparel production.* The second segment includes all the steps in turning fabrics into apparel, including the design process and garment manufacturing.
- *The retail segment.* The third segment includes all the business activities involved with selling fashion items to consumers. This ranges from showing customers what is new in designs, colors, and fabrics and convincing them to buy the new fashions.

85

Each of these segments is a separate field, but all relate to textiles and clothing. If you choose a career in textiles and clothing, it could be in one of these three areas.

Textile Production Segment

Textile production includes all the people and processes involved in making fibers and fabrics. The ranchers who raise sheep for wool and the farmers who grow cotton are part of this industry. The chemists who develop manufactured fibers are part of the textile industry, too.

In the United States, fabrics for clothing and accessories make up the largest share of textile production. Floor coverings—such as carpets and rugs—make up the second largest share. Industrial products utilize the third largest share of textile production. Use of textiles in industry ranges from making conveyor belts, to filters, and space suits. Other industrial textile uses include nose cones (for aerospace vehicles), football-field turf, and artificial hearts. The home furnishings industry uses the remaining share for various products. These include draperies, curtains, and upholstery fabrics, as well as bath and kitchen towels, blankets, sheets, and pillowcases. See **4-1** for a partial list of the many uses for textile fibers.

The Structure of the Textile Industry

The long road from fibers to fabrics requires many processes and thousands of workers. Four stages of production make up the basic structure of the textile industry.

- *Stage one: fiber production.* The first stage in producing textiles is fiber production. The natural fibers of cotton and linen come from cotton and

4-1 All of these items have something in common. They are all made of textiles.

Uses for Textiles		
Home Furnishings	*Medical Uses*	*Industry*
Sheets	Adhesive tape	Conveyor belts
Pillowcases	Bandages	Filters
Blankets	Antibacterial wound dressings	Safety nets
Bedspreads		Electronic circuit boards
Towels	Surgical gowns and masks	Protective garments for firefighters, police, and military
Rugs	Disposable sheets	
Carpets	Artificial hearts and arteries	
Lampshades	*Transportation*	Protective gloves for chefs
Tablecloths	Tire cords	Building insulation
Napkins	Seat belts	Hoses
Curtains	Seat covers	Mailbags
Draperies	Air bags	
Upholstery	Brake linings	
Flags	Boat sails	

flax plants. Texas grows most cotton in the United States. Wool comes from the fleece of sheep, and silk comes from cocoons spun by silkworms. Various chemical companies produce manufactured fibers.

- *Stage two: yarn production.* The spinning of fibers into yarns takes place in the second stage of textile production. Most of the mills remaining in the U.S. are in the states of North Carolina, South Carolina, and Georgia.
- *Stage three: fabric production.* Some textile mills also weave or knit yarns into fabrics during the fabric production stage. Looms and knitting machines produce unfinished cloth.
- *Stage four: fabric finishing.* During the final stage, fabric finishing occurs. Dyeing, printing, and other special treatments give fabrics the desired performance characteristics. Fabrics may be water repellent, fireproof, or wrinkle resistant. Some companies specialize only in this stage of production.

After the fourth stage, fabrics are ready for sale to apparel manufacturers or other companies requiring fabrics in their products. Some fabrics go to supply the needs of the home-sewing market. Coordination of this stage in the textile segment takes place in sales offices and showrooms usually located in New York City.

Textile Designing

Before fabric production begins, fabric designs must exist. *Textile designers* develop designs for fabrics, color combinations, patterns, prints, and weaves. In some textile companies, designers work at drawing boards to sketch their designs. Most designers today use computer design programs to create their designs, **4-2**. Finally, the designs go into the production of fabric.

The difference between textile designing and fashion designing is important. Textile designers produce fabric designs. Fashion designers work with finished fabrics. They design garments and accessories for men, women, and children.

Textile designers must have a technical background as well as creative skills. They need to understand what machines can and cannot do in the production of fabric. They must also be familiar with the latest changes in finishes, dyes, and equipment. They need to understand production costs. In this way, they can be creative and still meet the needs of the company.

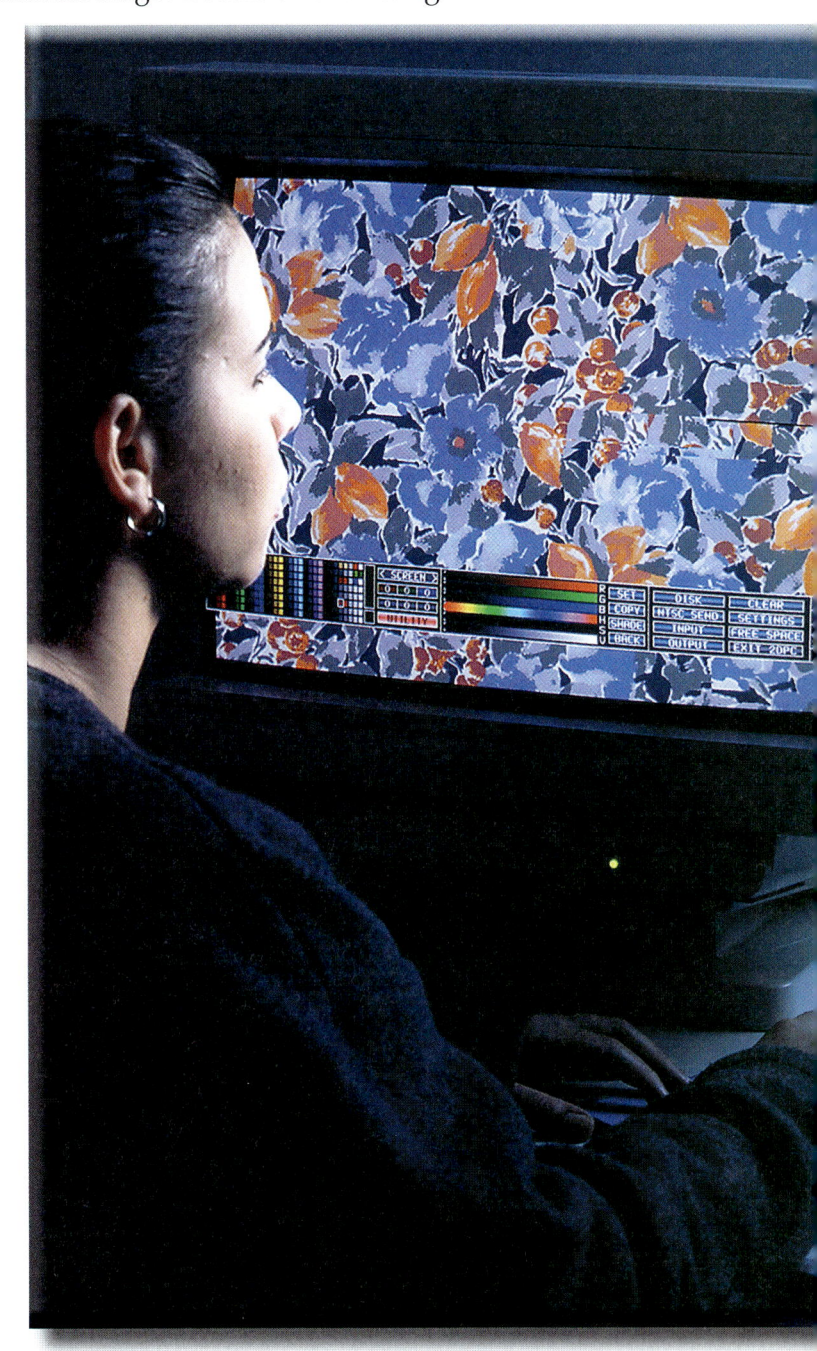

4-2 This textile designer uses CAD software to aid her in the creation of new textile patterns. *Fashion Institute of Technology*

Textile Converters

Many decisions about the production of fibers, yarns, and fabrics are the responsibilities of *textile converters*. They decide what fibers to use, what widths and weights of fabrics to weave or knit, and how many yards to produce. They select dye colors and choose finishes that will help the fabrics perform as expected. Some companies specialize only in this stage of fabric production.

Setting prices—or *costing the fabric*—is another task of textile converters. They compute all the costs involved in producing the fabric. Textile converters then add a margin of profit to the production cost to determine the fabric's selling price.

Manufacturing

Textile plant operations include many processes such as spinning, dyeing, weaving, knitting, and finishing. Each of these steps requires special machinery. The nature of each job varies with the kind of machine the job requires. Most operate by electronic or computerized controls.

Some employees who use machines in their work are *spinners*, *colorists*, *loom operators*, and *machine operators*. A high school diploma is often adequate background for some entry-level machine operators. They usually receive an hourly wage.

Textile Engineers

Textile engineers play an important part in textile manufacturing. Textile engineers may have a college degree in chemical, computer, electrical, industrial, or mechanical engineering. A *chemical engineer* might work in a department where fabric dyeing or printing occurs. A *computer engineer* often ensures correct programming for machines to properly make the fabrics. *Industrial engineers* oversee the performance of all production operations. They look for better and less costly ways of handling production without reducing quality.

Plant engineers make sure that all systems operate properly. These include machinery operation, heating, air conditioning, electrical, materials handling, and environmental control. They are expert problem-solvers in all areas of production.

Laboratory Technicians

Laboratory technicians perform tests on fibers, yarns, and fabrics in a laboratory, 4-3. They make sure the products meet certain standards of quality. Machines test how well and how long a fabric will wear under certain conditions. Lab technicians may perform various tests during many steps of production. This assures quality control throughout the process, resulting in a superior finished product.

Lab technicians learn textile technology programs in colleges or technical schools. They organize their own work and follow precise instructions. Lab technicians do detailed work and write accurate, thorough reports of test results.

Research and Development

Developing new products to meet consumer demand and finding ways to produce these products are important parts of the textile industry. **Research** is working to find new products such as fibers, weaves, dyes, and finishing techniques. **Development** means finding practical ways to use the products the researchers create. Another name for the combination of these processes is *R & D*.

A researcher generally has a college degree in chemical, mechanical, electrical, or textile engineering; physics; or textile chemistry. An advanced degree increases a researcher's value to the company and may be a requirement for some jobs, **4-4**.

Marketing

Marketing includes all of the activities involved in creating and selling profitable products. Before selling fabrics occurs, other processes take place. Purchasing the right raw materials—such as fibers and yarns—needs to occur. Manufacturers must decide what raw materials to buy and what fabrics to manufacture. They base their decisions on careful studies of what their customers want.

Market analysts are the people who study fashion changes and consumer demands. **Forecasting** is projecting future market trends for the coming months and years. Market-analysis information helps manufacturers decide what fabrics to buy for the new fashions. Because fabrics must be ready when clothing manufacturers want to buy them, analysts' must do their research far in advance of this need.

Textile sales associates are another part of the marketing division. Selling is the last step in the marketing process. Sales associates show fabric samples to manufacturers of men's, women's, and children's clothing. The manufacturers buy the fabrics they will use to produce garments for the next fashion season. Sales associates also sell their fabrics to fabric departments in stores and to fabric shops. Marketing and sales careers are highly competitive and often require a great deal of travel.

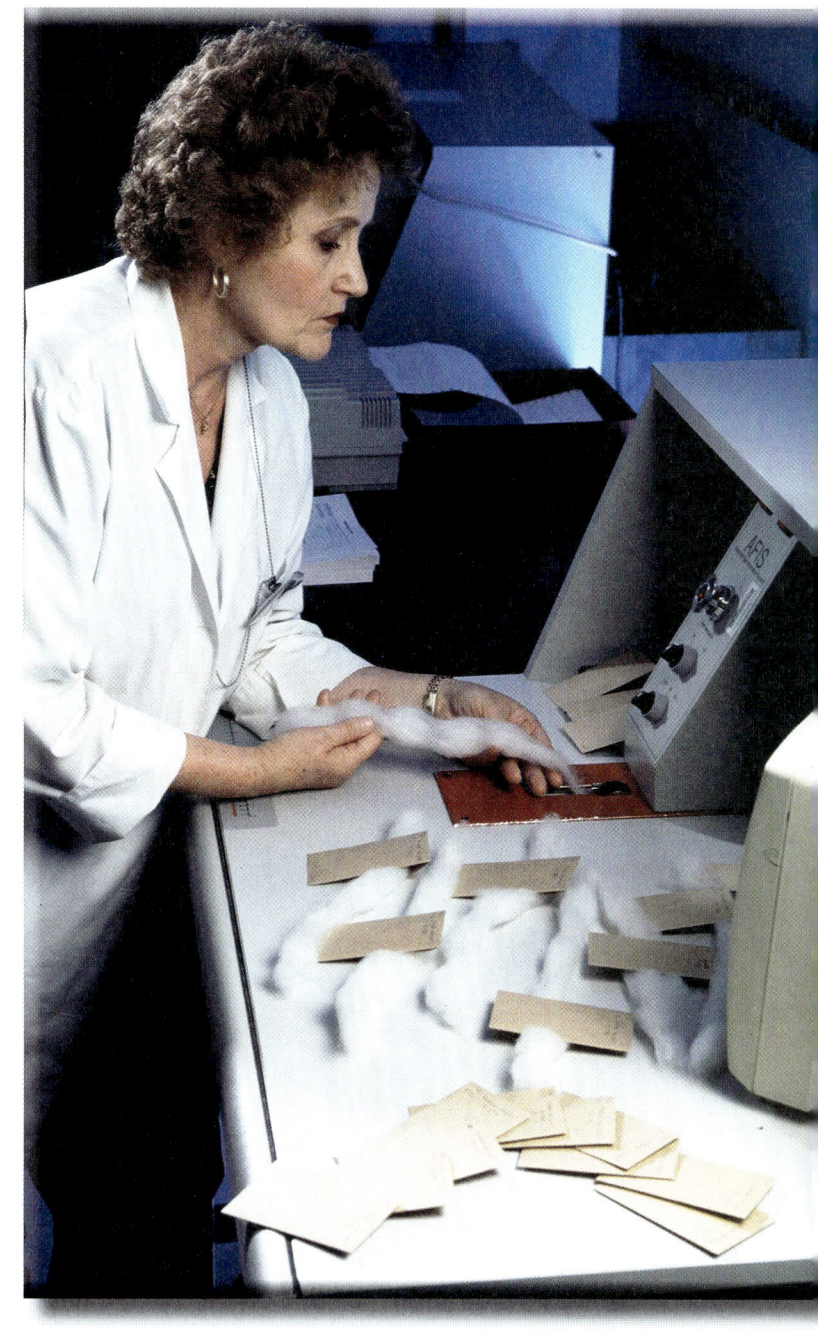

4-3 A laboratory technician is testing the quality factors of cotton samples. *Agricultural Research Service, USDA*

Apparel Production Segment

Apparel production includes all the people and processes involved in designing and making garments. It begins with the fabrics that eventually become items of apparel. The designing of garments, pattern making, cutting, sewing, assembling, and distribution of finished items to stores are all included in the process.

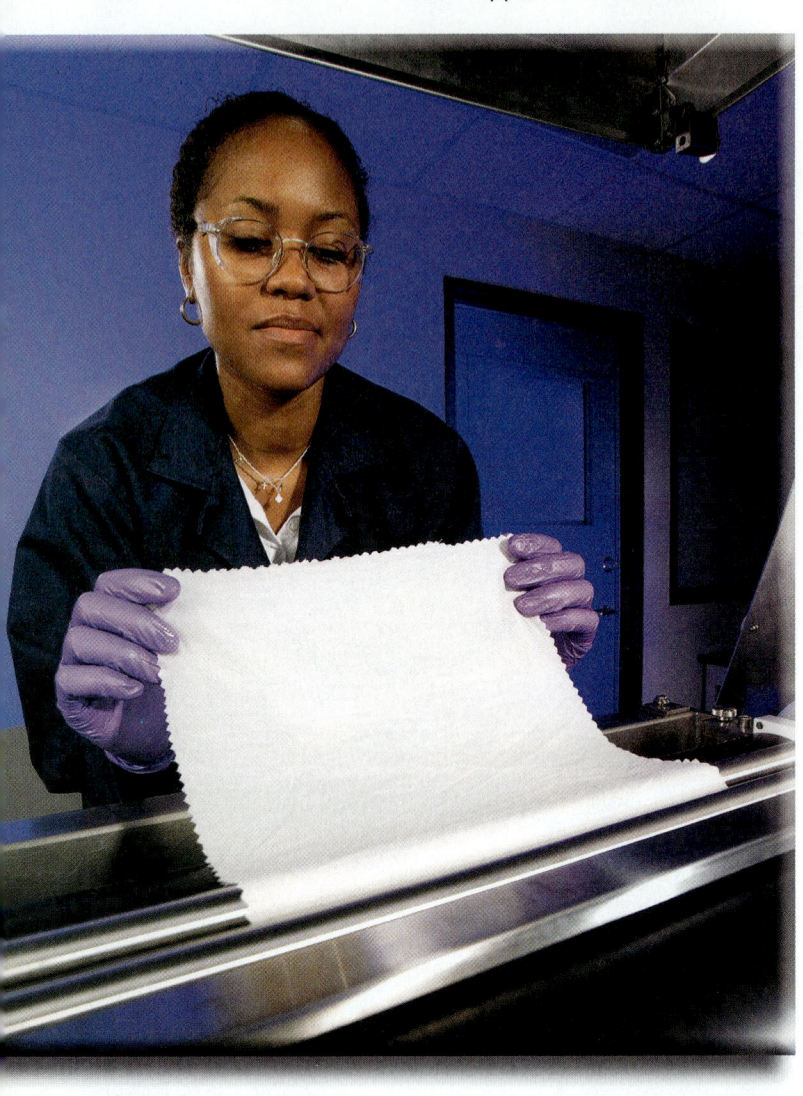

4-4 Advanced textile technology courses could lead to a career in research and development. *Agricultural Research Service, USDA*

The largest concentration of garment factories is in California. On the West coast, Los Angeles is the headquarters for the garment industry. The state of New York has hundreds of factories that produce garments. The leading manufacturers have design and marketing offices there, too. In addition, small garment factories are located throughout the United States.

The Structure of Apparel Companies

Apparel production companies have various departments or divisions within their companies. Each of these divisions has certain responsibilities that lead to shipment of garments to retail stores. The typical departments are responsible for:

- Research and merchandising
- Design and product development
- Production
- Sales and marketing

Research and Merchandising

Apparel production begins with research. A firm's staff tries to forecast what their customers will buy. Their goal is to have the right products, at the right price, at the right time so the company will be profitable.

Apparel designers interpret these trends and create sketches and sample designs. These become a part of a **merchandising plan**—the producer's plans for creating a line of designs for a given season. There are four production seasons: Spring, Summer, Fall I, and Fall II (Winter). Designers show the sample designs to retail buyers who then make their selections.

The selected designs are prepared for production. An apparel worker creates the master patterns in standard sizes for the design. Fabrics, fasteners, thread, and trims are ordered. The cutting and sewing typically begins about six months before the clothes appear in retail stores. The trend in recent years, however, is to reduce this time to four months.

Design and Product Development

Fashion designers create the designs and ideas for new clothes and accessories. They may specialize in women's, men's, or children's clothing. Others specialize further in certain types of garments such as men's coats, women's dresses, or children's sleepwear. Some may choose to specialize in an accessory such as shoes, hats, or handbags.

A fashion designer is the first person involved in making a garment. The first step is an idea. The designer makes sketches until he or she finds one satisfactory, 4-5. Then a *sample maker* sews the design together. A live model displays the sample garment for the designers and production managers. They consider the design itself, the latest fashion trends, and the costs of making garments from that design. If they accept the design, the garment is put into production.

Very few designers get a first job as a top designer. They usually begin in another position. Eventually they move up into a design position. Some entry-level jobs that may lead to designer positions are *sample maker*, *sketching assistant*, *sketcher*, and *design assistant*.

Becoming a designer requires special training. High school courses in art, clothing and textiles, computer science, history, and psychology are helpful. Fashion institutes, trade schools, and universities offer two- and four-year programs specializing in fashion design.

Production

The garment-making process involves many workers who perform the multiple steps for completing a garment. After the sample maker completes the designer's new garment, designers and producers may make changes or additions. Then a production *pattern maker* makes a perfect master pattern. *Pattern graders* take the master pattern and make it into a wide range of sizes. They make reductions or enlargements of each piece of the master pattern to get the different sizes. Most manufacturers, however, use computer programs to create the master patterns and the various sizes.

After grading or sizing the patterns, spreaders lay out the fabric on a long table. The fabric must be smooth and straight. A machine helps spreaders create many layers of fabric.

Markers are employees who decide how to place the pattern pieces to prevent as much fabric waste as possible. When making thousands of garments, saving a few inches of fabric per garment can add up to many yards. Most production plants have computer systems that place the pattern pieces electronically.

At this point, *cutters* cut through the layers of fabric with power saws or electric cutting machines. Computerized knife cutters, water-jet cutters, or lasers cut through layers of fabrics, 4-6. *Lasers* use intense beams of light that vaporize the fabric, making fast and precise cuts. Such cutters may cut through as many as 100 layers of fabric often a foot high at a time.

The hundreds of pieces of cloth are numbered, gathered, and put into bundles by sorters or assemblers. The bundles then move to the sewing room.

4-5 This fashion designer is sketching her ideas. *Shutterstock*

4-6 The high-speed computerized cutting machines of today can cut single layers or multiple layers of fabric quickly and precisely.
Gerber Technology

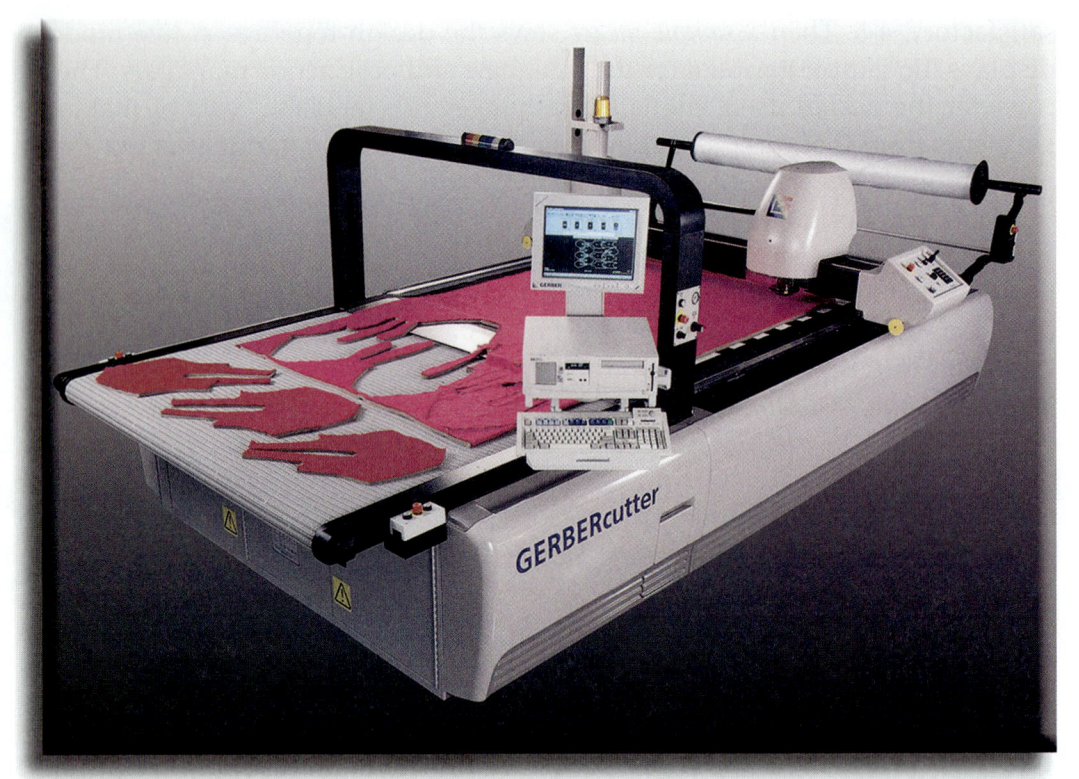

Here *sewing machine operators* sew the pieces together generally in assembly-line fashion. In this piecework system, one person does one specific task often using a specialized machine. For example, workers may sew bundles of collars at one station and sleeves at another. Later in the assembly line, other workers sew the parts together. With very expensive clothes, each sewing machine operator may sew an entire garment.

Finishers sew the final details on garments. They add outside stitching or any hand sewing the garments require. *Trimmers* remove loose threads, lint, and spots from the finished products. *Pressers* remove wrinkles and press creases and pleats in place on garments. The final task is attaching the labels or hangtags.

Many entry-level jobs in apparel production do not require education beyond high school. Because of the technical nature of most jobs on the production line, employers generally offer on-the-job training or apprenticeship programs. However, training from trade or technical schools could be helpful in obtaining a job or advancing to a better job.

Engineering and Management

In addition to production line workers, other people have careers in the production process. These people may have college degrees in apparel production, apparel management, or engineering. Workers in engineering and management have good communication and problem-solving skills which are essential for dealing with a variety of people and giving clear and accurate instructions. Engineering and management positions include

- *Plant managers.* These individuals have total responsibility for what happens in the company. Another name for plant manager is *chief engineer*.
- *Production managers.* Estimating production costs and scheduling work flow in the plant are primary responsibilities for production managers. They supervise all aspects of production activities in the plant.

- *Production engineers.* Managing a variety of engineering projects is the main responsibility of production engineers. They help select machinery and choose operation methods for top performance.
- *Costing engineers.* These individuals determine the price of producing an item of clothing or an accessory.
- *Quality control engineers.* Developing standards of quality for garments and meeting those standards are the key responsibilities of quality control engineers. They conduct tests of products at each step in the manufacturing process to check for quality.

Sales and Marketing

Marketing in the apparel industry is primarily wholesale. To understand wholesale, you must understand retail. **Wholesale** means to sell quantities of goods for resale. In contrast, **retail** means to sell small quantities of goods to consumers. In the apparel industry, manufacturers sell to retail buyers who represent shops and department stores (wholesale). Shops and department stores sell to individual customers (retail).

New fashions are in the process of production at least a *season* or six months before they are ready for sale in stores. When samples are ready, retail buyers view them in showrooms during market weeks. **Market weeks** are those time periods when apparel companies offer the next season's fashion lines.

During market weeks, retail-store buyers come to the **fashion centers** to view the new collections and make their selections. The U.S. fashion centers are New York, Los Angeles, Dallas, Chicago, Atlanta, and Miami. In several large cities, such as Atlanta, Dallas, and Chicago, there are also *apparel marts*. **Apparel marts** are buildings where many garment manufacturers have permanent showrooms and sales offices. They show their lines or collections and take orders from the buyers for their retail stores.

Manufacturers often hold special fashion shows for buyers. Models wear the new clothing designs to help convince buyers to order them. Fashion writers and fashion-promotion specialists also attend these invitation-only shows. They gather information about the new fashions. On returning to their home cities, they inform the public about the newest fashions and colors for the coming season.

As manufacturers receive orders from retail buyers, they schedule clothes for production. The stores receive deliveries in about three months. The clothes that buyers order in spring are in stores by summer so customers can buy them in time to wear for fall.

Custom Work in Apparel Production

Many people have their clothing **custom-made**. This means they ask someone to make garments especially for them. A desire to have one-of-a-kind garments could be one reason for wearing custom-made clothes. Figure features that prevent ready-made clothing from fitting well may be another reason.

Tailoring is a form of custom work. Suits and coats are the garments most often tailored. It is time-consuming, but many people are willing to pay high prices for well-tailored garments, **4-7**.

Tailors take a great deal of pride in their work. The finished garments often look nicer and fit better than most ready-to-wear clothing. The tailor's shop often sells fabric, too, which provides additional income for the tailor.

The Retail Segment

The third segment in the textile and apparel industry is the retail segment. After the garments are through production, they are ready for sale to consumers. **Retailers** are businesses that buy garments from manufacturers and sell them to customers. Retailers include department stores, discount chains, specialty stores (carrying specific kinds of apparel), and Internet and mail-order companies.

Fashion merchandising includes all phases of planning, buying, and selling of apparel. It is the central function of retailers. An important part of selling is fashion promotion. **Fashion promotion** includes advertising, setting up window and store displays, media publicity, and such special events as fashion shows. The intention of these efforts is to increase clothing sales and to move the merchandise the retailer orders.

Fashion merchandising and promotion involves many people. Some of their job titles are *merchandise managers, buyers, sales associates, market researchers, fashion coordinators, display directors, illustrators, writers,* and *models*.

Merchandise Managers

Merchandise managers are responsible for the operation of one or more departments within a store. This could be women's coats, children's wear, or men's shoes. New shops within the store such as boutiques may be the result of creative merchandise managers.

Merchandising managers plan seasonal sales, promotional sales, and special events. They are responsible for deciding what merchandise to sell and at what price. Long-range planning is necessary for successful events.

Merchandise managers work closely with sales associates to help them keep their departments looking attractive and up-to-date, 4-8. In-service meetings and training programs inform sales associates about the latest fashion trends and new methods of selling merchandise. The merchandising managers schedule these meetings.

Merchandising managers supervise and set budgets for the store's buyers. A budget tells the buyer how much money is available to spend at market for new merchandise.

A high school education could eventually lead to a merchandise manager's job after many years in retailing. However, a college degree with a major in

4-7 Tailors create custom-made garments for their clients.
Shutterstock

fashion merchandising, business, or marketing makes obtaining employment and advancement easier.

Buyers

Buyers are responsible for selecting the clothes and accessories to sell in the stores they represent. They may go to major fashion centers or markets several times a year. After viewing manufacturer's merchandise at the market, buyers order the items and amounts they want to be delivered to their stores. Buyers who work for large stores or chains of stores may travel worldwide looking for unusual merchandise for their customers.

In a specialty shop, a buyer may be responsible for all the merchandise the store sells. Large stores may have buyers for each department. In a small store, the merchandising manager and buyer may be the same person.

Keeping records about what customers are buying in their stores is a buyer's major responsibility. Computerization allows buyers to update such records quickly and easily. Buyers are interested in what styles, colors, and sizes are selling best. A store's profits depend largely on the decisions of its buyers. If items do not sell, it may take lowering the price—possibly several times—in order to move the merchandise. The store may not make any profit, or it may even lose money.

Buyers work closely with merchandise managers, display directors, fashion coordinators, and sales associates. Everyone must work together to maintain the image the store wants to present to the public. This image could be that of an exclusive boutique, a high-end department store, or the best budget-priced store in town.

A high school education is a must for buyers. However, postsecondary education from a university, technical school, or fashion institute is best. Business courses provide valuable background for the budgeting and pricing buyers do. Training in display and advertising make a buyer's job easier and advancement faster.

4-8 Merchandise managers are responsible for overseeing the operations of one or more departments within a store.
Shutterstock

Sales Associates

Sales associates are important employees in a store. They often develop long-term relationships with devoted customers. They learn the tastes of these customers and inform them when garments they might like arrive at the store.

Sales associates are the only store employees that most customers ever meet. Customers are also pleased when sales associates can answer questions about fabrics, fashions, garment construction, and care instructions. Pleasant and helpful associates leave customers with a lasting positive impression, *4-9*.

Good sales associates keep the merchandise displays attractive. They receive payments and package the items they sell. Sales associates may also be responsible for handling exchanges and returns.

4-9 A sales associate often determines whether or not a customer returns to shop again in the store.
Shutterstock

A high school diploma is a requirement for full-time sales associates. Many stores offer a short training period before a person starts to work as well as on-the-job training. Wages for sales associates may be at an hourly rate, salary, or salary plus a percentage of their total sales, or a **commission**.

A degree in merchandising, marketing, retailing, or a related area helps sales associates advance quickly in their positions. Colleges and fashion institutes offer courses in fashion merchandising, sales promotion, consumer motivation, retail store management, accounting, and business law.

Stock Clerk

A *stock clerk* is an entry-level position in retail. Although it is entry-level, it is an important job. Stock clerks keep any business running smoothly. Sales associates depend on stock clerks for such duties as receiving merchandise from the delivery trucks, comparing the delivery tickets with the merchandise received, and preparing price tags.

Market Researchers

Market researchers study what customers want and need. They survey boutiques, department stores, discount stores, and other retail outlets. They find out what is selling and what customers would buy if available on the market. Manufacturers, designers, and buyers receive this information. It influences the textile industry and apparel production as well as fashion merchandising and promotion. Market research generally requires a college degree in marketing.

Fashion Coordinators

Fashion coordinators promote their stores and merchandise. They visit wholesale and retail markets to gather information about what is happening in the fashion world. They relay this information to merchandise managers and buyers. Fashion coordinators also work with the advertising and publicity departments for their stores. This allows the stores to correlate advertising, promotional, and merchandising efforts.

Planning fashion shows is usually a responsibility of fashion coordinators. They select garments and accessories from different departments within their stores. They hire the models and write the scripts for the shows. The day of a show, the fashion coordinator is generally the person who presents the show, 4-10.

Other titles for fashion coordinators include *fashion directors, promotion directors,* or *fashion consultants.* They work for magazines, advertising agencies, and Internet and mail-order companies as well as retail stores. Most have degrees from colleges or professional schools of fashion, but a few advance from sales positions. Successful fashion coordinators work tactfully with people, speak to large audiences, and schedule time wisely.

Display Directors

Display directors create the attractive displays you see in store windows. When showing a suit or dress, all the accessories to go with it are also on display. A suit display may include a shirt, necktie, handkerchief, belt, socks, and shoes. A dress display may show jewelry, belts, scarves, and shoes. These displays may center on a theme such as vacation time or the beginning of spring. You are encouraged to buy not only the main garment, but everything that goes with it, too.

The fashion coordinator works closely with the display director to make sure the displays present the right fashion image for the store. Together they plan all displays.

A high school education is a requirement for display directors. Courses in technical art, design, and fashion illustration are valuable. Trade schools, community colleges, and universities offer these courses.

4-10 Fashion coordinators are responsible for putting on fashion shows that feature the store's apparel. *Shutterstock*

Fashion Illustrators

Fashion illustrators work for retail stores, pattern companies, and advertising agencies. The work of fashion illustrators is complex. In each illustration, they show construction details (seams, topstitching, trims), fabric textures (stiff, bulky, flimsy), fabric designs (prints, plaids, solids), and fashionable accessories (hats, shoes, jewelry). In addition, each one must be an attractive picture that will catch the eye of the viewer.

Successful fashion illustrators are artistic, creative, and have an interest in clothing. They generally receive training at a university or a special school of art or fashion. Useful courses include art, clothing and textiles, history, and psychology.

Fashion Writers

Fashion writers must keep in contact with manufacturers and leaders in the fashion industry. Then they can tell the public about new trends in fashion as soon as they occur. Manufacturers and advertisers send press kits to fashion writers that include detailed descriptions and photographs of new fashions.

Large newspapers have fashion writers and editors. Through regular columns or articles, they show and explain new fashions to readers. Many fashion writers and editors work for magazines and trade journals. Often their assignments are in a specific area such as clothing, textiles, accessories, hairstyles, or makeup. Successful fashion writers and editors have a flair for writing combined with a keen sense of fashion trends. Almost all jobs for fashion writers require a college degree in journalism and/or textiles and clothing.

Fashion Models

Fashion models serve many needs in photos for press releases, Internet and mail-order catalogs, pattern catalogs, and advertisements, **4-11**. Models are also essential in fashion shows. Fashion designers use models to show their latest lines in fashion shows during market weeks. Seminars, trade shows, and conventions are other popular places for fashion shows. Some large department stores and leading restaurants also feature them. They are often during midday for shoppers to see the latest fashions.

For models, beauty is not as important as posture. Their goal is to make the garments look their best. Successful models are well-groomed and have a flair for effective movements. They also have outgoing, pleasing personalities.

4-11 This successful model's personality helps sell the clothes he models. *Shutterstock*

Modeling school is recommended. Career opportunities in modeling are limited, and the competition is great. For those who succeed, the wages are high.

Alterations

Many clothing stores hire *alterations specialists*. Altering clothes can be more difficult than doing the original construction. Alterations specialists sew well, work fast, and fit clothing properly, **4-12**. Some their duties include

- deciding what fitting problems exist
- marking and pinning garments for alterations
- shortening or lengthening sleeves, hems, waistlines, and darts
- repairing damaged merchandise before a customer buys it
- changing trims or buttons to satisfy the customer

Alterations specialists often work for more than one store if the stores are small. Some work from home.

Vertical Integration of the Textile and Apparel Industries

Prior to the 1970s, the focus of most companies was on only one aspect of fabric or apparel production. For example, textile mills produced fabrics and then sold them to apparel manufacturing companies. With the formation of larger corporations, many handle all stages of production from producing the fibers to sewing the garments to selling them in stores. In such a **vertical integration** system, one company handles several or all steps in production and/or distribution. For example, Pendleton Woolen Mills processes the wool, weaves the fabrics, creates the garments, and sells them in their own stores. This allows the company to control all steps in the creation of their apparel, leading to greater cost control.

Vertically integrated companies may not be involved in all steps from fiber to garment sales. Some companies, for example, might produce specific fibers, make them into yarns, and then fabrics. These operations may take place at different plant locations, some in this country and others overseas. However, they all are branches of the same company.

4-12 Alterations specialists are needed to make final adjustments to bridal gowns. *Shutterstock*

Summary

- The textile and apparel industry consists of three segments: textile production, apparel production, and retail.
- The textile industry includes all the people and processes involved in making fibers and fabrics.
- Apparel production includes all the people and processes involved in designing and making garments.
- Retailers buy the garments from the manufacturers and sell them to customers.
- The structure of the textile industry is based on the four stages of production—producing fibers, spinning fibers into yarn, producing fabrics, and applying finishes to fabrics.
- Apparel production begins with a merchandising plan for creating a line or collection of designs for a given season. Buyers view designs at fashion centers and apparel marts during fashion week, and select those they want to sell in their retail stores. Garments are manufactured based on orders from the retailers.
- Fashion merchandising includes all phases of buying and selling clothes and accessories. Likewise, fashion promotion includes all efforts made to inform people of the newest fashions and convincing them to buy.
- A wide variety of job opportunities exists within the textile and apparel industry. As in any industry, production workers outnumber management personnel. Many jobs require college degrees; others are available with a high school education.
- Vertical integration is a system used by some large corporations that handle all stages of production from producing the fibers to sewing the garments to selling them in stores.

Graphic Organizer

On a separate sheet of paper, draw a T-chart. In the left column, write the main headings of the chapter. In the right column, note supporting details for each heading.

Main Headings	Supporting Details

Review the Facts

1. Which segment(s) of the textile and apparel industries includes market research?
2. Contrast textile designers and fashion designers.
3. What is included in fabric finishing?
4. What information do market analysts provide to textile manufacturers?
5. What happens during market weeks?
6. What is fashion merchandising and how does it relate to fashion promotion?
7. What is the job title of the person who plans sales, schedules in-service meetings for sales associates, and sets the budgets for buyers?
8. What types of records do buyers need to keep for their stores?
9. Identify at least four attributes that are most important for fashion models.
10. Describe the concept of vertical integration and how it applies to a textile or apparel company.

Think Critically

11. **Compare and contrast.** Which job or career described in this chapter appeals to you most? Compare and contrast these jobs and write a summary about your conclusions.
12. **Draw conclusions.** With advances in technology, computers are taking over more and more jobs in the textiles and apparel industry. Draw conclusions as to whether you think this is good or bad. Are there some jobs they cannot do? Summarize your response.
13. **Identify evidence.** How do you think the latest reality television shows influence the fashion industry? Use Internet and print resources to identify evidence to support your answer.
14. **Recognize advantages.** What do you see as the advantages of a vertically integrated company? What evidence can you provide to support your conclusions?

Apparel Applications

15. **Textile careers.** Search the Internet to find the names and addresses of textile manufacturers in your state or surrounding states. Then write to the manufacturers for information about jobs available, education requirements, job descriptions, and salaries, or obtain this information from their websites.
16. **Career research.** Choose a career in the textile and apparel industry that interests you. Use Internet resources, such as the *Occupational Outlook Handbook,* to locate information about job qualifications, duties and responsibilities, working conditions, and wages.

Academic Connections

17. **Writing.** In teams, outline the creation and production of a garment. Use text and Internet resources to identify all the people and all the steps involved in getting the garment to a manufacturer's showroom. Write a summary about your team's process.
18. **Reading.** Use Internet resources to research fashions presented for the most recent market week. Read two or more articles and write a summary of your findings.

Workplace Links

19. **Design garment.** Create a garment design. Sketch the design, or use a computerized drawing program. Recommend a type of textile for the design. How would you market this design? Who is the target consumer? Share your design with the class.
20. **Sales role plays.** Role-play situations in which sales associates interact with customers. Focus on how the attitudes and actions of sales associates influence the attitudes of customers.
21. **Fashion promotion.** Select a career in fashion merchandising or promotion and come up with a creative idea a person in that career could use. For example, as a merchandise manager, plan a seasonal sale. As a fashion coordinator, plan a fashion show. As a display director, design a store window display. Write an illustrated report showing the details about your creative idea.
22. **Education options.** Research trade schools, community colleges, fashion schools, and universities in your state that train people for careers in the textile and apparel industry. Compare course offerings, costs, and other factors important in selecting a school.

Careers in the Textile and Apparel Industry

As you learn more about the textile and apparel industry, you may have discovered you are interested in one or more careers. To help plan for your future, complete the FCCLA *Career Investigation* STAR Event. Review the *FCCLA STAR Events Manual* online for event details. See your adviser for information as needed.

Chapter 5

The Worldwide Apparel Industry

Chapter Objectives

After studying this chapter, you will be able to
- **summarize** factors that influence the U.S. apparel industry and world economies, including globalization, key trade agreements, laws, sourcing, and organizations.
- **describe** factors that affect the safety of work environments and workers, including the Fair Labor Standards Act and the Occupational Safety and Health Act.
- **determine** ethical and unethical practices in the apparel industry, including sweatshops and counterfeiting.
- **summarize** technological advances that impact the apparel industry.

Key Terms

globalization
exports
imports
balance of trade
trade surplus
trade deficit
quotas
tariffs
sourcing
domestic sourcing
global sourcing
offshore production
sweatshop
Fair Labor Standards Act
Occupational Safety and Health Act
recycling
renewable resources
nonrenewable resources
ethics
counterfeit goods
CAD (computer-aided design)
CAM (computer-aided manufacturing)
pattern grading
robotic machines
CIM (computer-integrated manufacturing)
Quick Response (QR)
Universal Product Codes (UPC)
e-commerce

Reading with Purpose

After reading each section, answer this question: If you explained the information to a friend who is not taking this class, what would you tell him or her?

Since its inception, the apparel industry has evolved and continues to change. Thankfully, many of the unhealthy factory conditions and exploitative policies that once characterized the industry are rare in the U.S. today. In recent years, many businesses, including textile and apparel producers, have focused on ways to reduce pollution and the waste of resources.

The use of computers, the Internet, and other technological advancements has dramatically changed textile and apparel production, marketing, and sales. Ideas and information can be transmitted from one part of the globe to another in a matter of seconds.

As the world has grown smaller, individuals, businesses, and nations have become more interdependent. The developing relationships among U.S. and foreign textile and apparel manufacturers have affected the economies of all countries involved. They are a part of the trend toward globalization.

Globalization is the flow of goods, services, money, labor, and technology across international borders. It is the result of the reduction or removal of trade barriers between countries.

U.S. Apparel Industries and World Economies

Take a look at a label in a garment you wear. Does it say *Made in the U.S.A.*? If so, it was manufactured in the U.S. of fabric made in the U.S., but the fiber and yarn may have come from another country. Although a garment is labeled with a single country of origin, multiple nations were probably involved in its production. For example, a garment with a *Made in Peru* label might use cotton that was grown in Texas and woven in North Carolina, **5-1**. It may have been cut and sewn in Lima, Peru, and washed and finished in Mexico City. The finished garment will be sold in the U.S. or another country. More than 60 countries are involved in some aspect of the garment industry. The industry employs over 30 million people worldwide.

Balance of Trade

Goods have always flowed back and forth across U.S. borders. Goods that are sent out of a country are called **exports**. Goods that come into a country from foreign sources are called **imports**.

5-1 Look at the labels on your clothes to see where they were made.
Shutterstock

The U.S. was once a major exporter of goods to countries around the globe. There were more textile-product exports than imports. Almost all of the early textile products—coarse and low-cost fabrics—were exported to China. Most of the cotton crop was also sold overseas. Finer clothes were imported.

In the U.S. during the 1700s, the value of exports exceeded imports so the U.S. had a favorable balance of trade. A country's **balance of trade** is the difference between the values of its imports and its exports. When the value of exports exceeds the value of imports, a **trade surplus** exists. Money flows into the U.S. in payment. By 1865, however, most of the textiles and cotton crops remained in this country to satisfy the growing need of American consumers.

Today—according to the Census Bureau's Foreign Trade Division—the U.S. exports about 11 billion dollars of textile and apparel products yearly. However, the U.S. imports of these products are nearly seven times greater than its exports. Therefore, the value of goods imported is *seven* times the value of goods exported. The result is a **trade deficit**, or negative trade balance. The U.S. has had an overall trade deficit since 1976. China has the largest trade surplus. This means more U.S. dollars are flowing into China allowing it to buy more U.S. goods, services, and businesses, **5-2**.

There are several reasons for this trade imbalance. One reason is the low wages some developing countries pay in comparison to the high wages U.S. companies pay. Low-wage countries can mass-produce garments at a lower cost. They can then sell these garments in the U.S. at lower prices than garments made and sold in this country. U.S. companies must also comply with government regulations—including those for worker safety, pay, and benefits—that are more stringent than those imposed by other governments. These regulations include those for worker pay, safety, and benefits, and environmental pollution.

For many countries, apparel manufacturing is a major revenue source. Often, apparel factories are the largest employers. Many people in developing countries rely on this industry for jobs that allow them to meet their basic needs. Some of these countries are China, India, Bangladesh, Costa Rica, and Guatemala.

Apparel production is labor intensive. The U.S. apparel industry is at a disadvantage when competing with their counterparts in countries offering lower wages. Also, clothing factories can be set up for less cost in some countries and factory owners do not need to make large investments in technology. The result has been a decrease in U.S. apparel production. As more garments are imported, unemployment in the U.S. apparel industry has increased.

5-2 U.S. ports are busy receiving goods from abroad and shipping goods overseas as well. *Shutterstock*

Trade Laws and Agreements

Between the years 2000 and 2010, nearly 557 U.S. textile plants closed and employment in the U.S. textile industry fell by 62 percent. The plant closings and reduction in jobs prompted the U.S. textile industry to urge the government to enact trade restrictions, particularly with China. Labor unions in the textile industry complained that overseas production was taking away their jobs. They favored a trade policy of *protectionism*. Governments that follow this policy create trade restrictions to protect businesses at home against foreign competition. They might establish **quotas**, for example, that limit how much of a good can be imported. They might also establish tariffs. **Tariffs** are taxes governments assess on imports that make them more expensive for consumers to buy.

Based on an international agreement signed in 1947, tariffs and quotas were allowed for certain textile and apparel products entering the U.S. It allowed for agreements between trading partners, but these were phased out in 2005.

Proponents of *free trade* are against these restrictions. Free trade is a policy by which governments limit trade restrictions. This allows countries to trade goods and services without restriction. Free trade permits all countries to do what they do best. They specialize in the aspects of production that are best suited to the skills and abilities of their people. They grow the crops that do best in their climates. The result is a greater selection of goods and services at lower prices worldwide.

World Trade Organization

In 1995, the World Trade Organization (WTO) was formed to govern world trade. The organization has 153 member countries. The WTO sets trade practices that are fair for all nations. It negotiates trade disputes between member nations. The *WTO Agreement on Textiles and Clothing* paved the way for phasing out quotas and tariffs on textiles and apparel between 1995 and 2005. The goal of the agreement was to allow more open access to consumer markets around the world.

Though most countries view the removal of quotas as positive, it brings severe challenges to others. Businesses in countries paying higher wages are at a disadvantage to those in countries paying lower wages. Therefore, some quotas still remain in effect for certain products from China, Russia, Ukraine, and Vietnam.

Free Trade Agreements

The U.S. has negotiated a number of additional Free Trade Agreements (FTA) with specific trading partners around the world. The goal is to reduce trade barriers among the participating countries resulting in economic benefits for all.

One of the most important of these is the *North American Free Trade Agreement (NAFTA)*. In 1994, the United States, Canada, and Mexico signed this agreement, 5-3. NAFTA lowered trade barriers and opened markets among the three countries. For the apparel industry, Mexico specializes in production while the U.S. and Canada focus on technology, design, and marketing. Many U.S. textile mills ship their fabrics to Mexico for garment production. Retailers often receive apparel shipments from Mexico more quickly than from Asian countries.

The *Dominican Republic-Central America-United States Free Trade Agreement (CAFTA-DR)* reduces tariffs and offers other economic incentives for trade. This agreement is between the United States and the smaller countries of Costa Rica, the Dominican Republic, El Salvador, Guatemala, Honduras, and Nicaragua. These countries had difficulty competing with the larger countries of China and India where wages are lower. This agreement also benefits U.S. businesses, farmers, and ranchers by opening up markets to their products. It reduces tariffs on certain items, along with other economic incentives.

5-3 The North American Free Trade Agreement encourages trade among Canada, Mexico, and the United States. *Shutterstock*

Global Sourcing

Many U.S. companies use the lower-cost labor supply outside of the United States for economic reasons. **Sourcing** is choosing how, when, and where a company will manufacture its goods or purchase its products. **Domestic sourcing** occurs within the United States. If a company looks beyond U.S. borders, this becomes **global sourcing**. When a company chooses to produce its products outside the U.S. using their own production guidelines, **offshore production** occurs. Companies continually review their sourcing options in order to be competitive. They may choose to keep some production facilities in the U.S., but use others that are offshore.

Most textile production has taken place in Mexico and in Asian countries—particularly China. Many companies open their own production facilities in foreign countries to manufacture their garments, 5-4. For example, Nike manufactures its products in more than 652 factories in 45 different countries. A garment might be designed in New York and cut in Hong Kong from fabric woven in Australia. Sewing of the garment may happen in China while marketing occurs in Germany.

Even with transportation and tariff costs (in some cases), retailers still often choose to do business offshore. For example, suppose a foreign-produced garment sells for $100. The retailer might receive $50 in the form of a markup, while $35 goes to the manufacturer, $10 to the contractor, and $5 to the garment worker. Foreign factories produce two-thirds of the apparel Americans wear.

Because so many garments are now imported, the law requires labels on textile and apparel products to show where they were made. However, labels may only indicate one stop in the production of garments.

5-4 This garment factory is located in Africa, but the apparel will be shipped to the U.S. *Shutterstock*

Creating Safe Work Environments

In the early days of the U.S. textile and apparel industry, working conditions and worker safety were not priorities for businesses. For example, workers could be required to work long hours without breaks. These conditions can no longer *legally* exist in the United States, although they continue in other parts of the world.

When the first textile mills were built in the U.S. in the late 1700s, labor was scarce. About 90 percent of Americans were farmers. To fill their factories with workers, mill owners recruited families and brought them to the mills to work. Children as young as four or five years old worked at the looms. Young, unmarried women were also hired to work in the mills. The *Lowell system* was a factory management system that brought the women to the mills. They were well paid by the standards for the period.

Due to increased immigration to the U.S. from Europe in the mid-1800s, the labor supply for textile mills and factories increased. Nearly three-fourths of the factory workers of that period were employed in the mills and factories of New England and the middle states. Most mills produced cotton, wool, and silk textiles.

As demand for goods from the factories increased and caused businesses to ramp up production, working conditions deteriorated. The mills were unsanitary, unhealthful buildings. The average workday was 12 to 15 hours long.

Highlights in History

The Lowell System

In the early 1800s, Lowell, Massachusetts, was the site of the largest textile factories in the U.S. that turned raw cotton into cotton textiles. Many workers were needed to run the machines and perform other functions in the factories. The Lowell factory owners tapped a source of labor that was unusual at the time—young, unmarried girls and women.

The "Lowell mill girls," as they were called, were the daughters of farmers and laborers. They lived together under supervision in boarding houses near the factories. They were paid well for the time, although they earned less than men. Most were between the ages of 13 and 25, and worked at the mills from one to three years before returning to their homes or getting married.

This system of factory management was called the Lowell system, or the Waltham-Lowell system. It created profits for its owners and new roles and opportunities for girls and women. At that time, girls lived with their families until they married. They did not work in factories for wages. In Lowell, many girls and young women were happy to be earning their own money, which they spent, sent home to their families, or saved to start their own households. When they were not working, the mill girls attended religious services, concerts, and classes. They started their own literary magazines and organized for better working conditions. They participated in other cultural and enrichment activities in the city that grew up around the factory.

Factories were often noisy, hot, damp, and dusty places. Workers labored long hours—12 to 14 hours a day with only a few short breaks. But working conditions were humane and pay was good compared with that of factory workers in Europe at that time. The Lowell factories attracted many visitors, including English novelist Charles Dickens. Dickens and others were impressed by what they saw, including the accomplishments of the mostly female workforce.

Factory owners and investors grew fabulously wealthy. As demand for factory produced fabric grew, new factories based on the Lowell model were built. The wealth created by the textile industry fueled development of the U.S. economy.

As competition among textile producers increased, the price of textiles and profits fell. The U.S. also suffered several economic downturns. Over time, working conditions and pay at the factories worsened. Workers were pushed to work harder, work longer hours, and to accept pay cuts. Many of the mill girls joined organized protests and went on strike.

As more factories opened, owners looked for other sources of cheap labor. They turned to immigrants from Ireland and Canada. By the 1850s, the Lowell system had been discontinued.

This photograph features a Mill Girl Boardinghouse and Boardinghouse Park in Lowell, Massachusetts. Mill owners provided supervised housing for the unmarried girls and women who worked in the mills. *NPS/Jonathan Parker*

The term *sweatshop* was coined for workrooms in New York City tenements where workers literally *sweated* under deplorable working conditions. Today, **sweatshop** refers to a manufacturing plant that may use child labor, pay lower than minimum wages, not pay overtime, or have unclean or unsafe facilities.

Labor Laws to Protect Apparel Workers

As long as there were many workers competing for jobs, wages stayed low. Early attempts to form labor unions were considered illegal acts by the courts. However, in 1900, the International Ladies' Garment Workers' Union formed. Its purpose was to improve working conditions for workers in the industry.

In the late 1800s and early 1900s, child labor was a serious problem, particularly in cotton mills. According to the 1900 U.S. census, one out of three workers in Southern cotton mills was a child under 16. Many children worked all night at the looms and industrial accidents were frequent. There were few safety devices on the dangerous looms, which easily caught long hair.

In the early 1900s, pressure from labor unions, child advocates, and others led to the passage of labor laws in many states. At least 38 states set a minimum age for workers of 12 years. Children in factories were prohibited from working more than 10 hours a day.

In 1938 the federal government enacted the **Fair Labor Standards Act**. It established a minimum wage and a maximum workweek of 40 hours. The act also forbade the employment of children under 16 in many jobs, particularly in jobs that might be hazardous to their health. These provisions were to protect the educational opportunities of the young. See Figure **5-5** for key features of the Child Labor Standards of the Fair Labor Standards Act. This law covers all employees who work for employers involved in interstate commerce. Individual states may have stricter laws that cover all workers.

As early as the 1920s, working conditions had improved in many companies. Safety devices were installed and sanitation was improved. It was not until 1970, however, with the passage of the federal **Occupational Safety and Health Act** that working conditions saw greater improvements. The Occupational Safety and Health Administration (OSHA) was created to set and enforce job safety and health standards. OSHA requires employers to provide safe workplaces. Employers must follow OSHA standards and make

Fair Labor Standards Act: Child Labor Provisions

- 18-year-olds can work at any job for any number of hours.
- 16- and 17-year-olds can work at any nonhazardous job for any number of hours. (Hazardous jobs include operating motor vehicles or power-driven machinery, working with explosives or nuclear materials, and many jobs in construction, demolition, meat processing, and other fields.)
- 14- and 15-year-olds may work outside school hours in various nonmanufacturing, nonmining, and nonhazardous jobs, but for no longer than three hours per school day or 18 hours per school week. Their work may not begin before 7 a.m. or extend past 7 p.m.
- Young people of any age may deliver newspapers or work for parents in a nonfarm business. They may also perform in radio, television, movie, or theatrical productions.

5-5 These provisions are important in safeguarding the health of young workers and preventing work from interfering with their education.

Sweatshops

Although most U.S. apparel manufacturers follow safe and fair employment practices, some unethical manufacturers do not. One way some employers keep their labor and manufacturing costs low is by hiring illegal immigrants. They may pay these workers less than the minimum wage or make them work long hours under poor conditions. Fear of deportation and the inability to speak and understand English keeps illegal immigrants from speaking out. Today, some small subcontractor businesses *illegally* operate sweatshops in the U.S. These may appear in cities with major apparel centers, such as Los Angeles, New York, Dallas, Miami, and Atlanta.

Garment workers employed in large factories often belong to unions. A union is an organization formed by workers to bargain with employers for better pay and work conditions. Federal and state agencies regularly inspected these factories for safety or employment violations.

By the 1980s and 1990s, some apparel companies began shifting certain production steps to small, specialized contractors in the U.S. and abroad. Contractors operating overseas may not be subject to U.S. regulations and inspections. As a result, inhumane conditions are still present in factories around the world.

President Bill Clinton established the *Apparel Industry Partnership* in 1996. This organization consists of representatives from apparel companies, unions, and human rights groups. It focuses on human rights issues throughout the global apparel industry in the hopes of eliminating sweatshops.

Though efforts continue to shut down sweatshops, they continue to exist. Garments made in these sweatshops may still bear the *Made in the U.S.A.* label.

5-6 Both employers and employees must do their part in keeping the workplace safe.

Responsibilities for a Safe Work Environment	
Employer Responsibilities	*Employee Responsibilities*
• Provide a workplace free from recognized hazards that could cause death or serious physical harm. • Comply with all standards, rules, and regulations under OSHA. • Make sure employees have and use safe tools and equipment. • Post signs to warn of potential hazards. • Establish and update safe operating procedures. • Provide health and safety-related training. • Keep records of work-related injuries and illnesses.	• Read the OSHA poster. • Comply with all standards. • Follow all employer safety and health rules. • Use or wear prescribed protective equipment. • Report hazardous conditions to supervisor. • Report job-related injuries or illnesses to employer.

Environmental Efforts of Textile Producers

With the development of synthetic fibers, came concerns about the release of toxic pollutants into the environment by chemical companies. The water supply and air around these factories drew special attention. Federal laws to address the release of pollutants began in the 1970s and include the following:

- Clean Air Act (1970)
- Toxic Substances Control Act (1976)
- Clean Water Act (1977)

There was also concern about the amount of energy and nonrenewable resources used in the making of synthetic fibers. In response, many textile producers made efforts to conserve water, energy, and electricity. In addition, more companies are recycling and using *renewable resources* instead of *nonrenewable resources*.

- **Recycling** is the process of converting waste material or unwanted existing products into new products. Recycling of textiles, paper, and plastic is common, 5-7.
- **Renewable resources** are natural resources—such as trees and plants—that nature can replenish.
- **Nonrenewable resources** are natural resources that can be used up. Nature cannot replenish them. An example is petroleum—used to make synthetic fibers, plastics, and gasoline.

Increases in all of these efforts are due, in part, to consumer awareness and demand. Many fiber manufacturers are now doing their part to protect the environment by developing *sustainable products*—those that do not deplete natural resources or cause environmental damage.

Environmentally Friendly Fibers

Many textile producers continually look for ways to protect the environment. Some producers use renewable resources in developing new fibers. Likewise, they may use recycled materials in other fibers and fabrics. Organically growing natural fibers is also a sustainable practice.

5-7 Bamboo trees, a renewable resource, have become important in textile production because they grow so rapidly. *Shutterstock*

Fibers from Renewable Sources

Lyocell—under the trade name is Tencel®—is a newer manufactured fiber made of wood pulp from eucalyptus trees grown in forests or tree farms that use sustainable farming practices. The chemical agents used to produce the fiber are recycled. The fiber itself is biodegradable, strong, and absorbent.

Sorona® is another new fiber made partially from corn instead of petrochemicals, reducing oil dependency. Because corn planting happens yearly, it is a renewable resource. The fabrics made from Sorona are soft, durable, and warm. Producers also use these fibers to make carpet and automotive products.

Another fiber that comes from a renewable source is rayon made from bamboo fibers. Bamboo grows rapidly and replanting occurs frequently. Rayon made from bamboo fibers has a silk-like feel.

Fibers from Recycled Materials

Some manufacturers are using recycled plastic bottles to make a polyester fiber. The bottles are sorted, cleaned, chopped, melted, and shaped into fibers. The fibers are made into fabrics used in sportswear, denim, thermal underwear, upholstery, and other items, 5-8.

Other manufacturers are making fabric out of recycled garments. For example, in some denim jeans, skirts, and shorts, 80 percent of the fabric is recycled cotton. One company, Patagonia, has a recycling program through which customers can return their worn Patagonia® fleece clothing and cotton T-shirts. The company processes the garments, breaking them down to the molecular level creating new polyester fibers. They then use these fibers to make new garments of the same quality as the original ones.

Organically Grown Fibers

Have you noticed the signs for organically grown foods when you visit the grocery store? Producers grow these foods without the use of chemical fertilizers and pesticides that might harm the environment.

In recent years, there has been growing concern among consumers about the amount of chemical pesticides and fertilizers used to grow cotton. This increased the market for organically grown cotton. Environmentally responsible growing techniques for cotton include the use of

- untreated seeds that are not genetically modified
- natural fertilizers that are biodegradable

5-8 By recycling empty plastic soda bottles, you can play a role in protecting the environment. *Source: National Association for PET Container Resources*

A New Life for Soda Bottles	
Products	**Number of 20-Ounce Soda Bottles**
T-shirt	19
Ski jacket (fiberfill)	14
Sleeping Bag (fiberfill)	114
Carpeting	19 per sq. foot OR 171 per sq. yard

- hand-weeding or cover crops for weed control
- crop rotation to different parts of the farmland to control disease
- beneficial insects to control destructive insects

Because organic cotton is more expensive to grow than regular cotton, organic-cotton clothing is more expensive and less desirable with consumers. The amount of organic cotton grown each year is still less than 1 percent of the total cotton grown, but that amount is expected to increase. Watch for apparel made of organically grown cotton when you shop. Manufacturers, such as Nike and Patagonia®, produce some garments from 100 percent organically grown cotton. Large retailers, such as Walmart and Gap, feature some items made of organic cotton. Small boutiques may specialize in environmentally friendly fashions.

Ethical and Unethical Practices Within the Industry

Ethics form the basis for many decisions companies make. **Ethics** are the moral principles that govern the behavior of a group or person. For example, a company with an ethical code that values human rights may stop working with a supplier that violates its workers' human rights. The ethics of business people may drive them to reduce the pollution levels of their factories. A company that believes in contributing to its community may sponsor events that benefit the local community.

Individuals and businesses sometimes behave or operate in unethical ways. For example, an unethical practice within the apparel and accessories industry is *counterfeiting*. **Counterfeit goods** are products that may appear identical to legitimate products, but the original manufacturer did not make them. Counterfeit goods often bear illegal copies of registered logos, brand names, or decorations. This is a violation of U.S. trademark laws. For instance, counterfeiters may copy prestige handbags by such makers as Louis Vuitton and Channel, which have distinctive features. Other items that are frequently counterfeit include sunglasses, watches, jeans, and status clothing items from such makers as Polo Ralph Lauren and 7 For All Mankind.

Counterfeiting increased in the mid-1980s when luxury fashion items became popular with consumers, **5-9**. Street vendors in large cities and in flea markets were the first to sell counterfeit goods. In recent years, online sales of counterfeit goods have skyrocketed. Buying online makes it more difficult for consumers to know if they are getting the real items. Only when their purchases arrive in the mail do they see that the items are not what they ordered. For example, counterfeit purses are often made of vinyl instead of leather. The quality of the topstitching is poor and the lining is made from cloth instead of leather. These differences were not visible in online photos.

Some people know they are buying counterfeits, but do so anyway. They consider it a victimless crime because they feel no one is harmed by it. They may tell friends about getting great deals, especially if they could not afford to buy the genuine items. They also feel they are not harming the authentic-brand companies.

There are victims, however. According to the U.S. Chamber of Commerce, counterfeiting annually costs U.S. companies between $200 and $250 billion. It results in the loss of 750,000 jobs. Counterfeiters pay no or few taxes, which results in a loss of government revenues. Designers get no return on their branded products. Legitimate retailers lose business from potential customers.

Counterfeiting is very profitable for the producers and sellers involved. Though it is illegal, few people are prosecuted. Consumers who knowingly purchase counterfeit items are directly supporting illegal businesses. The profits from these businesses may support organized crime, child labor, and sweatshops.

You and other consumers can end counterfeiting. If consumers stop purchasing counterfeit goods, the counterfeiters will soon get out of the business. Many websites are available to help consumers identify counterfeit items. In addition, consumers should be cautious when buying fashion items from unfamiliar online retailers. Purchase from reputable online retailers. Finally, remember if the price is too good to be true, the item is probably not authentic.

5-9 Counterfeit goods, such as sunglasses, are often sold by street vendors. *Shutterstock*

Technological Advances in the Apparel Industry

The development of computers was one of the most important technological advances of the twentieth century. Computers touched nearly every area of life, including textiles and apparel. Computers play a larger part in the design and manufacture of apparel than they do in most other industries. Since the 1990s, e-commerce has dramatically changed the retail end of the business.

Computer Use in Design and Manufacturing

A system called CAD/CAM revolutionized the garment industry, saving time and reducing costs in all areas. Designers use **CAD (computer-aided design)** software to create textile and garment designs. Likewise, workers using **CAM (computer-aided manufacturing)** software, control the steps in producing finished textiles and garments.

Textile designers develop designs, patterns, weaves, and suggest color combinations for fabrics. *Fashion designers* design clothing and accessories that use those fabrics. Both types of designers use CAD systems to help create the looks they want. Designers can easily change design details until they are satisfied with the design. For example, with the proper computer commands, they can easily change the design of a fabric—making plaids smaller or larger, or changing colors.

Many fashion designers use design software that has three-dimensional (3D) capabilities, **5-10**. It allows designers to turn a virtual image on the display screen so it can be viewed at any angle. The fashion designer can sketch a garment design on-screen and then rotate it to see all sides of the design.

Pattern makers use CAD systems, too. They can easily draw pattern pieces on the computer screen. Then designers may decide to change the shape of sleeves or move darts to a different location. When the pattern maker inputs these changes into the computer, it automatically adjusts all the pattern pieces and incorporates the changes. With only few keystrokes, the pattern maker can also create different sizes. This step is called **pattern grading**.

All areas of textile production utilize CAM systems. Textile makers use computerized machines for knitting, weaving, dyeing, and finishing fabrics.

CAM systems can control all areas of garment making, too. Many garment manufacturers use computers to determine the best layouts for pattern pieces on fabric. To do this, the computer operator enters data such as the fabric width and the length of each fabric roll. The pattern pieces appear on a display screen and the operator moves them into position. The computer can match plaids and stripes and automatically check pattern alignment with other fabric features. In order to avoid waste, the computer operator arranges the pattern pieces to make the best use of all the fabric.

Once he or she is satisfied with the layout, the computer operator creates a full-scale printout, or *marker*, **5-11**. The marker is a cutting guide. The marker printout lists the pattern size and name of each piece.

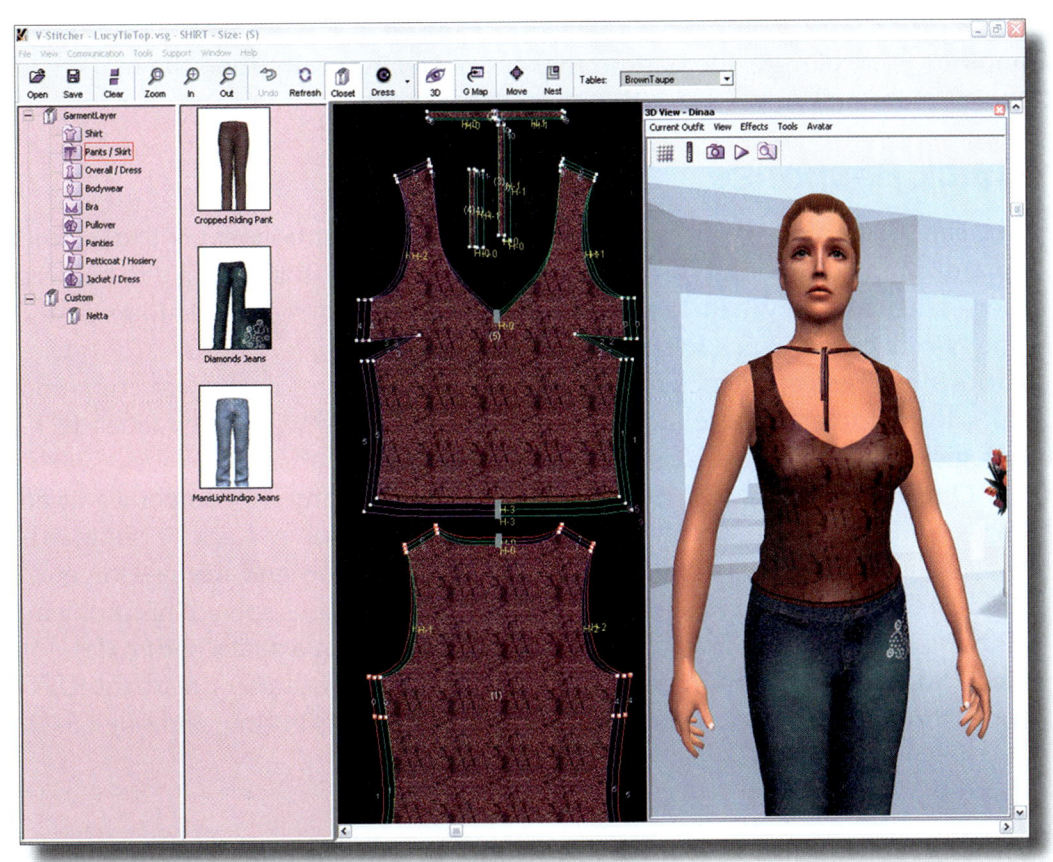

5-10 Three-dimensional pattern design software enables designers to view two-dimensional patterns on a three-dimensional human form to check fit and drape. The image can be viewed from all angles by rotating the form. *Gerber Technology*

A computer can control the knife cutters, water-jet cutters, and laser beams when cutting layers of fabric. The fabric thickness and the number of pieces to be cut influence the speed of the cutting device. The operator programs the sizes and shapes of garment pieces into the computer, and then presets the cutters to cut around the pieces.

Computers also control **robotic machines** to automatically assemble and package complete garments. An operator stationed at a computer terminal runs the system. Garment pieces move from one workstation to the next when the operator inputs commands. One machine sews, another trims, and another presses. At the end of the line, a machine labels and packages the garments.

5-11 CAD systems can automatically generate markers to maximize fabric use. *Gerber Technology*

CIM (computer-integrated manufacturing) is software that connects the CAD, CAM, and robotic machine systems. CIM helps coordinate the entire production process from design to finished product. Different terminals throughout a manufacturing plant feed information into the main system. CIM systems also track inventories, operating costs, and production information. At any time, plant managers can access information about anything and everything that is going on in the plant.

Garment manufacturing and pattern making may not occur at the same place. With CIM, companies can easily transfer data from one location to another. For example, the pattern maker can electronically send the marker to the garment maker.

Quick Response

The 1980s and 1990s brought increased competition from textile and apparel imports. In order for U.S. industries to survive, they needed to become more efficient. They had to find ways to get their garments to stores faster. The system called Quick Response was developed. **Quick Response (QR)** uses various business strategies to reduce the time between fiber production and sales to customers. These strategies require an investment in the latest technologies to improve quality and productivity.

Quick Response requires better communication among companies at all levels. Industry wide, there were two problems to solve. Lack of standards within the industry was one problem. The introduction and use of Universal Product Codes (UPC) on merchandise and shipping cartons solved this problem. **Universal Product Codes (UPC)** identify products using a series of *barcodes*—or black lines, bars, and numbers on labels. Computer scanners read the UPC codes throughout the various stages of production, distribution, and sales, **5-12**.

The other problem involved the incompatible computer systems that manufacturers and retailers were using. These systems could not communicate with each other. With the use of standardized software, computers of all companies can instantly communicate with each other. Fiber producers can communicate with fabric producers, and fabric producers can communicate with apparel manufacturers. Retailers can instantly inform manufacturers when inventories on certain garments are low. With QR strategies in place, the U.S. apparel industry is better able to compete worldwide.

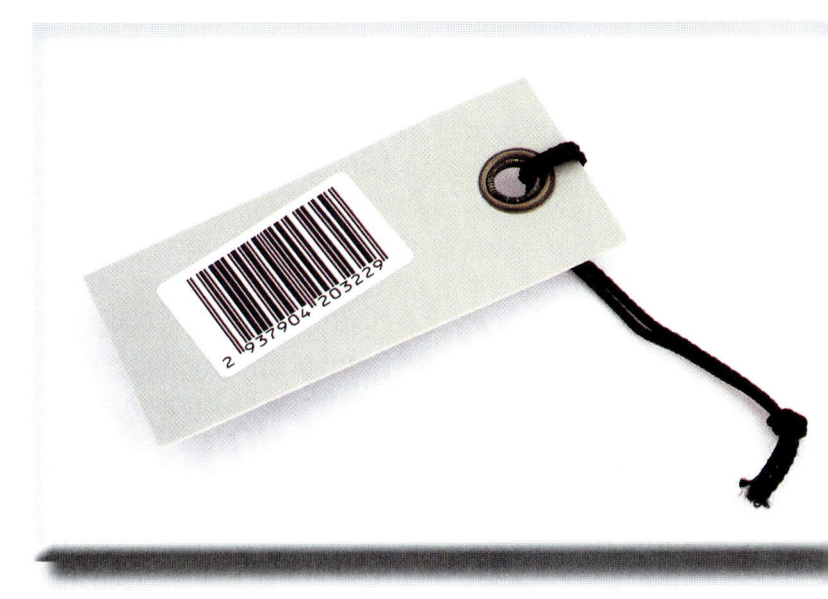

E-Commerce and Social Networking

Perhaps the greatest technological impact on the apparel industry in recent years is e-commerce. **E-commerce** involves conducting transactions electronically on the Internet. Almost all apparel companies today have their own websites to advertise their brands globally. Many retailers also sell their merchandise through their websites. In addition, they collect important data about their customers' likes and dislikes through their online activity. More and more people are making clothing purchases online rather than in retail stores. As consumer comfort increases with Internet buying, retailers expect this growth to continue.

To increase sales, many major apparel manufacturers and retailers are using social networking to reach their customers. Many use *YouTube, Twitter,* and *Facebook.* Some fashion designers use Twitter to communicate with their fans. This is one way they stay in touch with what their customers like and do not like, **5-13**. Manufacturer and retailer Facebook pages are common now. They allow consumers to share their reactions to the designs they see. Burberry®, for example, now provides a live webcast of their runway shows in London. Consumers can even place orders for the designs models are wearing. They no longer have to wait six months for the latest styles to appear in stores. This is appealing to those who want to be trendsetters or fashion forward.

5-12 The UPC on this garment label has followed it from production through to sales. *Shutterstock*

5-13 Social networking is being used by apparel manufacturers to stay in touch with their customers' likes and dislikes. *Shutterstock*

Summary

- Globalization is the result of reducing or removing trade barriers between countries.
- Importing more textiles and apparel than exporting resulted in a trade deficit in the U.S. and a decrease in apparel production.
- Free Trade Agreements (FTA) between the U.S. and specific trading partners around the world have the goal of reducing trade barriers and providing economic benefits for all.
- Sourcing choices influence how and where a company will manufacture its goods or purchase its products.
- Early abuses in child labor, long workweeks, and low pay in the textile mills impacted the passage of the Fair Labor Standards Act in 1938.
- The Occupational Safety and Health Act led to safer and healthier working conditions.
- Most apparel manufacturers follow safe and fair employment practices, however, some sweatshops still exist in this country and other countries.
- The release of toxic pollutants into the environment by chemical companies during the development of synthetic fibers brought about many concerns. Federal laws to address these concerns began in the 1970s.
- Apparel manufacturers are making efforts to use more renewable resources instead of nonrenewable resources.
- Some companies are developing new fibers by using renewable resources, recycled materials, and organically grown natural fibers.
- Ethics are the moral principles that govern a group's or person's behavior. Ethics may influence decisions companies make.
- Computers systems impact almost every aspect of apparel design and manufacturing. CAD, CAM, CIM, Quick Response, and e-commerce are examples.

Graphic Organizer

Draw a T-chart on a sheet of paper. Write each of the main heads in the left column of the chart and supporting details for each head in the right column.

Main Heads	Supporting Details

Review the Facts

1. Summarize globalization in your own words.
2. How do wages affect the balance of trade for textiles and apparel?
3. If a government believes in protectionism, describe two trade restrictions it might use.
4. What is the purpose of the North American Free Trade Agreement and what countries are involved?
5. Why do many companies use offshore production? How does this impact the U.S. textile and apparel industry?
6. Describe human rights violations that might occur in sweatshops.
7. List the three main provisions of the Fair Labor Standards Act.
8. What does the Occupational Safety and Health Act require?
9. What development in the textile industry led to increased pollution of water and air?
10. Name two products that are recycled into new garments.
11. Name three techniques used to grow organic cotton.
12. Give three reasons consumers should avoid buying counterfeit clothes and accessories.
13. Contrast three computer systems and how they have revolutionized the garment industry.
14. How does the fashion industry use social networking? Give an example.

Think Critically

15. **Draw conclusions.** Think about how globalization affects you personally. Summarize your conclusions for the class.

16. **Predict consequences.** What are the consequences of ethical choices some manufacturers make when moving their textile and apparel production facilities to developing countries? Discuss your predictions in class.

17. **Compare and contrast.** Research reliable resources for historical and present-day articles on sweatshops and other inhumane working conditions in the textile and apparel industry. Compare and contrast the conditions of each time period. What possibilities do you see for eliminating such conditions in the future?

18. **Analyze behavior.** What can you, as a wearer of apparel, do to save natural resources and protect the environment? What behaviors can you change? Discuss your thoughts in class.

19. **Analyze ethics.** What ethical choices are involved with knowingly buying counterfeit items? Predict the long-term consequences for the individual consumer, retailers, and original designers or manufacturers.

Apparel Applications

20. **Economic research.** Use reliable Internet sites to research the amount of the current U.S. trade deficit. How does the current deficit compare to the trade deficits five and ten years ago? In addition, research levels of textile and apparel imports and exports over the last five years. How do they vary from year-to-year? Is this a pattern that is likely to continue? Explain.

21. **Debate.** In two teams, debate the pros and cons of protectionism versus free trade. Give reliable evidence to support your team's view.

22. **Organic cotton survey.** Conduct a survey of retailers in your community to find who sells clothing or household items made of organically grown cotton. Prepare a report listing the names of the retailers, the items found made from organic cotton, and the names of the manufacturers that produce these items. Are there any stores in your community that sell only organic garments? How does this impact other retailers? Share your findings with the class.

23. **Manufacturer research.** Use school-approved social-networking sites to review several fashion manufacturers, such as Nike, Burberry, or Patagonia. What features do you like about these sites? How do the sites benefit consumers? Create a summary report using a school-approved blog application. Post your summary to the class blog.

Academic Connections

24. **Writing.** Research the effects of NAFTA on consumers, workers, businesses, and the economies of the three countries involved. Write a summary of your findings to share with the class.

25. **Social studies.** Research what life was like for the Lowell mill girls. Use such reliable websites as University of Massachusetts Lowell—Tsongas Industrial History Center or the National Park Service—Lowell National Historic Park for your research. Then write a short story from a mill girl's point of view about work at the mills and life in Lowell. Share your story with the class.

Workplace Links

26. **Worker rights.** Use Internet or print resources to research the Workers Rights Consortium and its efforts to eliminate sweatshops. Who belongs to this organization and how are they bringing about change? Use presentation software to create a report of your findings to share with the class.

27. **Discussion.** What are the costs and benefits of providing a safe work environment for employees? for employers?

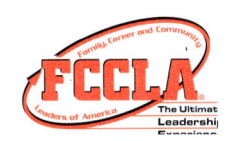

Take the Lead—Providing Clothes for People in Need

In many communities, nonprofit agencies collect and refurbish gently used clothing for people in need for little or no cost. As an FCCLA *Community Service* project, use your leadership skills and the *FCCLA Planning Process* to plan and implement a clothing drive at your school. Consider partnering with a nonprofit agency in your community for the clothing drive. See your adviser for information as needed.

Chapter 6

A Closer Look at Fashion Design

Chapter Objectives

After studying this chapter, you will be able to
- **contrast** ready-to-wear and couture.
- **describe** how knockoffs affect consumers and designers, including the role of licensing in the fashion industry.
- **identify** the main apparel categories and price points.
- **summarize** where fashion designers work, including the fashion capitals of the world.
- **state** sources of inspiration for fashion designers.
- **summarize** the final steps in the fashion design process.
- **identify** some of today's top fashion designers.
- **analyze** the role of the major fashion publications and trade associations in the apparel industry.

Key Terms

line	licensing	fashion week
collection	price points	croquis
couture	diffusion line	technical drawing
haute couture	store brand	prototype
prêt-a-porter	fashion capitals	trade associations
knockoff		

Reading with Purpose

Use a magazine search engine, such as MagPortal.com, to find a magazine article that relates to this chapter. Read the article and write four questions that you have about the article. Next, read the textbook chapter. Based on what you read in the chapter, see if you can answer any of the questions you had about the magazine article.

The world of fashion design is attracting the attention of a growing number of young people. Perhaps you are one of them. You may see yourself as a contestant in a fashion design reality show. Could you be the newest fashion designer to appeal to young Hollywood celebrities? Several young designers have become extremely popular in a short period of time. For example, the Mulleavy sisters from Pasadena, California, quickly hit the big time in high fashion. They began designing their Rodarte® brand in 2005 and showed their creations during New York's fashion week that fall.

The exciting world of fashion design has been centered in the fashion capitals of the world, such as Paris, New York City, and Milan. However, a career in fashion design can begin anywhere for anyone who has a talent for creating exciting new designs.

Ready-to-Wear versus Couture

Developing an understanding of the different levels of fashion and fashion industry terms is a good place to begin. Most of the apparel produced is ready-to-wear. *Ready-to-wear (RTW)* is apparel that is completely ready for a person to wear when purchased. Manufacturers mass-produce RTW in large quantities that require little or no hand sewing.

Apparel companies produce four to six lines or collections every year. A **line** is a group of styles designed for a particular fashion season, such as Spring or Summer. There is usually a new line for each season. In large companies, there may be as many as 40 to 75 new items in each line.

A **collection** is also a group of styles for a season, but of more expensive apparel. Well-known designers present their collections, while apparel companies offer their lines. Designers generally create two or more collections or lines each year.

The fashion seasons are Spring, Summer, Fall I, Fall II, Holiday, and Resort or Cruise (late fall or winter). The names of fashion seasons refer to the times when consumers buy garments, not when companies design or produce them. For example, Fall fashions begin appearing in stores in June. They are designed the September before, marketed in March, and manufactured in April.

Couture (koo-TOOR) is a French word meaning *sewing* or *dressmaking*. It refers to garments made to fit a particular customer. Only small quantities of couture garments are made and most of the work is done by hand. The fabrics are often expensive. Couture work originated in France and much of it continues there today. A very expensive gown bought in a local department store is *not* couture. It is ready-to-wear.

Haute couture (oat-koo-TOOR) means *high fashion* or *high sewing* in French. It is the most exclusive type of couture. Haute couture is for people who can spend over $100,000 for an evening gown. The haute couture industry began in Paris during the late 1850s. Charles Worth was the first designer to show his designs on live models. His customers then ordered certain designs to be made for themselves. Some famous haute couture designers include Coco Chanel and Christian Dior. They and other early designers created new fashions, and the rest of the fashion world followed. Each designer's business was called a *house*, such as the House of Worth and the House of Dior. When the founding designer retires or dies, former assistants or other designers may take over design responsibilities. There are 11 French haute-couture houses left. The houses show collections only twice a year: Fall/Winter and Spring/Summer. Figure **6-1** lists of some of the first and most famous haute-couture designers.

Many believe that couture fashion is on the decline. The haute couture houses reportedly are no longer profitable. Women today are more interested in casual styles as they have fewer occasions to wear formal attire. Celebrities wear haute couture gowns (on loan) during award-show events, such as the Oscars. However, the average person has little need for such gowns. Another reason that couture is on the decline is that the ready-to-wear industry has raised its quality and prices while keeping volume low. This is luring away the wealthy buyers who bought couture years ago. Most buyers of haute couture today are from the Middle East and Russia.

Nineteenth and Twentieth Century Designers and Their Fashion Contributions

Louis Vuitton: 1821–1892, France. Vuitton opened his first shop in Paris in 1854 selling luxury leather luggage. The use of his LV logo continues today. Under creative director Marc Jacobs, the line has expanded to womenswear and menswear, as well as leather goods and jewelry.

Charles Frederick Worth: 1825–1895, England. Born in England, Worth became a French designer and was considered the founder of haute couture. He opened his first design house in Paris in 1858. Early designs of the mid-1800s featured crinolines, trains, and bustles. In the late 1800s, his designs were more slender, without the ruffles and frills.

Mariano Fortuny: 1871–1949, Spain. Fortuny—whose design house was in Venice, Italy—was most famous for his loose-fitting, cylindrically shaped, silk pleated garment known as the "Delphos" gown. His special pleating process was patented in 1909.

Madeleine Vionnet: 1876–1975, France. Most famous in the 1920s and 1930s, she favored the use of crepe, satin, and gabardine cut on the bias to achieve simple, fluid shapes. She frequently used the cowl and halter neck styles.

Paul Poiret: 1879–1944, France. Poiret was responsible for the end of the tightly corseted look of 1908, creating simple, elegant, softly fitted gowns. He also designed the hobble skirt, which confined the ankles.

Guccio Gucci: 1881–1953, Italy. Gucci started a leather business in 1906, creating handbags, belts, shoes, and other leather goods. The House of Gucci was founded in 1921 and the "GG" logo developed. One of Gucci's most famous designs was the bamboo handle handbag. Gucci is still a global brand selling clothes as well as luxury leather goods. The current designer is Frida Giannini.

Coco Chanel: 1883–1971, France. Chanel is most famous for the "Boyish Look" she created following World War I and her collarless suits, often worn with a gilt chain bag and a string of pearls.

Elsa Schiaparelli: 1890–1973, Italy. Schiaparelli became known for her outrageous designs during the 1930s, merging art with fashion. She was best known for the "Shocking Pink" color she popularized. Her last showing was in 1953.

Cristobal Balenciaga: 1895–1972, Spain. Some of his more famous designs were the chemise dress (also called the "sack"); loose jackets with dolman sleeves; bodystockings; and large buttons and banded collars that stood away from the neck. He stopped designing in 1968.

Norman Norell: 1900–1972, U.S. In the 1960s, Norell became known for his culottes for day and evening, harem pants, and sequin-covered sheath dresses. He is considered to be one of the foremost U.S. designers.

Christian Dior: 1905–1957, France. Dior is most famous for the "New Look" he created following World War II featuring huge skirts, tiny waists, and stiffened bodices.

Claire McCardell: 1905–1958, U.S. McCardell is most famous for creating the look of American sportswear—practical clothing for everyday living. In 1944, she designed pumps based on ballet shoes. She is known for empire dresses, dirndl skirts, tube tops, and bare-back summer dresses.

Charles James: 1906–1978, England. Although born in England, as an American designer, James first became famous in 1932 for the culottes he designed, but later created sculpted ball gowns in lavish fabrics. He is also famous for his capes and coats, often trimmed in fur.

(Continued)

Ellen Endres

6-1 This list of the most famous fashion designers of the 19th and 20th centuries begins with the earliest designers, and includes the countries where they were born.

Continued

Oleg Cassini: 1913–2006, France. He became an American designer known for ready-to-wear sheath dresses, knitted suits, jackets, and cocktail dresses. He is most famous for the designs he created for Jacqueline Kennedy, creating her signature style.

Emilio Pucci: 1914–1992, Italy. In the 1950s, Pucci became famous for brightly printed silk blouses and shirts, capri pants, shorts, and mod tank dresses. His designs featured bold patterns and colors. The fashion house still continues today.

Bonnie Cashin: 1915–2000, U.S. Cashin was known for loose-fitting, functional, and clean designs. Her most popular designs were the poncho and funnel-necked pullover sweaters. She stopped designing in 1977.

Anne Klein: 1921–1974, U.S. Anne Klein began designing junior sportswear lines for young women, famous for matching dresses and jackets, battle jackets, and hooded blouson tops. Anne Klein & Co. was formed in 1968 and continues today.

Bill Blass: 1922–2002, U.S. Blass was a designer of elegant eveningwear as well as classic sportswear. He is most famous for ruffled collars, cuffs, and hemlines. He licensed many products.

Pierre Cardin: 1922–, Italy. Born in Italy to French parents, he became a French designer. He is best known for his "Space Age" collection consisting of catsuits, close-fitting helmets, and batwing jumpsuits. He also designed the "bubble dress" and unisex fashions.

Rudi Gernreich: 1922–1985, Austria. Gernreich, who became an American designer, did most of his designing in the 1960s for the young market. He is most famous for his topless bathing suit that featured straps from a high waist in front to the back.

Andre Courreges: 1923–, France. He became known for futuristic looks featuring very short skirts, mini dresses with trousers, and mid-calf white boots.

Geoffrey Beene: 1924–2004, U.S. He is most famous for elegant, superbly cut, couture apparel including empire dresses, shifts, and short skirts with long jackets. He licensed many products.

Hubert de Givenchy: 1927–, France. He designed women's eveningwear, suits, and dresses that were elegant and simple. He disliked decoration and concentrated on purity of line. He retired in 1995.

Liz Claiborne: 1929–2007, Belgium. Claiborne opened her own company in 1976, specializing in women's sportswear and officewear. She is best known for designing complete wardrobes of mix-and-match separates. The company still exists today.

Halston: 1932–1990, U.S. Halston was most famous for his knitwear, Ultrasuede dresses, sweater sets, wide-legged jersey trousers, and long slinky halter-neck gowns. The Halston label still continues to produce elegant designs.

Adolfo: 1933–, Cuba. He came to the U.S. and based his collections on knitted suits and tailored dresses for conservative clients. He stopped designing in 1993.

Ellen Endres

Mary Quant: 1934–, England. Quant designed for young people in the 1960s. She was best known for her miniskirts, skinny rib sweaters, low-slung hipster belts, and colored tights.

Yves Saint Laurent: 1936–2008, Algeria. As an Algerian-born French designer, Laurent was known for the trapeze dress, pea coats, tuxedo jackets, and safari jackets, as well as knickerbockers. He was most popular during the 1960s, creating sophisticated, restrained designs for men and women. He showed his last couture collection in 2002.

Perry Ellis: 1940–1986, U.S. Ellis began designing sportswear for men, then adapted the man's suit for women, creating a mannish but relaxed look. He often used textured wools and tweeds.

Willi Smith: 1948–1987, U.S. Smith opened WilliWear in 1976, specializing in oversized clothing, baggy trousers, and slouchy sweaters.

To survive, most French couture houses now produce their own RTW lines, or prêt-a-porter lines. **Prêt-a-porter** (pret-ah-pawr-TAY) means *ready-to-wear* in French. House boutiques (stores), specialty stores, and upscale department stores, such as Saks Fifth Avenue and Bloomingdales, sell these lines, 6-2.

Knockoffs

When people copy designers' high-priced designs and sell them at lower prices, they create **knockoffs**. The knockoffs may be made of less-expensive fabric or have less-complicated design details. The designs are similar, but not exact replicas. The gowns worn at the Academy Awards ceremonies are often copied immediately after the show.

In some countries, including the United States, it is legal. It is common to find exact line-for-line copies of designs. Copying a garment is illegal only if it has a unique *invention* that can be patented.

The practice is unfair to the original designers who receive nothing for the copied designs. Some designers in Europe are copyrighting their designs. However, with design copying occurring so quickly, by the time a designer obtains a copyright, the design is no longer in style.

Licensing

One way for designers and coutour houses to benefit from their design work is through licensing. **Licensing** occurs when the owner sells the right to use a particular name, image, or design to another party. The owner receives a *royalty*, or percentage of the profits, for this right. For example, a designer may give a manufacturer permission to use the designer's name on its product, such as a perfume. The manufacturer then pays a royalty to the designer. This practice is common and can be profitable for both parties.

Accessories and fragrances are often licensed. Other products that are licensed are eyewear, sportswear, children's clothes, home furnishings, and beauty products.

Celebrities may license their names for use on merchandise. Jessica Simpson, for instance, sold the use of her name to a manufacturer of a line of sportswear. Some designers have created merchandise for sale exclusively at certain retailers. Vera Wang's *Very Vera* brand sells only at Kohl's stores.

6-2 Upscale boutiques and exclusive department stores sell prêt-a-porter lines.
Shutterstock

Fashion Categories and Price Points

There are three major categories of apparel: men's, women's, and children's. Some companies manufacture garments in all three categories. Others may specialize in only one. Sometimes a company begins with one category, but expands to others as it grows. Retail stores also divide their apparel merchandise into these three categories.

Some companies divide these categories into additional subcategories, 6-3. Subdivisions in women's apparel, for example, may include

- outerwear (coats, jackets, and rainwear)
- dresses
- blouses
- career wear (suits, separates, and career dresses)
- sportswear (pants, sweaters, skirts, etc.)
- evening wear and special occasion
- bridal dresses
- maternity wear
- accessories
- intimate apparel

These categories are further broken down into size categories, such as misses, petites, and juniors. RTW fashion designers usually specialize in designing garments for just one category.

Price Points

The RTW apparel companies typically focus on one or more **price points**. These are categories based on either the wholesale or suggested retail price of the garments. These price points include the following:

- *Designer.* This is the most expensive price-point category for name designers.
- *Bridge.* This category falls between designer and better prices. It often is used for a name designer's less-expensive line, called a **diffusion line**. Examples of diffusion lines are *Marc for Marc Jacobs* and *D&G* by Dolce & Gabbana.
- *Better.* This category includes nationally known brand names, such as DKNY, or store brands, such as Banana Republic. A **store brand** is the name of a retail chain used as the store's exclusive label on their merchandise.

6-3 The category of women's apparel is further broken down into these subcategories.

Categories of Women's Apparel	
Outerwear (coats, jackets, and rainwear)	Evening wear and special occasion
Dresses	Bridal dresses
Blouses	Maternity wear
Career wear (suits, separates, and career dresses)	Accessories
Sportswear (pants, sweaters, skirts, etc.)	Intimate apparel

- *Moderate.* These reasonably priced lines include the sportswear brand names of Dockers. They also include less-expensive lines of companies with better merchandise, such as Lizwear.
- *Budget or mass.* Mass merchandisers and discount stores, or retailers who feature low prices, such as Old Navy, generally sell this merchandise.

Less-costly garments are often copies of more expensive ones. For example, an expensive suit may be made of silk. The less expensive one in a similar design may be made of polyester. Vinyl buttons and belts may replace the leather ones on a lower-cost suit. Less-expensive garments may require less fabric and fewer, less-detailed construction steps.

Where Do Fashion Designers Work?

Fashion designers are the people who create the designs and ideas for new clothes and accessories. They may specialize in women's, men's, or children's clothing. They may specialize further in certain types of garments such as men's coats, women's dresses, or children's sleepwear. Most designers work for ready-to-wear manufacturers.

Fashion designers usually begin their careers as assistants to higher-level designers in the RTW industry. Other entry-level jobs that may lead to designing are sample maker, sketching assistant, and sketcher. Eventually people in these jobs may move up into design positions.

Some designers begin their careers in retailing or at fashion magazines. This allows them to learn more about the fashion business before they go out on their own as independent designers.

A small number of unknown fashion designers begin by creating their own lines after receiving financial backing. This is a risky way to begin, but a few designers have been successful after opening their own businesses.

Fashion Capitals

Most new fashions originate in four cities, or **fashion capitals,** around the world. Most fashion designers eventually locate in these cities. They include the following:

- *Paris, France.* Haute couture began in Paris, and most people consider this city the fashion capital of the world. The couture houses are located here, and many designers seek the prestige of showing and selling their lines in Paris.
- *New York City.* In the United States, New York City is the fashion capital. During World War II, when travel to Paris was impossible, New York City emerged as a leader in fashion design. Most of the design studios and showrooms are located in the Seventh Avenue Garment District, 6-4.

6-4 Seventh Avenue in New York City, also known as the garment district, is the location of many fashion design studios. *Shutterstock*

- *Milan, Italy.* Milan was first known for its menswear, but now also creates beautiful textiles, knitwear, leather goods, and sportswear. Most of the RTW manufacturers in Italy are located in Milan.
- *London, England.* London is known for its *Savile Row* tailors who make classic men's business attire. Young designers who created the *punk* look in the 1960s also made London a fashion capital. Many of today's designers focus on styles that appeal to younger consumers.

Fashion weeks are held in these four cities. **Fashion week** is a fashion industry event that occurs twice a year and can last up to 10 days. During this time, fashion designers, brands, or houses present their latest collections in runway shows. Buyers, celebrities, and fashion editors are invited to see what styles will be available for the upcoming season. In New York City, tents are set up in Manhattan. As many as 50 shows may take place during fashion week, **6-5**.

Though most people consider these four cities to be fashion capitals, the fashion industry today has a global nature. In the United States, other important cities are San Francisco, Los Angeles, Dallas, Atlanta, Miami, Chicago, Portland, and Seattle. Montreal and Toronto are important fashion cities in Canada. Additional European fashion centers are in Germany, Spain, Denmark, Norway, Sweden, and Finland. Important fashion centers throughout the rest of the world are located in Australia, New Zealand, Japan, South Africa, India, Turkey, Brazil, and China.

The Fashion Design Process

Fashion design is a process. Good designers need to have certain qualities. They must be creative and imaginative, and must have artistic ability and a flair for clothing. Knowledge about fabrics is essential, along with familiarity with the processes used in making fabrics and garments. Sewing skills are a must. Designers use this knowledge to ensure the items they design can be produced within a given price range.

What Inspires Designers?

Where do designers get their ideas for new styles? Fashion designers look to various sources for inspiration. Many use museum exhibits of historical

6-5 The top designers of the world will show their collections during fashion week in New York City. *Shutterstock*

clothing, art galleries, and libraries as resources. World events often influence fashion trends.

Historic and Ethnic Costume Collections

Designers often study history to get ideas and create new designs using details from the past. They may look to the ancient Greek and Roman costumes, medieval costumes, or Victorian fashions. Some designers today are recreating styles—or *retro fashions*—from more recent decades, such as the 1940s or 1950s. They may also visit vintage clothing shops to find ideas to interpret for today's wearer.

Designers also get ideas by studying folk or ethnic costumes. They may recreate color motifs, lines, or shapes and incorporate them into their designs. Chinese and Russian folk costumes are a source of inspiration for some current designers. Carnival, a festival in Brazil, inspired a collection by designer Narciso Rodriguez.

The Arts

Fashion designers might visit art exhibits for inspiration. For example, the works of Brazilian artist Beatriz Milhazes and Art Deco artist Rene Gruau inspired Jason Wu's Spring 2011 collection. Current movies and popular television shows can inspire fashion ideas. Designers pay attention to what the top musical performers are wearing. Because teens often copy what their favorite popular celebrities are wearing, designers duplicate these fashions for the ready-to-wear market.

Textiles

Many designers get their inspiration from examining new swatches of fabrics from textile plants. These might have interesting prints or unique textures. A designer might see a beautiful fabric made into a certain garment style, **6-6**. The textile colors might inspire a complete line of apparel.

Nature

Designers also study nature for ideas to translate into fashion. The colors of nature—from sky and water to trees and fauna—are a source of inspiration to many designers. For example, the lapping water on the beaches of Dubai along with the shells he collected there, inspired William Tempest, a British designer. These visions inspired the colors and curves in his fashion collection.

6-6 This beautiful blue brocade fabric might have been the inspiration for this young designer. *Fashion Institute of Technology*

Observations

Designers also observe the world around them. They observe lifestyles and living patterns. They watch people on the streets or on their way to work. They take photos or make sketches on the spot. They want to design garments that meet the everyday needs of people. For example, designers who observe that exercise and fitness is a current trend create comfortable garments for people who work out. Their designs use fabrics that move with the body and absorb moisture.

Sometimes, instead of designers creating new fashion ideas, fashions come from the street. For instance, jeans and military surplus clothing started out as *street* fashions. Later, designers and trendsetters caught onto these fashions and made them *new* fashions.

Creating the Design Ideas

Once the designer has an idea or concept, he or she might begin by sketching designs. Some designers use a body sketch called a **croquis** (crow-KEY), 6-7. They draw onto the croquis or place an overlay sheet over the figure. Other designers do not use a body sketch. Instead, they utilize a **technical drawing,** or *tech drawing,* to show their garment designs. Designers often experiment with different versions, varying details such as seam lines and trimmings. A number of sketches and revisions might be necessary before a designer finalizes a design concept.

Most fashion designers today use CAD, computer-aided design, to develop their ideas. Many, if not all, apparel companies expect their designers to create tech drawings using CAD. CAD allows the designer to create, modify, and communicate pattern designs. Using a computer, a designer can change seam lines, move pockets, or change pleats into gathers. The designer can try different color combinations and different trims before achieving the right look. The ability to experiment is one of the advantages of using CAD. Another advantage is the time-saving that results.

An apparel-company designer may present as many as 60 design ideas to a review team to consider. The anticipated cost of producing garments is a key factor in the review process. The review team may recommend cost-cutting modifications, such as the use of less-expensive fabrics or trims. Of the original sketches, 30 or 40 will continue to the next stage.

6-7 Fashion designers may use a croquis, or body sketch, to draft their garment designs.
Ellen Endres/Steve Olewinski

Making the Samples

Once the review team selects a design, the next step is to make a sample, or **prototype**. Again using the CAD drawing, the designer plots a pattern on a screen and prints it out, 6-8.

A sample maker (who must have excellent sewing skills) creates the prototype in the company's sample size. He or she cuts the pattern from the specified fabric to make sure it is appropriate for the design. After the prototype is finished, the review team evaluates the style on a live fit model and a final decision is made. The designer and sample maker evaluate the overall style and construction details. Sometimes production engineers weight in with potential problems in factory production. If so, revision of the pattern may be necessary. The team may drop the style or make modifications. If the style is accepted, it receives a style number and moves to the production stage.

Today's Fashion Designers

The names of today's top fashion designers are frequently in the news. Watch a telecast of any film or television awards show and see celebrities on the red carpet wearing designer gowns. Reporters often ask celebrities, "Who designed your gown?" Read any fashion magazine and many designers are featured.

Figure 6-9 lists today's top fashion designers. Most of these designers have shown their collections for several decades and have established names in the industry. Only a few designers listed have become well known within the last decade. The names of most designers will never become synonymous with fashion. That is because they work in the ready-to-wear industry, designing apparel average people wear daily. There are many apparel industry designers worldwide. This industry employs the majority of fashion designers.

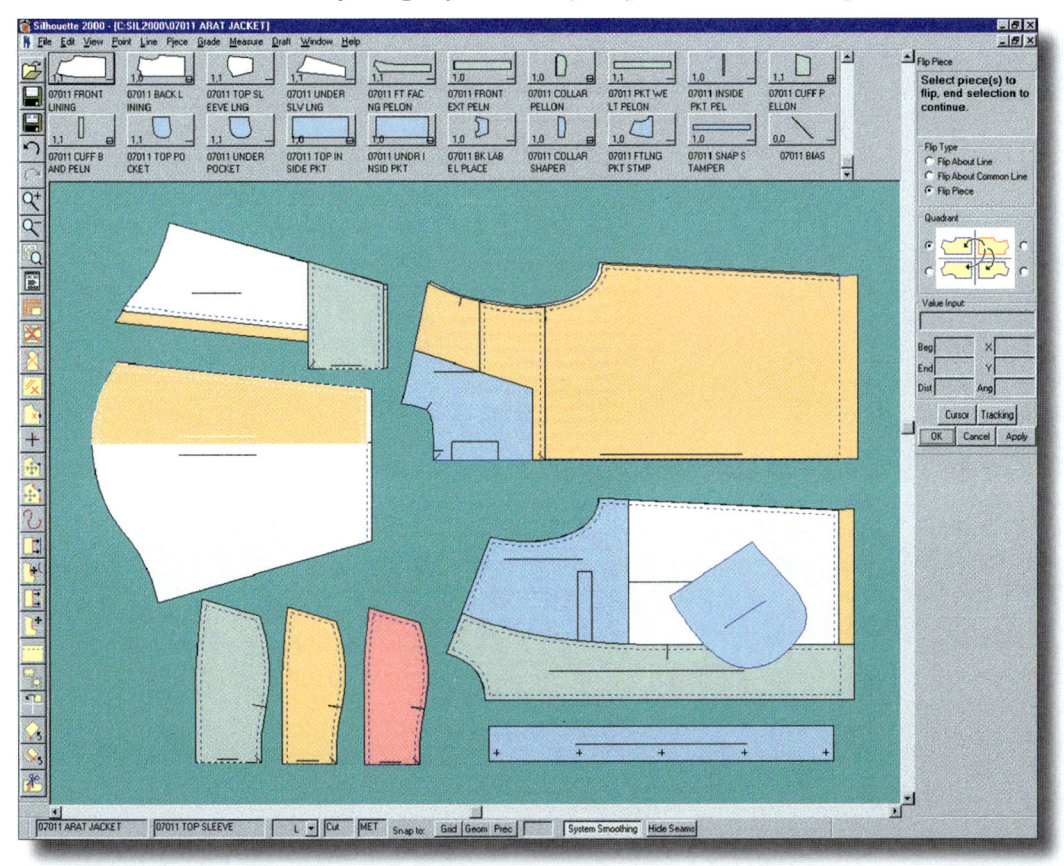

6-8 Pattern design is carried out electronically using CAD software. Revisions can be done quickly and easily.
Gerber Technology

Today's Top Fashion Designers

Giorgio Armani: Italian designer of menswear, especially unstructured suits, and some womenswear.

Badgley Mischka: Two American designers, Mark Badgley and James Mischka, teamed up in 1988 to form their label. They are best known for evening wear, fragrance, shoes, and handbags.

Monolo Blahnik: British designer of well-crafted and elaborate high heels.

Tory Burch: One of the newest American designers, Burch's fashion label began in 2004, and now is sold in 26 boutiques. Her designs are reminiscent of the 1950s and 60s, featuring caftans, tunics, sequined cardigans, and ballerina flats. They often feature the T-logo medallion.

Stephen Burrows: An American designer who popularized patchwork and visible use of machine-stitching. He is especially known for zigzag stitching along hems, creating the lettuce edge.

Oscar de la Renta: Designs elegant men's and women's clothes in New York and Paris.

Dolce and Gabbana: Two Italian designers, Domenico Dolce and Stefano Gabbana, formed their label in 1982. It became one of Italy's most successful ready-to-wear companies.

Jean-Paul Gaultier: Best known for his daring, form-fitting, controversial designs for younger men and women, Gaultier's designs are often unisex.

Caroline Herrera: Created her first ready-to-wear collection in 1981. Herrera's designs feature layered clothes of various fabrics in different lengths and is known for elegant day and evening wear.

Tommy Hilfiger: An American designer who began with menswear, Hilfiger now designs casual womenswear, accessories, and home fashions.

Marc Jacobs: Considered one of the hottest American fashion designers today, Jacobs began designing for Louis Vuitton in 1997. He created the grunge look in 1994, but his designs today are more luxurious.

Betsey Johnson: As an American designer of youthful clothes, Johnson created the disco look in the 1970s. She is known for extravagant, body-conscious clothes that are often made from stretch jersey.

Ellen Endres

Norma Kamali: Designing since 1968, Kamali considers her core pieces the jumpsuit, and a sleeping bag coat. She is known for her use of parachute cloth and her signature color scheme of black, white, and red.

Donna Karan: As an American designer of simple women's clothing, Karan's garments feature wraparound skirts and dresses and bodysuits of Lycra®.

Rei Kawakubo: Born in Japan, Rei is known for her torn, crumpled garments that drape around the body. Her knitwear is often tattered and ripped.

Calvin Klein: He first designed coats, blazers, and suits, as well as other sportswear, with simple, straight, pared-down looks. He became popular for his "designer" jeans in the 1970s and his underwear designs in the 1990s.

Michael Kors: Kors began his own sportswear label in 1981. His designs are considered minimalist. Kors is best known for his clinging dresses and jumpsuits, layered with jackets.

Christian Lacroix: A French designer, Lacroix opened his own couture house in Paris in 1987. He rocked the fashion world by launching a ready-to-wear line in 1988 and created the "pouf" skirt.

Karl Lagerfeld: Born in Germany, Lagerfeld began designing for Chanel in 1983, adding his unique touch to traditional Chanel. A year later, he launched his first collection under his own name.

Ralph Lauren: Created menswear under the Polo name, Lauren then expanded to include womenswear. He is known for his American-frontier fashion look.

Stella McCartney: After beginning her career designing for Christian Lacroix, McCartney created her own label in 2001. She features a complete line of womenswear, accessories, fragrance, skincare, eyewear, and perfume.

Alexander McQueen: A British designer who produced shocking, but creative designs, McQueen was head designer at Givenchy for five years before he left to create under his own label.

(Continued)

6-9 Here is a partial list of today's top fashion designers.

Continued

Nicole Miller: An independent American designer, Miller launched her first runway show in 1990. Her company sells all forms of apparel as well as eyewear, jewelry, cosmetics, and more. A line of novelty print ties for men were a huge success.

Rosita and Ottavio Missoni: A husband and wife team, Rosita and Ottavio launched a line of knitwear in bold patterns, colors, and designs. The company has now diversified into home furnishings.

Issey Miyake: Created a layered and wrapped look in the 1970s that became his hallmark. He is known for his minimalist designs using technology. For example, he created an outfit using a tube of cloth with the style and seams of the outfit embedded in it.

Isaac Mizrahi: An American designer, Mizrahi worked for Perry Ellis and Calvin Klein before forming his own company in 1987. He has designed baby-doll dresses, evening jumpsuits, and flounced tube dresses.

Claude Montana: A French designer who launched his first clothing collection in 1977, Montana is known for creating strong, masculine, broad-shouldered jackets and coats. He prefers working with leather.

Zac Posen: At the age of 21, Posen produced his first collection in 2002 and quickly became popular with young celebrities. His designs are influenced by the tailored look of the 40s, but with a feminine twist.

Miuccia Prada: An Italian designer, Prada designed her first clothing collection in 1988. Her clothes are described as highly designed, but body friendly, covered up, with boxy shapes.

Tracy Reese: A successful African-American designer with her own label and company, Reese launched her own line in 1996. She expanded her label and company in 2004 to include a line of bedding, curtains, and throws. The following year she added shoes and accessories.

Rodarte: Founded by sisters Kate and Laura Mulleavy in 2005, Rodarte is a brand of clothing and accessories

Narciso Rodriguez: A Cuban-American designer who worked for Anne Klein and Calvin Kline before launching his own collection in 1997, Rodriguez designed the dress Michelle Obama wore the night she and the then president-elect appeared for the first time in Chicago. He has a successful line of fragrances, as well.

Cynthia Rowley: She started by showing her designs in her own apartment in 1983, and incorporated her business in 1988. Rowley designs womenswear, menswear, shoes, handbags, and more, selling them in her shops in the major cities around the world.

Sonia Rykiel: Rykiel opened her first boutique in 1968 specializing in knitwear. Her figure-hugging designs feature soft wools, jersey, angora, and mohair.

Angel Sanchez: Born in Venezuela, Sanchez launched a bridal collection in 1999. He is known for his brightly colored cocktail dresses and evening gowns.

Jil Sander: Sander is one of Germany's most important designers. Her garments have a minimalist style and often resemble male garments in their simplicity.

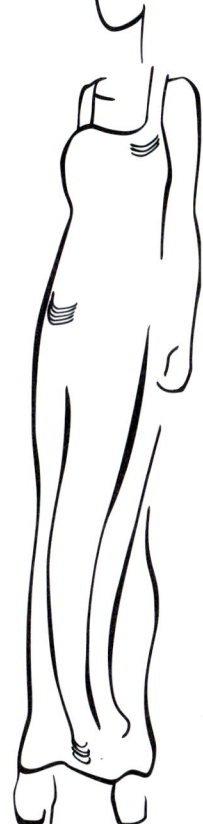

Ellen Endres

Anna Sui: Sui became well-known in 1991. Her designs show flair and humor, with a contemporary twist on vintage styles.

Emanuel Ungaro: Ungaro launched his company in 1965. He is best known for his soft, form-fitting apparel in many colors and patterns.

Valentino: In 1959, Valentino opened a couture house in Rome. His designs were elegant, glamorous, and gracefully cut, and often featured his initial "V." Though he is retired, his house continues to operate.

Versace: Gianni Versace (1946–1997) was one of the most important Italian designers of the 1980s and 1990s. He was known for his strong colors and clean lines. Following his death, his sister—Donatella—has designed for the label.

Diane Von Furstenberg: In 1972, Von Furstenberg opened her own business and created a jersey wraparound dress that became a best-seller. It had long sleeves, a fitted top, and a skirt that wrapped to tie at the waist.

Alexander Wang: As a young designer who launched his first clothing collection in 2007, Wang is known for designing of edgy clothing that is a bit punk rock.

Vera Wang: As an American designer known for exquisite bridal gowns and evening dresses, Wang has expanded her line to include evening wear, ready-to-wear, furs, and shoes.

Jason Wu: Wu is a young Asian-American designer who became famous after Michelle Obama wore his one-shoulder gown on inaugural night in 2008.

Fashion Publications and Associations

There are many ways to learn about the fashion industry today and to stay on top of the latest fashions. Traditionally, fashion magazines and newspapers, both print and online versions, have been the best sources of information for consumers. Fashion editors stay on top of the latest fashion trends and share them with their readers. They inform readers of where to find certain styles and how to wear and accessorize them.

The first fashion magazines were published in the late 1800s. Two of these, *Harper's Bazaar* and *Vogue*, are still available today. Some magazines target the young, contemporary buyer. These include *Elle*, *Teen Vogue*, and *InStyle*. Hundreds of fashion magazines are published today.

The most important trade publication is *Women's Wear Daily*. This newspaper is available five days a week in print or by online subscription. Industry people—fashion designers, manufacturers, and retailers—read this publication. Other trade publications specialize in specific segments of the industry.

Fashion News via Technology

Young buyers often prefer to find out the latest fashion news using technology. Fashion designers and manufacturers are taking advantage of these new ways of communicating with potential customers.

- *Websites.* There are numerous websites on fashion. Most of the major manufacturers and retailers have their own websites. In addition, countless other sites provide the latest fashion news. Many broadcast live runway shows over the Web.
- *Blogs and YouTube.* Blogs allow fashion designers to self-publish text, art, and links to their websites. YouTube offers short online-fashion videos to give customers new ways to interact with brands and view clothing in motion.
- *Apps.* One of the latest ways fashion designers are reaching consumers is through mobile-device technology. In recent years, at least a dozen fashion designers and labels have created apps for smartphone users. These apps showcase new collections, often to music, and offer style tips.
- *Twitter.* Dozens of fashion labels are using Twitter to communicate with potential customers. Tweets sent during Fashion Weeks provide designers instant feedback from attendees. Several designers tweet themselves, while others have staff members communicate with readers.
- *Facebook.* Though established as a social-networking site for staying in touch with friends, businesses use Facebook to communicate with their customers. Apparel manufacturers, retailers, and fashion designers have Facebook pages on which they share the latest information about their designs. They promote events, sales, and special offers to their customers. In return, their customers can post comments and provide immediate feedback.
- *Television shows.* With the advent of cable television, particularly the Style Network, people can view many fashion-related shows.

Trade Associations

People who work in the textile and apparel industry often belong to trade associations. **Trade associations** consist of member companies. Trade associations do research, promotions, and provide educational services for their industries. They usually sponsor trade shows. They also develop educational materials related to the apparel industry. Their research divisions may compile statistics important to association members.

The largest of the apparel associations is the American Apparel & Footwear Association (AAFA). This is an umbrella trade association for apparel companies. Other trade associations, such as the Children's Apparel Manufacturers Association, focus on specific divisions of the RTW industry.

The membership of the Council of Fashion Designers of America, Inc. (CFDA) includes more than 350 of America's best womenswear, menswear, jewelry, and accessory designers. In addition to giving design awards, they offer professional development programs and scholarships. Another key trade association is the Fashion Group International, Inc. (FGI). FGI has 5,000 members worldwide who have an interest in the business of fashion and design. Most members have careers in the fashion field. They use FGI to stay in touch with industry trends and issues. FGI also gives awards and scholarships.

Retailers are often members of the National Retail Federation (NRF). This is the largest trade association for retailers in the United States.

Highlights in History

Christian Dior: A Name Synonymous with Fashion

One of the most famous fashion designers of all time was Christian Dior. He was 31 years old when he began sketching fashion designs in Paris in 1938. Though his career was temporarily halted during World War II, in 1947 he opened his own fashion house for *truly elegant women*. His first collection was launched this same year. Fashions during and after the war were subject to fabric restrictions. These restrictions lead to short skirts and conservative designs. Christian Dior made a sensation with his truly feminine silhouette—wide rustling skirts with a daring mid-calf length setting off a tiny waist and rounded shoulders. The line became known as "The New Look" and symbolized the end of the war. The fashion look was an instant hit, and Dior's name became known worldwide.

Though The New Look dominated the fashion scene for several years, Dior continued to create variations on his basic theme throughout his twenty-two collections. All of his designs featured tasteful elegance, but were also in keeping with the demands of modern life, making his clothes easy to wear. Every garment Dior designed was fully lined to make sure the structure was well supported. Each design started with a study of the fabric, followed by a hundred or so sketches before it reached its final form.

Dior dressed the most elegant women of the time—the Duchess of Windsor, Marlene Dietrich, Britain's Princess Margaret and Princess Grace of Monaco, to name but a few. Dior felt his designs were for all women, for any day and any hour. He designed each garment for a particular time and place, whether a travel suit, an afternoon dress, a ball gown, or a tea.

Christian Dior died in 1957 at the age of 52. In only a very short time, he had become one of the most famous men in the world. The House of Dior continued after his death through another famous designer, Yves Saint Laurent.

Christian Dior's childhood home at Granville in France is now the Christian Dior Museum. *Goodheart-Willcox Publisher*

Summary

- Most of the apparel produced today is ready-to-wear (RTW). *Couture* refers to garments made to fit a particular customer.
- When the high-priced designs of name designers are copied and sold at lower prices, the copies are called *knockoffs*.
- Licensing is one way for designers and couture houses to receive payments from their designs.
- There are three major categories of apparel: men's, women's, and children's. Categories are further divided into subcategories of specific types of apparel, such as dresses, blouses, and sportswear.
- Fashion designers work in all apparel categories and at all price points. A particular designer may specialize in a certain category of apparel.
- Fashion designers begin creating their lines with a concept or idea. They use various sources for inspiration.
- Designers create sketches or technical drawings of their design idea.
- Fashion magazines, newspapers, technology, and trade associations relate fashion industry information to the public.
- Trade associations consist of member companies. They do research, promotions, and provide educational services for their industries.

Graphic Organizer

On a separate sheet of paper, draw a graphic organizer like the one you see here. Note the parts of the fashion design process and list two key facts about each.

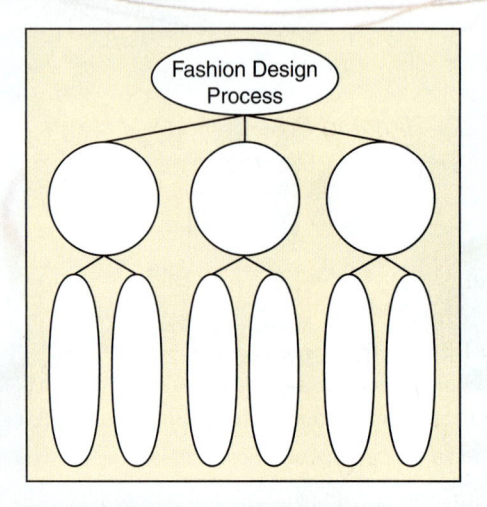

Review the Facts

1. Contrast the terms *ready-to-wear* and *couture*.
2. Who is considered the founder of haute couture?
3. How do knockoffs benefit consumers? How do they affect designers?
4. What is licensing? Give an example of a product that might be licensed. State who grants the license and who manufactures the licensed product.
5. List three price point categories. Give an example of a brand or label in each category.
6. What are the four fashion capitals of the world?
7. Describe what takes place during fashion week.
8. Give an example of a source of inspiration for a fashion designer. Then describe how it might translate into a design feature in a garment.
9. State three ways designers might create and present their fashion designs.
10. What is the difference between a croquis and a technical drawing?
11. Which fashion publication is the most important and influential in the fashion industry?
12. Name the trade association that covers all segments of the apparel industry.

Think Critically

13. **Debate.** In teams, debate the pros and cons of knockoff designs. Give evidence to support your reasoning.
14. **Draw conclusions.** What television shows and movies do you feel influence fashion design? What designs did they appear to inspire? Give a summary of your conclusions.
15. **Make inferences.** How do fashion designers benefit from such social networking sites as blogs or Facebook? Share your inferences with the class.
16. **Compare and contrast.** Compare and contrast the advantages and disadvantages you have observed about careers in fashion design. Would you choose this career? Why or why not?

Apparel Applications

17. **Fashion research.** Search the Internet for information on the Rodarte clothing brand and the two sisters who created it. Create an illustrated presentation to share.
18. **Compare garment quality.** As a class project, choose a garment style, such as jeans, that everyone wears. In teams, bring in samples of this garment style at four price points. How do the jeans differ in construction quality and fabric? Present your findings to the class.
19. **Fashion week technology.** Find out when the next fashion week will take place in New York City. Identify ways you can view the runway shows in real time and share with the class. What technology is necessary?
20. **Vintage clothing research.** Review several vintage clothing websites. Find an item of clothing or a garment feature that would appeal to you if you were designing a new garment. Print an example or post it to a school-approved class blog to share with the class.
21. **Designer report.** Choose one of the fashion designers listed in this chapter. Use Internet or print resources to create an in-depth illustrated report on this designer. Print and mount several designs. Share your report.
22. **Magazine evaluation.** Bring to class a fashion magazine that you read regularly. Compare it with magazines brought in by other students. Discuss what fashion designers are appealing to consumers today.
23. **Website review.** Tour the websites for the trade associations mentioned in this chapter. Compare the goals and mission statements for these associations. What are the similarities and differences? How do they benefit tradespeople and ultimately the consumer?

Academic Connections

24. **Writing.** Review the website for one of the 11 couture houses in Paris. Use a school-approved online blog application or presentation software to prepare a visual report about the couture house you chose to share with the class.
25. **Social studies.** Investigate what other countries, such as France, England, or Italy, are doing to prevent fashion knockoffs. Write a report summarizing your findings.

Workplace Links

26. **Research careers.** Locate the websites of apparel manufacturers in your state. Review the career links on the websites for fashion design jobs available. Choose two jobs. Identify the job descriptions, education requirements, and salaries. Share your findings with the class.
27. **Design inspiration.** Presume you are a fashion designer. Choose an item of inspiration for your next line. Share your design inspiration with the class. Explain how it will influence your design of an apparel item.
28. **Portfolio builder.** Meet with an art teacher or local fashion designer to learn how to draw a *croquis* or body sketch. Practice your drawing skills until the teacher or fashion designer feels you have mastered the skills. Then draw a simple fashion design you think will appeal to teens. Save a copy of your best design for your portfolio.

Fashion Design

For an individual event, use the FCCLA *Planning Process* to plan, carry out, and evaluate a project for the FCCLA *Fashion Design* STAR Event. The event conditions and requirements include

- developing a clothing label
- researching the intended target audience
- designing the label's first six-piece collection

Once you develop your sewing skills later in this course, you will select garment fabrics, sew a sample garment, and prepare your presentation. Use the FCCLA *STAR Events Manual* on the FCCLA website to identify specific competition requirements for your project. See your adviser for information as needed.

PART 2

Apparel Decisions

Chapters

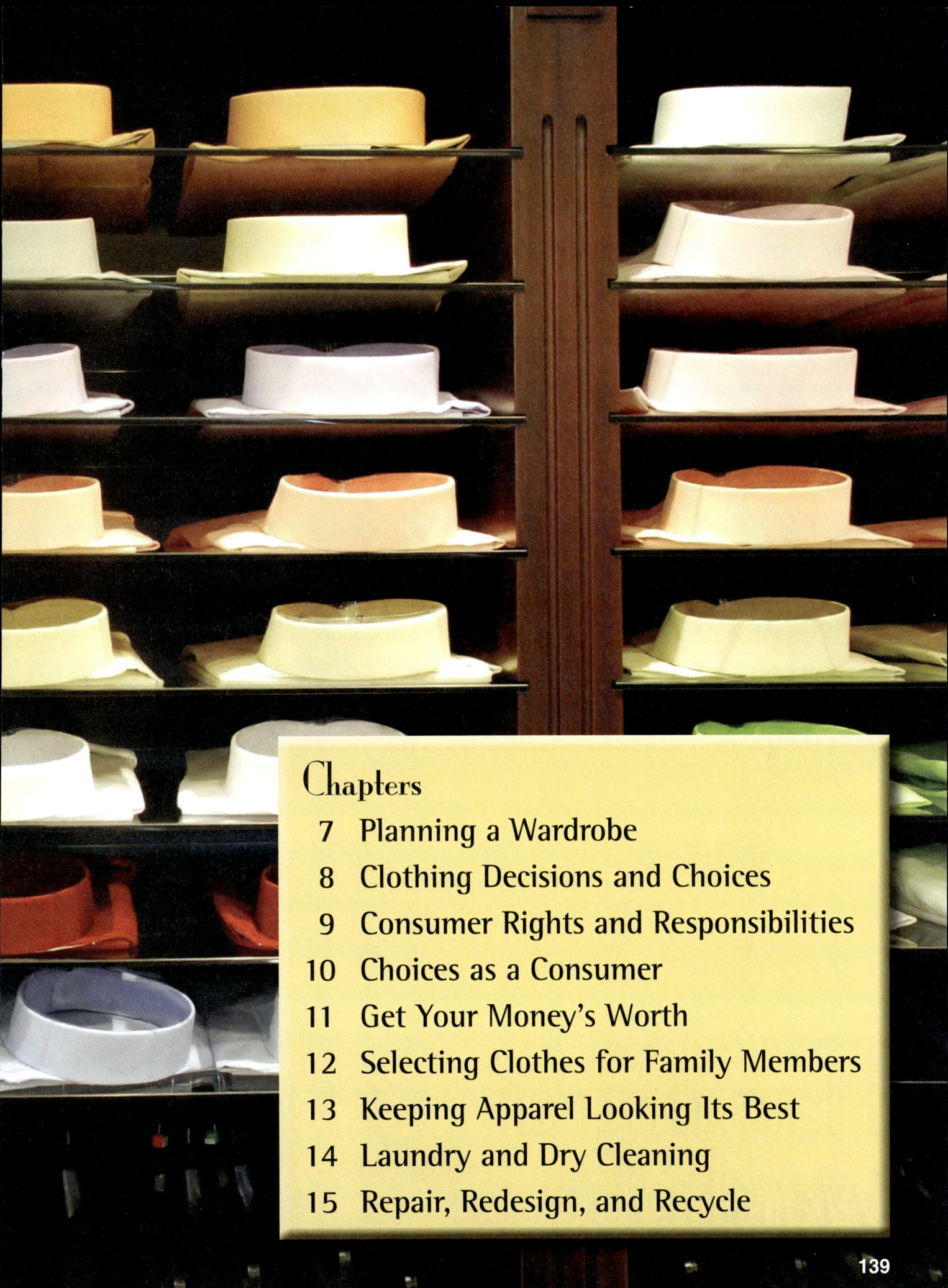

7 Planning a Wardrobe

8 Clothing Decisions and Choices

9 Consumer Rights and Responsibilities

10 Choices as a Consumer

11 Get Your Money's Worth

12 Selecting Clothes for Family Members

13 Keeping Apparel Looking Its Best

14 Laundry and Dry Cleaning

15 Repair, Redesign, and Recycle

Chapter 7

Planning a Wardrobe

Chapter Objectives

After studying this chapter, you will be able to
- **summarize** the benefits of wardrobe planning.
- **create** a clothing inventory.
- **evaluate** a clothing inventory to determine clothing needs and wants.
- **prioritize** clothing needs and wants.
- **demonstrate** how to mix-and-match clothing to create new outfits.
- **summarize** how accessories can extend a wardrobe.
- **select** appropriate clothing for different occasions and activities.

Key Terms

wardrobe
wardrobe plan
inventory
order of priority
mix-and-match wardrobe
accessories
dress codes

Reading with Purpose

On a sheet of paper, write the main headings in the chapter and leave space under each heading. As you read the chapter, write three main points that you learned after reading the information in each passage.

It has probably happened to you. A friend texts and invites you to go somewhere special. It suddenly hits you. You shout, "I have nothing to wear!" You look in your closet and shake your head. Nothing seems right for the occasion. That's when you think to yourself, "Why didn't I plan for something like this so I'd have the right clothes to wear?"

A simple solution to this dilemma could have been a wardrobe plan. In this chapter, you will learn how to review the clothes you have and evaluate what you need to add to meet your needs.

Making a Wardrobe Plan

A **wardrobe** is a collection of clothes and accessories a person has to wear. A good wardrobe does not just happen. It requires careful planning. A *plan* is a method a person uses to achieve a goal. With a **wardrobe plan**, you will know what clothes you currently have and which items you will need to add in the future.

The Benefits of a Well-Planned Wardrobe

In planning a wardrobe, the major benefit is having the appropriate clothes for any activity that might come your way. Your wardrobe should include suitable clothes for all your activities—at home, at school, at work, and for special occasions.

Another benefit of planning is to make better use of the clothes you already have. Before you buy a new garment, you should know how it will fit into your wardrobe. With planning, you will be able to identify which of your garments go well with others—seeming to double in number.

A third benefit of wardrobe planning is having a buying plan. When you go shopping, you will know what to look for—saving both time and money. You can avoid wasting time looking for items you do not really need, or wasting money buying clothes you forgot you already own or do not wear. You will know what additions your wardrobe requires so you can make smarter purchases.

Taking a Closer Look at What You Have

A good wardrobe plan will help you make better use of your present wardrobe. Most people are not aware of how many clothes they really have. Your first step in making a wardrobe plan is taking an inventory of the clothes you already own, **7-1**. An **inventory** is an itemized list of certain items—in this case, clothing and accessories. Have you ever made an inventory of all your clothing? Making a clothing inventory can give you a feeling of self-confidence and organization. You may even find a surprise in the back of your closet!

It is a good idea to take your clothing inventory at the beginning of a season or school year. The chart in **7-2** can serve as an inventory guide. You may want to add more rows or columns to the inventory. Include all of your clothes and accessories, grouping clothes and accessories by type. For instance, put all of your pants together, your shirts together, and your shorts together.

In addition to listing everything, ask yourself these questions: Which clothes are most enjoyable to wear? Which ones help you look your best? Which ones do you no longer wear and why? Your answers to these questions will depend on how the construction and quality of the clothes, how they fit, how you feel in them, the color, the type of fabric, and the design. The answers to these questions will help you have a better idea as to your clothing likes and dislikes.

7-1 Take a look at your wardrobe before you shop to see what you already have.
Shutterstock

Evaluating Your Wardrobe

When completing your wardrobe inventory, *evaluate* each item to determine its worth. After listing each item, note how you like it. Do you enjoy wearing the item, or do you seldom, if ever, wear it? Does it go with other items in your wardrobe, or do you need something to wear with it?

Evaluate the condition of each item. Is it like new, or is it wearing out? Does it need cleaning or repair? If there are garments that need repair, put them in a special section in your inventory. Indicate what repairs you need to make, such as stitching a seam that is coming loose or sewing on a button. As you find time, you can work on them. If items need to be dry cleaned, put these aside, too.

7-2 This partially complete chart of a young man's wardrobe may help you get started on a clothing inventory of your own.

Wardrobe Inventory				
List of My Clothes	*Description*	*How I Like It*	*Condition*	*What I Need to Add or Do*
Suits (guys)	none	don't like		
Sport Coats (guys)	1—plain brown	OK	like new	
Dresses (girls)				
Skirts (girls)				
Slacks	1—tan 1—plaid	like a lot don't like	good too small	1—pair plain—colored
Jeans	4 pairs	great	3—good 1—worn out	1—new pair
Shirts/Blouses	3—plain 5—pattern	like patterned ones best	2—too small	2—new shirts
Sweaters				
Jackets				
Coats	all weather	fits my needs	good	
Shoes/Boots	1—pair for school 1—pair boots	OK my favorite	beat up pretty good	new shoes
Underwear				
Socks				
Jewelry				
Belts				
Other				

Evaluate the fit of each item. Have you outgrown some of your clothes? Consider passing some of the clothing you have outgrown on to someone else.

When your inventory is complete, you can do an overall evaluation of your wardrobe. In the last column of the inventory, explain what actions you will take with each garment. For instance, you can now see what clothes you own and what, if any, new ones you need to add. You may find that you have more clothes in good condition than you thought. You may discover that you can combine more garments to create additional outfits. Also, make decisions about what to do with garments that need repair or you need to discard. Indicate who might welcome your discarded items.

Now look at the items under each category in your wardrobe inventory. Do you have too many clothing items of one type and not enough of another? For instance, are all of your shirts suited to jeans and only one to dress slacks? Do you have enough dress-up clothes for the number of times you need them?

What else can you learn from your inventory? Perhaps you can tell what type of clothing you like best from the comments under the heading, *How I Like It*. See 7-3. These garments probably best suit your figure or build, skin coloring, and personality. Deciding what you like best when there is so much to choose from is an accomplishment. In the future when shopping for new clothes, you will know the types of clothes that are most enjoyable to wear—helping you make savvy purchases.

Adding to Your Wardrobe

Now that you have a better picture of your current wardrobe, you can see what you need to add to it. Make a list of the clothes you need to replace because they no longer fit. Be sure to include the clothes that you have worn out. In addition, list the clothes that will help fill in some missing pieces in your wardrobe. As you make your shopping list, consider both your needs and your wants.

7-3 Take a close look at the clothes you like best to help you decide your likes and dislikes.
Shutterstock

Needs and Wants

You may find it difficult to distinguish between needs and wants. Few people would be happy if they had only things they need. Your actual clothing needs are few, but your wants are likely unlimited.

A *need* is something you require for existence. The most basic clothing need is covering your body for protection from the environment. For instance, you need a warm coat if you live in a cold climate. There are varying degrees of need, however. You may need to buy a required gym uniform for school, or your workplace may require a certain outfit. These are all examples of clothing needs.

A *want* is a desire for something that will give you more satisfaction than you currently have. Wants are endless. You may want clothes for attractiveness, enjoyment, variety, or self-confidence. Many wants result from the desire to have something because somebody else has it.

Your peer group and close friends also influence your clothing wants. Most teens like to dress as their peers do, and certain clothes help to accomplish this goal. Such clothes may seem like a need to you, but your parents may consider them wants.

Manufacturers use advertisements to make consumers want their products and fashions. Merchants set up attractive displays in stores to convince customers that they want certain merchandise. In 7-4, the display shows several styles of tops and pants. At first glance, you might think you would like to have one of the garments. However, if you refer back to your clothing inventory and the things you need, you might be able to resist the tempting display.

Prioritize Your Needs and Wants

As you review your list of wardrobe needs and wants, put them in **order of priority**, or list them from the *most* important to the *least* important. You may need some items right away, while others can wait. Because most people have a limited amount of money to spend on clothes, they need to buy the most important items first. These items are top priority. After purchasing the items you need, consider adding some of the items you want if money is still available. These items are lower on the priority list.

Stretching Your Clothing Dollars

7-4 Attractive window displays may cause you to confuse your clothing needs and wants.
Shutterstock

Few people have an unlimited amount of money to spend on clothes. Most people can benefit from finding ways to stretch their clothing dollars. This means finding ways to make the clothing you have work for more occasions. It also means buying new items that you will wear often instead of sitting in a drawer. Some of the following ideas may help.

Mixing and Matching

Mixing and matching is an easy way to make more outfits from the clothes you own. A **mix-and-match wardrobe** is one that includes garments that have been coordinated (put together) to add variety and to create more outfits. Even if you combine only a few garments in mix-and-match outfits, you can give the impression of having more clothes.

Look through your current wardrobe. Do you find that many of your clothes are a certain color? If so, consider using that color as a foundation for building your mix-and-match wardrobe. Review the garments in Figure **7-5**. The skirt, shorts, jeans, and slacks are all neutral colors. This allows any of them to be combined with any of the tops to create many different outfits.

Try New Combinations

Study your wardrobe carefully. Select a pair of slacks and see how many shirts and sweaters look good with them. Use your imagination to create combinations you have not thought of before. Hold the combinations together to observe the effect. How would a belt look with an outfit? With this try-and-see method, you may find new, unexpected combinations.

Males can interchange sport coats and slacks to make other outfits. For example, a neutral-colored sport coat helps create a variety of outfits when a person wears it with different pairs of slacks. Wearing the same coat with jeans

7-5 The neutral colors all combine well to create many different outfits. *Shutterstock*

offers a different look for some activities, **7-6**. Substitute a vest or sweater and you will have another outfit. Suppose a young man's wardrobe includes a pair of jeans, corduroy slacks, and khaki pants. He also owns a polo shirt, a colored T-shirt, a western shirt, solid color shirt, and jacket. How many different combinations could you make for him?

For young women, mixing and matching skirts, pants, blouses, vests, sweaters, and jackets creates a variety of outfits and different looks. Black pants are a good basic with which to start. You can team them with tops in a variety of styles and colors. If a young woman has a solid color suit, a plaid shirt, a dressy blouse, slacks, and jeans, how many different combinations could you make for her?

When you have the chance to add something to your wardrobe, get clothes that mix and match with those you already have. A few additions can create many new outfits.

Use Accessories

With the use of accessories, you can get more from your clothes. **Accessories** include belts, jewelry, scarves, hats, neckties, handbags, and shoes. They do not usually cost as much as other clothing items, and the choices are endless.

The primary advantage of using accessories is to add variety to your wardrobe. For instance, you can make the same outfit look either dressy or casual, depending on the accessories you wear with it. Low-heeled boots give a casual look when worn with pants, whereas strappy heels dress them up.

Another advantage of using accessories is that they can help you keep up with the latest fashions. Because they are less expensive than most garments, you can afford to buy them more often. Watch the Internet, magazines, and stores for the newest fashions. Then look for an accessory that will help give an old outfit that new look. Long scarves wrapped around the neck are currently popular. Depending on the weight of the fabric, you can wear them year-round. Belts are a popular accessory for giving an outfit a new look. Consider wearing a belt over a long tunic sweater for a fresh look.

Look through your wardrobe and decide what it will take to tie it all together. What could you select to wear with many outfits that will improve the look of each one? It is best not to want to spend money on items that you will seldom use or wear. This is when planning can really be worthwhile.

7-6 A sport coat for guys can be dressed up or down by combining it with different shirts and pants. *Shutterstock*

Trends Making News

Teens as Trendsetters

In today's booming economy, clothing manufacturers are targeting teens and preteens because of their huge numbers. In 2010, there were about 35 million 12- to 19-year-olds in the U.S. population. This number has been growing every year since 1992. Not only are there many teens, but their buying power is tremendous.

These two factors have made teens a prime target market. Every manufacturer and retailer wants a piece of this action. In addition, they want to establish a relationship with these young buyers to build brand loyalty that will stay with them into their adult years.

Because of the dollars at stake, retailers want to be sure they have what teens are buying when they are buying them. This means they have to plan ahead for the items to be designed, manufactured, and shipped to them. To be sure they don't miss this opportunity, manufacturers watch teen-age trendsetters. One way they do this today is through the Internet. For example, some manufacturers invite teens to fill out questionnaires on their websites. They also monitor the Internet, which plays an increasingly important role as tastemaker. In the past, consumers relied on fashion editors for magazines to report on trends, but now everyone can see everything via the Internet, often in real time. Inspiration and advice can come from professional websites as well as personal blogs whose authors share their love of clothes. A few trendsetting teens even dictate fashion from their bedrooms according to H&M's in-house magazine.

Selecting Appropriate Clothes

Dressing appropriately means wearing clothes that are suitable for the occasion. This includes clothes for school, relaxing with friends, a job, and special occasions. The accepted customs of your community will also affect what is appropriate clothing for you.

What you wear and how you appear can contribute a positive message about who you are. It means you know what suitable dress is and respect those cultural and social standards of your community. In contrast, inappropriate attire can distract from positive communication. The way you dress may cause people to see only what you are wearing and not who you really are. Which message do you want your appearance to convey?

During the teen years, people are trying to establish their own identities. For example, you want to make your own decisions and do things your own way. Pressure from your peer group is strongest at this time.

At this age, the selection and wearing of clothes often causes conflicts between parents and their teens. Parents may not understand why you want to wear the clothes that you select.

Teens want to convince the adults in their lives that they are growing up. Acting with maturity shows you accept responsibility for what you do. Dressing suitably for activities is one part of showing responsibility. This means you realize there are certain types of clothes that are appropriate to wear for the different things you do, 7-7. In most areas, you can wear jeans, T-shirts, and hoodies to school, the movies, or to a sports activity. However, these outfits might not be appropriate for a religious service.

School Clothes

Most of your clothing is likely for school wear. This same clothing can be appropriate for most other activities. It is impossible to dictate what clothes all teens should wear to which places. Different parts of the country accept more casual, informal wear than others.

Schools generally have some form of dress code. A **dress code** is a set of rules, usually written, that specifies the required manner of dress. Most school dress codes stress that student attire should be appropriate for the school environment. It should not interfere with the primary function of education. This means that certain types of clothes could be distracting. For instance, when a student's clothing distracts others, it is unsuitable for the educational environment. For example, if a teen female wore a skimpy top, it would be hard not to stare at her.

School dress codes today do not state what you must wear, but what you cannot wear. They often list items that are unsuitable for school. Examples of inappropriate items include pajamas, slippers, cut-offs, torn clothing, bare midriffs, halter tops, spaghetti straps, and any item of clothing that exposes skin in the torso area or undergarments. Clothing that is offensive or could be associated with gang activity, alcohol, or tobacco use is not appropriate.

Some schools require school uniforms. Many students do not mind wearing school uniforms because there is less peer pressure to buy the latest fashions. It makes getting ready for school much easier, as well. In addition, uniforms eliminate the decision about what to wear to school each morning.

Special Occasions

Some dress-up occasions call for clothes different than those a person wears to school. Although many after-school events are casual, some are specifically *dress up* events. They may require teens to wear sport coats, suits, neckties, or dresses. Homecoming dances and other school dances are usually dress up events.

7-7 Dressing appropriately for school and other occasions shows you are responsible. *Shutterstock*

Year-end proms are special events for high school students. The prom usually means *black tie* for guys and gals. When you see the words *black tie* on an invitation to a formal event, it means there are certain expectations for how to dress. These expectations include men wearing tuxedos and women wearing formal gowns or evening dresses, **7-8**.

Other occasions for wearing special clothing include weddings, funerals, and religious services. Clothing expectations for these events include the following:

- *Weddings.* Men traditionally wear suits or jackets and dress shirts with ties. Women generally wear dressier dresses or pantsuits.
- *Funerals.* Men wear suits and dress shirts with ties, while women wear more conservative dresses and pantsuits. Dresses, suits, and pantsuits in basic styles and colors are appropriate.
- *Religious services.* Conservative attire for men and women is also a typical requirement for religious services in churches, mosques, or temples.

If you are not sure what type clothing to wear to an event, ask someone who knows. The person who is responsible for the event is the best one to ask. Otherwise, ask several of your friends what they plan to wear. You might feel uncomfortable arriving at a party wearing a dress-up outfit if everyone else is in jeans. When you are dressed appropriately, you are able to relax and have a good time, knowing you are wearing the right clothes.

Work Clothes

If you work part-time after school, you may need to add special work clothes to your wardrobe. What you wear will depend on where you work. Some jobs require a uniform. Generally, your employer will provide your uniform, but you may be responsible for its care. If your employer only provides a special shirt and hat, you must provide the rest of the outfit such as black slacks. It is possible that you may need to spend your first paycheck entirely on work clothes.

7-8 For formal events, such as proms, evening gowns may be appropriate. *Shutterstock*

After you leave school, you will likely begin your full-time career. Again, depending upon where you work, you may have to wear a uniform. Industrial or construction work requires clothes that can stand up to hard use and provide protection from injury. Many jobs require business attire. Today, that could mean suits for men and suits, dresses, or pantsuits for women.

Many businesses today have adopted a more casual dress code. Casual dress for work began with the high-tech companies, however, by the early 1990s it started creeping into the rest of the work world. At first, companies allowed employees to forgo suits and ties on Fridays only. Now, more than half of large companies are casual five days a week.

The problem with casual attire for work is that everyone interprets *casual* differently. Some people believe its taking off your suit jacket and tie. Others show up for work in ragged T-shirts, bare midriffs, or gym clothes—items that are clearly inappropriate for work. Because of this, some companies hire consultants to teach employees what is appropriate for work and what is not.

Many companies have casual dress codes that help employees know what is appropriate and what is not. Most companies discourage the items listed in Figure 7-9.

Dressing casually at work is more comfortable and can be less expensive. It also gives people the chance to express their individual styles, but still requires use of good judgment. Dressing appropriately shows respect for coworkers and the workplace culture.

Community Customs

Communities vary in what is appropriate and acceptable clothing for different places and activities. Some communities are less formal. People can wear sportswear for most events. In other communities, you may see more dresses and pants outfits.

In some states, the law requires customers to wear shoes and shirts for admittance to restaurants and stores. Many restaurants display signs asking that customers wear shirts and shoes. A few elegant dining places require jackets and ties for men, although most now require only jackets. If you wish to eat there, you must accept the standard of dress. Most restaurants do not require such formal attire because people dress more casually today than in past years.

Wearing what the majority of people expect is important. This may not be what is most comfortable for you. However, you will feel more at ease when you are appropriately dressed.

Business Casual Don'ts

Don'ts for men and women include

- Worn-out sneakers
- Flip-flops
- Shorts
- Pool or beach clothes
- Jeans with holes in them

Don'ts for women include

- Very short dresses and skirts
- Pants that reveal the navel
- See-through clothing
- Low-cut upper clothing
- Halters, camisoles, and tank tops

Don'ts for men are

- Gym wear
- T-shirts or sleeveless shirts
- Ripped or unkempt clothing

7-9 In offices where dress is *business casual*, there are certain items of apparel that are not acceptable.

Summary

- A wardrobe is a collection of the clothes and accessories a person has to wear.
- A good wardrobe requires careful planning. It helps you know what clothes you have and what you will need to add.
- A wardrobe plan requires an inventory of your present clothes—identifying their condition, fit, and any gaps to fill in your wardrobe.
- List clothing needs and wants in order of priority to plan clothing purchases, making better use of time and money.
- Mix-and-match clothing items to make more outfits and wear different accessories to get more out of your wardrobe.
- Dressing appropriately means wearing clothes that are suitable for an occasion.
- School dress codes are designed to make sure that student attire does not interfere with the primary function of education.
- Many businesses have specific dress codes, and some are more casual than others.
- Accepted community customs impact what clothing is appropriate. Communities vary in what is appropriate and acceptable clothing for different places and activities.

Graphic Organizer

Draw a fishbone diagram like the one you see here to identify the four main chapter heads and key points under each head.

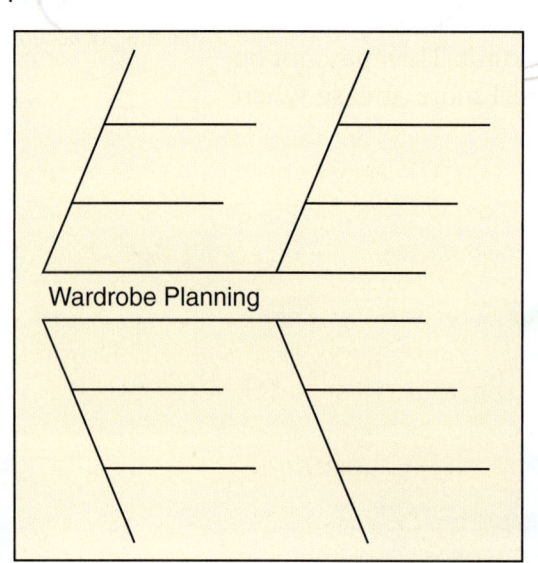

Review the Facts

1. List three benefits of wardrobe planning.
2. What is the first step in planning your wardrobe?
3. When is a good time to take a wardrobe inventory? What should it include?
4. Name three things to consider when evaluating each wardrobe item.
5. Contrast *needs* and *wants*. Give an example of each.
6. What is the most basic clothing need?
7. What does it mean to prioritize?
8. Explain how to mix-and-match four clothing items to make a number of different outfits. Describe the colors and styles.
9. How can accessories extend a wardrobe?
10. What is the primary goal of school dress codes?
11. Who should you talk to if you do not know what to wear to an event?
12. What problem can occur with casual dress codes in a place of business?

Think Critically

13. **Analyze outcomes.** Think about a clothing purchase that you regret. Analyze how a wardrobe plan may have helped you make a better clothing purchase. Share your analysis with the class.
14. **Recognize values.** Make a list of clothes you would like to buy. Identify which are needs and which are wants. How do your values influence your needs and wants?
15. **Identify evidence.** In teams, debate the pros and cons of school uniforms and school dress codes. Identify credible evidence to support each side of the debate.
16. **Draw conclusions.** How do spoken or unspoken expectations in your community impact the types of clothes people wear? Write a summary of your conclusions.

Apparel Applications

17. **Wardrobe priorities.** Make a list of the clothes that should be included in a student's wardrobe. List the number of garments and put them in an order of priority.
18. **Inventory/wardrobe plan.** Take an inventory of your clothes. Then make a wardrobe plan. Write a summary of the results of your clothing inventory and wardrobe plan. How can you put your plan into action?
19. **Listing needs and wants.** Make one list of clothing needs and one of clothing wants. In small groups, discuss the difference between needs and wants.
20. **Online wardrobe poster.** Use a school-approved online application to create an electronic poster for your mix-and-match wardrobe. Locate six photos of garments from online advertisements, magazines, or catalogs and copy and paste them into your e-poster. Number each item. List all the possible outfits you could make by mixing and matching the different items. Post your wardrobe collection to the class blog or website. Collaborate with your classmates about ways to improve your selections.
21. **Dress-code interview.** Interview a school guidance counselor or principal about the school dress code, or invite the counselor to speak to the class. Prepare questions before the interview.

Academic Connections

22. **Math.** Presume you have been given a $500 clothing allowance for a year. Make a wardrobe plan based on this amount of money. Use clothing catalogs or the Internet to see how much your clothing items will cost. Compare your plan with those of your classmates. What adjustments can you make to your plan to get the best value for the dollars you spend?
23. **Writing.** Use Internet or print resources to research the introduction and history of casual attire in the workplace. How has "business casual" changed over time? What practices do many top companies in the U.S. follow today? Write a summary of your findings to share with the class.

Workplace Links

24. **Workplace wardrobe plan.** Select an occupation and plan a suitable wardrobe for a person who works in that occupation. Explain the reasons for your choices.
25. **Make appropriate choices.** Collect pictures of people wearing different types of clothes—casual, business, and dress up. Post the pictures under two headings on the board—*Appropriate for Work* and *Inappropriate for Work*. As a class, discuss reasons why the clothing choices are appropriate or inappropriate for work.

Take the Lead—Providing Work Wardrobes

A number of nonprofit agencies collect gently used up-to-date clothes to help provide workplace wardrobes for people in need. These organizations, such as *Dress for Success*, work with disadvantaged people and provide them with appropriate clothing for interviews and work.

As an FCCLA *Community Service* class project, consider partnering with a community organization to sponsor a workplace clothing drive to serve people in need. Use the FCCLA *Planning Process* to develop your project. If you decide to organize this project on your own, consider stepping up to an FCCLA *STAR Event on Entrepreneurship*. See your adviser for information as needed.

Chapter 8

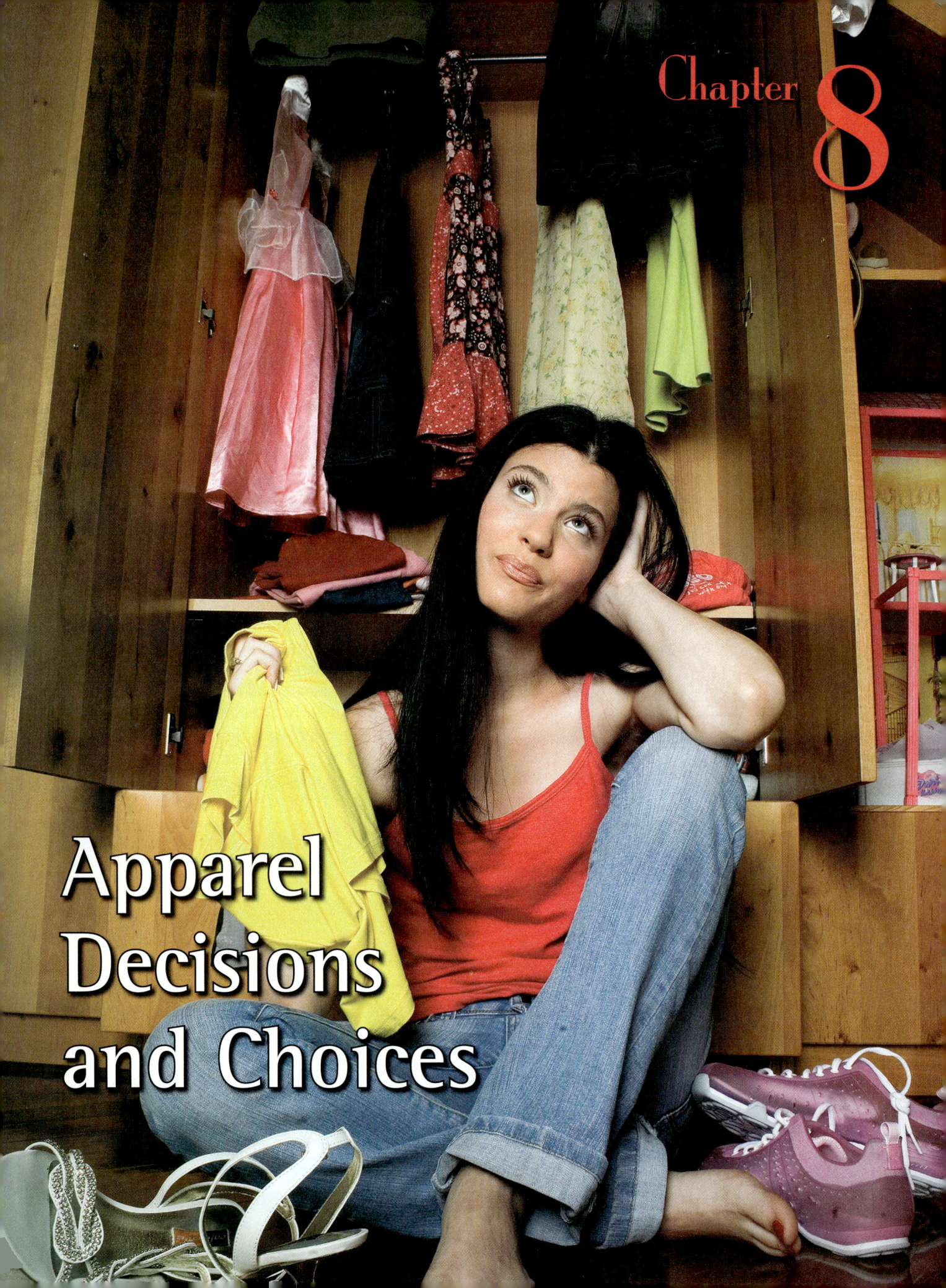

Apparel Decisions and Choices

Chapter Objectives

After studying this chapter, you will be able to
- **demonstrate** ability to use the decision-making process to make apparel decisions.
- **describe** factors affecting family apparel decisions.
- **summarize** the stages in the family life cycle and how they impact apparel decisions.
- **describe** various ways to meet family apparel needs.
- **analyze** impact of clothing care requirements on apparel selection.
- **analyze** factors to consider when deciding whether to sew or buy garments.

Key Terms

decision-making process	nonhuman resources	dual-career families
goals	alternatives	priorities
resources	family life cycle	compromise
human resources	multiple roles	budget

Intentional Reading

Before you read the chapter, read all of the chart and photograph captions. What do you know about the material covered in this chapter just from reading the captions?

Making clothing decisions and choices is like putting together a jigsaw puzzle. You have to add the pieces one-by-one. A good wardrobe plan will help you see which parts fit together. You do not want any extra pieces that will not fit into the final product—a wardrobe that works. You must decide which pieces to add and how to arrange them for proper fit.

A few of the right additions to any wardrobe can make a big change. Learning to use the decision-making process to make wise clothing decisions can help create a wardrobe that works for all occasions.

Decision Making

Decision making is the process of making a choice. Most people make many decisions about clothing every day. Some are minor decisions, while others are major decisions. What to wear to school each day is a minor or simple decision for most teens. Whether to wear a sweater or a jacket may not be a major decision either. However, what clothes to buy and how much to spend may be more important decisions, 8-1. Whether to sew some garments and what to give away to someone else may also be in the important decision category. You may make some of these decisions quickly, while others might require some thought.

The Decision-Making Process

Making decisions is usually easier if you have a plan for making them. If you follow the decision-making process, it will be easier to make decisions. The **decision-making process** is a series of steps to go through when making choices. These steps are useful for making minor or major decisions. Here are the steps to follow:

1. State the problem to solve.
2. Set goals for what you want to accomplish.
3. Identify resources.
4. List the alternatives.
5. Make the decision.
6. Carry out the decision.
7. Evaluate the results of the decision.

State the Problem

Be specific about what you must decide. Otherwise, you may have trouble deciding how to solve the problem. The problem could range from what to wear to school tomorrow to how you will coordinate your wardrobe. State the problem in clear and precise terms. For instance, "I need to decide what to wear with my new shirt" or "I need a jacket, another pair of jeans, and a pair of school shoes to round out my wardrobe" clearly state your needs. These are better statements than saying, "I need new clothes for school." Stating the problem in detail will help you know what to consider when making your decision, resulting in a better decision.

8-1 Buying a winter coat is a more important decision because coats can be costly. *Shutterstock*

Set Goals

Goals are what you want to accomplish. Establish specific goals for what you want to attain. Then determine the goal to reach from the decision you will make. For instance, a goal may be to add a jacket, a pair of jeans, and a pair of school shoes to your wardrobe before school starts.

Identify Resources

Resources are the objects or abilities people can use to reach their goals. All people have both human resources and nonhuman resources. **Human resources** are all the resources you have such as skills, knowledge, and experience.

Nonhuman resources are the material things you have or can use to achieve your goals, including money, tools, time, and community resources.

Make a list of all your resources. Do you know how to sew? This is a human resource. Do you have money available from a part-time job or an allowance? Do family members or friends offer you secondhand clothes? Do you have time to sew or carefully shop for the items you want? What types of stores are present in your community? These are all types of nonhuman resources, **8-2**.

List the Alternatives

There are usually several **alternatives**, or ways to solve a problem or reach a goal. Explore all of the options and weigh their advantages and disadvantages. A good way to test alternatives is to ask yourself some questions. Would you want to make a jacket? Do you want to shop for jeans and shoes now or wait until they go on sale? What are your feelings about wearing secondhand jeans or a secondhand jacket? Do you have the skills necessary to mix and match new garments with those in your present wardrobe to create new outfits? This could extend your wardrobe.

Make the Decision

After carefully thinking about the advantages and disadvantages of each alternative, decide which is best. Perhaps you will make the decision to sew the jacket and buy the shoes on sale. A relative, who has grown several inches this year, may offer you a pair of good secondhand jeans. Making the right decisions is easy when you use the right process.

Carry Out the Decision

To carry out a decision means to turn words into actions. The quicker you carry out your decision, the quicker you will meet your goal. For example, since you know you will be making a jacket, you can shop for fabric that will coordinate with other items in your wardrobe. You can also begin looking for shoes that are on sale. Perhaps, with the money you saved by getting the jeans secondhand and sewing the jacket, you could buy accessories to further extend your wardrobe.

8-2 The time you have to shop and carefully compare merchandise is a type of nonhuman resource. *Shutterstock*

Evaluate the Results

Think about the decisions you have made. Were they successful decisions? Did the decisions solve the problem? Did you meet your goal? Are you satisfied with the results? What would you have done differently? By carefully evaluating your decisions, your future decision-making skills will improve. When you evaluated your decisions about the jacket, jeans, and shoes, were you happy? Although it took a lot of thought, you now have three great additions to your wardrobe.

Factors Affecting Family Clothing Decisions

In making family clothing decisions, use the same decision-making process. However, instead of applying the process to just your needs, apply it to the needs of the family.

Several factors affect family clothing decisions. These include the stage in the family life cycle; family values, goals, and priorities; family resources; and the budget for clothes. How a family manages all of these factors will determine how successful its clothing decisions will be.

Stage in the Family Life Cycle

Families change through the years. From being newly married couples to being grandparents, families grow in size. Households often grow from two people to many people. After a few years it is back to two again, and then possibly one. These changes occur in stages that make up the **family life cycle**. Clothing needs change as families go through these stages, **8-3**.

Beginning Stage

The first stage of the family life cycle is the *beginning stage*. It begins when a couple first marries and establishes a home together. Employment of both the husband and wife provides them with money to spend on themselves. They

8-3 Family life cycle follows a series of stages, and clothing needs change throughout these stages.
Goodheart-Willcox Publisher

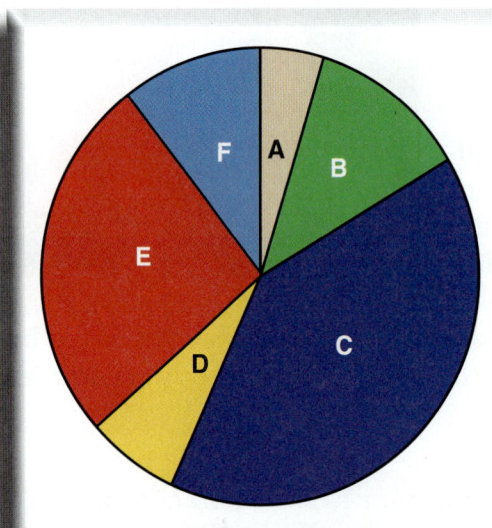

Family Life Cycle
A. **Beginning Stage:** Married couple without children.
B. **Childbearing Stage:** Couple with child(ren) up to 2½ years old; couple with child(ren) 2½ to 6 years old.
C. **Parenting Stage:** Couple with child(ren) 6 to 13 years old.
D. **Launching Stage:** Couple with child(ren) leaving home; couple with child(ren) living away from home.
E. **Midyears Stage:** Couple before retirement, but after all children left home.
F. **Aging Stage:** Couple during retirement until death of both spouses.

also have time to pursue leisure activities. The couple will buy clothes that suite their work needs and clothes for special occasions and leisure activities.

Childbearing Stage

The second stage of the family life cycle begins when a couple has a child and enters the *childbearing stage*. Couples make many adjustments during this stage as they assume their new roles as parents. They have more demands on their time, money, energy, and freedom. This stage continues until all children are born. The first baby will have many clothing needs. The next child can wear some of the clothes of the firstborn. Because babies and young children grow fast, they need clothes more often than adults do.

Parenting Stage

The family enters the third stage, or *parenting stage*, of the family life cycle when the first child begins school. More changes occur in the family. School activities, sports events, and social activities lead to a busy family life making more demands on time, money, and energy. When children go to school, their clothing needs often increase. In addition to play clothes, children need clothes for school. When children become teens, they spend more time with their friends and less time with their families. Teens are involved in more social activities and may work part-time. They will sometimes need more clothes for their many activities.

Family members with involvement in organizations or sports may need special clothes. For instance, if members of a family down-hill or cross-country ski, they might need hats, gloves, jackets, pants, and boots. If children belong to organizations such as Scouts or Little League, special uniforms may also be a requirement, 8-4. Also, consider family members' hobbies and activities when determining family clothing needs.

Sometimes, special clothing needs arise for special occasions or holidays. For instance, a wedding often calls for special clothes. Families may also need special clothes for a family vacation.

8-4 Little League uniforms might be required by children involved in baseball.
Shutterstock

Launching Stage

The fourth stage, or the *launching stage*, of the family life cycle begins when the first child leaves home. Young adults may leave for school, work, or marriage. Those planning to attend college often need clothes for their college wardrobes. Young adults entering the job market will need clothes appropriate for their jobs.

Mid-Years Stage

As the children leave, parents have more time and space for themselves. They may have more money to spend on their own interests. Since a couple's income is usually highest at this stage, they may do more traveling which may involve additional wardrobe needs.

Aging Stage

When couples retire, they enter the *aging stage*. Depending on their health, many couples continue to be active in a variety of ways. Couples may pursue hobbies, do volunteer work, or participate in sports, 8-5. People in their retirement years may need more casual clothes. When couples experience declining health, their need for special services may increase. Clothing needs in the aging stage often relate to health.

As you can see, throughout the various stages of the life cycle, family clothing needs change. New clothing needs arise at each life-cycle stage.

Multiple Roles of Family Members

As you read about the family life cycle stages, you may have noticed the different roles family members play at different times in their lives. Sometimes the role is of a student; sometimes the role is of an employee, or a wife or husband. Throughout your life, you will have **multiple roles**. This means you combine two or more family roles with roles outside the family at the same time. Currently you are a student, a son, or a daughter. You may also be a brother or a sister, a friend, a class officer, or an employee. Each role requires fulfilling certain responsibilities, and each may have different clothing needs. As a student, you may participate in a school sport that requires a uniform. Maybe you have to pay for a costume as a singer in a madrigal group. Perhaps you also have a part-time job that requires special attire.

In the future, you will likely take on parenting and career roles. In **dual-career families**, both parents work outside the home. Meeting both family and career responsibilities is challenging. These multiple roles will strongly influence clothing needs.

8-5 Retirees need clothes suited to their activities. *Shutterstock*

Family Values, Goals, and Priorities

A family's values and goals will affect clothing decisions. Family attitudes about clothes, their tastes, and their activities will all influence a family's priorities. Families set **priorities** based on what is most important to them.

Setting family clothing priorities and achieving goals are most effective if each member of the family has a part in the process. Parents usually lead the planning process. When children reach a level of understanding, parents generally encourage them to participate, too. The family should decide what is most important to the family as a unit and to each member. Family members should think and talk about their values as they relate to their clothing needs and wants. How does what the family values influence clothing decisions? Is the appearance of family members more important than saving money for college? What does the family value most?

Setting family clothing priorities and goals has advantages. Each family member learns to balance his or her own needs and wants against those of others. Everyone learns to compromise. In a **compromise**, everyone agrees to give up a little to reach a mutual agreement.

Family members should begin by listing clothing items each member needs and wants most. Then estimate the cost of each item and when the family member will need it. This will help in establishing priorities and goals.

It is a good idea to try to find a balance among family goals. For instance, it may be nice to buy each member new summer clothes, but winter coats may be a need later in the year. Perhaps one family member wants an expensive outfit for a special occasion while another wants clothes for school or work. In such cases as this, a family decision-making session is important. Discussing the family needs, values, goals, and priorities will help the family reach a decision that is best for all.

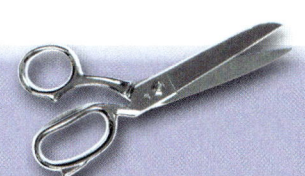

Trends Making News

Backpacks—A Real Pain in the Back

Backpacks came on the school scene because they were a great way to tote home stacks of books. Unfortunately, books are getting heavier and homework demands require students to carry them back and forth to school almost daily. It is not unusual for some preteens to carry packs that weigh as much as 50 percent of their body weight. This kind of weight can cause muscle strain, neck and shoulder pain, low back pain, or acquired scoliosis (curvature of the spine).

Most backpacks were not designed for carrying the amount of weight placed in them. There is a disconnection between the weight the bags are carrying and the design of the pack.

To avoid back pain, check the weight of your backpack by placing it on a bathroom scale. It should weigh less than 10 percent of your body weight. Also check to see if the backpack has an internal frame to help distribute the weight. The shoulder straps should be tight enough so the pack touches your back. Do not wear the pack over one shoulder. This shifts all the weight to one side, which causes pain and muscle spasms. Better still, try one of the new wheeled backpacks, which looks like small carry-on luggage, and avoid the pain altogether.

Some schools are finding other ways to address the problem. For example, a set of textbooks is kept in each classroom for in-class use only. Each student also has a text at home to use for homework assignments. In this way, books do not have to be carried back and forth. It saves wear and tear on the books so they last longer, and students have fewer back problems. This has also been a solution for those schools that are doing away with lockers for security reasons.

Meeting Family Clothing Needs

After family clothing values, goals, and priorities have been discussed, a family should consider their resources. Resources are the objects or abilities that families can use to reach goals. Skills, time, and money are all resources that can help meet family clothing needs.

Identify Family Resources

Just as families differ, the resources available to each family differ. If a family lacks a resource such as money, perhaps family members can use other resources such as time or skills to compensate. For instance, sewing clothes or careful shopping could save the family money. Family members can learn to do their own clothing repairs and alterations instead of paying someone else to do them. Recycling or redesigning garments can save money and enlarge wardrobes. Sharing clothes among family members or handing them down from one family member to another are other options.

Making a Spending Plan or Budget

Used wisely, money is an important resource. A **budget** is a spending plan that can help families manage money. It gives a family a clear picture of how much money is available to meet needs. The family budget includes many items. Keep in mind that clothing is only one of these items. Other items include food, housing, health care, transportation, personal items, and recreation, **8-6**.

Some families set up clothing budgets on a monthly, seasonal, or yearly basis. However the budget is set up, family members need to consider the

- total amount of money the family has to spend
- total amount of nonclothing expenses
- amount the family can budget for clothes after meeting essential needs such as housing and food

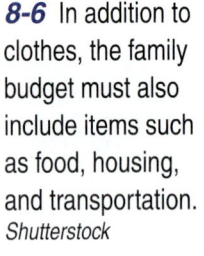

8-6 In addition to clothes, the family budget must also include items such as food, housing, and transportation.
Shutterstock

Once a family decides how much money is available for clothing, it is important to keep a record of clothing expenses. Clothing expenses include the cost of all garments plus their regular upkeep—laundry, dry cleaning, and repairs. A periodic review of this list can help a family see if spending patterns need to change. For example, a family may want to reduce spending on clothes or reduce spending in such other areas as recreation in order to meet clothing needs.

Families can save money on clothes by buying well-made garments that require replacement less often. Although these well-made garments may cost slightly more, the extra expense pays off in the long run. Inexpensive clothes are often poor quality. Seams may not be sturdy, hems may come loose, and fasteners fall off. If garment repairs are not easy or too costly, it may be necessary to discard them after only a few wearings. The dollars saved in the purchase price will be lost if the garment is only worn a few times.

The list of expenses reflects family spending patterns and helps in planning future expenses. Big-budget items like winter coats or a new career wardrobe may require extra planning and saving. A family can start preparing for these needs several months in advance. Setting aside a certain amount of money weekly, helps ensure it is available when it is time to purchase the items in need.

Every few months, the family budget requires re-evaluation. A budget is not rigid, but is adaptable and subject to change. When there is a need to alter the budget, family members should discuss it and make the necessary adjustments. A budget is a useful tool in meeting family needs when family values, goals, and priorities are the foundation, 8-7.

Consider Costs of Clothing Care

It is a good idea to buy clothes that you can launder to avoid dry cleaning bills. Dry cleaning a garment each time it is soiled adds to the total cost of that garment. It is far less expensive to launder a garment at home. Consider this factor when purchasing clothes. Read the labels to determine care requirements. If many items need to be dry cleaned each year, this will impact the clothing budget.

8-7 This couple is re-evaluating the family budget and making adjustments. *Shutterstock*

Consider how often you will wear the item when you think about care costs. A jacket you wear to school every day for several months will need frequent cleaning. If the jacket is washable, it will cost only a few cents to clean each time. If it requires dry cleaning, it could cost between five and ten dollars each cleaning. Do the math and you will see a significant difference. To do so, first determine the *cost-per-wearing*. Add what you paid for the garment to the estimated cleaning costs for the year. Divide this total by the number of times you wear the garment. This will give you the cost-per-wearing.

Is Sewing an Option?

Now that you have learned about the decision-making process, you can apply it to sewing or buying decisions for clothing. How do you decide whether to make a garment or buy one? It is a good idea to consider several factors. These include

- your sewing skills
- how much money is available
- the type of design you want
- whether or not you enjoy sewing
- obtaining a good fit
- the amount of time available before you need the garment

Answering the questions in Figure **8-8** may help you to make your decision. After answering these questions, apply the decision-making process to your decision.

You may find that each option has both advantages and disadvantages. You may choose to sew some items and buy others ready-made. For example, you may want to sew clothes that are easier to make, such as pants, skirts, and T-shirts. You may want to buy items that may be more difficult to sew, such as shirts, blouses, and jackets.

You may choose to sew some of your clothes because sewing is one of the best ways to build up a wardrobe. Sewing is a skill, as is playing the guitar, throwing a football, or riding a horse. Certain skills are easier for some people than for others. However, with patience and practice, you can learn any skill, including sewing.

If you sew, you could have many more clothes for the same amount of money. Many times, you can sew clothes of better materials for less money than if you buy the same types of ready-made clothes. You would also know how well they are constructed.

Sometimes, sewing is the only way to get the garment you want—the right color, style, and fit. You could make garments that reflect your interests and personality by adding your own design details to make your garments totally unique. Your clothes would look great, and you could have fun making them.

Fit is one of the most important factors in a clothing decision. When you buy ready-to-wear clothes, you can try them on before you buy them. If you sew, you can take careful measurements to help ensure a good fit. You can also make adjustments to the fit while you construct the garment.

To Sew? To Buy? Factors to Consider	
	How would you rate your sewing skills?
	How much money would it cost to make the garment? How much money would it cost to buy the garment at a store?
	How do the current fashions in the stores look on you? Would you rather wear a personal, original design?
	Do you see sewing as a fun activity or as a chore?
	Do you wear a standard size that requires little, if any, alterations? Are you "in between" sizes, or do you find that ready-made garments just don't fit you like they should?
	When do you need the garment? What would require the most time—shopping for the garment or sewing the garment? Do you have enough time to shop for a pattern, fabric, and notions and to make the garment?

8-8 Before making a decision about sewing or buying a garment, ask yourself these questions.

Both shopping for ready-made garments and sewing garments take time. When deciding whether to sew or buy, you need to know how soon you will need the garment, **8-9**. If you need a garment tomorrow, you will probably have to buy it. If you have some spare time, sewing may be a wise choice. If the design is simple, it may not take long to sew. See Figure **8-10** for some other advantages of sewing.

Other Options for Meeting Clothing Needs

Buying new clothes or sewing them are only two ways of meeting your clothing needs. There are other options you might consider.

- *Recycling and redesigning.* Recycling is not only environmentally friendly, but it can be fun to make something out of a garment you were going to throw away. Be creative! If you have even basic sewing skills, you can put them to use in this way. For inspiration, visit a store that sells trims and decorative *appliqués*—cutout, sew-on decorations. You may be able to restyle some of last year's outfits to have this year's new fashion.
- *Altering a garment.* It may be possible to save a garment you can alter it in some way to fit you or another family member. See if you can lengthen or shorten pants or skirts if necessary. Maybe you can let out some seams to increase the size or move some buttons over. Again, basic sewing skills are all that you need.

8-9 Sometimes sewing is the only way to have the garment you want. You can have fun making and wearing your own clothes. *Photo courtesy of McCall Pattern Company*

8-10 These are just some of the advantages of being able to sew. Can you think of others?

Why Sew

- Have an interesting hobby and outlet for your creativity.
- Have a feeling of pride and accomplishment.
- Make accessories for your own room and home.
- Make gifts and garments for your family and friends.
- Earn money by sewing or altering clothes for friends.
- Select ready-made clothing more intelligently.
- Alter your ready-mades so they will fit better.
- Consider a future career in the fashion field and perhaps a part-time job very soon.

- *Repairing a garment.* Too often people discard garments because they need repairs. If you can learn to make simple garment repairs, you can make clothes last much longer. The most common repairs are restitching a seam that has split or sewing on a button, **8-11**. Sometimes zippers require replacement or holes require patching.
- *Sharing.* It might be possible to share an article of clothing or accessory with another family member. Sisters (and even best friends) often share some of their clothes, especially items they may only wear for special occasions, such as dressy shoes or handbags. Just be sure you take care of any shared items.
- *Trading.* Also known as *clothes swaps*, this latest craze in trading clothes with friends is another way to add to your wardrobe. Some people organize clothes-swap parties using online at websites designated for this purpose. Each guest brings clean, fashionable clothing items they no longer wear, and trades them for items their friends no longer want. Everyone benefits without spending any money.
- *Renting.* You may already be using this method of meeting your clothing needs. Perhaps you or another family member has rented a tuxedo for a wedding or prom. You can rent other types of garments for special occasions, too. Renting is often the best option if a person will wear the garment only one time. If you see a need for wearing the same garment several times, it may pay to buy the garment instead.

Depending on your needs, you can use any or all of the options presented in this chapter to meet personal and family clothing needs.

8-11 Making simple repairs can give new life to clothes you already own. *Shutterstock*

Summary

- Decision making is the process of making a choice. You make minor and major decisions about clothing every day.
- Follow the steps in the decision-making process to help develop a plan for making clothing choices.
- Goals are what you want to accomplish. The decisions you make and the resources available help you reach your goals.
- Alternatives refer to several ways to solve a problem or reach a goal.
- Families go through changes that occur in stages of the family life cycle. Clothing needs change as families go through these stages and take on roles that may require different clothes.
- Families need to consider their values, goals, and priorities when making clothing decisions. All of these factors will influence the resources and amount of money they set aside to meet their clothing needs.
- Use the decision-making process to help choose whether to sew a garment or buy it ready-made. Other options for meeting clothing needs are recycling, repairing, altering, sharing, trading, and renting.

Graphic Organizer

Draw a T-chart on a sheet of paper. Write the steps in the decision-making process in the left column. Allow space for writing. In the right column, note specific actions that occur during each step.

Decision-Making Steps	Specific Actions

Review the Facts

1. Give two examples of minor decisions and two examples of major decisions related to clothing. Label each decision as minor or major.
2. What are the steps in the decision-making process?
3. Contrast human resources and nonhuman resources.
4. List three human and three nonhuman resources to consider when making clothing decisions.
5. Summarize stages of the family life cycle. Identify clothing needs families might have during each of these stages.
6. What are three examples of family resources?
7. Name three factors families should consider when setting up a budget.
8. How can reading the clothing care label save you money?
9. What are six factors to consider when deciding whether to sew or buy a garment?
10. What is a clothes swap?

Think Critically

11. **Draw conclusions.** Think of an important decision you recently made. Draw conclusions about how using the decision-making process would have helped you make a better decision. Share your conclusions with the class.
12. **Analyze resources.** What human and nonhuman resources do you have? Analyze how you might use these resources. Write a short summary.
13. **Identify relevant information.** In which stage of the family life cycle is your family? Identify ways family clothing needs differ at this stage than in previous stages. How do values and resources impact clothing choices?
14. **Analyze impact.** Analyze the short-term and long-term impact of clothing-care requirements on the clothing budget.

Apparel Applications

15. **Debate.** In two teams, debate which is better—sewing clothes or buying clothes. Identify credible evidence to support your team's viewpoint.
16. **Purchase planning.** Identify an article of clothing you will need to purchase in the next six months. Plan your purchase using the decision-making process.
17. **Budget interview.** Interview one or more families you know about how they budget for clothing purchases each year. What factors influence the budget amount most—individual needs, family needs, or money? What advice do they have for managing clothing costs?
18. **Wardrobe planning.** Presume that you are going to college and that you have $300 to spend on new clothes. Your wardrobe inventory indicates you will need several clothing items, including a warm jacket. Identify the items and create a plan for meeting these clothing needs. Share your plan with the class.

Academic Connections

19. **Math.** Presume you have a monthly clothing allowance of $35. Create a clothing budget for the next six months. List your goals and the total amount you have to spend. Estimate how much you can spend per item to meet your clothing needs during this time frame. How will this budget help you reach your goals?

20. **Writing.** Plan a clothes-swap party with other members of your class. Analyze the success of the clothes swap and write an article about it for the school paper.

Workplace Links

21. **Career wardrobe.** Identify a career you might like in an apparel or textile industry. Use the steps in the decision-making process to help select clothing options for your career wardrobe. List your choices and identify how the decision-making process helped you make them.
22. **Portfolio builder.** Presume that you want to pursue an apparel and textiles career. Where might you go to school to get your two- or four-year degree? Search the Internet for three accredited colleges or universities that interest you. Use the decision-making process to choose which school to attend. Record your decisions and actions for each step of the process using a computer. Save a copy of your decision on a CD or flash drive for your portfolio.

Using the Planning Process

Compare and contrast the decision-making process with the FCCLA *Planning Process*. How are they similar and different? Write a summary of your conclusions.

Chapter 9

Consumer Rights and Responsibilities

Chapter Objectives

After studying this chapter, you will be able to
- **explain** the information provided on labels and hangtags.
- **summarize** federal legislation that deals with textile products.
- **identify** consumer protection agencies and organizations.
- **describe** your rights and responsibilities as a consumer of goods and services.
- **summarize** how to effectively complain about a product that does not perform as you expected.

Key Terms

consumer
labels
hangtags
Textile Fiber Products Identification Act (TFPIA)
generic groups
trademark name
Wool Products Labeling Act
Fur Products Labeling Act
Care Labeling Rule
Flammable Fabrics Act
Federal Hazardous Substances Act
standards
Fair Credit Billing Act

Reading with Purpose

On separate sticky notes, write five reasons why the information in this chapter is important to you. Think about how this information could help you at home or work. As you read the chapter, place the sticky notes on the pages that related to each reason.

Teens are important consumers in today's economy. A **consumer** is a person who uses goods and services. A *good* is a physical item and *service* refers to work performed. You are a consumer of goods every time you buy an article of clothing. You are a consumer of services when you have a garment dry-cleaned.

As you grow older, you will be given more freedom. You will choose and buy more of your own clothes. Freedom comes with responsibility; especially the responsibility to make wise choices. Getting your money's worth in the clothes you buy will be an important goal.

Labels and Hangtags

Do you read the labels and hangtags attached to the textile items you buy? Time, effort, and money were used to develop them, **9-1**. Laws were passed to require them. Labels and hangtags tell you what to expect from products and how to care for them properly. Understanding them will help you make wiser clothing decisions.

Fabrics and garments are labeled for four basic reasons:

- to identify them
- to help businesses sell them
- to help consumers make wise purchases
- to explain how to properly care for them

Labels are small pieces of ribbon or fabric that are firmly attached inside of garments. They provide important information. Labels remain attached to garments as they are used. In some types of garments, labels are stamped onto the fabric through heat-transfer technology. The required information about these tagless garments is printed inside the clothing. By law, garment labels must list the fiber content, care instructions, and country of origin. They may also list fabric construction, special finishes, performance standards, sizes, brand names, and guarantees.

9-1 Reading the labels and hangtags on clothes can help you make wise buying decisions. *Shutterstock*

Hangtags, which are also attached to new clothing, are removed before the clothing is worn. They are larger than labels and are usually made of heavy paper or cardboard. Manufacturers are not required by law to provide them. Some of the information on garment labels may be repeated on hangtags. Manufacturers' trademarks, garment sizes, style numbers, prices, and special features may also be listed. See samples of labels and hangtags in **9-2**.

Using Labels and Hangtags

Labels are attached so they will not be seen while the garment is worn. They are usually found at the back of the neckline of shirts, blouses, dresses, and sweaters. Look for them at the back center of the waistband on skirts and slacks. Sometimes they are located in a side seam close to the hem. Men's suits and sport jackets often have labels on the inside pocket at chest level. Some jackets and coats have the label on the front facing below the waistline. You may have to search, but the labels can be found.

Tagless garments are shown in **9-3**. They usually include T-shirts, knit tops, and underwear. More clothing items will be tagless in the future.

Labels and hangtags are meant to help you and other consumers. Make use of them. Smart shoppers save hangtags. On each hangtag, they write the date and place of purchase, and a short description of the garment. Hangtags can be kept in the laundry area for easy reference.

Federal Legislation to Help Consumers

At one time, consumers did not have hangtags and labels to reference. They became necessary after manufactured fabrics appeared on the market. People did not know how to care for the new fabrics. They could not look at the fabrics and determine what fibers they were made of. Consumers and clothing manufacturers were confused.

9-2 Note the many kinds of information provided on labels and hangtags. *Jack Klasey*

The government created regulations to require textile manufacturers to identify the fiber content of their products. Regulations that deal with clothing are the

- Wool Products Labeling Act, 1939
- Fur Products Labeling Act, 1951
- Textile Fiber Products Identification Act, 1960
- Care Labeling Rule, 1971
- National Organic Program (NOP) Regulations

Amendments were added to many of these acts. Additional acts were passed to protect consumers, particularly children, from unsafe products, including clothing and textiles. These are the

- Flammable Fabrics Act, 1953
- Federal Hazardous Substances Act, 1960
- Consumer Products Safety Act, 1972, and Consumer Products Safety Improvement Act, 2008

9-3 Tagless garments include required label information, but are more comfortable to wear. *Jack Klasey*

Textile Fiber Products Identification Act

Manufacturers are required by the **Textile Fiber Products Identification Act (TFPIA)** to provide information about most of the fibers that make up garments and other textile products. The Federal Trade Commission (FTC) enforces this act and created **generic groups** for manufactured fibers. Each group contains fibers that are chemically alike. When a new fiber is created, it is added to an already existing generic group. If the composition of the new fiber is unlike any existing group, a new group is created. The most common of the 22 generic groups of fibers used in apparel textiles are listed in **9-4**.

Each generic group can include many different fibers. Although the fibers in a particular generic group are chemically alike, there are slight differences. Manufacturers want their fibers to have unique characteristics. They give each fiber a **trademark name** to set it apart from others. This may include an identifying name, symbol, or design that sets a manufacturer's product apart from similar products or competitors. For instance, olefin is a generic name. The olefin fibers used to make indoor-outdoor carpeting are different from the olefin fibers used in upholstery fabrics. Manufacturers give each type of olefin fiber a different trademark name. Herculon and Spectra are two of the olefin trademark names. Study **9-5** for other examples.

The TFPIA requires that all clothing and many household textile products be labeled to show

- the generic name of every fiber in the item, unless a fiber weighs less than five percent of the total fiber weight
- the percentage of each fiber, by weight
- the name or other identification of the manufacturer
- the country of origin, if the textile product is imported

9-4 The Federal Trade Commission has assigned 25 generic names to the various types of manufactured fibers according to the chemicals used to make them. The 22 fiber groups listed here are used in apparel.

Generic Fiber Groups

Acetate	Glass	Nytril*	Spandex
Acrylic	Lyocell	Olefin (polypropylene)	Triacetate
Anidex	Melamine	PLA	Vinal*
Aramid	Metallic	Polyester	Vinyon
Azlon*	Modacrylic	Rayon	
Elastoester	Nylon	Saran	

*Not currently produced in the U.S.

If a label states *Made in the U.S.A.*, all—or virtually all—of the product must be made in the United States.

Wool Products Labeling Act

Clothing and household items that contain wool are subject to the **Wool Products Labeling Act**. The FTC also enforces this act. It covers items made of sheep's wool and other wool fibers, including cashmere, llama, camel hair, and mohair.

Product labels are required to contain the fiber content of the item (wool type and amount), the country of origin, and the name of manufacturer or marketer. In addition, wool clothing labels must list a cleaning method. If the wool is recycled, that information must also be given.

Fur Products Labeling Act

The **Fur Products Labeling Act** requires that products made from animal fur must fulfill FTC's labeling requirements. The product label must include the name of the animal, the country of origin of imported fur products and products made of imported fur. The label must also indicate whether or not the fur was bleached, dyed, or artificially colored.

Care Labeling Rule

The **Care Labeling Rule** requires garment manufacturers to provide clear, uniform, and detailed instructions for the care and maintenance of garments. The information must be given on the labels of apparel items, with some exceptions. This rule was issued by the Federal Trade Commission. The care label must be attached firmly to the garment, be easy to find, and be readable for the useful life of the garment.

Labels can be any color, style, or shape as long as they follow the standards set by law. They can be fused, glued, or sewn to the garment, **9-6**. They must not unravel. The instructions may be printed directly on the fabric, but must remain readable for the life of the garment.

The rule requires labels to include the following information:
- method of washing (by hand or machine)
- water temperature (cold, warm, or hot)
- method of drying (machine, hang, or lay flat)

Generic Name	Trademark Name
Acetate	Estron
	Celanese
	Chromspun
	MicroSafe
Acrylic	Acrilan
	Creslan
	Duraspun
	Wear-Dated
Lyocell	Tencel
Modacrylic	SEF
Nylon	Anso
	Antron
	Enka
	Zeftron
Olefin	Herculon
	Spectra
Polyester	Dacron
	Fortrel
	Coolmax
	Microlux
Rayon (viscose)	Modal
	Bemberg
	Zantrel
Spandex	Lycra
	Glospan

9-5 Within each generic group there are several trademark names. Each one represents a fiber with slight variations.

- drying temperature (low, medium, or high)
- type of bleach when all types cannot be used safely
- use of iron and ironing temperature when necessary (cool, warm, or do not iron)

This rule applies to fabrics as well as to ready-made garments. The ends of fabric bolts are coded with care instructions.

National Organic Program Regulations

The National Organic Program is run by the U.S. Department of Agriculture (USDA). Through this program, the USDA regulates the use of the term *organic* as it is applied to agricultural products. Agricultural products include raw natural fibers, such as cotton, flax, and wool. NOP regulations require that these fibers, and clothing made from them, meet government standards before being labeled as organic. Clothing made from textiles that meet these standards can be labeled as *organic* or *100 percent organic*.

9-6 This care label contains both written care instructions as well as the newer care symbols. *Shutterstock*

To be considered organically grown, crops must be grown without the use of most pesticides and certain types of fertilizers. Wool labeled *organic* or *100 percent organic* must be from livestock raised under certain conditions. For example, the animals cannot be given antibiotics or growth hormones. NOP regulations also cover the processing and handling of organic products.

Consumer Products Safety Act and Consumer Products Improvement Act

The Consumer Products Safety Act created the U.S. Consumer Product Safety Commission (CPSC). The agency sets national safety standards for many hazardous substances and products found in and around homes. It requires manufacturers to label products to inform consumers about hazardous substances and give safe-handling instructions. The CPSC bans unsafe products and works with manufacturers to take them off the market. Consumer education is another one of its roles.

In 2008, Congress passed the Consumer Products Improvement Act which increased the funding and authority given to the CPSC. The agency created new regulations and tougher standards for many children's products. For example, the amount of lead in children's products—jewelry, furniture, toys, and other products—was lowered. Manufacturers must test their products and certify that they are safe. The act required CPSC to create and maintain a database containing safety information about products. This database is available to consumers.

Flammable Fabrics Act

The **Flammable Fabrics Act** was first passed in 1953 to regulate the manufacture and sale of highly flammable clothing and fabrics. It was directed at prohibiting the sale of hazardous *torch-type* fabrics. These are fabrics that burn easier and quicker than others. The act is enforced by the U.S. Consumer Product Safety Commission, which sets mandatory flammability standards. Before the CPSC was created, the act was enforced by the FTC.

The Flammable Fabrics Act has been expanded many times. Specific standards have been added for carpets, rugs, mattresses, children's sleepwear, and some upholstery fabrics.

Treating fabrics to reduce flammability does not prevent them from burning. Almost every fabric will burn when exposed to a flame. Flame-resistant fabrics will stop burning when they are removed from a small flame. These fabrics are less flammable or they are treated with substances that make them less flammable. Consumers still need to take precautions and reduce fire hazards.

Consumers must be warned if the flame-resistant properties of a garment will be destroyed by laundering methods. For instance, children's sleepwear must be washed using a detergent instead of soap. This is because soap can destroy the flame-resistant properties of the fabric.

In the future, there may be more flammability standards. Many manufacturers are working on new fibers and finishes to make more fabrics flame-resistant.

Federal Hazardous Substances Act

The **Federal Hazardous Substances Act** focuses on the issue of child safety and covers toys and many other products intended for the use of children. It has strict labeling requirements for products and bans the sale of others that contain hazardous substances. Among its many requirements, this act requires that some children's clothing pass a use and abuse test. These include items

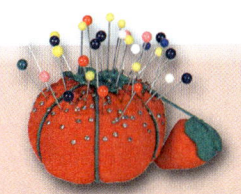

Did You Know?

Flammability Standards for Children's Sleepwear

Many children are seen in emergency rooms each year because the clothing they were wearing caught fire. The government's flammability standards for children's sleepwear are especially strict. Children's sleepwear must be either snug-fitting or made from flame-resistant fabrics.

The standards do not apply to infants' sleepwear in sizes nine months and under. This is because infants this young cannot walk over to a range or strike a match.

Snug-fitting garments are less likely to catch fire if a child goes near an open flame, such as a match, candle, or range burner. Since snug-fitting children's sleepwear may not be made of flame-resistant fabrics, it must hug the child's body. This requirement should be stated on hangtags and permanent labels affixed to these garments.

Children should never be put to sleep in loose-fitting, cotton or cotton-blend clothing. This type of clothing, such as over-sized T-shirts, can easily catch fire.

with decorative buttons or other attached items. This test assures that children will not choke on or become injured from sharp points and edges. Lead paint, which is toxic and can cause illness, cannot be used on children's items.

Consumer Protection Agencies and Organizations

You have learned about laws that were passed to guide and protect consumers. States may pass their own laws, which may be more restrictive than federal laws. Federal and state government agencies and organizations were created to enforce these laws. Some of these organizations also set safety standards. **Standards** are a set of criteria, established by authorities, used to judge whether or not products meet certain levels of performance and quality. The following are some of the government agencies involved in regulating the products of the textile and apparel industries:

- The *U.S. Consumer Product Safety Commission (CPSC)* protects the public from the risks of serious injury or death from consumer products. The CPSC sets safety standards for many products and investigates product-related injuries and deaths. It informs the public about dangerous products and issues recalls of dangerous items.
- The *Federal Trade Commission (FTC)* promotes free and fair competition by preventing deceptive practices, false advertising, and unfair trade practices. It enforces consumer protection legislation.
- The *U.S. Food and Drug Administration (FDA)* protects the public against impure and unsafe foods, drugs, tobacco products, cosmetics, and other products.
- The *National Institute of Standards and Technology (NIST)*, previously called the National Bureau of Standards, works with industry to develop and apply technology, measurements, and standards. NIST is an agency within the U.S. Department of Commerce.
- The *U.S. Department of Agriculture (USDA)* is the government agency that promotes U.S. agriculture and international trade. It is responsible for the safety of much of the country's food supply. It educates the public about nutrition and food safety. It also regulates the production and marketing of organic products, such as the organic cotton used to make clothing.

In addition to these government agencies, several private nonprofit groups help consumers. Trade organizations representing various industries also benefit consumers through their work. These include the following:

- *Better Business Bureaus (BBB)* are private organizations supported by business and professional groups. They provide reports on businesses to help consumers with purchases and help resolve consumers' disputes with businesses. They promote ethical business standards and self-regulation of business practices.
- The *International Organization for Standardization (ISO)* is a network of national standards institutes of more than 150 countries. They develop and publish standards to certify the quality of goods and services internationally. These standards include those for textiles.

- *ASTM International*, formerly known as the American Society for Testing and Materials, develops voluntary standards for products and materials. These standards are used by industries and governments around the world.

These groups work to improve standards in many fields, including textiles and clothing. They conduct research to find which new products consumers want. They test fabrics and garments for quality and durability. By helping businesses develop better products, these groups aid both producers and consumers.

Your Rights as a Consumer

As a consumer, you have the right to expect certain things from the businesses that provide the goods and services you use. During the 1960s, President John F. Kennedy defined the rights of consumers as: the right to safety, the right to be informed, the right to choose, and the right to be heard.

- *Right to safety.* The right to safety is the right to expect protection from dangerous goods and services. These are goods and services that may be harmful to a person's health or life.
- *Right to be informed.* The right to be informed is the right to be given accurate facts and information about products and services. This enables consumers to make wise choices. Advertising, online and print articles, and product labels are some sources of information.
- *Right to choose.* The right to choose is the right to free choice in the marketplace. Consumers should be able to choose what to buy and where to buy it from. This requires the marketplace to provide a wide variety of goods and services from more than one producer.
- *Right to be heard.* The right to be heard is the right to speak out if a product or service is unsatisfactory. People and agencies in business and government should listen and help consumers settle their complaints.

During the 1970s, President Richard Nixon added another right—the *right to redress*. This is the right to be compensated for defective products, poor service, or the broken promises of sellers or manufacturers. For example, suppose you buy a product that turns out to be unsatisfactory. You should be able to get a replacement, a store credit, or a refund.

Another consumer right was added by President Gerald Ford—the *right to consumer education*. This is the right of consumers to acquire the skills and knowledge needed to make informed choices. Several government agencies and consumer education programs were created to help consumers buy wisely. They provide classes and educational materials online and in print. They also warn consumers about fraud and unethical practices and how consumers can either avoid or take action against them.

Your Responsibilities as a Consumer

Consumers have responsibilities as well as rights. The people who make and sell goods and services have the right to expect certain things from you as a consumer. See 9-7 for a list that outlines consumer rights and responsibilities. You have the responsibility to do the following:

Consumer Rights and Responsibilities

- The right to safety…and the responsibility to use products safely and to guard against carelessness, especially around fire hazards.
- The right to be informed…and the responsibility to seek out information and to use it when buying.
- The right to choose…and the responsibility to buy wisely from the wide variety of goods and services available.
- The right to be heard…and the responsibility to let legitimate complaints be known.
- The right to redress…and the responsibility to make sure that fair compensation is received.
- The right to consumer education…and the responsibility to seek it out and use it.

9-7 Consumers should be aware of their rights and responsibilities.

- *Use products safely and to guard against carelessness.* Keeping safety in mind, especially around fire hazards, is the consumer's responsibility. For instance, you should not reach over a burning flame, especially if you are wearing a garment that could easily catch fire.
- *Seek out information and to use it when buying.* When manufacturers or businesses provide information about a product or service, you have the responsibility to seek it out. You also have the responsibility to use this information when buying the product or paying for the service. For example, read labels and hangtags that provide product information.
- *Buy wisely from the wide variety of goods and services available.* Smart consumers are smart shoppers. They compare the offerings and prices from different sellers before buying. They look for features they want and prices they can afford. See **9-8**. They only buy the garments that meet their standards. For example, they check that buttons are securely attached,

Trends Making News

Shoplifting—A Cost to Everyone

Theft of goods cost U.S. retailers nearly $13 billion a year, according to the non profit National Association for Shoplifting Prevention (NASP). The losses would be even higher without antitheft systems such as electronic article surveillance (EAS) devices and closed circuit television systems.

Shoplifting hurts more than just retailers. All consumers are impacted. To make up for shoplifting losses, retailers raise their prices. Everyone pays more.

Who is stealing and what are they taking? About one out of four shoplifters are kids and teenagers. Younger shoplifters are most likely to steal items they cannot afford or are prohibited from buying. These include compact discs, cosmetics, trendy clothes, cigarettes, and consumer electronics.

Why do people steal? Simply stated, they steal to get something for nothing. This is like getting a gift, which gives them a *lift*. For teens, the reasons often relate to pressures they feel from family, peers, or school. Most teens who steal say they do not know why they do it. Some say they want nice things or cave in to pressure from friends. Others just want to see if they can get away with it. Some shoplifters are motivated by anger, depression, or boredom.

Many people know that stealing is wrong and can usually resist the temptation to do it. But when life is stressful, some people give in to the temptation. Shoplifting is one of many inappropriate ways of coping with stress. Other unhealthy ways of coping include overeating, drinking, using drugs, and withdrawal.

What can be done to reduce shoplifting? New technology is making it possible to catch more shoplifters. Retailers are installing more technologically sophisticated loss-prevention systems. Manufacturers are applying thin label-like electronic circuits directly to apparel.

buttonholes are neatly made, zippers zip without catching, and stripes match at the seams. They ask questions before they buy. Study the list of shopping tips in **9-9**.

- *Let legitimate complaints be known.* If a product does not perform as advertised and expected, the buyer should inform the seller or the manufacturer. They may not be aware of the problem.

As a consumer, you are also responsible for following care instructions recommended on hangtags and care labels. This makes it more likely that products will perform as intended. For example, suppose a care label in a shirt says, *Dry clean only*. If you wash the shirt and it shrinks, you cannot make a claim to anyone about the shrinkage.

9-8 Examine clothes before you buy. Careful shopping will assure you of getting the quality you want.
Shutterstock

Handling a Complaint

Your responsibilities as a consumer are to be well-informed and to properly care for your purchased goods. If a product does not perform as it should, you should notify the appropriate party. When buyers and sellers work together, products can be improved.

You may buy something that you cannot wear because it is of poor quality or has a defect. For example, suppose you discovered that a button was missing on a new shirt or cardigan sweater? If an extra button is not supplied, all of the buttons must be replaced. In cases like this, a complaint is in order. You may not like to complain, but you do not want to feel you made a *bad buy*. There are several things you can do.

9-9 Smart consumers find the answers to these questions before they buy clothes.

10 Easy Tips to Follow Before You Buy

- Is the fiber content right for your needs? (Look at labels.)
- Is the garment washable? Does it have to be dry-cleaned? (Look at labels and tags for instructions.)
- Is the garment colorfast? (Look at labels and tags. Ask questions before you buy.)
- Is the garment wrinkle-resistant? (Look at tags for claims. Then, just to make sure, crumple a corner in your hand. Does it bounce back? It should.)
- Will the fabric pill? (Look at a small area after you have rubbed it together in a circular motion. Hold it at an angle. Any fuzziness or pilling?)
- Will the fabric snag? (Look for long stitches or loose loops in fabric.)
- Is the garment well-constructed? (Look at buttons, buttonholes, stitching, dangling threads, width of seams, hem.)
- Will the garment sag or bag? (Look at fabric after you have wrapped it tight around your fist. It should flatten right out without buckling.)
- Is there a guarantee or warranty? (Look at tags, and read the fine print carefully.)
- Are you buying from a reliable retailer? (Look up a store's return policy before purchasing. Why be sorry later?)

Return the Item

Go back to the store where you bought the item. Bring the item and the sales receipt with you. Return the garment to the proper person. This could be the manager, department head, or customer service representative. These people want to know about customer complaints so they can correct problems before they occur again. Most stores will gladly replace your purchase or refund your money. The item is often returned to the manufacturer for credit on the store's account.

If you purchased the item online or from a catalog, check the return policy. The policy should be stated on the website or in the catalog. Most companies send return labels with their merchandise to make it easier to return items. Some even provide return envelopes. They usually provide a form that asks you why the item is being returned. If the item is defective, state so in an enclosed letter. You could also phone or e-mail the company.

Write a Letter

What should you do if you are not satisfied with how your problem is handled? Write a letter to the store or retailer. Do so as soon as possible. Do not wait weeks or months to act. Read and study the sample complaint letter in **9-10**. Notice the information that should be included in such a letter. Be sure to include the following:

- Purchase information (date, price, style number, and other details)
- The problem, clearly stated
- The action you have already taken
- The action you would like the company to take
- A time frame in which you expect results

If you are not contacted within the time specified in your letter, write to the manufacturer. You can use the Internet to do a search for the company. Many manufacturers have their own websites that provide you a way to contact them.

Contact Your Credit Card Company

If you paid for the defective item with a credit card, the credit card company may be able to help you. This step can be taken after you have contacted the seller and not received satisfaction. Follow the dispute directions on the back of your credit card bill. Submit your complaint in writing. The credit card company may stop payment to the retailer until the problem is resolved.

The **Fair Credit Billing Act** protects consumers against unfair billing practices and defective merchandise. Customers have 60 days after receiving the first bill containing the error to notify the creditor. Creditors must acknowledge receiving complaints within 30 days, and resolve problems within 90 days. Customers do not have to pay for the item in question until the issue is resolved.

Consumer Assistance

If the above suggestions do not work, you can contact a consumer protection agency for help. You may contact the consumer reporter at a local newspaper, radio, or TV station. The Better Business Bureau can also advise you.

Consumers, retailers, and manufacturers must work together for the benefit of everyone. Manufacturers want their products to perform well so retailers

Chapter 9   Consumer Rights and Responsibilities   183

will want to continue to sell them. Retailers want to offer quality products and services so they will have satisfied, happy customers. Consumers want to feel they have made good buying decisions.

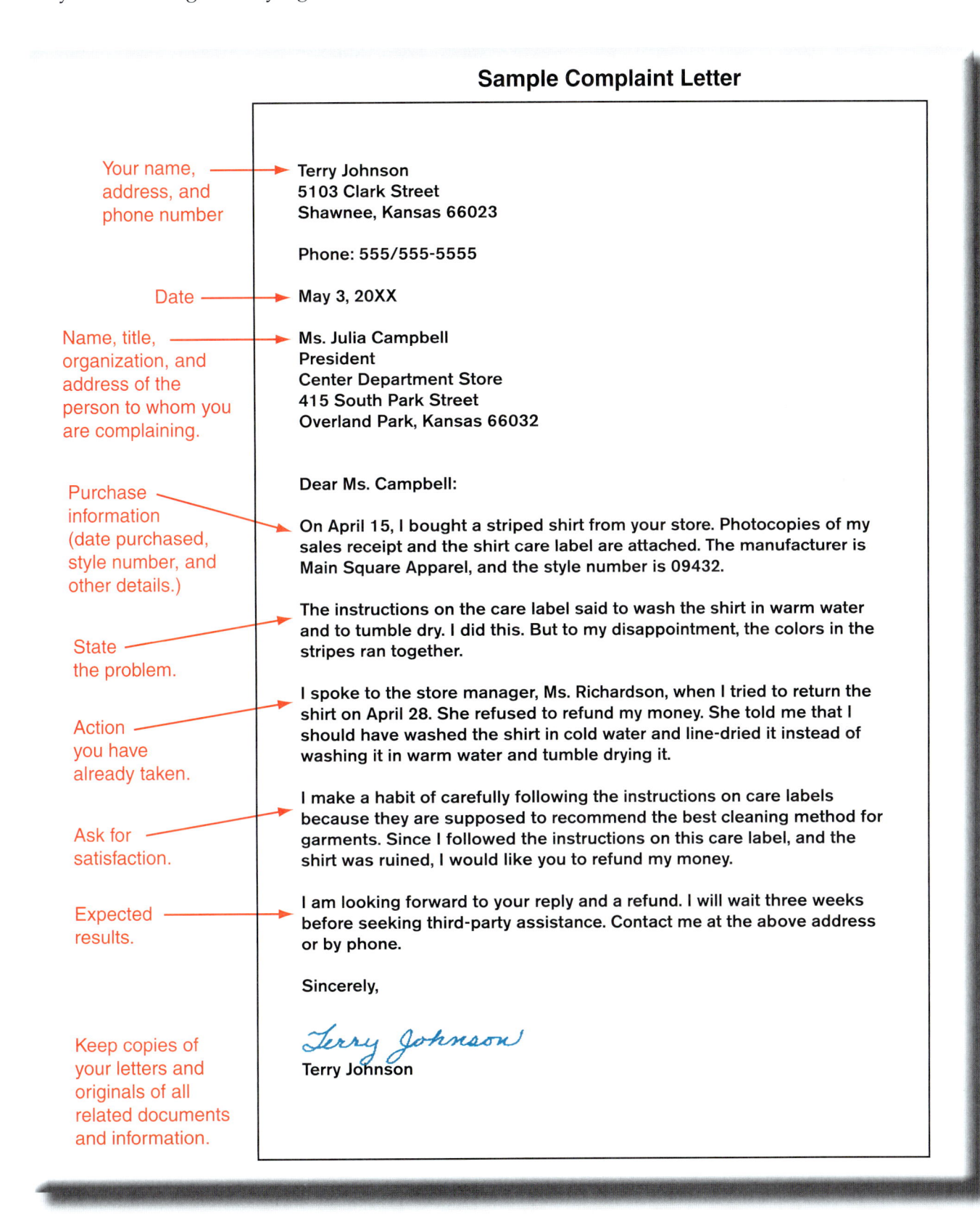

Sample Complaint Letter

Your name, address, and phone number →
Terry Johnson
5103 Clark Street
Shawnee, Kansas 66023

Phone: 555/555-5555

Date →
May 3, 20XX

Name, title, organization, and address of the person to whom you are complaining. →
Ms. Julia Campbell
President
Center Department Store
415 South Park Street
Overland Park, Kansas 66032

Dear Ms. Campbell:

Purchase information (date purchased, style number, and other details.) →
On April 15, I bought a striped shirt from your store. Photocopies of my sales receipt and the shirt care label are attached. The manufacturer is Main Square Apparel, and the style number is 09432.

State the problem. →
The instructions on the care label said to wash the shirt in warm water and to tumble dry. I did this. But to my disappointment, the colors in the stripes ran together.

Action you have already taken. →
I spoke to the store manager, Ms. Richardson, when I tried to return the shirt on April 28. She refused to refund my money. She told me that I should have washed the shirt in cold water and line-dried it instead of washing it in warm water and tumble drying it.

Ask for satisfaction. →
I make a habit of carefully following the instructions on care labels because they are supposed to recommend the best cleaning method for garments. Since I followed the instructions on this care label, and the shirt was ruined, I would like you to refund my money.

Expected results. →
I am looking forward to your reply and a refund. I will wait three weeks before seeking third-party assistance. Contact me at the above address or by phone.

Sincerely,

Terry Johnson
Terry Johnson

Keep copies of your letters and originals of all related documents and information.

9-10 Sometimes it may be necessary to write a complaint letter.

Summary

- Fabrics and garments are labeled for four basic reasons: to identify the product, to help businesses sell products, to help consumers make wise purchases, and to explain proper care methods for the product.
- Two important pieces of legislation that help consumers select and care for clothing are the Textile Fiber Products Identification Act and the Care Labeling Rule. Two acts that protect the safety of consumers are the Flammable Fabrics Act and the Federal Hazardous Substances Act.
- Each fiber has a generic name and a trademark name. Many manufacturers may produce the same generic fiber, but each will have its own trademark name for their fiber.
- Care labels stating how garments are to be cleaned must appear on all clothing items. Care labels must be attached firmly to garments, be easy to find, and be readable for the useful life of garments.
- Manufacturing or treating fabrics to reduce flammability does not prevent them from burning. Almost every fabric will burn when exposed to a flame. Treating fabrics reduces the danger of burning. Consumers must always be vigilant about fire hazards.
- As a consumer, you have the right to expect certain things from the goods and services you use. Several government agencies and organizations assist consumers and enforce consumer-related legislation.
- Consumers have responsibilities as well as rights. The people who make and sell goods and services expect certain things from you as a consumer.
- If a product does not perform as it should, you should inform the right people. When buyers and sellers work together, products can be improved.

Graphic Organizer

Draw a graphic organizer like the one you see here to outline the process for handling a consumer complaint.

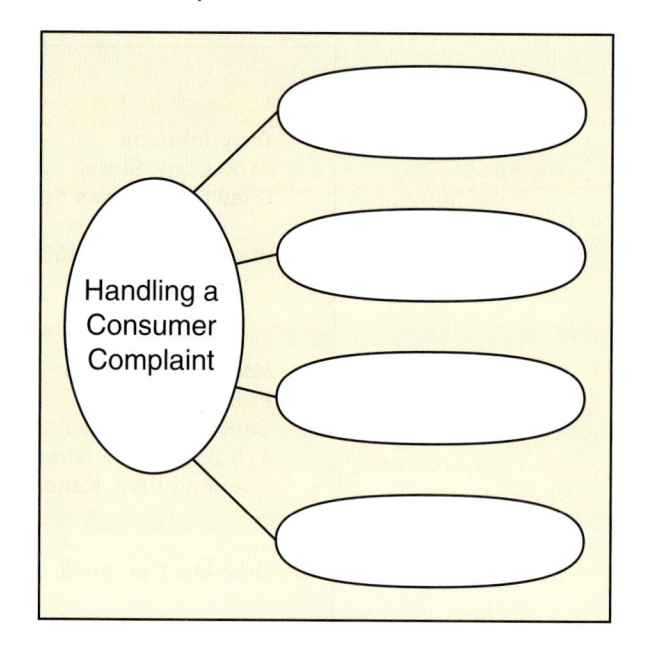

Review the Facts

1. What are the differences between hangtags and labels?
2. What information is required to be on a label?
3. All manufactured fibers are divided into 25 ____.
4. What information does the TFPIA legislation *not* require that labels include?
5. List the six items of information required on care labels according to the Care Labeling Rule.
6. Where is care information found for fabrics sold by the yard?
7. Name three specific products covered by the Flammable Fabrics Act.
8. List the six rights of consumers.
9. Name the responsibilities of consumers.
10. Which federal agency is responsible for enforcing consumer protection legislation?
11. If an item does not perform as expected, explain what should be done first.

Think Critically

12. **Predict consequences.** Identify possible consequences of having no laws to protect consumers regarding apparel and textiles. Discuss these possible consequences in class.
13. **Analyze outcomes.** Imagine what it would be like to buy clothes and other textile items without any labels or hangtags on them. What kinds of problems could consumers have?
14. **Draw conclusions.** In pursuing the *right to redress*, draw conclusions about why it is important for customers to follow the return policies of stores and manufacturers.
15. **Analyze behavior.** Think about an experience you have had with a fabric or garment that failed to wear or perform as you expected. What could you have done differently as a consumer?

Apparel Applications

16. **Electronic bulletin board.** Collect hangtags and labels for an electronic bulletin board display. Scan the labels into a computer and use a school-approved web-based application to create an electronic bulletin board. Have classmates identify information that is required and not required on the labels and hangtags.
17. **Hangtag file.** Create a file box for storing garment hangtags and place it in the laundry area. Decide how you will categorize the file box. On the back of each hangtag, write the date of purchase, description of garment, etc., and place in the file box. As an alternative, scan the above information into your computer and keep an electronic file box for this information.
18. **Create a resource listing.** As a class, research and develop a brochure listing local sources for consumer assistance. Review the business section of the local phone directory. Also use the Internet to see what services your community offers. Consider posting the brochure to the school website.
19. **Consumer role-play.** Role-play correct and incorrect ways to return defective merchandise to a store.

Academic Connections

20. **Writing.** Write a sample letter to a store manager about a disappointing purchase. Follow the guidelines given in the chapter. Compare your letter with those of your classmates for clarity and detail.
21. **Reading.** Choose one of the laws related to textiles and apparel addressed in this chapter. Review the law and its most recent amendments. Write a summary of your findings to share with the class.
22. **Social studies.** Consumers have responsibilities as well as rights. Review each of the consumer responsibilities again. How do you carry out these responsibilities as a consumer? Then review the history of the Consumer Bill of Rights and write a summary of your findings.

Workplace Links

23. **Investigating return policies.** Investigate the merchandise-return policies and the do's and don'ts of returning merchandise for at least three businesses in your area. Give an oral report to the class about your findings.
24. **Writing care labels.** Presume you and your team work for a garment manufacturer who is coming out with a new line. Your team is responsible for writing the care labels for the new garments. Choose one garment and fabric content. Then write a care label that could be applicable to this garment and fabric. Compare with other teams.

Investigating Consumer-Related Careers

Is a career as a consumer advocate of interest to you? Would you find it interesting and challenging to provide such assistance to consumers?

In your continuing career search, take the interactive *Career Scan* which is part of the FCCLA *Career Connection* program. This tool helps you rate your career development experiences and focuses your attention on *Career Connection* units that meet your career goals. See your adviser for information as needed.

Chapter 10

Choices as a Consumer

Chapter Objectives

After studying this chapter, you will be able to
- **analyze** the features of different types of stores.
- **compare** the features of nonstore shopping.
- **analyze** effective shopping strategies to help manage apparel dollars.
- **summarize** various ways to pay for purchases.

Key Terms

department stores
specialty stores
chain stores
discount stores
off-price discount stores
factory outlet stores
overruns
irregular

seconds
resale shops
thrift shops
consignment
comparison shopping
impulse buying
infomercials
advertorials

bargain
finance charge
debit card
credit
regular charge account
revolving charge account
layaway buying

Reading with Purpose

Read the summary at the end of the chapter before you begin reading. Reading the summary helps identify main points and important information.

You have to make many choices when you buy clothes. One of these choices is deciding where to purchase your clothing. Most clothing purchases are made in retail stores. As you know, there are many types of stores that sell clothes and accessories. Each type presents consumers with advantages and disadvantages.

You can also shop for clothes from your home almost 24-hours a day. All you need is a phone, or a television or computer with an Internet connection. A growing number of consumers are also shopping on the go. They use mobile, handheld devices to view merchandise and make purchases no matter where they are.

Another choice you make when buying clothing is how to pay for it. Consumers also have more options today when they are ready to pay for their purchases. With so many choices, it pays to be an informed consumer.

Types of Stores

Why do you like one store better than another? Is it because it carries a wider selection of clothes? Are the salespeople more helpful? See **10-1**. Do they treat you as an important person rather than as an inexperienced young person? Maybe you shop in a certain store because your friends shop there. Perhaps your favorite store is located in a shopping mall close to your home.

10-1 Courteous and helpful salespeople can attract customers to a store. *Shutterstock*

There are many types of stores that carry clothing. By comparing the features, as well as the prices, you can find which type of store suits you best.

Department Stores

Department stores offer one-stop shopping. They sell a variety of clothing, shoes, and accessories in a wide range of styles, qualities, and prices. A department store offers clothing for infants, children, teens, and juniors, as well as older persons. In addition, many sell products for the home such as furniture, carpet, lamps, and linens. Luggage, jewelry, and cosmetics are also sold.

Much of the merchandise department stores carry comes from designers and manufacturers that consumers associate with quality. They may also carry *private label*, or house-brand, merchandise that is made specifically for a store. This allows stores to specify the qualities they want in these products. Many large department stores also have budget-priced clothing departments.

Department stores provide good service for their customers. Their salespeople can provide personal assistance. They help customers find their sizes, get the proper fit, and arrange for alterations. In most department stores, customers pay for merchandise in the same area of the store or department where they found it. Customers can easily return merchandise if they are unhappy with what they bought.

Many services may be offered such as credit accounts, alterations, gift wrapping and mailing, and home delivery. Department stores usually charge fees for these services. Customers should decide if using them is worth the cost.

Specialty Stores

Specialty stores sell specific kinds of merchandise. For instance, they may sell only junior-size dresses, boys' and men's pants, or infants' wear. Shopping centers and malls are good places to find specialty stores, **10-2**. If you need a certain item that is not available in most stores, a specialty store may be able to get it for you. The service is usually good, and the salespeople are knowledgeable about their merchandise. For people with limited time to shop, specialty stores are ideal. Prices are sometimes higher than those in other stores.

A *boutique* is a type of specialty store that features a limited amount of unique apparel or accessories. These stores are small, pricey, and give much personal service.

Chain Stores

Chain stores are groups of 12 or more stores owned and managed by a central office. The stores carry the same lines of products at similar prices. Some chains are department stores, such as Sears and JCPenney. Other chains are more like specialty shops, selling a single-product category, such as men's or women's clothes. Banana Republic and Gap are examples of chain clothing stores.

All the stores in a chain have a similar look. Private-label merchandise may be made exclusively for the stores. Manufacturers offer lower prices to chain stores because of their buying power. This leads to lower retail prices.

Discount Stores

Discount stores have lower prices than department stores. One reason they get better prices from manufacturers is because they buy in large quantities. Target and Walmart are examples of discount stores. Such stores carry a wide range of clothing and household items. The quality of clothing can range from high to low. Lower-quality items are still wearable although many have slight defects such as pulled threads or uneven fabric color. Discount stores also buy clothes from manufacturers who produced more than their dealers ordered. These may include first-quality clothes that are sold at lower prices because they are extras.

Discount stores are the department stores' greatest competition. In recent years, discount stores have done more to improve their image. Some are signing up well-known designers to create stylish clothes. Isaac Mizrahi created a line for Target. Walmart has a Norma Kamali line of clothes. Some stores have greeters to welcome you when you enter. They may have film developing, snack bars, and banking facilities within them. They have convenient hours and are open in the evenings, on weekends, and most holidays.

Generally, discount stores offer less personal service than department stores. You are on your own to find your style preferences and sizes. Large overhead signs direct you to the proper department. Once you select your items, you take them to the checkout counters at the front of the store. The buildings are large and simply decorated. Dressing rooms may be sparse. Special services, such as home deliveries, are not offered.

10-2 Malls offer climate-controlled shopping. A variety of specialty shops are often located in malls.
Shutterstock

Off-Price Discount Stores

Another type of discount store is becoming more common. These stores—or **off-price discount stores**—feature brand-name or designer merchandise at below-normal prices. You may have a T.J.Maxx, Marshalls, Syms, or Designer Depot store near you. Off-price discount stores sell moderate- to higher-priced merchandise. Sometimes the labels are removed to protect the manufacturers' products sold in other stores at full price. Some retailers operate their own stores with their own lower-priced merchandise. Examples of these stores are Nordstrom Rack, Ann Taylor Loft, and Saks Fifth Avenue OFF 5th.

Buyers who work for off-price discount stores do not place orders for their merchandise. Instead, they buy what is available during the season when most other buyers are placing orders for the next season. They buy whatever they can and sell it immediately. These are clothes that stores ordered but returned when they did not sell. They are often *overages*, or merchandise a designer produced too much of. As a consumer, you can enjoy reduced prices for brand-name goods at these stores. However, you cannot predict what you will find when you shop.

Factory Outlet Stores

Factory outlet stores are stores operated by manufacturers that sell only their own merchandise. See **10-3**. The prices are often lower than those at department stores because the clothing comes directly from factories. There are no wholesalers or *middle people* involved. The stores are often located near the manufacturers' factories and away from stores that sell their full-price merchandise. Factory outlet malls feature only stores of this type. They are usually located in outlying areas.

Some factory outlet stores offer first-quality items from the current season, shipped only weeks after the same items went to the department stores. They also sell last season's lines and manufacturers' overruns. **Overruns** are items produced by manufacturers, but not ordered by retailers. Half of all outlets carry clothes produced specifically for those stores.

Not all items at outlet stores are bargains. You should be familiar with the prices of items you are looking for before going. The return policies of outlet stores are not as liberal as those of full-price stores.

10-3 Some name-brand manufacturers run factory outlet stores. You can find some very good buys at these stores. *Shutterstock*

Outlet stores also carry irregulars and seconds. Garment labels or price tags indicate if they are irregulars or seconds. An **irregular** garment has a slight defect. Before buying, find the defect and determine if it will prevent you from wearing the garment. **Seconds** are items that are soiled or have flaws. A garment with a poorly sewn seam or a hidden flaw can still be a good buy. The seam may be repaired. The flaw may not show as the garment is worn. Soiled garments can be cleaned.

Resale Shops

Resale shops are just what their name implies. The clothing has been owned and worn before. It is being sold again. Clothing that has been outgrown or is no longer worn is brought to these stores by consumers. They also carry leftovers from retail stores and some out-of-style garments.

Some resale shops sell donated items. **Thrift shops** are resale shops that are often run by not-for-profit organizations to raise money for charitable causes. Most of the clothing, accessories, household goods, furniture, and other thrift-shop items are donated by the public. However, some items may be leftovers donated from other stores. People who make donations may sometimes receive tax benefits.

Other resale shops sell on **consignment**—a form of resale in which a portion of the sale price goes to the shop and the rest goes back to the owner. Shops often carry an item on consignment for about 30 days. If the item does not sell in that time, the price is reduced. If it still does not sell, it is returned to the owner or donated to charity.

Many resale shops have *no-return policies*, so shoppers should try on items before buying. Shoppers should also carefully examine garments for flaws and signs of quality. Inspect clothes for stains, missing buttons, and broken zippers.

Nonstore Shopping

If you want to shop without leaving your home, or if store hours are inconvenient, you may prefer nonstore shopping. If so, you have several choices: catalog shopping, online shopping, and television shopping. Personal selling is another form of nonstore shopping.

A growing number of consumers are turning to nonstore shopping to make many of their purchases, **10-4**. There are several reasons for its popularity. One is the widespread use of credit cards, online payment services, and gift cards, which can be used to make nonstore purchases. Another is the number of people who now have less time for shopping at retail stores. With mail-order and online shopping, they can take their time choosing the items they want when they have the time to shop.

Catalog and Online Shopping

Catalog shopping is one way to shop at home. Catalogs are usually mailed to customers' homes. Consumers flip through the catalogs to find the items they want and order these items by phone or mail. Catalogs often offer a better assortment of clothing than local stores. Prices vary, but they are usually comparable to those of department stores. See **10-5** for some catalog shopping hints.

10-4 Online shopping gives consumers the convenience of shopping from their homes. *Shutterstock*

> ### Helpful Hints for Catalog Shopping
>
> - When ordering, ask about special services, like free color swatches, hemming, or advice on coordinating outfits.
> - Sizes differ from one catalog to another, so take your measurements and follow the sizing directions on the order form. Ask the operator if the style runs full or snug, long or short. Also watch for sizing clues such as *fitted*, *relaxed fit*, or *oversize*.
> - Factor in mailing charges, which add to costs. A low-priced item may not be a good buy after postage and handling are added. If ordering several items, do so at one time to keep these charges as low as possible.
> - Ask the operator when your order will be shipped (usually within a day or two) and the approximate arrival date. In case of problems, write down the date ordered, item details, and order number.
> - Ask about the return policy. Most catalogs accept returns, but you will not get your original mailing charge refunded. Many catalogs now offer free returns and enclose a labeled package for your use.

10-5 Catalog shopping can be a convenient way to shop, but follow these helpful hints.

The fastest growth in nonstore shopping is occurring online. It involves the use of the Internet to select and make purchases. A majority of households have Internet access, and more than half make purchases online. The most popular things sold online are travel services, books, and computer equipment, but apparel sales are growing. Even designer apparel can now be purchased online.

For online shopping, you need a computer with a modem and an Internet service provider. Almost all retailers have websites where they sell their merchandise. Visitors to these websites can view pictures of clothing styles and read descriptions of items. At some sites, pictures are three-dimensional or can be rotated and magnified. Information on colors, sizes, styles, and prices are given. To purchase an item, the buyer keys in a selection and pays by entering a credit card number. Merchandise is delivered within a few days.

Online shopping can be hassle free if a website is well-designed. Some websites are easier to navigate than others, **10-6**. They connect buyers to the products they want with just a few key strokes or taps on a screen. Some sites can send customers electronic notices of sales and special offers. Sites may provide *wish lists* where people can *window shop* and create an online record of items they like, making gift shopping easier. A recent addition is online videos, such as fashions shown on runway models.

Pros and Cons of Catalog and Online Shopping

There are advantages and disadvantages to catalog and online shopping. The following are some of the advantages:

- ***Convenience.*** Shopping by mail, phone, or online is convenient. There are no parking problems and shopping is not restricted to store hours. Orders are easily placed by phone, practically any time, day or night, through toll-free numbers and credit cards. Orders can also be mailed or faxed.
- ***Service.*** Catalog and online services are usually quite good. Returns can usually be made with no questions asked. (Check the company policy to see if you can return items for a refund or credit.)
- ***Product information.*** Each item of clothing is shown and described. The fabrics, sizes, colors, prices, and details are listed. This catalog or online information is often more complete than what a store salesperson could give you.
- ***Selection.*** The selection is much larger than what can be found in stores.

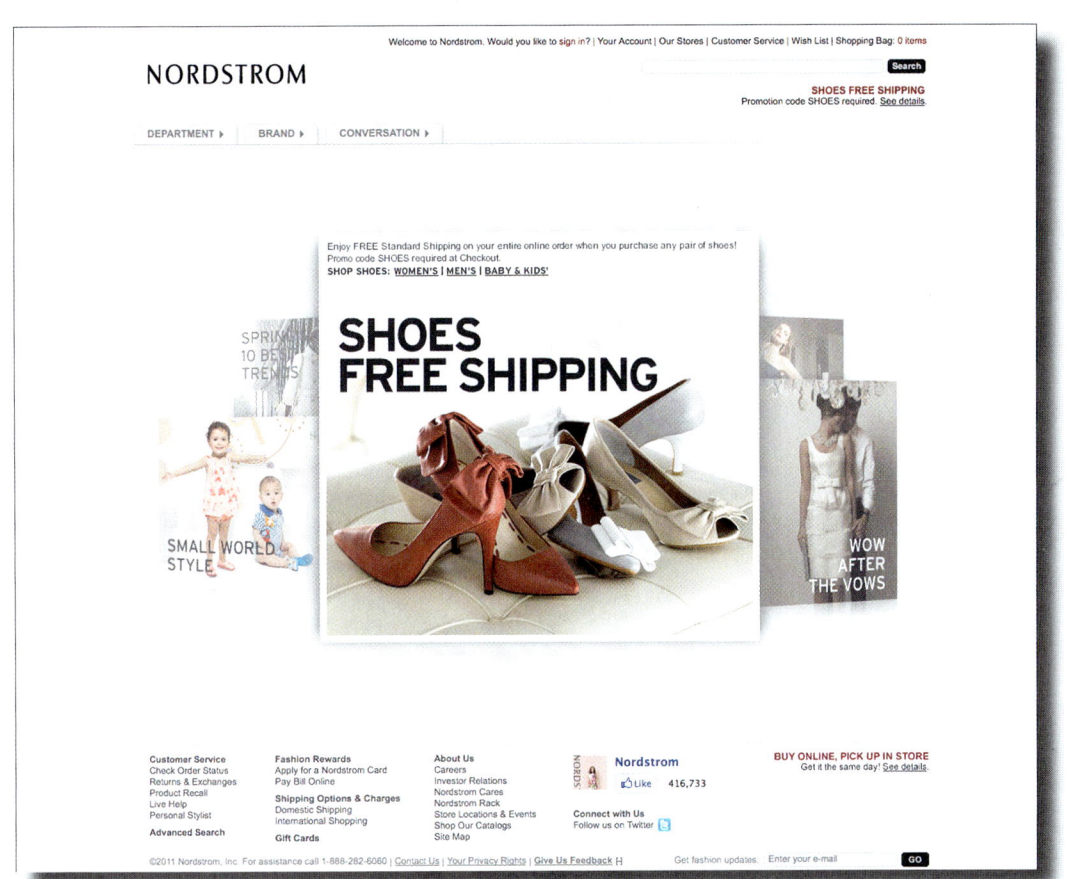

10-6 Shopping online is more satisfying if a retail website is easy to navigate. *Nordstrom.com*

Some disadvantages are the following:

- *Delivery charge.* There is often a delivery charge added to the price of your purchase. However, due to competition, some merchants are dropping delivery charges.
- *Garment fit.* Perfect fit may be a problem, as you are not able to try the garment on before you buy it.
- *Garment color.* There may be a slight difference in color when the garment arrives. Photos are taken of each item, but the exact color is difficult to reproduce on paper or online.
- *Returns.* If you have to return an item, you will have to repackage it and return it for an exchange, a refund, or credit. You may have to pay the shipping cost of returning the item.
- *Wait.* You will have to wait for your order to be delivered, which is inconvenient if you need something right away. Faster delivery is available at a higher price.

A disadvantage in buying clothing online is that you cannot feel the fabric or try on the clothes. Some retailers attempt to overcome this problem by allowing customers to try clothes on a personal model created on screen to mimic the shopper's own body traits. Some sites allow you to view fabric swatches up close. Others allow you to see both the front and back of a product. At some sites, if you select one item, other items will be shown that coordinate with your initial selection.

Many consumers are anxious about providing financial information, including their credit card numbers, online. Most established online retailers' use software that protects their customers' personal information by encrypting

Trends Making News

.com Shopping—Buyer Beware

In 1996, electronic commerce (e-commerce) began with a relatively small number of shoppers making purchases over the Internet. E-commerce has exploded since then. Well-designed websites made shopping online a popular alternative to shopping at traditional brick-and-mortar stores.

Yet there are problems with shopping online that you, the consumer, need to be aware of. There are honest merchants and there are dishonest merchants. There are safety and security concerns, just as there are when you shop at your local mall. This is especially so if you search for a specific item and end up at the website of a company unknown to you. Remember, anyone can set up shop on the Internet. Very few safeguards are currently in place to protect consumers. Therefore, you need to be extra cautious when shopping online. Be sure of the following before making any purchase and entering your credit card number. Does the site

- provide complete information about the company? (This includes the type of company, what it sells, where it is located, and how it can be contacted.)
- provide enough details about products so you know exactly what you are buying?
- provide complete information on the cost of the item, including shipping and handling, and any taxes?
- provide any warranties or guarantees?
- allow you to print a record of the transaction?
- provide confirmation by e-mail within one business day that your order has been received?
- notify you of stock status and approximate delivery time?
- explain the return policy and how you can receive a credit?
- provide credit card transactions through a secured server?
- list a phone number or e-mail address for customer service if you have any complaints or problems?

If you can answer yes to all of these questions, then you can be fairly sure your online shopping experience will be a positive one.

it into bits of code that only they and the customer can view. Experts say consumers should only buy from reputable online retailers. They should restrict the information they give out and update their virus protection software regularly.

Another option is to set up an account with an online payment service, such as PayPal, that can be used at multiple sites. This account establishes a direct link to your bank account, debit card, or credit card. You do not provide the retailer with your credit card number. Your financial information may be more secure.

When you make a clothing purchase at a local mall, the retailer must collect sales taxes from you. The taxes collected are paid to the government. The taxes you pay depend on the sales tax rate in your area. Taxes make purchases more expensive. Tax collection rules vary from state to state, but they tend to be lenient for catalog and online retailers. For example, these businesses may not be required to collect sales taxes from their out-of-state customers. Some state governments rely on residents to report their online purchases and pay the taxes they owe. New laws are being considered to force online retailers to collect sales taxes from all of their customers.

Television Shopping

Several television channels show products that are available for purchase. A wide variety of products, including clothing and accessories, are sold in this manner. Many home shopping programs feature jewelry. The products are displayed, modeled, and described in detail. Viewers call toll-free numbers to place their orders. Most merchants require payment by credit card, and the orders are shipped to your home.

Television shopping is convenient, but some people are tempted to order items they do not need or cannot afford. Celebrity hosts entice people to buy. Personal testimonials by satisfied customers are also used to promote the sale of products.

Personal Selling

Clothing items, jewelry, accessories, and cosmetics are also sold in peoples' homes through *personal selling*. Parties or showings are scheduled in private homes, either for groups or individuals. Items are modeled or displayed, and orders are taken by a sales representative. The items are then delivered in person or through the mail. The merchandise is generally of a high quality, but may also be high in price. Customers sometimes feel pressure to buy if the party is held by a friend. Before you attend a party, be sure you can do so without feeling pressured to buy something you do not need.

Shopping Strategies

Few people have unlimited funds for clothing purchases. When you shop, a number of strategies can help you get the most for your money. Using some of these strategies will help your clothing dollars go farther.

Do Comparison Shopping

A smart shopper compares qualities and prices in different retailers before buying. This is called **comparison shopping**. The young woman in **10-7** is comparing tops. She wants one with the right details at the right price.

Begin your comparison shopping by studying advertisements for items you need and keep prices in mind. Mail-order catalogs are a good reference in comparison shopping. Then when you visit stores, you are ready to compare garments. Read the labels to be sure you are comparing items with similar qualities.

Many consumers comparison shop online to find the best prices for the products they want to buy. Once they have narrowed down their choices, they often make the purchase at a local retail store. Some websites even consolidate listings from reliable merchants. They show a range of retailers and prices for each product.

10-7 After comparison shopping, this young woman has found the top she wants. It is the right style, size, color, and price. *Shutterstock*

Comparison shopping takes time. You must be patient and have a desire to get the best value for your money. The results make it worthwhile. They include a feeling of satisfaction when you know you made the right purchase.

Avoid Impulse Buying

People often buy clothes without a plan. **Impulse buying** occurs when people buy something as soon as they see it, without stopping to think about their needs. They do not consider whether or not they have items in their wardrobe that can be worn with it. They buy something because it is pretty, because someone else has one, or because they happen to have enough money with them.

Do not let yourself be influenced by advertising displays or special sale signs. Impulse buying will cause you to spend too much money and you may not be happy with your purchase when you return home. It is smarter to make a list of planned purchases before you begin to shop. Then if you find a sale price on a garment you had planned to buy, you will have found a true bargain.

Use Advertisements Wisely

Advertising can create wants by making products seem desirable. Clever slogans, songs, and phrases are composed to catch your attention. Photos and videos are shown to heighten your interest. Advertisements are placed in magazines and newspapers. They also appear on television and the Internet. When using the Internet, pop-up windows often appear containing links to sellers' websites.

Many clothing ads are aimed at young people. Teens can be fashion leaders. They may begin new clothing trends. They spend much of the money they have on clothes.

The advertising industry gives major financial support to newspapers, magazines, radio, television, and the Internet. These methods of communication help the advertiser reach you, the consumer, 10-8. Competition between companies is stiff. They want you to spend your money for their products. They also want you to be satisfied so you will buy their products again.

10-8 Attractive magazine ads are designed to draw you into a store to make a purchase. *Shutterstock*

Ads Provide Information

Advertisements can also help you. They often contain information that can help you with your buying decision. For instance, if you are buying a pair of pants, you may want to know its fiber content, care requirements, brand name, available sizes, and price. You need to know what stores carry the item. Informational ads also tell you the advantages of a product and show you how to use products correctly. New products are often introduced in this manner. Ads also announce sales, which can help you save money.

Advertising Appeals Used

Advertisers look for ways to entice you to buy their products. They try to appeal to the needs most people have for individuality, adventure, and fantasy. Words such as *just in*, *latest designs*, and *new* encourage you to buy. Some of the appeals used to sell apparel are the following:

- *Insecurity appeal:* Words can tap into people's insecurities, such as being unpopular or unattractive to the opposite sex. The message is: Wearing this garment will make you attractive, popular, or sexy.
- *Bandwagon:* This technique leads you to believe that everyone is buying the advertised item—*jumping on the bandwagon*. The message is: If you want to be fashionable and trendy, you should buy this.
- *Celebrity endorsements:* Advertisers pay well-known celebrities—actors, musical performers, or sports figures—to model their garments. The message is: If you buy this product, you will be like your favorite celebrity.

Infomercials and Advertorials

Infomercials and advertorials blur the lines between advertising and information. Television **infomercials** advertise a product under the guise of a product demonstration by a host or *expert*. These are a half-hour to an hour in length. They look like regular television shows.

Advertorials attempt to hide advertising by presenting it in the form of a newspaper article or magazine story. (Look for the word *Advertisement* in small letters at the top of the page.) No matter how convincing the expert or how appealing the article, remember that infomercials and advertorials are forms of advertising.

Know Your Sales

People are more likely to buy something when they think they are getting a good deal. When stores plan sales, they advertise them as opportunities for consumers to find great bargains. However, a sale is a **bargain** only when consumers save money on items they need. Items that are not needed are not bargains, even when prices are lowered. Learning how to evaluate sales will help you save money and be a better shopper, **10-9**.

Most stores have many sales during a year. They are often scheduled when sales are slow to lure shoppers into stores. Sometimes stores hold sales at the same times, such as before and after holidays. Other sale days are chosen by individual stores. Sales are labeled *Store-Wide Sale, Bargain Days, Anniversary Sale, Manager's Sale,* and other catchy titles. Some stores have sales each week. Free gifts and door prizes are sometimes offered to entice customers into stores during sales.

You can save money at sales if you understand sales and are familiar with prices. You should plan your purchases before you go to a sale. It is hard to think clearly when you are surrounded by people. It is easy to be tempted to spend money on things you do not need.

Look at the hangtags to see if the prices have really been lowered. See **10-10**. A 50 percent markdown may be a bargain if a garment is still in good condition. But 10 percent off is not a great savings. It would be a bargain only if it is exactly what you want.

Clearance, inventory, and end-of-season sales can be real money-savers. Look for these types of sales:

- *Clearance sales* are planned when a store wants to sell items to make room for new merchandise.
- *Inventory sales* are held before stock is counted or after it is counted. In either case, an inventory sale is held to reduce a store's inventory.
- *End-of-season sales* are held to make room for new merchandise for a new season.
- *Coupon sales* allow customers to receive discounts on the last ticketed prices. Coupon deductions may range from 5 to 20 percent off. Coupons are usually mailed to people who have charge accounts with stores. Some coupons are printed in newspapers and magazines. They can also be printed from retailers' websites or used for online purchases.
- *Preseason sales* feature items that are ahead of the season, such as coats sold at the end of summer. Since items are purchased early, stores offer them at sale prices. After these sales, prices return to full retail prices.
- *Special-purchase sales* offer products that were bought especially for these sales. By buying large amounts of these products, stores can buy and sell them for less than their regular prices. This type of sale usually offers fewer bargains than other sales.
- *Preferred customer sales* are for people who have charge accounts with a specific retailer. They are a way of thanking their customers for their loyalty.
- *Going-out-of-business sales* indicate that store owners are closing their businesses for some reason. All of the merchandise must be sold. Prices may be good, but items cannot be returned.

10-9 Clearance sales can be real money-savers for consumers when products include what they want and need. *Shutterstock*

Irregulars or seconds are sometimes good buys. Take your time and inspect any item before you buy it. If it has an imperfection you will not accept, it is best to find it before leaving the store.

Some sale items cannot be returned. They may be marked as *final sale*. Ask before you buy. There also may be a time limit, such as 30 days, for returning items for refunds. Check to see if you can get your money refunded. You may be given a *store credit* instead. This means that the amount you paid for the returned item can only be used to purchase another item at the store.

Sales can help both stores and consumers. Stores need to sell the products. They have to make room for the newer ones. Consumers like to get the products they need at reduced prices. Study the sale ads and online sites of stores near you to find those that offer real sale bargains.

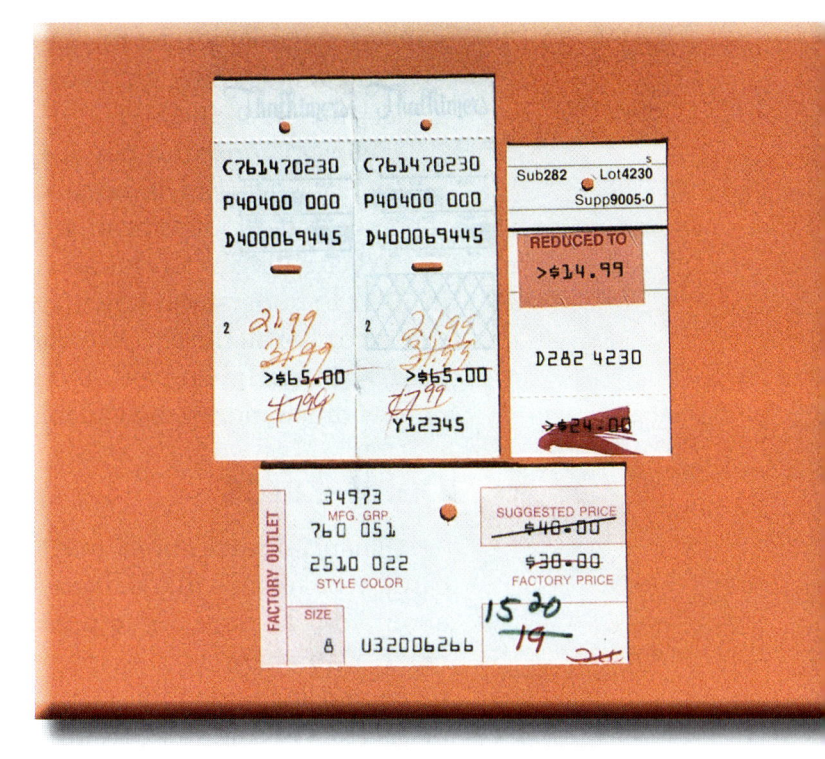

10-10 Check sale markdowns to see if you are really getting a good deal. Remember, a sale is a bargain only if it is something you really need and want.
Goodheart-Willcox Publisher

Paying for What You Buy

After careful shopping, you are ready to pay for your purchases. The cashier may ask you how you intend to pay—by cash, check, or credit. You may want to put your purchases on layaway. The decision is yours, but you need to know the pros and cons of each option.

Paying with Cash

Paying for clothing with cash is the quickest and easiest way to buy. You can buy what you like no matter where you shop because all stores take cash as payment. Paying with cash has other advantages. There are no finance charges when you pay with cash. (A **finance charge** is the price you pay for credit.) Also, you cannot spend more money than you have. You are less likely to go into debt by spending money you do not have.

If you are under 18, paying with cash may be the only payment method you can use. Some alternative methods—payment by check, debit card, and credit—may require a minimum age or the involvement of a parent or guardian.

Paying with a Check

As with cash, you can avoid finance charges by paying by check. The easiest way to obtain checks is to open an account at a financial institution, such as a bank. With a basic checking account, you can make deposits, or put money into the account. You can then write checks on the account to pay for your purchases. The check amount should not exceed the account balance. When you use a check, you let the bank pay your bill from your account. Your check gives the retailer the right to collect the money you owe. Guidelines for writing a check are given in **10-11**.

Before planning to pay for your purchases by check, find out the store's policy. Some stores will not accept checks. Others may require that you show several pieces of identification, such as a credit card and a driver's license.

When filling out a check, write clearly in ink. Study the details of the check in **10-12** to understand how to write a check correctly. Be sure to keep an accurate record of all the checks you write. This will help you remember whom you paid, how much you paid, and when you paid. It will also help you keep track of how much money is available in your account.

Debit Cards

Financial institutions may also provide you with a debit card (or check card), which looks much like a credit card. The card is coded with information about your account and a personal identification number, or PIN. When you make a purchase, you swipe the card through an electronic scanner and are prompted for your PIN. When you use a **debit card**, money is immediately deducted via computer from your bank account. If you do not have enough money in your account to cover the charge, the transaction will not go through.

If you use a debit card, you need to record the transaction in your checkbook to keep track of your balance. When you receive your bank statement, also check these transactions for accuracy. Your PIN ensures that others cannot use your card, so memorize it and do not reveal it to anyone.

10-11 Study these guidelines to learn how to write a check.

How to Write a Check

- Write clearly with ink.
- Date the check with month, day, and year.
- After words "Pay to the order of," write the name of the recipient of the check. Ask the clerk for the correct name or title to use. If you are unsure of spelling, ask for help.
- Write the amount of the payment in numerals, close to the dollar sign. Make your first number as close as possible to the sign.
- Write the amount of the payment in words at the beginning of the next line. After the dollars amount, write the word, "and." The amount of cents may be written as 25/100, or 00/00, or no/100. Draw a line through the space that is left in the line.
- Sign the check exactly as you signed the signature card when you opened the account.
- Record the check number, amount, date, and recipient of the check. You may also record what you purchased.

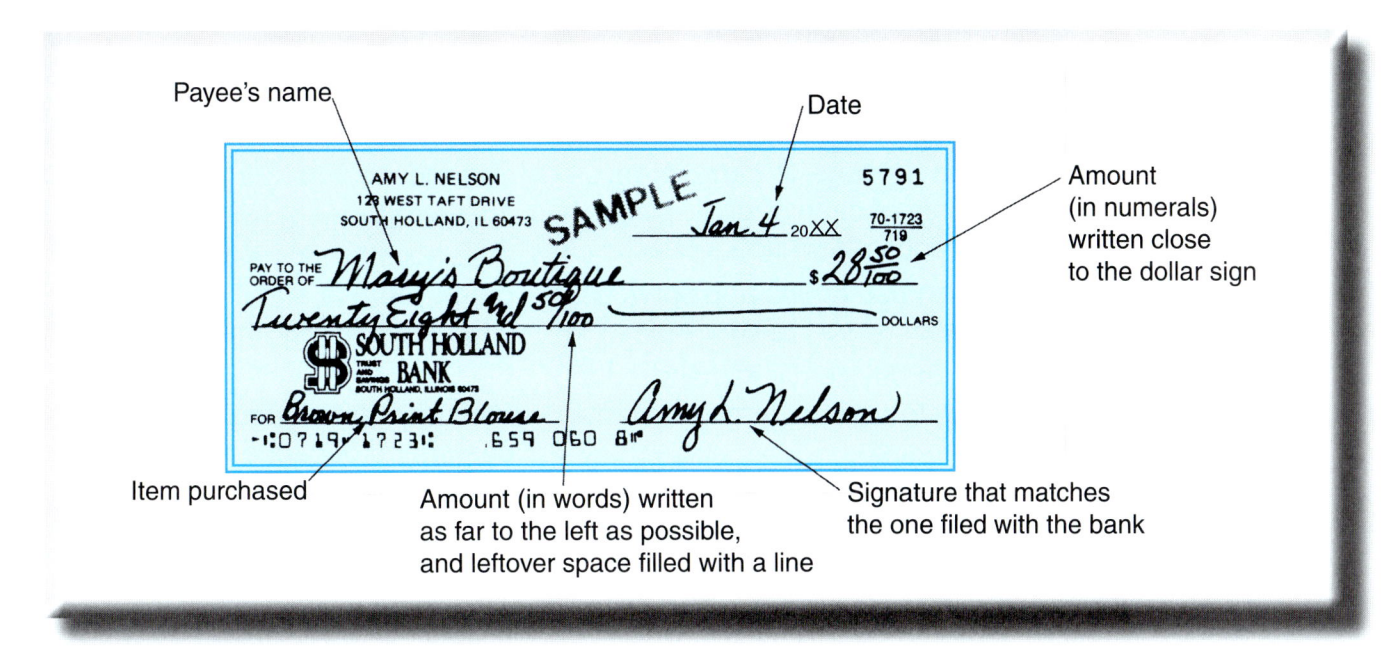

Payee's name — *Date* — Amount (in numerals) written close to the dollar sign

Item purchased — Amount (in words) written as far to the left as possible, and leftover space filled with a line — Signature that matches the one filed with the bank

10-12 Checks should be written neatly and correctly to avoid errors.
Goodheart-Willcox Publisher

Using Credit

Buying on **credit** is a promise to pay in the future for what you buy today. People often purchase clothing on credit because it can have several advantages. Buying on credit can have disadvantages, too. For a list of advantages and disadvantages of using credit, see **10-13**.

Types of Credit

The two major types of retail credit are the regular charge account and the revolving charge account. With the **regular charge account**, you may charge purchases in exchange for your promise to pay in full within 10 to 30 days after the billing date. You will receive a bill or statement. If you pay on time, there is no finance charge.

The **revolving charge account** allows you to make purchases up to a limit set by the creditor when the account was opened. You can make multiple purchases as long as the total of all the purchases does not exceed the limit. Bills are usually received monthly. If the bill is paid in full by the due date, there is no finance charge. If the bill is not paid in full, there is a finance charge on the unpaid balance. You are required to make at least the minimum payment each month. This amount is specified on the bill.

Credit Cards

Credit cards are most often used to make credit purchases. There are several types of credit cards:

- *Store credit cards.* A merchant may issue credit cards to eligible customers who can then use the card to purchase goods and services from the merchant. These cards cannot be used to buy goods or services from other merchants. Finance charges and other fees are charged.

10-13 Using credit has both advantages and disadvantages.

Buying on Credit

Advantages	Disadvantages
• You do not have to carry large amounts of cash or go through the process of writing a check. • You can use goods and services before or as you pay for them. • You can buy costly items without having to save up large amounts of cash first. • It can simplify exchanges and returns. • It allows you to pay for items you purchase by phone or online.	• You reduce your future income. • It is usually more expensive than buying with cash. The more credit you use and the more time you take to repay, the more you must pay in finance charges. • You may be tempted to overspend because of impulse buying. • Failure to pay promptly could result in a poor credit rating.

- *Financial-institution cards, such as Visa and MasterCard.* These cards are issued by financial institutions and can be used to make purchases from any merchant who accepts them. Finance charges and other fees are charged. Sometimes an annual fee is charged for these cards.
- *Travel and entertainment cards, such as American Express.* Cardholders must usually pay their entire credit card balance each month. A membership fee is charged for these, as well as other fees.

Credit cards often specify a *credit limit*. This is the maximum amount of money a customer can owe the credit card company at one time.

When you apply for credit, you must complete an application form. The lender uses the information you provide, as well as other information obtained, to assess your creditworthiness. Someone who is creditworthy has the ability to pay their bills and a history of repaying their debts. The form asks questions about an applicant's income, bank accounts, address and length of residence, and other debt, including credit cards. You must be at least 18 years old in order to have a card in your own name.

Read the credit contract before signing. Sign only when you are sure you understand all the terms and obligations and can meet those terms and obligations. You should know the annual percentage rate applied to unpaid balances. You should also note the minimum amount you must pay each month and the number of days you have to make your payments. Penalties can be added if payments arrive after the due date. These can add up quickly, 10-14.

10-14 Before using a credit card, be sure you can meet all the terms and regulations.
Shutterstock

Layaway Buying

If a store's customers do not have the money to pay for their purchases, they can sometimes use layaway buying. **Layaway buying** allows a store's customers to place small deposits on purchases that the store then holds for them. At some stores, the deposit must be at least 10 percent of the cost of the layaway item. Customers make payments each week or month until the full amounts are paid. When the last payments are made, the customers receive their items. Interest is usually not charged on the unpaid balances of layaway purchases. However, there may be service charges.

Layaway buying can be an advantage if you need an expensive item. Suppose you need a coat for next season. You find a coat that is a good buy, but you do not have enough money to buy it now. You could put the coat on layaway. The disadvantage of layaway is the wait. You have to wait weeks or months before you can get your item. Also, if you fail to complete the payments, you lose the item, and in some cases, the money you already paid. Be sure to check the store's layaway policy before making a layaway purchase.

Summary

- Most clothing purchases are made in retail stores. There are many types of stores that sell clothes and accessories. Each type has advantages and disadvantages.
- If you want to shop from your home, you can use a nonstore shopping option, such as catalog shopping, online shopping, television shopping, or personal selling.
- To get the most value for your money, you should comparison shop—comparing qualities and prices in different stores—before you buy. Avoid impulse buying to help stay within your budget.
- Advertisements can help you learn more about a product, but they can also create wants by making products seem more desirable.
- There are many kinds of sales, but a sale is a bargain only when you can save money on items you need.
- You have many options for paying for your purchases. You can pay with cash, a check, a debit card, or a credit card. Some retailers offer layaway buying.

Graphic Organizer

Use the fishbone diagram to identify four important shopping strategies and two or three details about each.

Review the Facts

1. What is the main feature department stores offer their customers?
2. What is the difference between a regular discount store and an off-price discount store?
3. Why are prices usually lower at factory outlet stores?
4. Name three advantages and three disadvantages of catalog and online shopping.
5. How have online merchandisers made it safe for customers to give their credit card numbers when making purchases?
6. When comparison shopping, what two things should you compare?
7. Why is it a good idea to avoid impulse buying?
8. How can consumers benefit from reading advertisements?
9. How do sales help both stores and consumers?
10. What methods of paying for purchases do not have finance charges?
11. Contrast regular charge accounts and revolving charge accounts.
12. When applying for a credit card, what is a company looking for in a potential customer?

Think Critically

13. **Draw conclusions.** In light of increasing online shopping, draw conclusions about whether consumer protection is of lesser or greater importance now than in the past. If necessary, use Internet resources to locate evidence to support your conclusions.
14. **Analyze behavior.** How do advertisements influence consumer behavior? How do they impact your behavior? Are items on sale always a bargain for you? Analyze actions you and other consumers can take to avoid such influences. Discuss your analysis in class.

Apparel Applications

15. **Compare store policies.** Use Internet resources to investigate the policies of at least three stores related to returned merchandise, sales, shoplifting, etc. How are the policies similar and different? Share your findings with the class.
16. **Comparison shopping.** Select different types of stores for comparison shopping. Choose one item that can be found in each store type. In pairs, compare garment prices, quality, and store services for each. Based on your comparison, where would you purchase the item?
17. **Online shopping.** Select an item of clothing that you could buy online. Review three websites that offer the item. Compare the offers and such items as cost, availability, qualities, shipping charges, shipping date, return policy, and method of delivery. From which online vendor would you buy the garment? Why?
18. **Online display.** Review clothing advertisements from the websites of five stores. Use a school-approved Web application to create an attractive display to post to the class Web page. Note the kinds of information each store gives and terms designed to create wants.
19. **Analyze TV shopping.** Watch a home shopping TV show. What methods are used to entice consumers to buy? How do these methods compare to those used with online and catalog shopping? What are the advantages and disadvantages of shopping in this way?
20. **Evaluate credit applications.** Obtain a credit card application. Why do you think each question is asked?

Academic Connections

21. **Reading.** Read the apparel advertisements in several newspapers and/or fashion magazines. Compile a list of advertising slogans that you think influence people to buy.
22. **Math.** Calculate the differences in cost and convenience for a coat that you can buy for $150 cash; buy on credit at 18 percent annual interest; buy on layaway, paying $25.00 per month.

Workplace Links

23. **Create a commercial.** Presume you work for a major department store. You and your team have been assigned to write a TV commercial to sell a new garment or accessory. Write the script and locate a garment or accessory to use in the commercial. Use a digital camcorder to video-record your commercial. Present the commercial to the class.
24. **Research ethics.** Use Internet or print resources to investigate the code of ethics used in advertising copy. If possible, interview the manager of a local newspaper to identify how the paper applies ethics in advertising. Write a summary of your findings.
25. **Critique retail websites.** What makes an effective retail website? Review several websites and make a list of the strengths and weaknesses of each one. What ideas would you use if you were designing your own retail website?

School Resale Shop

Many students in your school may have unmet clothing needs for a variety of reasons. As an FCCLA *Community Service* project, establish an in-school clothing resale shop for the school community. Be sure to get permission from school officials to start this project. Use the FCCLA *Planning Process* as a planning tool. Here are a few things to think about:
- garment types the shop will sell
- garment conditions that are acceptable for resale
- pricing guidelines the shop will use
- times the shop will be open and scheduling people to operate the shop

See your adviser for assistance as needed.

Chapter 11

Get Your Money's Worth

Sale
end of season

Chapter Objectives

After studying this chapter, you will be able to
- **select** clothes that fit properly.
- **evaluate** standards of quality construction in garments.
- **judge** the appearance and fit of a garment.
- **make** decisions concerning alterations.
- **make** the best clothes-buying decisions considering care, price, and quality.
- **select** quality accessories.

Key Terms

quality
ease
vanity sizing
alterations
fine jewelry
costume jewelry

Reading with Purpose

After reading each section (separated by main headings), stop and write a brief summary about what you just read. Be sure to paraphrase and use your own words.

Have you ever had to choose between two items you liked when shopping for clothes? The decision is easier when you know which key factors to compare.

One key factor to consider is fit. Which item fits you the best? Even clothes that are the same size may fit you differently. You need to evaluate points of fit in a garment to make the best selection.

To get your money's worth in clothing, you also need to understand the term quality. The **quality** of an item depends on the degree to which it meets certain standards of excellence. The words high, medium, and low are used to describe quality. A garment of low quality will not perform as well as one of high quality. A low-quality garment may not look as good, fit as well, or wear as long as a high-quality garment.

Quality and fit are only two of the factors you should consider when buying clothes. These are some other questions you may ask yourself. Does it look right on me? Is it appropriate for my activities? Will I wear it often enough to get my money's worth? Does it fit into my wardrobe plan? How will I care for it? Do I have accessories that will go with it?

Getting the Right Fit

You may have noticed that some garments in your size seem to fit and others do not. This is because apparel manufacturers in the U.S. do not interpret standard sizes in the same way. Also, the sizes used on garment labels and tags are based on average body measurements that have changed over time.

Standard measurements for the garment industry were established more than 30 years ago. The average woman today, however, weighs 164 pounds, up from 140 pounds in 1960. People have also become more tubular in shape. Though height has increased, so have the average sizes of the hips and waist.

Each manufacturer has its own target market. This is the subgroup of consumers that make up its customer base. For example, some target teens, while others design for career women. Different populations have different body proportions and preferences. Therefore, some manufacturers design more ease into their garments. **Ease** is extra space to allow for movement and livability. Others design for close-fitting looks.

Some manufacturers engage in the practice of **vanity sizing** where they cut clothes larger, but the sizes they are labeled are not increased. A woman who is a true size 14 might fit comfortably into a size 10. If she prefers to be a smaller size, this makes her feel good about her figure. She is probably more likely to buy the apparel.

Find the Right Size

Begin your search for the right fit by finding the size category for your body structure. Height, weight, build, and key body measurements are used to determine size categories. Within these categories, a range of sizes is offered. The chart in **11-1** gives descriptions and size ranges of various categories for both men and women.

Try on for the Best Fit

When you try on a garment, it should feel comfortable. It should not be too tight, too loose, too long, or too short. You can perform a few simple tests to check the fit. For example, if you try on a jacket or shirt, cross your arms in front of your body. If you feel a lot of pull across the upper back and shoulders, you need a larger size or a different style. Otherwise, when you wear the garment you will not be comfortable. If you bend your elbows, long sleeves should not hike up above your wrists. Raise your arms to make sure shirts and dresses fall back in place when your arms are lowered.

When you try on pants, be sure to sit down to make sure there is enough room in the seat. While seated, check to see that the pant waistline does not gap in the back. Try on garments with the shoes you plan to wear with them. When trying on pants, make sure the length works with the shoes or that the length can be altered.

View yourself in a three-way, full-length mirror. Once you are satisfied with the fit, you can look closer at the quality of the construction.

Judging Garment Quality

The quality of a garment must be considered when making a buying decision. Quality often determines how a garment looks, how well it fits, and how long it will wear.

Size-Range Categories

Female Size Categories

Figure Types	Sizes	Proportions
Preteen (girls)	6–16	For girls whose figures are average; undeveloped in bust and hips. Height approximately 4'2" to 5'.
Slim girls	4S–16S	For girls whose figures are slim; undeveloped in bust and hips.
Girls plus	8½–20½	For girls whose figures are heavier; undeveloped in bust and hips.
Young Junior	3–13	For girls whose figures are beginning to mature and becoming longer in the waist. Height approximately 5'1" to 5'3".
Junior	1–15	For girls and women who are short waisted, have fully developed bust and hips, and small waist. Height approximately 5'4" to 5'5".
Junior petite	1JP–15JP	Junior figure with height 5'1" and under.
Junior tall	3T–17T	Junior figure with height 5'7" to 5'11".
Misses	4–18	For girls and women, fully developed, with average figures and proportions. Height approximately 5'5" to 5'9".
Misses petite	4P–16P	For short and slim girls and women. Height under 5'4".
Tall misses	6T–20T	Height over 5'9".
Women's	14W–26W	Large proportions. Height 5'5" to 5'9".
Half sizes	12½–24½	Heavier, short waisted girls and women. Height under 5'5".

(Sometimes Misses sizes are: Small, sizes 2–6; Medium, sizes 8–10; Large, sizes 12–14; Extra Large, sizes 16–18; XX Large, sizes 20–22.)

Male Size Categories

Figure Types	Sizes	Proportions
Boys regular	6–20	For boys of average frame and proportion.
Slim boys	6S–20S	For small frames and thin body.
Husky boys	8H–20H	For boys who have a fuller body in proportion to height.
Student	26–32	Average frame to proportions; physique is beginning to mature; narrower seat in proportion to waist.
Men's (related to chest measurement)	34–48	For boys and men who are fully developed. Height 5'7" to 5'11".

(Sometimes Men's sizes are: Extra small, sizes 30–32; Small, sizes 34–36; Medium, sizes 38–40; Large, sizes 42–44; Extra large, sizes 46–48. Short men, for men of heights 5'3" to 5'7"; Tall men, for men of heights 5'11" to 6'3".)

11-1 Getting the right fit begins by finding the right size category for your body structure.

Part 2 Apparel Decisions

Levels of Quality

The quality of apparel can generally be described as high, medium, or low.

- *High-quality.* These garments have the best construction features, use the best materials, and reflect good design. Attention to detail is seen in the construction of the garment. For example, plaids and stripes are matched at the seams. The fabrics and trims are some of the best available. The styling of the garment follows the principles of good design. The higher prices of these garments reflect these quality features.
- *Medium-quality.* The construction features in these garments are good and reliable. Garments are well made and durable. Quality fabrics are used. They generally reflect good design. These garments are in the medium price range.
- *Low-quality.* The quality of garment construction is poor, and fabrics may not hold up well when worn and cleaned. Principles of good design may not be followed. These are generally the lowest-priced garments.

Although high-quality garments are more durable than low-quality ones, they are also more costly. Durability may not be an important consideration in some clothes purchases. You may want different levels of quality for different garments. You would be smart to buy a high-quality coat or jacket because you probably plan to wear it for several seasons. When shopping for a shirt that is the latest fad, however, one of lower quality with a lower price could be your best buy. You do not need it to be durable because it will probably be out of style by next year. You must decide which quality meets your needs.

Price is sometimes an indication of quality, but not always. Alert and educated shoppers often find good-quality products at low prices. Before making purchases, they compare the quality and price of similar items offered by several retailers.

General Standards of Quality

You should look at a number of construction details when judging the quality of a garment. A checklist for judging quality construction is given in **11-2**.

First look closely at the fabric. Evaluate its evenness of color and pattern. Check to see that it has no defects. Also consider the appropriateness of the fabric for the garment. For example, a tailored suit should be made of a tightly woven fabric of medium to heavy weight. Pajamas should be made of fabrics that are comfortable next to the skin.

The cut of the garment should be evaluated. If the fabric has texture like corduroy, does it run in the same direction? Is there ample fabric used in the garment? Do plaids, stripes, and checks match?

Seams, seam allowances, and stitching are important to check. Seams should be neat and smooth with ample seam allowances. Stitching should be straight and neat. Thread color should match the fabric and be suitable in weight.

Hems are also important to check. They should be an even width and an appropriate depth for the design of the garment. If you may lengthen the garment at some time, check to see if this would be possible. Hemming stitches should not show on the outside of the garment.

There are other features to check as well. Look again at the checklist shown in 11-2.

Judging Quality

Construction Features	Quality Indicators
Cut and Fabric	• Fabric free from flaws and irregularities. • Garment pieces cut with the grain. • Fabric appropriate for garment type and style. • Stripes, plaids, checks, and other designs matched at seams.
Seams	• Generous allowances for seams. • Flat, even in width, wide enough to withstand strain and permit alterations. • Double-row stitching to reinforce stress points, such as underarms, crotch, waist, neckline.
Stitching	• Short, continuous, and straight. • Securely fastened at the ends. • Thread of the right weight, color, and fiber for the fabric.
Reinforcements	• Extra stitching, bar tacks, metal rivets, or tape at points of strain. • Reinforced underarm seams, openings, slits, pockets, knees and elbows in work clothes, sportswear, and children's play clothes.
Hems	• Flat, even in width, invisible on the right side. • Carefully finished and evenly stitched on inside. • Even in length.
Buttonholes	• Cut with grain of fabric. • Smooth and properly placed. • Right size and type for the garment. • Firmly stitched and trimmed, with no loose threads or frayed edges. • Evenly spaced with reinforced corners.
Buttons, Hooks and Eyes, Snaps	• Firmly attached and properly spaced. • Right size and type for garment. • Extra buttons often included for high-quality clothes.
Trim and Decoration	• Suited to the garment, well placed, and firmly attached. • Same care requirements as garment.
Zippers and Closures	• Smooth, flat, securely stitched. • Right size, type, strength, and color for garment. • Smooth-sliding zippers and easy-to-operate closures.
Linings	• Smooth, properly inserted. • Right weight and texture for garment with same care requirements.

(Continued)

11-2 Become familiar with these items for judging the quality of garment construction.

Judging Quality *(continued)*	
Construction Features	*Quality Indicators*
Interfacing	• Properly placed, hidden, and securely attached. • Materials right for the garment and its care requirements.
Pockets	• Flat, smooth, and properly matched to garment. • Reinforced corners and firmly woven linings.
Collars and Lapels	• Collar points neatly finished, no curling. • Collar top slightly turned over undercollar around seam edges. • Lapels lying flat to the chest with graceful roll and smooth edge.

11-2 *Continued.*

Specific Points to Check for Quality and Fit

The following pointers may help you evaluate specific styles of garments the next time you shop. Check the quality, fit, performance, and price of any garment before you buy.

Shirts and Blouses

When choosing a shirt or blouse, look for

- ample room across the chest or bust, back, and shoulders
- shoulder seams that extend to the shoulder edge unless the garment design calls for a different placement
- tops that are long enough to stay tucked in jeans, skirts, or slacks
- armholes that are large enough to allow arms to move freely
- collars with even, sharp points
- smooth topstitching
- buttons sewn on securely and placed directly under buttonholes
- well-made buttonholes
- neat, even cuffs that fit comfortably around wrists
- pockets that are securely sewn on and are flat without wrinkles

Sport Jackets and Suits

Before you buy a sport jacket or suit, as in **11-3**, be sure

- it fits smoothly across the upper back and shoulders, with no wrinkles or bunching
- armholes are large enough for an undershirt, shirt, and sweater to be worn underneath the jacket
- outside stitching is smooth
- it fits smoothly across the chest area when buttoned
- pocket corners are reinforced

- shirt cuffs extend about ½ inch beyond jacket sleeves
- the collar fits closely around the neck without gaps
- any pattern in the fabric matches at the center, side seams, and pockets
- buttons are sewn on securely with a shank beneath so they button easily and smoothly
- linings and interfacings are used as needed to give strength, support, and better shape to the garment

Jeans and Slacks

When shopping for jeans or slacks, check to see that

- you can walk and sit comfortably in them
- the seat area fits smoothly without bagging or binding
- the crotch length is just right—not too long or too short
- the waistband has a double thickness of fabric
- stitching is reinforced at the bottom of the zipper and corners of pockets
- a locking pull tab on the zipper will keep it from unzipping by itself
- seams are straight and not puckered
- the slacks hang straight without wrinkling
- you can follow the instructions given on the care label

Dresses and Skirts

Before choosing a skirt or dress, as in **11-4**, see if

- it is cut with enough fabric so it does not look skimpy
- the garment feels good on your body
- it hangs straight from the waistband without cupping under the hips
- the waistline fits snugly at your natural waistline
- the waistline does not roll up (It rolls if it is too tight in the hip area.)
- the bustline darts (if present) point toward the highest point of the bust
- the zipper works smoothly and has a lock tab
- the seams are wide enough to alter, if needed

11-3 Check for quality construction when buying suits or sport jackets. *Shutterstock*

Consider Alterations

Suppose you want to buy a garment, but it does not quite fit. Perhaps it can be altered. **Alterations** are changes made in the size, length, or style of a garment. They can make a garment larger, smaller, shorter, or longer. Buttons and trims can be added, moved, or changed.

Before you buy a garment that needs alterations, there are some factors to consider. Some alterations are easy to do, while others are more complicated and are seldom effective or successful. If you can make the alterations yourself, it may be worthwhile. If you have to pay someone to make the alterations, you need to consider this cost in the overall cost of the garment.

It is important to check seam widths. If a garment is to be made larger, the seams must be wide enough to accomplish this. If a garment will be lengthened, make sure there is sufficient width in the hem to let it down.

Easy alterations include lengthening or shortening a garment, leveling an uneven hem, shortening sleeves, or taking in some seams.

Major alterations in ready-to-wear clothing may not be effective or worthwhile. For instance, if a jacket is too full or too tight across the shoulders, major alterations would be required, **11-5**. The sleeves might have to be removed and adjusted. The lining and shoulder pads would need to be adjusted. Unless you are an experienced sewer, these alterations are usually not recommended. If you hire someone to make these alterations, it will be expensive.

11-4 Carefully check the construction and fit of a dress before making a purchase.
Shutterstock

If a skirt or a pair of pants is too large in the waistline, you will probably have to remove the waistband. The seams and the waistband would need adjustments. The zipper area may also need alteration.

Unless ready-to-wear garments requiring major alterations are exceptionally good buys, it is best to avoid them. Too much altering can change the looks of a garment, and it may never look just right.

Making the Buying Decision

Once you find a garment that fits and evaluate its quality, you are almost ready to make a buying decision. There are just two more factors to consider.

Care Requirements

Take a look at the clothing label that describes how you are to care for the garment. Can you wash the garment? If so, can it be machine washed or must you wash it by hand? Being able to wash a garment in a washing machine along with your other clothes is most convenient. It will save you both time and money. If you have to wash the garment by hand, it will take more of your time. Do you have this time to spare? Hand washing clothing is not costly, but it is time-consuming.

Does the label state that the garment must be dry-cleaned? If so, you should consider this cost in addition to the initial price you will pay for the garment. Even if an item is on sale, it will cost you more in the long run if it must be dry-cleaned frequently. Wool winter coats must be dry-cleaned, but only a few times during the wearing season. A shirt or pair of pants that must be dry-cleaned after each wearing will be more costly overall.

Also consider the color of the garment and the fabric used to make it. A white or light-colored garment shows spots easily. If you can easily wash the soiled garment, this might not be a problem. If it has to be dry-cleaned, it will take time and money, **11-6**. Some clothes have special fabric finishes that reduce stains and spots. If this appeals to you, look for information about special finishes on garment hangtags.

Another factor to consider is wrinkling. Does this garment wrinkle easily, requiring frequent pressing? Does it have to be ironed after laundering? Some garment labels and hangtags state that garments are wrinkle resistant, or have an anti-wrinkle fabric finish. Garments with this finish require little, if any, ironing after they are removed from the dryer. They also wrinkle less when worn. Some fibers are naturally wrinkle resistant. Nylon, for example, resists wrinkling, but cotton and rayon do not. Clothes made of knit fabrics are less likely to wrinkle. If you will be packing the garment in a suitcase or do not have time for ironing, wrinkling might be an important consideration.

11-5 Jackets such as this one are far more difficult to alter than most dresses or skirts.
Shutterstock

Compare Price Versus Quality

Is the lowest-priced item of clothing always the best buy? Does buying the most expensive item always mean you are getting the best quality? The answer to both of these questions is no. The lowest-priced garment is not the best buy if it falls apart after only a few wearings. The most expensive garment may not be the best buy if you are really paying for a designer's name on the label. The best buy is the garment you buy after careful evaluation of its price and quality. This includes comparing its price and quality with those of other garments sold by other retailers.

Most consumers want to get the best quality for the least amount of money. You have learned how to judge the quality of clothing. The quality features described in Figure 11-2 may add to the cost of a garment. Other factors also add to the price. The retailer may want a higher profit margin and may price garments accordingly. Unusual design features or trims might increase the price. You must decide if it is worth paying more for these features.

Before buying apparel, consider how often you will wear the garment. If you will wear it frequently, the quality of the fabric and construction is important. You might be willing to pay more for something you will wear often. If you will only wear the item a few times, perhaps a lower-quality garment that costs less is the best buy.

You are the judge. If you have done some comparison shopping, the decision will be easier. If you have looked over your wardrobe and identify items you really need, the decision will be easier. When you know you have tried to find the best item for the best price, you feel more comfortable with your buying decisions.

11-6 This sweater and plaid vest will not show spots easily. This will save on dry-cleaning costs.
Shutterstock

Buying Accessories

Accessories are fun to choose and wear. Accessories include shoes, handbags, neckties, jewelry, and belts. They are the items you need to complete an outfit. Accessories add variety to your wardrobe. The right ones can change a plain, dull outfit into the latest look, **11-7**. You can take the same outfit and make it casual or dressy, depending on the accessories you wear with it.

Before you shop, examine your wardrobe and decide what kinds of accessories you can use. Consider the main colors in your wardrobe. You can achieve a coordinated look by repeating outfit colors in the accessories you wear with the outfits.

11-7 Choosing the right accessories can give an outfit a complete look.
Shutterstock

Keep your size and body build in mind when selecting your accessories. For instance, small accessories are more flattering on people who are petite or small. Large accessories seem to overpower them.

Many accessories—scarves, ties, costume jewelry, belts—cost less than clothes. People often buy accessories that appeal to them. When they get home, however, they find that the items do not go well with any of their outfits. In this way, buying accessories results in wasted money. With some planning, however, well-chosen accessories are an inexpensive way to stretch a wardrobe.

Shoes

Shoes are the most important accessory in your wardrobe and should be chosen with care. Shoes can be expensive. The ones you wear most often should be comfortable and of good quality. You can spend less money on the shoes you seldom wear.

Good fit is the most important feature of shoes. Good-fitting shoes are comfortable and support the feet. If fitted correctly, they are not too short, too loose, or too tight. Poorly fitted shoes can cause discomfort and foot disorders. These include bunions, corns, calluses, and ingrown toenails. They can contribute to poor posture.

There are many things you can do while shoe shopping to make sure you get a good fit. Do not rush when buying shoes. Try to do your shoe shopping toward the end of the day when your feet are their largest. Feet tend to swell during the course of the day.

At better shoe departments, a sales associate can measure your feet. You should stand during the measurement. A person's feet are usually slightly different in size, with one foot larger than the other. Make sure to fit your shoes to the larger foot. You can place innersoles or pads in the shoe of your smaller foot for better fit and comfort. When trying on shoes, wear the same type of socks or hose that you plan to wear with the shoes you buy.

Highlights in History

A Sneaking Success

You probably have a pair of sneakers in your closet. You may even have several pairs, each designed for a different sport or activity. You might use one pair for playing basketball and a different pair for walking. Where and when did sneakers first appear?

The first shoes that combined canvas uppers with rubber soles were made in the United States in the late 1800s. American tire companies Goodyear and U.S. Rubber developed the manufacturing process called *vulcanization*. This process used heat to meld rubber to cloth in a sturdy, permanent bond. The first rubber-soled shoes were called *plimsolls* because the thick, rubber sole looked like the Plimsoll line. This was the load-line marking around the side of cargo ships.

From 1892 to 1913, U.S. Rubber was manufacturing 30 different brands of shoes. The company decided to make just one brand. When choosing a name, the first choice was Peds, from the Latin word meaning foot. Since that name was already trademarked, they selected the name Keds. Keds® were the first mass-marketed canvas-top *sneakers*. An advertising agent nicknamed them sneakers because the rubber-soled shoes allowed the wearer to sneak up on people! All other shoes at that time made noise when the wearer walked.

The first athlete to endorse a sneaker was Charles (*Chuck*) Taylor in 1923. Sales of Converse All Star sneakers increased dramatically when the Chuck Taylor ankle patch was added to the shoe. By the beginning of this century, Nike was paying Tiger Woods and Michael Jordan tens of millions of dollars to wear their shoes.

Sneakers have come a long way from their humble beginnings. Today's shoes are designed to assist athletes in the specific demands of their sports. Knowledge gained from sports medicine influenced shoe design to improve performance while preventing injury. Motion-control devices, new shock-absorbing materials, and many other features are now incorporated into sneakers. One brand continuously adjusts the shoe's cushioning while you run.

Walking in shoes helps you to judge the comfort and fit. Try on both shoes and walk in them. The widest part of the shoe should fit the widest part of your foot. When you stand, shoes should be ½ to ¾ of an inch longer than your foot. Check the fit in the instep, in the heel, and over the arch. Examine the material and construction. Will this style, color, and quality fit your needs?

Never buy shoes that have to be broken in. Shoes should not be a bit uncomfortable when you buy them. Do not accept a sales associate's reassurance that the shoes will feel better after you have worn them a few hours.

Handbags

Most young women have at least one handbag or purse in their wardrobes. Your activities, body size, and personal taste are the main factors in choosing a handbag.

Handbags are available in all sizes and shapes, 11-8. They are made of various materials including leather, vinyl, fabric, and cord. Before you buy a purse, examine it closely. Look for rough seams or edges. Check the fastener.

It should open easily and close securely. Look for handy compartments that help keep your belongings in order. Check how securely the handles are attached to the purse. Handles attached to rings are often more durable.

Brightly colored purses might be fun to carry. If your budget is limited, a purse in a neutral or basic color would be a better choice. It would look right with more of your outfits.

Scarves

People wear scarves to keep their necks warm, to protect their coat collars from soil, and to add interest to their outfits. Scarves are available in wool, wool-blends, cotton, silk, and other fibers. The fabrics range from thick, warm, and bulky to thin and flimsy.

As fashions change, so do scarves and the ways people wear them. Shapes, colors, and sizes vary with the seasons and with what is fashionable at a particular time. Scarf shapes often include squares, triangles, and rectangles. They are sometimes small and sometimes large. What scarf shape is now most popular?

Adding a scarf to an outfit can give it a new, lively look. Scarves add individuality to clothing. They can also stretch your wardrobe by helping you create more outfits from the same garments. Scarves are usually inexpensive. They are available in a wide selection of fabrics, styles, and colors. You can use these fashion accessories as your imagination and creativity dictate.

Neckties

Neckties express the wearer's individuality and personality. A conservative man may prefer to wear dark-colored ties, in either solids or small patterns. An outgoing man will select bolder patterns and brighter colors.

Neckwear fashions change just as other fashions do. Neckties change in width, color, design, and fabric. They can be tricky to tie. Study **11-9** until you can tie a perfect tie.

A necktie's care label gives instructions for cleaning. Many neckties are washable. Others must be dry-cleaned.

11-8 Handbags come in a variety of shapes, sizes, and materials. They can be used for several years.
Shutterstock

11-9 Here is one way to tie a perfect tie.

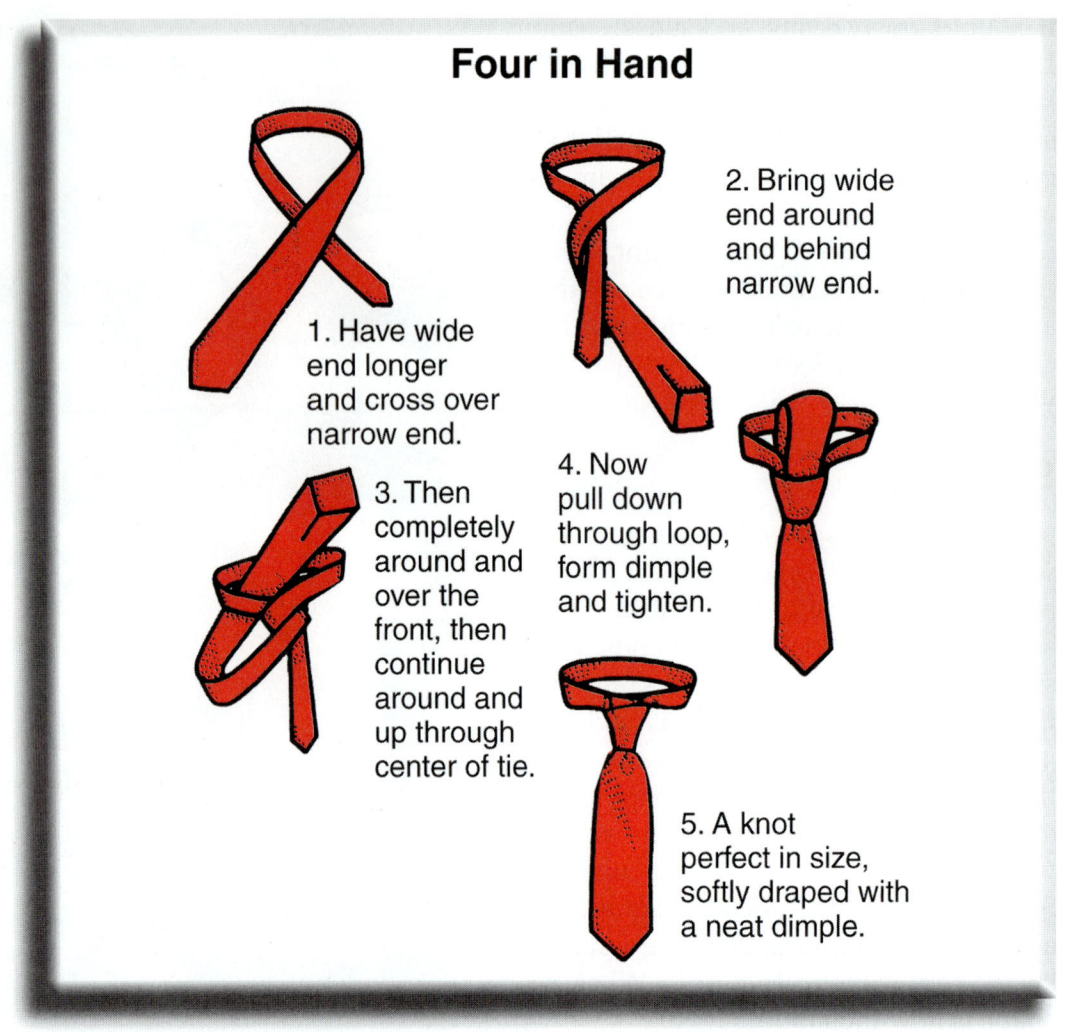

Four in Hand

1. Have wide end longer and cross over narrow end.
2. Bring wide end around and behind narrow end.
3. Then completely around and over the front, then continue around and up through center of tie.
4. Now pull down through loop, form dimple and tighten.
5. A knot perfect in size, softly draped with a neat dimple.

Jewelry

Jewelry is usually divided into two categories: costume and fine jewelry. The difference between fine jewelry and costume, or fashion jewelry, is the material used to make it. **Fine jewelry** is usually made from gold, silver, or platinum. It may contain precious or semiprecious stones. Diamonds, rubies, sapphires, and emeralds are types of *precious stones*. Jade, garnet, opal, and amethyst are types of *semiprecious stones*. Fine jewelry is expensive.

Costume jewelry is designed to wear with current fashions. It is usually made from inexpensive materials. Most costume jewelry is affordable.

Jewelry can be both functional and ornamental. Watchbands, cuff links, and tie tacks are types of functional jewelry. Ornamental items are rings, bracelets, necklaces, and earrings.

Although looking at jewelry is fun, making a choice can be difficult. Jewelry comes in a wide variety of designs, colors, and shapes. To make the best choices, planning will help. Before shopping, decide what you need and what will go with several outfits. Know how much money you can afford to spend. Then look for the jewelry that will show your individuality, **11-10**.

Belts

Belts can be functional, decorative, or both. They are available in many materials, including leather, vinyl, metal, and fabric. Belts come in styles that are wide, narrow, stretchy, thick, thin, heavy, and lightweight. Designs are varied.

Belt sizes usually correspond to waist measurements, but men should buy belts two inches larger than their waist size. Try on a belt before buying it. Keep your overall body size in mind. A belt that is wide and heavy might overwhelm a person who is short and small. It would look better on someone who is tall or large.

11-10 Costume jewelry is popular because of its affordability. *Shutterstock*

Summary

- Two key factors to consider when buying apparel are fit and quality. To find the right size, begin with the size category for your body structure. Then find the size closest to your measurements. Try on garments before you purchase them as sizes can vary with each manufacturer.
- The quality of a garment can be described as high, medium, or low. You may want different levels of quality for different types of garments. Price is sometimes an indication of quality, but not always.
- Evaluate the following construction details when judging the quality of a garment: fabric, cut, seams, seam allowances, stitching, reinforcements, buttonholes, hems, fasteners and closures, trim and decoration, linings and interfacings, pockets, collars, and special features.
- When deciding whether or not to buy a garment that needs alterations, consider the complexity of the alteration. You may be able to make simple alterations yourself. Paying someone to make them will add to the overall cost of the garment.
- Consider the care requirements of garments before you buy them. Garments that must be hand washed or dry-cleaned may require more time or money than you want to spend. Also compare price versus quality.
- Accessories, which are often inexpensive, can update and add variety to a wardrobe. With the right accessories, the same outfit can be either casual or dressy. Plan accessory purchases to avoid wasting money on items that do not go with your wardrobe.

Graphic Organizer

Draw a T-chart on a sheet of paper. Write the seven headers under *Judging Garment Quality* in the left column. In the right column, write at least two supporting details for each header.

Judging Garment Quality	
Headings	Supporting Details

Review the Facts

1. The _____ of an item depends on how well it meets certain standards of excellence.
2. Why does the same size not always fit you the same way?
3. Give two suggestions to follow when trying on garments.
4. How does a high-quality garment differ from a low-quality garment?
5. What should you look at when evaluating the fabric in a garment?
6. List five points to check before buying jeans or slacks.
7. Name three alterations that are easy to do.
8. Being able to machine wash a garment instead of dry cleaning it will save you both _____ and _____.
9. Is a low-quality garment ever a good purchase? Explain your answer.
10. _____ is the most important consideration when buying shoes.
11. What is the purpose of wearing neckties?
12. Name an example of functional jewelry.

Think Critically

13. **Identify evidence.** Should manufacturers be required to follow strict standards in sizing their garments? Use reliable resources to locate evidence to support your conclusions.
14. **Draw conclusions.** Can you get better quality in a garment if you sew it yourself? Why or why not?
15. **Predict outcomes.** Is it wise to pay more for high-quality accessories than for high-quality clothing? Predict possible outcomes of this action.

Apparel Applications

16. **Determine size.** Measure your hips, waist, and chest or bust following the guidelines in your favorite catalog. Use the catalog size chart to determine your size category or figure type and your size. Have you been buying the right size?
17. **Evaluate garment quality.** Bring a garment to class and evaluate its construction using the checklist in Figure 11-2. Rate the garment's quality as high, medium, or low.
18. **Judge price and quality.** At several different stores, shop for a similar garment, such as a shirt or blouse. Note the price of each garment and compare the quality features. Decide if price is an indication of quality. Write a report stating which garment you would buy and why.
19. **Assess fit and quality.** Bring a suit to class and model it. Have the class judge the fit using the points listed for checking quality and fit to evaluate these garments. In addition, have other class members model blouses, shirts, jeans, skirts, and dresses. Assess the quality and fit of each according to chapter guidelines.
20. **Alterations decisions.** If some of the items in activity 19 do not fit, decide if they could be altered. What alterations would be necessary? Could they be done by a beginning sewer, or would they need to be done by an alterations expert?
21. **Shoe tour.** Tour a shoe department or store. Ask the sales associate to discuss materials used, proper foot measurements, and shoe fit. Examine the quality of shoes on display. Compare prices.

Academic Connections

22. **Math.** Find out what it would cost to dry-clean a lined, corduroy jacket at a local dry cleaner. Determine how many times you would need to have the jacket cleaned during the year. Multiply the cost of dry-cleaning by the number of times you will need it cleaned in one year. Compare this cost with a jacket that can be laundered.
23. **Writing.** Use Internet or print resources to investigate the latest information about three-dimensional body scan measurement systems used to provide consumers with accurate measurements for fitting clothes? How do these scanners work? Are they safe? How do the scans benefit consumers and the apparel industry? Write a summary of your findings, noting the resources used.

Workplace Links

24. **Scarf practice.** Presume you are a sales associate at a local department store. Your supervisor has assigned you to learn the latest trends in scarf-tying to teach customers. Use Internet or print resources to investigate how to tie scarves. Then practice several different ways to wear a scarf until you are comfortable to teach others.
25. **Interview.** Interview a representative from a local department store about buying clothes and accessories. Ask the person about how to choose quality items. Write a summary of your findings to share with the class.

Learning About Consumer Clout

As an individual or as a team, investigate the FCCLA *Financial Fitness* program Consumer Clout unit. Use the FCCLA *Planning Process* to develop a peer-education presentation on becoming a savvy consumer. Share your presentation at school and other peer-group organizations. See your adviser for information as needed.

Chapter 12

Selecting Apparel for Family Members

Chapter Objectives

After studying this chapter, you will be able to
- **analyze** factors that affect apparel decisions for family members of all ages.
- **choose** appropriate clothing for children, adults, and older adults.
- **evaluate** garment features and fabrics appropriate for people with disabilities.

Key Terms

flame resistant
self-help features
hook-and-loop tape
disability

Reading with Purpose

Imagine you are a business owner and have several employees working for you. As you read the chapter, think about what you would like your employees to know about these topics. When you finish reading, write a memo to your employees and include key information from the chapter.

People have different clothing needs as they pass through the various stages of life. For instance, a baby's clothing needs are different from those of a preteen. Your clothing needs are a lot different from those of an older adult.

All members of a family want clothes that are comfortable, safe to wear, and attractive. They also want clothes that are suitable for their activities and require little care, **12-1**.

Suppose you want to select a clothing item for a baby, a parent, a grandparent, or a person with a disability. What would you buy or make? What factors would you consider? With a few guidelines, your selection can be both useful and pleasing.

12-1 Family members of all ages need clothes to fit their lifestyles.
Shutterstock

Selecting Clothes for Children

Years ago, children were dressed like small adults. We now know that children have clothing needs all their own. Although some adults are willing to sacrifice comfort and freedom of movement for fashion, children should not have to.

Children in different stages of growth and development have different clothing needs. Yet there are some common guidelines for all children's clothing. For example, it should allow them to move freely. It should have room for growth built in. It must be safe for children to wear and minimize the risk of injury. Also important, children's clothing should be durable, comfortable, and easy to care for. Whether you are selecting or making clothes for an infant, a toddler, a preschooler, or a school-age child, read more about factors to consider.

- *Proper fit.* Apparel sizes are not standardized in the U.S. For example, a size 4 garment from one manufacturer may be larger than a size 4 in a similar garment made by another company. The best way to check for proper fit is to have the child try on the garment at the time of purchase. When this is not possible, use the child's current measurements, including height and weight, to select the proper size. Using the measurements will give a better fit than using the child's age.

  To identify the correct size, find the child's measurements on the manufacturer's size chart. These are usually found on garment packaging and tags. Look for clothing that provides for normal growth. For example, choose garments with adequate sleeve and garment lengths that a child will not outgrow within a few weeks or months. Choose clothing that is not so tight that it restricts a child's movements or so loose that it may cause a child to trip and fall.

- *Comfort.* Consider the wearing comfort of the garments. Children like smooth, soft clothing best. They will not wear clothes that are rough textured, scratchy, or itchy. Sleeves, neckbands, and waistbands should fit snuggly, but not bind. Knit fabrics are good choices because they give and stretch.

Highlights in History

Pink and Blue for Children's Clothing

Pink for girls and blue for boys. People often use this guideline as they select clothes for babies and decorate their nurseries. Where did this idea come from, and how long has it been around?

Pink and blue were first associated with gender in 1916. An article in *Infants' and Children's Wear Review* stated, "the generally accepted rule is pink for the boy and blue for the girl." Believe it or not, little boys wore pink as recently as the 1940s. The colors were used interchangeably for boys and girls until after World War II.

By 1950, a combination of public opinion and manufacturers' clout ordained pink for girls and blue for boys. Even with this mandate, it was still permissible for girls to wear blue, but not for boys to wear pink. If a garment's trim or color was equated with feminine clothing, it was unacceptable for boys. This notion exists today.

A nonsexist child-rearing movement grew in the 1970s. Garment features associated with femininity, such as the color pink and ruffles, were considered sexist. Many parents pressed manufacturers for gender-neutral children's clothes. Gender-neutral clothing were those that had colors and trims previously acceptable for boys only.

During the 20th century, boys' attire became increasingly less feminine and girls' clothing became more masculine. For example, before 1970, trousers were viewed as garments to be worn by males only. In the 1970s, school and office dress codes were revised to allow girls and women to wear pants. Trousers are accepted attire for women and girls in nearly every social situation today.

- *Safety.* Safety is a critical factor to consider. Injuries and deaths of infants and children have been attributed to the garments they were wearing. For example, in 1995, children's clothing with drawstrings was banned by the Consumer Product Safety Commission. The drawstrings were usually located at the neck or waist of garments. Some young children were strangled when their garments' drawstrings caught in cribs or playground equipment. A recall was placed on any clothing made prior to 1995 that still had these drawstrings. Parents and caregivers are advised to cut or remove drawstrings in older items of children's clothing.

    While shopping for children's sleepwear, you will notice tags or labels on these garments stating they meet flame-resistant standards. These are standards set by the federal government. This does not mean that these garments are fireproof. **Flame resistant** means if they were accidentally ignited, they would burn very slowly. When removed from the flame, they would be either self-extinguishing or easy to extinguish. Sleepwear for children nine months to size 14 is required to be flame resistant or snug fitting.

- *Care.* Infants and children often soil their clothes with spilled food and drinks, dirt, markers, and other materials. Clothing should be machine washable—for both convenience and economy. Easy-care, soft, durable fabrics that require little or no ironing are good fabric choices for children's clothes, **12-2**.

Infants

People shopping for infant clothing can be easily tempted to buy the many cute outfits available. Some infant apparel, however, does not meet the needs of a growing baby. Many factors influence the selection of baby clothes. They include comfort, ease of care, fabric type, construction, size, season of the year, and climate.

- Your major concern should be the baby's comfort. Keep in mind that a baby's skin is sensitive and delicate. Good choices include clothes that are easy to change and those that do not chafe. Fabrics used for baby clothes should be soft, absorbent, and lightweight. Knitted fabrics offer more comfort and ease of movement than woven ones. Knit garments are also popular because of the built-in stretch that *grows* with the baby.

- Since babies are often changed several times a day, baby clothes should be easy to wash and dry.

- Most infants double their weight in the first three or four months. Select clothes with growth features that adjust to a baby's rapidly increasing size and weight. For instance, some two-piece sleepers have a double set of snaps at the waist. The sleeper can be lengthened by using a second set of snaps.

- Dressing and undressing a baby is easier if clothing has neck openings, zippers, snaps, or buttons, **12-3**. Pullover garments should have stretchable necklines. Pants should have snap crotches for easy diaper changing.

12-2 Children are active. They need clothes that are easy care and durable.
Shutterstock

- For safety reasons, avoid loose buttons or snaps that can be pulled off garments and swallowed. All trims should be firmly attached.
- Stretch terry coveralls and baby jogging suits are suitable for play. Be sure they allow lots of room for movement and growth. Most coveralls have a snap closure that extends down the legs for easy dressing. For greater warmth, blanket sleepers are available. These are useful in cooler weather when a baby is likely to kick off the covers and needs extra warmth. For older babies, sleepers should have rubber-soled feet to prevent slipping and falling.

When selecting baby clothes, the garment label and package information are good guides. Age, weight, height, or general sizes are often given. For infants, clothing sizes may be listed by age in months or by descriptive terms, such as small, medium, or large. Weight is usually a more accurate guide than age or general size. When trying to decide between a newborn size or a larger size, it is usually best to choose the slightly larger sizes for growing babies.

12-3 For infants, look for soft, knit garments with snaps. The snaps make it easier to change diapers.
Shutterstock

Toddlers and Preschoolers

Infants do not care what they wear as long as they are comfortable. Toddlers and preschoolers are more interested in their clothes. The main determinants of their clothing needs are their growth, active movement, and improving ability to self-dress. Comfort is still important, however. Toddlers' and preschoolers' clothes should be comfortable, safe to wear, durable, functional, and attractive.

When selecting clothes for toddlers and preschoolers, growth features are important. At this stage, children tend to grow faster in height than in width. Therefore, the length of the torso, arms, and legs change more quickly than the width of the shoulders, chest, and hips. Built-in growth features include

- adjustable or stretchable shoulder straps
- raglan or sleeveless styles
- elastic inserts
- stretch or knit fabrics
- undefined waistlines in one-piece garments
- large hems that can be let down as the child grows
- two-piece outfits

Comfort and safety are of special concern when selecting clothes for toddlers and preschoolers. Soft, absorbent, and flame-resistant fabrics should be used for making children's clothes. The garments should fit properly and have nonbinding, simple designs. For safety reasons, clothing, especially outdoor

Chapter 12   Selecting Apparel for Family Members   **229**

clothing, should be brightly colored so children can be clearly seen by motorists. Hoods and hats should not hinder the child's vision.

Toddlers and preschoolers like bright colors and designs. These give children an opportunity to learn to recognize colors, shapes, and symbols.

Toddlers

Toddlers have not developed waistlines and some still wear diapers. Simple styles that allow for fullness and maximum freedom of movement should be selected. One-piece garments that fall from the shoulders are practical. Snap inseams on pants help make changing diapers easier.

Design features should be functional as well as decorative. For instance, shoulder straps should cross in the back to prevent them from sliding off the shoulders.

During the toddler stage, children strive to become independent. They begin to learn to dress themselves. Clothing with **self-help features** encourages independence for children at this stage. Easy-to-work openings and closures for quick changes are necessary during toilet learning. Elastic waistbands are especially good for these children. Pull-on garments with large neck and armhole openings are easiest for toddlers to handle, **12-4**. Shirts that have an obvious front and back help toddlers dress themselves. When toddlers learn to snap, button, or zip clothing, they are proud of the new skills they have mastered.

Toddlers clothing sizes are 1T, 2T, 3T, and 4T. These sizes are based on age, but it is best to go by children's height, weight, chest, and waist measurements. Toddlers do not always wear the size based on their age. See Figure **12-5** for toddler clothing sizes.

Preschoolers

Preschoolers are still growing quickly and moving actively. When selecting clothes for preschoolers, look for styles that allow them to move freely. Jumpsuits are practical because they allow for mobility. Preschoolers can also wear belts or pants with elastic waistbands because their waistlines are now more defined.

Dressing skills improve during the preschool years. Preschoolers can manipulate fasteners such as buttons, snaps, nylon tape closings, and zippers. They may still have trouble with small fasteners or with fasteners on the backs of garments. Look for design features that help children identify the fronts from the backs of garments. These features include V-necklines at the fronts of shirts or appliqué designs on the fronts of pants.

12-4 Tops with large necklines and elastic pull-on pants are ideal for active toddlers.
Shutterstock

12-5 These measurements are used to determine clothing sizes for toddlers.

Clothing Sizes for Toddlers				
Toddler Size	Height (in inches)	Chest (in inches)	Waist (in inches)	Approximate Weight (in pounds)
1T	29½ to 32	20 to 20½	19½	25
2T	32½ to 35	21 to 21½	20	29
3T	35½ to 38	22 to 22½	20½	33
4T	38½ to 41	23 to 23½	21	38

Allowing preschoolers to help select their clothing ensures they will wear it. A color-coordinated wardrobe is a good idea. This way, almost any combination of garments will look good. Preschoolers like garments with pockets. Pockets should be easy to reach and big enough to hold favorite small toys or other items.

Preschoolers wear sizes from 2 to 6X. Though these numbers are related to a child's age, it is again best to go by height rather than age, **12-6**.

School-Age Children

School-age children are most comfortable when they wear clothes similar to those of their friends. Older brothers and sisters and celebrities also influence what they like to wear. Dressing like others helps school-age children to feel they belong. Conforming to certain styles of dress is an important aspect of belonging to a group.

It is a good idea to allow school-age children to help select their own clothes. By helping to choose what clothes to buy and what to wear each day, children develop decision-making skills.

Consider the opinions of school-age children regarding clothing colors and styles. Children notice what other children, especially their friends, are wearing. They enjoy wearing similar clothing, **12-7**. Select items that will fit into a child's wardrobe. Children should know which outfits are for school, play, or special occasions.

12-6 Garments in sizes 2 to 6X are for preschoolers. They are taller and more slender than toddlers.

Clothing Sizes for Preschoolers				
Children's Size	Height (in inches)	Chest (in inches)	Slim Waist (in inches)	Regular Waist (in inches)
2	32½ to 35	21	18	20
3	35½ to 38	22	18½	20½
4	38½ to 41	23	19¼	21¼
5	41½ to 44	24	20	22
6	44½ to 47	25	20½	22½
6X	47½ to 49	25½	21	23

Clothes for school-age children should be appropriate for their activities. For example, since they like to play, their clothes should hold up under rough wear. Select clothes that are durable and require little care.

As children become more skillful with self-dressing, you can choose clothing with smaller buttons and zippers. These features help children develop coordination with their fingers and hands.

Safety is another factor to consider when choosing clothes for school-age children. Clothes should be in bright colors that motorists can easily see. Caps or hats that do not obstruct children's vision are good choices. Reflective-fluorescent tapes that reflect car headlights are helpful safety features that can be added to garments. They can be used for a decorative effect. Stitch them to children's outdoor wear, rainwear, and Halloween costumes.

12-7 School-age children notice what their peers wear and want to dress like them.
Shutterstock

Clothes for Adults

When selecting clothing for adults, a number of factors should be considered. These include their occupations, interests, and activities.

Occupations Influence Clothing Needs

Adults' occupations, or the kinds of work they do, often determine their clothing needs. For example, bankers, salespeople, receptionists, and managers often come into contact with the public. The way they dress influences how people perceive them and their companies. Their companies want them to make a good impression because this could affect the success of the company.

Many professional and business people wear suits. Men often wear ties. Office workers may wear dress slacks or dresses, shirts or blouses, and sweaters or blazers. Most people who work in the same office wear similar types of clothing. In some offices, clothing styles are more casual than in other offices.

People who do physical work need durable clothes. They include farmers, painters, factory workers, auto mechanics, and construction workers. Their clothing must be sturdy enough to withstand hard wear and frequent laundering. Well-made garments in wash-and-wear fabrics are suitable.

Some adults are employed in jobs that require safety clothing and accessories such as hard hats, earplugs, eye goggles, and safety shoes. Welders, miners, brick masons, and certain factory workers need these types of items. Medical workers need clothes made of fabrics that can be sanitized, **12-8**.

Special clothing or uniforms may be needed in some jobs, such as those in medical fields, airlines, restaurants, and some government jobs. The clothing identifies employees. It may be furnished by employers or purchased by employees.

12-8 An adult's occupation often determines his or her clothing needs. Medical workers need clothes that can be sanitized.
Shutterstock

Interests and Activities

Many adults have leisure interests and activities that require special clothes. The clothing needs of adults who spend a lot of time outdoors fishing or golfing are different from those of people who prefer reading or attending plays and concerts.

Many adults have special interests or hobbies that require certain gear. This gear may include gardening gloves, beach towels, tennis racket covers, chef's aprons, sun hats, or athletic socks.

People who do chores outside their homes, such as shoveling snow and mowing the lawn, need clothes that are appropriate for the climate.

For men, shirts come in sizes according to the wearers' neck and sleeve measurements. Men's slacks are labeled by their waist and inseam measurements. The inseam measurement is taken from the crotch of a pant leg to the edge of the pant hem. Sweaters are usually sized as small, medium, large, and extra-large.

Women's dresses, skirts, and slacks often range in sizes from 4 to 20. Some specialty shops and department stores offer larger sizes, petite sizes, and half-sizes. Blouses may be sized according to the bust measurement. Women's sweaters come in small, medium, large, and extra-large.

Some adults work from home. Some remain at home to care for their children or their aging parents. People who spend most of their time at home need fewer and more casual clothes than people who work outside of the home. These adults may need clothes for caring for children, shopping, caring for the home, gardening, and preparing food. Clothes should be casual and easy to clean. Many stay-at-home parents are active in volunteer work. They may need clothes similar to those of office workers or more casual outfits, depending on what type of volunteer work they do.

Clothes for Older Adults

When older adults select clothes, they should consider their lifestyles. How do they spend most of their time? If they are usually at home, they may need only casual clothes. If they are always on the go, attending community events and religious services or traveling, they may need more extensive wardrobes.

Older adults are generally more conservative in their dress, **12-9**. They usually avoid the latest styles and fads. They often prefer basic garments that stay in style longer and are easily updated with accessories. Jewelry, scarves, or belts can give an outfit a new look.

Clothing for older adults has many of the characteristics of clothing for young children. These include safety features, large openings, fabrics that feel soft to the skin, and fasteners that open and close easily. This is because many older adults develop physical limitations that can make dressing and undressing difficult. For example, arthritis, which causes pain and stiffness in the joints, affects many older adults. They may not be able to raise their arms over their heads to manipulate back closures. They may have problems with zipper pulls or buttons. Clothing and accessories that makes dressing and undressing easier, such as slip-on shoes and pre-tied neckties, are appropriate. Pull-on slacks and pants with elastic at the waistline are good choices. Wraparound garments that tie in front are easy to wear. Hook-and-loop tape fasteners can be used in many areas instead of buttons. **Hook-and-loop tape** has tiny hooks on one strip and loops on the other that hold together when pressed with the fingers. Hook-and-loop tape fasteners on belts are easier to fasten than buckles.

As people become older, they may be less active. The lack of physical activity and other health problems can contribute to poor blood circulation. As a result, many older adults become more sensitive to cool temperatures. They may need more items such as sweaters, robes, and warm slippers.

Selecting Clothes for People with Disabilities

A **disability** is a condition that interferes with a person's ability to perform tasks like walking, lifting, or getting dressed. Some people are born with disabilities. Others develop disabilities as a result of illness or injury. Disabilities may last a lifetime or a limited period of time.

People with disabilities want to be as independent as possible. Part of being independent is being able to get dressed and undressed with minimal assistance from others. Certain clothing styles are easier to put on, take off, and wear than others. Clothes selected for people with disabilities should promote comfort and independent living, 12-10. Clothing should be as attractive and fashionable as possible. At the same time, it must be functional. Clothing should contribute to the dignity of people who depend on others for personal care.

Finding ready-to-wear garments or home-sewing patterns that meet the needs of people with disabilities can be difficult. Alterations or adaptations may be necessary to make clothing easier to put on and more comfortable to wear.

12-9 Older adults are generally more conservative in their dress and need clothes suited to their activities.
Shutterstock

Helpful Apparel Design Features

When selecting clothing for people with disabilities, remember their unique clothing needs. Select something they can manage conveniently. Clothing can

12-10 Clothing that is comfortable and easy to put on can help people with disabilities lead independent lives. *Shutterstock*

12-11 Finding clothes that fit over a cast can be especially challenging. *Shutterstock*

also be altered, adding features that make it easier to put on, take off, and wear.

- *Arm openings and sleeves.* Some people with physical disabilities do not have the full use of their hands and arms. They may have trouble reaching back to fasten garments with back openings or slip their arms into set-in sleeves. This is why larger arm openings and styles with raglan sleeves are better choices.

- *Garment closures and fasteners.* People with limited hand movements or limited vision may have trouble aligning and buttoning buttons and other fasteners. Hook-and-loop tape can make it easier for them. It is available in long strips that can replace zippers. It is also available in small pieces to use in place of snaps or buttons.

- *Garment fronts and backs.* People with limited vision may have trouble distinguishing the back of a garment from the front. Design features, such as a V-neckline or a design on the front of a garment, can help them identify the garment's front. If someone has limited vision and cannot identify colors, garments can be marked. Stitch small pieces of rickrack or other trim to the inside of garments. Garments that can be worn together can be marked with the same size or type of trim.

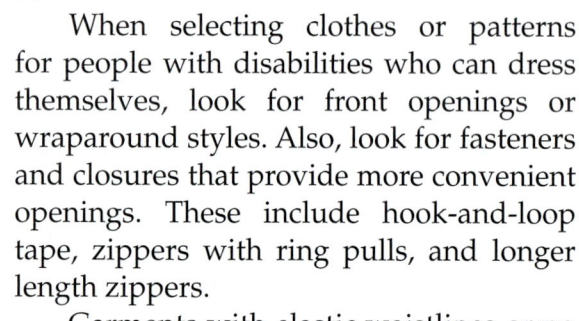

When selecting clothes or patterns for people with disabilities who can dress themselves, look for front openings or wraparound styles. Also, look for fasteners and closures that provide more convenient openings. These include hook-and-loop tape, zippers with ring pulls, and longer length zippers.

Garments with elastic waistlines or no waistlines are more comfortable for people who must be in one position for long time periods.

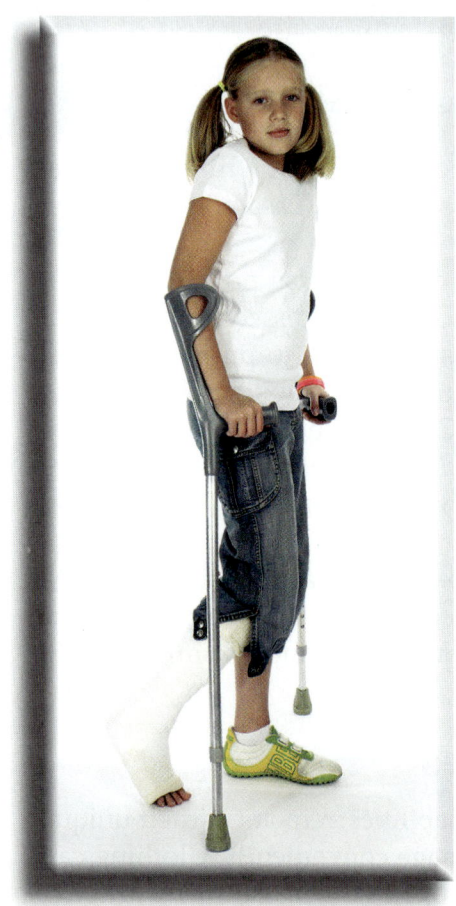

Often clothing must fit over braces and casts, such as a cast on a leg, **12-11**. Slacks with elastic waists can be pulled over casts and braces. Adding zippers to the inseams of slacks also aids in dressing. Choose durable fabrics, especially if an individual wears a brace. The friction caused by braces can be hard on most fabrics. A garment can be adapted by fusing or stitching an extra layer of fabric to the inside to reinforce areas that receive a lot of wear. Consider adding leather patches or large appliqués to the outside of garments to reinforce areas that receive friction.

Select easy-care fabrics. Heavy fabrics may be too bulky for people who use wheelchairs, crutches, or walkers. Fabrics that cling are not suitable because they do not allow adequate freedom of movement. Moderate-weight knit fabrics are a good choice because they provide comfort and ease of movement. When selecting or adapting clothes for people with physical disabilities, look for the features listed in **12-12.**

Apparel Features for People with Disabilities

When buying apparel for people with physical disabilities, look for the following features. Sometimes garments can be modified to add some of these features. Also consider these points when constructing garments for people with disabilities.

Garment Features	Fabrics
• Large arm openings • Raglan or dolman sleeves • V-necklines • Large necklines with drawstrings • Front or side openings • Wraparound styles • Elastic waists, drawstrings, or no waistline at all • Few fastenings, especially above mid-chest level • Hook-and-loop fasteners or large hooks • Longer length zippers • Zippers with ring pulls, or add to existing pull • Large pockets and long shirttails • Reinforced areas that receive wear	• Durable • Soft and absorbent, but not scratchy • Moderate weight that provides warmth • Knits that give but do not cling • Prints that do not show stains • Easy to launder; requires little or no ironing

12-12 Look for these features when buying clothes for people with disabilities.

Summary

- Clothing needs for children vary with their stages of growth and development.
- Many factors influence the selection of baby clothes. Comfort, ease of care, fabric type, construction, size, and season of the year or climate are all important.
- Toddlers and preschoolers are more interested in their clothes. Their clothing needs are based on growth, active movement, and their improving abilities to dress themselves.
- School-age children are most comfortable when they wear clothes similar to those of their friends. Dressing like others helps school-age children to feel they belong.
- Adults consider a number of factors when selecting their clothes, including their occupations, interests, and activities.
- Clothing for the older adults and young children may have similar characteristics. These include safety features, large openings, fabrics that feel soft to the skin, and fasteners that open and close easily.
- People with disabilities have unique clothing needs. Select, alter, or construct clothing that someone with a functional limitation can conveniently manage.

Graphic Organizer

Draw a fishbone diagram like the one here and note two key points for each header under *Selecting Clothes for Children*.

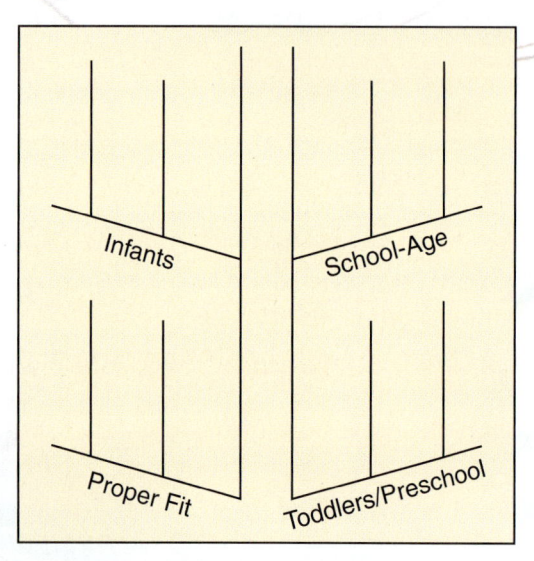

Review the Facts

1. List five factors to consider when selecting clothes for children.
2. For proper fit, select clothes for a child according to the child's _____ and _____.
3. What are three features to look for when buying clothes for an infant?
4. List three types of built-in growth features in clothes for toddlers and preschoolers.
5. Clothing with self-help features will encourage _____ as children learn to dress and undress themselves.
6. Why should school-age children be allowed to help select their own clothes?
7. Often, adults' major clothing needs are determined by their _____.
8. What is the main factor that determines the clothing needs of older adults?
9. Describe three general characteristics of clothes selected for people with disabilities.
10. Name three construction features you would look for when selecting a garment for a person who has limited vision.

Think Critically

11. **Make inferences.** What are some ways parents help their children learn to dress themselves? Discuss your inferences in class.
12. **Analyze behavior.** At what age do you think children start to become aware of how their clothes look to others?
13. **Compare and contrast.** Think about the clothing needs of children and older adults. In small groups, compare and contrast how they are similar and different. Discuss your answers with the class.
14. **Identify relevant information.** If a friend of yours broke an arm, what suggestions could you give to modify his or her clothes?

Apparel Applications

15. **Analyze garment features.** Bring to class several children's garments. Discuss the features that are good and those that could be improved.
16. **Interview parent.** Interview someone who has a small child. Ask what factors he or she considers in selecting clothes for the child. Write a summary of your findings.
17. **Choose children's garments.** Interview three school-age children about their choices in clothing. Ask about their favorite colors, styles, and fabrics. Then identify garment choices you would make for these children. Write an illustrated report, showing your garment selections, to share with the class.
18. **Interview workers.** Interview two people in different occupations—one who must wear a uniform to work and another who does not. How are their wardrobe needs different? How do their occupations affect the amount of money they spend on suitable work clothes?
19. **Invite speaker.** Invite a person with a disability to speak to the class about the adaptations or alterations that must be made to his or her clothing for comfort, convenience, and/or proper fit.
20. **Evaluate clothes for disabilities.** Using the Internet, find companies that sell clothing for people with physical disabilities and review their catalogs. Compare the variety, quality, and cost of items offered for sale. Do you think it will be more cost-effective to modify traditional clothing for people with disabilities? Discuss your responses.

Academic Connections

21. **Writing.** Interview someone who has had a broken leg, foot, or arm. Write a short report about how the disability affected the person's clothing selections.
22. **Reading.** Use Internet or print resources from a reliable organization such as *AARP*, to research clothing choices for older adults. Read two or more articles and write a summary of your findings.

Workplace Links

23. **Portfolio builder.** Presume you work with alterations at a local department store. Your supervisor has asked you to come up with a way to modify pants to make them easier for someone who uses a wheelchair to put on without assistance. Write a summary explaining how you would make the alterations to the pants. If possible, illustrate your report. Save a copy for your portfolio.
24. **Choose workplace wardrobes.** Plan a weeks' wardrobe for one person who works in apparel retail and another person who works in a physically demanding job, such as carpentry or electrical work. Use Internet or print catalogs to locate garment examples for each person. Create a poster display showing each wardrobe and explain your choices to the class.

Working with an Older Adult

Do you like being around older adults and listening to the stories they tell? If you do, you may enjoy working with an older adult who has clothing needs. Contact a local social service organization to find out about older adults who need assistance. Plan an FCCLA *Power of One* project using the *FCCLA Planning Process*. Plan your project according to the needs of the older adult, such as for shopping assistance or making alterations. See your adviser with questions as needed.

Chapter 13

Keeping Apparel Looking Its Best

Chapter Objectives

After studying this chapter, you will be able to
- **explain** how to care for clothes on a daily basis.
- **describe** daily and seasonal methods of storing clothes.
- **choose** the laundry product best suited to a certain laundry task.
- **select** and use clothing care equipment.

Key Terms

stain
detergents
source reduction
water hardness
water softener
prewash soil and stain removers
enzyme presoak
bleach
fabric softeners
starch
sizings
solvent
agitation

Reading with Purpose

Arrange a study session to read the chapter with a classmate. After reading each passage independently, stop and tell each other what you think the main points are in the passage. Continue with each passage until you finish the chapter.

You have probably taken a great deal of time to select, purchase, or sew the clothes you wear. In order to save your investment of time and money, you need to take good care of your clothes. To keep them looking their best for a long time, there are simple clothing care practices you need to follow every day. Your clothes also need to be laundered properly to maintain their appearance.

Most clothing items are easier to care for today than they were in past years. New fibers and fabric characteristics that are used in clothing make laundering them easier. Laundry care products have improved through the years, and new products appear regularly. All are designed to do a better job of keeping your clothes looking their best. You need to learn about these products and how to use them. Then you will always have clean clothes whenever you need them.

Daily Clothing Care

What do you do with your clothes at the end of the day? Some people toss them onto a chair or on the floor. People who want their clothes to last, however, take the time to put them where they belong. Do they need to be cleaned? Do they need a repair? Can they be worn again? There is no better time than the end of the day to make these decisions. See **13-1**.

After you wear a garment, do a quick inspection.
- First, check for stains. If you remember spilling food or liquids on your clothes, now is a good time to do some preliminary stain removal. For most washable items, a quick rinse in cool water will go a long way to prevent permanent stains from forming.

> **Keeping Your Clothes Ready to Wear**
>
> - Decide if a garment is to be worn again before cleaning.
> - Remove any stains or spots.
> - Place garments that need repairs in a special place. You will know where they are when you have time to work on them.
> - Put dresses, jackets, shirts, and coats on hangers.
> - Fold pants over plastic hangers, or use pants hangers.
> - Fold sweaters and place them in drawers or on shelves.
> - If shoes are damp from wearing, let them dry before putting them away.
> - Wipe dust or dirt from shoes before putting them in the closet.

13-1 Keep your clothes ready to wear by following these tips.

- Next, check garments for any repairs they might need. Is a button starting to come loose? Did you catch your heel in a hem, causing a few stitches to come loose? If so, set the garment aside so you will remember to make the repair before you need to wear it again.
- If the garment can be worn again, put it on a hanger or in a drawer. Heavier garments should be placed on padded hangers or wide, shaped wood or plastic hangers. Fold sweaters carefully and put them in drawers. They could stretch out of shape on hangers.
- Empty all pockets. Close zippers and button closures to keep garments from becoming wrinkled or twisted in crowded closets.
- Use a clothing brush or lint roller to brush dust and lint off garments.
- Place soiled clothing items that need laundering in a clothes basket or hamper. Having a place designated for dirty laundry in a bedroom or bathroom is important. When it fills up, it reminds people to do their laundry. It also helps some people resist the temptation to toss their dirty clothes on floors or chairs.

Some soiled items need to be dry-cleaned. Some families have a special place for clothing items that need to be taken to a dry cleaner.

Remove Stains

You may discover a stain when you inspect your clothes. A **stain** is a spot or discoloration caused by various liquids or solid materials. You will not see some stains until they have been in the garment for a while. Then they appear as yellow spots.

Treat a stain as soon as you see it. A fresh stain comes out more easily than an old one. Ironing over a stain will often make it impossible to remove.

Removing stains is easier than you may think. Most common ones can be removed if you are prompt, patient, and persistent. Try to find out what the stain is. Use the stain-removal procedure that is recommended for the stain and the type of fabric it is on. Otherwise, you may damage your garment or set the stain. If it is worth saving, it is worth a little extra time and effort.

You may have to try to remove the stain several times before you succeed. If the first treatment does not work, try a different method. Knowing what caused the stain will speed the process. Stains on durable press fabrics are sometimes difficult to remove because of the chemical finish that is on them.

You are more likely to remove a stain if you use the right products. In the laundry area, you should keep detergents, prewash soil and stain removers, bleaches, solvents, clean white cloths, and white paper towels or facial tissues. Also, keep a chart, listing stains and their removal procedures in this area, **13-2**.

A Guide For Removing Stains

Adhesive tape. Scrape with a dull knife. Apply cleaning fluid or prewash stain remover. Rinse, and then wash with detergent.

Ballpoint ink. Laundering will remove some types of ballpoint ink, but it sets other types. To see if stain will wash out, find a similar scrap of fabric. Mark it with the ink and wash it. Pretreat with a prewash stain remover. Denatured (rubbing) alcohol will remove some types of ink. Place stain face down on paper towels and apply alcohol. When stain is removed, wash as usual.

Blood. Soak fresh stains in cold water. Rinse. For dried stains, pretreat or soak in warm water with enzyme product. Rub a heavy-duty detergent into the spot, and then launder as usual. If the stain remains, rewash using a bleach product that is safe for the fabric.

Candle wax. Rub the stain with ice and scrape off as much wax as possible. Then place the stain between several layers of white paper towels. Press with warm iron. If any stain remains, apply cleaning fluid or prewash stain remover. Launder.

Car grease, oil. Most of these stains can be removed by rubbing a heavy-duty detergent or prewash stain remover into the stain. Wash in hottest water safe for fabric. If the stain remains, put cleaning fluid on it and wash again.

Chewing gum. Make the gum hard by putting ice on it. Remove as much as you can with a dull knife. Put prewash stain remover or cleaning fluid on the remaining spot. Then launder.

Chocolate. Soak stain in warm water with a product containing enzymes, or treat with prewash stain remover. Rinse. If stain remains, work heavy-duty detergent into the stain. Then rinse thoroughly. If the stain looks greasy, apply cleaning fluid.

Coffee or tea. Soak in enzyme presoak product or oxygen bleach. Use the hottest water safe for the fabric. Wash.

Cosmetics. Apply undiluted, heavy-duty liquid detergent to stain. Work with your fingers to form suds. Rinse well. Or, pretreat with prewash stain remover. If the garment is not washable, use a spot remover. Rub the edges of the stain lightly with a cloth. This will prevent a circle from forming.

Deodorants and antiperspirants. Rub liquid detergent on stain. Wash in the hottest water safe for fabric. Pretreat heavy stains with prewash stain remover. Allow to stand 5 to 10 minutes.

Grass. Pretreat or soak in product containing enzymes. Wash garment as usual. If stain remains, use bleach according to manufacturer's directions.

Ice Cream or milk. Pretreat or soak stains using product containing enzymes. Soak for at least 30 minutes or several hours. Launder. Repeat if necessary.

Nail polish. Use nail polish remover. Before using, test a scrap or small area to be sure it will not cause damage. Do not use remover on acetate or triacetate fabrics. Place stain face down on paper towels and apply remover to back of stain.

Fruit—Fruit Juices, Soft Drinks, Punches. If possible, sponge with cool water as soon as stain occurs. Soak with enzyme presoak, rinse. Bleach the garment, if possible. Apply white vinegar if bleach cannot be used. Launder again.

Perspiration. Presoak by wetting the area and applying heavy-duty detergent or use a prewash stain remover. Wait one hour. Then wash in hot water. Stubborn stains may respond to product containing enzymes or oxygen bleach.

Scorch. Launder using bleach that is safe for fabric in hot water.

13-2 This guide lists some methods you can use to remove common stains.

Clothing Storage

If garments are clean, they are ready to be stored. Garments can be placed on hangers and hung in closets or folded and stored in drawers or on shelves.

Daily Storage

If you wish to hang a garment, select a hanger based on the garment's style and weight. Wire hangers may be used, but check for rust, peeling paint, or rough edges that can snag delicate items. Plastic tubular hangers are preferred for lightweight, firmly woven shirts and blouses. Padded hangers are better for sheer fabric blouses and dresses.

Jackets, suits, and tailored garments call for wide, shaped wood or plastic hangers that provide more support. Slacks can be suspended from cuffs or hems using specially designed hangers. Otherwise, place slacks over the horizontal bar of a plastic tubular hanger, instead of a wire hanger, to prevent creases from forming at the thigh. If closet space is limited, you can purchase special hangers that hold several skirts, pants, or shirts.

Sweaters and stretchable garments should not be placed on hangers. They should be folded and stored in drawers or plastic boxes, or on shelves, 13-3. Hanging these garments would cause them to stretch and lose their shape. Fold garments at construction lines. If boxes are used, label them so you can find items easily. Boxes can be placed on closet floors or shelves. If garments must be stacked, place heavier items at the bottom. Some smaller items can be rolled rather than folded, reducing wrinkles and saving storage space. This works well for underwear and socks.

13-3 Knits can stretch out of shape on hangers. They keep their shape if stored in drawers or on shelves. Originally published in Lowe's Creative Ideas magazine. Copyright 2006 SPC Custom Publishing.

Seasonal Clothing Storage

You may need special clothes and accessories if you live in a cold climate. These coats, sweaters, and other items need to be stored when winter is past.

Select a storage area that is dry and away from direct sunlight. Attics are usually better than basements. Dampness in basements can cause mildew and musty, unpleasant odors, which are difficult to remove.

Cloth garment bags and cardboard boxes are good containers for storing out-of-season clothes. If boxes are labeled, needed items can be found quickly. To prevent wrinkling, place tissue paper between folds.

The most important thing to remember about storing clothing is to store it clean. It is impossible to see all the soiled spots on a garment. A soft drink spill may not show, for example. It can turn yellow or brown during storage and be impossible to remove later. If insects find the spot, they will eat it as well as some of the fabric. It is smart to have winter clothing dry-cleaned before storing it.

Storing winter garments takes more effort than storing summer clothes. Wool is the warmest fiber, so it is used in many winter garments. Wool is expensive and requires special care if it is to look nice for several seasons, **13-4**.

Moths are pests that attack woolen garments. They appear mysteriously in closets and storage areas and lay eggs on clothing. When the eggs hatch, the larvae eat the wool. Dry cleaning destroys moth eggs and larvae. This is another reason to clean clothes before storing them. Tightly seal bags and boxes of clean garments with tape to keep moths out.

Repellents for moths are available. There are cake, flake-crystal, and marble forms. All are effective if used according to manufacturers' directions. Garments must be placed in sealed containers for the products to be effective. Many have an odor, so clothes have to be aired before wearing.

Silverfish is another pest that eats soil spots, as well as fabrics. Cleanliness is the best treatment for keeping them away. An all-purpose insect spray may be needed for closets and storage areas. When using these products, be sure to follow directions.

Clothing Care Products

To keep clothes looking their best, it is a good idea to keep some laundry and stain-removal products on hand. At the minimum, you should have a good laundry detergent. Some additional laundry aids, however, can solve specific laundry problems. Knowing what these products are and what they can do will help you select what you need. Some products are designed to remove stains on clothing.

13-4 Wool coats should be dry-cleaned before they are stored for the summer.
Shutterstock

Laundry Detergents

Detergents are made from petroleum and natural fats and oils. Their primary purpose is to remove dirt from laundry items. There are many types of detergents on the market. Choose the one best suited to your needs. Some are high-sudsing and others are low-sudsing, but suds are not needed to clean clothes.

- *General-purpose detergents.* These products are suitable for all washable fabrics, from heavily soiled work clothes to lightly soiled lingerie.
- *Ultra detergents.* These detergents are concentrated and come in smaller packages. They provide the same amount of cleaning power as general-purpose detergents, but you use less product. The advantage of ultra detergents is that they contribute to source reduction. **Source reduction** is a decrease in the amount of materials or energy used during the manufacture and distribution of products and packaging. Concentrates require 15 to 50 percent less packaging material than non-concentrated products. Many ultra detergents are available as refill containers that also use less packaging material than the primary containers. This also helps with source reduction.
- *Light-duty detergents.* These detergents are designed for lightly soiled items and delicate fabrics, as well as baby clothes.
- *Combination detergents.* These are detergents that do two jobs, such as removing dirt as well as bleaching or softening. Combination detergents contribute to source reduction because fewer products are needed.
- *Cold-water detergents.* This category of detergents is designed for use in cold water. These detergents help consumers reduce their energy bills by using cold water instead of hot water.
- *Fragrance-free or dye-free detergents.* These detergents do not contain fragrances or dyes that can be irritating to people who have certain allergies.
- *High-efficiency (HE) detergents.* The newest category of laundry detergents are designed for high-efficiency, front-loading washers and top-loading washers. These washers use less water. They require the use of detergents formulated to be low-sudsing and quick-dispersing. Using high-sudsing detergents in HE washers can result in improper cleaning.

13-5 Measure the recommended amount of detergent for your type of washer and your wash load. *Shutterstock*

Detergents are available as liquids, powders, or premeasured tablets. Follow the directions on the package to find the amount of detergent to use. For best results, measure the detergent as in **13-5**, rather than just pouring it into the machine.

Water Softeners

The advantage of detergents is that they can be used in both hard and soft water. **Water hardness** refers to the amount of minerals, usually calcium and magnesium, contained in the water. Some sections of the country have hard water, and other areas have soft water. Hard water, which is preferred for drinking, can cause problems when washing clothes. It can make clothing look dingy and feel rough to the touch.

How do you know whether or not your home has hard water? A soap scum or film often forms when you use soap-based products in hard water. Do you find a ring around your bathtub after the water is drained? If so, you probably have hard water.

Many families in hard-water areas use a **water softener**, which is a product or device used to soften the water. Some families have a water-softening system installed in their homes if their water is very hard. By doing this, all the water that enters their homes is softened. Other families add white vinegar to the rinse cycle or purchase packaged water softeners that remove or inactivate minerals in the water. These products are sold as powders or liquids. Powders are added to the wash or rinse water when doing the laundry. Liquids are usually added to rinse water only. The result is whiter, cleaner, and softer clothes.

Prewash Soil and Stain Removers

Products that help remove oily stains and heavy soil are called **prewash soil and stain removers**. They are available as sprays, liquids, gels, sticks, wipes, or foams. They contain solvents that penetrate the fibers and dissolve grease and oil stains. Prewash products are especially effective on oil-based stains on polyester fabrics. For instance, when a prewash spray is used on the neck edges of shirt or blouse collars, they become cleaner. To get the best cleaning action, be sure to follow the directions on the label.

Wipes can be applied while wearing garments and are safe for all dry-cleanable fabrics. They can be carried with you and used in an emergency. Sticks are also convenient to use soon after stains occurs. This makes stains easier to remove when garments are laundered at a later time, **13-6**.

13-6 Little children often get stains on their clothing. Treat stains as soon as possible so they are easier to remove. *Shutterstock*

Enzyme Presoaks

An **enzyme presoak** is used for soaking the laundry before washing. These products help remove many difficult stains, especially those with a protein base. Baby formula, blood, dairy products, eggs, and grass stains can be removed with the use of an enzyme product. Though these powders are usually used to soak laundry before washing, they can also be added to the wash cycle in addition to the detergent. This boosts the cleaning power of the detergent.

Bleach

Bleach is a chemical mixture that removes stains and whitens or brightens fabrics. With proper laundering, bleach is seldom necessary for the weekly wash. Bleach can shorten the life of garments by weakening the fibers if it is used too often. There are two types of bleaches: chlorine bleach and oxygen bleach.

- *Chlorine bleach* is identified by the word *hypochlorite* or *liquid household bleach*. It is the more powerful of the laundry bleaches. It disinfects, as well as cleans and whitens. Use it in wash water according to the manufacturer's directions. Caution! Check care labels on garments before using bleach on them. Many advise *Do Not Bleach*. Never use bleach on wool, silk, spandex, or any garment with a label that warns against its use, **13-7**.

  Chlorine bleach can be used on white fabrics and colorfast washables. Do not pour chlorine bleach directly on clothes. Instead, put it in the water before you add the clothes. Follow the directions on the container to decide how much to use.

- *Oxygen bleach* is identified by the words *perborate* or *all-fabric*. It may also be referred to as nonchlorine bleach. It is mild and can be used on most colored fabrics. Follow directions from the manufacturer. You may need to soak the garment.

13-7 Be sure to check a garment's care label to see if chlorine bleach can be used. *Shutterstock*

Fabric Softeners

Fabric softeners, a popular laundry aid, give softness and fluffiness to fabrics. Fabric softeners cause a thin, invisible, lubricating coating to form over each fiber. As a result, garments are soft and have few wrinkles. Many products add a pleasing fragrance. Clothes are easier to iron and nicer to wear. Fabric softeners should not be used on some children's sleepwear, however, since it may reduce the effectiveness of flame retardants on fabrics.

Fabric softeners can also reduce static electricity in garments. Sometimes in cold, dry weather, garments made from manufactured fibers cling to the body or other fabrics. This is caused by static electricity. It causes the snapping noises you sometimes hear when you remove a shirt, sweater, slip, or skirt. Besides fabric softeners, other antistatic products are available. Some can be sprayed from aerosol cans.

Fabric softeners are available in two forms. Liquid products are added to the final rinse cycle. To be effective, they should not be used with any other laundry products in the rinse cycle. They should be diluted and added directly to the rinse water. Do not pour directly on fabrics because staining can occur. Always use the amount suggested by the manufacturer. Fabric softeners are available in concentrated forms.

Other fabric softeners are added to clothes in the dryer. Some are in the form of small nonwoven sheets of synthetic fabric or polyurethane foam. These are saturated with a softener, and the heat of the dryer transfers the softener to the clothes. A new sheet is used each time. A packet-type fabric softener is attached to a fin of the dryer drum.

Starch and Sizings

Starch produces a crisp, smooth surface on fabrics. It is available in dry, liquid, or spray forms. If collars or cuffs appear wrinkled or puckered, a light application of spray starch before ironing should give them a smooth look. The dry and liquid forms are mixed with water before applying to fabrics. Starch is most effective on cotton or cotton-blend fabrics. Sizings are designed for use with synthetic fabrics. It makes ironing easier and adds body to fabrics.

Solvents or Cleaning Fluids

A solvent is sometimes used to dissolve stains, especially those caused by makeup and grease. There are many brand names for solvents, but most are labeled *cleaning fluid* or *spot remover*. Read all label warnings before buying, using, and storing. Some are flammable, and some are poisonous. Use them only in well-ventilated places.

Clothing Care Equipment

Special equipment is needed to care for clothing. These include washing machines, clothes dryers, irons, and ironing boards, 13-8. Many people have this equipment in their homes. It is also available for use in self-service laundries. Apartment buildings and college dorms may have laundry rooms where this equipment is available for residents' use.

13-8 A washer, dryer, an iron, and an ironing board are needed to care for clothes at home. *Shutterstock*

Washers and Dryers

Many families have their own washing machines and dryers. Traditional automatic models have touch screens, dials, or push buttons that can be set according to the wash load. These settings include:

- water fill level
- water temperatures for wash and rinse cycles
- soak time
- wash cycles that determine agitator speed and length of washing time

Most models offer at least three cycles: regular, gentle, and permanent press. Each cycle is usually characterized by its length and the amount of agitation to clothes. **Agitation** is the action that traditional automatic washers use helps to loosen and remove soils from the clothes during the wash cycle.

Top-loading washers are the most common. In most top-loaders, laundry is completely submerged in water. An agitator moves the laundry back and forth to loosen soils. Deluxe models also include features for dispensing fabric softener, presoak product, and bleach, as well as detergent. These models also offer a wider range of water levels and more temperature combinations. Less expensive models have fewer features. They are less convenient, but they can clean clothing as well as the deluxe models.

High-Efficiency (HE) Washers

Front-loading, high-efficiency (HE) washing machines operate differently than traditional automatic washers. These washers use a tumbler system with no agitator. The tub rotates back and forth, moving the water and detergent through the laundry to remove soil. Only a small amount of water is used, saving water and energy. These machines can use 20- to 50-percent less energy than other top-loading models because there is much less water to heat. They remove more water, thus cutting drying time which also saves energy.

Top-loading, high-efficiency washers are also available. These washers use a gentle motion that cleans using very little water. Spinning, rotating, and/or *wobbling* wheels, plates, or disks achieve the wash action. These washers either have no center post or a smaller post instead of a traditional agitator.

When using high-efficiency washers, use the dispensers provided for adding detergents, fabric softeners, and bleach. It is best to avoid pretreat and presoak products in HE washers because these products may be normal- to high-sudsing. This can cause excess sudsing, reducing the effectiveness of the HE detergents.

Dryers

Automatic washing machines often have matching automatic dryers. Some are designed to stack on top of one another, thus conserving space. Dryers usually have regular, permanent press, and air fluff cycles. The regular cycle is for items that are not sensitive to heat. The permanent press cycle provides a cool-down time with no heat at the end to reduce wrinkles. The air fluff cycle provides tumbling in unheated air. Some new dryers have as many as five heat settings and 20 drying cycles. Many have moisture sensors that turn off the heat when the laundry is dry. Newer models provide a removable drying rack for items that need to be laid flat to dry.

Some families take their clothes to self-service laundries. The commercial machines there are coin-operated. Several can be used at one time. This can reduce the time spent doing laundry.

Irons and Ironing Boards

In addition to a washer and dryer, an iron and ironing board may be needed. Irons generally have both dry and steam settings and a wide variety of fabric settings. The dry setting is used at low temperatures for fabrics sensitive to heat. If the fabric is already damp, a dry iron setting can be used. Steam settings are used when a fabric must be ironed or pressed with steam. The soleplate of the iron has holes that allow steam to escape, 13-9. Some models have a button that is pushed to give the fabric a shot of steam or water. Most irons use distilled water to avoid the buildup of mineral deposits, but some can use tap water.

Soleplates of irons can be shiny or have a Teflon® coating. This coating helps prevent scorching, sticking, and shine on fabrics. The iron also glides easier across the fabric. Some irons have an automatic shut-off as a safety feature. If the iron is left unattended for a period of time, it will shut off automatically.

An ironing board is an asset. Most adjust to the user's height for comfort. Make sure the board is sturdy and does not rock. Use a padded cover. Padding is usually foam or a felted pad. Most covers have a silicone treatment to prevent burning and to extend wear. Replace both when wear starts to show, because tears and burned areas can damage clothes during ironing.

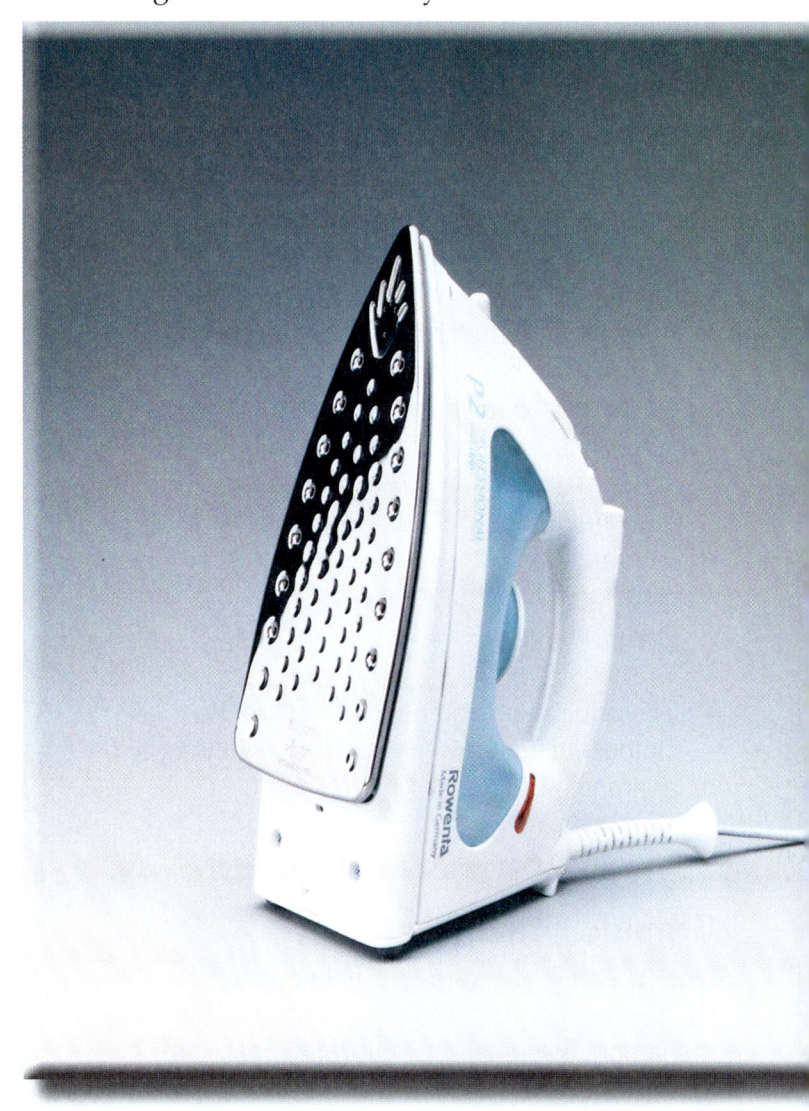

13-9 Steam irons have holes that allow steam to escape. The combination of heat and moisture effectively removes wrinkles.
Rowenta

Summary

- To keep clothes looking their best for a long time, you should perform some simple clothing care practices every day. These include checking for stains, making repairs, and hanging or folding clothes properly.
- Most common stains on clothing can be removed if you are prompt, patient, and persistent. The key is to remove stains as soon as you see them.
- Clean clothes should be placed on hangers, or folded and stored in drawers and boxes, or on shelves. If clothes are to be stored for a period of time, they require some special care.
- Keep some laundry and stain-removal products on hand, such as laundry detergent. Some additional laundry aids can solve specific laundry problems. These include water softeners, prewash soil and stain removers, enzyme presoaks, bleaches, fabric softeners, starches and sizings, and solvents and cleaning fluids. Learn how and when to use these products to keep your clothes looking their best.
- The equipment you need to care for your clothes include a washer, a dryer, an iron, and an ironing board.

Graphic Organizer

Draw a T-chart diagram on a sheet of paper. In the left column, list the types of clothing care products. In the right column, list several supporting details for each.

Clothing Care Products	
Product Types	Supporting Details

Review the Facts

1. State at least four things you should do daily to keep your clothes looking their best.
2. Why is it important to remove stains as soon as possible after they occur?
3. What two types of hangers are best for slacks?
4. Why should you store only clean clothes when seasons change?
5. State two ways laundry-product manufacturers are helping with source reduction.
6. What type of detergent must be used in front-loading washers and why?
7. If you have hard water, how will a water softener improve the look and feel of your clothes?
8. Contrast chlorine bleach and oxygen bleach.
9. Name the three most common wash cycles available on automatic washers and explain how they differ.
10. Describe the permanent press cycle on a dryer.

Think Critically

11. **Analyze behaviors.** Analyze your daily clothing care practices. What improvements could you make?
12. **Draw conclusions.** Draw conclusions about what can you do as a user of clothing care products to help reduce pollution and protect the environment. Share your conclusions with the class.
13. **Recognize alternatives.** When it comes to clothes and their care, what recycling options might you consider? Make a list of your alternatives and post them in your closet.

Apparel Applications

14. **Plan garment care.** Do an inventory of the clothes in your closet. Determine if any clothes have stains, need minor repairs, or need to be laundered or dry-cleaned before you can wear them again. Make a list of these garments. Then make a plan for correcting these problems so all your clothes are available to wear when you need them.

15. **Storage research.** Review a website of a retailer that sells products designed for clothes storage and closet organization. What items could help you take better care of your clothes and make better use of clothes storage space? Write an illustrated report on what you would buy and why. Share your findings with the class.

16. **Speaker.** Invite a professional closet organizer to visit the class and give pointers on how to best organize a closet.

17. **Laundry practices.** Talk with your family members whether your laundry practices are helping to conserve energy and reduce pollution. What changes, if any, would you recommend? Why?

18. **Laundry product research.** To further research laundry product information, use reliable websites, such as the *American Cleaning Institute (ACI)*. Use school-approved Web application software to post links or reproducible information to the class blog or Web page.

19. **Investigate appliances.** Visit a local appliance center or home improvement center to investigate appliances. Compare features of different washers and dryers. Study prices and energy-efficiency ratings. Decide which would be a better buy. Share your findings with the class.

Academic Connections

20. **Reading.** Do an Internet search on source reduction in the cleaning product industry. What are cleaning product manufacturers doing to aid the environment? Prepare a report for the class.

21. **Writing.** Review the websites of two or more stores that sells laundry products. Compare prices of the various laundry products and what they are designed to do. Are the new combination detergents and products a better buy? Write a summary of your findings.

Workplace Links

22. **Design storage.** Presume your employer has assigned you to design the perfect closet—one that would solve all or most of the storage needs for all people. What would it look like? Use a CAD program or other design software to create your closet system. Save a copy of your design as a portfolio example.

23. **Communicate laundry information.** Newsletter editor, it is your responsibility to write a monthly article on clothing care for your apparel company's online newsletter. The target market for your company is the teen market. This month's topic is on laundry methods that support the environment. As you gather information for your article, remember to use *who, what, when, where, why,* and *how*. Keep your target audience in mind as you write your article.

Investigating Laundry Appliance Careers

With your interest in keeping apparel looking its best, does a career related to laundry-appliance design and engineering of interest to you? Perhaps a career as a public relations specialist who promotes energy-efficient laundry appliances may be another option.

In your career research, take the interactive *Career Scan* which is part of the FCCLA *Career Connection* program. This tool helps you rate your career development experiences and focus your attention on *Career Connection* units that meet your career goals. See your adviser for information as needed.

Chapter 14

Laundry and Dry Cleaning

Chapter Objectives

After studying this chapter, you will be able to

- **summarize** how using information on care labels can help you obtain good laundry results.
- **demonstrate** how to remove various types of stains.
- **summarize** how to properly and safely wash and dry clothing.
- **explain** the difference between pressing and ironing.
- **utilize** the services of a professional dry cleaner.

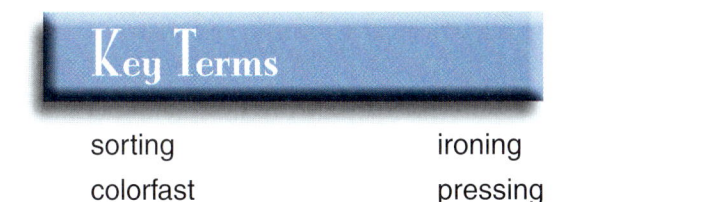

Key Terms

sorting
colorfast
ironing
pressing
dry cleaning

Reading with Purpose

Find a reliable magazine article on the Web that relates to this chapter. Read the article and write four questions that you have about the article. Next, read the text chapter. Based on what you read in the chapter, see if you can answer any of the questions you had about the magazine article.

In many families today, all of the adult members work outside the home. They have limited time and energy for household tasks that must be done. Everyone must help with these tasks. If you are like many teens, you perform certain household tasks on a regular basis. Perhaps you help with the family laundry. *Laundering* is the washing of clothes with water and laundry products. You can learn how to launder clothes so they get clean, look good, and last longer.

Understanding Care Labels

Before washing, drying, or ironing garments, you need to read the care labels. You often find care labels at the center neckline or in a seam. They are permanently attached to garments. These are the manufacturers' recommended methods of safely caring for the garments. They are your best guide for what to do and what not to do. See **14-1** for an explanation of these terms.

Prior to 1972, there were no care labels in garments. Instructions for care were on the hangtags consumers removed before wearing the garments. In 1972, the Federal Trade Commission (FTC) issued the Care Labeling Rule. This law required the manufacturers of most wearing apparel to attach permanent labels to their products. The labels had to give clear and complete directions for regular care and maintenance.

Understanding Care Labels

	When label reads...it means:
Machine Washable	**Machine wash**—Wash, bleach, dry, and press by any customary method including commercial laundering and dry cleaning. **Home launder only**—Same as above, but do not use commercial laundering. **No chlorine bleach**—Do not use chlorine bleach. Oxygen bleach may be used. **No bleach**—Do not use any type of bleach. **Cold wash; cold rinse**—Use cold water from tap, or cold washing machine setting. **Warm wash; warm rinse**—Use warm water, or warm washing machine setting. **Hot wash**—Use hot water, or hot washing machine setting. **No spin**—Remove wash load before final machine spin cycle. **Delicate cycle; gentle cycle**—Use appropriate machine setting; otherwise wash by hand. **Durable press; permanent press**—Use appropriate machine setting; otherwise use warm wash, cold rinse, and short spin cycle. **Wash separately**—Wash alone or with like colors.
Non-Machine Washing	**Hand wash**—Launder only by hand in lukewarm (hand comfortable) water. May be bleached, may be dry-cleaned. **Hand wash only**—Same as above, but do not dry-clean. **Hand wash separately**—Hand-wash alone or with like colors. **No bleach**—Do not use bleach. **Damp wipe**—Clean surface with damp cloth or sponge
Home Drying	**Tumble dry**—Dry in tumble dryer at specified setting–high, medium, low, or no heat. **Tumble dry; remove promptly**—Same as above, but in absence of cool-down cycle, remove at once when tumbling stops. **Drip-dry**—Hang wet and allow to dry. **Line dry**—Hang damp and allow to dry. **No wring; no twist**—Hang dry, drip-dry, or dry flat only. Handle to prevent wrinkles and distortion. **Dry flat**—Lay garment on flat surface. **Block to dry**—Maintain original size and shape while drying.

(Continued)

14-1 This explanation of care terms will help you understand them. *American Apparel Manufacturers Assoc.*

Care instructions are printed on labels or woven into them. The instructions may be printed directly on the fabric, but must remain readable for the life of the garment. Many manufacturers print the care instructions on the

Understanding Care Labels	
	When label reads...it means:
Ironing or Pressing	Cool iron—Set iron at lowest setting. Warm iron—Set iron at medium setting. Hot iron—Set iron at hot setting. Do not iron—Do not iron or press with heat. Steam iron—Iron or press with steam. Iron damp—Dampen garment before ironing.
Miscellaneous	Dry-clean only—Garment should be dry-cleaned only. No dry-clean—Use recommended care instructions. No dry-cleaning materials to be used.

14-1 *Continued.*

backs of their own brand labels. This is legal if the labels state *Care Instructions on Reverse Side*. Exemptions may be granted for

- articles, such as hosiery, in which utility or appearance may be impaired by permanent labels
- articles that are completely washable under normal circumstances
- articles that are intended to sell at retail for $3.00 or less
- apparel made of suede or leather

In 1984, the Care Labeling Rule was revised. The information listed on labels had to be more detailed and complete. A label that recommends washing, for example, must state the washing method. Only a few exceptions were allowed.

The rule requires labels to include the following information:

- safe washing method (by hand or machine)
- safe water temperature (cold, warm, or hot)
- safe drying method (machine, hang, or lay flat)
- safe drying temperature (low, medium, or high)
- type of bleach (if all types of bleach cannot be used)
- safe use of iron and ironing temperature when necessary (cool, warm, or do not iron)

The care label should warn consumers about cleaning method(s) that cannot be used. If a care label gives washing instructions, but does not warn against dry-cleaning, the garment should be dry-cleanable. If a dry-cleanable article can be damaged by particular cleaning solvents, the label must specify the best type of solvent to use.

In 1997, the Care Labeling Rule was revised to allow manufacturers to use standard care symbols in place of words on labels. These symbols are shown in **14-2**. This allows American-made products to be marketed with the same care labels throughout North America. Consumers make fewer laundry mistakes because of the Care Labeling Rule.

Care Label Symbols

Wash

MACHINE WASH CYCLE
- Normal
- Permanent Press/wrinkle resistant
- Gentle/delicate
- Hand wash

WATER TEMPERATURE
- ••• Hot (50C/120F)
- •• Warm (40C/105F)
- • Cold/cool (30C/85F)

WARNING SIGNS
- Do not wash
- Do not wring

Dry

TUMBLE DRY CYCLE
- Dry
- Normal
- Permanent Press/wrinkle resistant
- Gentle/delicate

HEAT SETTING
- High
- Medium
- Low
- No heat/air

SPECIAL INSTRUCTIONS
- Line dry/hang to dry
- Drip dry
- Dry flat
- In the shade

WARNING SIGNS
- Do not tumble dry
- Do not dry (used with do not wash)

Bleach

BLEACH SYMBOLS
- Any bleach (when needed)
- Only non-chlorine bleach (when needed)

WARNING SIGNS
- Do not bleach

Iron

IRON—DRY OR STEAM
- Iron
- High
- Medium
- Low

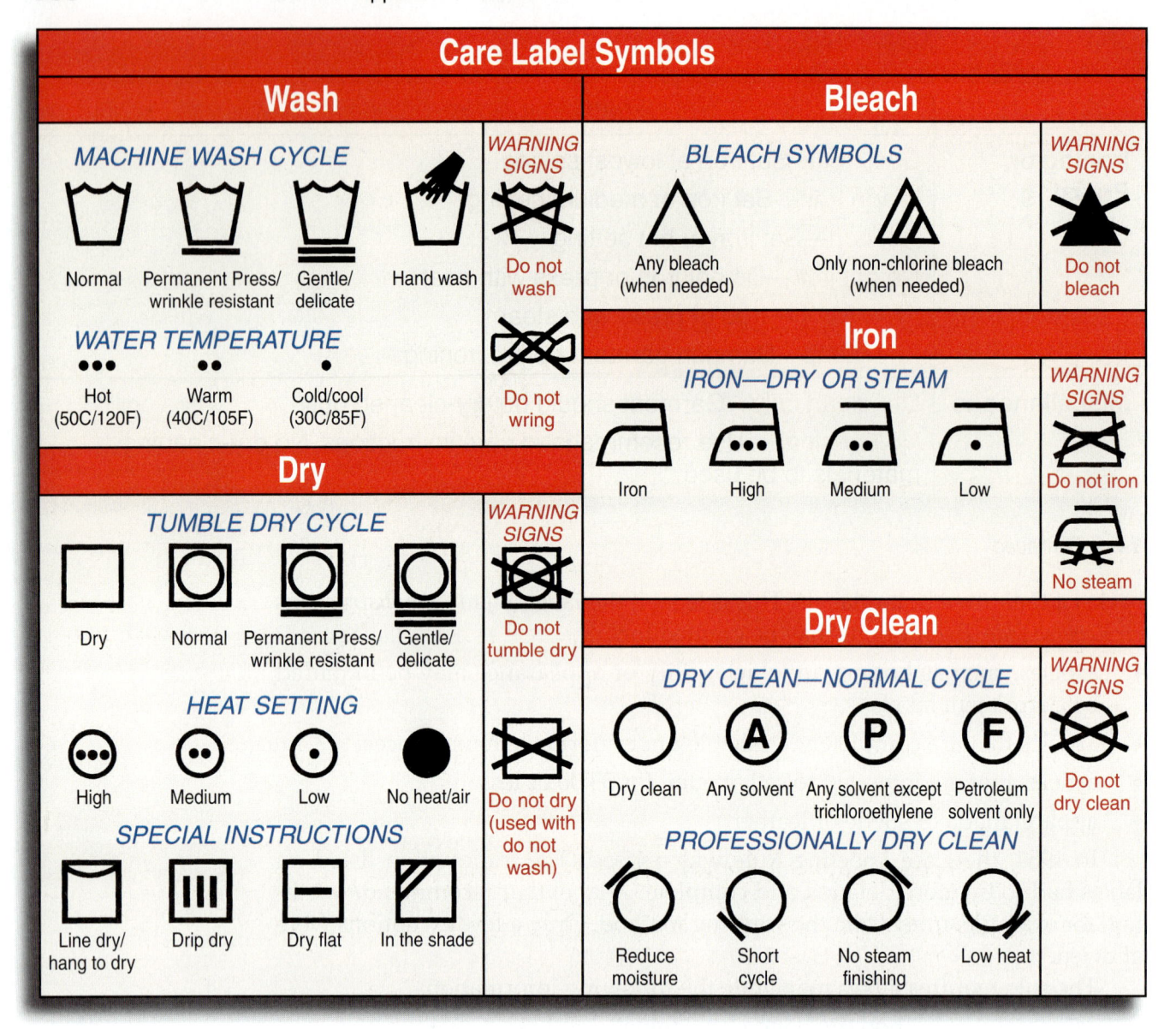

WARNING SIGNS
- Do not iron
- No steam

Dry Clean

DRY CLEAN—NORMAL CYCLE
- Dry clean
- A — Any solvent
- P — Any solvent except trichloroethylene
- F — Petroleum solvent only

PROFESSIONALLY DRY CLEAN
- Reduce moisture
- Short cycle
- No steam finishing
- Low heat

WARNING SIGNS
- Do not dry clean

14-2 Look for these symbols on care labels in your clothes. *Federal Trade Commission*

Preparing Clothes for Washing

Look over each garment carefully before washing it. Remove all items from the pockets. A facial tissue left in a pocket will cover clothes with lint.

Remove or secure fasteners. Close zippers, fasten hooks and eyes, and shut buttons. Sometimes fasteners can be secured inside a pocket. This prevents damage to the washer basket, to other clothes, and to the item. If a large metal fastener or buckle cannot be removed from an item, it can be tucked inside the fabric and basted in place.

Loosely tie together long belts, strings, sashes, or stockings. Turn knits inside out to prevent snagging. Shake dirt from cuffs of slacks. See **14-3** for tips on preparing clothes for washing.

Pretreatment and Stain Removal

Check garments for stains and remove them before washing. Stains can set permanently if stained garments are exposed to hot water and dryer heat.

There are water-based stains and oil-based stains. Water-based stains include fruit, vegetables, soft drinks, coffee, and tea. Oil-based stains include cosmetics, grease, candle wax, motor oil, and tar. Water-based stains are

Preparing Clothes for Washing

- Make sure all pockets are empty. Turn them inside out.
- Turn down cuffs and brush away lint and dirt.
- Remove pins, buckles, and other hard or sharp objects to avoid scratching the washer basket or snagging other items.
- Close zippers and fasten snaps and hooks to avoid snagging other items in the load.
- Tie strings and cords so they will not tangle.
- Mend tears, loose hems, and seams. Sew on missing buttons and fasteners.

14-3 Taking steps like these before washing can pay off with better results. *Shutterstock*

removed using a *wet process* (one with water), usually detergent and water. Stains are generally soaked in cool water for a period of time. To remove oil-based stains, use a *dry process* (one without water) with a solvent or spot remover if you cannot wash the garment.

Many oil-based stains can be removed from washable garments if pretreated with a liquid laundry detergent. First, wet the stained area. Then pour undiluted detergent on it. Wait a few minutes before washing or rinsing the garment. You may need to soak it longer (up to 30 minutes) or use a heavy-duty detergent.

If you cannot wash a garment, use a solvent or spot remover. When using a solvent or dry-cleaning fluid, first place the stained area on an absorbent surface—a soft cloth, paper towels, or facial tissues. Put the stained side down so the stain will move out of the garment, not through it.

Dampen a soft cloth or pad of cotton with the solvent. Apply the solvent to the stain using a soft brushing or tapping motion. Work outward from the center. Brush the edges often to prevent a circle from forming around the stained area. Frequently changing the absorbent pad under the fabric will prevent the stain from going back into the fabric.

Stain Removal Cautions

Keep the following safety precautions in mind when removing stains:

- Read instructions on all products and keep them in their original labeled containers.
- Always store cleaning materials beyond the reach of children.
- Do not mix or combine stain removal products, such as ammonia and chlorine bleach. Some mixtures can release harmful, sometimes deadly, gases.
- Solvents, such as cleaning fluids and denatured alcohol, should be used only in well-ventilated rooms. Keep them away from open flames and pilot lights.
- Clothes treated with solvents should be rinsed before washing.

Sorting Clothes

Sorting clothes involves grouping them according to how they should be laundered. Sorting is necessary to get good results in laundering. When sorting clothes:

Focus on Technology

What's New in Cleaning Clothes?

While textile manufacturers are finding new ways to improve stain and wrinkle resistance, manufacturers of laundry appliances are coming up with new innovations, too. Appliance manufacturers are continually developing new features to improve the performance of washing machines and dryers. The following are some of the latest features available on today's washing machines:

- **Steam.** To improve overall cleaning, remove stains, and sanitize fabrics, steam is the latest method of choice. Steam can remove such stains as ketchup, grape juice, grease, and grass, thus saving the time spent in pre-treating clothes. Steam can also be used into the wash cycle to help loosen dirt and hard-to-remove stains. A steam-only tumbling cycle removes wrinkles and odors from clothes. This cycle can also be used to remove stubborn wrinkles from clothes when they are left in the dryer from the day before.

- **Silver ions.** Washers that use silver ions (small particles of silver) can sanitize clothes even when washed in cold water. The introduction of silver ions into the wash water removes 99 percent of odor-causing bacteria for up to 30 days. This is ideal for delicates, colors, and special care items that can be damaged by bleach and high water temperatures.

- **Temperature controls.** Automatic temperature controls allow the washer to determine the right temperature needed to wash clothes. Previously you could select from just three to four water temperatures. Now washers select the temperature for you. In addition, some washers have internal water heaters that can boost the water temperature to 160°F to help achieve sanitation.

- **Sensors.** Instead of selecting a desired water level yourself, sensors can detect how much water to use based on the size of the load.

- **Overnight feature.** An *overnight ready* feature allows you to put a small load of laundry into the washer and remove it 8 hours later, washed, dried, and ready to wear. There is no need to move the laundry from the washer to a dryer.

Some of the features found on today's dryers include the following:

- **Moisture sensors.** Moisture sensors minimize the possibility of over-drying your clothes. Over-drying can damage or shrink clothes. This feature also saves energy because the dryer shuts off automatically when the clothes are dry.

- **Drying rack.** A drum rack to use when drying items you do not want to tumble dry, such as athletic shoes.

All of these features are available today, but they can add substantially to the cost of the appliance. Decide carefully what features will benefit you the most when selecting these appliances.

- *Sort by color.* This is the most important consideration, **14-4**. Avoid mixing a colored item that is not colorfast with a white load. (**Colorfast** means that an item retains its original color without fading or running.) Separate laundry into several groups: (1) white or white-background prints that are colorfast, (2) light colors, (3) medium and bright colors, and (4) dark colors. If a garment's care label says it should be washed separately, the item is likely not colorfast and will probably lose color. Be sure to wash it separately, or with similar colors, until you are sure it will not leave dye in the water.

- *Sort by construction and fabric type.* Separate loosely knit or woven fabrics, sheers, laces, and delicate garments from sturdy items. Wash more delicate items separately because they require a shorter wash time and gentle agitation. Also separate heavy lint-producers from other items. These include flannel pajamas, terry cloth robes, and fuzzy sweatshirts. They will transfer lint to other items, especially dark socks and clothing made of corduroy and permanent press fabrics.
- *Sort by amount and kind of soil.* Place heavily soiled or greasy clothes in a separate pile. If washed with lightly soiled items, they will make them dingy. Whites may look gray or yellow, and colors may become dull.

If possible, include large and small garments in each pile. This allows for better washing action.

If you have a heavily soiled, white garment, it may be wise to wash it by itself. Many light-colored, manufactured fibers (especially nylon) absorb dirt from wash water and become gray or dingy.

Washing Clothes

After sorting the laundry into baskets, or wash loads, you are ready to begin. Most laundry can be washed in automatic washers. Some will require hand washing.

Machine Washing

For best results, use the following guidelines when washing clothes with a traditional top-loading machine. The order of these steps may vary with front-loading HE washers. It is always best to read and follow the manufacturer's recommendations for the washing machine you use.

14-4 This woman needs to sort her laundry—a necessary step before washing clothes. *Shutterstock*

Choose and Add Laundry Products

A variety of products are available for use in machine washing. First, you need a detergent to remove dirt. Read and follow the directions on the product's label for best results. Measure the recommended amount of detergent using the specially designed bottle cap or other device provided with the detergent. If a device is not provided, use a standard measuring cup. Pour the detergent into the washer tub or detergent dispenser following the manufacturer's instructions.

The amount of detergent recommended is based on an average load. This is five to seven pounds of clothes, moderately soiled, and washed in moderately hard water. If any of these conditions are not met, adjust the amount of detergent.

When using other laundry additives, follow the container instructions for their use. Add some products, such as oxygen bleaches, to the wash water before putting clothes in the washer. Fabric softeners are usually added to the rinse water. Many washers have dispensers for these products.

Load the Washer

When you load the washer, be careful not to add too many clothes. It is better to underload than to overload a washer. Garments need room to move about easily in the water and detergent to get their cleanest. Do not wind large items around the agitator or the tub. They can become tangled.

If the garments are heavily soiled, wash only a few at a time. Bulky clothes take up room even if they are lightweight. If you launder a blanket, wash it by itself.

Select the Water Level and Temperature

In agitator-type washers, the water level should match the size of the load. There should be ample water for the movement of the clothes. Choose a lower water level for smaller wash loads. This saves energy and water. High-efficiency (HE) washers are designed to use less water.

The water temperatures you select will be based on the items you are washing, **14-5**. Water temperature affects cleaning, wrinkling, and color and size retention. Hot water (120°F and above) does the best job of removing soil and disinfecting. Hot water, however, can cause colors to run and garments to shrink. It also increases wrinkling. Use hot water with sturdy whites, diapers, colorfast items, and heavily soiled, permanent-press items.

In contrast to using hot water, using warm water (about 105°F) produces less shrinkage, color loss, and wrinkling. Water at this temperature, however, does not sanitize clothes. To sanitize clothes; you need to add a disinfectant to the wash water. The most common disinfectant is chlorine bleach, but disinfectants containing pine oil can also be used. Use warm water for moderately soiled, permanent press, and non-colorfast items. Some silks, washable woolens, and manufactured fibers are washed in warm water.

Cold water (85°F or cooler) does not clean as well as hot or warm water. Cold water does reduce wrinkling and color-fading. Wash only non-colorfast and lightly soiled items in cold water. Cold water is not recommended for use in HE washers.

There are cold-water detergents specifically formulated for washing all types of clothes. These detergents have improved in recent years. Studies show

Correct Water Temperatures	
Water Temperature	**Items to Wash**
Hot Water	Sturdy whites, diapers, colorfast items, and heavily soiled permanent-press items.
Warm Water	Moderately soiled, permanent press, and non-colorfast items. Silks, washable woolens, and manufactured fibers.
Cold Water	Non-colorfast, lightly soiled items. Dark colored items that are lightly soiled.

14-5 Laundering clothes in correct water temperatures will help clothes retain their colors and appearance.

that some cold-water brands clean all clothes as well as general-purpose detergents. Some people use cold-water detergents to reduce their energy use.

Using cold water for rinsing reduces wrinkles. It also helps to conserve energy used in heating water. Even when using hot or warm water for the wash cycle, use cold water for rinsing to save energy.

Select the Agitation Speed or Wash Cycle

Choose an agitation speed or wash cycle suitable for the items you are washing. Most washing machines give you a selection of wash cycles to choose from. Basic wash cycles include *regular* or *normal*, *delicate*, and *permanent press*. Other machines have a "wash speed selection" with *regular* and *gentle* selections. Some washers have as many as 10 automatic wash cycles.

In traditional top-loading washers, agitation is necessary for soil removal. Use normal or regular agitation for all but delicate items, which can be damaged by too much agitation. Choose gentle speeds for delicate loads. The permanent press cycle usually has normal agitation, but includes a cool-down rinse to minimize wrinkling. Wrinkling of permanent press items may occur at higher speeds.

> **Laundry Safety**
> NEVER put your hand inside the washer while it is running. Motors are powerful, and parts move at high speed. *You can be hurt!*

In front-loading HE models, the door is locked shut after the wash cycle starts. Most top-loading washers shut off when the door is opened. Still, never put your hand inside the washer until it has stopped. For a review of steps in laundering, see **14-6**.

Hand Washing

A garment's care label may state that it should be hand washed. Hand washing is recommended for various reasons. A garment may have delicate trims or colors that run when washed. A garment that is loosely knitted, such as a sweater, may look better and last longer if washed by hand. Many wool garments have care labels that suggest they be washed by hand. Machine washing may cause them to shrink or the fibers to become matted.

When you wash clothes by hand, wash only one or two garments at a time. Pretreat spots and stains. Use the water temperature suited to the fabric. Add the detergent in the amount suggested on the package label. Swish the detergent around with your hand until it has dissolved. Force the water through the garment by squeezing it several times with your hands. This dissolves the soil and lifts it out of the garment into the water. Badly soiled areas may need to be rubbed between your fingers to remove the soil.

Rinse several times to get all of the detergent or soap out of the garment. Rinse as many times as necessary until the water is clear and no suds remain. Rolling the garment in a large towel can remove most of the water. To dry the garment, either hang it on a rustproof hanger or lay it flat on a clean towel according to manufacturer's directions.

> **Steps in Laundering**
>
> 1. Read care labels.
> 2. Treat spots, stains, and very dirty areas.
> 3. Sort clothes.
> 4. Choose and add the right amount of laundry products.
> 5. Load the washer.
> 6. Select the water level (unless the machine does so automatically).
> 7. Select the appropriate water temperatures.
> 8. Select the appropriate wash cycle.

14-6 If you follow these steps, you will have good laundry results.

Drying Clothes

Most clothes that are washed together can be dried together. An automatic dryer is the easiest and quickest way to dry clothes. Clothes can also be dried without using a dryer. Line drying, drip-drying, and drying flat are other recommended methods of drying clothes.

Machine Drying

Drying clothes using an automatic dryer seems simple. Just throw the clothes in, set the dial, and come back later. Doing a good job, however, requires a few more steps.

First, learn how to use the dryer. Study the information from the manufacturer that came with the dryer, if it is available.

Before putting garments into the dryer, read their care labels. Some garments cannot be dried in a dryer. Labels may recommend other methods of drying, such as line drying, drip-drying, or drying flat.

Labels also include a recommended dryer temperature, such as high, low, or no heat. High temperatures can ruin buttons and trims and shrink some clothes. Cotton garments can withstand higher temperatures than those made of manufactured fibers. Set controls for *regular*. Fabrics with wrinkle-resistant finishes require low temperatures. Heat can dissolve the chemicals used for these finishes. Set the control on *permanent press*. The permanent press cycle provides a cool down period at the end to minimize wrinkling. For fine fabrics that require more gentle heat and tumbling, set the control to *delicate*. Do not overload the dryer. Overloading the dryer causes clothing to become wrinkled and twisted.

An average load of clothes needs about 25 to 30 minutes of drying time. Heavier items, such as jeans, sweatshirts, and towels, may need more than 30 minutes. Lingerie and other delicate garments require a lower temperature and about 10 to 15 minutes of drying time.

Remove the clothes as soon as the dryer stops, 14-7. This prevents wrinkling and most garments will be ready to wear. If clothes lie in the bottom of the dryer until they are cool, they will probably need to be ironed. Some dryers have a wrinkle-control cycle that keeps the dryer tumbling until the laundry can be removed. Be sure to clean the lint filter after each use.

Hang any garments you can on hangers. Smooth the seams, collars, and cuffs. Fold flat items—such as T-shirts, towels, and sheets—while they are still warm to prevent even more wrinkles. Clothes should be completely dry before they are put away. Dampness can cause mildew and foul odors.

Line Drying

Many care labels suggest line drying or state *hang to dry*. This can be done outside on a clothesline. If your home does not have a yard or clothesline, you can dry line-dry items indoors using plastic hangers. Or you can string up a temporary clothesline in a basement or over a bathtub. If you suffer from allergies, you may want to hang garments indoors. Items dried outside may pick up pollen from the air.

As you hang the clothes, shake them, smooth out the wrinkles, and straighten the seams. When wet clothes are hung using clothespins, the pins can leave imprints. To minimize imprints, pin clothes in places, such as the bottoms of shirts or along waistbands, where imprints will not show.

If the garments are outside, take them from the line as soon as they are dry. Long exposure to the sun may cause some clothes to fade.

Flat Drying

Some garments cannot be hung to dry or tumbled in a dryer because they will shrink or stretch out of shape. Their care labels may state that they should be laid flat to dry. First remove much of the rinse water by rolling the garment in a towel and pressing out the water. The garment should then be unrolled and shaped on a clean, flat, absorbent surface, such as a clean bath towel.

Removable drying racks are a feature with some automatic dryers for flat drying garments. The garments are laid on the racks and the dryer temperature is set to the appropriate setting.

Drip-Drying

In drip-drying, garments are not squeezed, wrung, or twisted to remove the water. After rinsing, lift the garments from the water and place them on plastic or rustproof hangers. Hang garments over an area that will not be damaged by water. You may want to drip-dry garments over the bathtub, in the shower, or outdoors.

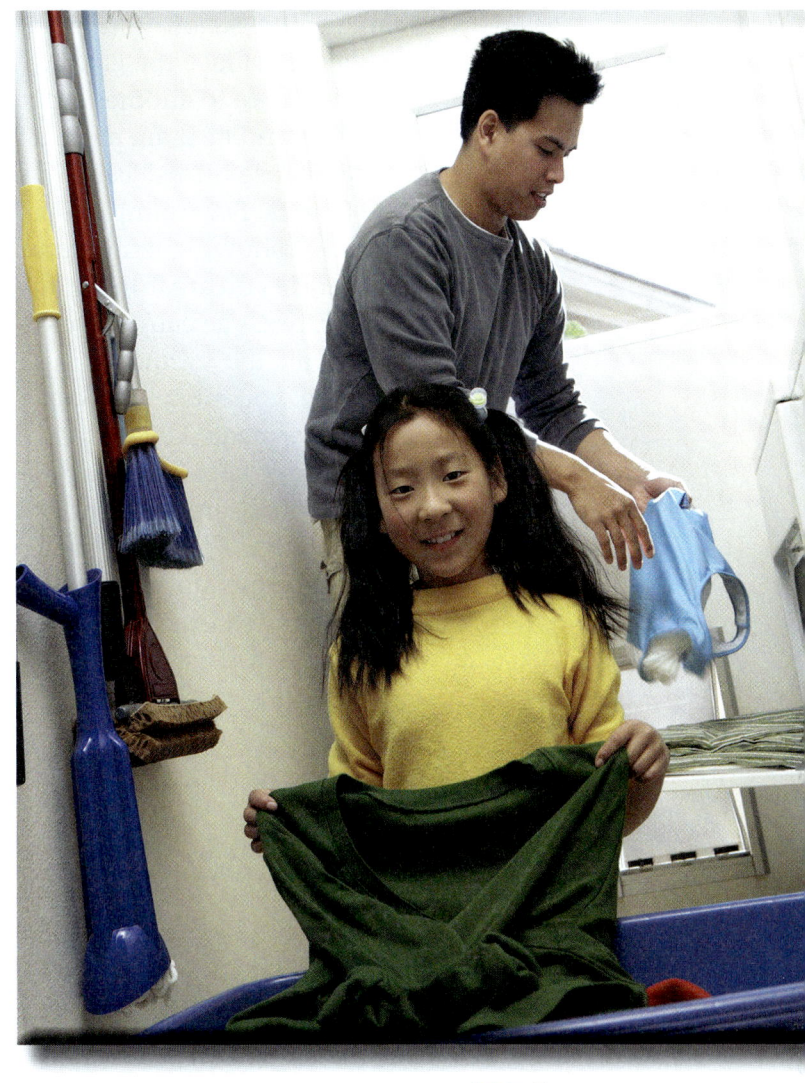

14-7 To prevent wrinkling, promptly remove clothing from the dryer and fold items neatly or hang them on hangers. *Shutterstock*

Pressing and Ironing

What is the difference between pressing and ironing? The terms are sometimes used to describe the same task.

After several washings, even minimum-care garments look better after ironing. **Ironing** is the process of removing wrinkles from damp, washable clothing. Heat and pressure are used to smooth the fabric. The iron is moved over the fabric in a gliding motion. Garments are dampened and then ironed after laundering.

Pressing is the process of removing wrinkles from clothing using steam and a lifting motion. The iron does not glide across the fabric. This could be done just before wearing a garment. It is used for wool items. Pressing is also done when people sew clothes. They press seams open after they sew them.

A steam iron makes the job easier. Some steam irons have spray buttons that supply an extra mist of moisture when pushed. This helps remove stubborn wrinkles. If a steam iron is not available, ironing using a damp cloth works equally well. Place the cloth carefully over a small section of a garment, iron, and then move to another section.

Steam and heat are more effective than pressure in removing wrinkles, but they can cause burns. Use irons and steam irons safely. Heat can also damage some fabrics. For example, some synthetics melt under a hot iron. Most irons have a dial showing temperature settings according to fabric types. Set the dial to the fabric you are ironing. If you think the heat of the iron may damage your garment, press a seam first as a test.

Iron all the garments that are delicate or require low-temperatures first. Otherwise, you must wait for the temperature of the iron to adjust up and down between garments. Cottons and linens require higher temperatures. Ironing on the wrong side of fabrics prevents shine on the face of the garment.

Iron small areas, such as sleeves, collars, and cuffs, before going to the large sections. There will be less wrinkling of parts already ironed. Iron with the grain of the fabric (usually from top to bottom). The garment will be less likely to stretch out of shape. Use a light, gliding motion. Let the heat of the iron remove the wrinkles, **14-8**.

Firmly insert the plug into the electrical outlet before turning on the iron. When finished, turn off the iron. Unplug it by grasping the plug and not by yanking the cord. Yanking the cord can damage it, leading to a possible electrical shock.

Dry Cleaning

The care labels on some clothes state they must be dry-cleaned instead of laundered. **Dry cleaning** is a process of cleaning clothes using organic solvents instead of water. This type of cleaning is done by professional dry cleaners.

Garments that must be dry-cleaned include those made of wool and silk, as well as many suits, coats, and some dresses. Professional dry cleaners can also clean special materials such as leather, suede, fur, and imitations of these materials.

Professional dry-cleaning services can be expensive. You can cut costs by doing some dry cleaning at home in your own dryer. Special kits can be purchased that contain all the supplies you need, including a stain remover. One popular kit provides a reusable bag in which you place up to four garments and a specially moistened cloth. The chemicals in the cloth are activated by the heat of the dryer. Within 30 minutes, clothes are smooth and most odors and stains removed.

14-8 Use a gliding motion when ironing, and let heat instead of pressure do the work for you. *Corbis*

Laundry Safety

Follow these safety precautions when using a steam iron:
- Fill the iron with water before plugging it in. Do not overfill or the water may boil out.
- Make sure you cannot trip over the iron cord or pull the iron off the board.
- Keep your hands and face away from the steam. Steam is extremely dangerous!
- Place the iron on its heel rest after each use.
- Turn off the iron and allow it to cool before unplugging it. Unplug the iron after each use.
- Empty any remaining water before storing the iron.

Professional Dry Cleaning

Professional dry cleaners use large machines that look like washing machines. The clothes are placed in the machine and are tumbled. The chemical solvent flows through the clothes and removes the dirt and soil. After a period of time, the solvent drains from the machine, and the clothes tumble dry.

Professional dry cleaners remove stains and spots before garments are cleaned. Different stains require different chemicals and cleaning methods. This is why it is important to point out stains to the dry cleaner and, if possible, identify them, 14-9. Be sure to point out light-colored stains. If overlooked, these stains could turn brown with the heat used during dry cleaning.

Professional dry cleaners offer services other than cleaning. For example, some plastic trims and buttons must be removed from garments before cleaning because the chemical solvent may melt or misshape them. A dry cleaner will remove them and then replace them after the garments are cleaned. If a water-repellent coat no longer repels water, the cleaners can add a new finish for an additional cost.

Dry cleaners press most garments after they are cleaned. Pressing is done with special equipment. Garments are placed on forms. Steam is released from inside the forms and blown through the garments. Wrinkles are pressed or blown out in this manner. Garments that have pleats and creases, such as skirts and pants, are pressed with large pressing machines that use pressure and steam.

14-9 Professional dry cleaners remove stains and spots from garments. Identify stains when you drop garments off. *Shutterstock*

Summary

- Garment care labels provide the information you need to properly care for your clothes. Read them for washing, drying, ironing, and dry-cleaning recommendations.
- Check for stains and remove them before washing. Otherwise, they may set permanently into fabrics exposed to hot water and dryer heat.
- Washing clothes involves making many decisions. Laundry is sorted into piles and various laundry products are used. The appropriate wash cycles are selected, as well as water temperatures for washing and rinsing. Some washing machines require users to select water levels.
- Clothes can be dried using machine drying, line drying, flat drying, or drip-drying. Some garments require ironing.
- Some clothes need to be dry-cleaned. You can use a professional dry cleaner, or do it yourself using a clothes dryer and a dry-cleaning kit.

Graphic Organizer

Use the spider diagram to note the methods for drying clothes. List two key points for each method.

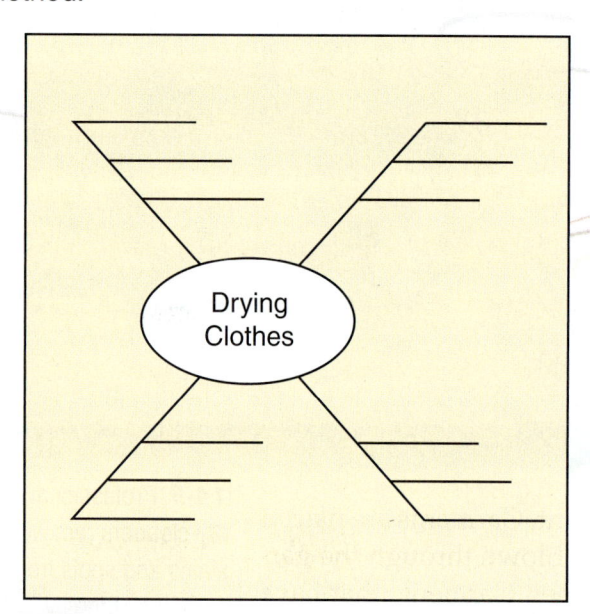

Review the Facts

1. What change was made in the Care Labeling Rule in 1997?
2. Remove _____ stains by the wet process and _____ stains by the dry process.
3. Give two safety precautions you should use when removing stains.
4. What three factors determine how clothes should be sorted before washing?
5. Why should a heavily soiled white garment be washed separately?
6. Which water temperature does the best job of removing soil and disinfecting?
7. Give an important safety rule you should always remember when loading a washer.
8. Why should permanent press garments be dried at low temperatures with a cool-down period at the end?
9. Contrast ironing and pressing.
10. When having your clothes dry-cleaned, why is it important to point out any stains to the dry cleaner?

Think Critically

11. **Make inferences.** Assume someone removed all of the care labels from your clothes. Make inferences about what process would you use to determine how to care for your clothes.
12. **Assess outcomes.** Have you ever had a laundry disaster? Describe what happened and assess the outcomes. Then describe what you should have done to avoid this outcome.
13. **Compare and contrast.** Compare the cost of owning laundry equipment versus doing your laundry in a commercial establishment. Discuss advantages and disadvantages.
15. **Identify evidence.** Investigate the environmental concerns regarding dry cleaning solvents. What evidence can you find for or against the current use of dry cleaning solvents? Discuss your findings with the class.

Apparel Applications

16. **Examine labels.** Bring a variety of garments to class. In groups, examine the care labels and describe how to clean each garment.
17. **Garment care blog.** Locate examples of garments ruined as a result of improper clothing care methods. Take digital photos of the garments and use a school-approved Web-based application to create a blog display of these items for class. Collaborate with your classmates online about how the damage to the clothes could have been prevented.
18. **Demonstrate stain removal.** Obtain three 8-inch by 8-inch swatches of different fabrics—permanent press, cotton or linen, and wool. Stain each fabric with the same food stain. Allow the stains to set for at least 15 minutes. Using the text guidelines, demonstrate to the class how to remove the stain from each fabric. Note the products and procedures you used for removing the stains. From which fabric was the stain most easily removed. Why?
19. **Summarize garment care.** Write a summary explaining how you would care for each of the following garments: A white 100 percent cotton shirt with a ballpoint-pen mark; beige wool slacks with a soda stain; a red hoodie with a ketchup stain.
20. **Determine product safety.** Assemble a variety of laundry products. Read the safety precautions on the labels. Formulate a set of safety guidelines when using certain laundry products.
21. **Demonstrate pressing and ironing.** Choose two garments that require pressing or ironing. Then demonstrate each technique for the class, when and why you are using each. What safety precautions should people follow when using either technique? Ask the class to critique your demonstration.

Academic Connections

22. **Math.** Locate prices of several brands of laundry detergent—both regular and high efficiency. Choose the same size packaging for each brand. Divide the total cost by the number of ounces in the packaging. This will give you the cost-per-ounce and help you determine which detergent is the better buy.
23. **Reading.** Use Internet and print resources to learn about self-service laundry facilities. How does the heavy-duty, commercial equipment function? Share your findings with the class.

Workplace Links

24. **Laundry article.** Presume you are an editor of the online newsletter for a major manufacturer of washers. Your assignment is to write an article on how to do laundry that is targeted at teens. What key points would you include to help them through the process?
25. **Field trip.** Tour a commercial laundry and dry-cleaning plant. Inspect products used. Ask questions about spot and stain removal. Have the workers explain what they are doing to preserve the environment and safely dispose of solvents. Is this a career that interests you? Why or why not?

Sustainable Laundry Practices

Use the FCCLA *Planning Process* to plan and carry out an FCCLA STAR Event *Illustrated Talk* on using sustainable laundry practices in the home. Use the FCCLA *STAR Events Manual* online for details on developing your project. See your adviser for information as needed.

Chapter 15

Repair, Redesign, and Recycle

Chapter Objectives

After studying this chapter, you will be able to

- **expand** your wardrobe by repairing, altering, redesigning, and recycling garments.
- **demonstrate** clothing repair techniques.
- **alter** garments to adjust their fit.
- **restyle** and update garments to better fit your wardrobe needs.
- **utilize** garment-redesigning methods such as dyeing, painting, or adding appliqués, embroidery, and trims.
- **summarize** ways to recycle clothes.

Key Terms

patching
redesigning
restyling
embroidery
appliqué
fusible fabric
tie-dyeing
patchwork

Reading with Purpose

Rewrite each chapter objective as a question. As you read, look for the answers to each question. Write the answers in your own words.

Do you have garments in your closet that hang there month after month without being worn? Perhaps some of these items have loose buttons, rips, or tears that need to be repaired. Others are in good condition, but are not worn because they are the wrong color or style. Perhaps other items have been outgrown.

You can save money and revive your wardrobe by learning how to repair, alter, redesign, and recycle. By applying your creative abilities and sewing skills, you can bring many garments back to life.

15-1 Some stitches came loose along a seam in this skirt. Repairing the seam right away means the skirt can be worn when needed. *Shutterstock*

Repairing Clothes

What do you do with your clothes that need repairs? Do you hide them in the back of your closet? A better solution is to repair the garments when you first notice problems. See **15-1**. If that is not possible, you should put them in a special place, along with the supplies you need to make repairs. Then when you have time, you can repair all of the items at once.

269

Small holes and rips often grow in size. Repairs tend to become more difficult to make the longer they are delayed. This is especially true if damaged clothes are not repaired before laundering. After washing, rips and holes are often larger. Stretching may also occur.

Fix That Hole

When a hole appears in a garment, it needs to be patched. **Patching** is the technique of sewing a small piece of fabric over a hole in a garment. Patches are often used on garments to add color and interest. No one has to know about the holes beneath the patches.

Patches come from many sources. For example, a decorative appliqué can be used to patch a small hole. Leftover scraps of fabric can be cut into various shapes and used as patches. Iron-on materials, sold in fabric and craft stores, can be used to cover holes quickly and easily. Choose them in colors that match garments or try new designs.

First, trim the damaged portion of the garment to a square or rectangle shape. Cut a fabric patch from a piece of similar or contrasting fabric. Make the patch about 1 inch larger than the hole it is to repair. Turn under the edges around the patch, and topstitch for extra strength. See **15-2**. A sewing machine gives faster and stronger repairs than hand sewing, but you can use either method.

Repair That Rip

A few stitches by hand, or with a sewing machine, may be all that is needed to repair a rip. If the rip is in an area that receives much stress, such as the seat or crotch of pants, a double row of stitches is a better choice. Use a double strand of thread for extra strength if you sew by hand. If the color of the fabric does not match that of your thread exactly, go with a darker shade rather than a lighter one.

Look at **15-3**. The seam in the pants is ripped. To mend the rip, turn the pants inside out. Pin the seam together and sew with short stitches. A second row of stitches placed close to the first row will reinforce the seam to prevent future rips. See **15-4**. Do not pull stitches too tight if you are hand sewing. Tight stitches may break again under stress.

15-2 After the garment edges around the patch have been turned back, topstitching is done to add strength.
Goodheart-Willcox Publisher

15-3 Rips in a seam are easy to repair. *Frank Zosky, Photographer*

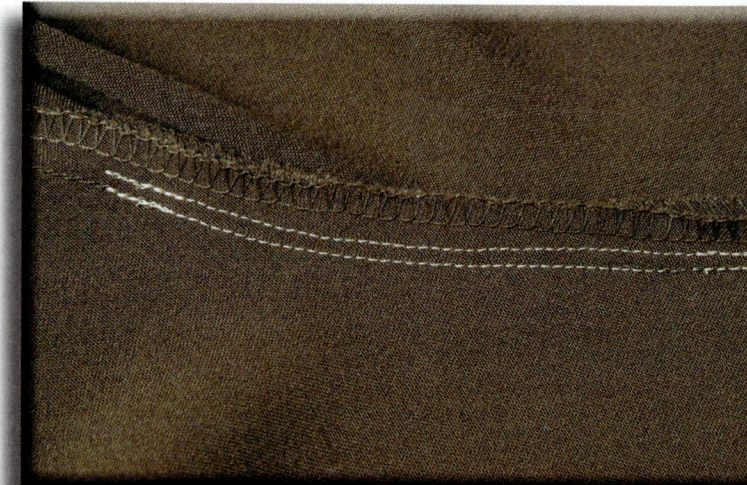

15-4 A double row of stitching reinforces the seam. (Note: Lighter thread used for illustration purposes only.)
Frank Zosky, Photographer

Another quick way to fix a tear or hole in a garment is to use the zigzag stitch on a sewing machine. A patch is not needed. Simply stitch the edges of the tear together. This is quick and easy to do, but should only be used on work or play clothes.

Quick Repairs

Other quick repairs include the following:

- *Loose buttons.* When loose buttons fall off, they are often lost for good. It is difficult to find buttons that are identical to lost ones. When buttons are loose, resew them immediately. If you do not have time, remove the loose buttons and put them where you can find them later. See 15-5 for a list of steps to sew on buttons.
- *Loose fasteners.* Hooks and eyes, as well as snaps, should be kept in good repair on your clothing. Study 15-6 to see how they should be attached.
- *Loose hems.* Hems often come loose. People often catch the heels of their shoes in hems and rip out the stitching. Many ready-to-wear garment hems are sewn using a chain stitch, which can easily unravel when a loose thread is pulled. Fortunately, restitching a hem is an easy repair. Use a fine needle with a single strand of thread that is knotted at one end. Then restitch using any of the following: a hemming stitch, slip stitch, blind stitch, or catch stitch. Overlap the old stitching with the new. Do not pull the stitches too tight.
- *Snags.* A snag in a knitted garment, such as a sweater, is usually simple to repair. A snag should be repaired right away because if it catches on something, it can become a big hole. To repair a snag, insert a small crochet hook, snag fixer, or needle threader through the wrong side of the fabric directly under the snag. Hook the loop of the snag and pull it through to the underside. Then smooth any puckers by gently pulling the fabric.

Having a clothing repair box can save you time and effort. Most repairs can be made in a few minutes if the equipment is handy. Scissors, needles, buttons, snaps, hooks and eyes, light and dark thread, and a thimble are some of the items you need.

(A) Button placement: Close opening of garment. To mark placement of button, place a pin through buttonhole. Slip buttonhole over the pin to open.

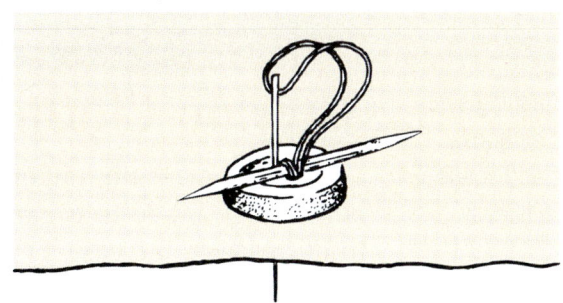

(B) Sew-through button: Place a pin or toothpick on top of the button. Bring needle and thread through the fabric and button, over the pin and back through the fabric. Repeat five or six times.

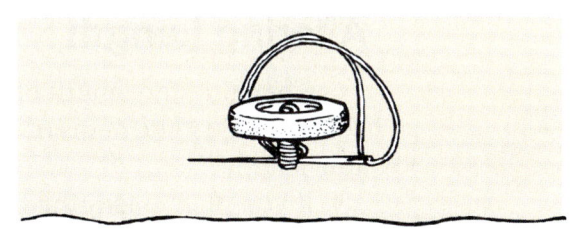

(C) Remove pin and pull button up. Bring threaded needle between garment and button. Wind thread around stitches several times to make a shank. (Shanks raise buttons from garment to allow room for the button hole to fit smoothly beneath it.) Pass thread to underside of garment and fasten securely.

(D) Shank button: Shank buttons need an additional thread shank, but it can be smaller than the shank for sew-through ones. Sew the button on loosely. Then wind the thread under the button to form the thread shank.

15-5 Mark the placement of the button. Then follow these steps to secure it.
Goodheart-Willcox Publisher

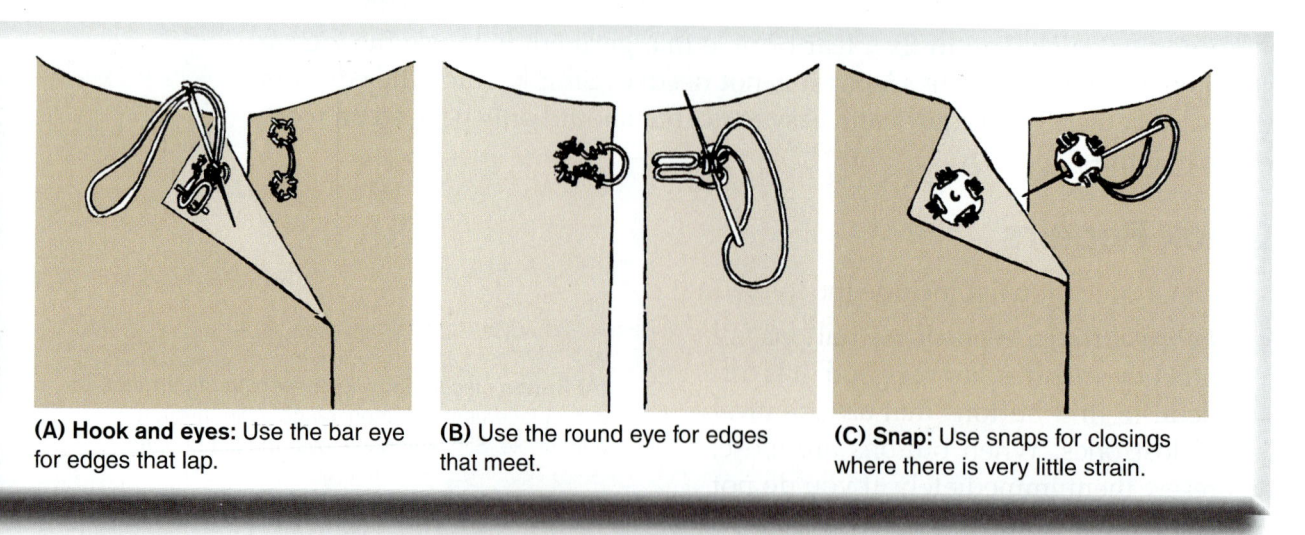

(A) Hook and eyes: Use the bar eye for edges that lap.

(B) Use the round eye for edges that meet.

(C) Snap: Use snaps for closings where there is very little strain.

15-6 Attaching such fasteners as hooks and eyes and snaps to clothing is easy.
Goodheart-Willcox Publisher

Altering Clothes

If a garment no longer fits well, it may need to be altered. An alteration is a change made to a garment so that it fits properly. A garment is altered to decrease or increase its length or width. A pair of slacks that are not worn because they are too long may be a candidate for alteration. They can be shortened. A nice skirt that is too loose or too tight in the hips may also be altered. Some simple alterations make garments fit better so you can enjoy wearing them more often.

Altering Length

Changing the length of a garment is one of the easiest alterations to make. You can adjust the hems of pants, dresses, skirts, tops, and sleeves to a comfortable length.

If you plan to lengthen a garment, be sure to check the existing hem allowance. It should be deep enough to allow for the extra length. If the hem allowance is too narrow, you may have to add wide hem facing tape to the garment edge. If you are shortening a garment, and the new hem is too deep, you may need to trim away some of the hem depth.

To alter the hem of a garment, remove the existing hem. Press out the crease. If you are lengthening the garment, be sure you can remove the crease in the fabric. To do so, you may have to clean the garment or use a spot remover. Next, try on the garment. Ask a friend or family member to pin the hem in place. Follow the instructions for hemming given later in the text.

Altering Width

Changing the garment width can be a minor or a complex task. Sometimes, all that is needed is to move a hook or button. Other times, both sides, or the front and back of a garment, need to be changed.

Remove the stitching in areas that need adjustment. Pin new seams in place. Be sure to evenly distribute the decrease or increase among all seams. The more seams a garment has, the easier it is to alter its width. Try on the garment, and check the fit.

When letting out a garment, or making it larger, sew the new seam outside the old seam in the seam allowance. It is important to always check the width of a seam allowance to be sure it is wide enough to sew a new seam. When taking in a garment, or making it smaller, sew the new seam inside the old seam or within the garment itself. After sewing the new seams, remove the old stitching and press.

Redesigning Clothes

Redesigning a garment means to change its appearance or function. Redesigning is a good way of expanding a wardrobe at little or no cost. Garments can be redesigned by restyling them, adding decorative features, or changing their colors.

Redesign shirts and blouses by changing long sleeves to short sleeves. You can add decorative trim to an old garment, or dye it a new color. Liven up a tired-looking jacket by adding a decorative touch, such as an appliqué. Tie-dyeing or painting T-shirts can give them an updated or original fashion look. Through redesigning, you can add personal touches to any garment.

Restyling

By **restyling** a garment, you can give it a new and different look. For example, the easiest way to restyle jeans that are too short in length is to cut them off above the knees. Jeans then become a pair of *cut-offs*. See **15-7**. You can also restyle pants that are too short. Cut them off to the length you like best for shorts. Be sure to allow enough length for a hem. If pant legs are flared and the current fashion calls for straight legs, make the legs straight. Restitch both the outer and inner seams. Be sure the amount you take in is exactly the same for both legs.

By removing the sleeves from a sweater or jacket, you can make a vest. The armholes have to be finished with overcasting or by sewing a folded trim over the edges. Change long sleeves into short sleeves by cutting off the old sleeves and hemming the edges. New buttons may be added for an updated look.

Some dresses may be made into jumpers by removing collars and sleeves. Finish the cut edges. If a dress has a full skirt, you may want to slim it down with larger side seams. If the skirt is too narrow, you could make side slits starting at the hem. Belts can create a slimmer silhouette to a full dress.

Embroidery, Trims, and Appliqués

A garment can also be restyled by adding embroidery. **Embroidery** is decorative stitching that creates patterns or designs on fabric, **15-8**. It can be

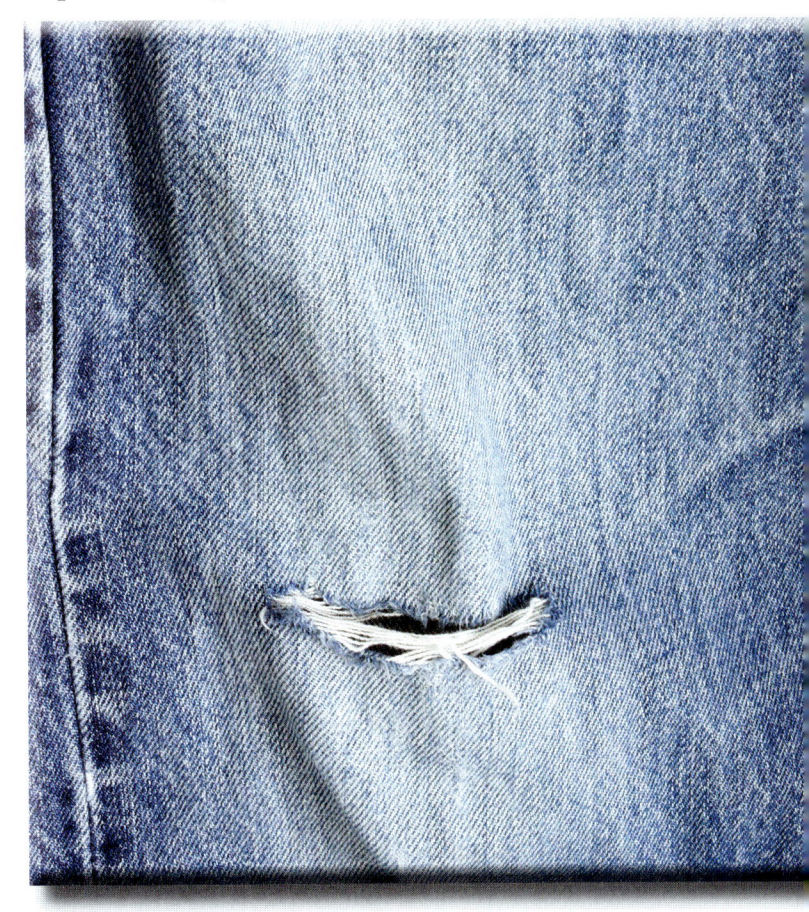

15-7 Making *cut-offs* of jeans that have holes at the knees is easy to do. *Shutterstock*

15-8 Embroidery can add a special touch to denim jeans. *Shutterstock*

done by hand or by machine. Many sewing machine models have decorative stitches programmed into them. Other machines use cards containing different design motifs that are inserted into them. Embroidery using either of these methods can give garments a personal touch.

Trims can also be used to give clothes a unique look. Trims are purchased by the yard or in packages. They include braids, rickrack, bias tape, foldover braid, and knitted bands. Some trims are designed to give a decorative edge to a garment. These include fringe, piping, and pre-gathered ruffles.

Whenever you use a decorative technique, such as trim application, consider the total effect it creates. For instance, if you use decorative trim at the hem of a garment, repeat the use of the trim on the sleeves or the collar. Trims can also be used to cover crease lines created when hems are lowered. When estimating how much trim is needed, measure the area to be trimmed, then add at least ½ yard. This provides extra trim that may be needed to join ends and to go around corners and curves.

Appliqué is the process of sewing one or more small pieces of contrasting fabric onto a larger piece of fabric or a garment. Appliqués add a decorative touch to clothing. They are made of small pieces of fabric that are cut into any shape, **15-9**. The appliqués can be made from a pattern. You can buy appliqué patterns in fabric stores, or you can draw your own designs.

Finish the edges of an appliqué using a zigzag stitch on a sewing machine or a serger. For a neat look, trim close to the stitching. When you sew the appliqué to the garment, fewer stitches will be needed to keep the edges from fraying.

Another way to apply an appliqué to a garment is to use **fusible fabric**. This sheer fabric has a thin layer of plastic adhesive. Cut a piece of fusible fabric the same size or a bit smaller than the appliqué. Place it between the appliqué and the garment. Apply steam with an iron and the fusible fabric will fuse (join) the other two fabrics. The appliqué will stay attached to the garment even when it is washed or dry-cleaned.

15-9 A colorful, sequined appliqué gives this pair a jeans a unique look. *Shutterstock*

Dyeing

One of the easiest ways to change the look of clothes is by dyeing or recoloring them. You can make light garments darker, or make dull apparel brighter.

Dye can be bought in liquid or powder forms. Many colors are available. Interesting effects can be achieved using combinations of colors. Use your creativity.

Only clothes that are washable can be dyed. Some fibers will not take dye. Check product packages for directions. Use hot water, rinse thoroughly, and dry.

Tie-Dyeing

Tie-dyeing is a method of dyeing fabric and one of the earliest known methods of decorating fabric. It is still popular today, **15-10**. Before the fabric is exposed to dyes, sections are folded or gathered and tied tightly with string or wrapped with rubber bands. When the fabric is immersed, the tied or wrapped portions do not absorb the dye. Tie-dyeing is a resist type of fabric dyeing. When the strings, folds, and rubber bands are removed, they leave designs behind.

Tie-dyeing can be done before or after a garment is made. It is a thrifty way to update tired-looking garments and a neat way to create something that is one-of-a-kind. It is also exciting because the tie-dyed design is always a surprise. All types of garments can be tie-dyed, as well as fabric handbags, backpacks, belts, shoelaces, and socks. To get the best results and to use products safely, always follow the directions of dye manufacturers.

Fabric Painting

Another fun way to add color to clothes is to paint them. Colors can be applied with a brush, pen, marker, or directly from a tube. Designs can be painted with acrylic fabric paints. These paints are washable and come in ready-to-use tubes. Many colors are available. Some paints are designed to create a raised area on the fabric.

You can have fun creating your own designs on items such as jogging outfits, T-shirts, jeans, or canvas bags. You can also purchase patterns to follow.

Recycling Clothes

How many clothes do you throw away each year? Studies show that each person annually discards 54 pounds of clothing and other textile items. This amounts to an annual total of about 9 million tons in the U.S. alone. Though many items are donated to charities, most go into the trash and end up in landfills.

15-10 The fabric used to make this top was tie-dyed to give it a unique look. *Shutterstock*

There are companies, however, that recycle textile products. Recycling means to reuse. About 25 percent of discarded textile products are recycled by these companies. Some communities have collection sites especially for textiles. Perhaps your community is one of them.

Instead of discarding clothes, find ways to extend their usefulness. There are several ways to do this. You can pass clothing along for others to use. You can also make something entirely new out of a garment. Recycling clothes is a way to conserve resources as well as save money.

Passing Clothes Along

You may have some garments that are in good condition. If you cannot wear them or redesign them, you may want to consider passing them along to someone else.

In many families, older children pass clothes along to younger siblings, 15-11. This helps families save money. When family members outgrow them, they often pass the clothes on to relatives or friends. Clothing sizes often change at a rapid rate until people are well into their teen years. Therefore, clothes are usually outgrown before they wear out completely.

Many charitable groups give away or sell clothing at a small cost. These groups include Goodwill, the Red Cross, the Salvation Army, and various religious groups. In many cases, they help families who have lost their belongings in a flood, fire, or other disaster. Low-priced used clothing is also sold at thrift shops, which are often run by not-for-profit organizations. Store profits are used to assist struggling families and individuals.

Your usable but unwanted clothing can help others. It may be satisfying to know that your unwanted clothing is being used by someone who needs it. Some organizations have a pick-up service to collect donations of clothing. Such donations are usually tax deductible.

Organizations such as Goodwill and the Salvation Army evaluate the used clothing they collect. They will not sell defective clothes or shoes in their stores. Worn and defective items are sent to textile recyclers. These businesses either ship them to other countries to be worn or sort and resell them to textile recovery facilities. The textile recovery industry prevents 2.5 billion pounds of textile products from entering U.S. landfills annually. This averages about 10 pounds per person in the United States. The recycled textiles may become cleaning cloths, paper, insulation, or upholstery.

You may want to sell your unwanted clothes if they still have some fashion value. You can earn money by selling clothes to consignment shops. If these shops sell your item, a portion of the sale price will come back to you. The remainder of the sale price goes to the shop. If your item does not sell within a

15-11 Clothes are often recycled among family members. Since children outgrow more clothes than they wear out, the clothes are often passed on to younger sisters and brothers. *Shutterstock*

specified time, the price is reduced. If it still does not sell, it will be returned to you or donated to charity.

Yard and garage sales, flea markets, and bazaars are other venues for selling clothes. Yard and garage sales are often held by several people or families working together.

Online auction sites, such as eBay, are a good option if you have a unique garment. Like-new designer clothes are often sold online.

New Life for Old Clothes

When a garment can no longer be worn by you or anyone else, what can you do with it? You may be able to recycle the usable sections. For example, perhaps you might use the fabric to make small purses, makeup pouches, or shoe bags. If you do not use these items yourself, you can sell or give them away. They cost little or nothing to make, **15-12**.

Sometimes fabric from old adult clothes can be recycled into clothing for children. For instance, the skirt of an old dress may be fashioned into a small child's shirt.

If you have outgrown a pair of jeans, you might use them to make a tote bag or backpack. Simply cut off the legs just below the crotch, turn the garment inside out, and sew the legs together. Tote bags and backpacks are popular for carrying school supplies. Other outgrown clothes can also be used to make tote bags.

Patchwork

Patchwork can give you an opportunity to use your artistic talents. **Patchwork** involves sewing pieces and shapes of different fabrics together. The fabrics are often of different textures and designs. Patchwork quilts are popular and attractive. Many are displayed in homes and museums as works of art. Many teens use their old T-shirts to make quilts that preserve memories of past events or clubs they belonged to. If you do not want to create a quilt, you can make a patchwork bedspread. You can also make tote bags, place mats, stuffed toys, and pillows from patchwork. Clothing, such as vests, can be made using patchwork designs.

Patterns and ideas for patchwork projects are available in craft stores and magazines. Be sure to use fabrics that are firmly woven. Each object should be made from fabrics that require the same care. For instance, denim and heavy cotton flannel would require the same care.

15-12 You can recycle fabric from garments into useful items, such as this organizer made from the legs of cut-off jeans. *Reproduced courtesy of Coats & Clark*

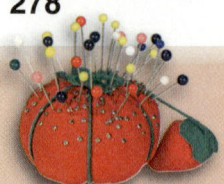

Did You Know?

Patchwork Is a Work of Art

Patchwork can be a fun way to use fabric scraps in a creative way. Patchwork is sewing small pieces and shapes of fabric together to form larger pieces. Once you have a larger piece of fabric to work with, there are any number of ways you can use it.

In earlier times, patchwork was a way of reusing old pieces of fabric. They were often made into quilts. Today, patchwork can be used to make sections of a garment, such as a collar or pockets, or an entire garment, such as a vest. It can also be used to make accessories, such as purses and ties. Home accessories often feature patchwork in pillows, bedspreads, place mats, and wall hangings.

Patchwork does not have to be a way of using scraps of fabric. Many patchwork fabrics are specifically designed around certain colors and fabric patterns. When selecting fabrics to create a patchwork design, keep the following points in mind:

- All fabrics should have the same care requirements.
- All fabrics should be of a similar weight for even wear.
- The colors and patterns should coordinate or complement each other.
- The fabric patterns should be in proportion to the size of the patches. The larger the patch, the larger the pattern can be.

Choose a simple design for your first project that uses squares and triangles. The size of each patch should be no smaller than 2 inches and no larger than 8 inches. Cut a pattern out of cardboard allowing ¼-inch seam allowances.

Make sure your fabrics are on grain. Use your pattern to mark the pieces on the wrong side of the fabric. Cut the pieces out using shears.

Sew all seams using a ¼-inch seam and 12–15 stitches per inch. If using triangles in your design, sew these first to form squares. Then sew the square patches together to form rows. Press all seams open before joining the rows. Finally, sew the rows together to form the fabric. Your patchwork is now ready to be made into a garment or home accessory.

You can create a dramatic effect with patchwork using simple squares and triangles. *Shutterstock*

15-13 Some old clothes can be recycled for a children's prop box. *Bananastock*

Other Uses for Old Clothes

Children love to play *dress-up*. A box of old clothes can provide them with many hours of fun, **15-13**. Old clothes make good Halloween and masquerade costumes, too.

When garments are too worn to be recycled into other useful items, they can be used for cleaning. Household rags may be needed for polishing woodwork, dusting furniture, or washing cars. Be careful to first cut off buttons and other fasteners that can scratch furniture or the paint on a car. Old buttons and fasteners can also be recycled for later use.

Fabrics made of 100 percent cotton or cotton blends often make the best rags because they are soft and absorbent. Fabrics made of other fibers that are not suitable as rags can be used to stuff pillows and toys, **15-14**. Use your imagination to come up with new and different ways to recycle clothes.

15-14 Some fabrics can be recycled to make stuffing materials for stuffed animals. *Simplicity Pattern Co., Inc.*

Summary

- There are several ways to revive your clothes. These include repairing, altering, redesigning, and recycling.
- Repair holes and rips and reattach loose buttons, fasteners, and hems when you first notice them. Then they will be ready to wear when you next need them.
- A garment can be altered to decrease or increase its length or width so it fits better.
- Redesigning includes restyling for a new look, adding decorative features such as appliqués or trims, or changing the color of a garment.
- Recycling means to reuse. With clothing, this means finding ways and methods of extending the use of garments. This includes passing clothes along to others, such as family members or friends. There are charitable groups that give away or sell used clothing at a small cost to those in need. These groups send defective clothes to textile recyclers.
- Recycling also includes finding new uses for the fabric in the clothes. Sometimes fabric from old clothes is used to make clothes for children. Patchwork is sewing pieces and shapes of fabric together. Old garments can be used for patchwork projects, such as quilts or tote bags.
- When garments are too worn to be recycled into other useful items, they can be used as cleaning cloths or stuffed into pillows and toys.

Graphic Organizer

Draw a star diagram to outline the main types of redesigning clothes. Note two key points about each.

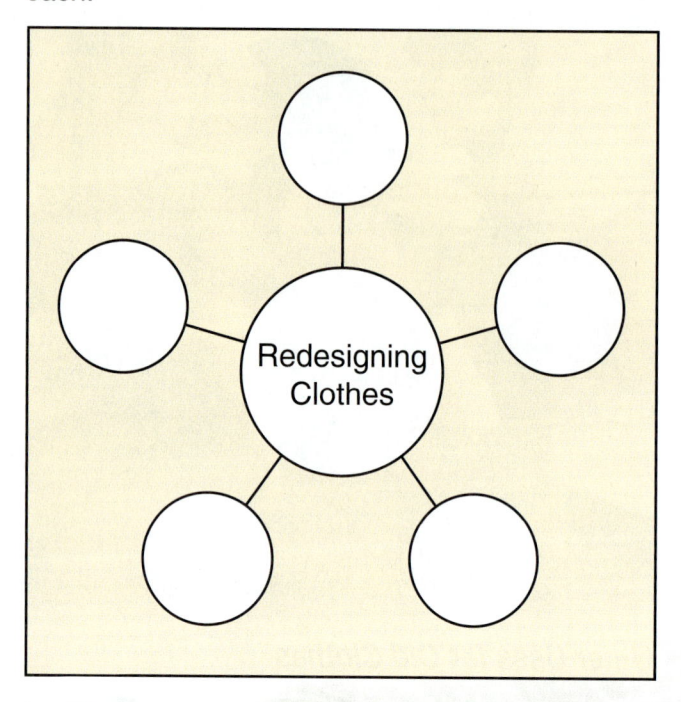

Review the Facts

1. If you do not have the exact color of thread that matches a garment you are repairing, should you use a lighter or darker color thread?
2. How would you fix a snag in a sweater?
3. If there is not enough depth in a hem to lengthen a garment, what can you do to add length?
4. (True or False) When letting out a garment, or making it larger, sew the new seam inside the old seam allowance.
5. How can you restyle a long-sleeved shirt with sleeves that are too short for you?
6. What kind of paint can you use to *paint* fabric?
7. List three ways you can restyle or recycle worn jeans.
8. List four ways you can recycle garments you no longer wear.
9. What do organizations such as Goodwill and the Salvation Army do with the clothes they collect?
10. List all of the options available to resell unwanted clothes.

Think Critically

11. **Draw conclusions.** Do fewer people repair their own clothing today than in earlier times? Draw conclusions about possible reasons for this.
12. **Predict outcomes.** Why do you think teens took to the worn and frayed look in jeans? Predict whether you think this is a fad or will it remain popular for some time and explain your reasoning.
13. **Analyze decisions.** Do you think it is important to recycle everything you can? Why or why not? How do you make decisions on what to recycle and what not to recycle?

Apparel Applications

14. **Discussion.** Do you have any clothes you cannot wear because they need simple repairs? What skills do you need to do these repairs? Discuss your thoughts with the class.
15. **Brainstorm ideas.** Bring an article of clothing to class that you no longer wear. As a class, brainstorm ways to repair, redesign, or recycle each garment brought to class.
16. **Oral presentation.** Bring a garment to class that you have repaired, redesigned, or recycled. Describe the technique you used for the class.
17. **Assemble sewing tools.** Assemble a clothing repair box. Give a reason for including each item you add to the box.
18. **Electronic bulletin board.** Use a school-approved Web-based blog or bulletin board application to display pictures of garments you and your classmates have redesigned. Title the bulletin board *Cures for Sick Clothes*.
19. **Class donation.** Bring clean clothing that you no longer wear to class. As a class, sort it according to age groups. Deliver the clothing to a charitable organization.

Academic Connections

20. **Reading.** Use Internet or print resources to read at least two articles on redesigning clothes through one or more of the methods in the chapter. What are the latest trends? What skills do you need to do these redesigns? Write a summary citing your sources of information.
21. **Writing.** As a class, brainstorm a list of recycling ideas. Then research textile recycling services in your area. Write a brief summary about each service. Combine the list of recycling ideas with your summaries about the textile recycling services into a public service announcement (PSA). Get permission from school authorities to publish your PSA in the school newspaper.

Workplace Links

22. **Entrepreneur opportunity.** Invite an entrepreneur to class to demonstrate a new electronic embroidery machine. How does this person use the machine in his or her business? What is the job outlook for entrepreneurs in such a business?
23. **School resale shop.** As a class, collect used prom dresses. Repair items, if necessary. Arrange to resell them at the school resale shop or school store. Donate the money to a charity of class choice.

Teamwork—Reclaiming Shoes

What happens to shoes you and others outgrow or wear only for a short time? Do usable shoes end up in a landfill? Attend a meeting of a charitable organization to find out what needs they fill in the community and around the world.

Present your findings to your FCCLA chapter. Then use the FCCLA *Planning Process* to plan, carry out, and evaluate a *Community Service* project involving the collection of gently used athletic shoes for the charity. Perhaps your team can partner with the organization members to distribute the shoes. See your adviser for information as needed.

PART 3

Color and Design

Chapters

16 Color

17 The Elements and Principles of Design

Chapter 16

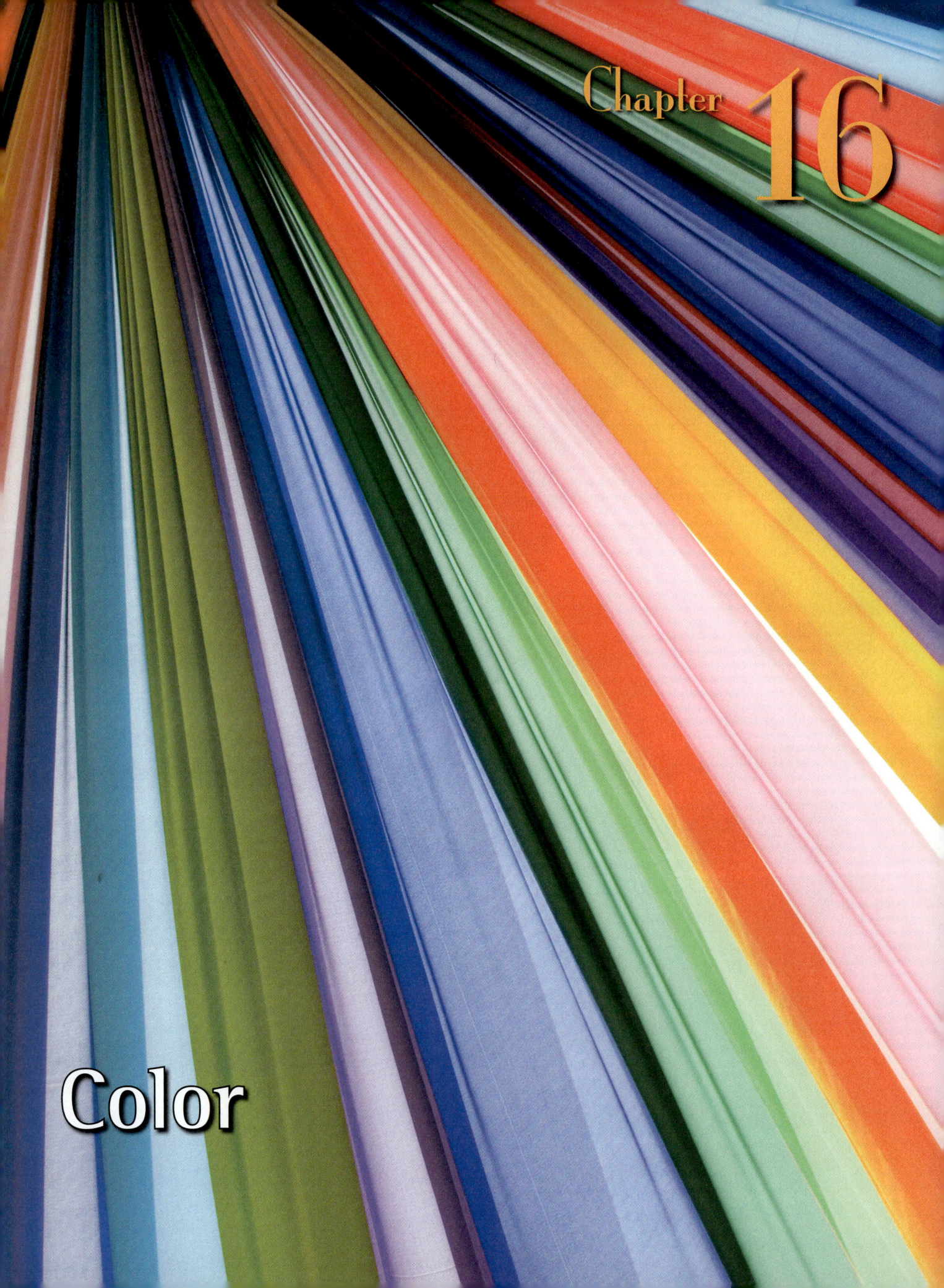

Color

Chapter Objectives

After studying this chapter, you will be able to
- **define** basic color terms.
- **describe** the relationship of the colors in the color wheel.
- **identify** the basic color schemes.
- **choose** colors that enhance your skin tone, hair, eye color, and body shape.
- **select** colors that reflect your personality, moods, and feelings.

Key Terms

hue
value
tint
shade
intensity
neutrals
color wheel
primary color
secondary color
tertiary color
complementary color
warm color
cool color
color scheme
monochromatic color scheme
analogous color scheme
complementary color scheme
split-complementary color scheme
triadic color scheme
accented neutral color scheme

Reading with Purpose

Write all of the chapter terms on a sheet of paper. Highlight the words that you *do not* know. Before you begin reading, look up the highlighted words in the glossary and write the definitions.

16-1 Can you imagine what our world would be like without color?
Shutterstock

Color affects you in many ways. Look at Figure **16-1**. Try to imagine how the world would look if everything were colorless. Color is everywhere. It is hard to visualize life without it.

Few people are aware of the power of color. For instance, studies show that the color red can increase your appetite. Have you ever seen red carpets or furniture in a restaurant? This color choice was not accidental. It was planned to encourage you to order more food! Red is also used in many store displays to attract shoppers to certain areas.

When shopping for clothes, color may be the first thing that attracts you to a particular garment. The range of colors is almost limitless. Some are light; others are dark. Some are bright; others are dull.

285

Part 3 Color and Design

Understanding the properties of color can help you choose colors that will best enhance your features. You can make better clothing decisions when you choose colors that are best for you.

Color and Its Meanings

Some colors are associated with certain feelings or moods. Studies show that people associate certain traits and emotions to specific colors, too. Here are some examples.

- *Red.* As a vibrant color, red is associated with anger, power, danger, passion, war, and love. It makes people feel good and full of energy.
- *Orange.* A warm, lively color, orange expresses courage, friendliness, hospitality, and energy, **16-2**.
- *Yellow.* Yellow is cheerful and bright. Over the years it has been associated with prosperity, cowardice, deceit, wisdom, and warmth.
- *Green.* While it is restful and refreshing, green is the color many people connect to spring. Green has been associated with luck, envy, life, and hope.
- *Blue.* Cool, calm, and dignified, blue expresses serenity and formality, and gives a feeling of spaciousness. It is often associated with depression, as a *blue Monday*.
- *Purple.* While expressing opulence, wisdom, and suffering, purple also is the color of royalty, mystery, humility, and dignity.
- *Black.* A mysterious, sophisticated, and strong color, black may symbolize wisdom, evil, and death. In U.S. culture, people often wear black for funerals.
- *White.* White is serene and cool. It is the symbol of innocence, purity, faith, and peace. This is why white is worn for weddings and other religious ceremonies.

16-2 Orange is a warm, lively color that expresses friendliness and energy. *Shutterstock*

Understanding Color Terms

Color has three properties or qualities. The first is hue. **Hue** is the name of a color, such as red, green, or blue. The other two qualities of color are value and intensity.

Value is the lightness or darkness of a color. Each color has a wide value scale from light to dark. Different values form when white or black is added to a color. A **tint** is made by adding white to a color. For instance, pink is a tint of red. A **shade** is made by adding black to a color. Maroon is a shade of red, navy is a shade of blue, and brown is a shade of orange.

Intensity is the brightness or dullness of a color. Flag blue is bright and denim blue is dull, but both are blue. A bright color is more intense than a dull color. Adding more of the dominant color makes a color more intense. Adding some of a color's complement will make the color less intense. For instance, adding a little bit of green to the color red will make the red look *grayed*.

The color blocks in **16-3** and **16-4** will help you compare tints and shades. The color blocks in **16-5** and **16-6** will help you compare bright and dull intensities.

16-3 The value (lightness or darkness) of any color can be changed. When white is added to a color, the result is a tint. *National Institute of Standards and Technology*

16-4 A shade is made by adding black to a color. *National Institute of Standards and Technology*

16-5 Colors look more intense when more of the dominant color is added. *National Institute of Standards and Technology*

16-6 A color looks less intense (grayed) when some of its complement is added to it. *National Institute of Standards and Technology*

Black, white, and gray are **neutrals**. White is the absence of color. It reflects light. Black absorbs all color and light. When white and black are used together, the contrast produces a dramatic effect, **16-7**. A blend of white and black forms gray—another neutral. In clothing, beige is also considered a neutral.

You can wear black, white, gray, and beige with all colors. Many people use neutrals as basic colors in planning a wardrobe. You can mix and match them with various hues to produce a pleasing look. When you use a small amount of color in an outfit with a neutral, the color becomes more vivid.

White and light-colored clothing feel cooler because white reflects light. This is why people often wear white clothes in tropical climates or in the summer. Since black absorbs light, it makes black and dark-colored clothes feel warmer. This is why dark clothes are popular in cold climates.

The Color Wheel

The **color wheel** shows the relationship among colors or hues, **16-8**. Red, yellow, and blue are the basic or **primary colors**. Each is a pure hue. No other colors can be combined to make any of them. They are placed equal distances from each other on the color wheel, forming a triangle. All other colors are made from the three primary hues.

Orange, green, and violet are the **secondary colors**. Mixing equal amounts of two primary hues forms the secondary colors. To form the secondary colors, red and yellow make orange; yellow and blue make green; and red and blue make violet (purple). They are located evenly between each primary hue on the color wheel.

Combining equal amounts of a primary and a secondary hue form a **tertiary color**. These colors are red-violet, blue-violet, blue-green, yellow-green, yellow-orange, and red-orange. Locate them between a primary and secondary hue on the color wheel. Another name for these tertiary colors is *intermediate colors*. See **16-9** to locate the primary, secondary, and tertiary colors on the color wheel.

Complementary colors are colors located opposite one another on the color wheel. They have the greatest contrast and look brightest when used together. Red and green are complementary colors, as are yellow and violet. Look at the color wheel to identify other complementary colors. To lower the intensity of a color, you add some of its complement. When mixed together, as in paints or dyes, any pair of complementary colors in equal amounts will produce gray.

16-7 A dramatic effect is achieved when black and white are used together. *The McCall Pattern Co.*

16-8 Colors in a color wheel are arranged in a circle to show how they relate to one another. Each color seems to "belong" between its neighbors. The inner ring shows tints of the colors. The outer ring shows shades of the colors. *Goodheart-Willcox Publisher*

16-9 Primary, secondary, and intermediate colors can be determined by their location on the color wheel. *Goodheart-Willcox Publisher*

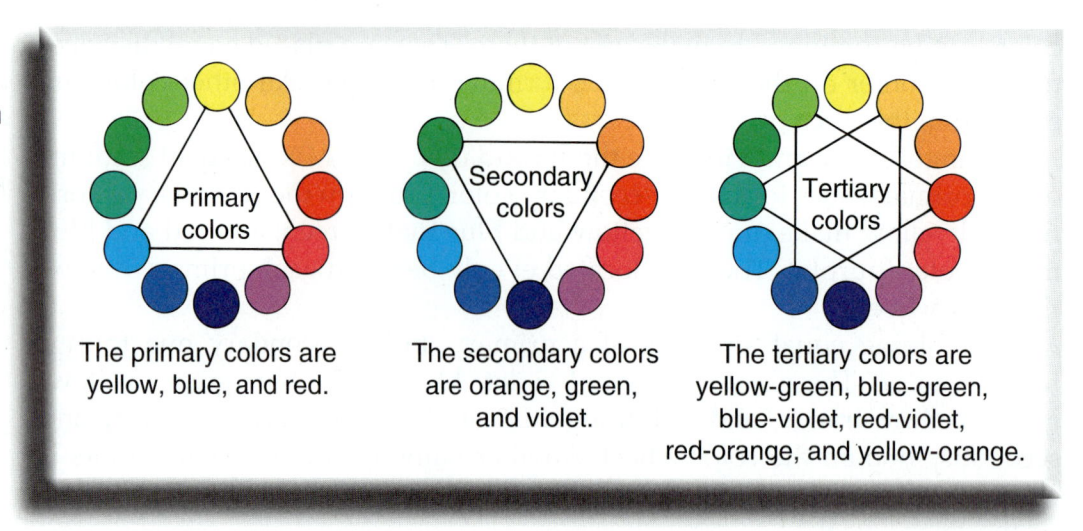

Primary colors
The primary colors are yellow, blue, and red.

Secondary colors
The secondary colors are orange, green, and violet.

Tertiary colors
The tertiary colors are yellow-green, blue-green, blue-violet, red-violet, red-orange, and yellow-orange.

Warm and Cool Colors

Look at the color wheel again. You will notice that one side looks cool and one side looks warm. Red, orange, and yellow are considered **warm colors**. They are bright and cheerful, and suggest activity. Many people like to wear warm colors.

Blues, greens, and purples are the **cool colors**. Restful, relaxing, refreshing, cool, soothing, and serious are terms often used to describe these colors. Long-term hospital patients may stay in rooms painted soft green or blue-green. These colors are relaxing and they offer a feeling of comfort.

Warm, light, and bright colors appear to *advance*, or come toward you. When an object moves closer to you, it becomes larger in appearance. Notice your surroundings. Warmer colors are likely to catch your eye first. This is why warm colors are used for traffic signs and danger signals. Hunters must wear orange caps so that others can easily see them. Red and orange flags are used on construction projects. Traffic police wear yellow raincoats.

Advertising designers use this knowledge of color in their work. Notice how many food products have yellow or red in their labels when you are in a food store. The advancing colors quickly attract your attention.

Cool, dark, and dull colors appear to *recede*, or move away. As an object moves away from you, it appears smaller. That is why a person looks slimmer in a blue outfit than in a red one. Slacks made in dark, cool colors have a slenderizing effect. Notice how warm colors appear to advance and cool colors recede in Figure **16-10**.

16-10 Notice how the warm colors in this photograph catch your eye before the cool colors or neutrals. *Shutterstock*

Color Schemes

Appealing combinations of colors form **color schemes**. Figure **16-11** shows how you can use the color wheel to see the formation of various color schemes. Designers often base fabric and clothing designs on these time-tested color schemes.

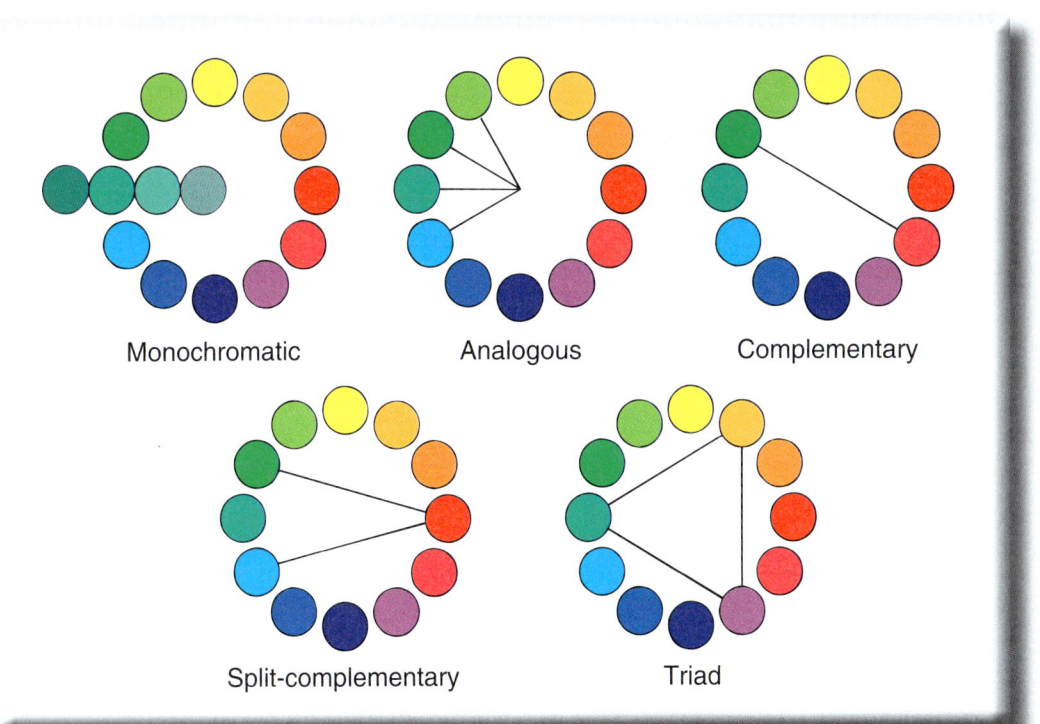

16-11 These examples illustrate the various types of color schemes.
Goodheart-Willcox Publisher

Monochromatic Analogous Complementary

Split-complementary Triad

Monochromatic

Using several tints, shades, and intensities of one color together forms a one-color scheme, or **monochromatic color scheme**. For instance, you might use pink, red, and maroon together to form a monochromatic scheme. Someone wearing a pale blue shirt, navy jeans, and pure blue socks is displaying a monochromatic outfit.

Analogous

Using adjacent colors together forms an **analogous color scheme**, 16-12. *Adjacent* colors are next to each other on the color wheel. They are closely related and always blend well. You can find analogous color schemes in nature. Autumn leaves in yellows, oranges, and reds exemplify a natural analogous color scheme.

Complementary

A **complementary color scheme** combines colors that are opposite each other on the color wheel. When put side by side, complementary colors make each other look brighter. For instance, the complement of blue is orange. When using the two colors together, both seem brighter. Red and green are stronger when you use them together, as are yellow and violet. If you want others to notice you, this is a combination to choose. Using tints and shades in complementary colors make a subtle, but pleasing combination.

16-12 An analogous color harmony is created when the yellow-green scarf is worn with the blue-green top. *Shutterstock*

Split-Complementary

A **split-complementary color scheme** combines one color with the two colors on the sides of its opposite complement. An example is the combination of red with yellow-green and blue-green. This combination is a little less bold than a complementary scheme, but still provides vivid contrast.

Triadic

The **triadic color scheme** uses three colors that form an equal-lateral sided triangle on the color wheel. Using the three primary colors (red, yellow, and blue) or the three secondary colors (green, orange, and violet) together makes a triad color scheme, **16-13**. When using this vivid color harmony, it is best to use a large amount of one color and lesser amounts of the other two. You can also use less intense colors for an attractive combination.

Accented Neutral

When combining a neutral color with a bright color accent, an **accented neutral color scheme** forms. You can use black, white, gray, or beige with any bright color for a pleasing look. This is also a very versatile combination when mixing and matching various pieces in a wardrobe. By changing the accent color, you can give an outfit an entirely new look. A black sweater and slacks changes instantly with a bright-colored belt or scarf.

16-13 The sweater and scarf combination shown here illustrates the triad color scheme. *Shutterstock*

Choosing Your Best Colors

There are hundreds of colors in your life; each is a little different. *Color sense* is having knowledge about color. You were not born with it, but you can easily acquire it. See **16-14** for some helpful guidelines.

Your choice of color depends on your personal coloring, body shape, personality, and present wardrobe. The season of the year or a special occasion may also be a factor. Select colors that look good on you, give you self-confidence, and make you feel your best.

> **Color Selection Guidelines**
>
> - Decide which color is most flattering.
> - Select a neutral or a basic color as a wardrobe foundation. Beige, navy blue, or black are often used.
>   - *With beige*—try using brown, orange, rust, black, dark green, blue-green, white, and coral.
>   - *With navy blue*—use bright green, red, white, pink, yellow, coral, and light blue.
>   - *With black*—use any color. Because of the sharp contrast, some tints and shades will be better than others.
> - Use the basic color selection for items that cost the most money and can be worn several years—coats and suits.
> - Use light and bright colors to play up your best features. Use dull, dark colors to minimize other features.
> - Use bright colors in small amounts to add interest and for accent. Using too many at a time results in a spotty effect.
> - Plan your clothes so that you will be able to *mix-and-match*. This way you will have several different outfits and save money.

16-14 Follow these guidelines to help you choose your best colors.

Colors for Your Skin Tone

How can you decide which colors are best for you? Your personal coloring, which includes your skin tone, is one factor to consider. Choosing the right clothing colors can enhance your skin tone.

Skin contains brown, yellow, and red pigments that determine skin tone. Your skin tone will reflect more of one pigment than of another. People with darker skin have more brown pigment than people with lighter skin. There are many variations of skin tone ranging from very fair to very dark.

Skin color also has blue or yellow *undertones*. You may be able to see these undertones in the coloring on the inside of your wrist.

People with blue undertones look generally best in cool colors. People with yellow undertones usually look best in warm colors. Some cosmetic manufacturers market products designed for warm and cool skin tones.

Colors for Your Hair and Eyes

Another important consideration in selecting your best colors is the color of your hair and eyes. Your hair can take on a new glow with the right colors. Color can also affect the color and brightness of your eyes.

You can emphasize your hair and eye color in two ways. First, choose clothes in tints or shades of your hair or eyes. For instance, beige or tan emphasizes brown hair color. Blue eyes may seem bluer when a person wears a blue garment.

The second way to emphasize hair and eye color is to choose clothes in complementary colors. For instance, a red shirt helps emphasize green eyes.

Most eyes contain a touch of several colors. Some eyes seem to change color when an individual wears different colors. For instance, hazel eyes will seem greener when a person wears green clothing. Color does not influence brown eyes as much as other eye colors.

Your Seasonal Coloring

Your personal coloring is sometimes described as one of the four seasons of the year. If you have winter or summer coloring, you have blue undertones in your skin color. If you have spring or autumn coloring, you have yellow undertones, **16-15**.

- *Winter coloring.* More people have winter coloring than any other seasonal coloring. People with winter coloring usually have dark hair and eyes. They wear true black or pure white well. Bright, vivid, contrasting colors with blue undertones are their best colors. Faded or muted colors are generally not good choices. Silver or pewter jewelry tones look best.

- *Summer coloring.* People with summer coloring have hints of pink in their skin. They might easily sunburn. Their eyes are normally very blue; some might have shades of green or hazel. Their hair is usually ash to light blond with light to golden-blond highlights. Soft, cool colors usually look best on people with summer coloring. Silver- or pewter-toned jewelry also flatters their skin tones.

- *Spring coloring.* People with spring coloring have the most delicate coloring of any season. Their hair color is often light to strawberry blond, pale brown, or reddish brown, while eye coloring is usually blue but can be shades of blue-green. People with spring coloring generally look best in clear, bright colors in medium to light shades. They should avoid muted or faded colors. Gold jewelry tones best enhance their skin.

- *Autumn coloring.* People with autumn coloring can have ivory or peach colored skin, and they may have freckles. Their hair may be light or dark brown with auburn or red highlights. People with autumn coloring often have brown eyes, but hazel, green, or blue-green eyes are also common. These people can wear muted and vivid colors, but generally look best in the colors of fall foliage. Gold jewelry looks great with the autumn colors and enhances skin tones.

Your personal coloring determines the colors that look best on you. If you have winter or summer coloring, you look best in cool colors. If you have spring or autumn coloring, warm colors are best for you to wear. Many colors will look great with your personal coloring.

What is your seasonal coloring? Here is a simple way to check out your coloring. Try draping fabrics representing different seasonal colors around your shoulders. Be sure to cover any clothes you are wearing. Study the effects in a large mirror to determine which colors look best on you. Do some colors enhance the blue or yellow undertones of your skin? Do the colors that look best on you seem to fall into a warm or cool category? The best colors for you enhance your personal coloring.

The Seasonal Approach to Your Personal Coloring

Your Season	Winter	Summer	Autumn	Spring
Skin Coloring	**Blue Undertones** Milk white (colorless) White (with slight undertone) Beige (with slight sallowness) Rosy beige Olive Black Freckles: dark brown, gray	**Blue Undertones** Light beige (with a little tinge of pink) Light beige (no color, slightly pale) Rosy pink Dark brown Freckles: medium to dark brown	**Yellow Undertones** Pure ivory Peach Golden beige Coppery beige Coppery brown Golden black Freckles: golden blond or light brown	**Yellow Undertones** Ivory Peach Peachy pink Peachy beige Light beige Golden beige Peachy brown Brown Freckles: light Golden brown
Hair Coloring	Black (with blue cast) Brown (medium to dark, maybe red highlights) Blond (white) Salt and pepper Silver-gray white (snow)	Platinum Blond Ash blond Smoky blond Smoky brown (or reddish cast) Dark brown (taupe cast) Blue-gray	Red Reddish brown Golden brown Golden blond Charcoal black Bronze or metallic gray	Yellow blond Golden blond Strawberry blond Redhead Auburn Golden brown Golden gray
Eyes	Black Dark brown Brown (with a reddish cast) Hazel (with varying shades of gray, green, blue) Green (with blue or green combination) Medium blue Dark blue	Blue (clear, sky blue, aqua, may have white flecks) Gray-blue (may be chameleon) Soft pale gray Green (may have white flecks) Hazel (with flecks)	Dark brown Golden brown Hazel (brownish-green) Deep to pale green (gold, brown, or citron flecks) Jade green Peacock blue	Clear/bright blue Aqua blue (with turquoise) Bluish-green Clear green Light brown Golden to topaz brown

16-15 Find your personal colors in this chart to determine your seasonal coloring.

Colors for Your Body Type

Color is one of the best ways to make the most of your body type or shape, 16-16. You can use colors to enhance your best features if you follow some simple guidelines.

Light, warm, and bright colors make an object appear larger. Most people can wear white and off-white, but it will make some body features appear larger. If a person wants to emphasize broad shoulders, he or she should select a garment with white or a light color in that area.

The dark, cool, dull colors tend to make objects appear smaller. People who want a slimmer look can use this to their advantage. Blue jeans are more slimming than light-colored khaki slacks. A dark green shirt gives a smaller appearance than a bright red one.

Using a single color in an entire outfit can give a slimmer look. This is because the eye travels from top to bottom without a break, giving the illusion of greater height. The traditional business suit shows this effect. When using two contrasting colors in an outfit, the eye will stop where one color ends and

16-16 Choosing the right colors for your clothes accentuates your personal coloring and your body shape.
Photo courtesy of McCall Pattern Company

Chapter 16 Color 297

the other begins. This tends to give a shorter appearance. When a person wears a shirt or jacket with a contrasting color in the slacks or skirt, the figure appears shorter. You can use these guidelines in making your figure appear taller or shorter, **16-17**.

You can also choose colors to emphasize your best features. For example, to draw attention to a narrow waist, use subdued colors elsewhere. The eye automatically moves to the area of emphasis.

Perhaps you have found a color that you like and that is right for your body type. However, you find little of this color in your wardrobe. It is unreasonable to toss everything out and start over. Plan carefully to add this color to your wardrobe. Which clothes in your current wardrobe could you wear with new clothes in this color? See **16-18**.

16-17 Notice how the matching jacket and pants on the right gives the illusion of more height compared to the contrasting jacket and pants outfit on the left. *Photo courtesy of McCall Pattern Company*

Effects of Color on Body Shape

- Wear neutrals to draw attention away from the body. Add color in accessories.
- Wear black and navy blue for a slenderizing effect.
- Wear two- or three-piece outfits in contrasting colors if you are tall and thin.
- Wear an outfit of only one color, especially a cool color, to appear taller.
- Wear bold, bright colors and white to draw attention to a certain body part, such as the shoulders. These colors give the visual appearance of added weight.
- Wear separates that are one color or are an analogous color scheme if you are a person who is small. A scattered look will result if too many different colors are worn.
- Select colorful tops that continue below the waistline if you are short-waisted to give the illusion of length or height.
- A one-color outfit is slenderizing for a person who is heavier.
- Note the following when choosing accessories:
  - Multicolored or light shoes draw attention to the feet and make them appear larger.
  - Wide, light-colored belts make a waistline appear larger.

16-18 These are some of the effects of color on your body shape.

Did You Know

Blue Rules as the Most Popular Color

The color blue came in as the country's most popular color in a study done by Pantone, Inc., a color communication company. Nearly 35 percent of the 2000 people polled chose the color that evokes a soothing, calming tranquility. Perhaps this color choice reflects the stressful state of today's world.

Second to blue was green, chosen by 16 percent of those polled. It is considered fresh, clean, and revitalizing. It also signifies ecology and the preservation of nature—a current social concern.

The third most popular color was—surprisingly—purple, which just edged out red by 1 percent. The 18- to 29-year-olds consider purple to be sexy. Red is still viewed as the most exciting color, while black is considered mysterious and sophisticated.

When it comes to apparel, 37 percent of the people surveyed chose blue as their favorite color for casual clothing. Grays and blacks were preferred for business suits, but were the second favorite color for casual clothing (13 percent). Blues were the second favorite color for business attire.

Bright orange was the least favorite color overall, but found its highest acceptance among teens. Young people like this in-your-face, look-at-me color. A sulfuric yellow-green was the second most disliked color among adults, but it, too, was a favorite with teens.

So what's your favorite color? Whatever it is today may change as you get older as color preferences do tend to reflect a person's age.

Colors and Your Personality

Your personality often influences colors you wear. People who wear more warm colors than cool colors are often more outgoing. They are often lively, active, and energetic. They love bright colors. They feel light-hearted and cheerful when wearing bright colors.

Other people may feel shy and uncomfortable in such bright colors. Orange or red could overshadow their personalities. Cool or conservative colors often make them feel more at ease. They feel better in the calming look of blues and greens.

Look at the clothes you own. You may be able to tell whether you prefer warm or cool colors. Do you see more of one type of color than another?

Some colors make you feel good because you are sure you look nice in them. Suppose you receive a compliment on what you are wearing. The color of the outfit probably flatters your personal coloring. The color of a garment should enhance the appearance of the person who wears it. Your personal likes and dislikes and your tastes influence the colors you select to wear. Wearing colors that enhance your appearance generally have a positive effect on your personality, **16-19**.

16-19 The colors you choose to wear often reflect something about your personality.
Shutterstock

Summary

- Colors can be associated with certain feelings or moods.
- Understanding the properties of color can help you choose colors that enhance your best features and help you make better clothing decisions.
- Color has three properties or qualities: hue, value, and intensity.
- The color wheel shows the relationship among colors or hues.
- Colors on the wheel are classified as primary, secondary, or tertiary colors. Half of the colors are warm colors and the other half are cool colors.
- Colors opposite each other on the color wheel are complementary colors.
- The most appealing color combinations fall into six basic color schemes: monochromatic, analogous, complementary, split-complementary, triad, and accented neutral.
- Your best colors are those that enhance your personal coloring and body type. Consider your skin tone, hair, and eye color when choosing wardrobe colors.
- Using a color selection system based on the four seasons of the year can help you choose the right colors for you.
- Light, warm, bright colors tend to increase size, while dark, cool, dull colors tend to decrease size.

Graphic Organizer

Draw a T-chart on a sheet of paper. In the left column, list the topics found under the header Choosing Your Best Colors. In the right column, note significant details for each topic.

| Choosing Your Best Colors ||
Main Topics	Significant Details

Review the Facts

1. The brightness or dullness of a color describes its _____.
2. Name the secondary hues.
3. In a complementary color scheme, the color _____ is used with yellow.
4. An analogous color scheme uses colors that are _____ on the color wheel.
5. Give an example of a triad color scheme.
6. Everyone has either _____ or _____ undertones in their skin coloring.
7. Name two ways to use color to emphasize your hair and eyes.
8. What skin tone do people with summer coloring have?
9. What three types of colors should you choose if you want to appear smaller?
10. Give an example of how color can indicate your mood.

Think Critically

11. **Draw conclusions.** Use Internet or print resources to find out what colors are *in* this season. Do these colors enhance your features? Draw conclusions about what can you do to be fashionable and still look your best if these are not your best colors.

12. **Analyze decisions.** What color would you wear to an important job interview? How does this color enhance your skin, hair, eyes, and body shape? Explain your decision.
13. **Predict outcomes.** Think up some descriptive color names that would affect people's emotions. Predict which color names would entice people to buy garments in these colors. Share your predictions with the class.

Apparel Applications

14. **Create a color wheel.** Using tempera paints, make a color wheel of primary, secondary, and intermediate colors.
15. **Bulletin board.** Arrange a color wheel on the bulletin board. Group samples of fabric or paper under such words as value, intensity, cool, and warm. Title the bulletin board: *Put a Little Color in Your Life.*
16. **Create color schemes.** Use fabric or tempera paint to create examples of a complementary color scheme, an analogous color scheme, and a monochromatic color scheme. How can you use your color schemes in the future when selecting clothing?
17. **Analyze color schemes.** Bring samples of fabric prints and plaids to class. Identify the color scheme that was used in each fabric.
18. **Choose garment colors.** Select three garments. Describe the colors, and explain how they enhance your features. Discuss your choices in class. Do your classmates agree or disagree with your choices? Why?

Academic Connections

19. **Reading.** Locate reliable Internet or print resources on color and read about one or more of the following: color used as symbols; color used to reflect tranquility and peace; color that arouses passion; and colors that are used for warnings. Discuss your findings with the class.
20. **Writing.** Select a color scheme of your choice. Write a *word picture* describing an outfit in this color scheme. Would this be a good outfit for you to wear? Explain.

Workplace Links

21. **Analyze color choices.** Suppose you work for a trendy boutique. One of your clients is having trouble choosing a garment for a special occasion. You note the problem appears to be choosing the right color. Work with your client (a classmate) to determine his or her best color. Hold different-color fabric swatches next to your client's face. Which colors enhance your client's features?
22. **Portfolio builder.** Use Internet or print catalogs to select clothing colors for a mix-and-match wardrobe that enhances your best features. Plan enough wardrobe items for one week. Create a digital or print photo essay showing your wardrobe choices. Write a summary about your decisions, including how these clothing items enhance your skin, hair, eyes, body type, and personality. Save your photo essay in your portfolio.

Leading the Way with Color

Do you find the psychology of color fascinating? Are you interested in the impact of color on clothing choices? If you are, consider joining forces with a local nonprofit group that assists its clients with choosing clothes for work. Such groups often work with people who have low incomes. For an FCCLA *Community Service* project, consult a leader in the organization about working with one or more clients to help choose clothing colors that work well and the client(s) feel good in. See your adviser for information as needed.

Chapter 17

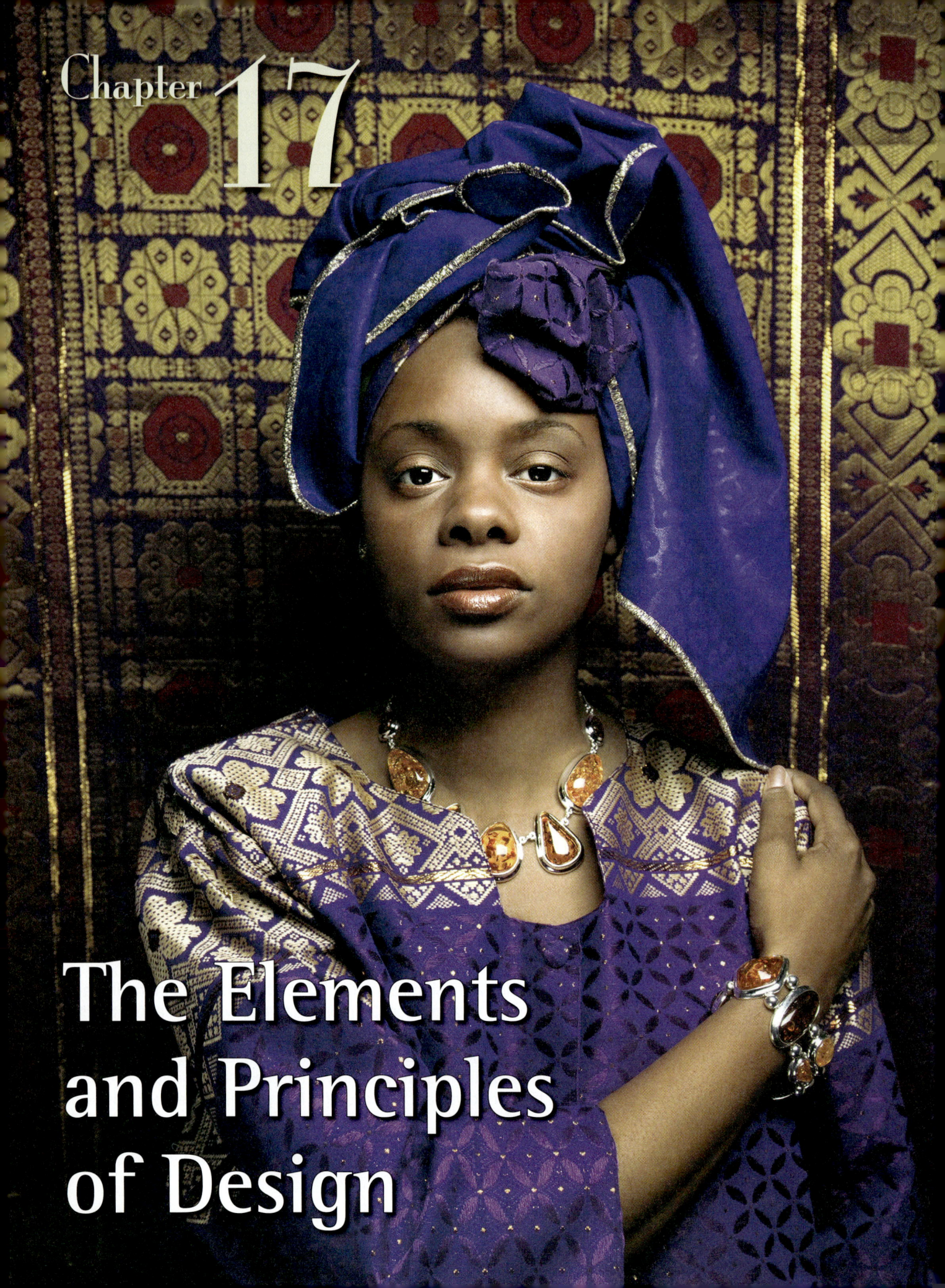

The Elements and Principles of Design

Chapter Objectives

After studying this chapter, you will be able to
- **identify** five basic body types.
- **describe** the elements of design and their use in clothing design.
- **describe** the principles of design and their use in clothing design.
- **explain** how the principles of design relate to the design elements.
- **use** the elements and principles of design in selecting clothes and accessories appropriate for your figure type and size.

Key Terms

design
optical illusion
elements of design
line
structural lines

decorative lines
shape
form
texture
principles of design

balance
proportion
rhythm
emphasis
harmony

Reading with Purpose

Before reading, skim the chapter and examine how it is organized. Look at the bold or italic words, headings of different colors and sizes, bulleted lists or numbered lists, tables, charts, captions, and boxed features.

A **design** is an arrangement of elements or details in a product or work of art. Paintings, buildings, and even cities are designs. The clothes people wear are designs. *Designing* is the art or practice of creating designs.

You may be attracted to a certain outfit because it is well designed. The overall effect is pleasing; all of the elements seem to belong together. The colors are right, the fabric is right, and the design is right. (A fashion designer, who is using the *elements* and *principles* of design you will study in this chapter, is carefully planning the outfit in 17-1.)

How can knowing about good design help you? First, it will help you to recognize a well-designed garment or ensemble. Second, it will help you select the designs that look best on you. With clever use of design, you will be able to show off your best features. If you know you look good, you will feel good about yourself.

Figure Types

Few people are ever totally happy with their body shapes. Some think they are too skinny or too heavy—too tall or too short. Others think their shoulders are too big or their hips are too broad when they look in a mirror. You may recall that the colors a person wears can give the illusion of increased or decreased

17-1 A fashion designer uses the elements and principles of design to achieve an attractive result. *Fashion Institute of Technology*

height or size. This does not mean a person is actually bigger or smaller; the color just creates that illusion. Understanding figure types and body shapes is key to developing a sense of design, which in turn will help you look your best.

A good place to begin is by identifying some basic body shapes. Body shape is called *figure* for females and *physique* for men. These figure and physique types are often compared to geometric shapes—particularly the triangle, rectangle, and circle. You may also see them referred to as objects, such as a pear, apple, and hourglass. These geometric shapes and objects represent the common shapes found in the human form. See figure **17-2**. The following are the five most common figure and/or physique types:

- *Triangle.* This shape is narrow on top and wider at the bottom. This means a person may have narrower shoulders, average to small bust/chest, and broader hips and thighs. Some people describe this figure as pear-shaped.
- *Inverted triangle.* This person has a large upper body and a smaller lower body. Shoulders are wide, but hips and thighs are narrow. The bust or chest is average to large. This shape may be described as apple-shaped. The typical man's physique is an inverted triangle.
- *Rectangle.* A person with this figure type has shoulders, waist, and hips of a similar width. The body shape has few curves. The chest is usually small and there is no defined waist.
- *Hourglass.* When you picture an hourglass, you envision an object that is wide at both the top and bottom, but narrow in the middle. This also describes the hourglass figure type. This person generally has a larger bust, a well-defined waist, and wider hips.
- *Circle or Rounded.* This body shape has more weight around the mid-section and often a large chest. As a result, the shoulders and hips appear narrower.

No matter what figure or physique type, people can use the elements and principles of design to create an **optical illusion**—a misleading image or visual impression presented to the eyes—of a slightly different shape and, therefore, enhance their best features.

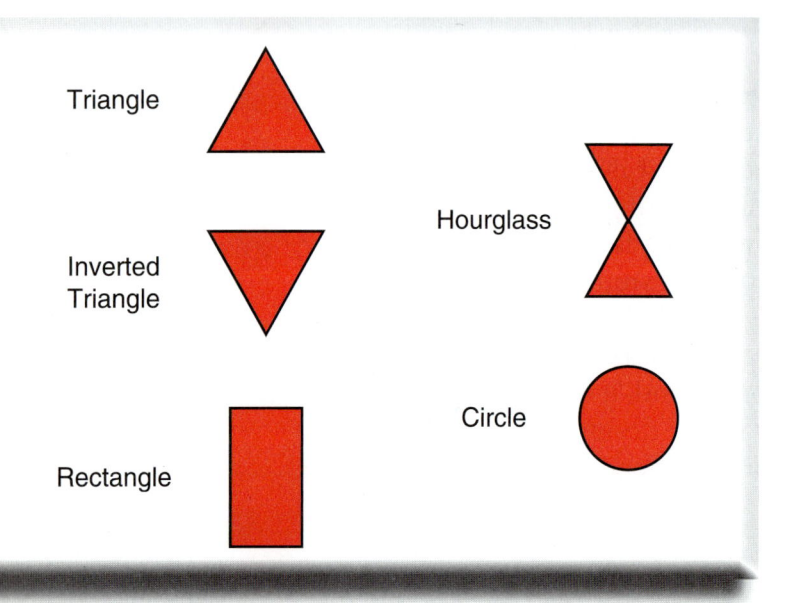

17-2 These five geometric shapes and objects represent the most common figure types. *Goodheart-Willcox Publisher*

Elements of Design

The **elements of design** are color, line, form, and texture. They are sometimes referred to as the building blocks of design. Each of these elements plays an important role in forming the structure of clothing designs. You can apply your knowledge of the elements of design as you select, buy, or construct clothes.

Line

Lines give direction to a design and break larger areas into smaller ones. Lines also create movement in a design, carrying the eye from one area to another. They can be vertical, horizontal, diagonal, or curved, **17-3**.

- *Vertical lines* lead the eye up and down. They give the feeling of height, dignity, and strength.
- *Horizontal lines* carry the eye from side to side. Such lines suggest a feeling of calm relaxation, but can add width.
- *Diagonal lines* are angled or slanted. They suggest activity, movement, and excitement. Because they are less common, they attract attention.
- *Curved lines* gently bend. They create the appearance of softness and fullness.

The lines found in garments can be either structural or decorative. **Structural lines** form as the pieces of a garment are sewn together. Seams, darts, pleats, tucks, or the edges of the garment may form these lines. They are easy to see in plain fabric. Sometimes structural lines are the main design element in a garment, **17-4**.

Decorative lines are applied to a garment to add interest. Braid, fringe, ruffles, edgings, top-stitching, lace, tabs, flaps, appliqués, and buttons all form decorative lines. The designer adds these features to a garment to create the design. Sometimes decorative lines accent structural lines. For instance, top-stitching along a neckline, seam, or cuff emphasizes the structural lines.

The line most important to a person is the *silhouette* or outline of the body. Knowing his or her silhouette helps a person decide how to use line in clothing to enhance appearance. See **17-5.**

17-3 These are just a few of the types of lines found in clothing.

Vertical Lines

Wearing clothes with vertical lines can make a person look taller and narrower. Study the illustrations in **17-6**. Notice how the eye moves upward, giving the illusion of slim height. A vertically striped dress can make a female seem taller because of the unbroken line the stripes create. Likewise, a vertically striped shirt or jacket can make a male seem taller.

The stripes in the fabric can form vertical lines, as well as any fabric design that is up and down—circles, dots, or prints. The structural and decorative lines of the garment may be vertical. Seams, buttons, pockets, cuffs, and trimmings may be in a vertical line.

Not all vertical lines make a figure appear narrower. If the lines are wide or spaced far apart, the figure will appear larger. This is because the eye goes back and forth between the lines, giving the illusion of more width. In 17-7, notice how the wide panel gives a wider look to the body. The narrow panel has a slenderizing effect.

Horizontal Lines

Horizontal lines cause the eyes to move from side to side, and tend to make a figure appear shorter and wider. Look at the illustrations in 17-8. If a garment has horizontal stripes, the body appears wider and therefore larger or heavier.

People with body shapes that seem too tall and thin can select garments that have horizontal stripes. For example, a wide contrasting belt can make a figure seem shorter because it divides the body into two parts, 17-9. Wide, bold stripes across narrow shoulders give the illusion of broader shoulders. Large people will seem even larger in bold plaids than in clothes with narrow, vertical stripes.

17-4 The structural lines are quite visible in this dress where the white center panel contrasts with the black.
Photo courtesy of McCall Pattern Company

17-5 An optical illusion causes your eye to sense that the left rectangle is shorter than the right one.

Using Lines to Create Illusions

Garment lines can create optical illusions. Look at the illustration. Though each rectangle is the same, the one on the right looks longer and narrower than the one on the left.

The clever use of line can give an illusion that people have different body types than they really have. With the correct use of line, a person can look shorter, taller, larger, or smaller.

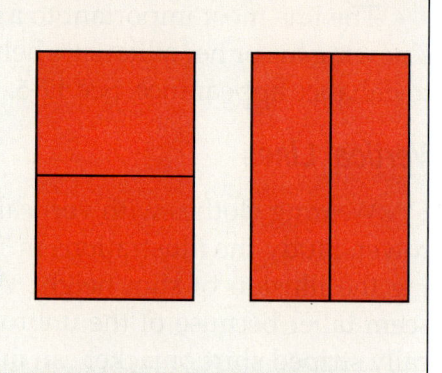

Chapter 17   The Elements and Principles of Design   **307**

17-6 For a taller and narrower look, select vertical lines that keep the eye moving upward.

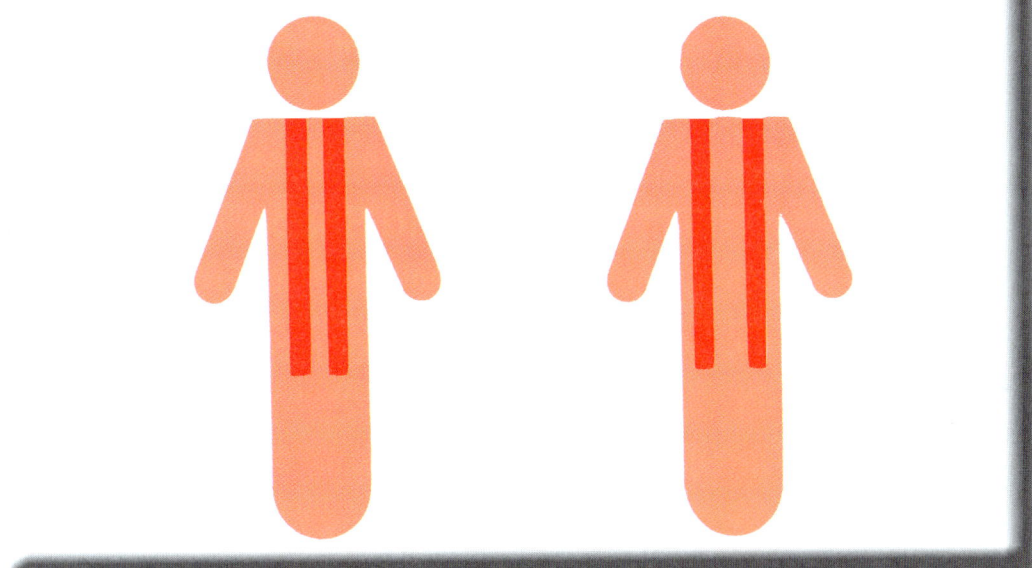

17-7 Not all vertical lines have the same effect. If they are spaced far apart, the figure will appear wider and heavier.

17-8 For a shorter, more rounded look, select lines that keep the eye moving from side to side.

Diagonal Lines

If a garment has diagonal lines and they are nearly vertical, they give the illusion of height. If they are mostly horizontal, they add width. However, the effect is not as strong as with strictly vertical or horizontal lines.

Curved Lines

Rolled collars on sweaters and round collars on garments are popular uses of curved lines. Pockets, trims, necklines, scarves, and caps or hats can also use curved lines.

Different effects can be achieved by using curved lines. For example, a person's square face will look less square with a rounded neckline. A long, thin neck appears shorter if a person wears a turtleneck or rolled neck sweater. A V-neckline draws emphasis to a pointed chin, while a high or round neckline softens this feature.

Form and Shape

The outline of an object is its **shape**, which is made up of lines. If you stand in front of a lighted area near a wall, you can see your silhouette on the wall as a shadow. When people see you from a distance, they see only your shape.

When a two-dimensional shape takes on a third dimension, it becomes a *form* or *mass*. **Form** is the three-dimensional shape of an object. If an object has height, weight, and depth, it has form. Form makes up the enclosed area of a design. Along with body shape, the clothes people wear help to create form.

Many factors determine what form or silhouette will be in fashion from year to year. One year the form may be a *natural* look. Clothes may follow the shape of the body. Another year, padded shoulders—which give a squared form—may be popular.

Several forms or shapes are common in clothes. These include the following:

- *Natural form.* The natural form follows the shape of the body. Clothes fit close and reveal the natural waist and hips.
- *Full form.* Some clothes, such as a full skirt or pants with wide legs, produce a full form. These clothes tend to visually increase size and weight.
- *Tubular form.* Clothes with a tubular form are more vertical. They include a straight dress without a defined waistline, straight-leg pants, or a suit. The tubular form creates the illusion of height and slenderness, 17-10.
- *Bell form.* Clothes that produce the bell-shaped form look good on most people. Flared skirts and pants are examples of bell forms.

17-9 The horizontal lines created by the contrasting belt, skirt color, and patch pockets cause the figure to appear shorter and wider. *Photo courtesy of McCall Pattern Company*

Texture

Texture refers to how a fabric feels and looks on the surface. The yarn, weave, and finish determine a fabric's texture. Some words that describe texture are smooth, dull, rough, shiny, nubby, soft, fuzzy, delicate, crisp, pebbly, scratchy, swishy, and shaggy.

Awareness of physique or figure type can help people choose textured fabrics that help enhance their best features. The following guidelines are helpful to note when choosing texture:

- Fuzzy, loopy, or shaggy surfaces are usually thicker and bulkier. They increase visual size.
- Stiff, crisp textures also increase the illusion of size because the fabric stands away from the body. They can, however, help conceal some body features.
- Soft, clingy fabrics reveal the body's entire silhouette.
- Smooth, flat textures give the illusion of decreased size.
- Shiny textures reflect light and emphasize body curves. They tend to add the illusion of weight or size.
- Dull surfaces tend to decrease size because they absorb light.

Combinations of textures are interesting. A bulky sweater to emphasize the shoulders can be worn with smooth-textured, slenderizing pants.

Fabrics may have a design woven into them or printed on them, creating a pattern. The fabric may be a stripe, plaid, floral, or geometric print. The designs may be large or small, light or dark, bold or subdued. If the pattern or design is large and bold, the texture will be secondary. The applied design will be more important than the texture.

Large, bold patterns call attention to the area where they are worn, **17-11**. This increases apparent size, especially when using bright or contrasting colors. Quiet, small, overall prints tend to decrease apparent size.

17-10 The tubular form of this dress gives the appearance of height and slimness.
Photo courtesy of McCall Pattern Company

Principles of Design

The **principles of design** are guidelines for combining and using the elements of design (color, form, line, and texture). *Balance, proportion, rhythm,* and *emphasis* are the principles of design. When these are used correctly, the result is *harmony*—the goal of design.

The principles of design are used in both creating and judging a design. Designers also use these principles as they work.

17-11 Large plaid fabrics in contrasting colors tend to increase apparent size. *Simplicity Pattern Co.*

Learning how to use each design principle helps people analyze the clothing designs they select. By assessing particular combinations of colors, forms, lines, or textures, they can make choices that enhance their body types.

Balance

When looking at something that has **balance**, you see objects that are arranged in an even, pleasing way. There is equal visual weight on both sides of an imaginary center line. Proper use of the elements of design creates balance in garments and outfits. Color, line, form, or texture can be used separately or together to achieve balance. There are two types of balance: formal and informal.

Formal Balance

With *formal balance*, or symmetrical balance, both sides of a garment are identical, 17-12. Formal balance is easy to achieve and observe in garments and outfits. Many shirts, blouses, pants, jackets, coats, and sweaters have formal balance. For example, skirts with the same number of pleats on each side of the center have formal balance. A shirt with an identical breast pocket on each side also has formal balance.

Informal Balance

Balance can also be achieved when the design elements are different on either side of an imaginary line. This unequal kind of balance is called *informal balance*, or asymmetrical balance. Informal balance is not as easy to create as formal balance, but it is usually more visually interesting. The sides are not alike, but neither side overpowers the other. With informal balance, there is less monotony while maintaining equal visual weight. Although each side is different, to the eye, the design appears to be balanced. A jacket with an off-center closing on one side balanced with a pocket on the other side is an example of informal balance, 17-13.

Proportion

Proportion is the relationship of one part to another and of all the parts to the whole. This includes sizes, spaces, shapes, and visual weight. When an outfit has pleasing proportion, it looks right for the person wearing it.

Clothing and accessories should be in proportion to a person's size and body shape. For example:

- If a person has a small body shape or is short, he or she should avoid styles that seem overpowering. Garments with huge pockets, big collars, large buttons, and wide lapels are not in proportion to body size.

17-12 A classic Western-style shirt is an example of formal balance with both sides of the garment identical on either side of center. *Photo courtesy of McCall Pattern Company*

17-13 This dress is an example of informal balance. The one shoulder sleeve balances the longer hem and jewelry on the opposite side. *Photo courtesy of McCall Pattern Company*

- If an individual has short legs, a short jacket will make his or her legs appear longer. A longer jacket makes the upper body seem longer and legs shorter.
- If a person is tall and slender, a large plaid sports shirt looks just right. In contrast, the same shirt will look out of proportion on a smaller, shorter person.
- If a female is smaller, a large handbag or other large accessories will look completely out of proportion to her size.
- If a person is tall, a wide, large belt looks proportionately appropriate. A narrower belt is more in proportion for smaller body shapes.

Unequal proportions are usually more visually interesting than equal ones, **17-14**. When a jacket or shirt is exactly the same length as the skirt or pants length worn with it, the effect is uninteresting. Stripes on fabrics that are equal in width are not as interesting as those that vary in width. An uneven number (three or five) of buttons on a jacket or coat is more pleasing than an even number (two or four).

Learning to identify good proportion requires examining many garments and outfits. Reviewing pictures in newspapers and magazines will give you practice. Study your own clothes and the clothing you see others wear. With practice, you will be able to achieve the best proportion for you.

Rhythm

Rhythm is the feeling of movement created by line, shape, or color in a design. It causes the eye to move smoothly from one part of the design to another. With rhythm, each part of the design seems to belong to or go with another part.

Rhythm in design is somewhat like rhythm in music. In music, a sound is repeated, a regular beat is heard, and rhythm is produced. However, in design, we *see* rhythm rather than hear it. Rhythm in design is achieved by repetition, gradation, and radiation of colors, lines, shapes, and textures, 17-15.

- *Repetition.* To achieve rhythm through repetition, lines, colors, forms, or textures are repeated in a design. For example, a designer may choose one color in a plaid for use in trim or buttons. Because of the repetition of color, your eye moves from one area to another and causes you to look at each part of the outfit. Likewise, when lines are repeated, rhythm is achieved, 17-16. Curved pockets on a coat go with the curves of the coat hem or the rounded lapels. Contrasting trim on a suit may be repeated on both the lapels and sleeve hems.

17-14 The short contrasting top shows good use of proportion in this outfit.
Simplicity Pattern Co.

- *Gradation.* Varying rhythm through gradation also achieves movement. For instance, stripes may be close together at the top of a sweater and gradually become wider apart at the bottom. Gradation also occurs with other types of movement—from light to dark colors, from small to large sizes or large to small, or from horizontal to vertical lines.
- *Radiation.* Another way to achieve rhythm in design is by radiation. Radiation occurs when lines extend outward from a central point. In clothing, gathers at the neckline of a sweater or dress create lines toward the waistline. These same gathers also draw the viewer's eye to the person's face because it is close to the center of interest or where the lines form.

With rhythm, your eye moves steadily from one part of an outfit to another part. This is why it is important for plaids and stripes to match at seams. Unmatched stripes and plaids can destroy the rhythm of an outfit. The uneven breaks in the fabric design cause the eye to stop at that point.

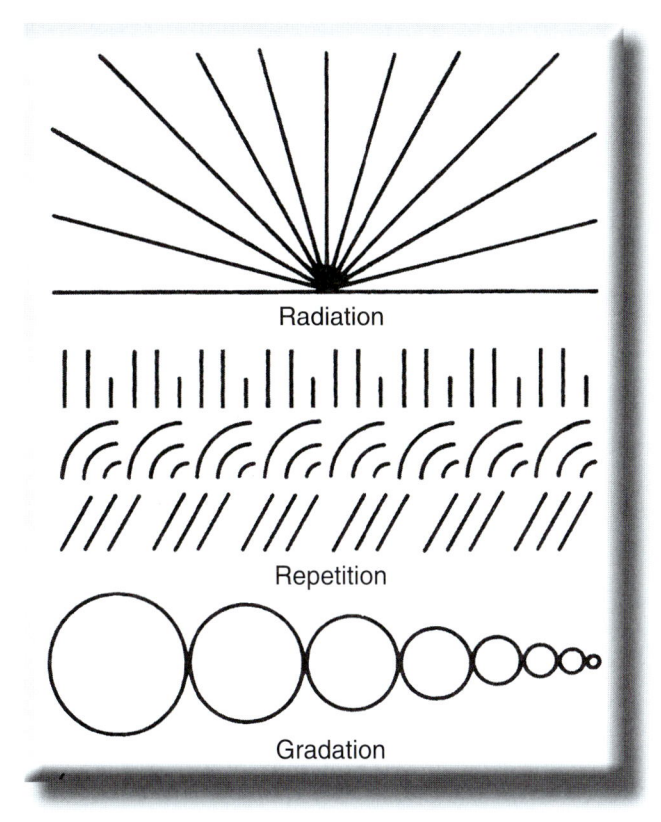

17-15 Rhythm can be achieved in a variety of ways.

17-16 The repetition of lines in this skirt creates rhythm, which causes the eye to move the length of the skirt. *Photo courtesy of McCall Pattern Company*

Emphasis

Interesting designs have one part that stands out more than any other part. They have a center of interest or **emphasis**. The eye is drawn to this area and it is the first thing people see.

Emphasis should be used to draw attention to a person's best features, 17-17. Color, design details, texture, and accessories all help achieve emphasis. Lace, ruffles, and unusual shapes in buttons and trims draw attention to the areas of placement.

Accessories can add emphasis to a plain blouse and skirt or a shirt and pants. A tie, a pin, or neck jewelry can improve the looks of any outfit by providing a point of emphasis.

A contrasting belt emphasizes the waistline. A person who is thicker through the middle will likely choose another area of his or her body to emphasize. For example, a bright print tie or scarf at the neckline pulls attention away from the body shape and draws it to the face.

If a person desires to give the illusion of decreased height, he or she may choose an area of emphasis at the waistline or hemline. To give the optical illusion of increased height, place the area of interest high on the body. This draws the eye upward instead of downward.

Achieving Harmony

Using the elements of design according to the principles of design creates harmony and a pleasing visual image. In achieving **harmony**, all parts of a design look as if they belong together as in **17-18**. The line, color, form, and texture harmonize with each other. The design is harmonious when it is well balanced, has a sense of rhythm, and is in good proportion. Everything looks suited to the whole—there is a sense of unity. The design also enhances the coloring, body type, and personality of the wearer.

Consider all parts of an outfit when striving for harmony. Jeans and leather jackets go together. A leather jacket over a fancy party dress is less harmonious. A plaid, cotton flannel sports shirt looks better with the collar open than with a necktie.

Accessories can help achieve harmony in an outfit. However, too many accessories can also spoil the effect. Repeating colors from a garment in an added belt or jewelry can be pleasing. Both males and females can wear boots, jeans, a western belt, and shirt for a harmonious, casual look.

Just as harmony is the goal of good design, wearing garments and outfits that help you look your best should be your goal. You can use your knowledge of the design elements and design principles to enhance your best features. The bottom line is to select clothing that creates the best total look for you and that you find pleasing.

17-17 The contrasting scarf worn with this coat provides a point of emphasis and calls attention to the face.
Simplicity Pattern Co.

17-18 Harmony is achieved when all aspects of an ensemble create a pleasing visual image and all parts of the design seem to belong together. *Simplicity Pattern Co.*

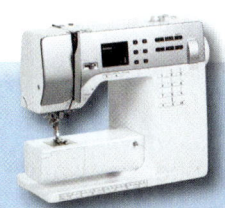

Focus on Technology

Virtual Reality Puts You in the Fashion Picture

One of the drawbacks of shopping for clothes online is the inability to try them on to see how they look and fit. That may be less of a problem now that there are Virtual Dressing Rooms™. This latest technology, available now at some websites, allows you to virtually *try on* clothing and accessories. You can even apply makeup and experiment with new hairstyles and colors on a model that reflects your own measurements, features, and skin tone. You can sample and mix and match an entire digital inventory of clothes, accessories, hairstyles, makeup, and eyeglasses.

To get started, use your own face and body measurements to create a photorealistic lifelike image. Body shapes (triangular, hourglass, pear, apple, lanky) and types (petite, misses, women's, men's) are selected. A built-in fashion advisory offers advice on fashion selections. Recommendations for appropriate styles and colors based on your figure or physique type and skin tone are provided. Accessories to go with an outfit might also be suggested. Finally, the correct garment size based on the manufacturer's clothing lines is provided. Shopping for clothes online can be more fun and satisfying when you can put yourself on the computer screen.

Other new features to look for on fashion websites include

- shopping services that keep a file of your sizes, tastes, and past purchases
- ability for two shoppers at two different computers to browse together and add items to a single *shopping cart*
- e-mail announcements of special sales and promotions
- the mailing of free fabric swatches if you want to check out the color or feel of a fabric
- *zoom* technology that allows shoppers to see product details
- a *live chat* option that allows you to talk directly to a customer service representative, receive outfit suggestions, or help in finding certain items
- talking by phone (if you have a second line) or by live text

What other innovations await the online shopper?

Summary

- A design is an arrangement of elements or details in a product or work of art. The clothes people wear are designs.
- Figure and physique types are often compared to geometric shapes, particularly the triangle, rectangle, and circle. These geometric shapes and objects represent the common shapes found in the human figure.
- The elements of design are color, line, form, and texture.
- Lines in garments can be vertical, horizontal, diagonal, or curved. They may be structural or decorative. Lines can create optical illusions that may mislead the eyes.
- The form or shape of a garment can give the illusion of larger or smaller size. Fabric texture also influences visual shape and size.
- The principles of design are balance, proportion, rhythm, and emphasis.
- The goal of good design is harmony. Correctly using the elements and principles of design achieves harmony.

Graphic Organizer

Use a Venn diagram to show how using elements and principles of design well leads to harmony in good design.

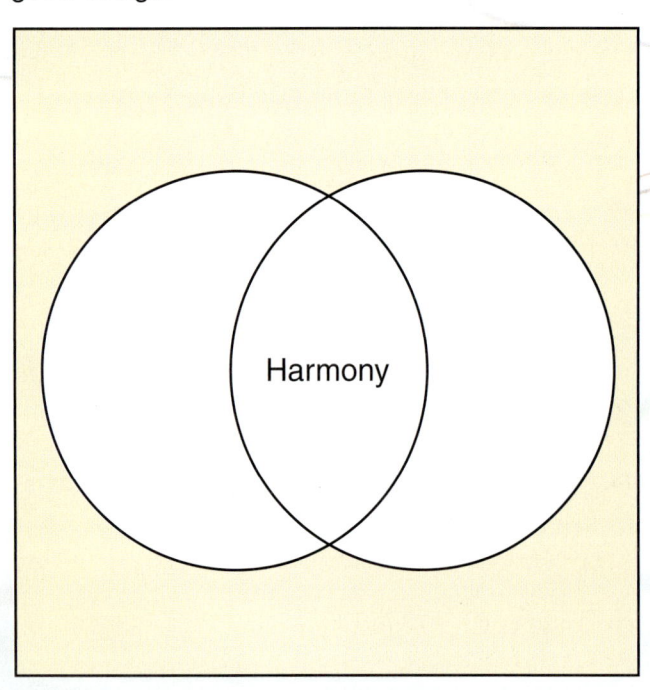

Review the Facts

1. Which body type has a larger upper body and a smaller lower body and represents a man's physique?
2. Explain the difference between structural lines and decorative lines in garments.
3. Give three examples of lines in garment features that give the illusion of height and slenderness.
4. Name two fabric textures that tend to give the appearance of increased size.
5. Explain how the principles of design relate to the design elements.
6. Contrast formal and informal balance.
7. Name three design features to avoid when choosing clothes or accessories that are in proportion for a smaller figure.
8. Give an example of how to achieve rhythm in a garment. State the type of rhythm used in your example.
9. A bright red tie worn with a white shirt is an example of which principle of design?
10. Summarize how to achieve harmony in a design.

Think Critically

11. **Make inferences.** Is there a difference between good design and bad design? Identify evidence to support your inferences.
12. **Draw conclusions.** If you were a fashion designer, which element of design would you consider most important? Why? Share your conclusions with the class.
13. **Make predictions.** Review a number of fashion magazines or websites. Identify which form or silhouette seems to be in fashion for the current season. Predict which factors may influence silhouettes for the following season.

Apparel Applications

14. **Electronic bulletin board.** Plan an electronic bulletin board titled *Select the Right Designs*. Locate electronic pictures of fabric examples with various textures, lines, forms and colors. Use a school-approved web application to group them according to different body shapes noted in the text—triangle, inverted triangle, rectangle, hourglass, and circle or rounded. Post your electronic bulletin board to the class website.

15. **Identify fabric effects.** Collect as many fabric samples as possible of textures and designs. Describe each texture and design in class. Identify those that give the illusion of increased size and those that offer a narrowing effect.

16. **Photo essay.** Create a photo essay illustrating the different principles of design. Use clothing photos from magazines, pattern books, or from print or online catalogs. Mount pictures on paper or insert digital pictures into presentation software. Share your examples with the class. Are your examples excellent, fair, or poor? Support your choices.

17. **Identify balance.** Examine your wardrobe. Choose two items that show formal and informal balance. Take a picture of these items. Write a summary indicating why these articles of clothing are good examples of formal and informal balance.

18. **Demonstrate proportion.** With a classmate of a different height, demonstrate the principle of proportion by trying on several sweaters or jackets of different lengths.

19. **Analyze harmony.** Collect ten pictures of people in various outfits. Decide which outfits have harmony and which do not. Give reasons for your answers. Also decide which outfits would make a person look taller and slimmer and which would make a person look shorter and heavier.

Academic Connections

20. **Reading.** Read articles relating to the elements and principles of design in one or more recent fashion magazines. How do the articles describe the use of the elements and principles of design in current fashions? Share your findings with the class.

21. **Writing.** Choose one of the five basic figure/physique types. Review the elements and principles of design. Then make a list of colors, garment features, styles, and accessories that would be appropriate for this figure or physique. Create another list of items to avoid. Write a summary explaining your rationale for these choices.

Workplace Links

22. **Design fabric.** Create a fabric design on paper or with a CAD program on a computer. Analyze the design. Does it use the elements and principles of design to achieve harmony? Ask class members for comments.

23. **Show emphasis.** Presume you work in a clothing retail shop. Your assignment is to come up with creative ways to highlight points of emphasis in the new line of garments just delivered to the store. Choose one garment, identify the point of emphasis, and explain how you will display the garment to its best advantage.

24. **Portfolio builder.** As a fashion writer for your school newspaper, it has come to your attention that your classmates want to know more about how to choose clothes to enhance their appearance. Write an article about using the elements and principles of design to enhance various figure types and physiques. Save a copy for your portfolio.

Using the Elements and Principles of Design

Prepare an FCCLA STAR Event *Illustrated Talk* on a topic related to using the elements and principles of design. For example, you might use the elements and principles to organize a presentation on choosing a low-cost wardrobe for a teen or someone starting a new job.

Use the *Illustrated Talk* guidelines found in the FCCLA STAR Events Manual on the Web. See your adviser for information as needed.

PART 4

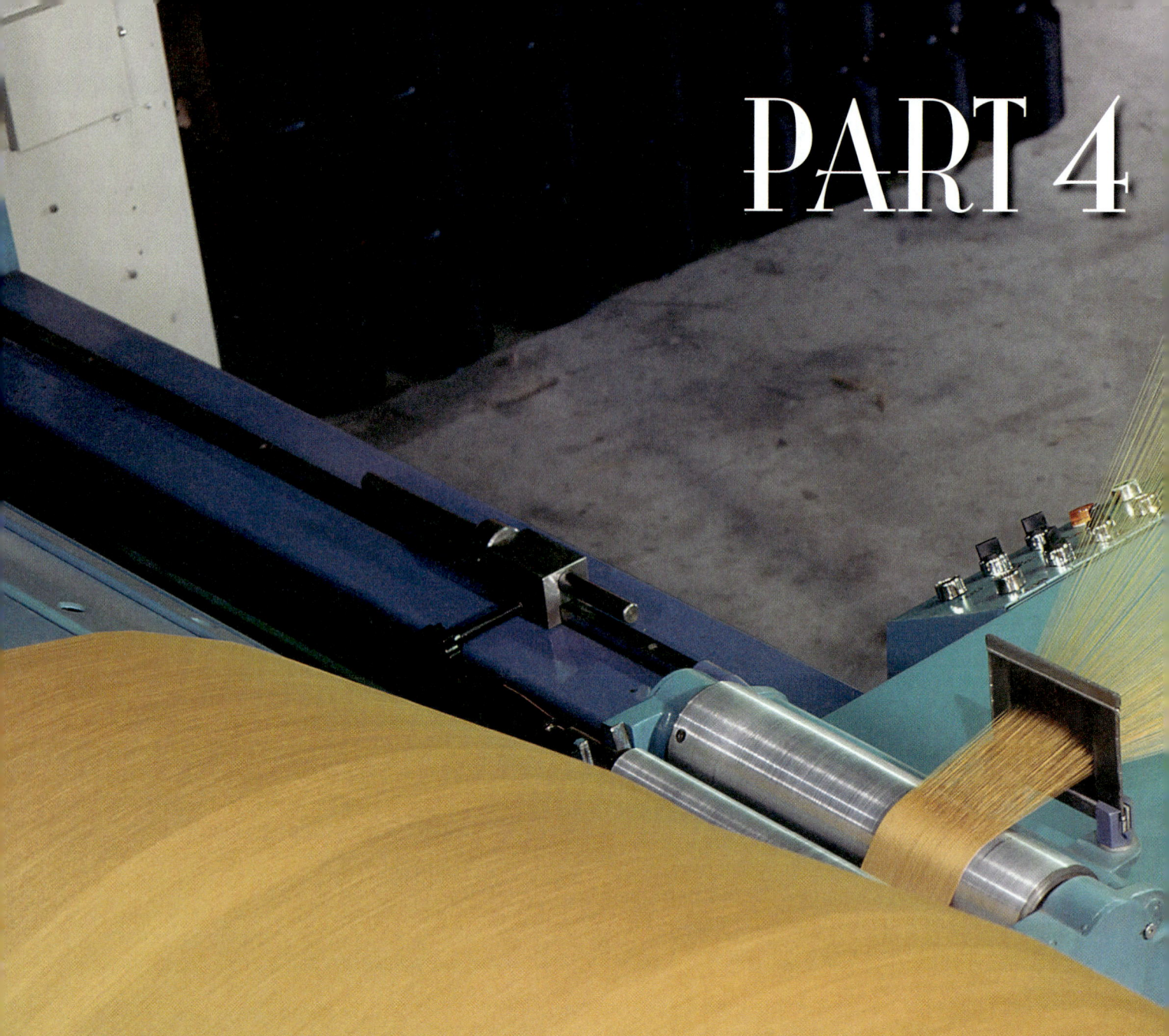

From Fibers to Fabrics

Chapters

18 The Natural Fibers
19 The Manufactured Fibers
20 From Yarn to Fabric
21 Fabric Color and Finishes

Chapter 18

The Natural Fibers

Chapter Objectives

After studying this chapter, you will be able to
- **identify** fiber characteristics that affect appearance and performance of fabrics.
- **summarize** the sources, production steps, and characteristics of the natural fibers.
- **summarize** the characteristics, care, and end uses of natural fibers.

Key Terms

yarn	mildew	woolen yarns
fabrics	linen	worsted yarns
cellulosic fibers	ramie	virgin wool
protein fibers	jute	recycled wool
cotton	wool	silk

Reading with Purpose

Make a list of everything you already know about the topic of this chapter. As you read the chapter, check off the items that are covered in the chapter. Then make a list of facts that are new to you.

Fibers are the basic units of all textiles. When fibers are put together to form a continuous strand, a **yarn** is made. Yarns are woven or knitted together to make **fabrics**.

Look at **18-1** to see the relationship among fibers, yarns, and fabrics. You can see the same thing by pulling a *thread* from any scrap of fabric. This is a yarn. Untwist the yarn to find the tiny, individual fibers.

There are two main groups of fibers. *Natural fibers* are made from natural sources—plants and animals. Common natural fibers are cotton and wool. *Manufactured fibers* are made from chemicals in factories. Common manufactured fibers are nylon and polyester.

Fiber Characteristics

Each fiber has its own characteristics and properties, depending on its source or chemical composition. The fiber may also be short, long, straight, or curly. These fiber characteristics greatly affect the appearance and performance of the fabrics they become.

Knowledge of fiber characteristics will help you select the fiber most appropriate for its end use. The characteristics you look for in a fiber used for sportswear are different from one you select for evening wear. Fibers chosen for carpets or bed linens will require different characteristics than those chosen for bath towels.

18-1 Fibers are combined to make yarns, and yarns are combined to make fabrics. *Agricultural Research Service, USDA*

As you read about the various fibers, you will learn about their characteristics, 18-2. Keep these characteristics in mind as you learn about the natural fibers as well as the manufactured fibers. Then you will be able to select the best fiber for your particular apparel or household need.

Natural Fibers

The most common natural fibers are cotton, linen, wool, and silk. Natural fibers vary in quality depending on the kind of animal or plant and the growing conditions. The fibers must be cleaned before they can be made into yarns. Supplies of natural fibers vary, according to the season. They each have unique characteristics that cannot be copied by science. Therefore, natural fibers are still an important part of today's textile story.

There are two categories of natural fibers: cellulosic fibers and protein fibers, 18-3. **Cellulosic fibers** come from vegetable (plant) sources. There are many kinds of cellulosic fibers, but few are used in clothing. Cotton, flax, and ramie are the main cellulosic fibers used for apparel.

Protein fibers come from animal sources. Wool and silk are the main protein fibers. Others are called *specialty hair fibers*. These include mohair and cashmere fibers from the goat family; camel, llama, alpaca, vicuña, and guanaco hairs of the camel family; and angora hair from the rabbit family. Supplies of the specialty hair fibers are smaller than wool supplies, so they are more expensive.

Cotton

Cotton is the natural fiber obtained from the cotton plant. Throughout history, cotton has played a major role in everyday life. It was and still is the most widely used natural fiber.

Cotton has many features that make it great for clothing and household items. It is inexpensive and has many uses. Cotton is strong and launders well, though it may shrink unless given a special treatment. It is soft and absorbent, making it a good choice for towels and undergarments. It keeps the body cool in warm weather, so it is a popular choice for summer apparel.

Two disadvantages of cotton are that it wrinkles easily unless given a special finish, and it mildews if stored when damp. **Mildew** is a discoloration caused by a fungus that grows on some fabrics when they are moist for a period of time.

Fiber Characteristics

Strength—the ability to withstand pulling and twisting
Shrinkage—the ability to maintain size
Warmth—the ability to maintain body temperature
Durability—the ability to hold up to repeated usage
Absorbency—the ability to take in moisture
Wicking—the ability to pull moisture away from the body and toward the surface of the fabric where it can evaporate quickly
Wrinkle resistance—the ability to resist creasing
Resiliency—the ability to spring back when crushed or wrinkled
Elasticity—the ability to return to its original size
Shape retention—the ability to retain the original shape
Abrasion resistance—the ability to withstand rubbing
Luster—the natural sheen or shine of some fibers
Static resistance—the ability to withstand the buildup of electricity

18-2 Knowledge of fiber characteristics will help you select the right fabric for your needs.

Natural Fibers

Cellulosic		Specialty Hair Fibers	
Cotton	Jute	Cashmere	Alpaca
Hemp	Flax	Camel's hair	Vicuña
Ramie		Llama	Guanaco
Protein			
Wool	Silk		

18-3 Of all the natural fibers, cotton, linen, wool, and silk are used most often in clothes.

The cotton plant can grow in any part of the world where the growing season lasts six or seven months. China leads in cotton production, followed by the U.S. and India.

Cotton comes from the seedpods of the cotton plant. After the blooms fall from the plant, the seedpod or *boll* grows. Snow-white fibers form from the seeds inside. When it is ripe, the boll bursts open. Many bolls are on one stalk or plant, **18-4**.

After picking, cotton is taken to a *gin*. This machine separates the fibers from the seed. The cotton is compressed into 500-pound bales. Once cotton reaches the mill, it goes through many steps before becoming yarn, including the following:

- After removal of most impurities, the fibers are shaped into a lap. The *lap* is a continuous layer of fibers that is wrapped into a cylindrical package.
- *Carding* pulls the fibers from the lap, cleans them, and straightens them into a *carded sliver*—a soft rope of fibers.
- *Drawing*—a process that begins to make the fibers parallel—combines many carded slivers into a single drawn sliver. Blending the fibers this way helps make them more uniform. The drawn sliver is *stretched*.

- *Combing* may be done to make fibers even more parallel and to remove any short fibers. This leaves longer fibers, which make smoother, stronger yarns. Combing is an extra step that adds cost to the final product. The product of combing is *combed sliver*. See **18-5**.

- At this point, the combed (or drawn) slivers are fed into a roving frame where the cotton is twisted slightly and pulled to become a smaller strand. This strand is called *roving*. It is about the size of a pencil.

- Finally, spinning machines pull the roving finer, add more twist, and wind it on bobbins. The tightly wound yarns are ready to be formed into fabric. See **18-6**.

Cotton has had a great deal of competition from manufactured fibers. New treatments and finishes have helped cotton retain its popularity. For instance, shrinkage of cotton denim has been controlled so the jeans you buy will not shrink as much. In addition, combining cotton with manufactured fibers greatly improves garment performance.

Previously, you learned about organic cotton. Many people are concerned about the amount of chemical pesticides and fertilizers used to grow cotton. They prefer to buy garments and household textiles made from organically grown cotton. Organic cotton is more expensive to grow than regular cotton, so it will cost more. It makes up less than one percent of all cotton.

18-4 When the cotton ball is ripe, it bursts open and is ready to harvest. *Shutterstock*

18-5 The combing machine further straightens the fibers to make smoother, stronger yarns called combed slivers. *National Cotton Council of America*

18-6 Cotton yarns are wound onto bobbins and are ready to be made into fabric. *Shutterstock*

Trends Making News

Recycled Jeans

Recycling clothing used to mean taking items to a thrift shop or a consignment store to be bought and worn again by others. But a growing concern about dwindling natural resources and environmental pollution is driving businesses to devise new ways to recycle apparel. Some companies have been turning old clothing into new products.

For example, "denim drives" are held by student groups and major retailers. Some retailers offer discounts on new merchandise in exchange for customers' used denim jeans. Thousands of pairs of jeans can be collected in a single drive and turned over to manufacturers for processing. After the zippers, snaps, buttons, and any decorations are removed, the jeans are broken down into cotton fibers. The fibers are used to create new products, such as the insulation used in the walls of homes and commercial buildings.

Repurposing materials in this way can help conserve raw materials. It can be good for the environment in other ways. For example, by insulating their homes, people reduce their use of nonrenewable energy sources, including coal and natural gas. Although insulation made from recycled blue jeans can be expensive, manufacturers claim the use of natural fibers makes it less toxic.

In the future, clever entrepreneurs will likely create other new ways to recycle jeans and other apparel.

Shutterstock

Flax (Linen)

Flax is the fiber used to make **linen** fabric. It was probably the first cellulosic fiber used for making fabric. The Egyptians grew fields of flax along the Nile River over 4000 years ago and made it into fine cloth. Pieces of linen have been found in the tombs of the Pharaohs. Egyptian mummies, wrapped in linen, are still seen in museums. Today, Belgium, France, the Netherlands, and Poland produce most of the linen fabric.

Linen is known for its durability and absorbency. Flax fibers are the strongest of the natural fibers. They are also smooth and lustrous. Since flax fibers are longer than cotton ones, there are fewer fiber ends in a yarn. There is less lint from fiber ends on the fabric surface. This means that linen does not attract or hold soil like cotton does. For this reason, linen is a good choice for tablecloths, kitchen towels, draperies, upholstery, and clothing, **18-7**.

Linen has an added plus as a fabric for summer apparel since flax is the coolest of wearable fibers. This is because it absorbs body heat, carries it away from the body, and dries quickly.

A disadvantage of linen is that it wrinkles easily. A special finish can solve this problem, but the finish reduces the absorption and coolness of the fabric.

Linen is often an expensive fabric. This is because making linen from flax takes much time and effort. Machines pull flax plants from the ground. Threshing machines remove the seeds, and the flax stalks are allowed to dry in the sun. Then they are tied into bundles and soaked in dew or water for one or two days. This loosens the outside woody stalk from the flax fibers. The bundles are dried again and rollers crush the stalks. This completes the separation of the soft flax fibers from the harsh straw.

Next, the fibers are combed. This process separates the short fibers from the long fibers. Then they pass through a machine in which they are combined into a continuous wide ribbon, or sliver. The drawing process is repeated until all the fibers are parallel in small, ropelike strands.

Finally, the linen yarns are spun. The method used depends on the kind of fabric that will be made. Finishes can be applied to give linen different properties, 18-8.

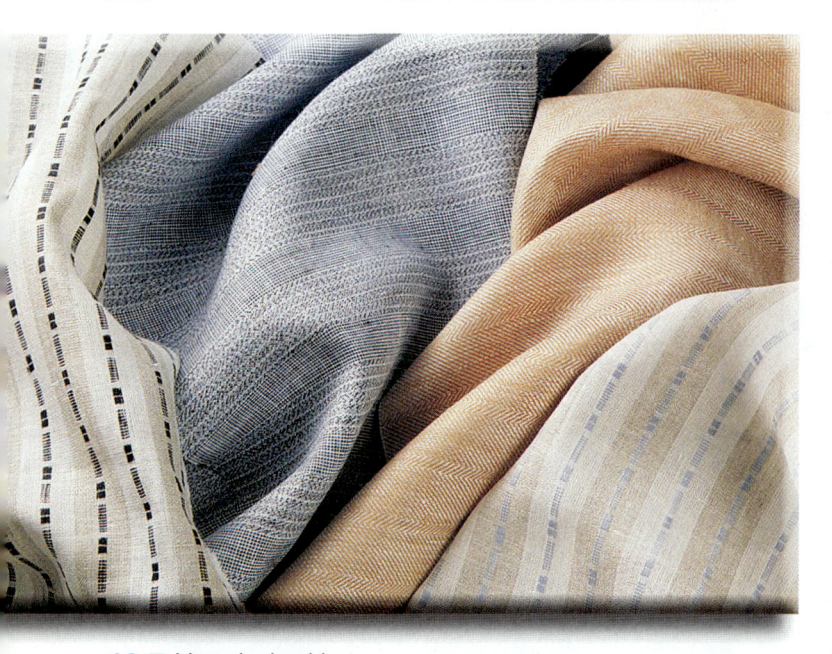

18-7 Linen is durable and extremely beautiful and has a distinctive texture. *Irish Linen Guild*

Other Plant Fibers

Ramie comes from a shrubby plant that grows often in China and India. The fibers come from the stems of the plants, similar to harvesting of flax for linen.

The ramie fiber is strong, lustrous, absorbs moisture, and dries quickly. In the past, it was mainly used for making ropes, canvas, and fire hoses because of its strength. Today, in combination with other natural fibers and manufactured fibers, ramie is used in clothing. Ramie adds strength to fabrics such as cotton, rayon, and silk, while these fibers give a soft feel to the fabric.

18-8 Different finishing treatments can produce the crisp elegance of a fine damask tablecloth or the cool comfort of linen clothes. *Irish Linen Guild*

Jute also comes from a plant. It is a rough, coarse fiber and has a natural odor. The main use of jute is for making burlap bags, but it is also used for decorative household items and accessories. Bulletin boards and lampshades often have a burlap fabric covering.

Jute is not a strong fiber, and the fiber weakens with age. It wrinkles easily and produces lint. Jute takes dyes readily and is quite inexpensive.

Wool

Wool is made from the fleece (hair) of sheep or lambs. It is the most common animal fiber people wear today, but its use goes back to early times. Crude wool fabrics have been found in ruins of the Stone Age. Even then, people knew that the fleece of sheep was softer and warmer than the skins of other animals. Sheep were the first animals to be domesticated (raised for their fleece).

Wool is the warmest of the natural fibers. It is a natural insulator, so it protects the body from changes in temperature. The fibers trap air, preventing the transfer of heat and cold. A wool fabric is strong and durable, but lightweight. It can absorb moisture without making a person feel wet. It is also *resilient*, recovering its original shape and size after stretching. The wrinkle-resistance of wool is another desirable characteristic. These factors make it a comfortable fabric for clothes.

The first step to produce wool is to shear the sheep, 18-9. If possible, the fleece is removed in one piece. The quality varies from different areas on the sheep. The best comes from the shoulders and sides, the poorest from the lower legs. Quality also depends on the health of the sheep and the climate.

At the wool mill, many steps are needed to produce yarn. First, the fibers are graded and sorted according to quality. To remove the natural *lanolin*, or oil, the fibers are *scoured* or washed in detergent or soap. Lanolin is refined and used in cosmetics, shampoos, and ointments.

Wool is carded to straighten fibers. After carding, the longer fibers are combed. The carded sliver is made into **woolen yarns** that use the short fibers (less than two inches). Yarns made from combed sliver (called top in the case of wool) are called **worsted yarns**. Worsted yarns are made using longer fibers.

The fibers in woolen yarns lie in all directions, giving a twisted, loose look. They have a somewhat fuzzy surface. These yarns are used for making flannels, tweeds, and soft fleece fabrics.

The longer fibers in worsted yarns are tightly twisted. This produces a closely woven, hard-surfaced fabric. Worsted fabrics are lighter in weight and smoother than woolen fabrics. Gabardine, challis, and sharkskin are examples of worsted fabrics. See 18-10 to compare woolen and worsted yarns.

Consumers cannot know how much and what type of wool is in a fabric simply by looking at it. To protect consumers and manufacturers, the *Wool Products Labeling Act* was passed in 1939. The law helped overcome confusion and misinformation about the wool used in products. Any textile product that

18-9 Once a year, fleece is taken from the sheep by an expert shearer using an electric clipper. *Shutterstock*

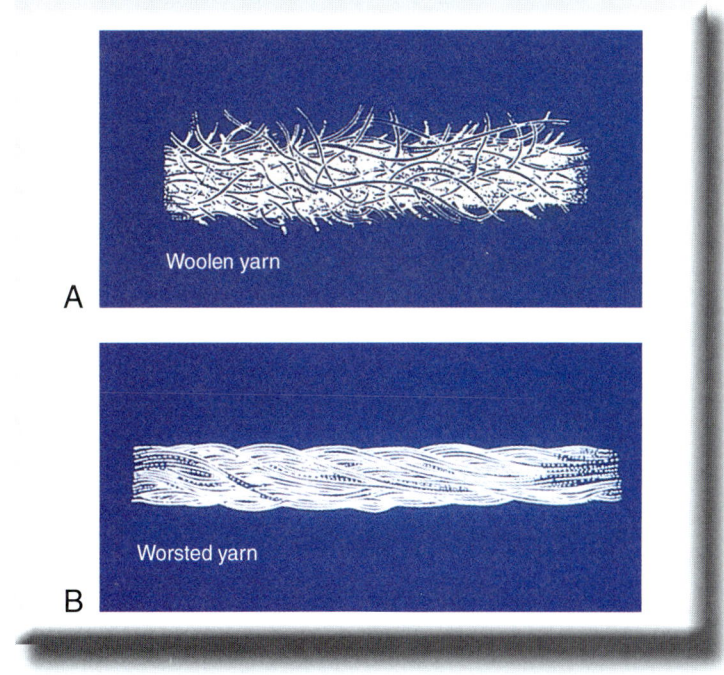

18-10 Woolen yarns are made from carded sliver (A). Worsted yarns are made from combed sliver called "top" (B). *International Wool Secretariat*

contains some wool must list the percentage and type of wool present and the country of origin. The term *wool* means that the fiber has never been used before for a fabric or garment. Some manufacturers call this **virgin wool**.

Recycled wool contains wool fibers from previously made wool fabrics. Recycled wool can come from two sources. It might come from a product that was made but never used. This is called *reprocessed wool* and may come from unused garments or cutting scraps. If made from wool that was previously used, it is called *reused wool*.

When wool is recycled, the quality can be lower. A low price may be more important than appearance or durability. Uses for recycled wool may include winter gloves, interlinings of coats, and picnic blankets. A small amount of recycled wool mixed with other fibers does not mean the product is inferior. You must decide how you will be using the product. It may meet your particular needs.

Australian Wool Innovation Ltd and its affiliates currently own the Woolmark brand. All apparel products (fabrics and garments) legally displaying a Woolmark symbol must have passed Woolmark quality standards, which requires products to be made from 100 percent new wool and to meet a range of performance standards, **8-11**. Products made of no less than 50 percent wool, and no more than two others fibers, use the *Woolmark Blend* logo. *Woolmark* and *Woolmark Blend* branding is also available for home/interior and laundry care products.

Silk

Silk is a protein fiber that comes from the cocoons of silkworms. Manufacturers unwind the cocoons to obtain the fiber. The silk fiber is the longest natural fiber, sometimes reaching a thousand yards or more.

Silk is one of the strongest fibers. A strand of silk is two-thirds as strong as an iron wire of equal size. While it is strong, it also has a natural shine or *luster* giving fabrics a luxurious look. It is very elastic and resists wrinkling. Silk is so smooth that dirt does not cling to it. Though silk is washable, the dyes used often are not. Most care labels advise dry cleaning garments made of silk.

Japan is the leading producer of raw silk today. China, Italy, France, and India also produce large amounts of silk. The United States does not produce raw silk because of the high cost of labor. However, it is the world's largest manufacturer of silk products.

Some of the steps in silk production are shown in **18-12**. A silk moth lays from 200 to 500 eggs early in the summer. As soon as the tiny worms hatch, they begin eating mulberry leaves. They eat their own weight in leaves each day. After about five weeks, they have grown to about 3 inches long and ½-inch thick.

At this time, the silkworm stops eating and begins to spin its cocoon. First, it spins

18-11 The Woolmark label is used on fabrics made of pure wool. The Woolmark Blend mark is used on fabrics made predominately of wool. *The Woolmark, Woolmark Blend & Wool Blend logo are registered trade marks of The Woolmark Company which is owned by Australian Wool Innovation and indicates high quality of woolen products. End products carrying these symbols have been quality tested by The Woolmark Company for compliance with its performance and fiber content specifications. The Woolmark is one of the most recognized symbols globally and represents the world's largest fiber quality assurance scheme.*

A Silk moths come out of their cocoons and mate.

B This female has laid her clutch of eggs from which caterpillars, also called silkworms, will hatch.

C The silkworms grow by eating mulberry leaves.

D Full-grown silkworms find an empty "frame" provided by the silk farmer to spin their cocoons. These frames make harvesting of the cocoons quick and efficient. Threads from four or five cocoons are wound together on a reel. Later, they can be either wound onto cones or twisted into skeins.

18-12 Silkworms produce silk strands as they spin their cocoons. The silk yarns are then sent to cloth manufacturers.
SERICULUM, Sebastopol, CA

the outer covering of the cocoon. Then it begins to wind the silk strand around its body. The silkworm is soon out of sight. If left undisturbed, the worm will turn into a tiny moth and force its way out of its cocoon in two or three weeks. Since this would break and ruin the silk thread, it is killed by heat before this can happen.

The cocoon is unwound either by hand or by machine. A few threads are put together and wound on a reel. Later, the silk from these reels is twisted tightly into skeins, tied in bundles, and baled. It is then ready for the manufacturers of silk cloth.

Silk is covered by a natural gum, which must be removed by washing. This is done so dyes will give brilliant, uniform colors. The washing process makes some yarns very thin and lightweight. To make the yarns heavier, some manufacturers add salts from tin, lead, or iron. This fabric is called *weighted silk*. One way to tell if silk is weighted is to shake the fabric and see if it rustles. Too much weighting weakens the silk.

Manufacturers also use the short threads from broken cocoons. They are spun in much the same way as cotton fibers. This *spun silk* is used in making rough-textured fabrics. Spun silk is not as strong or lustrous as reeled silk.

See Figure 18-13 for a summary of the advantages, disadvantages, uses, and care of the natural fibers. Reviewing these fiber characteristics will help you select the best fiber for your particular use.

\multicolumn{4}{c	}{**Natural Fibers: Care, Characteristics, and Uses**}
Fiber and Care	*Advantages*	*Disadvantages*	*End Uses*
Cotton *Care:* Washable; withstands high temperatures; does not scorch easily when ironed; can be boiled to sterilize	Inexpensive; supply plentiful Comfortable—cool in warm weather Absorbent—soaks up water easily; good for towels and underwear No static electricity buildup Versatile; dyes and prints well Can be combined with other fibers Wide variety of uses	Mildews if put in damp storage area or put away damp Wrinkles easily unless a special finish is added Shrinks in hot water if not treated Weakened by wrinkle-resistant finishes, perspiration, and long exposure to sun	Clothing—all kinds of underwear and outerwear; socks, shirts, dresses, jeans, coats Home furnishings—towels, washcloths, sheets, bedspreads, curtains, slipcovers, tablecloths, rugs
Flax (Linen) *Care:* Washable; withstands high temperatures, will not scorch easily when ironed; withstands frequent laundering	Strongest of natural fibers Comfortable; absorbs moisture from skin and dries quickly Smooth, lustrous Durable Lint-free; used for dishtowels, cloth for medical profession	Expensive if of good quality Wrinkles easily unless treated Creases hard to remove Shines if ironed on right side Mildews, rots, and has color loss	Clothing—suits, dresses, handkerchiefs Home furnishings—draperies, kitchen towels, tablecloths, upholstery

Continued.

18-13 This chart summarizes the care, advantages, disadvantages, and end uses of the natural fibers.

Natural Fibers: Care, Characteristics, and Uses

Fiber and Care	Advantages	Disadvantages	End Uses
Ramie *Care:* Washable; can be ironed at high temperature	Strong Lustrous Dries quickly Durable Absorbs moisture	Wrinkles easily Stiff and wirelike Coarse Expensive	Cords, twine, rope, canvas, fire hoses Combined with other fibers for draperies, upholstery fabrics, and wearing apparel
Wool *Care:* Most fabrics must be dry cleaned; if washable, use warm/cool water; press at low temperature	Warmest of all fibers, but lightweight Highly absorbent (absorbs moisture without feeling wet) Wrinkle resistant Holds and regains shape Creases well Durable Combines successfully with other fibers	Expensive will shrink and mat when moisture and heat are applied Attracts moths and carpet beetles Absorbs odors Burns slowly, self-extinguishes	Clothing—outerwear, sweaters, suits, skirts; athletic socks Home furnishings—rugs, carpets, upholstery, blankets
Silk *Care:* Usually requires dry cleaning; if washable, use cool water; requires low temperature for pressing	Luxurious look and feel Strong but lightweight Very absorbent Comfortable in all climates Resists wrinkling Soil resistant Combines well with other fibers	Yellows with age Weakened by long exposure to sunlight, detergents, and perspiration Attacked by insects such as silverfish Spotted by water unless specially treated Expensive	Clothing—wedding dresses, evening gowns, blouses, scarves, neckties, and lingerie Home furnishings—lampshades, pillow cushions, wall hangings, draperies, upholstery

18-13 Continued.

Summary

- Fibers are the basic units of all textiles. There are two main groups of fibers. Natural fibers are made from plants and animals. Manufactured fibers are made from chemicals in special manufacturing processes.
- Depending on its source or chemical composition, each fiber has its own characteristics and properties. Understanding fiber characteristics helps people select the fiber most suitable for its end use.
- Cotton, linen, wool, and silk are the most common natural fibers.
- There are two categories of natural fibers: cellulosic fibers from plant sources and protein fibers from animal sources.
- Natural fibers go through a process of harvesting, cleaning, carding, and spinning to produce yarns.
- The Wool Products Labeling Act was passed to help consumers know how much and what type of wool is in the fabrics they buy.

Graphic Organizer

Draw a fishbone diagram. List four natural fibers and note two characteristics of each.

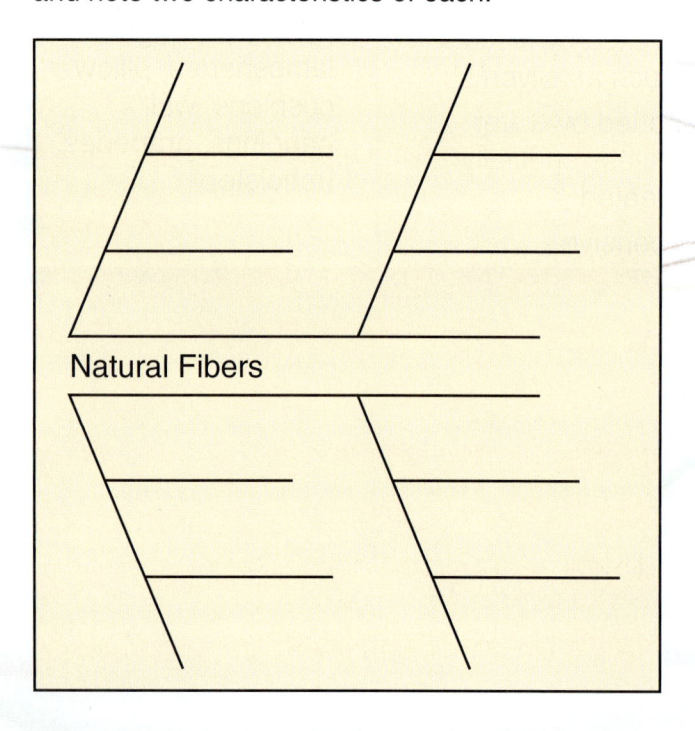

Natural Fibers

Review the Facts

1. Summarize the relationship among fibers, yarns, and fabrics.
2. What is absorbency, and why might you want this characteristic in a fabric?
3. List two advantages of cotton.
4. Which fiber is used to make linen?
5. _____ is the coolest natural fiber; _____ is the warmest.
6. The major natural protein fibers are _____ and _____.
7. What is the oil obtained from processing of wool? Name two uses for this oil.
8. Contrast reprocessed wool and reused wool.
9. Why is silk not produced in the United States?
10. Name two key characteristics of silk.

Think Critically

11. **Recognize bias.** Do you or any of your friends or family members have any fiber biases? For example, does anyone ever say "I hate polyester" or "I only choose clothes made of natural fibers"? If so, why do you think people have such biases?
12. **Draw conclusions.** The popularity of cotton declined a few decades ago. Draw conclusions about what you think happened to cause this decline.
13. **Analyze behavior.** Would you buy a wool product that contained recycled wool? Why or why not?
14. **Recognize assumptions.** What do you think about when someone says they are wearing a garment made of silk? What assumptions do your make?

Apparel Applications

15. **Identify fibers and fabrics.** Collect samples of fabrics made from various natural fibers. Identify and compare the characteristics.
16. **Electronic bulletin board.** Locate digital pictures showing the end uses for the different fibers. Use a school-approved Web-based application to post them on the class blog or electronic bulletin board. Discuss the uses with your classmates online.
17. **Field trip.** Take a field trip to a fabric store and compare prices of fabrics made from different fibers. Which seem affordable for most consumers? As an alternative, take an online field trip to the websites of one or more fabric sellers and compare fabrics. Write a summary of your findings.
18. **Test wrinkle-resistance.** Hold a piece of cotton fabric in one hand and a piece of polyester fabric in the other. Squeeze both for five seconds, then compare. Which is more wrinkle-resistant? Why?
19. **Test shrinkage.** Cut two identically sized samples of wool fabric. Record the size measurements. Wash one sample in cold water and the other one in hot water. Dry the samples by squeezing in a towel. Measure each again. Was there a change? What characteristic of wool caused this difference? Discuss in class.
20. **Evaluate textile products.** Identify five textile products in your home (kitchen or closet) that are made of natural fibers. Describe each item and state the natural fiber used in each. Evaluate and explain why it *was* or *was not* a good fiber choice for this item. Consider the care, appearance, and performance.

Academic Connections

21. **Science.** Place a tablespoon of water on each of two plates. Place a linen sample on one plate and a nylon sample on the other. Which absorbed more water? Write a summary of your conclusions.
22. **Science.** Look at three natural fibers and yarns under a microscope. Identify and compare them. Write a detailed description of each fiber. How do the features of each fiber contribute to their best properties?

Workplace Links

23. **Make recommendations.** Presume a new client is shopping in the apparel store at which you work. Your client is soon traveling to a South American country for work. What fibers and fabrics would you recommend for your client's work and casual wardrobes? Present your recommendations to your client (the class).
24. **Portfolio builder.** Create a vignette of *natural-fiber fabrics* you would choose for two garment designs. Show photographs or drawings of the designs. Label each fabric, identifying its fiber content, finishes, care method, and proposed use. Save your vignette in your portfolio.

Informing Others About Eco-Friendly Natural Fibers

Are you concerned about the environmental impact of natural-fiber textiles used for clothes and home use? If you are, consider planning and preparing a presentation to share your concerns with others. Use the speaking and presentation guidelines in the FCCLA *Dynamic Leadership* program to prepare an oral and visual presentation about eco-friendly natural fibers. Follow the *FCCLA Planning Process* for developing your presentation. See your adviser for information as needed.

Chapter 19

The Manufactured Fibers

Chapter Objectives

After studying this chapter, you will be able to
- **outline** the processes involved in the production of manufactured fibers.
- **summarize** the characteristics, care, and end uses of manufactured fibers.

Key Terms

spinneret
filament
staple fibers
texturing
pilling

Reading with Purpose

As you read the chapter, take notes in presentation software. Make one slide for each heading. List three to four main points on each slide. Use the finished presentation to study for a test.

Manufactured fibers surround you. They are in clothes, on furniture, at school, and in cars. They can be as small as a spider's web or as large as the ropes that moor an ocean vessel.

Rayon was the first commercially produced fiber. It was followed by acetate. These fibers, along with triacetate and lyocell, are made from cellulose, the fibrous substance in plant life. They are called *cellulosic fibers*.

Combining molecules of nitrogen, oxygen, hydrogen, and carbon makes most other manufactured fibers. The molecules are linked in various ways to form chemical compounds called *polymers*. These manufactured fibers are called *synthetic fibers* since they are made from chemicals. See **19-1** for a list of the generic names of the most common manufactured fibers. New manufactured fibers are being developed through research efforts all of the time.

19-1 These are the generic names of the most common manufactured fibers used in apparel.

Manufactured Fibers			
Cellulosic Fibers			
acetate	lyocell	rayon	triacetate
Synthetic Fibers			
acrylic	elastoester	nylon	saran
anidex	glass	nytril	spandex
aramid	metallic	olefin	vinal
azlon	modacrylic	polyester	vinyon

335

Manufacturing Fibers

The raw materials and chemicals used to make manufactured fibers can vary. They all go through the same basic steps before they become fibers:

1. The solid raw material is changed to a liquid.
2. The liquid is *extruded* (forced or pushed) through a **spinneret**—a small nozzle with many tiny holes, similar to a bathroom showerhead, 19-2.
3. The liquid hardens in the form of a fiber.

In step one, the raw material becomes a thick liquid (like honey). Softwood trees are the most common source for rayon and acetate. The wood is cut into small wood chips. These are dissolved by chemicals to form the thick liquid. More recently, bamboo is a material source for making rayon.

The other manufactured fibers begin as a solid mass of chemicals, which is chopped into small pieces. These are either melted or dissolved by chemicals to form the liquid.

The second step is to extrude the liquid through a spinneret. As the thick liquid is *extruded* (forced) through the spinneret, each tiny hole forms one fiber. Several fibers join to make a filament, 19-3.

A **filament** is a continuous strand of fiber. Any manufactured fiber can be made in filament form; however, silk is the only natural fiber that is a filament. Other natural fibers are short and are called **staple fibers**. Manufactured filaments can be cut to make staple fibers.

In the third step, the filament is hardened. *Spinning* is the process of extrusion and the formation of filaments. Some filaments pass from the spinneret directly into a chemical bath where they become solid (*wet spinning*). Others harden after the chemical that was used to liquefy it to liquid evaporates in warm air (*dry spinning*). Some filaments harden as soon as they come in contact with cool air (*melt spinning*).

The next step varies, depending on the type of yarn that will be made. To make filament yarns, a few filaments are twisted together into yarns. Then the yarns are wound onto spools. To make staple yarns, filaments are cut into short lengths and later spun into yarns.

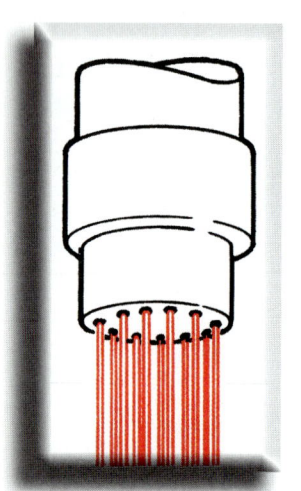

19-2 The metal spinneret has very tiny holes. Thick liquid solutions are pushed through the holes to form fibers.
Goodheart-Willcox Publisher

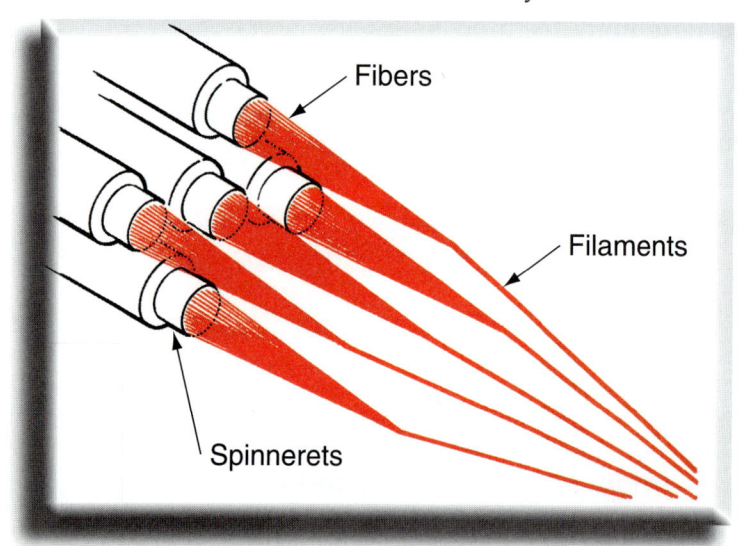

19-3 Fibers formed by the holes of the spinneret combine to form a filament.
Goodheart-Willcox Publisher

Fiber Modifications

Two factors affect the properties of manufactured fibers. One is the chemicals used to make the fiber. This factor remains fairly constant. The other is the way the fiber is treated during production.

Before, during, and after the three basic production steps, there are countless ways to alter the fiber. The cross-sectional shape can be changed. It might be round, trilobal, pentagonal, or octagonal. Each shape results in fibers with different characteristics. The fiber can be thick or thin. The color, luster, wrinkle-resistance, absorption, strength, and pliability can all be varied during the fiber-making process.

Fibers can be twisted, crimped, coiled, or looped to vary the appearance and stretch. This is called **texturing**, 19-4.

The list of fiber modifications grows longer each year. Also, scientists in textile labs continue to find new and better fibers to meet new needs and requirements.

Characteristics of Manufactured Fibers

Although there are many ways to modify manufactured fibers, each kind of fiber has some typical characteristics. The following passages identify the characteristics of some of the most popular manufactured fibers that are used in apparel and household textiles. There are other manufactured fibers, but these are used more for specialized protective clothing. This clothing might be used by the military, firefighters, or astronauts.

19-4 The filament yarn shown at the top in this illustration has not been textured. The same yarn after being textured adds bulk and stretch to fabrics.
American Enka Corp.

Rayon

Rayon is much like cotton. It is soft, comfortable, absorbent, inexpensive, and versatile. It is easy to dye and drapes well. A special treatment increases its strength and resistance to shrinking and wrinkling.

Manufacturers use rayon for almost all kinds of clothing. Lingerie, shirts, blouses, dresses, slacks, coats, and work clothes are some of the common uses, 19-5. In the home, usage of rayon may include bedding, rugs, curtains, draperies, upholstery, and tablecloths. It is also a main use in many nonwoven, industrial and medical products.

Care instructions for rayon garments vary. Some require dry cleaning, others require washing by hand. Some can be washed and bleached like cotton. Check the care labels.

Bamboo

Bamboo is now a fiber source for making rayon. Bamboo is not a separate fiber class—it is another source of cellulosic fiber and requires legal identification as rayon on labeling. You may find labels stating *100 percent rayon from bamboo* or *100 percent viscose from bamboo*, both of which are legally acceptable.

Because of bamboo's fast growth rate and renewability, environmentalists prefer its use. Rayon made from bamboo is durable and soft. It has a natural sheen, is breathable, and biodegradable. Though advertising may label it as antibacterial, this property is often lost during chemical processing. It has

19-5 Rayon is often used in clothing. It is soft, easy to dye, and drapes well. Here it is blended with nylon.
JCPenney Co., Inc.

excellent wicking ability, pulling moisture away from the skin. It is also very absorbent, and is a good fiber for making bath towels. Some manufacturers blend it with cotton.

Lyocell

Though *lyocell* has a separate generic name, the Federal Trade Commission classifies it as a subcategory under rayon. It has similar characteristics as rayon, as well as similar uses. Many people consider the manufacturing process more environmentally acceptable than that of other rayon fibers. A common trademark name for lyocell is Tencel®.

Lyocell is a versatile fiber with many desirable properties. It is breathable and generally comfortable to wear. It is also very absorbent, and can take high-ironing temperatures—but will scorch. Lyocell has moderate resiliency and does not wrinkle as badly as cotton or linen. Some wrinkles will hang out by placing the garment in a warm, moist area. Slight shrinkage is common. Lyocell has strength and durability. It dyes well, has a luxurious feel, and a soft drape.

Lyocell was initially expensive to manufacture, so its use was mainly in designer apparel. As costs came down, it is now found in more affordable apparel. Common uses include fabrics for denim and gabardine and fabrics for women's garments and men's shirts. You may also find it in some home products, such as towels and sheets.

Most lyocell garments require hand or machine washing and tumble drying. However, some fabrics are best dry-cleaned. Other garments may need touch-up ironing at a medium to high temperature.

Acetate

Acetate looks and feels luxurious. It is crisp and drapes (handles) well. It can be dyed in a wide range of colors. With special dyes, acetate will not fade or change color. It is resistant to moths and mildew. It is inexpensive, but is a weaker fiber.

Clothing uses for acetate include neckties, scarves, shirts, blouses, dresses, evening gowns, lingerie, and garment linings. Home use may include draperies, upholstery, and such quilted products as comforters and mattress pads.

Most acetate garments should be dry-cleaned. (Check the care labels.) If you do launder them at home, handle them with care. Use warm water with mild suds. Do not twist the garment. Press while slightly damp on the wrong side of the fabric. Use a cool iron. Acetate melts under high heat.

Triacetate

Triacetate is similar to acetate in appearance. It can be very lustrous. It is more resistant to sunlight, wrinkling, and shrinkage than acetate. Permanent creases and pleats can be made in triacetate fabrics using a special heat treatment.

Triacetate is often used in lightweight knits. Garments of triacetate include dresses, shirts, blouses, and clothes that require permanent pleats.

Caring for triacetate garments is easy. Most are machine washable and dryable, although pleated garments require hand washing. Use a low iron temperature for garments that need ironing.

Nylon

Nylon is very strong and durable. It is elastic, but keeps its shape. It is lightweight, lustrous, and easy to dye. Because nylon is low in absorbency, static electricity is a problem. It also is uncomfortable in hot weather, and provides little warmth in cold weather. Pilling may also be a problem if the fabric is made from nylon staple. **Pilling** is the formation of small balls of fibers on the fabric surface due to wear.

Nylon is the fiber source for many garments, 19-6, including hosiery, lingerie, casual tops, dresses, raincoats, and skiwear. Carpets, draperies, and upholstery are home uses. Nylon has many other uses such as thread, seat belts, racket strings, ropes, tents, and tire cord.

Most nylon garments are machine washable and dryable at low temperatures. They dry quickly. Use warm water and a fabric softener. Remove garments from the dryer as soon as it stops. Wash light-colored nylon items alone. They pick up colors from darker items if washed together.

Polyester

Polyester is very resistant to wrinkling, stretching, shrinking, bleach, sunlight, moths, and mildew. It is strong and easy to dye. With a special heat treatment, it will hold permanent creases. Polyester is versatile. Manufacturers can achieve almost any texture and appearance in polyester fabrics. It also has disadvantages. Pilling may be a problem. Oily stains are difficult to remove. Moisture absorption is quite low which makes these fabrics uncomfortable in hot, humid weather. Static electricity is also a problem because of low moisture absorbency.

Polyester can be used alone or blended with other fibers (especially cotton) in clothing, 19-7. Shirts, blouses, children's wear, dresses, insulated garments, lingerie, permanent press garments, slacks, and suits are common uses for polyester. Carpets, curtains, and sheets are common household uses. Thread, fiberfill, fire hose, ropes, tire cord, and sails are other uses.

19-6 Nylon skiwear is lightweight, durable, and comfortable.
Shutterstock

Most polyester items are machine washable and dryable. Use warm water and a fabric softener. Remove promptly from the dryer to prevent wrinkles.

Olefin

Olefin is the lightest fiber made. It floats on water and has very low moisture absorption. It resists wrinkles, soil, water-based stains, mildew, and insects. Olefin is a strong, durable fiber and is inexpensive. The fiber does not absorb

19-7 Polyester is often blended with cotton to create comfortable, easy-care clothing.
JCPenney Co., Inc.

moisture, but wicks it away from the body. Athletes who work out in extreme hot or cold weather prefer garments made of olefin. The disadvantages are that it absorbs oily spills, is difficult to dye, and melts at fairly low temperatures.

Knitted sportswear and sweaters are made of olefin. In the future, more garments will be made of olefin. Indoor/outdoor carpeting is the largest single use of the fiber. Carpet backing, slipcovers, and upholstery are other home uses. Industry uses olefin for filters, sewing thread, envelopes, and rope.

When laundering olefin items, machine wash them in lukewarm water and use a fabric softener. If you machine dry, use a very low setting and remove items promptly.

Acrylic

Acrylic is often a replacement for wool in garments. It is soft, warm, and lightweight. It keeps its shape well and resists sunlight damage, chemicals, and wrinkles. Special treatments help keep permanent creases when desirable. Pilling and static electricity may be problems.

Many sweaters are made of acrylic. Other uses are dresses, infant wear, slacks, athletic wear, and socks, 19-8. Blankets, carpets, draperies, and upholstery are some home uses. Hand-knitting yarns are another use.

Wash delicate items by hand in warm water. Gently squeeze out water. Smooth out wrinkles, and hang to dry. (Lay sweaters flat to dry.) If the care label suggests machine washing, use warm water and a fabric softener. Machine dry at a low setting, and remove promptly.

Modacrylic

Modacrylic is flame resistant. It also resists shrinkage and chemicals. It is soft, warm, and easy to dye. Fibers can be molded and keep their shape. One disadvantage is the fiber does soften at low temperatures.

A common use for modacrylic is in manufacturing fake fur. Other common uses for these fabrics include deep-pile coats, trims, and wigs. In the home, uses for modacrylic include blankets, carpets, flame-resistant draperies, and wall coverings. Other uses include filters, paint rollers, and stuffed toys.

Dry-clean furlike items. Check the care label. If a modacrylic item is washable, use warm water, mild suds, and a fabric softener. Use a very low setting on the dryer, and remove promptly, or air dry and brush lightly.

Spandex

Spandex is elastic, like rubber, but is made entirely from chemicals. Spandex has good stretch and will go back into shape easily. Spandex is resistant to sunlight, oil, perspiration, and abrasion. It is used for both woven and knitted fabrics. Fabrics for many garments contain a small percentage of spandex to allow give during wearing. Previously, its main use was in swimsuits, undergarments, ski pants, and other articles requiring stretch, **19-9**.

High temperatures in washing machines and dryers can cause spandex to lose some of its stretching power, and cause it to take on a gray tint. Bleach and the chlorine in swimming pools may also damage it. That is why it is important to rinse a swimsuit thoroughly as soon as possible after swimming in a chlorine pool if the suit contains spandex.

Elastoester

In 1997, the Federal Trade Commission recognized *elastoester* as a new generic fiber. This fiber is similar to polyester, but is stretchy like spandex. It retains dyes better than nylon or spandex and is less susceptible to chlorine damage, an important characteristic for swimwear. Its excellent stretching qualities make it a good substitute for spandex.

19-8 Fleece for athletic wear is often made of acrylic. *Shutterstock*

19-9 Swimsuits and exercise wear often contain spandex where stretch is desired. *Shutterstock*

Elastoester washes well and withstands high temperatures when wet. The major uses for elastoester are sweaters, hosiery, socks, foundation garments, knitwear, swimwear, activewear, athletic wear, ski pants, and sportswear.

See figure 19-10 for a summary of the characteristics, care, and uses of these manufactured fibers.

Manufactured Fiber Care, Characteristics, and Uses

Generic Name	Advantages	Disadvantages	End Uses
Rayon *Care:* Some need dry cleaning; others are hand washable.	Very absorbent Drapes well Dyes and prints well Soft Comfortable Versatile Inexpensive	Wrinkles easily unless treated Low resiliency Heat sensitive Mildews Shrinks in hot water unless treated Stretches Weak when wet	Blouses Dresses Shirts Lingerie Sportswear Bedding Curtains Tablecloths
Lyocell *Care:* Hand or machine washable; tumble dry. Some require dry cleaning.	Soft Strong Absorbent Dyes well Drapes well Biodegradable Luxurious hand	Susceptible to mildew Moderate resiliency Slight shrinkage	Dresses Shirts Blouses Bedding Towels
Acetate *Care:* Most require dry cleaning; if washable, use warm water, drip dry, low iron temperature.	Silklike luster/feel Drapes well Resists moths, mildew, pilling Inexpensive Easy to dye	Poor abrasion resistance Weak Heat sensitive Special care for cleaning	Dresses Blouses Linings Lingerie Shirts Scarves Neckties
Triacetate *Care:* Machine wash and dry.	Resists wrinkles and fading Easy care Resilient Can be heat set Lustrous Does not shrink	Nonabsorbent Weak Static buildup Low abrasion resistance	Blouses Dresses Lightweight knits Pleated garments

Continued.

19-10 The advantages, disadvantages, care, and end uses for many manufactured fibers are summarized in this chart.

Manufactured Fiber Care, Characteristics, and Uses

Generic Name	Advantages	Disadvantages	End Uses
Nylon *Care:* Machine wash and dry at low temperature.	Very strong Lightweight Dries quickly Durable Resilient Resists mildew, moths, chemicals, wrinkles Retains shape Colorfast Easy care	Low absorbency Surface pills Damaged by sun Picks up oils and dyes in wash Static buildup Heat sensitive	Casual tops Hosiery Lingerie Skiwear Slacks Windbreakers Dresses Raincoats Carpets Upholstery
Polyester *Care:* Machine wash and dry.	Resilient Colorfast Strong/durable Easy care Resists wrinkles, abrasion, bleach, perspiration, mildew, moths Can be heat set Does not stretch or shrink	Low absorbency Spun yarns pill Takes oily stains Static buildup	Permanent-press fabrics Fiberfill insulation Shirts and dresses Suits Undergarments Sportswear Children's wear Carpets
Olefin *Care:* Machine wash and dry at low temperature.	Resists abrasion, chemicals, water borne stains, mildew, pilling, wrinkles, static buildup Not affected by weather, aging, perspiration Strong, durable Very lightweight Inexpensive	Heat sensitive Poor dyeability Nonabsorbent Easily stained by oil substances	Knitted socks, sportswear, sweaters, shirts Nonwoven fabrics for industrial apparel Filler in quilted goods Disposable diapers Carpets

Continued.

19-10 Continued.

Manufactured Fiber Care, Characteristics, and Uses

Generic Name	Advantages	Disadvantages	End Uses
Acrylic *Care:* Hand or machine wash and dry at low temperature.	Resembles wool Lightweight Soft, fluffy Warm, bulky Resilient Resists sunlight, moths, chemicals, mildew, wrinkles	Low absorbency Static buildup Surface pills Heat sensitive	Sportswear Sweaters Infant wear Knitted garments Blankets Carpets Draperies
Modacrylic *Care:* Some require dry cleaning; others machine wash and dry at low temperature.	Bulky, warm Easy to dye Resists wrinkling, flames, chemicals Retains shape Soft, lightweight	Heat sensitive Static buildup Weak Surface pills	Furlike fabrics Coats Knitwear Sportswear Fleece fabrics Wigs
Spandex *Care:* Machine wash and dry at low temperature.	Very elastic Resistant to lotions, oils, perspiration, sun, abrasion Lightweight Strong, durable Soft, smooth Easy care	Nonabsorbent Yellows with age Heat sensitive Harmed by chlorine bleach	Swimwear Skiwear Undergarments Support hose Exercise and dance wear
Elastoester *Care:* Machine wash and dry.	Very elastic Retains dyes well Not damaged by chlorine bleach Withstands high temperatures when wet		Sweaters Hosiery and socks Foundation garments Knitwear Swimwear Activewear

19-10 Continued.

Trends Making News

Tie-Dyeing: A Fun Way to Design Your Own Fabric

Be your own textile designer with a package or two of dye. Use the stripe, donut knot, and rosette knot to create interesting patterns.

- **Stripe.** Lay fabric on a flat surface. Mark the places where you want stripes. Gather the fabric and tie tightly. Use many strings or rubber bands for a wide stripe, or a single string or band for a narrow stripe.

- **Rosette knot.** Pull a section of fabric. Fasten tightly with string or rubber bands. Add more ties to get the sunburst variation shown here.

- **Donut knot.** Begin as if you were making a rosette knot. Then push the center through to the other side. Secure tightly with string or rubber bands.

Let your imagination run wild and create unique designs on fabrics you can then sew into garments or frame as pieces of art.

For more ideas and specific instructions, visit the *Rit* dye website.

Summary

- There are two categories of manufactured fibers—*cellulosic fibers* (rayon, acetate, lyocell, and triacetate) and *synthetic fibers* (nylon, polyester, spandex, and others).
- Molecule combinations of nitrogen, oxygen, hydrogen, and carbon make manufactured fibers. The molecules are linked in various ways to form chemical compounds called *polymers*.
- Manufactured fibers are called *synthetic fibers* because they are made from chemicals.
- Manufactured fibers go through a process of melting, extruding, and spinning to form yarns.
- Manufactured fibers can be modified in many ways to change their color, luster, wrinkle-resistance, absorption, strength, and pliability.
- Although manufactured fibers can be modified in many ways, each kind of fiber has some typical characteristics.

Graphic Organizer

Draw a T-chart on a sheet of paper. In the left column, list the manufactured fibers found in the chapter. In the right column, note at least two characteristics of each fiber.

Manufactured Fibers	Characteristics

Review the Facts

1. What are the sources for the manufactured cellulosic fibers and the synthetic fibers?
2. List the three basic steps in manufacturing fibers.
3. How does a filament differ from a staple fiber?
4. What two factors influence the properties of manufactured fibers?
5. When yarns are textured, they can be _____.
6. Summarize the relationship between rayon and bamboo.
7. Name three features of lyocell that make it desirable for apparel.
8. What problem might occur when washing light-colored nylon clothes?
9. What characteristics of polyester make it preferable to cotton?
10. Why does elastoester replace spandex in many garments requiring stretch?

Think Critically

11. **Identify evidence.** Some fiber manufacturers are making efforts to save the environment. Do you think enough is being done? Use reliable Internet or print resources to locate evidence to support your thinking.
12. **Recognize values.** Would you look for fiber manufacturers who make special efforts to conserve natural resources? How do your values influence your choices?
13. **Make predictions.** If you were a textile chemist, predict what new fiber characteristic would you try to develop? Why?
14. **Draw conclusions.** Make a list of end uses for fibers. Include both clothing items and household uses. Then recommend a fiber for each use. Draw conclusions about why you made each choice.

Apparel Applications

15. **Analyze fibers.** Gather samples of several fabrics made from manufactured fibers. Unravel some of the fabrics and loosen the fibers. Have the fibers undergone texturing? If so, by what method? How does texturing influence the fabric characteristics?

16. **Discuss fibers.** From a selection of fabric remnants, identify the fiber(s) used and list the characteristics of these fibers. Then discuss suitable and unsuitable end uses for each fabric and determine the care requirements for each.

17. **Choose fabrics for fashions.** Locate apparel photos in online magazines and pattern company sites. Select an appropriate fabric for each item. Use a school-approved Web application to copy and paste photos of your selections into a class blog. Collaborate with your classmates about your fabric choices. What other suggestions do they have?

18. **Photo essay.** Locate pictures of household items made from fabric. Mount the pictures for your photo essay neatly on poster board. Select an appropriate fiber for each item and write it under the appropriate photo. Explain why you chose each fiber. As an alternative, take digital photos of household items made from fabric. Create your photo essay using presentation software to share with the class.

Academic Connections

19. **Reading.** What fiber names have you seen recently on garment labels that are new to you? Use a reliable Internet resource, such as the *American Fiber Manufacturer's Association* website, to read more about these fibers. Share your findings with the class.

20. **Science.** Look at various natural and manufactured fibers and yarns under a microscope. Identify and compare them. How are their characteristics similar and different? Write a summary of your findings.

21. **Writing.** Search the Internet to find some of the most recent innovations in fiber manufacturing and characteristics. Write a report about your findings using presentation software and illustration. Share your report with the class.

Workplace Links

22. **Fiber research.** Research the other generic fibers not covered in this chapter. These fibers often have specialized uses other than everyday wearing apparel. Make a chart of these fibers. How are many of the specialized fibers used in the workplace?

23. **Job shadowing.** Many fibers look the same. Research various tests used in laboratories to identify fibers in fabrics. Then, if possible, make arrangements to job shadow a textile research chemist to see how these tests are carried out.

24. **Portfolio builder.** Create a vignette of *manufactured-fiber fabrics* you would choose for two garment designs. Show photographs or drawings of the designs. Label each fabric, identifying its fiber content, finishes, care method, and proposed use. Save your vignette in your portfolio.

Fibers, Fashion, and the Workplace

To learn more about how fashion designers use fibers in their everyday work, complete an FCCLA *Power of One* unit called *Working on Working*. Contact a fashion designer in your area. Make arrangements to spend a day with him or her to learn more about how the designer uses fibers and fabrics in daily work. How does knowledge of fibers and fabrics help the designer to effectively develop garment designs for clients?

Use the FCCLA *Planning Process* and *Working on Working* unit activities to plan, carry out, and evaluate your project. See your adviser for information as needed.

Chapter 20

From Yarn to Fabric

Chapter Objectives

After studying this chapter, you will be able to
- **summarize** how fibers are combined to make various types of yarns.
- **describe** the three basic weaves and the most common variations of these weaves.
- **describe** the two methods of knitting and the most common variations of weft and warp knits.
- **summarize** other fabric constructions.

Key Terms

spun yarns	woven fabric	nap
monofilament yarns	warp yarns	knitting
multifilament yarns	filling yarns	weft knitting
single yarn	selvage	warp knitting
ply yarn	grain	felt
cord yarn	plain weave	films
blend	twill weave	bonding
combination yarn	satin weave	quilting
weaving	pile fabric	

Reading with Purpose

Read through the list of Key Terms at the beginning of the chapter. Write what you think each term means on a separate sheet of paper. Then look up the terms in the glossary and write the text definition.

Before a yarn becomes part of a finished fabric, it goes through many steps. The yarn itself can vary in size, strength, and texture. It can be made into fabric in several different ways.

The appearance and performance of a textile product depends on its fiber content, type of yarn, fabric construction, added color, and finishes. These factors can be varied to make millions of different fabrics. In this chapter, you will learn how fibers are made into yarns and yarns into fabrics.

Yarns

Fibers are combined together to make yarns, **20-1**. Yarns are combined to make fabrics. The type of yarn used has a tremendous effect on the finished product.

20-1 Spinning machines combine fibers to make yarns, which will then be woven into fabrics.
Shutterstock

Types of Yarns

Spun yarns are made from short, staple fibers. They have a rough surface. Some of the tiny fiber ends stick out and make the yarn look fuzzy. Cotton, flax, and wool are made into spun yarns. Silk filaments can also be cut into staples and made into spun yarns as can all manufactured fibers

Monofilament yarns are made from a single filament. The clear, plasticlike thread used to hem some ready-to-wear garments is a monofilament yarn. Hosiery is another use for these yarns.

Group of filaments form **multifilament yarns**. Manufacturers can make silk and all manufactured fibers into multifilament yarns for most kinds of clothing.

Twist in Yarns

The amount of *twist* added to a yarn varies. Twist holds the fibers or filaments together. The addition of twist also increases the strength of the yarn.

- *Very low twist* yarns are often used for multifilament yarns. The fibers used in this kind of yarn are strong, so the twist is used only to hold the filaments together.
- *Low twist*, spun yarns are *fluffy*. Manufacturers use them to make bulky, soft, and fuzzy fabrics. They are fairly weak and pill easily.
- *Average twist* is the most common twist for yarns made of staple fibers.
- *High twist* yarns are hard and compact. These yarns are less common today. Voile and crepe fabrics require high twist yarns.

Textured Yarns

Filament yarns from all manufactured fibers (except rayon and acetate) can be *textured*. This makes the yarns less smooth. They are crimped, looped, or coiled to achieve some properties of the spun yarns.

Texturing yarns makes them more absorbent and more comfortable with more bulk and stretch. They have less static buildup. The development of texturing is a major factor in the widespread acceptance of manufactured fibers.

Single, Ply, and Cord Yarns

The relationship among single, ply, and cord yarns is shown in **20-2**. The product of the first twisting step is a **single yarn**.

Twisting two or more single yarns together makes a **ply yarn**. Each part of the yarn is called a *ply*. Ply yarns are larger and stronger than single yarns. Home knitting or crocheting is done with ply yarns. Examine a knitting yarn closely. You can easily see the various yarns that have been twisted together.

When ply yarns are twisted together, the result is a **cord yarn**. Ropes are often made from cord yarns.

Blends and Combinations

Many textiles are a mixture of natural and manufactured fibers. These are called *blends* or *combinations*.

When different types of staple fibers are spun together into a single yarn, the result is a **blend**. A resulting spun yarn benefits from the desirable qualities of each fiber. Any type of fiber can be blended with another—both natural and manufactured fibers—to get the best result.

Combination yarns result from twisting two or more different yarns into a ply. Combining spun yarns and filament yarns in different ways form *novelty yarns*. These yarns are unusual combinations of different sizes, colors, and textures of yarns.

Blends and combinations help make fabrics with better performance, better appearance, or lower prices. For example, adding acrylic to a wool fiber or yarn can reduce the yarn cost. Since acrylic neither shrinks nor attracts moths, this combination can lessen both of these problems.

Many shirts are a blend of 65 percent polyester and 35 percent cotton. The amount of each fiber used is important. This 65-35 blend takes advantage of the good characteristics of both fibers and lessens the effect of the negative characteristics. Cotton feels good next to the body. It is cool and absorbent, and it does not pill. However, cotton wrinkles easily and shrinks. Polyester is strong and wrinkle-resistant. It dries quickly and does not shrink. A blend of these fibers results in a fabric with the best characteristics of each.

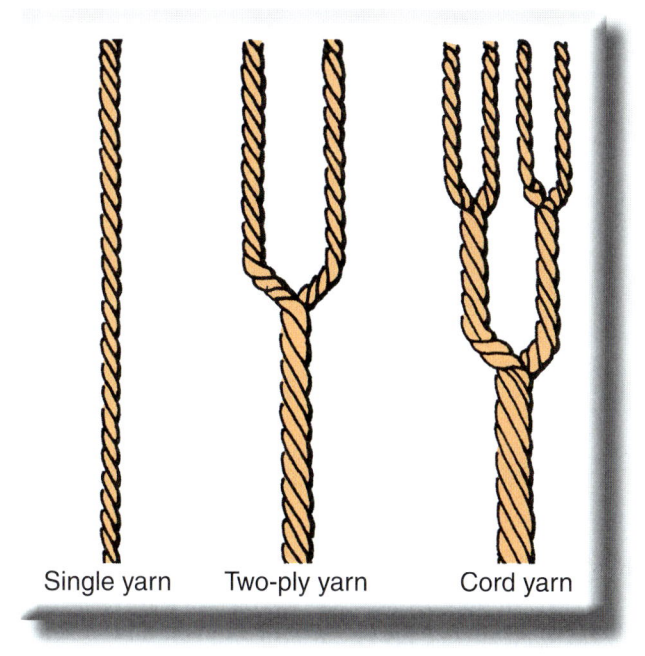

20-2 Fibers are first twisted into single yarns. Another twisting step combines single yarns into ply yarns. A third twisting step forms cord yarns.
Goodheart-Willcox Publisher

Woven Fabrics

The two most common methods of making fabric are weaving and knitting. Other methods include felting and bonding. From only a few construction methods come many different fabrics.

Weaving

Weaving is the process of interlacing yarns at right angles to each other to create a **woven fabric**. It is done on machines called *looms*, as in **20-3**. For generations, weaving was done by hand. Your great-great-grandparents may have had a loom in their home. A few people use handlooms today. Some are large, but most handlooms are small. Hand-woven products are usually costly, specialty items.

Weaving requires the use of two sets of yarns. The lengthwise yarns are the **warp yarns**. The crosswise yarns are the **filling yarns** (also called *weft* yarns). The warp yarns are threaded onto the loom. They must be strong and durable to withstand the strain of the weaving process.

20-3 High-speed looms can weave thousands of yards of fabric in a very short time. *American Sheep Industry Assoc.*

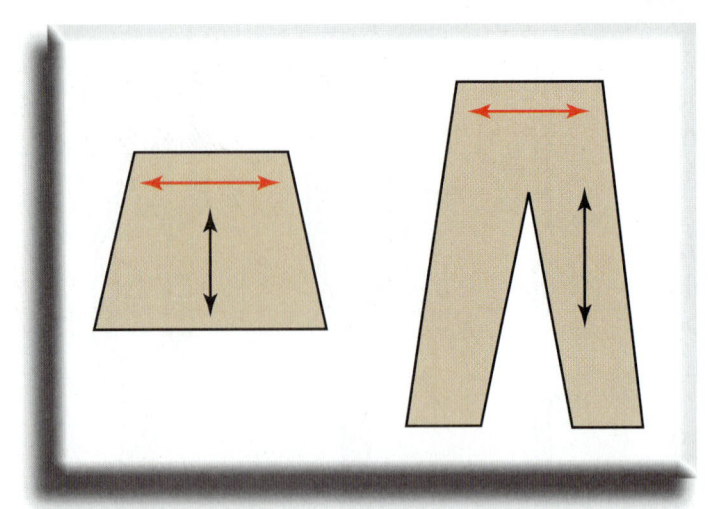

20-4 Because filling yarns (blue) stretch more than warp yarns (black), garments are made with the filling yarns going around the body. Warp yarns are used in the lengthwise direction.
Goodheart-Willcox Publisher

The filling yarns pass over and under the warp yarns. When they reach an edge, they turn back and weave across the warp yarns in the other direction. The turned filling yarns along each side of the woven fabric form the **selvage**—the fabric edge that is very strong and will not ravel. Most modern high-speed looms do not return the yarn. The yarns are fed from one or both sides and cut. This results in the fringe-like selvage found on many fabrics.

The filling yarns are usually weaker than the warp yarns. Therefore, if the fabric has low-twist or *special effect* yarns, they will be in the filling.

In woven fabrics, the filling yarns stretch more than the warp. This is why the grain of fabric is important in clothing. **Grain** refers to the direction the yarns run. Garments need to stretch more across your body than up and down. Therefore, the *crosswise grain* is along the filling. The *lengthwise grain* is along the warp, 20-4.

Basic Weaves

Through the weaving process, passing the filling yarns over and under different numbers of warp yarns can create various types of woven fabrics. There are three basic types of weaves. They are the *plain weave, the twill weave,* and the *satin weave*. Review Figure 20-5 as you read about the various weaves.

Focus on Technology

Microfiber Textiles

More and more garments and fabrics state word *microfiber* on their labels. Whenever you see this word on a label, you will notice the fabric is extra smooth, soft, and silky, and the fabric weave is barely visible. Microfibers are one of the most important developments in textiles in recent years. The technology to extrude extremely fine filaments that are still strong and uniform led to their development. These microfibers are even finer than silk as you can see in this diagram.

In addition to a luxurious feel, microfibers have some outstanding performance characteristics. They are popular for raincoats and jackets because they are lighter and more comfortable than conventional fibers. The small filaments are packed so close together that they form an effective wind barrier. This barrier prevents loss of body heat. In addition, the nonwetting surface of the fibers causes water to bead up. These beads are larger than the spaces between the yarns so the water is locked out. Moisture vapor can still escape, keeping the wearer dry and comfortable. Fabrics made of microfibers can breathe well. Chemical treatments and coatings are not needed to provide water resistance.

Microfiber yarns are made from most major generic fibers, particularly nylon, polyester, acrylic, and rayon. Watch for this term to show up more and more in the apparel and fabrics you buy.

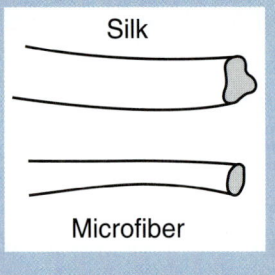

Weaves	Fabric Names
Plain Weave	Organdy, Gingham, Voile, Percale, Taffeta, Poplin, Grosgrain, Batiste, Chambray, Chiffon, Muslin, Broadcloth, Faille, Oxford (basket weave)
Twill Weave	Serge, Gabardine, Herringbone, Surah, Denim, Flannel
Satin Weave	Satin, Sateen

20-5 Compare these magnified views of the various weaves. *American Textile Manufacturers Institute*

Plain Weave

Passing a filling yarn over one warp yarn and then under one warp yarn makes the **plain weave**. The netting of a tennis racket is an example of the plain weave.

Generally, plain weave fabrics are strong, durable, and easy to sew. They wrinkle more and absorb less moisture than fabrics of other weaves.

Using large yarns with small ones, textured yarns, different colors, or a special finish can change the effect. You can also get a different look by working with more than one yarn at a time. The *basket weave* is made by passing two or more filling yarns over and under two or more warp yarns.

above the fabric surface. The nap lies in one direction on a pile fabric.

- *Leno weave.* In the leno weave, two warp yarns cross over each other before each filling yarn, 20-8. A special loom attachment produces this weave. Leno-weave fabrics are lacelike in character. Uses include sheer curtains and thermal blankets.
- *Jacquard weave.* Large and complex designs are woven on Jacquard looms. Before computers were used, the design of the fabric is programmed on a series of punch cards. The cards controlled the warp yarns, raising or lowering them to create the woven design. Most factories today have computerized the programming. Designs are scanned into the computer and the computer manipulates the loom. Damask, brocade, and tapestry fabrics are made on the Jacquard loom. They are used for clothing and home furnishings such as bedspreads and upholstery. Towels with hotel names as the woven design are also made on these looms.
- *Dobby weave.* Smaller geometric patterns can be woven into a fabric with a dobby attachment that is added to a regular loom. A plastic tape is punched with holes for the weave pattern. These holes control the warp yarns to produce the design.

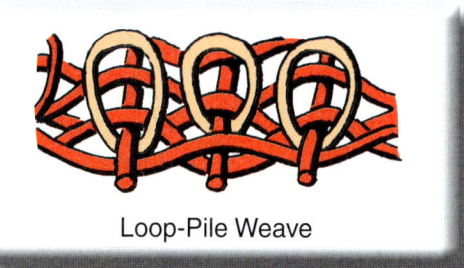

Loop-Pile Weave

20-7 Notice how loops of the pile extend above the fabric surface.
Goodheart-Willcox Publisher

Leno Weave

20-8 In the leno weave, you can see how two warp yarns cross each other before going over or under a filling yarn.
Goodheart-Willcox Publisher

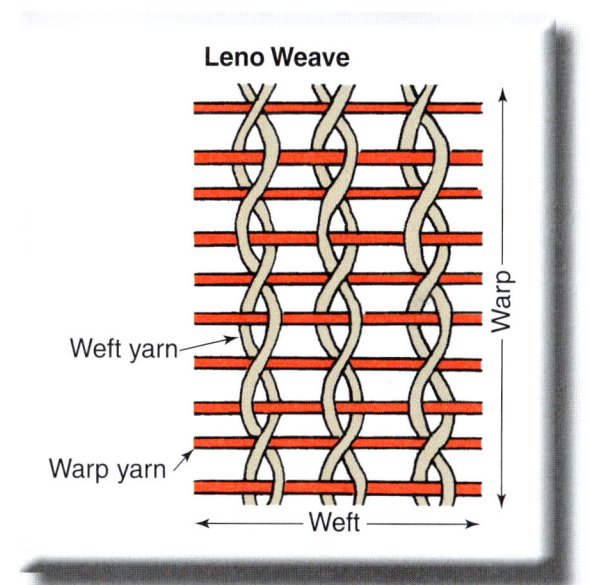

Knitted Fabrics

Knitting is a process that loops yarns together. One loop of yarn is pulled through another loop, just as you would knit at home. The loops or stitches can be varied to create different patterns and textures. Different yarns produce different effects. Textured filament yarns are often used in knits. Figure 20-9 shows a close-up view of knitted fabric. You can see that the construction is not like a woven fabric.

20-9 This drawing shows the looping of yarns for knitting.
American Textile Manufacturers Institute

Knits	Fabric Names	
Knitting	**Weft knit fabrics:** Double knit Jersey Rib-knit Pile-knit jersey Velour Fisherman's knit Purl knit Stockinette Knitted terry cloth	**Warp knit fabrics:** Tricot jersey Lace Power net Raschel knit

In comparison to weaving, knitting is a newer process. It was first done by machine in the 16th century. Today, modern knitting machines move faster than the eye can follow. Machines use complex patterns and fine yarns. An idea and pattern is developed with the use of a computer. The computer then controls the knitting machine. Knits are a large and exciting part of today's textile industry.

Why are knits popular? One reason is the development of manufactured fibers. They are well-suited for knitting. Another reason is that most people today want clothes that are comfortable to wear. Knits answer that need for comfort. They adjust to the shape of a person's body. They stretch when a person sits, walks, reaches, and bends, **20-10**.

Knitted fabrics can be warm in the winter or cool in the summer, depending on the fiber, yarn, and finish used. Caring for them is easy, too. They resist wrinkling and most are washable—if you follow the care instructions—and require little or no ironing.

Knitted fabrics are very versatile. They can be made from any fiber and yarn. Most woven fabrics can be copied by a knitted one.

Two methods of knitting are *weft* (filling) and *warp*. The difference between the two is in the formation of the loops.

Weft Knitting

In **weft knitting**, the loops are made as yarn is added in the crosswise direction. This can be done by hand or by machine.

Weft knitting machines can be either circular or flat. Circular machines knit the fabric in the shape of a tube, **20-11**. Specially designed circular machines make socks, tights, and hosiery. These machines are computerized and can produce hundreds of shapes and sizes.

Generally, flat knitting is more complex than circular knitting. Flat knitting can be done in various ways to produce different effects. Stitches can be added or dropped, changing the fabric width. This creates the garment shape, so production of the final garment requires little sewing. Sweaters, dresses, and other knit garments are knitted on these machines, as well as separate collars, cuffs, and trims.

The most common type of weft knit is the *single knit*. These knits are made on a single-needle knitting machine. Single knits stretch in both directions and can stretch out of shape. The right side will look different from the back side. The cut edges may curl or roll. Single knits can run if snagged. Pantyhose, T-shirts, and lingerie are usually made of single-knit fabrics.

20-10 Knitted garments are popular because they stretch, resist wrinkling, and are easy to care for.
Shutterstock

Another kind of weft knit is the *double knit*. Two sets of needles are used on a weft knitting machine. Although it is called *double knit*, it cannot be separated into two layers. The result is a sturdy fabric that will not stretch or sag. It has enough *give* to be comfortable. Double knits are useful in children's, men's, and women's clothing as well as in household goods.

Types of Weft Knits

There is a wide variety of weft knits. These include the following:

- *Jersey knits.* The most common type of single knit is jersey. The front and back of the fabric differs in appearance. The fabric curls when cut and can run. There is little lengthwise stretch. T-shirts, sportswear, sleepwear, and pantyhose are made of jersey knit.
- *Purl knits.* Purl knits differ from jersey knits in several ways. Purl knits appear the same on both sides of the fabric and stretch both lengthwise and crosswise. They are heavier in weight and do not curl when cut. Sweaters are usually purl knits.
- *Rib knits.* Rib knits have visible vertical ribs on both sides of the fabric. Two alternating types of stitches create these ribs. They have considerable crosswise stretch but little lengthwise stretch. Rib knits are used in sweaters and dresses, particularly neckbands and cuffs.
- *Interlock knits.* This is a double-knit fabric that looks like jersey on both sides. It will not run and cut edges lie flat.
- *Pile knits.* Pile knit fabrics have a knitted base fabric with a pile or nap. *Fleece* is a popular pile knit. These fabrics are used frequently for outerwear garments such as sweatshirts and jackets.

20-11 A circular knitting machine produces fabric in a tubular form. *Shutterstock*

Warp Knitting

In **warp knitting**, the loops are made by one or more sets of warp yarns. Each set of warp yarns is as wide as the fabric. An entire course of loops is made at one time. Then the warp yarns are raised to make the next course. With each course, the stitches must move to the left or right to connect the loops.

Warp knitting is the fastest way to make cloth. Warp knits are made on flat machines, **20-12**. The knit designs and colors are programmed by computer. Review figure 20-9 for a list of warp-knit fabrics.

Warp knits tend to be less elastic and lighter in weight than weft knits. Warp knits will not run, but any knit will snag when a loop is pulled. Bringing the pulled loop to the inside of the garment where it will not show can solve this problem.

Common warp knit fabrics are tricot and raschel knits.

- *Tricot knits.* Tricot knits have fine lines on one side and cross ribs on the other. They are usually made from very fine filament yarns, creating soft fabrics. Tricot knits are used for clingy dresses, lingerie, and undergarments.

- *Raschel knits.* Raschel knits contain an inlaid connecting (sometimes textured) yarn in addition to the columns of knit stitches. The result can be crochetlike fabrics, as well as laces and nettings. Raschel knits have less stretch.

Seamless Knit Garments

One of the newest trends in knitting is making seamless garments. This may be the next generation of clothing because these garments feel good, are comfortable, and have a slimming effect on the body. The current fashion trend is for tighter-fitting clothes for both men and women.

Regular knitting machines produce yards of fabric that have to be cut and sewn. A normal garment may require 17 different operations and each stage must undergo a quality check. The seamless machines produce individual garments from yarn that is fed into the machine. Computer commands allow for different stitching patterns in various sizes. These special knitting machines can create a garment in one or two operations. Seamless garments take 30- to 40-percent less time to make than cut-and-sew versions. Knit tops, skirts, and T-shirts are also popular seamless garments.

20-12 Warp knitting provides lighter and more delicate material than weft knitting. Lingerie, swimsuits, and exercise wear are often made in this manner. *American Textile Manufacturers Institute*

Other Fabric Constructions

Yarns are made of fibers, and fabrics are made of yarns, right? Well, that is a good rule. But like all rules, it has exceptions. Not all fabrics are woven or knitted. Some fabrics are made directly from fibers. A few fabrics do not even have fibers!

Felt

Felt is made from short wool fibers. Wool fibers have overlapping scales. Under a microscope you can see they look like fish scales. As heat, moisture, and pressure are applied to the fibers, the scales interlock to form a solid mass.

Felt fabrics are thick, stiff, and warm. They are not as strong as woven or knitted fabrics. Felt is easily molded into any shape. It is used for hats, handicrafts, and household items, **20-13**.

Nonwoven Fabrics

Fibers other than wool can be made into a web fabric much like felt. In some cases, adhesives hold the staple fibers together. For many of the manufactured fibers, heat is used to *melt* the fibers together.

Nonwoven fabrics are often used for disposable items. They are less costly than woven or knitted fabrics. Some uses of nonwoven fabrics are diapers, hospital sheets, operating gowns, bandages, towels, and cleaning cloths. A nondisposable use is for *interfacings* in garments—a layer of fabric under the outer fabric that prevents stretching and provides shape.

Most nonwoven fabrics are made in the U.S. because of the technology involved in producing the fabrics. The largest growth in the use of nonwovens is for personal and household *wipes*. Many people buy wipes because of their antibacterial and disinfecting qualities. One third is sold as baby wipes, one third for personal use, and the other third are used for cleaning. Floor cleaners, glass cleaners, and mop heads are popular uses.

Films

Films are not made of fibers. They are thin sheets of vinyl and urethane. They are often used as a coating on other fabrics. Films are low cost and waterproof. They can be finished to look like leather or any woven fabric.

Fabrics with a urethane coating are easy to sew and easy to clean. They are durable and will remain soft in cold weather. They will not crack or scuff.

Films and film-coated fabrics are used for raincoats, umbrellas, purses, shoes, tablecloths, and upholstery.

Bonded Fabrics

Bonding is the process of permanently fastening (gluing) one fabric to another. A bonded fabric is often more stable.

Tricot knit is often used as the backing fabric. It is inexpensive and allows some stretch. Sometimes a layer of foam is attached to a layer of fabric to add warmth. Bonded fabrics have more body than single fabrics, and they wrinkle less. They are easy to sew. They will not fray or ravel, and they do not require lining.

Bonded-fabric garments are warm without being heavy. They are often used for skiwear and winter coats.

Quilted Fabrics

Quilting is the process of adding a layer of padding (batting) between two layers of fabric, 20-14. Rows of machine stitching hold the three layers together, creating a pattern. Sometimes a machine that uses heat to weld the layers together creates a quilted look without the stitching.

20-13 Felt is commonly used to make hats because it can be molded into the desired shape. *Shutterstock*

20-14 The fabric used in this coat is quilted. There is a layer of padding between two fabric layers. *Shutterstock*

A Dictionary of Fabrics

Batiste (buh-teest). A fine soft sheer fabric of plain weave made from such fibers as cotton, cotton-polyester blend, silk, and manufactured fibers.

Boulcé (bool-SAY). A medium-weight woven or knitted fabric of irregularly twisted yarns; small spaced loops on the fabric surface are distinguishing marks. Boulcé can be made from natural and manufactured fibers.

Broadcloth. A fine, mercerized cotton fabric made in plain and rib weaves with a soft semigloss finish. The fabric is made from silk and manufactured fibers.

Brocade. A fabric characterized by raised designs, such as Jacquard. Fabric often has multiple colors and can be made from natural or manufactured fibers.

Calico. A plain-weave cotton fabric that is coarse, but lightweight. The fabric can be white, but often is printed with a small motif.

Challis (SHA-lee). A soft, lightweight fabric made in a plain or twill weave of natural or manufactured fibers. These fabrics have either a solid color or floral-type pattern.

Chambray (SHAM-bray). A lightweight plain-weave cotton or cotton-blend fabric with a variegated surface due to the use of dyed lengthwise yarns and white crosswise yarns.

Chiffon (shih-FAHN). A very sheer and gauzy plain-weave fabric made from highly twisted yarns, often made from silk and manufactured fibers.

Chino (CHEE-noh). A sturdy, lustrous plain- or twill-weave fabric made from cotton or manufactured fibers, often khaki in color.

Chintz. A plain-weave cotton fabric usually with a glazed colorful print.

Corduroy. A durable, cut pile fabric with narrow or wide raised lengthwise ribs, or *wales*, often made from cotton or manufactured fibers.

Crepe (CRAYP). A light, plain-weave fabric with a crinkly surface made by using highly twisted yarns in either or both the warp and filling. Natural and manufactured fibers can be used to make crepe.

Damask (DAH-muhsk). A firm, lustrous fabric made from a one-color Jacquard weave. The characteristic flat design has a satin finish with a dull background. Both natural and manufactured fibers are used for damask.

Denim. A firm, durable twill-weave fabric with distinguishing colored warp yarns and white filling yarns, usually cotton.

Dotted swiss. A crisp, sheer, plain-weave fabric with a soft slub of heavier yarn brought to the fabric surface at evenly spaced intervals. The dots may also be added through flocking.

Faille (FYUHL). A crosswise-ribbed fabric that is made with a heavy crosswise yarn and a fine lengthwise yarn during weaving and is made from either natural or manufactured fibers.

Fake fur. A woven or knitted pile fabric that resembles fur.

Felt. A nonwoven fabric with a dull, flat finish. It can be made from wool or wool and synthetic blends.

Flannel. When made from cotton or blends, flannel is a plain-weave fabric with a soft, brushed surface. When made from wool, it is a twill-weave fabric with a soft, brushed face.

Fleece. A plain-weave fabric of soft yarns, brushed to create a thick, deep nap. This fabric can be made from wool or manufactured fibers.

Gabardine (GAH-buhr-deen). A twill worsted fabric woven with diagonal lines that show on the right side of the fabric only. This hard finished, hard-wearing fabric can be made from wool or manufactured fibers.

Gingham. A medium-weight, closely woven plain-weave fabric. It is typically yarn dyed and woven to create checks, plaids, and stripes.

Lace. An open, ornamental fabric with a design that is formed by a network of threads. Lace can be made from natural or manufactured fibers.

Lamé (lah-MAY). An ornamental, brocaded fabric into which metallic threads are woven. This fabric can be made from natural or manufactured fibers.

Madras (MAH-druhs). A brightly colored, plain-weave fabric usually in bold plaids, stripes, or checks. May bleed when washed. Madras from India is usually hand woven.

Moiré (MAW-ray). A fabric with an irregular, wavy, watermark appearance on the surface.

Muslin. A plain-weave cotton fabric that is fairly strong and durable. Muslin can be purchased as finished cloth and in unbleached form.

Organdy. A sheer, stiff transparent fabric made in a plain weave. It is available in cotton, silk, and manufactured fibers.

Organza. Similar to, but much stiffer than organdy. This sheer fabric can be made from silk and manufactured fibers.

Oxford cloth. A basket-weave fabric made from cotton that comes in a variety of weights. It has a soft luster when mercerized.

Percale. A fine, closely woven cotton fabric that is medium in weight. It is often used for sheeting and comes in plain colors and prints.

Piqué (pih-KAY). A durable, corded cotton fabric. The cords run lengthwise and form ribs. Some piqué fabrics have a birds-eye or waffle pattern.

Plissé (plih-SAY). A type of crepe with puckered designs formed by treating with a chemical solution, such as sodium hydroxide.

Poplin. A strong fabric in a plain weave with fine crosswise ribs. It is usually made from cotton, but can be made from wool, silk, and manufactured fibers.

Sateen. A cotton fabric made in a satin weave.

Satin. A lustrous, satin-weave fabric. The high luster is produced by floating yarns on the surface on the right side of the fabric. It is generally made from silk or manufactured fibers.

Seersucker. A light, cotton or manufactured fiber fabric that has permanently crinkled surface stripes on the right side of the fabric. The crinkled effect is produced by a plain weave-crepe variation.

Shantung (shan-TUHN). A plain-weave fabric with a slightly irregular surface produced by heavier, rough-textured crosswise yarns.

Suede cloth. A woven fabric with a short, napped finish that resembles suede. It can be made from cotton, wool, and rayon fibers.

Taffeta. A crisp, plain-woven lustrous fabric with a stiffness that rustles with movement. It is made from silk and manufactured fibers.

Terry cloth. A heavy, absorbent cotton fabric made from heavy lengthwise threads woven into loops on one or both sides of the fabric. Loops are often uncut.

Tricot. A plain, warp-knitted fabric. It can be made from such fibers as nylon, wool, rayon, silk, or cotton.

Tulle (TOOL). A sheer, stiff fabric that is woven in a fine mesh. It can be made from silk or manufactured fibers.

Tweed. A sturdy, rough-textured fabric usually made in a plain or twill weave for suits and coats. It has a mixed-color effect. Usually made from wool, although cotton, silk, and manufactured fibers are also used.

Velour (veh-LOOR). A pile or napped fabric that resembles velvet. In lighter weights it is used for clothing; heavier weights can be used for upholstery and draperies.

Velvet (VEHL-vuht). A pile fabric woven from silk or manufactured fibers. The pile may be cut or uncut (or both). *Cut velvet* has a design cut into it. Silk and manufactured fibers are generally used for velvet.

Velveteen (vehl-vuh-TEEN). A twill or plain weave with a short weft pile. It is often made from cotton or cotton/manufactured fiber blends.

Voile (VOYUHL). A fine, crisp, sheer, lightweight fabric made in a plain weave. It may be plain or printed and made of cotton or manufactured fibers. It is similar to organdy, but less crisp.

Summary

- Fibers are combined to make yarns. Yarns are combined to make fabrics. Fabrics can utilize spun yarns, monofilament yarns, or multifilament yarns.
- The amount of twist added to a yarn affects the strength of the yarn.
- Filament yarns can be textured, making the yarns less smooth.
- Two or more yarns can be twisted together to form ply yarns.
- When different staple fibers are spun together into a single yarn, a blend results. When two or more different yarns are twisted into a ply, a combination yarn results.
- The two most common methods of making fabric are weaving and knitting. Other methods include felting, bonding, and quilting.
- Weaving is the process of interlacing yarns at right angles to each other to create a woven fabric. Different effects are achieved by passing the filling yarns over and under different numbers of warp yarns.
- Knitting is the process of looping yarns together to form a knitted fabric. The loops or stitches can be varied to create different patterns and textures.
- Knitted fabrics can be warm in the winter or cool in the summer, depending on the fiber, yarn, and finish used. They resist wrinkling and most are washable and require little or no ironing.

Graphic Organizer

Create a KWHL chart identifying what you know, what you want to know, how you are going to learn what you want to know, and what you have learned about the chapter content.

What I Know	What I Want to Know	How I Will Learn	What I Have Learned

Review the Facts

1. Which yarns are made from staple fibers?
2. Name two reasons for adding twist to a yarn.
3. Contrast single, ply, and cord yarns.
4. When different staple fibers are spun into a single yarn, the result is a _____.
5. In woven fabrics, the lengthwise yarns are the _____ yarns. The crosswise yarns are the _____ yarns.
6. Name the three basic weaves and one fabric made from each.
7. What is the basic difference between weaving and knitting?
8. How do jersey knits differ from purl knits?
9. List three uses of nonwoven fabrics.
10. Which type of fabric is *not* made of fibers?

Think Critically

11. **Analyze decisions.** If you were creating a blended yarn, which two fibers would you choose? Why? What characteristics would they bring to a fabric?

12. **Make inferences.** Read the labels on the clothes you are wearing. Are any of them blends? If so, infer why you think each fiber was used in the garment. What characteristics does each fiber contribute?
13. **Compare and contrast.** What are the advantages and disadvantages of woven fabrics versus knitted fabrics? Which do you prefer for garments and why?

Apparel Applications

14. **Digital fabric dictionary.** Unravel some fabric samples. Identify the kinds of yarns used. Take digital photos of the fabrics and yarns. Use desk-top publishing software to create your own fabric dictionary.
15. **Analyze fiber blends.** Look through a catalog of ready-to-wear clothing. Make a list of the fiber blends that are listed. Why do you think these particular blends are popular? Discuss your thoughts in class.
16. **Create weaves.** Use narrow strips of colored paper to construct small samples of basic weaves. Create a display and discuss characteristics of each.
17. **Examine fabric weaves.** Look at samples of fabrics made from the plain weave, twill weave, and satin weave. Locate the distinct diagonal lines found in the twill weave and notice the angle of the wale. Locate the floating yarns in the twill and satin weaves. Based on your examination, make a recommended use for each.
18. **Examine pile fabrics.** Look at samples of pile fabrics. Determine if they are cut or uncut pile fabrics. Are the base fabrics woven or knit? Make a recommendation for using each.
19. **Analyze stretch.** Compare the stretch of various knits. Cut five-inch squares of each knit. Lay each square on a piece of ¼-inch scale graph paper. Stretch each knit square lengthwise and crosswise and mark the amount of stretch each has. Compare results. Also notice which knits curl at the edges when cut.

Academic Connections

20. **Writing.** Choose a type of fabric to research. Use Internet or print resources to locate additional information and possible photos or illustrations. Be sure to include the fabric construction and characteristics. Write an illustrated summary of your findings.
21. **Social studies.** Research the earliest types of woven and knitted fabrics. Locate image examples if possible. Use presentation software to create an illustrated report. Share your findings with the class.

Workplace Links

22. **Fabric recommendations.** Presume you are a fashion designer with three new types of garments for the coming season (*Note:* Use magazine or catalog photos for this activity). A client is coming in to review your sketches or photos of your designs. What kind of fabric construction would you recommend for these garments? How would you explain your reasoning to your client.
23. **Create a sample book.** Locate various samples of felt, films, nonwoven fabrics, bonded fabrics, and quilted fabrics. Mount each on a separate sheet of paper and secure in a binder. Label each sample and include pictures for the end uses for each.

Informing Others—Technology and Fabrics

Choose a technological innovation such as microfibers or nanofibers to research. How are these high-tech fibers produced? Use the speaking and presentation guidelines in the FCCLA *Dynamic Leadership* program to prepare an oral and visual presentation about your fabric of choice. Follow the FCCLA *Planning Process* in developing your presentation. If possible, step up to the next level and use your presentation for an FCCLA STAR Event *Illustrated Talk*. See your adviser for information as needed.

Chapter 21

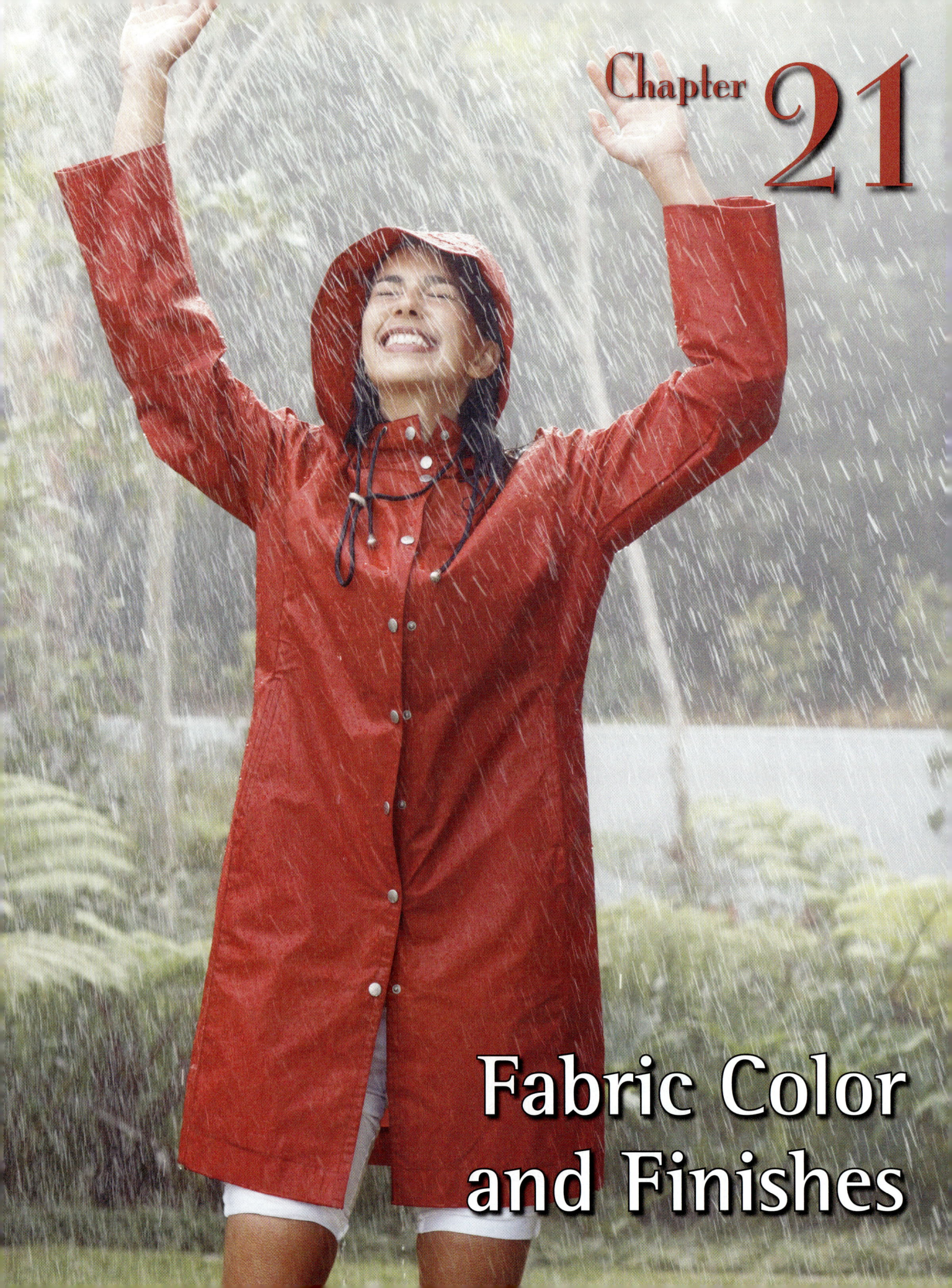

Fabric Color and Finishes

Chapter Objectives

After studying this chapter, you will be able to

- **describe** various ways to add color to fabrics.
- **summarize** methods used to print designs on fabrics.
- **explain** the performance to be expected from different finishes applied to fabrics.
- **summarize** finishes that affect the appearance and texture of fabrics.

Key Terms

greige goods
dyes
fiber dyeing
solution dyeing
stock dyeing
yarn dyeing
piece dyeing
garment dyeing
printing
fabric finish

Reading with Purpose

As you read the chapter, record any questions that come to mind. Indicate where the answer to the question can be found: within the text, by asking your instructor, in another book, on the Internet, or by reflecting on your own experiences. Pursue the answers to your questions.

After the cloth is woven or knitted into fabric, it is still in an unfinished state. The unfinished fabric is called **greige** (*gray*) **goods**. The fabric still has a way to go before it is ready to be sewn into finished garments. Color needs to be added if it was not added earlier in the process. A design may need to be printed onto the fabric in some way.

The fabric also may not have the final feel or performance characteristics consumers expect of the fabrics they wear or purchase for the home. The fabric needs to have finishes added.

Adding Color

Color is a major part of any textile item. As you shop for clothes, the first thing you notice is color. You want colors that are in fashion and that look good on you.

Dyes are coloring agents that are used to add color to fibers, yarns, fabrics, or garments. Some dyes come from natural sources, and some are manufactured. Today, dyes are used to produce five million different colors. Computers are programmed to match these colors. This system saves time and prevents mistakes.

Dyeing

Dyeing is one way to add color to textile products. Fiber dyeing, yarn dyeing, and piece dyeing are the basic dyeing methods.

Fiber Dyeing

If fibers are dyed before they are spun into yarns, the process is **fiber dyeing**. This can be done in two ways:

Manufactured fibers are solution dyed. In **solution dyeing**, the dye is added to the thick liquid before it is forced through the spinneret.

Natural fibers, usually wool, may be stock dyed. In **stock dyeing**, the dye is added to the loose fibers. This gives a tweed effect to the final fabric.

Yarn Dyeing

Before some yarn is knitted or woven into fabrics, it goes through a process called **yarn dyeing**. After spinning, the yarns are tightly wound on tubes, and then placed in the dye bath. Most fabrics that are plaid or striped, as in **21-1**, are yarn dyed. Generally, yarn dyeing costs less than fiber dyeing, but more than piece dyeing.

Piece Dyeing

The most common method of dyeing is piece dyeing. During the **piece dyeing** process, color is added after the fabric has been made. Piece dyeing allows manufacturers to follow fashion trends closely. They can wait until the last minute to choose dye colors. Most, but not all, piece-dyed fabrics are solid colors.

21-1 These warp yarns have been dyed. The finished, woven fabric is striped Jacquard. *Somet S.p.A., Bergamo, Italy*

Some dyes will color one type of fiber, but not another. It is possible to combine different dyes in a single dye bath. When placing a fabric consisting of more than one fiber in that dye bath, it can become a stripe or check, or other pattern through this *cross-dyeing* process. For example, suppose a manufacturer mixed a red dye for acetate and a blue dye for rayon in a dye bath for a specially woven acetate/rayon fabric. When placing this fabric in the dye bath, the result might be a red and blue striped fabric. This is the magic of cross dyeing.

Garment Dyeing

A more recent trend is garment dyeing. With **garment dyeing,** an undyed finished garment is dyed after construction. The manufacturer must be certain the thread, buttons, zippers, and other trims will take the dye in the same way so the color is consistent. The advantage of garment dyeing is that it allows manufacturers to make fast deliveries to retailers of particular popular colors.

Colorfastness

For most people, if they purchase a garment that is washable, they want to be certain the color will remain the same after laundering. They also want to be certain the dye will not bleed onto other garments in the same wash load. In other words, they want a garment that is colorfast. *Colorfast* means the color will remain in spite of a certain influence such as washing, dry cleaning, perspiration, sunlight, or rubbing.

Unfortunately, no dye is colorfast to everything. The permanence of a color depends on the chemical makeup of the dye, the fiber composition, and the method of adding the dye. These factors must all work together.

You cannot be sure a garment is colorfast just by looking at it. Read the care label. It should warn you if the item is not colorfast under certain conditions. This information is important to consider when making a purchase decision. For example, when buying a swimsuit, you do not want one that chlorine or sunlight negatively affects. When buying children's clothes, you want the color to hold up well under washing many times.

Some fabrics are designed to fade or *bleed*. A fashion designer might select such a fabric because it imparts a certain desired look over time, 21-2. If this is the case, the label will warn you to expect this change. The label might also give special care instructions, such as washing the garment separate from other articles of clothing that might absorb the dye.

Printing

Printing also adds color to fabrics. **Printing** is the process of adding color, pattern, or design to fabric surfaces. You can easily tell whether fabrics have been colored in a dye bath or by printing. The wrong (back) side of most printed fabrics is much lighter than the right side. Both sides of dyed fabrics are the same color.

There are many ways to print cloth. Some methods have been used for hundreds of years. Others take advantage of the latest technology. They include the following:

- *Roller printing.* In roller printing, the design is etched on copper rollers. Each color in the design requires a separate roller. As the cloth passes through the rollers, each one transfers its color and pattern to the fabric. This is a simple and fast method of applying design to a fabric, but it is expensive.
- *Screen printing.* Screen printing is one of the earliest known methods of applying design to fabric. A woven-mesh screen attached to a wooden frame suspends an ink-blocking stencil over the fabric. The areas of the design that are not to receive color are blocked off. As a roller or squeegee moves across the screen, ink is pressed through the open areas of the woven mesh onto the fabric. Each color requires a separate screen.
- *Rotary screen printing.* This is one of the newest and fastest printing methods. It combines both roller and screen printing methods. The design is transferred onto a cylinder-shaped screen—one screen for each color. Dye is forced through a pattern of holes in each screen. The cylinders roll over the fabric, leaving the design.
- *Heat transfer printing.* In this printing method, the dyes are first printed on paper. With the application of heat and pressure to the paper and fabric, the dyes change to gases that move from the paper base onto the fabric. This process results in clean, fine lines in elaborate designs, but fabrics are sometimes stiff. T-shirts are often printed in this manner.

21-2 Jeans are often meant to fade in color. Be sure to read the care labels before you launder a new pair of jeans. *Shutterstock*

- *Digital printing.* This process creates printable designs on a computer that are then sent directly to fabric printing machinery. The use of screens and color separation is not necessary. Ink-jet printers apply the designs directly to the fabric. The advantage of this method is that changes in colors and designs can be made quickly, responding to the latest fashion trends. Another advantage is that it uses much less water than traditional methods, making it more environmentally desirable. This type of printing is replacing many of the older methods of printing.

Finishes

All fabrics receive some kind of finish. A **fabric finish** is any treatment to fibers, yarns, or fabrics that make the final products look, feel, or perform differently. Finishes can be applied with heat, pressure, or chemicals.

Not all fabric finishes last for the life of the garment. The following terms indicate how long a finish will last:

- *Permanent finish*—lasts for the life of a garment
- *Durable finish*—lasts through several launderings or dry cleanings
- *Temporary finish*—lasts only until the fabric is washed or dry-cleaned
- *Renewable finish*—a temporary finish that can be replaced or reapplied

Another key to look for when reading labels is any word ending in *proof*. This indicates there is complete protection, such as waterproof. If the words *resistant* or *repellent* are used, you know the finish gives only partial protection. Examples are *stain-resistant* and *water-repellent*.

Although finishes make textile items more beautiful and more useful, they cannot improve the quality of the fabric itself. Fabric quality depends on the quality of the fibers and yarns and on the method of construction.

Each of the many different finishes gives certain characteristics to a fabric. Read the labels to see what finishes have been applied. Some of the finishes are designed to affect the performance of the fabric. Others affect the appearance or texture of the fabric.

Finishes That Affect Performance

The following finishes are designed to affect the performance of the fabric. Children's play clothes often have several of these finishes applied.

Antibacterial and Antimicrobial

This finish suppresses the growth of odor-causing bacteria, fungi, and mold spores. Fabrics that create warm, moist conditions next to the body lead to ideal conditions for the growth of bacteria and fungi. The result is perspiration that can lead to odors and stains. These finishes act as built-in deodorants. Antibacterial fabrics are also suitable for use in healthcare settings where hygiene is extremely important, **21-3**.

Antistatic

Antistatic chemical treatment prevents static electricity. This process prevents garments from clinging to the wearer. This finish is also important for use in upholstery and carpets.

Crease-Resistant and Wrinkle-Resistant

Crease-resistant and wrinkle-resistant finishes are much the same. They involve treating fabrics with resins, a special group of chemicals. Resins are *baked* onto cotton, rayon, and linen fabrics. They help fabrics resist wrinkles, but they also make fabrics weaker and less absorbent. Stains are more difficult to remove from fabrics with resin finishes.

Fabrics may be *precured* before they are made into garments, but the garments will not retain creases that are created during the construction process. A completed garment may be pressed and then *postcured* to permanently hold creases, pleats, and hems.

Durable Press and Permanent Press

Many manufactured fibers achieve a durable-press or permanent-press finish without resins. With this process, manufacturers use high temperatures to *heat set* fabrics or garments. The heat-setting process permanently creates the desired shapes, creases, and pleats; however, the fabrics resist wrinkles. By following the care instructions, ironing is unnecessary. However, it is important to remove garments from the dryer as soon as the tumbling stops or wrinkles may form.

Fade-Resistant

Labeling a fabric fade-resistant means the colors remain true for a longer period of time. This is particularly important when selecting drapery and upholstery fabrics, especially for outdoor use.

Flame-Resistant and Flame-Retardant

The *Flammable Fabrics Act (FFA)* lists general requirements for all clothing and specific ones for children's sleepwear, carpets, rugs, and mattresses. As a fabric burns, this chemical finish works by cutting off the oxygen supply or changing the chemical makeup of the fibers. This causes the flame to extinguish itself. These finishes also inhibit the rate of ignition, slow the spread of flames, and encourage a fabric to self-extinguish. Because these finishes add cost and may have environmental implications, their use on children's sleepwear is uncommon. They can, however, be found on some specialty work-wear items.

A fabric need not have a finish on it to meet the requirements of the FFA. Several fibers are flame-resistant and will meet the standards, **21-4**.

21-3 All members of the hospital medical staff benefit from antibacterial finishes on their uniforms.
Shutterstock

21-4 Children's sleepwear must meet the regulations established by the Flammable Fabrics Act.
Shutterstock

Mildew-Resistant

The application of a metallic chemical to fabrics helps prevent mildew. Usage of such fabrics includes shower curtains and outdoor furniture.

Mercerization

To improve luster, strength, and absorbency, cotton and rayon fabrics undergo the chemical treatment of mercerization. This process uses a solution of caustic soda or lye. Mercerized fabrics also absorb dyes better.

Moth-Repellent

Manufacturers can add chemicals that repel moths to dye baths to slightly change wool fibers. Because of the changes in the fibers, moth and carpet beetle larvae will not eat them.

Shrinkage Control

Fabrics labeled as *preshrunk* have been shrunk by moisture and heat. When consumers buy these fabrics or garments, they will not shrink more than three percent unless the label states otherwise. You may also see the name Sanforized® on labels. This trademark means that fabrics have been processed so they will not shrink more than one percent in either direction when washed.

Soil-Release

Soil-release finishes allow fabrics to be more easily *wetted*, helping detergents release soil. Manufacturers often use this finish with durable-press finishes.

Stain-Resistant

Stain-resistant finishes cause fabrics to repel food, water, and other substances by reducing absorbency. You can sponge or wash the stains off easily.

Water-Repellent and Waterproof

The application of a water-repellent finish to tightly woven fabrics helps them resist water. The finish cannot resist heavy rain or long exposure to rain. It is a renewable, but not a permanent, finish, **21-5**.

21-5 A water-repellent finish is often applied to coats designed to wear in the rain. *Shutterstock*

Focus on Technology

Nanotechnology in the Apparel Industry

Apparel that battles bugs, soothes with aloe vera, and fends off odors! Can it be? Yes, thanks to fiber innovations brought to us through the science of nanotechnology. **Nanotechnology** involves the transformation of materials at the molecular level, atom by atom. In other words, finishes are not added to the fabric. These characteristics result from alterations to the molecular structure of the chemicals that are used to form the fibers.

Most fiber enhancements are developed to address common consumer complaints about fabrics. Though some of these enhancements have been around for years, they were not durable. After a few washings, the treatment was no longer effective. They also compromised the style, drape, comfort, and feel of the fabric. Today, consumers can have it all.

The complaints and their innovative solutions include the following:

- **Static electricity.** When applied to polyester, this treatment reduces static cling and repels statically attractive substances, such as dog hair, lint, and dust. Your clothes won't cling to you, and no more static shocks.
- **Stains.** New innovations have led to fabrics that repel stains as well as release stains, so you're protected on defense and offense. Spill resistance keeps stains from soaking in, while stain release allows them to easily come clean. If coffee spills on your pants, it just beads up and rolls right off.
- **Insect bites.** When heading for the woods, clothes treated with a substance from chrysanthemums will repel insects. No more bites from mosquitoes, ticks, ants, flies, and chiggers! Look for *Buzz Off* clothing by Orvis.
- **Moisture.** You will look and feel cool all day long with new natural and synthetic fabrics that provide moisture wicking. Fabrics pull perspiration away from the skin, keeping the body cooler, dryer, and more comfortable. The fabrics *breathe*. When it's hot, they let air in. When it's chilly, the fibers close up.
- **Odors.** No one wants smelly socks, so you can get ones that have a new odor-fighting component. Gore-Tex even makes scent-suppressing clothing for hunters. Towels treated with Microban fend off mold, mildew, and odor-causing bacteria. Antimicrobials inhibit the growth of the micro-organisms that cause odors and stains.
- **Irritation.** Moisturizing socks and aloe-enriched intimates soothe the skin thanks to technology that involves microcapsules. Microcapsules included in the fabric rupture on movement, contacting the skin.

Who knows what lies ahead as science continues to tackle common consumer complaints.

Water-repellent finishes are not the same as waterproof fabrics. Waterproof fabrics are films or film-coated fabrics. No water can soak into these fabrics. They are lower in cost, but less comfortable than fabrics with a water-repellent finish. To be sure a garment is waterproof, the seams must also be sealed.

Finishes That Affect Appearance and Texture

Sometimes manufacturers need to change the appearance or texture of a fabric for a customer's specifications. The following finishes are just a few they use to change the appearance or texture of the fabric, **21-6**.

Calendering

Calendering is the application of heat and pressure with rollers on fabrics to produce a smooth, polished surface. Sometimes the rollers have engraved sections that create a raised design on the fabric. This is called *embossing*. A watered effect can also be created. The result is a *moiré* (maw-RAY) fabric. Another variation is *glazing*, in which a resin is applied before the fabric goes between the rollers. This results in a polished look on the fabric surface.

Napping

Napping raises the short, loose fibers on the fabric surface. Fiber ends are pulled from low-twist, spun yarns to create a soft, fuzzy surface on the fabric.

Sizing

Sizing involves the application of starch or resin to fabrics to increase weight, body, and luster. It is a less expensive way to improve the appearance of a fabric, but it often washes out.

Stone Washing and Acid Wash

Just as the name implies, the stone-washed fabric is placed in an industrial washer that is filled with pumice stones. As the cylinder rotates, the stones repeatedly beat against the fabric. The result is a softer fabric that has a worn, faded appearance. Its main use is on canvas and denim. Soaking the pumice stones in chlorine causes an *acid-wash* finish. The chlorine creates sharper color contrasts on denim.

Weighting

To increase the fabric weight and crispness, some manufacturers add metallic salts to silk—a process called *weighting*. Because too much of the metallic salts will cause severe damage to the fiber, laws regulate how much manufacturers may add to this fabric finish.

21-6 Select fabrics with finishes that will meet your various performance requirements. *Comstock*

Did You Know?

Coloring and Finishing the Green Way

Some substances and processes used to add color and finishes to fibers, yarns, and fabrics can contribute to environmental problems. They can cause harmful chemicals and gasses to be released into the environment. Other manufacturing processes waste energy, water, and other valuable resources.

Manufacturers have found many ways to make their products greener, or more environmentally friendly. Following are a few of them.

- **Minimizing the use of toxic substances in dyes and finishes.** This is being done by using dry finishes instead of wet finishes on textiles. Wet finishes involve the application of chemicals to fabric. Dry finishes involve the use of heat and machines instead of chemicals. Other manufacturers are using formaldehyde-free finishes; formaldehyde has been linked to health problems. Using hydrogen peroxide instead of chlorine for bleaching and using vegetable and other natural dyes instead of harsh chemicals are other changes manufacturers are making.

- **Using manufacturing processes that conserve water and energy.** Using ink-jet printers instead of dye baths to apply color conserves water and energy. If dye-baths are used, reuse of the dye-bath saves water by recycling it. A foam finishing process saves water by using foam instead of water to apply chemicals. Using dyeing processes that work in cool water instead of hot water also conserves energy.

- **Creating products that require less laundering or can be washed in cold water.** Water-repellent and stain-resistant finishes protect clothing from dirt and stains. Bacterial-resistant finishes keep odor-causing bacteria from growing on fabrics. Garments with these finishes need less laundering to stay clean. This saves water and energy. It also lessens environmental pollution caused by detergents and chemicals used for cleaning clothes. Other finishes applied to clothes allow them to be washed and cleaned at lower temperatures.

Summary

- Greige goods are either dyed or printed to add color and pattern to the fabric. There are many methods used to dye and print fabrics.
- Dyeing is one way to add color to textile products. The methods include fiber dyeing, yarn dyeing, and piece dyeing.
- Colorfast means the color will remain in spite of a certain influence such as washing, dry cleaning, perspiration, sunlight, or rubbing.
- Printing is the process of adding color, pattern, or design to the surface of fabrics.
- There are many ways to print cloth. Some methods have been used for hundreds of years. Others, such as digital printing, take advantage of the latest technology.
- A fabric finish is any treatment given to fibers, yarns, or fabrics that make the final product look, feel, or perform differently. Not all fabric finishes last for the life of the garment.
- Many finishes affect the performance of the fabric. Some performance finishes are wrinkle resistant, durable press, flame-resistant, and mercerization.
- Other finishes affect the appearance or texture of the fabric. These include calendaring, napping, sizing, and stone washing.

Graphic Organizer

Draw a T-chart and list the main headings of the chapter in the left column. Write at least three supporting details for each heading in the right column.

Main Headings	Supporting Details

Review the Facts

1. Explain the difference between solution dyeing and stock dyeing.
2. Which two methods of dyeing allow a quick response to changing fashion trends?
3. In _____ printing, the design is etched on copper rollers.
4. Which method of printing combines two older methods of printing?
5. Explain how computers are now used in fabric printing.
6. Contrast water-repellent and waterproof finishes.
7. What two finishes would you look for if you did not want a garment to shrink?
8. How are stone-washed jeans made?

Think Critically

9. **Analyze outcomes.** Name an item of clothing that should be colorfast. Analyze the importance of colorfastness for this garment. Why is it important for it to be colorfast? What might be the negative outcomes from lack of colorfastness? If you are not sure if a garment you plan to launder is colorfast, what would you do?

10. **Analyze behavior.** If a garment has a flame-resistant label on it, do you think people are more likely to be careless around open flames? Why or why not?
11. **Draw conclusions.** What conclusions can you draw about why more garment manufacturers are now using the term durable press instead of permanent press?

Apparel Applications

12. **Identify color application methods.** Examine several fabric samples. Discuss which ones were dyed and which ones were printed. Then examine a variety of T-shirts that have sayings or logos on them. What printing method was likely used on these shirts?
13. **Identify dyeing method.** Look at a sample of cotton chambray fabric. Pull off a filling yarn and a warp yarn. Notice that the filling yarns are white and the warp yarns are a color. What method of dyeing was used?
14. **Experiment with dyeing.** Obtain samples of undyed wool and cotton fibers and a package of commercially made fabric dye. Follow the package directions for mixing the dye. Place the dye in two glass bowls. Label one bowl *wool* and the other *cotton*. Place the wool and cotton fibers in each bowl. Check the fibers at 5, 10, and 15 minute intervals and note how well the dye has absorbed into the fibers. Repeat this experiment using undyed manufactured fabric swatches from such fibers as rayon and polyester. Compare the results of each experiment.
15. **Develop a finish dictionary.** Use the Internet to find trademark names for the finishes described in this chapter. Use a pocket-size notebook to create a *finish dictionary*. List one finish type per page with a brief description of the finish. Add the trademark names you find for each finish. Use your finish dictionary when shopping for specific clothing items or fabrics.

Academic Connections

16. **Social studies.** Research the history of various natural-dyeing techniques used generations ago. Choose two of the processes and experiment with them using pieces of cotton muslin fabric. Create a display of the fabrics along with a description of how they were dyed.
17. **Reading.** Research the use of organic dyes in the American textile and apparel industry. When is it best to use organic dyes? What makes the dyes organic or sustainable? Prepare an oral report about your findings to share with the class.

Workplace Links

18. **Job shadowing.** Find a local entrepreneur who operates a screen-printing business and ask if you might observe the screen-printing process. What does this individual like and dislike about the business? What clothing products do customers request most? Share your experience with the class.
19. **Informing customers.** Imagine that you work in the marketing department of a national clothing store chain. Part of your job responsibility is to write articles on new products for the store's website. The store is promoting a new line of lightweight outdoor wear that is water-repellant. Write an article describing the features of this new clothing line. Use text and Internet resources to identify key information about these features. Share your article.

Informing Others About Textile Finishes

Are you concerned about the environmental impact of textile coloring methods and finishes? What sustainable methods are used for coloring clothing and applying finishes to clothing?

Use the speaking and presentation guidelines in the FCCLA *Dynamic Leadership* program to prepare an oral presentation about sustainable coloring and finishing methods for fabrics. Follow the FCCLA *Planning Process* as you develop your presentation. See your adviser for information as needed.

PART 5

Sewing Techniques

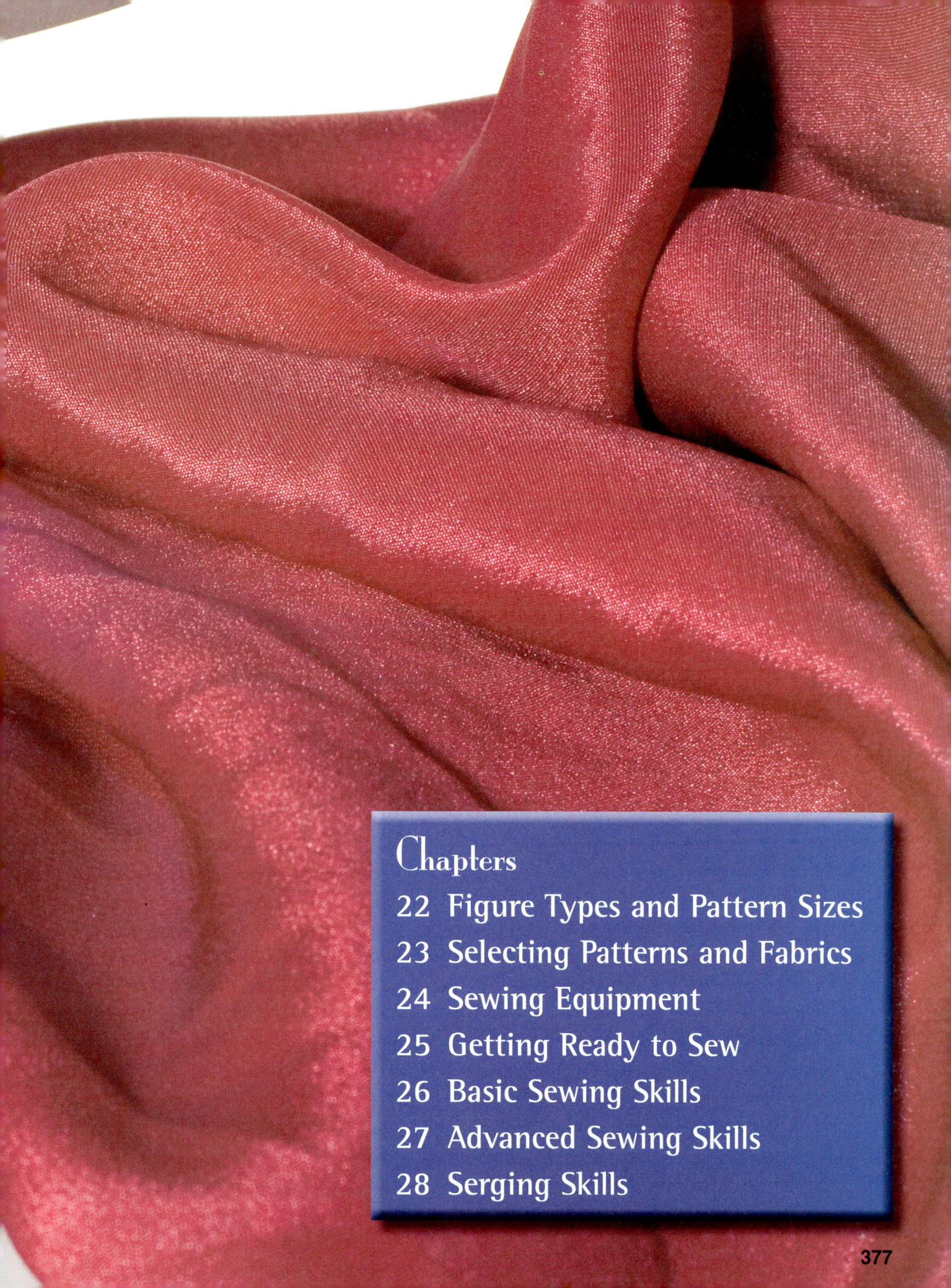

Chapters
22 Figure Types and Pattern Sizes
23 Selecting Patterns and Fabrics
24 Sewing Equipment
25 Getting Ready to Sew
26 Basic Sewing Skills
27 Advanced Sewing Skills
28 Serging Skills

Chapter 22

Figure Types and Pattern Sizes

Chapter Objectives

After studying this chapter, you will be able to
- **determine** appropriate figure type and pattern size.
- **take** accurate body measurements.
- **select** a pattern size based on garment type.
- **summarize** the importance of pattern ease.

Key Terms

figure types
standard sizes
unisex
body measurements
multisized patterns
wearing ease
design ease

Reading with Purpose

As you read the chapter, put sticky notes next to the passages about which you have questions. Write your questions on the sticky notes. Discuss the questions with your classmates or teacher.

When you look around the classroom, you see students of all sizes and shapes. Some are more mature in growth than others of the same age. You can find tall, short, thin, and curvy people all in the same group.

You may not be able to wear the same size clothing as the student beside you. Ready-to-wear clothes as well as clothes patterns are made in many sizes to suit the many types of people. The difficult part of choosing clothes or patterns is getting ones that fit.

Determining Figure Type

All pattern companies group patterns under figure types according to height and proportion. Your **figure type** is based on your height, proportions, and body type. Your back waist measurement can also be useful in determining figure type. The female figure types are Girls', Girls' Plus, Misses', Miss Petite, Women's, and Women's Petite, **22-1**. (Patterns for a *Junior* figure type are seldom available from pattern companies today.) For males, the figure types are Boys', Teen Boys', and Men's.

Some of the figure types have their own sections in the pattern catalogs. This helps you quickly find the section you want without flipping through the entire catalog.

Figure Types for Females and Males

Girls'	Girls' Plus	Misses'	Miss Petite
No defined bustline. Short waist length. For the growing girl who has not yet begun to mature.	Slightly developed bustline. Short waist length. Young, growing girls' figure, over the average weight for their age and height.	Height 5'5" to 5'6". Average bust position. Average waist length. Fully-developed, well-proportioned figure considered to be the "average" figure, also the tallest.	Height 5'2" to 5'3". Average bust position. Short waist length. Fully-developed, but shorter than Misses' figure.

(Continued)

22-1 These are the descriptions of the basic figure types for girls, boys, women, and men. *The McCall Pattern Company*

Determining Size

All pattern companies use the same set of body measurements for their **standard sizes**. Standard sizes also remain the same from issue to issue of the catalogs. Pattern sizes may or may not correspond to ready-to-wear sizes. The sizes of ready-to-wear garments vary from one garment manufacturer to another.

Bust or chest, waist, and hip or seat measurements determine pattern sizes. There are different sizes in each figure type. Once you know your figure type, you can easily determine your pattern size. All you have to do is measure carefully.

Some patterns are designed for either males or females. The styles are often more classic and look good on either a male or female figures. These sizes are called **unisex**. They are made for figures within the Misses', Men's, Teen Boys', Boys', and Girls' size ranges. See 22-3 for these measurements.

Figure Types for Females and Males

Women's	Women's Petite	Boys'/Teen Boys'	Men's
Height 5'5" to 5'6". Average bust position. Average waist length. Proportionately larger, more mature figure with slightly longer back waist length measurement due to fuller back.	Height 5'2" to 5'3". Low bust position. Short waist length. Short, fully-developed figure with narrow shoulders. Bust is smaller in proportion to waist and hips. Sometimes called half-size.	Height 4' to 5'8". Boys who have not yet reached full stature. Shoulders and hips are not as developed as those of a man.	Approximately 5'10". Adult male figure of average build with fully developed shoulders, hips, and neck.

22-1 Continued.

Taking Body Measurements

Body measurements are the actual dimensions of your body. Take body measurements over undergarments or a well-fitting garment. Remove any bulky garments, sweaters, or belts. You may want to have a family member or friend take your measurements. Stand or sit erect and still. The tape measure should be snug, but not tight.

Make a chart of your own to record your measurements. You will use the chart later to make any needed adjustments on your pattern. It will also be helpful when you select patterns in the future.

The measurements for each figure type for girls and women are shown in 22-2. The measurements for men's and boys' sizes are also listed in 22-3.

Female Pattern Sizes and Body Measurements

Inches

Girls'/Girls' Plus—For growing girls who have not yet begun to mature.
Girls' Plus are designed for girls over the average weight for their height and age.

	Girls'					Girls' Plus				
Sizes	7	8	10	12	14	8½	10½	12½	14½	16½
Chest	26	27	28½	30	32	30	31½	33	34½	36
Waist	23	23½	24½	25½	26½	28	29	30	31	32
Hips	27	28	30	32	34	33	34½	36	37½	39
Back waist length	11½	12	12¾	13½	14¼	12½	13¼	14	14¾	15½
approx. height	50	52	56	58½	61	52	56	58½	61	63½

Misses'/Miss Petite—For well-proportioned, developed figures.
Misses' about 5'5" to 5'6" without shoes. Miss Petite under 5'4" without shoes.

Sizes	4	6	8	10	12	14	16	18	20	22	24	26
Bust	29½	30½	31½	32½	34	36	38	40	42	44	46	48
Waist	22	23	24	25	26½	28	30	32	34	37	39	41½
Hip–9" below waist	31½	32½	33½	34½	36	38	40	42	44	46	48	50
Misses-Back waist length	15½	15½	15¾	16	16¼	16½	16¾	17	17¼	17⅜	17½	17¾
Miss Petite-Back waist length	14	14½	14¾	15	15¼	15½	15¾	16	16¼	16⅜	16½	16⅝

Women's/Women's Petite—for larger, more fully mature figures.
Women's about 5'5" to 5'6" without shoes. Women's Petite under 5'4" without shoes.

Sizes	Women's	16W	20W	22W	24W	26W	28W	30W	32W
	Women's Petite	36	38	40	42	44	46	48	50
Bust		40	42	44	46	48	50	52	54
Waist		33	35	37	39	41½	44	46½	49
Hip–9" below waist		42	44	46	48	50	52	54	56
Women's back waist length		17⅛	17¼	17⅜	17½	17⅝	17¾	17⅞	18
Women's Petite back waist length		16⅛	16¼	16⅜	16½	16⅝	16¾	16⅞	17

22-2 Pattern sizes and body measurements for female figures are given in this chart.

Measuring Females

To take female measurements, tie a string, cord, or narrow elastic around the waist—the narrowest part of the midsection at the navel. Bend over from side to side. The string will fall at your natural waistline. Keep the string in place while taking your measurements.

Male and Unisex Pattern Sizes and Body Measurements

Inches

Boys' & Teen Boys'—For growing boys and young men who have not reached full adult stature.

Sizes	7	8	10	12	14	16	18	20
Chest	26	27	28	30	32	33½	35	36½
Waist	23	24	25	26	27	28	29	30
Hip	27	28	29½	31	32½	34	35½	37
Neck band	11¾	12	12½	13	13½	14	14½	15
Approx. height	48	50	54	58	61	64	66	68
Shirt sleeve	22⅜	23¼	25	26¾	29	30	31	32

Men's—For men of average build; about 5'10" without shoes.

Sizes	32	34	36	38	40	42	44	46	48	50	52
Chest	32	34	36	38	40	41	44	46	48	50	52
Waist	27	28	30	32	34	36	39	42	44	46	48
Hip	34	35	37	39	41	43	45	47	49	51	53
Neck band	13½	14	14½	15	15½	16	16½	17	17½	18	18½
Shirt sleeve	31	32	32	33	33	34	34	35	35	36	36

Unisex—For figures within Misses', Men's, Teen-Boys', Boys' and Girls' size ranges.

Sizes	XXS	XS	S	M	L	XL	XXL
Chest/Bust	28-29	30-32	34-36	38-40	42-44	46-48	50-52
Hip	29-30	31-32	35-37	39-41	43-45	47-49	51-53

22-3 Pattern sizes and body measurements for male figures, as well as unisex sizes, are given in this chart.

Measurements to Determine Pattern Size

The following measurements are needed to determine pattern type and size. Measure the body as shown in 22-4.

- *Height*—Figure types are based on measurements without shoes. Stand against a wall. Mark height level at the top of the head lightly on the wall. Then measure from mark to floor to determine height.

- *Back Waist Length*—Measure from the prominent bone you can feel at the base of your neck to the string at the waistline.

- *High Bust*—Take this measurement with the tape straight across the back, directly under the arms, and above the fullest part of the bust.

- *Bust*—Measure across the fullest part of the bust, holding the tape measure straight across the back at the tips of the shoulder blades. Keep arms down at the side of the body.

- *Waist*—Measure over the string or elastic at the waist to obtain the waist measurement.

1. Height (without shoes)
2. Back Waist Length-from prominent bone at back neck base to waist
3. Neck (males only)-at the Adam's apple. Add ½" (1.3 cm) to neck body measurement. This measurement is now the same as ready-to-wear collar size.
4. High Bust (female only)-directly under the arms, above the bust and around the back
5. Bust/Chest-around the fullest part
6. Waist-over the string
7. Hips/Seat-around the fullest part. At these distances below waist: Misses' and Women's-9" (23 cm), Miss Petite, Women's Petite, and Teen-Boys'-7" (18 cm), Men-8" (20.5 cm), Girls'-5½" to 7" (14 cm to 18 cm), Boys' 6" (15 cm).
8. Front Waist Length-from shoulder at neck base to waist (over bust point on females)
9. Shoulder to bust (females only)-from shoulder at neck base to bust point
10. Shoulder Length-from neck base to shoulder bone
11. Back Width-across the midback. At these distances below neck base: Miss Petite, Misses, Women and Women Petite-5" (12.5 cm), Men-6" (15 cm), Teen-Boys'-4½" (11.5 cm), Girls' and Boys'-4" (10 cm)
12. Arm Length-from shoulder bone to wristbone over slightly bent elbow
13. Shoulder to elbow (female only)-from end of shoulder to middle of slightly bent elbow
14. Upper Arm-around arm at fullest part between shoulder and elbow
15. Crotch Depth-from side waist to chair. Sit on a hard, flat chair and use a straight ruler
16. Crotch Length-from center back waist, between legs, to center front waist
17. Inseam length-from crotch to desired length
18. Thigh-around the fullest part

Garment measurements that are nice to have:

19. Back Skirt Length (females)-from center back at waist to desired length
20. Pants Side Length-from side waistline to desired length along outside of leg

22-4 In order to sew garments that fit, you need to take accurate measurements. *Simplicity Pattern Co., Inc.*

- *Hips*—Measure around the fullest or largest part of the body—usually 7 to 9 inches below the waist with the tape measure parallel to the floor—to obtain the hip measurement.

Measurements to Determine Alterations

The following list contains some measurements that you may not find on pattern-size charts. These measurements will help you make a garment that fits well and looks good. By comparing these measurements with the same areas on pattern pieces, you will see what, if any, alterations you will need to make. (Remember that pattern pieces are slightly larger than body measurements so you can move comfortably in your clothes.) Be sure to make alterations to the pattern before cutting your fabric. You will save time and get a better fit by altering patterns instead of garments. Use the following directions to take these measurements:

- *Front waist length*—Measure from the base of the neck to the waistline.
- *Shoulder to bust*—Measure from center of the shoulder to the highest point of bust.
- *Shoulder length*—Measure from the base of the neck below ear to the tip of shoulder. This is the length of the shoulder seam.
- *Back width*—Measure the distance from armhole to armhole across the back with the tape measure 4 to 5 inches (depending on figure type) below the base of the neck.
- *Arm length*—Measure from the shoulder bone to the wrist bone, over a slightly bent elbow.
- *Shoulder to elbow*—Measure from the end of shoulder to the middle of a slightly bent elbow.
- *Upper arm*—Measure around the arm at the fullest part between the shoulder and elbow.
- *Crotch depth*—Sit flat and straight on a chair. Use a ruler to measure from side waist to the chair surface.
- *Crotch length*—Measure from the center back waist between the legs to the center front waist.
- *Inseam length*—Measure the inseam of the leg to the desired length. As an alternative, measure the inseam of a pair of pants that fit you well to get this measurement.
- *Thigh*—Measure around the fullest part of the thigh.
- *Back skirt length*—Measure from the elastic around the waist to the desired length at the center back. Remember to allow for the hem when comparing measurements on your pattern.

Measuring Males

Tie a string, cord, or narrow elastic around the waist over a shirt. Then measure the body as in 22-4.

Measurements to Determine Pattern Size

Take the following measurements to determine the correct pattern size for males.

- *Height*—Stand tall, without shoes, against a wall. Put a ruler on top of the head and lightly mark the position on the wall. Measure the distance between the mark and the floor to obtain the height.
- *Chest*—Measure around the fullest or largest part of the chest.
- *Waist*—Measure at the exact waistline because this determines size.
- *Hips*—Measure around the fullest part of the seat—about 7 inches below the waistline for boys and 8 inches for men.

- *Neck band*—Measure around the neck at the Adam's apple. Add ½ inch to the neck measurement. This is the shirt neck size. It is also a ready-to-wear shirt measurement.
- *Shirt sleeve or arm length*—Measure from the large bone at the back of the neck along the shoulder, over a bent elbow, and down to the wrist bone. This is also a ready-to-wear shirt measurement.

Measurements to Determine Alterations

The following additional measurements are helpful when determining alterations. You do not need them to determine pattern size. When sewing pants, you will need the inseam and pants side length measurements to help determine alterations.

- *Back waist length*—Measure from the prominent bone you can feel at the center-back neck base to your waistline.
- *Front waist length*—Measure from the base of the neck to the waistline.
- *Shoulder length*—Measure from the base of the neck below ear to the tip of shoulder. This is the length of the shoulder seam.
- *Back width*—Measure the distance from armhole to armhole across the back with the tape measure, 4 to 5 inches below base of the neck (depending on figure type).
- *Upper arm*—Measure around the arm at fullest part between the shoulder and elbow.
- *Crotch depth*—Sit flat and straight on a chair. Use a ruler to measure from side waist to the chair.
- *Crotch length*—Measure from center back waist between the legs to center front waist.
- *Inseam length*—Measure the inseam of the leg to the desired length. As an alternative, measure the inseam of a pair of pants that fit you well to get this measurement.
- *Thigh*—Measure around the fullest part of the thigh.
- *Pants side length*—Measure from the natural waistline down the outside of the leg to the desired pants length.

Selecting a Pattern That Fits

After determining your figure type and taking your measurements, you are ready to choose patterns that will fit you. Compare your measurements to the pattern measurements listed under your figure type in the pattern catalog or on the back of a pattern envelope. (Refer back to 22-2 or 22-3.)

Most people are not a perfect size. If you fall between two sizes, keep the following points in mind:

- If you are small boned, choose the smaller size. If you are large boned, choose the larger one.
- If you like a close fit, choose the smaller size. If you prefer a loose fit, choose the larger size.
- If the silhouette is close fitting, choose the larger size.

Most patterns are multisized. **Multisized patterns** have several sizes printed on the same pattern tissue. Select the cutting line for the size that fits your body. These patterns help if you are different sizes on the top and bottom. You can follow the cutting lines for the size of each body area.

Garment Type Determines Size

Sometimes you will need to choose a size based on the garment you are making. Consider the following for females:

- *For tops, blouses, dresses, coats, or jackets.* The bust is the most important measurement for these garments. Females should look for the size with the bust measurement closest to their own if they do not fit any group exactly. Waist and hip sections of a pattern are easier to alter than shoulder and bust darts. The pattern will lose its original look if you make too many alterations.
- *For skirts, slacks, and shorts.* Use the waist measurement for these garments. Adjust the hip, if necessary. If the hip measures two or more sizes larger than the waist, use the hip measurement. Choose the size closest to your hip measurement and adjust the waist.

If you are buying a pattern that includes both blouses or jackets and skirts or pants, select the size by the bust or chest measurement. Alter the waist and hips, if necessary.

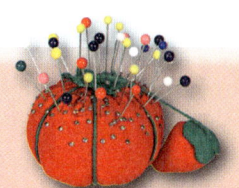

Did You Know?

You Can Learn to Sew with Kit Projects

If you are just learning to sew, a kit project may be a good choice for you. Kits are available for both sewing and home decorating projects. Kits for sewing projects include such items as jackets, vests, sweatshirts, shorts, pants, bags, comforters, and toys. Kits can also be purchased to make pillows, wall hangings, baby clothes, and many other items.

Kits come ready to assemble to make a professional-looking item. They include fabric, yarn, or other materials needed to construct the project. They also contain all notions such as buckles, snaps, buttons, zippers, and trims. Polyester fiberfill or down is often included for stuffed articles. Step-by-step directions are included with each kit. Kits are sold in a range of prices and are designed for a variety of skill levels.

Pineapple Appeal

An advantage of using a kit is the quickness with which you can finish a project. You can choose kits that match your skills, and you can learn new techniques as you progress. You must follow directions carefully in order not to damage a part or section of the item. Extra fabric is not provided for mistakes!

Pattern sizes for Boys', Teen Boys', and Men's are different. Consider the following for males:

- *For slacks or shorts.* Buy a pattern using the waist measurement.
- *For shirts.* Use the neck measurement for choosing a pattern size.
- *For sport coats and vests.* Buy these patterns using the chest size. For a snug fit, pick a smaller size pattern; for a looser fit, choose a larger size pattern. Some young men might prefer a closer fit while older men might prefer extra room.

Unisex styles are designed and sized to look good on both males and females. Unisex patterns are selected by the chest, bust, or hip measurement and sized for a looser fit than female and male patterns, 22-5. If you prefer a closer fit, you might select a smaller unisex size. Likewise, if you prefer more room or an extremely baggy look, you might choose a larger unisex size.

Pattern Ease

It is not possible to wear pants that measure exactly the same as your body. When measuring the hip area of a pattern, you may find it to be 2 to 3 inches larger than the hip measurement listed on the pattern envelope. This extra room is called **wearing ease**. It is planned so clothes fit comfortably. Ease is important in patterns for both males and females. Without ease, garments are too tight, uncomfortable, and unattractive. Unflattering wrinkles and pulls often occur, making it impossible to sit, walk, or bend in your clothes.

Larger pattern sizes have more ease, as do coats and jackets. Wearing ease varies from measurement to measurement, but generally includes the following:

- *Waist*—1 inch of wearing ease
- *Hips*—generally 2½ inches of ease
- *Bust or chest*—generally between 2½ and 3½ inches of ease

22-5 These unisex patterns are designed with a looser fit to suit both male and female figures. *Photo courtesy of McCall Pattern Co.*

Another type of ease is called **design ease**. This is an extra amount of fullness the designer uses to give a garment its special look or silhouette. When a fashion look features a body skimming fit, there is less design ease in the patterns, **22-6**. When a looser look is in style, there is more design ease built into the patterns. Design ease varies from a little extra—a few tucks or pleats—to a lot. For example, trouser styles may have flat fronts, small tucks at the waistline, or deeper, fuller pleats. The resulting hip width will be different in each style.

There are several ways to determine the amount of design ease in a pattern. First, study the artwork or photographs on the pattern envelope to see how close or full the garment appears. You can also read the written descriptions of the garment on the pattern envelope. Look for the following descriptive terms: *close-fitted*, *fitted*, *semi-fitted*, *loose fitting*, or *very loose fitting*. These terms will give you an idea of the amount of ease in the garment. A close-fitted garment may have no design ease allowed. A very loose fitting garment may have over 8 inches of ease in the bust area and over six inches in the hips. Another way is to compare your actual body measurements to the finished garment measurements. These are printed on the tissue pattern and/or on the back of the pattern envelope.

Patterns designed only for knitted fabrics have less ease allowance than other patterns. Some *give* is supplied by the fabric itself. A regular amount of ease is too much. In addition, people usually wear knitted garments closer to the body than garments made of woven fabrics. This is true for both male and female patterns.

22-6 The designer of this pattern allowed some design ease for a body skimming fit.
Simplicity Pattern Co., Inc.

Summary

- Pattern companies group patterns under figure types according to height and proportion.
- All pattern companies use the same set of body measurements for their standard sizes.
- Body measurements are the actual dimensions of your body. Take these measurements over your undergarments or a well-fitting garment.
- Most people are not a perfect size. Choose a size based on your bone structure, the fit you prefer, the closeness of the silhouette, and the type of garment you are sewing.
- All patterns have a certain amount of ease added to them to make them comfortable and attractive.

Graphic Organizer

Use a spider diagram to identify two key points for each main heading in this chapter.

Determining Figure Type | Determining Size
Figure Types/Pattern Sizes
Taking Body Measurements | Selecting Patterns

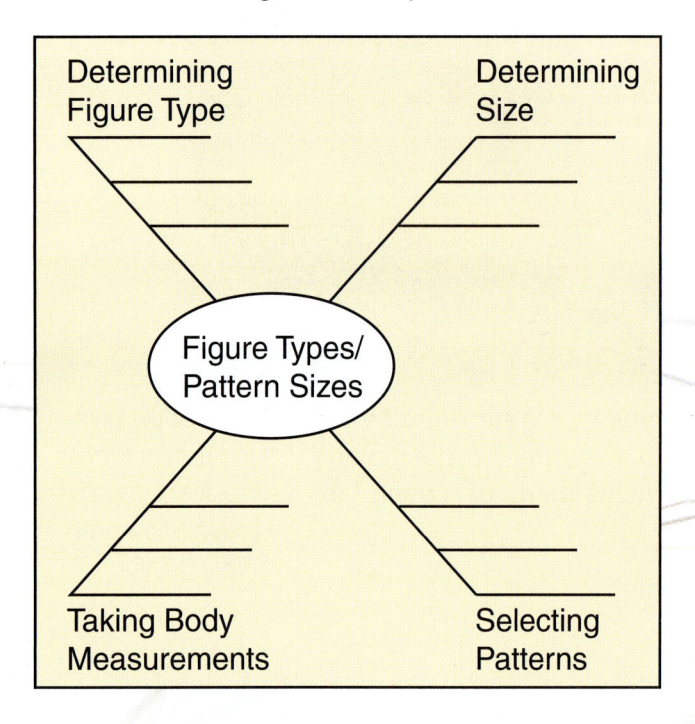

Review the Facts

1. List five terms used to identify pattern figure types.
2. How are figure types determined?
3. Are pattern sizes the same as ready-to-wear sizes?
4. What is the correct method for measuring height? waist?
5. What are the advantages of altering a pattern to fit rather than altering a garment?
6. Explain how to determine shirt neck size for men and boys.
7. Why should females select patterns closest to their bust size?
8. By what measurement should you buy men's slacks?
9. Contrast wearing ease and design ease.
10. Name three ways to judge the amount of design ease in a pattern.

Think Critically

11. **Draw conclusions.** Ready-to-wear garment manufacturers have attempted to standardize sizes, but there still is a great deal of variation. In contrast, the major pattern companies have agreed on a set of standard body measurements for their sizes. Draw conclusions about why you think garment manufacturers have not shown this same willingness to make their sizes consistent.

12. **Analyze outcomes.** After taking your measurements and determining your pattern size, you may notice it is one or two sizes larger than your customary ready-to-wear size. What are some reasons for this outcome? Is this a concern for you? Once you make your garment, how will anyone know the size?

13. **Identify evidence.** What evidence can you locate that shows design ease in current fashions? What evidence shows future trends for design ease in fashions? Are garments today more close-fitting or loose-fitting? Which do you prefer? Why?

Apparel Applications

14. **Make a chart.** Make an oversized chart showing how to take measurements for males and females. Post it on a bulletin board.

15. **Take measurements.** With a family member or friend, take each other's measurements. Take each measurement in the same body place to assure accuracy. Create a personal measurement chart and record your measurements.

16. **Determine ease.** Bring ready-made garments to class. Measure them in the same areas as your body measurements. Compare the measurements and determine the amount of ease allowed. Decide if each measurement is wearing ease or design ease.

17. **Compare patterns and ready-to-wear.** Measure your pattern pieces and the corresponding areas of a similar ready-made garment of the same size. How much difference do you find? Does the difference account for wearing ease, design ease, or both?

18. **Evaluate pattern ease.** Compare two patterns of the same size—one designed for knitted fabrics only and one designed for woven fabrics. (Make sure the styles are somewhat alike.) How much difference in ease do you find?

Academic Connections

19. **Reading.** Read at least three Internet or print resources about the history of sewing patterns. When were patterns first available to consumers? How were sizes determined? Who was responsible for creating these patterns? Why? Write a short report of your findings.

20. **Math.** Analyze pattern sizing methods for U.S. sewing patterns and those available from another part of the world, such as Europe. How do the measurements for pattern sizing compare? What are the similarities and differences? Share your findings with the class.

Workplace Connections

21. **Determine pattern size.** Create a role-play with a classmate for the following situation: Imagine you work at a fabric store. You have a new customer who is just learning how to sew. Your customer has a personal measurement chart, but is concerned about choosing the right pattern size because her figure type and measurements indicate a much larger size than her ready-to-wear size. How will you help your customer buy the right pattern size?

22. **Customer communication.** Presume you are the owner of a custom sewing business. You have a new customer who wants you to sew a special-occasion dress that is close-fitted. Your customer brought in her basic measurements and assures you she took them accurately. How would you explain to your customer the necessity and benefit of taking more detailed measurements for this garment?

Leading the Way on Fashion Tours

Some community organizations sponsor yearly fashion tours or shows for historic or new fashions. These events help raise money for worthy causes. Consider volunteering to help write the narration for such an event. Work along side the community organizers and learn as much as you can about the fashions for the event. If possible, research historical data about the fashions that add interest to your narration.

Use the FCCLA *Planning Process* to plan, carry out, and evaluate experience for this community event. Your project can also work as an FCCLA *Interpersonal Communications* STAR Event. See your adviser for information as needed.

Chapter 23

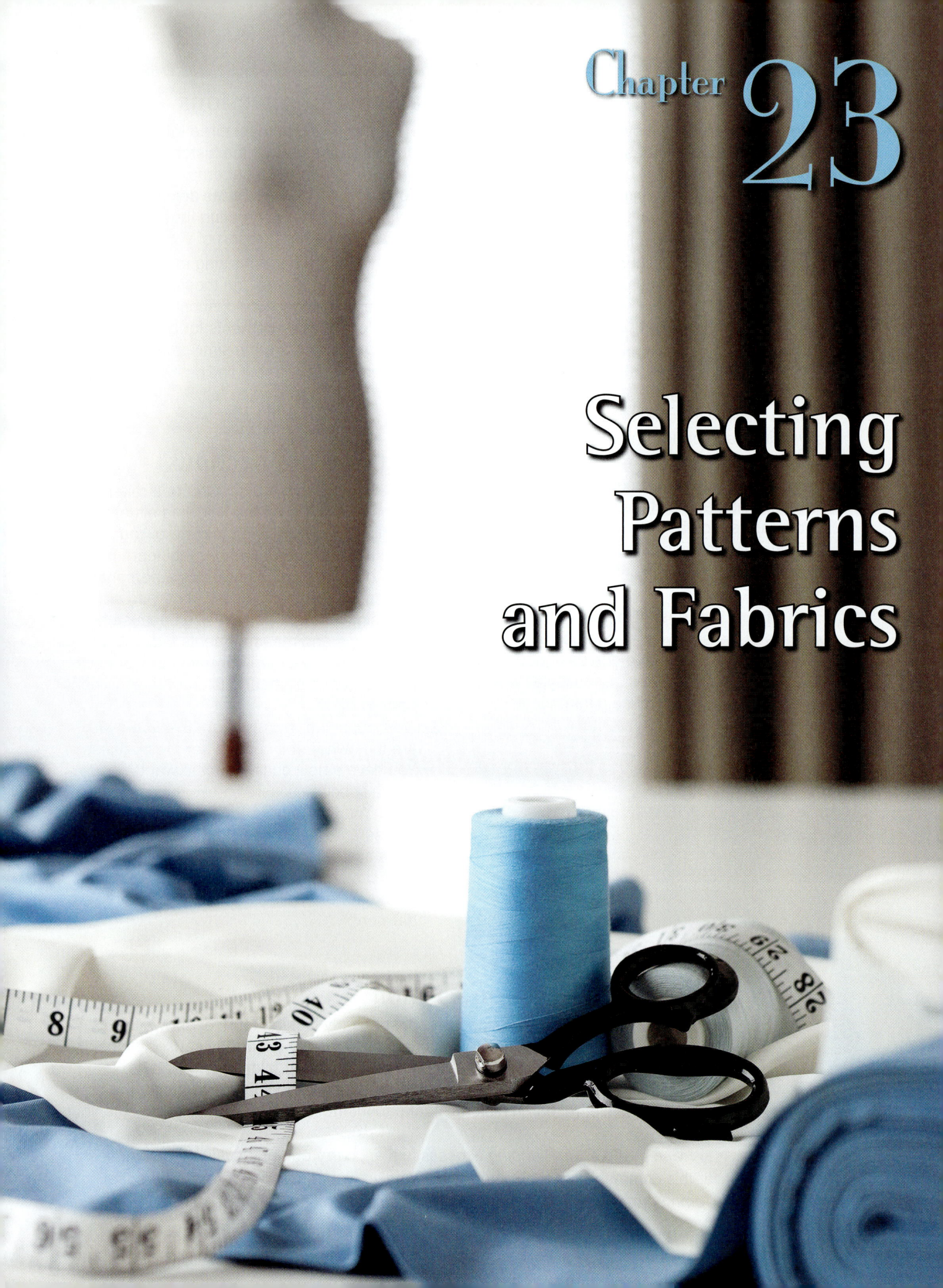

Selecting Patterns and Fabrics

Chapter Objectives

After studying this chapter, you will be able to
- **summarize** the information provided in pattern catalogs.
- **explain** what is included in a pattern and describe the purpose of each component.
- **identify** the symbols found on a pattern piece.
- **choose** a pattern based on your skill level and needs.
- **choose** a fabric based on your skill level and needs.
- **identify** items that can be sewn for personal use and home decorating.

Key Terms

pattern	grain line	shirred curtains
notions	adjustment lines	café curtains
cutting and sewing guide sheet	notches	duvet
	dots	dust ruffle
cutting line	valance	pillow sham
stitching line		

Reading with Purpose

Predict what you think will be covered in this chapter. Make a list of your predictions. After reading the chapter, decide if your predictions were correct.

The pattern catalog and your pattern give you ideas about styles, fashions, possible fabrics, and accessories. A **pattern** includes tissue paper pieces to follow when cutting out your fabric. It also includes step-by-step instructions for constructing the garment or item. With the help of a pattern, you can buy the supplies and cut, mark, and sew your garment successfully.

Pattern Catalogs

Each of the major pattern companies has its own catalogs. They are all similar in format and size. Many popular patterns remain in the catalogs for months or even years. The pattern companies drop other patterns that do not sell well. Although four major catalog issues come out each year, the pattern companies introduce new patterns monthly.

Pattern catalogs show many photographs and detailed drawings. They give you ideas for garment variations and possible fabrics. The catalogs show many outfits with accessories so you can see how to complete the outfits.

The garment sketches in pattern catalogs show the shape or form of the garment. This helps you better determine if a particular style is good for you. The sketches also show textures, colors, or designs that enhance the visual appearance of the garment, **23-1**.

In the back of the catalogs, you will find a measurements page. In addition, there are charts that show the different pattern sizes and illustrations to show how to take body measurements correctly. If you are not sure which pattern size to buy, this is the place to look.

You can also look at patterns online. All of the major pattern companies have websites that show the patterns you see in their store catalogs. These websites provide other helpful information, too, such as how to take body measurements to determine pattern sizes. Links are provided to other sewing websites and sewing machine companies. One pattern-company website even provides a special place for sewing students to post photos of their finished projects. You can also purchase patterns through these websites.

Some of the major pattern companies also publish their own magazines. New issues come out several times a year. They feature styles that are popular for the upcoming season along with helpful sewing tips. You can purchase the magazines at newsstands and fabric stores, or subscribe to the magazines.

Understanding the Pattern

A pattern is to a person making a garment what a blueprint is to a carpenter building a house. The pattern shows the *what*, *when*, and *how*. Just like a blueprint, a pattern gives you a basic plan. This helps you successfully build or put together a product—a garment.

Most stores will not let you return or exchange patterns. Study the pattern in the pattern catalog until you are certain it is the one you want.

Your pattern has three main parts. Each part contains helpful information. The parts include the

- envelope front and back
- cutting and sewing instructions
- tissue pattern pieces

23-1 This sketch was made by a graphic artist at the pattern company. It will be used in the pattern catalog and for the pattern envelope.
Photo courtesy of McCall Pattern Company

Pattern Envelope

The front of the envelope gives the pattern number, figure type, size, and price. It also shows a sketch and sometimes a photograph of the garment, **23-2**. You often see more than one view, as in **23-3**. These views give you an idea of different fabrics, designs, and details that you can use. For instance, a shirt pattern may show long sleeves, short sleeves, and no sleeves; collar and no collar. You can choose the combination you prefer. Most of the information on the envelope front is also available in the catalog.

23-2 The front of a pattern envelope can give you important information as well as show you what the finished garment should look like. *Photo courtesy of McCall Pattern Company*

23-3 Pattern envelopes sometimes show photographs or sketches of different garments that can be made from the same pattern. *Photo courtesy of McCall Pattern Company*

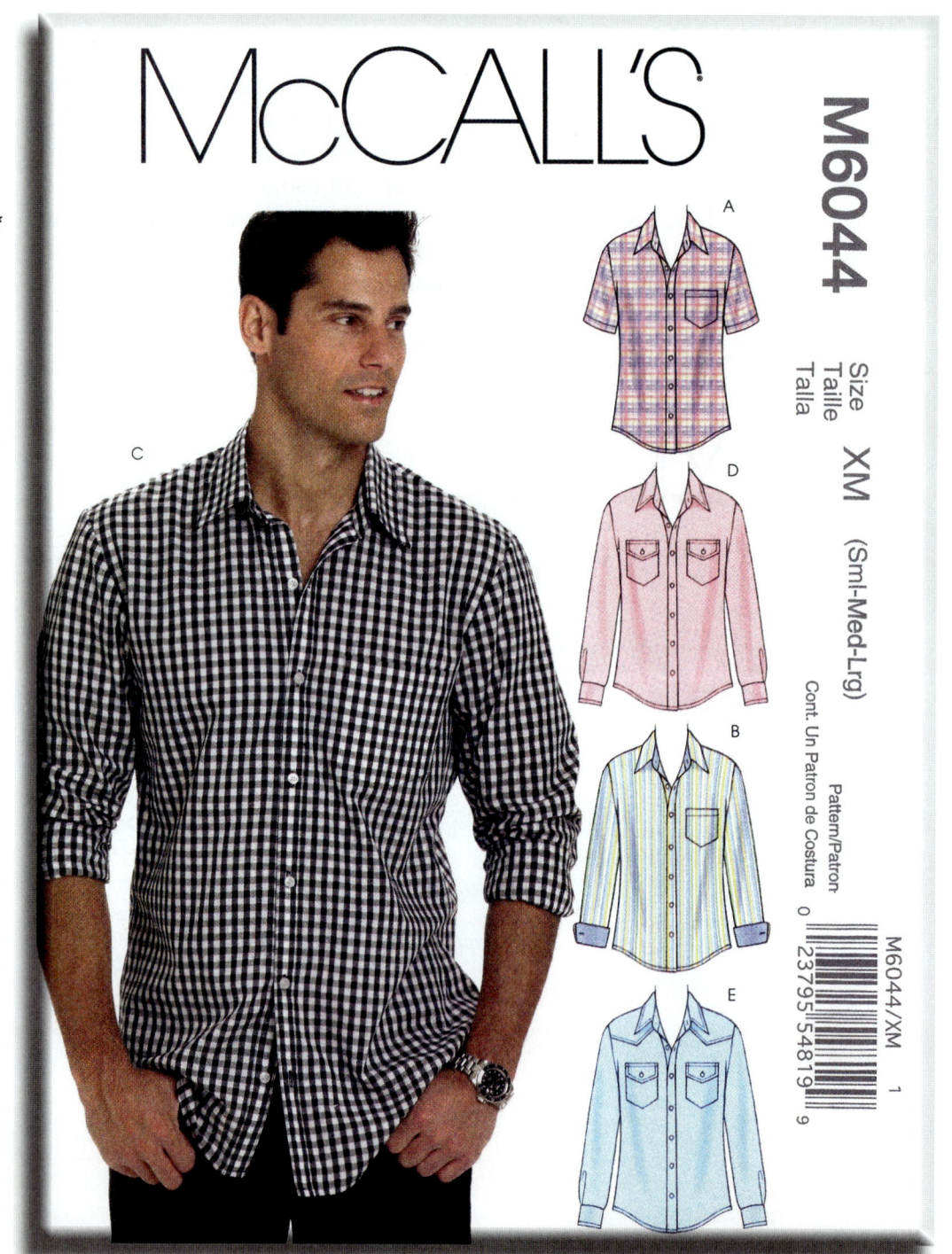

On the back of the pattern envelope is a chart that states the amount of fabric you need to make the garments. Usually, the chart lists the fabric width so you can easily find the length you need. The most common widths are 36 inches, 45 inches, and 60 inches. If your fabric width is not on the list, use a conversion chart like the one in **23-4**. The pattern companies usually provide a fabric conversion chart in their catalogs and online.

The back of the envelope also holds many other kinds of information. For example, if your pattern requires lining or interfacing, the amount needed is listed. Standard body measurements are also given. You can use them as a reference if you make pattern adjustments for your body shape.

The information on the back of the pattern envelope also includes the notions you need to complete your garment. **Notions** are items other than fabric

Conversion Chart for Different Widths of Fabric

Fabric Width	35"–36"	39"–42"	44"–45"	52"–54"	58"–60"
Yardage	1¾	1½	1⅜	1⅛	1
	2	1¾	1⅝	1⅜	1¼
	2¼	2	1¾	1½	1⅜
	2½	2¼	2⅛	1¾	1⅝
	2⅞	2½	2¼	1⅞	1¾
	3⅛	2¾	2½	2	1⅞
	3⅜	2⅞	2¾	2¼	2
	3¾	3⅛	2⅞	2⅜	2½
	4¼	3⅜	3⅛	2⅝	2⅜
	4½	3⅝	3⅜	2¾	2⅝
	4¾	3⅞	3⅝	2⅞	2¾
	5	4⅛	3⅞	3⅛	2⅞

23-4 If your fabric is narrower or wider than your pattern shows, this chart can help you select the amount you need to buy. For example, if your pattern envelope calls for 1¾ yard of 36-inch fabric and your chosen fabric is 60 inches wide, you will need only 1 yard.

that become part of a garment. These include such items as thread, fasteners, and interfacing. They are under the headings *Notions* or *Supplies Needed*. The size and amount you need of each notion are also listed. Read the back of the pattern envelope carefully to make sure you buy the necessary notions and supplies, **23-5**.

Cutting and Sewing Guide Sheet

In your pattern envelope, you will find one or more printed sheets. These **cutting and sewing guide sheets** give detailed instructions on how to make your garment. The first page gives the cutting layouts, explanations of marking symbols, and a few general directions. Also on the first page, you will find line drawings of all pattern pieces. Each piece has a letter or number on it. This makes it easier to identify the pieces you need for the view you are making.

The next section usually includes some general directions. A pattern markings section explains the symbols on pattern pieces such as cutting lines, grain lines, notches, and dots. Another section shows how to lengthen or shorten pattern pieces for a proper fit. The directions may also give suggestions for preparing your fabric and pattern, as well as any special cutting notes. A fabric key generally explains the meaning of various shadings on the guide sheet. Using the fabric key, you will be able to see the different layers of fabric and the printed and reversed sides of pattern pieces in the cutting layouts.

Cutting layouts show you how to correctly place the pattern pieces on your fabric. The guide sheet gives layouts for different views and sizes. It also shows layouts for various widths of fabrics and fabrics with nap. Find the layout for your garment and draw a circle around it. Often there are special notes in the cutting layout section to make cutting and marking easier. Be sure to read these carefully before you begin.

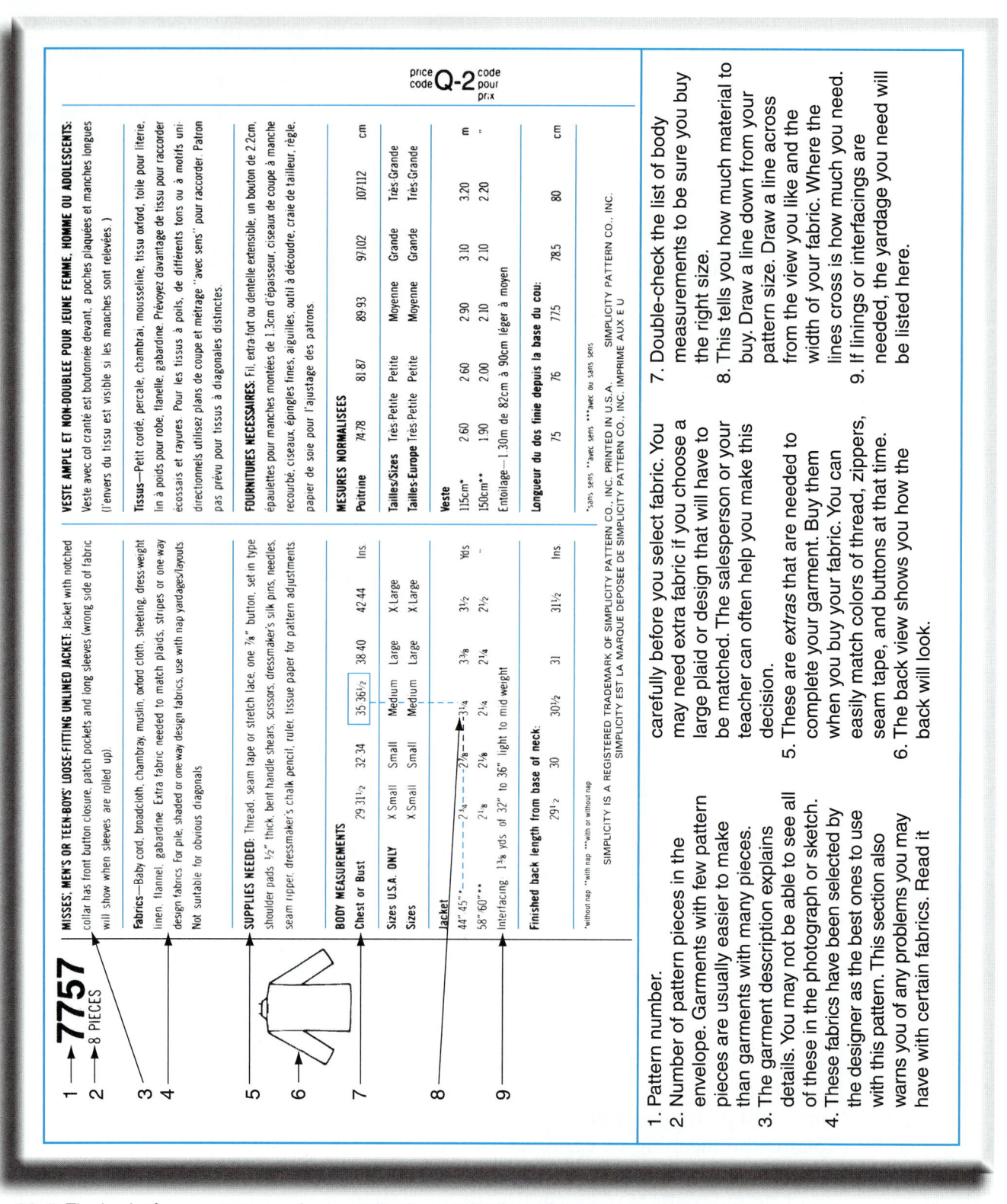

23-5 The back of your pattern envelope contains important information. *Simplicity Pattern Co., Inc.*

The sewing directions in the guide sheet takes you step-by-step through the process of making your garment, **23-6**. Complete each part before going on to the next. It will make the construction of your garment easier if you read through all the steps before you begin sewing. You will have a better idea of what to do and how to do it.

Pattern Pieces

Inside your pattern envelope you will also find the pattern pieces necessary for making your garment. Select the pieces you need by referring to the guide sheet. Refold the others, and put them back in the envelope.

Each pattern piece lists the pattern number, size, view number, name of piece, and identification letter. In addition, pattern pieces use many symbols, **23-7**. The bold line around each piece is the **cutting line**. Most patterns have several sizes printed on one pattern piece. If so, you will see several cutting lines representing each pattern size. Use the cutting line for your size. If you are not using a multisized pattern, just inside the cutting line may be a broken line that represents the **stitching line**. Multisized patterns do not show a stitching line.

A line with triangles on both ends indicates the **grain line**. This line helps you correctly locate the pattern on the fabric grain. Thin, solid lines indicate center fold lines, hemlines, and placements for pockets or trims that go on the outside of the garment. **Adjustment lines** show where to shorten or lengthen the pattern piece.

Notches are the diamond-shaped symbols along the cutting line. They help you join pieces together at the right place. **Dots** are also aids for matching seams and other construction details.

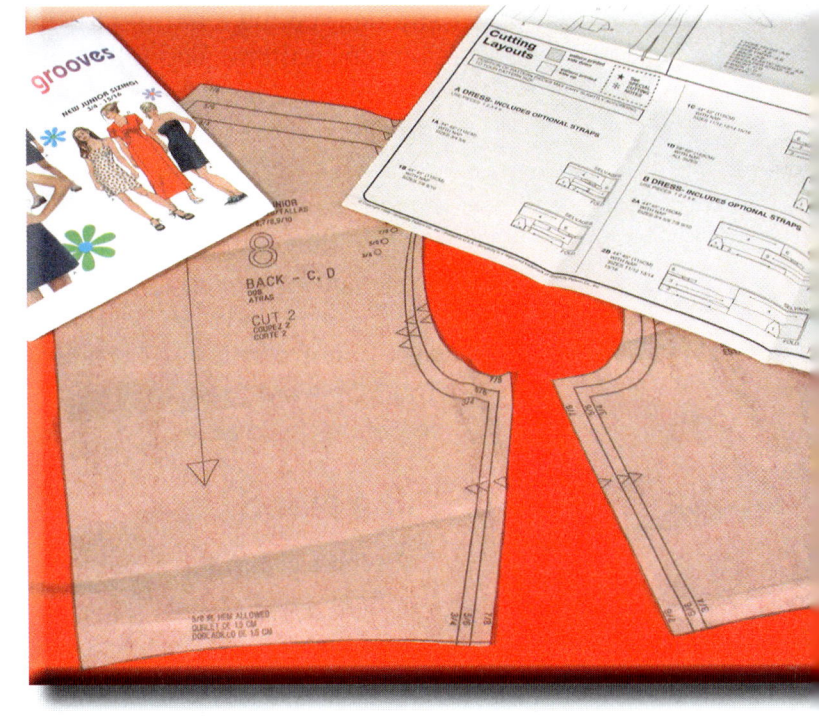

23-6 Your guide sheet gives step-by-step directions for making your garment. Sketches are shown to help you understand procedures.
Jack Klasey

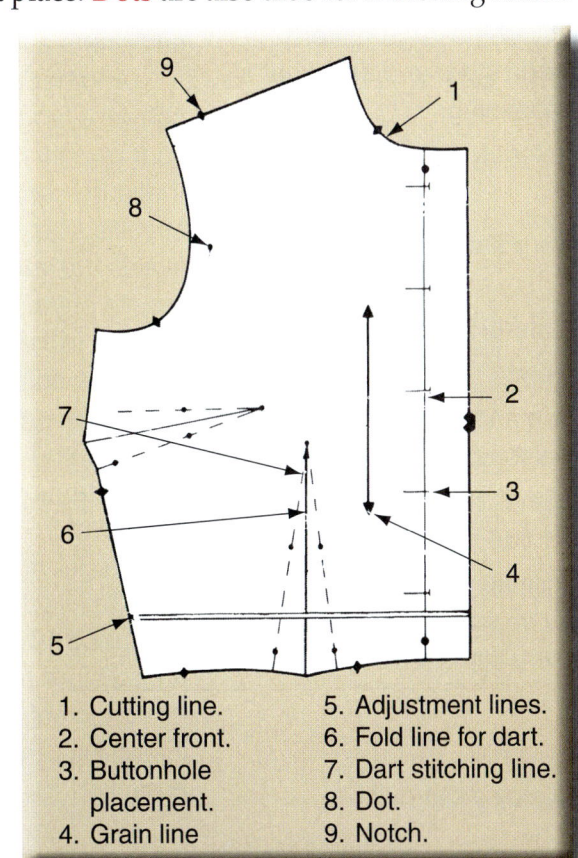

23-7 These pattern symbols are found on most pattern pieces. Multisized patterns may show as many as five cutting lines.
Goodheart-Willcox Publisher

1. Cutting line.
2. Center front.
3. Buttonhole placement.
4. Grain line
5. Adjustment lines.
6. Fold line for dart.
7. Dart stitching line.
8. Dot.
9. Notch.

Choosing a Pattern

There are several factors to consider when choosing a pattern. These include the following:

- matching your sewing skill level to pattern complexity
- filling a need in your wardrobe
- choosing a design that flatters your body shape

Match Your Skill Level

If you have very little sewing experience, you will want to choose a pattern that is fairly simple. Making a garment using a simple pattern takes less time than a more complex pattern. The following terms are used in catalogs to identify simple patterns: *Yes! It's Easy, See & Sew, Easy Stitch 'n Save,* and *It's So Easy.* Some will indicate a short time period, such as 60 minutes, 90 minutes, or two hours.

Generally, simple patterns have few pieces, and fit loosely. They do not have pleats, curved yokes, collars, or pockets. These garments need little fitting, so they are good for beginners. Sweatshirts, sweatpants, shorts, and tops are usually quick and easy to make.

If you already have some sewing experience, you may choose a more complex pattern. This can increase your sewing-skill knowledge and techniques. You may want to try making more fitted garments that require more advanced sewing techniques.

Fill a Need

When choosing a pattern, consider what you need. Do you need new sweats? Could you use a new pair of pull-on pants? Do you need a new vest to go with your jeans? Look again at your wardrobe inventory. Sewing a garment makes more sense if you know that you need it in your wardrobe.

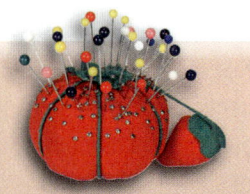

Did You Know?

Patterns—New Kinds, New Places

Someone new to sewing may be surprised at the many kinds of patterns available for home sewing. Look through any of the large pattern catalogs at your local fabric store and see what all you can sew. Here is a sampling:

- bridal gowns and tuxedos
- maternity clothes
- children's clothes from baby layettes to christening gowns
- scrubs and other apparel for medical workers
- lingerie and sleepwear
- costumes for children and adults, from Halloween costumes to historical clothes
- vintage women's clothes from earlier decades, such as the 40s and 50s
- home decor items including pillows, slipcovers, bedspreads, window treatments, placemats, chair cushions, nursery items, and more
- purses, backpacks, hats, and gloves
- stuffed toys and beanbags
- craft items from doll clothes to quilts
- pet accessories

If you cannot get to a store to look at pattern catalogs, you can view most pattern selections online. All of the major pattern companies have websites on which you can browse their pattern selections and then order patterns online.

Another option is to purchase a computer-software program that allows you to create your own custom patterns. You enter your exact measurements to create a pattern drafted to your specific size. Then choose from a library of basic styles and various necklines, sleeves, etc. See the results of your design selections on screen. When you are satisfied with the results, print your pattern using the computer.

There are also many websites that offer free patterns and sewing-project directions. You can find patterns for simple items that you can print or download from the Web. Many sewing machine and serger manufacturers provide projects at their websites, including *Baby Lock, Elna, Janome, Pfaff,* and *Viking Husqvarna.* Craft and quilt projects are also available online. It does not take much of a search online to find all types of interesting and easy sewing projects and patterns. Have fun!

Flatter Your Body Shape

Keep in mind what you learned about the principles and elements of design. Which styles, lines, and colors were best suited to your body shape?

Visit a clothing store and look at ready-to-wear garments. Try on several garments in a style you think you like. Is the style flattering to your body shape? Do the colors look good on you? Do you like loose styles or more fitted ones? Observing how you look in these styles will help you in your decision making.

Choosing a Fabric

Once you have selected the pattern, you are ready to choose a fabric. Fabric stores have many bolts of fabric from which to choose. They are organized by fabric types. You will notice that some are called *decorator fabrics*. These are designed for such household items as pillows, window treatments, and slipcovers, and are generally not suitable for clothes. *Fashion fabrics* are designed for sewing clothes.

Within the fashion fabrics section, bolts of fabric are generally organized by fiber content or fabric style, **23-8**. For example, wools and wool blends will be together. You will also find a section of fabrics suitable for bridal gowns or special occasion wear. Knit fabrics will also be together.

Notice the labels on the ends of the bolts of fabric. This is where you will find the fabric name, such as denim or gabardine, and the fiber content. This label also states the fabric width and special finishes the fabric may have, such as *preshrunk* or *wrinkle resistant*. The care information is also important. If you want a washable garment, this is where you will find the care instructions. All of this information is essential to your selection.

The pattern illustration can help you decide a fabric design to buy. If the illustration shows a garment in a stripe or plaid, it means you can use that fabric design if you wish. Suppose you want to use a stripe and the picture does not show stripes. Look on the back of the envelope for a list of any fabrics and designs that are *not* suitable for the garment. For example, fabrics with a nap or one-way design are not suitable for some patterns. If so, the pattern envelope will provide this information. You will also find a list of suggested fabrics. This is a good place to begin.

The yardage chart on the back of the pattern envelope may list yardage for fabrics *With Nap* and *Without Nap*. If a fabric has a nap or one-way design, the garment generally requires more yards of fabric. This is because the major pattern pieces must all be cut so the pile runs in the same direction. If not, sections of the garment may look like they are a slightly different color. Examples of fabrics with a nap or pile are corduroy and velvet. Garments you make from striped or plaid fabrics often require more fabric in order to match the fabric design at the seams and openings.

23-8 The bolts of fabric in a fabric store will be organized by fabric type. *Shutterstock*

Some patterns are suitable for knit fabrics only. Knit fabrics stretch more than woven fabrics. There are many different types of knits available. Select the weight and type of knit recommended for your pattern.

- Lightweight knits include single knits, jerseys, and tricots. These knits stretch more crosswise than lengthwise. They are suitable for softly styled garments with fluid lines, **23-9**.
- Medium-weight knits such as cotton knits and wool jerseys are used mainly for sportswear.
- Heavier knits include double knits and sweatshirt knits. These stretch very little and hold their shape well.

Some patterns designed for knits have a stretch gauge on the pattern envelope. Hold a piece of the fabric against this gauge to see if the knit stretches the necessary amount. Fold over the fabric along a crosswise course several inches from a cut end. Pull the knit in the crosswise direction. If it stretches as much as the stretch gauge indicates, then it is suitable for use with your pattern.

Consider Your Skill Level

Just as you chose a pattern to match your skill level, you should also choose a fabric at your skill level. Some fabrics are more difficult to sew than others. If you are just learning to sew, it is best to choose a fabric that is easy to sew. Your best choice is a firmly woven fabric of medium weight. You might want to avoid the following:

- fabrics that are loosely woven and ravel easily
- fabrics with a nap or one-way design
- pile or fake-fur fabrics
- stripes and plaids that require matching at the seams
- slippery or sheer fabrics
- bulky or thick fabrics

23-9 Garments made of lightweight knits are soft and fluid.
Simplicity Pattern Co., Inc.

Other Items to Sew

Patterns are available for a wide range of sewing projects. For some simple items, you may even want to make your own patterns. The ideas that follow are all fairly easy projects.

Bags

It seems that almost everywhere people go, they take some of their belongings with them. People need messenger bags, book bags, reusable shopping bags, beach bags, lunch bags, duffle bags, and computer bags to help them carry their possessions. You can give bags for cell phones, cameras, and game systems a custom look. Making bags can be a quick and easy sewing project.

Use your creativity to make your own patterns in the shapes and sizes you like. Since these items are small, you can even use leftover fabric scraps. Consider adding embroidery, bright trims, or special fabrics for a personal touch.

Sports Equipment

Clothes and accessories for a wide variety of sports activities make great sewing projects. You can save up to half the cost of ready-made items if you sew your own. Some items you can make are vests, sweaters, jackets, pillows, backpacks, hoods, and ski mitts. You can also make swimwear, tennis and bicycle bags, exercise mats, and head covers for golf clubs. Seat cushions make an excellent project for spectator sports.

Stuffed Toys

Stuffed toys give you a chance to express your creativity and use your imagination. Use your originality to create one-of-a-kind designs. Then use these items as gifts for friends and children.

A wide variety of patterns for toys can be found in pattern catalogs. These include balls, clowns, and a wide variety of animals and other items, 23-10. With extra time, you can create your own pattern. If time is short, use a kit for stuffed toys.

When making stuffed toys for small children, select a sturdy fabric. Use polyester fiberfill for the stuffing so you can launder the toy safely. Use fabrics to add such details as eyes and noses you can sew onto the toy. If you use button eyes, be sure to attach them securely so children cannot pull them off and swallow them.

Home Décor Items

Many people today are using their sewing skills to decorate their living spaces. The ever-increasing number of home decorating shows are sparking the interest of would-be interior designers. You can save substantial money with these do-it-yourself projects. Depending on the project, the changes a person makes in a room can range from simple to dramatic.

23-10 Any child would love receiving one of these cute, cuddly stuffed toys.
Simplicity Pattern Co., Inc.

Pattern catalogs can provide inspiration. Look in the sections marked *Home Décor*. You can get ideas here, and even purchase patterns. You can also buy magazines and books that feature sewing projects for the home. Such resources often include instructions and patterns. The Internet is also a great resource. Many sites offer step-by-step instructions for many projects with photos or video. Home decorating projects are easy enough for beginning sewers because the seams are often straight lines.

Pillows

Making pillows can be one of the fastest ways to add a decorative touch to a room. Consider making them in a variety of shapes. You can also use your imagination to create pillows from various fabrics. Firmly woven or medium- to heavyweight knit fabrics work best for pillows, and so does patchwork.

Stuff pillows with polyester fiberfill, or use ready-made pillow forms. Stitch a zipper into one seam of the cover to easily remove it for washing. Add machine-washable trims and fabric paints to personalize pillows.

Large floor pillows provide a comfortable place to sit while reading or watching television. Make these pillows firmer than other types of pillows. This ensures the pillows keep their shape and last longer. Like other pillows, you can stuff floor pillows with polyester fiberfill or a pillow form.

Window Treatments

Giving windows a new look is not as difficult as it may seem. The stitching lines are straight on most treatments. If you can sew a straight seam, you can easily give your windows a new look.

Window treatments range from curtains and draperies to shades and valances. Your choice will depend on the type of window you have and the amount of privacy you want. Be sure the fabrics you select are fade resistant to sunlight.

The easiest window treatments to sew are curtains and valances. A **valance** is a horizontal fabric treatment across the top of a window. It is often used over or with shades or curtains, but can be used alone. **Shirred curtains** are panels gathered onto rods. These curtains require hemming the bottom and sides. Then you make a rod casing by folding and stitching the top. Insert the rod and hang it up. You can make a simple valance with the same method.

Café curtains are hung from clip-on rings that slide along a rod. They may cover only the window bottom with a matching valance at the top. Full-length curtains can also be hung with rings that clip onto the top of each of two curtain panels. Make curtain panels by measuring, pressing, and stitching hems along all four sides of the panels.

Bedding

The popularity of comforters with duvet covers makes for an easy decorating project. A **duvet** is a removable cover that fits over a comforter, 23-11. Select a decorator fabric that is washable and feels comfortable next to the skin. The fabric should be at least 54 inches wide. Careful measuring and straight seams lead to satisfying results.

23-11 A duvet cover is a simple sewing project that can be the focal point of a bedroom. *Shutterstock*

Sew matching pillows and dust ruffles to complete the look. Place a **dust ruffle** (or bed skirt) between the mattress and the box spring. It serves as a covering for the box spring. Pleated dust ruffles are the easiest to sew.

Pillow covers can be made in a variety of shapes and sizes to match the duvet. A **pillow sham** is a decorative cover you place over the bed pillow, but remove from the pillow for sleeping. A pillow sham is easy to make. Two overlapping pieces of fabric form the backside and make it easy to remove the pillow.

Tabletop Accessories

Perhaps the simplest items to sew for the home are for the table. Table runners, place mats, and napkins are easy to sew. The shapes are usually rectangular, although you can make round place mats, too. These items make great gifts for all times of the year. You can also make oven mitts and covers for small appliances.

Be sure the fabrics you choose for these items are washable. Stain release and durable-press finishes are also worth considering. Be creative with the trims you choose, but make certain they have the same care requirements as the fabric you choose.

Summary

- Pattern catalogs show patterns available in a variety of sizes, along with ideas for garment variations and possible fabrics. They also have measurement charts.
- All patterns have three parts: the pattern envelope, the cutting and sewing guide sheet, and the pattern pieces. Each provides important information.
- Pattern envelopes may show several views giving ideas for using different fabrics, designs, and details.
- The cutting and sewing guide sheet gives detailed instructions on how to make a garment.
- Each pattern piece has a pattern number, size, view number, name of piece, and identification letter printed on it.
- Choose patterns to match your sewing skill level, fill a need in your wardrobe, and flatter your body shape.
- The pattern illustration can help you decide a fabric design to buy. Some patterns are designed for knit fabrics only. Knit fabrics stretch more than woven fabrics.
- Choose a fabric that matches your skill level. If you are just learning to sew, choose an easy-to-sew fabric.
- Patterns are available for a wide range of sewing projects, including bags, sports equipment, stuffed toys, and various items for the home.

Graphic Organizer

Create a T-chart and list the chapter headings and subheadings in the left column. Then list at least two supporting details for each in the right column.

Headings/Subheadings	Supporting Details

Review the Facts

1. When looking for a pattern, you may have forgotten your figure type although you remember your measurements. How can you use the pattern catalog to solve your problem?
2. List four things you can learn by looking at the front of the pattern envelope.
3. Where can you find suggestions for the type of fabric to use with your pattern?
4. What directions are given in the cutting layouts section of the cutting and sewing guide sheet?
5. Why should you read through all the steps of the sewing instructions section before beginning to sew?
6. Which pattern symbol shows you where to shorten or lengthen the pattern piece?
7. Name three factors to consider when choosing your own pattern.
8. Name three features generally found on simple patterns.
9. What information is provided on the ends of bolts of fabric?
10. What is the best fabric choice for someone just learning to sew?

Think Critically

11. **Draw conclusions.** Most pattern companies have switched to multisized patterns in recent years. Draw conclusions about why you think they made this change.
12. **Make inferences.** Infer why you think it is important to choose a pattern suited to your skill level. What results might happen if you do not?
13. **Compare and contrast.** Compare and contrast the use of a sewing kit with the use of a standard pattern and fabric. What are the advantages and disadvantages of each?
14. **Make predictions.** Predict what items you could sew for a room to give it a new look. What factors would you consider to validate your predictions?

Apparel Applications

15. **Compare catalogs.** At a fabric store, look through the pattern catalogs. Become familiar with the format and all sections. Then compare them to their online catalogs. What are the similarities and differences? Which would you prefer to use? Share your findings with the class.
16. **Project blog.** Collect print or digital pictures of garments or items that are easy first projects to sew. (Scan print pictures into your computer.) Use a school-approved Web application to create an attractive online bulletin board or blog page with your suggestions. Collaborate online with your classmates to determine the ease of the projects.
17. **Create a display.** Select patterns for teen males and females from pattern catalogs and magazines. Make a display using a *Now* caption for beginning projects and a *Later* caption for more difficult patterns.
18. **Compare fabrics.** Divide a selection of sample fabrics into two groups. Label the groups *More Difficult to Sew* and *Easier to Sew*. Compare the fabrics. What features make some more difficult to sew? Discuss your thoughts with the class.

Academic Connections

19. **Writing.** Select a pattern from a pattern catalog you feel flatters your body shape. Write a paragraph explaining the type of fabric you would use. Identify reasons for your selections.
20. **Math.** Choose a pattern for a garment you would like to make. Identify the fabrics and notions necessary to make the garment. Make a list of these items. Then obtain prices of the fabrics and notions at a fabric store or gather the information from the website of a fabric store. List the prices for each item including your pattern and total the cost. Compare the cost to a similar ready-to-wear garment? How do the costs compare? Would you still choose to sew the garment if it was more costly? Share your findings in class.

Workplace Connections

21. **Write an article.** Imagine you are a fashion writer for a pattern company magazine. Your assignment for this issue is to choose several of the hottest-selling patterns and write about ideas for individualizing them for a one-of-a-kind look. Share your article.
22. **Showcase new patterns.** Presume you work in a fabric store. Your supervisor wants you to put together a display showcasing several popular patterns and fabrics for the coming season. Use actual pattern envelopes or print pattern envelope information off the Web. Select fabric samples to go with each pattern. Create an attractive display to entice customers to make a purchase.

Community Service—Clothes for Protection

In many areas of the world, lack of clothing for protection and modesty is a real problem. Think about the natural disasters in Haiti and Indonesia and the needs they created among the inhabitants.

As an FCCLA *Community Service* project, use your leadership skills and the FCCLA *Planning Process* to develop a project to sew clothes for people in need. Consider partnering with a local nonprofit organization to sew clothes for a specific group of people. For example, you might sew garments for children of preschool age. See your adviser for information as needed.

Chapter 24

Sewing Equipment

Chapter Objectives

After studying this chapter, you will be able to
- **describe** the sewing equipment needed for sewing.
- **describe** the various types of notions that may be needed for sewing a garment or project.
- **identify** the parts and functions of the parts of a sewing machine.
- **recognize** minor sewing machine problems that might occur and solve them.
- **summarize** how to care for a sewing machine.

Key Terms

shears
scissors
rotary cutter
pinking or scalloping shears
thread clipper
seam ripper
tape measure
skirt marker
sewing gauge
thimble
fasteners
interfacing
press cloth
sleeve board
seam roll
pressing ham

Reading with Purpose

Read the review questions at the end of the chapter *before* you read the chapter. Keep the questions in mind as you read to help you determine which information is most important.

Every kind of job requires special equipment. Some tools are necessary to do the job—others just make it easier. The list of basic supplies is not long. Other tools can be added as you need them. See Figure **24-1** for a list of the basic supplies plus additional supplies you might want to add later on.

Cutting Tools

Many types of shears and scissors are available for sewing, **24-2**. The list of basic supplies includes a pair of shears. Other cutting tools are helpful additions.

Shears and scissors are not the same. **Shears** are longer than scissors and usually have blades that are 7 to 8 inches long. The handles are not the same size—they are shaped to fit your hand. Left-handed persons should use left-handed shears.

Use shears to cut pattern pieces from the fabric. Bent-handled shears are the most popular cutting tool for fabric. The bent handle allows the fabric to lie flat as it is cut. This results in more accurate cutting.

Scissors are usually short and the handles have small, matching holes. Blades are different widths, but about 4 to 6 inches long. Use scissors to clip around curves, trim seams, and clip threads. They are lightweight and easy to handle.

409

Sewing Supplies	
Basic Supplies	**Additional Supplies**
Shears	Scissors
Tape measure	Pinking or scalloping shears
Tracing wheel and paper	Thread clipper or seam ripper
Needles	Sewing gauge
Pins	Yardstick or meter stick
Pincushion	Tailor's chalk
Thread	Thimble
Iron	Sleeve board
Ironing board	Press cloth
Sewing machine	Pressing ham

24-1 A successful sewer needs these supplies.

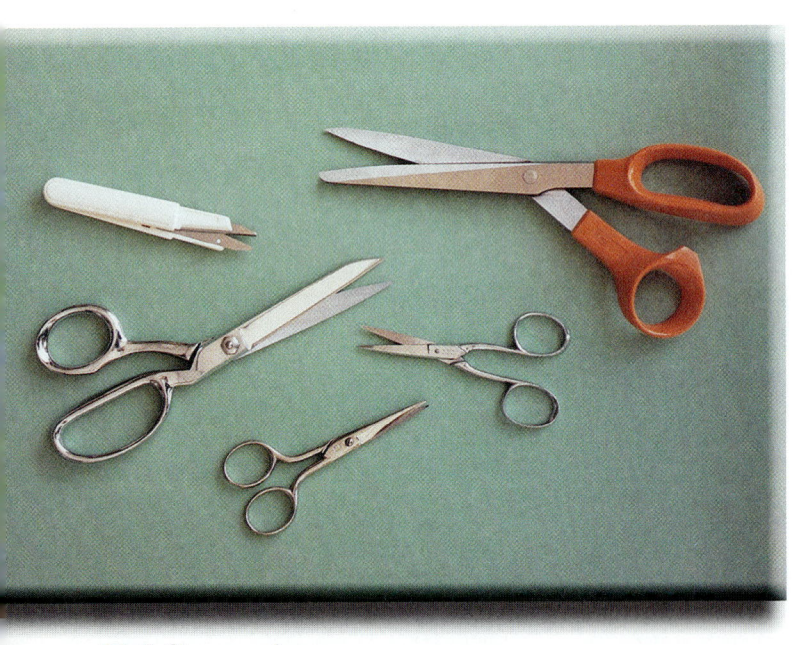

24-2 Shears, scissors, and thread clippers come in various shapes and sizes. *J. Wiss & Sons Co.*

A good pair of shears will cost more than most other basic supplies. If you care for shears properly, they will last for years. Use them only for cutting fabric—not for cutting string, paper, or anything else. If they become dull, have them sharpened by a professional who knows the correct way to do this.

Another useful tool for cutting fabric is a **rotary cutter.** It has a round blade and looks like a pizza cutter. A locking mechanism retracts the blade for safety. The rotary cutter is good for cutting straight lines—especially those for quilt pieces. Use this cutter with a special *self-healing* mat that protects both the work surface and the blade.

Pinking or **scalloping shears** have a zigzag cutting edge or a scalloping cutting edge. They are useful for giving seam edges a finished look. You can also use these shears to achieve a decorative look on nonwoven fabrics. Do not use them to cut garment pieces from fabric. The uneven edge is difficult to follow when sewing. Seam edges can be pinked after stitching the seams.

A **thread clipper** is used to clip threads at the start and end of every stitching line. The clippers spring action reopens the blade after each cut. You can also use this tool as a seam ripper to undo sewing mistakes or remove basting stitches.

Another handy cutting tool is a **seam ripper**. This is a small gadget with a hook-like blade that is useful for removing stitches. It can quickly remove an entire row of stitching. You have to be careful, however, that you do not cut the fabric or yourself.

Measuring Tools

To sew accurately, you need the proper measuring tools, **24-3**. A **tape measure** is a requirement for taking body measurements. It is 60 inches long. One made of plastic or strong fabric does not stretch. Metal ends protect it for longer use.

To mark an even hem on a dress or skirt, you can use a **skirt marker**. This device is useful for measuring and marking hemlines on garments using either pins or chalk. To use this device, wear the garment to be hemmed and stand beside the skirt marker. Another person marks the placement of the hem with pins or powdered chalk, measuring an equal distance from the floor.

A yardstick is also useful for marking hems and making sure pattern pieces are laid on the fabric grain. For marking buttonholes, pleats, and tucks use a 12-inch, transparent-plastic ruler.

A **sewing gauge** (or seam gauge) is a 6-inch ruler with a sliding marker. You can use it to measure hems, seam widths, cuffs, space between buttons, and other short distances. Although this tool is not necessary, it is inexpensive and handy. A *hem gauge* can also be used for measuring hems. It is a thin curved metal or plastic plate with graduated markings.

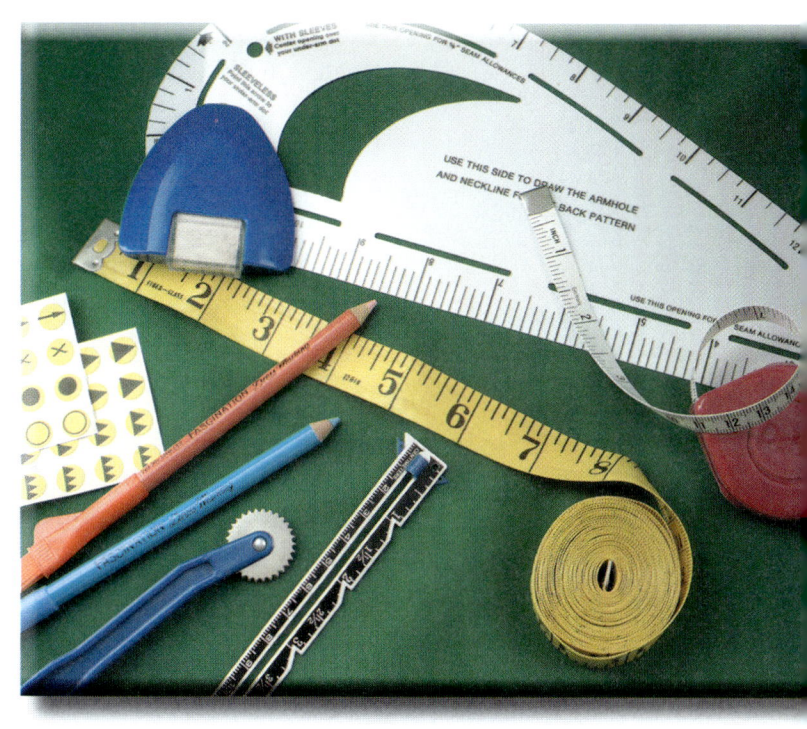

24-3 A tape measure, skirt marker, and sewing gauge are helpful measuring tools. *Prym-Dritz Corp.*

Marking Tools

Marking tools are useful for transferring pattern markings to the fabric. You will use these markings to put the pattern pieces together in the right way. Tracing wheels, dressmaker's carbon paper, marking pens, and tailor's chalk are types of marking tools, **24-4**. They are inexpensive and you can find them in fabric and craft stores. Do not use ballpoint pens—the ink will soak through and can permanently mark the fabric.

- *Dressmaker's carbon paper and tracing wheel.* These items are frequently used to transfer markings. You can purchase a package of several colors of a special waxed paper. The tracing wheel can have a smooth edge or a serrated edge. Place the colored side of the paper next to the wrong side of the fabric. When you apply pressure and roll the wheel, it marks any pattern markings that you need to transfer. Choose a color close to the color of your fabric. If the color shows through on the right side, it will not be noticed. The marks usually can be removed when the garment is washed or dry cleaned. It is best to test the carbon paper on a scrap of the garment fabric first.

- *Fabric marking pens.* One of the easiest and fastest ways to mark fabric is with fabric marking pens. These pens contain disappearing ink that makes it possible to mark on either the right or wrong side of the fabric. There are two types: water-soluble pens and evaporating marking pens.

24-4 Choose from these various marking tools to transfer pattern markings to fabric.

Water-soluble pens contain a blue ink that disappears when the marks are treated with water. *Evaporating* marking pens contain a purple ink that evaporates in less than 48 hours. To be sure your markings will still be there when you need them, do not use this type of pen until just before you are ready to sew.

- *Tailor's chalk.* This clay chalk comes in red, white, and blue. It is available in a small square form or as a pencil. You can generally brush away the chalk marks when you no longer need them.

Needles

There are many sizes and types of hand-sewing needles. Hand sewing is easier when you use the right needle. Coarse needles are for heavy fabrics, and fine needles are for delicate fabrics. A package of assorted sizes and types is a good choice.

The sizes for coarse needles are low numbers. The sizes for fine needles are high numbers. Therefore, a size 1 needle is larger than a size 12 needle. Size 7 or 8 is used for most common hand sewing tasks.

Three types of hand-sewing needles are sharps, betweens, and crewel.

- *Sharps* are most often used for hand sewing. They are average in length and have a small eye.
- *Betweens* are very short needles with a small eye. They are useful for fine stitches.
- *Crewel* or *embroidery needles* have larger eyes. They are used for crewel and embroidery projects as well as hand sewing.

Sewing machine needles also come in a range of sizes from size 9 to size 18. The lower numbers are the finer needles and the higher numbers are coarser needles. The weight of the fabric and the size or type of thread determines the size needle to use. Use a size 9 or 11 for fine fabrics and a size 16 or 18 for heavier fabrics.

Three basic types of machine needles are ballpoint, sharp, and universal.

- *Ballpoint needles.* Use a ballpoint needle for knits and stretch fabrics. A rounded tip allows the needle to slip between the yarns. It pushes the fabric aside instead of piercing it.
- *Sharp needles.* Use a sharp needle for woven fabrics. It is designed to pierce heavyweight, densely woven fabrics.
- *Universal needles.* The universal needle has a specially rounded point. It is sharp enough to pierce tightly woven fabrics yet rounded enough to push aside the yarns of a knitted fabric. It is a good all-purpose sewing machine needle.

Replace sewing machine needles when they become dull or bent. A damaged needle can harm fabric and cause stitching problems.

Pins

Straight pins are useful for attaching pattern pieces to fabric and pinning garment pieces together before sewing. Avoid marking pattern details with just pins because the pins fall out of place before you use the marking. The following are several types of pins:

- *Dressmaker's pins* are medium in diameter with sharp points. Since they are brass, they will not rust.
- *Silk pins* are very slender. They have the sharpest points and were first designed for use with silk or very fine fabrics which resulted in the name *silk* pins. These pins are made of stainless steel or brass.
- *Ballpoint pins* are recommended for use with knit fabrics. The rounded point slides between the yarns instead of cutting through them, preventing snags.
- *Ball-headed pins* have large, round heads. They are easy to see and to handle.

Pincushions

Pincushions make it much easier to pick up pins and replace them when pinning a pattern to fabric or when joining garment sections together. They also keep pins from falling into the sewing machine as you remove them.

Pincushions come in many shapes and sizes. Some can be worn on your wrist to keep the pins handy. Some are magnetic. Others have a small strawberry-shaped emery bag attached to them. You can remove a rough spot or a dull point on a needle or pin by pushing it into the bag several times, **24-5**.

Thimbles

When sewing by hand, a needle can damage your finger if you are working with thick layers or tightly woven fabric. A **thimble** is a metal or plastic device that is placed over the middle or ring finger of your sewing hand. You use it to push the needle through the fabric. Thimbles are also available in leather. These may be more comfortable and easier to fit. Some leather thimbles have a circle of textured metal over the pad of the finger.

Choose a thimble with deep enough grooves to hold the needle securely. Try on a thimble when you buy it. It should be snug but not tight. If it is too loose, you will not be able to use it successfully. It may feel awkward the first time you use it, but it will soon become a helpful tool, **24-6**.

24-5 This pincushion has an emery bag attached for use in sharpening needles and pins. *Prym-Dritz Corp.*

Notions

Notions are items other than fabric that become part of a garment or project. Thread, zippers, buttons, snaps, hooks and eyes, hook and loop tape,

24-6 Choose a thimble that has deep grooves and fits your middle finger of your sewing hand. *Shutterstock*

tapes, trims, elastics, and interfacings are notions. The pattern envelope lists the notions for a project under *notions* or *supplies*.

Buy notions at the same time you buy the fabric. This way you can match colors. When you are selecting notions, keep in mind the care of the finished garment. If the garment is washable, make sure that the notions are also washable.

Thread

Thread comes in a wide variety of colors. If you are using solid-colored fabric, select thread that is slightly darker. (Thread looks lighter when it is stitched into fabric.) If the fabric is a print or a plaid, try to select thread that matches the background color in the fabric, **24-7**.

Choosing the right fiber content of thread is just as important as choosing the color. There are three main types of thread available. They are polyester/cotton, polyester, and mercerized cotton. There are several types of specialty threads also available.

- *Polyester/cotton thread.* This all-purpose thread can be used for sewing almost all fabrics. It is strong, stretchable, and has minimum shrinkage. This thread is often used to sew on knit and stretch fabrics because of its strength and ability to *give*. It has a polyester core that gives the thread strength. This core is then wrapped with cotton to give it smoothness and luster. It comes in an extra-fine weight for sewing lightweight fabrics. An all-purpose weight is useful for medium to heavyweight fabrics.
- *Polyester thread.* This thread is also considered an all-purpose thread. It is strong, abrasion resistant, and has the ability to stretch and recover.
- *Mercerized cotton thread.* This thread is used to sew on woven fabrics made of natural fibers. It is smooth and lustrous. Although it sews well, it has limited stretching ability. If there is excess strain on the seams you sew, the seams could rip. *Mercerization* is a process that increases the strength, luster, and colorfastness of threads.

Specialty threads are useful for specific projects. These include the following:

- *Silk thread.* Recommended for sewing on sheer and delicate fabrics, silk thread is also used on wool and silk fabrics.
- *Nylon thread.* Heavy fabrics such as upholstery are the main use for nylon thread.
- *Rayon thread.* This thread is lustrous and silklike, making it appropriate for decorative stitching. Size 40 rayon thread is suitable for free-hand machine embroidery. Size 30 is a heavier thread that gives bolder topstitching and

greater fill-in when using programmed decorative stitches on your sewing machine.

- *Heavy-duty thread.* This thread is also used for heavier fabrics that require heavy thread.
- *Buttonhole twist.* Used for topstitching and hand-worked buttonholes, buttonhole twist is thicker than other threads.
- *Basting and quilting.* Basting and quilting threads are used to make quilts and other craft items.
- *Metallic thread.* These threads add sparkle to decorative stitches.

Fasteners

Fasteners close the openings on garments. They include zippers, buttons, hooks and eyes, snaps, and hook and loop tape. The pattern envelope will list the type of fastener a garment requires under *notions*.

24-7 Choose a thread color that is slightly darker than the fabric color or matches the background color in a plaid. *Shutterstock*

Highlights in History

Inventions We Can't Live Without

For thousands of years, buttons and belts were the only fasteners used to hold clothes together. Then an engineer named Whitcomb Judson invented his *clasp locker* in 1893. It was really a series of hooks and eyes that closed mechanically. It was not a real hit, however, because it was rather crude and tended to come open—not a real advantage.

In 1913, Gideon Sundbach developed a similar fastener using metal teeth—the prototype of today's zipper. He sold these fasteners to the U.S. Army for use on soldiers' clothing and gear during World War I. Sundbach is considered the father of the zipper industry.

The word *zipper* was actually coined by B.F. Goodrich in 1923, whose company sold rubber galoshes equipped with zippers. Goodrich named them zippers because of the zipping sound they made when opened and closed.

Velcro® is another fastener that has found many uses. A Swiss engineer named George de Mestral invented it in 1948. He got the idea while hiking. George noticed how burrs (burdock seeds) stuck to his clothing due to their hooklike protrusions. He used this concept to develop Velcro, which consists of one strip of nylon with loops and another with hooks. Though used mainly in apparel, Velcro is also used to fasten many other items. Can you name some of them?

Zippers

Zippers are available in various colors, types, and lengths. Like thread, you need to match the color of the zipper to the fabric. Check your pattern envelope for the type and length zipper you need. Zippers are available with both nylon and metal teeth in various weights and thicknesses, 24-8. The zipper tapes may be made of cotton or manufactured fibers. They may be firmly woven or stretchable.

Different types of zippers have different uses. These include the following:

- *All-purpose zippers* are used most often. They open only from the top.
- *Separating zippers* can come apart at the bottom. They are used on jackets and parkas.
- *Invisible zippers* look like regular seams from the right side of the garment. No stitching is visible. The special way they are sewn gives them this appearance.
- *Two-way zippers* have sliders at the top and the bottom. They can be opened at either end.
- *Trouser zippers* have wider tapes and teeth than other zippers. The teeth are often made of brass.

24-8 Zippers come in a variety of widths, lengths, and colors. The teeth may be made of metal or nylon.
Shutterstock

Buttons

Buttons can be decorative or functional. The size and number of buttons you need are listed on your pattern envelope. A button's size is its diameter. There are two common types of buttons:

- *Sew-through buttons* have two to four holes in them. Thread is stitched through the holes.
- *Shank buttons* have a loop underneath the button. You stitch the thread through the loop.

Hooks, Eyes, and Snaps

Hooks and eyes come in a variety of sizes. Regular hooks and eyes have curved or straight eyes. *Curved eyes* are used on edges that just meet, such as the edge of a collar. *Straight eyes* are used when edges overlap, such as on a waistband. Trouser hooks and eyes are wider and flatter.

Snaps also come in many sizes. Smaller snaps are used in areas with little strain. Larger snaps can withstand heavy-duty use. They can be used covered or uncovered depending on the garment, 24-9.

Hooks and eyes and snaps usually come in black and silver. Black is usually used on dark-colored fabrics. Silver is often used on light-colored fabrics.

Hook-and-Loop Tape

Hook-and-loop tape is made up of two pieces of nylon. One piece has tiny nylon loops. The other has a fuzzy surface. When the two pieces are pressed together, they stick to one another. Hook-and-loop tape may come in precut shapes such as circles and squares. It is also available in strips by the yard. A common brand of hook-and-loop tape is Velcro®.

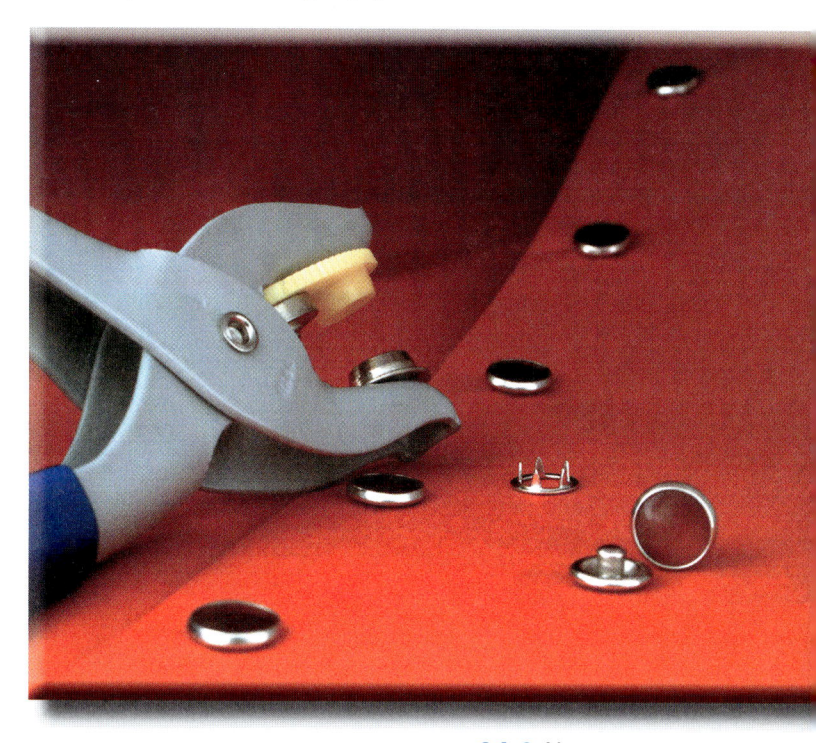

Tapes and Trims

Tapes and trims are available in a variety of types, widths, and colors. They may be firmly woven or stretchable. The type you choose depends on how you will use it.

Tapes and trims can be functional and decorative. For instance, you can use colorful seam tape to finish hems and facing edges. Other colorful trims, such as ribbon, lace, and braid, are made into designs to decorate garments. Tapes can be used to cover fabric edges or reinforce seams to keep them from stretching.

A number of tapes and trims are available. They include

- *seam tape*—a woven tape used to finish hem and facing edges
- *twill tape*—a firm tape used to reinforce seams
- *bias tape*—a single-fold or double-fold tape that stretches; use it to bind curved or straight edges or for casings and ties
- *hem facing*—a wide type of bias tape used for hems and binding edges
- *piping*—a corded bias strip that can be inserted into a seam for a decorative effect
- *ribbing*—a knitted band used for necklines, sleeves, or lower edges

Check the package directions for how to use these tapes and trims and how to apply them. Your pattern may tell you what type and how much to buy for the garment you are making.

24-9 No-sew decorative snap fasteners are applied with a special type of pliers. *Prym-Dritz Corp.*

Elastics

Elastic is used to give better fit to garments. It is available in different widths and types. When buying elastic, check to make sure you get the kind you need. Different types of elastics include the following:

- *Woven elastic* can be used in a casing (an enclosure to hold elastic) because it stays the same width when stretched. It can also be stitched directly to a garment. It is usually thicker than other elastics so it is good to use with heavier fabrics.
- *Braided elastic* becomes narrow when it is stretched. It is only used in casings.
- *Knitted elastic* is soft and lightweight. It resists curling when stretched. It is best suited for lightweight fabrics and swimwear.

- *Transparent* (clear) *elastic* is a synthetic product that stretches three to four times its length with complete recovery to its original size. It is sewn directly onto the fabric and is a good choice for swimwear and lingerie.

Interfacings

Interfacing is a fabric used under the outer fabric to prevent stretching and provide shape to a garment. It also adds strength to necklines, buttonholes, and front closings. It gives shape to collars, cuffs, waistbands, and pockets.

When choosing interfacing, consider the weight of your fabric. As a rule, choose interfacing the same weight or a little lighter weight than your fabric. Make sure your interfacing has the same care instructions as the other fabric you are using. Interfacings come in both woven and nonwoven types. They are also either sewn into the garment or have a *fusible backing*. Fusible interfacings bond to another fabric when pressed with an iron.

Pressing Equipment

As you construct a garment, it is important to press with an iron as you sew. Irons vary in features and cost. A dry iron can be used successfully if you use a damp pressing cloth to supply steam when needed. A steam iron is more convenient and produces a lot of steam. The moisture, not the heat, shapes the garment.

To prevent iron shine and possible water drops on the fabric, cover your garment with a **press cloth** before you press. You can use an absorbent, light- to medium-weight cotton or linen fabric for a press cloth. A press cloth allows you to remove wrinkles without making the fabric surface shiny. To provide more steam, simply dampen the press cloth.

A **sleeve board** is handy for pressing small details. It looks like a small ironing board. A **seam roll** is a long tubular cushion that allows you to press seams open without leaving marks from the seam allowances. Curved seams and darts can be easily pressed with a **pressing ham** (a firm, round cushion), **24-10**. The garment lies flat against its rounded shape and curved edges.

An ironing board should be sturdy, level, and adjustable for different heights. A smooth absorbent padding with a tight-fitting cover is best. A cotton cover absorbs moisture. Keep the cover smooth and clean.

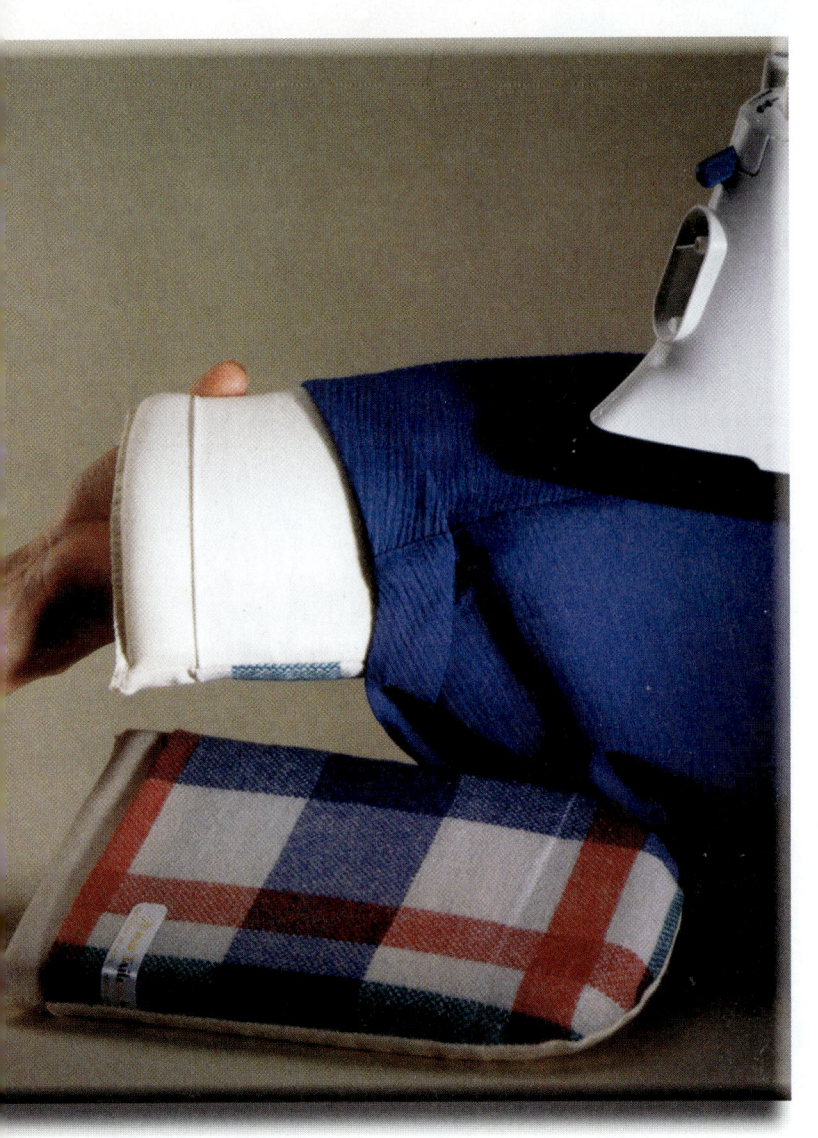

24-10 A small pressing mitt helps you get good results when pressing curved areas and seams. *June Tailor, Inc.*

The Sewing Machine

Since Elias Howe patented his sewing machine in 1846, sewing machines have had many changes in shape and features. The latest change has been the addition of computer technology. Thread tension, stitch length, and buttonhole size can be automatically set. Many more stitches are often available.

If you have ever sewn a seam by hand, you can appreciate the efficiency of a sewing machine. It is a complex piece of machinery. Before you sew, you should learn how the machine you will use works. Different models and brands vary in some ways. They may thread differently. Some may have special features. Regardless of the model you use, you must know some basics: threading, starting, controlling the speed, backstitching, and stopping at the desired spot.

The Parts of the Sewing Machine

In order to learn how to operate a sewing machine, it helps to have a basic knowledge of its parts. Figure 24-11 shows the head of a sewing machine. It holds many moving parts that help the machine operate.

There are many makes and models of sewing machines. The following are the main parts of most sewing machines. Locate these parts on the sewing machine you will be using.

- *Hand wheel* (also called the balance wheel) controls movement of the take-up lever and needle. It turns as the machine runs. You can move the needle up and down by turning the wheel toward you with your hand.
- *Bobbin winder* guides the thread when filling the bobbin with thread.
- *Spool pin* holds the spool of thread.
- *Presser foot pressure adjustment* controls the amount of pressure the presser foot places against the feed system.
- *Stitch width dial* controls the width of zigzag stitching. It also positions the needle for straight stitching.
- *Thread guides* lead the thread to the needle.
- *Bobbin winder tension disc* regulates thread tension for bobbin winding.
- *Take-up lever* controls flow of needle thread. It must be at its highest position each time you start to sew. If it is not, the thread will be pulled up and away from the needle as the lever rises and you will have to thread the needle again. It also must be at its highest position when you end a line of stitching. If not, you may have difficulty removing the fabric from under the presser foot. Some newer machines automatically stop with the take-up lever in the highest position.
- *Face plate* swings open for access to movable parts and light on some machines.
- *Thread tension dial* lets you set the tension for your particular project. Your fabric, stitch, and thread will determine the tension setting you need. Some newer machines automatically adjust thread tension.
- *Presser foot* holds fabric against feed system teeth.
- *Feed dog* moves fabric under the presser foot.
- *Needle plate* has guidelines to help you sew straight, even seams. It also supports the fabric during sewing.

420   Part 5   Sewing Techniques

1	Pre-tension stud
2	Thread tension adjustment dial
3	Thread guide
4	Red stitches (decorative stitches)
5	Green stitches (sewing stitches)
6	Selector lever
7	Spool pins
8	Bobbin winder
9	Hand wheel
10	Stitch width dial
11	Needle position dial
12	Buttonhole dial
13	Power/light switch
14	Reverse lever
15	Stitch length dial
16	Stitch program color indicator (red – green)
17	Stitch program selector dial
18	Sewing/Darning selector dial
19	Bobbin door
20	Feed dogs/stitch plate
21	Presser foot
22	Thread guide
23	Thread take-up

24-11 This illustration identifies the various parts of a sewing machine. *Photo courtesy of BERNINA International/BERNINA of America, Inc.*

- *Needle clamp* holds the needle in place.
- *Stitch length dial* regulates the length of the stitches. Some models have a special setting for stretch stitching.
- *Reverse lever* lets you stitch backward.
- *Presser foot lifter* allows you to raise and lower the presser foot.
- *Thread cutter* is on the back of the presser bar for convenience.
- *Bobbin cover* plate covers the bobbin and bobbin case.
- *Speed controller* is used to operate the machine. Press down on it to stitch.
- *Power* and *light switch* turns on machine and sewing light at one time.
- *Stitch selectors* allows you to choose decorative or sewing stitches.

An important item that comes with your sewing machine is the *instruction manual*, 24-12. It shows the parts of the machine and explains what they do. It describes any accessories that come with the machine and any special features. Be sure to read the instruction manual thoroughly before you begin using a sewing machine.

Using the Sewing Machine

Machines operate with two threads: the needle thread and the bobbin thread. The needle thread runs from the spool pin, around the tension discs and through the take-up lever, thread guides, and needle. The bobbin thread runs from the bobbin plate up through the throat plate. Study the machine diagram to see how to thread the sewing machine.

Begin to sew using some fabric scraps. Use two layers since most sewing is done with two pieces of fabric. Keep your fingers away from the machine needle. Learn to control the speed of the machine.

Study the chart of sewing machine problems and cures in 24-13. It will help you determine the source of any problems that might occur and how to correct them.

24-12 Before you begin to sew, reading through the instruction manual that comes with your machine is important. *Steve Olewinski*

Minor Problems and Cures for Sewing Machines

Problem	Cause	Cure
1. Loud noise as you start to sew and matted threads in seam line.	• Machine threaded wrong.	• Thread machine again.
2. Lower thread breaks.	• Lower tension too tight. • Knot in bobbin thread.	• Adjust tension screw. • Check thread.
3. Puckered seam line.	• Tension too tight. • Thread too heavy or too light for fabric. • Pulling on fabric. • Tail ends of threads caught in presser foot.	• Check by sewing on different weight fabric. • Make sure threads are under presser foot and to the back when starting.
4. Machine locks. Needle will not go up and down.	• Thread caught in bobbin.	• Turn hand wheel backward to release thread.
5. Skipped stitches.	• Needle bent, blunt, too long or short. • Needle threaded wrong.	• Check needle. • Thread needle again. • May need a stretch needle.
6. Looped stitches. Top line. Bottom line.	• Top tension adjusted wrong. • Bottom tension adjusted wrong. • Thread not fully in tension dial.	• Check tension.
7. Needle picks or pulls thread in line of stitching.	• Point of needle bent when it hit a pin.	• Insert new needle.
8. Needle breaks.	• Presser foot loose and needle hit it. • Pulling fabric while stitching.	• Tighten presser foot. Do not pull fabric.
9. Machine runs "hard."	• Needs cleaning and oiling.	• Clean and oil according to instruction booklet.
10. Machine will not run at all.	• Machine may be unplugged. Cord or outlet may be defective.	• Check to see if plugged in tightly. • Check another outlet to see if cord is okay.

24-13 You can save time and frustration by learning to recognize common sewing machine problems and knowing how to solve them.

Caring for the Sewing Machine

A sewing machine is a precise instrument that will stitch well if you give it the proper care. You will need to do your part in keeping the machine clean and running smoothly. Follow these guidelines:

- Unplug the sewing machine before cleaning it.
- Remove lint and fluff from the exposed parts using a soft cloth. Clean the machine head, tension discs, take-up lever, thread guides, presser foot bar, and needle bar.
- With a small lint brush, clean behind the face plate and around the feed dog and bobbin case. You may need to remove the entire bobbin case, **24-14**.
- Check to see if you are to oil your machine. Many newer machines never need to be oiled. If your machine is to be oiled, follow the instruction manual. Be sure to only use sewing machine oil. Use only the amount recommended, which is usually just a drop. Then sew a few lines of stitching on a scrap of fabric to remove excess oil.
- Cover the sewing machine when it is not in use to keep dust away from the machine.

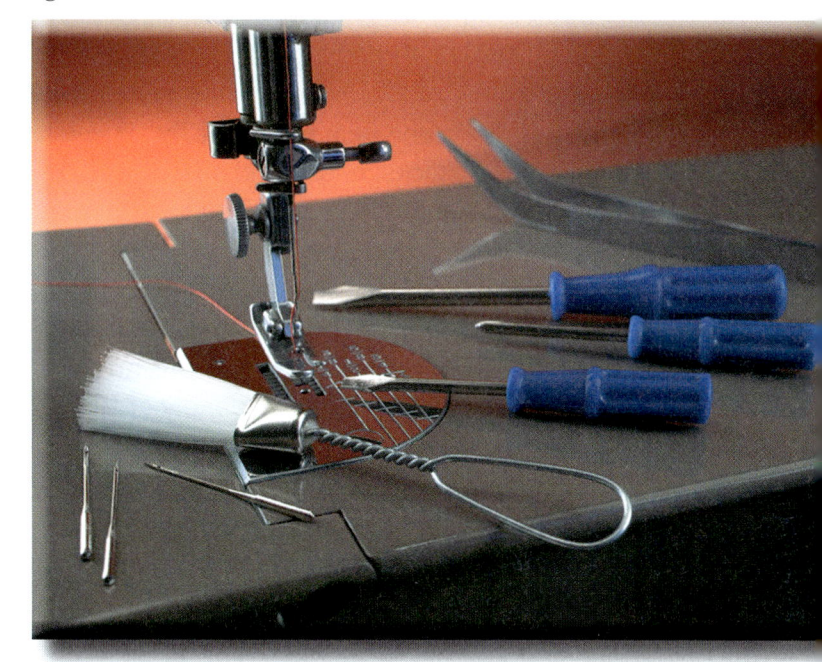

If you have a sewing machine at home, check the use and care manual that came with your machine. It will tell you how to care for your machine each time it is used. It will also tell you what needs to be done every few months to keep your machine running well for many years.

24-14 Use a lint brush to clean the face plate, feed dog, and bobbin case. Change machine needles whenever they become dull. *Prym-Dritz Corp.*

Summary

- Special equipment is necessary for successful sewing. Some tools are necessary to do the job. Others just make the job easier.
- Cutting tools include shears, scissors, pinking or scalloping shears, thread clippers, and seam rippers.
- Measuring tools include tape measures, skirt markers, yardsticks, rulers, and sewing gauges. You will need to have a tape measure.
- Marking tools help transfer pattern markings to the fabric. Many people use dressmaker's carbon paper and a tracing wheel for this task.
- Both needles (hand and machine) and pins are needed for sewing. They come in a variety of types and sizes.
- Notions are items other than fabric that become part of a garment or project. Thread, zippers, buttons, snaps, hooks and eyes, hook and loop tape, tapes, trims, elastics, and interfacings are examples.
- It is important to press as you sew using an iron and ironing board. In addition, you may want to use a press cloth, sleeve board, seam roll, and pressing ham.
- The sewing machine is a complex piece of machinery. Different models and brands vary in some ways. Regardless of the model used, you must know some basics: threading, starting, controlling the speed, backstitching, and stopping. You also need to know how to care for the sewing machine.

Graphic Organizer

Create a star diagram and note the types of sewing equipment.

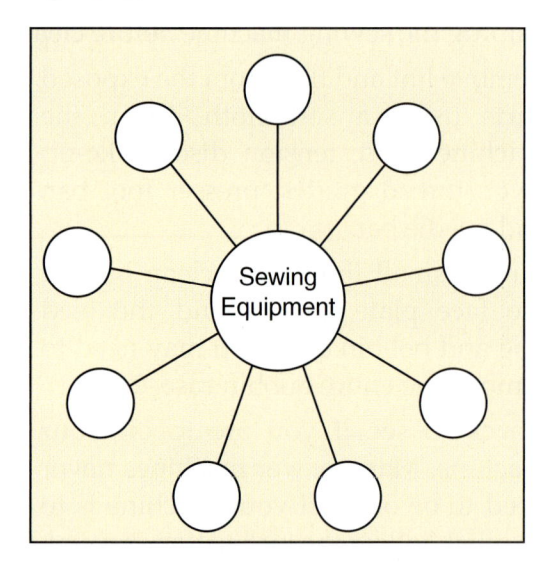

Review the Facts

1. Explain the difference between scissors and shears.
2. What is the advantage of bent-handled shears?
3. Describe pinking shears and their use.
4. List two factors to consider in buying a good tape measure.
5. Describe a marking tool and how to use it.
6. Explain the numbering system for machine- and hand-sewing needles.
7. Name the best all-purpose sewing machine needle and why it is a good choice for most fabrics.
8. Which pins should you use with knitted fabrics?
9. When is a thimble used and why?
10. Why is polyester/cotton thread a good choice for sewing almost all fabrics?
11. Which type of zipper would you choose if you were sewing a jacket and why?
12. When using hooks and eyes, which type of eye would you use if you want the edges of your garment to just meet?
13. When choosing interfacing fabric, explain how you decide what weight to buy.
14. Which pressing tool would you use to press a curved seam and a dart?
15. What should you use to clean a sewing machine each time it is used?

Think Critically

16. **Compare and contrast.** Compare the various tools for transferring pattern markings to fabrics. What are the advantages and disadvantages of each?
20. **Analyze sources.** When sewing for the first time, there are supplies you may need to buy. Brainstorm ways to obtain these supplies if funds are not available.
21. **Make inferences.** Review the basic sewing supplies in Figure 24-1. Which of these would you need to use to make simple clothing repairs and alterations? What does this tell you about the supplies needed to construct a new garment?

Apparel Applications

22. **Equipment review.** Team up with a classmate and choose a piece of sewing equipment. One team member summarizes factors to consider in purchasing it. The other explains how to use and care for it.
23. **Experiment.** Try removing a rough spot on a pin or sharpening it by using an emery bag attached to a pincushion. What was the pin like before using the emery bag? What were the results?
24. **Notions report.** Visit notions departments in a fabric store or look through sewing magazines or catalogs in print or online. Find unusual equipment and items. Prepare a report for the class.
25. **Thimble practice.** Learning to use a thimble can take time, but it is worth the effort to prevent unnecessary wear and tear on your fingertips. Use a scrap of fabric and a threaded needle to practice using a thimble.
26. **Safety bulletin board.** Prepare a list of safety guidelines for using sewing equipment, the sewing machine, and pressing equipment. Post it on the bulletin board.
27. **Demonstrate equipment proficiency.** On a classroom sewing machine, demonstrate filling a bobbin, threading the bobbin, changing a needle, controlling speed, following lines, turning corners, and storing the machine.

Academic Connections

28. **Writing.** Some people find it awkward to use a thimble. Write a letter about what you would say to them about its use and usefulness. What alternatives to the standard thimble would you suggest? What advice would you give for using a thimble successfully?
29. **Social studies.** Conduct an oral-history interview with an older adult you know about sewing equipment they and their grandparents used. Was it different? What changes have they observed in equipment over the years? Share with the class.

Workplace Connections

30. **Job shadow.** Make arrangements to job shadow a sewing machine salesperson. Have this individual tell you about the various machines he or she sells and why. Share your experience with the class.
31. **Machine care demonstration.** Presume you are an instructor at a local sewing machine shop. You have a new group of beginning sewers in class this week. Prepare a demonstration showing how to care for one of the sewing machines your business (the class) sells. Follow the instruction manual for the machine.

Service Project Display

Do some students in your school community lack resources to purchase necessary sewing equipment? Would some like to sew at home, but do not have a sewing machine? Think about ways your class can help support others by providing necessary equipment.

Develop and implement an in-depth service project for a *Chapter Service Project Display STAR Event*. Use the FCCLA *Planning Process* to help you determine ways to obtain sewing equipment and sewing machines for your school community. See your adviser for information as needed.

Chapter 25

Getting Ready to Sew

Chapter Objectives

After studying this chapter, you will be able to
- **evaluate** the fabric grain and prepare the fabric for cutting and sewing.
- **make** alternations to the pattern as needed.
- **lay** out a pattern and properly pin it to the fabric.
- **cut** out a garment.
- **transfer** pattern markings to fabric.

Key Terms

preshrinking
true bias
off-grain
layout

Reading with Purpose

Before you read the chapter, interview a person who works with alterations and sewing. Ask this person why it is important to know about the chapter topic and how it relates to the workplace. Take notes during the interview. As you read the chapter, highlight the items from your notes that are discussed in the chapter.

The more you know about something, the more at ease you feel working with it. This is true if you are caring for children, playing baseball, talking before a group, or sewing a garment.

Sewing is a complex task, but it seems easier once you know more about it. By learning about fabrics, patterns, equipment, and basic sewing techniques, you will avoid frustration and mistakes. Instead, you will enjoy sewing and have success with your projects.

This chapter explains many preliminary sewing steps. The sewing guide sheet for your pattern gives step-by-step directions for your specific garment. Together, they tell you all you need to know to make your sewing project a success.

Preparing the Fabric

Before pinning the pattern to the fabric, there are some preliminary steps you must follow in preparing the fabric. The fabric may need to be preshrunk. You may also need to straighten the grain of the fabric. Both of these preparation steps help assure a properly fitted garment when it is finished and ready to wear.

Preshrinking the Fabric

Many of today's fabrics have already gone through a preshrinking process. **Preshrinking** means the fabrics were put through a process (washing or dry cleaning) to minimize shrinking when you wash or dry clean them. Check the label on the end of the bolt when you buy your fabric. If it does not say *preshrunk*, you should do it yourself. This will ensure that your finished garment will not shrink.

To preshrink your fabric, treat it as if it were the finished garment. If you will machine wash and dry the garment, machine wash and dry the fabric. (You do not need to add detergent.) If you are to hand wash the garment and lay it flat to dry, do this to the fabric, too. If the garment will be dry-cleaned, dry-clean the fabric before you sew your garment.

Also check the notions. You may need to preshrink zippers and trims, too. If you do not preshrink them, they may shrink after you attach them to the garment, causing the garment to pucker.

Understanding Fabric Grain

As you know, woven fabrics have two sets of yarns—warp and filling. The direction the yarns run is called grain. The warp yarns form the *lengthwise grain*. An easy way to find the lengthwise grain is to look for the selvages of the fabric. The lengthwise grain runs in the same direction as (or parallel to) the selvages, 25-1. When your pattern refers to *straight grain* or *grain line*, it is referring to the lengthwise grain.

The filling yarns run straight across the fabric from one selvage to the other. This is the *crosswise grain* of the fabric.

The other fabric grain is *bias grain*. This runs diagonally across the fabric. **True bias** runs at a 45 degree angle, 25-2. It offers the greatest amount of stretch in a woven fabric. To find the true bias, pick up a corner of the fabric. Fold it so the cut edge is parallel to the selvage. The diagonal fold forms the true bias.

The grain in knitted fabrics is slightly different. Instead of two sets of yarns, these fabrics have rows of loops in two directions. The rows of loops running the length of the fabric form the lengthwise grain. The rows of loops running

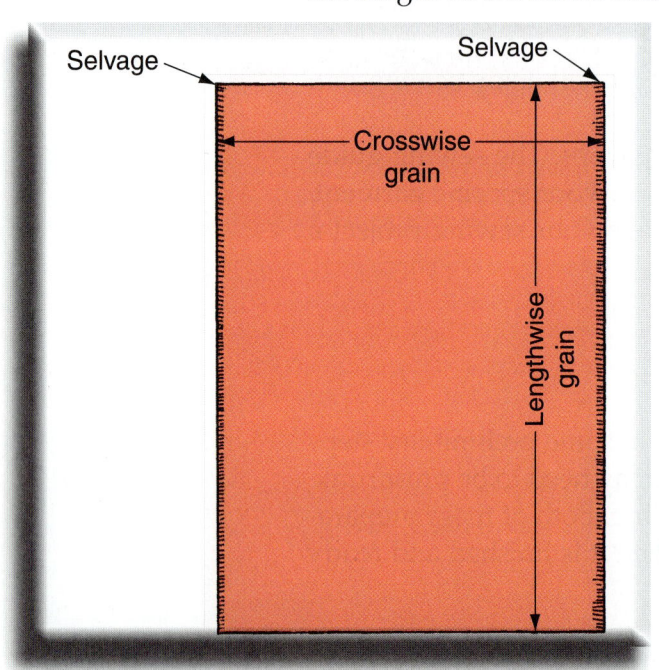

25-1 The lengthwise grain runs parallel to the selvages. The crosswise grain runs between selvages. *Goodheart-Willcox Publisher*

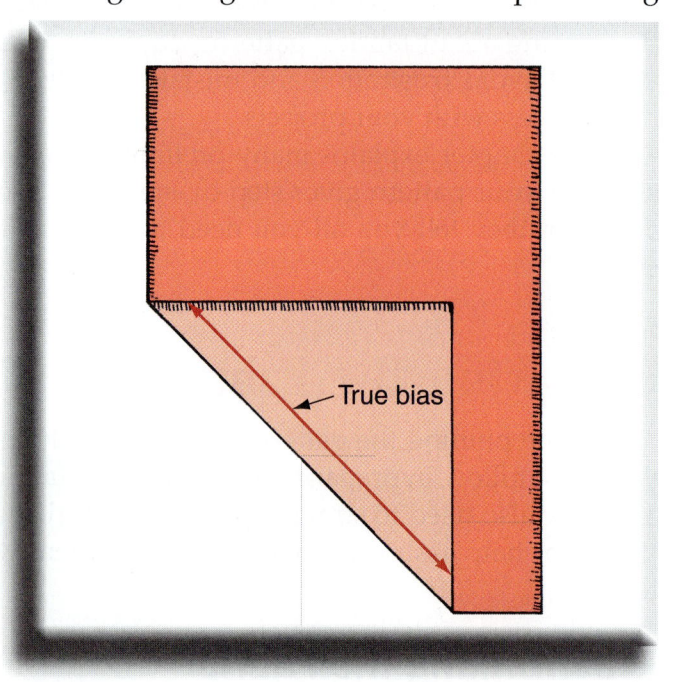

25-2 The true bias runs at a 45-degree angle across the fabric. *Goodheart-Willcox Publisher*

across the fabric form the crosswise grain. In knitted fabrics, the crosswise grain allows the most stretch.

Checking the Grain

If the fabric is **off-grain**, the lengthwise yarns and the crosswise yarns are not at a perfect 90-degree angle to each other. The fabric grain is crooked, and it will be difficult to handle. It may not lie flat as you cut out the pattern pieces. The finished garment will twist, pull to one side, and the hem may be uneven. The fabric grain must be *straight* to make a garment look right.

The first step in checking the straightness of the grain is to see if the fabric was cut along the crosswise grain. (The fabric may not have been cut on the grain when it was cut from the bolt of fabric in the store.) You may be able to see one of the filling yarns. Cut along one of these filling yarns close to the end of the fabric. If you cannot see the yarns clearly, clip through the selvage near the cut edge. Inside the clip, pick up one filling yarn and pull it gently. With your other hand, push the fabric along the pulled yarn, 25-3. This leaves a mark that you can use as a cutting line. If the yarn breaks in the middle of the fabric, cut as far as you can see the line. Pick up the yarn and pull it again. Continue until you have cut all the way across the fabric.

Lay the fabric on a large, flat surface. Bring the two selvages together, making a lengthwise fold. If the grain is straight, the fold will be smooth and straight. The selvages will match, and the cut edges on each end will match. The cut edges and the selvages will meet in a right angle, 25-4.

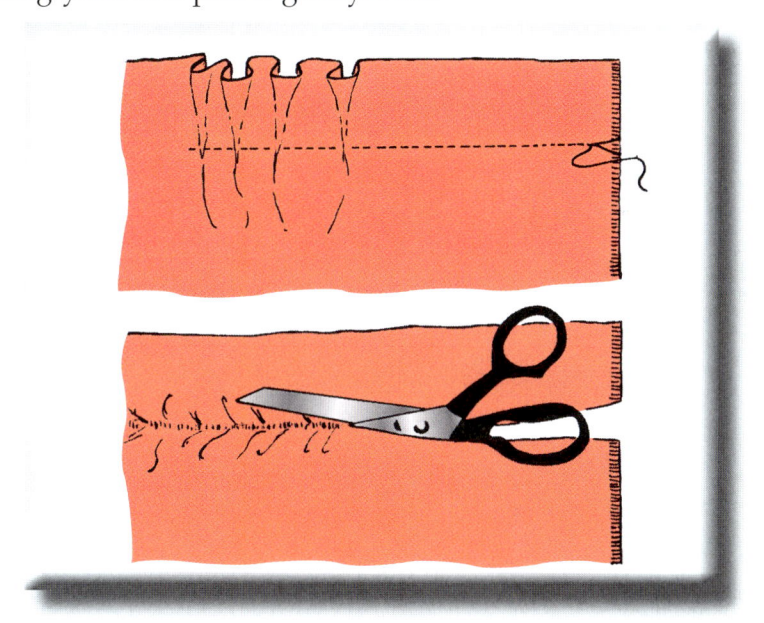

Straightening the Grain

Suppose the fold is not smooth and straight or that the edges do not match. This may happen if the fabric was twisted as it was rolled onto bolts. It can be straightened by pulling the fabric on the bias. Two people can do this better than one. Hold the two opposite corners that are too short. Pull along the bias. Check often to see if you have pulled enough to straighten the grain.

Sometimes the finishing process forces the yarns off-grain. In durable-press fabrics, chemicals and heat are added to help resist wrinkling. If unevenness occurs during the finishing stage, it is *baked* into the fabric. You will have to use the fabric as it is. Pulling the fabric to straighten the grain will not work because it will return to the off-grain shape after pulling.

25-3 One way to find the straight crosswise grain is to pull a filling yarn, leaving a mark you can follow when cutting. *Goodheart-Willcox Publisher*

Pressing the Fabric

If your fabric needs pressing, do it before you place your pattern pieces on it. Accurate cutting is impossible on wrinkled fabric. Press carefully and thoroughly. Give special attention to the center fold. The crease may be difficult to remove. A damp pressing cloth or a steam iron is often helpful.

Press in the direction of the lengthwise grain. This will keep the fabric grain in line. Fabric stretches very little in the lengthwise direction.

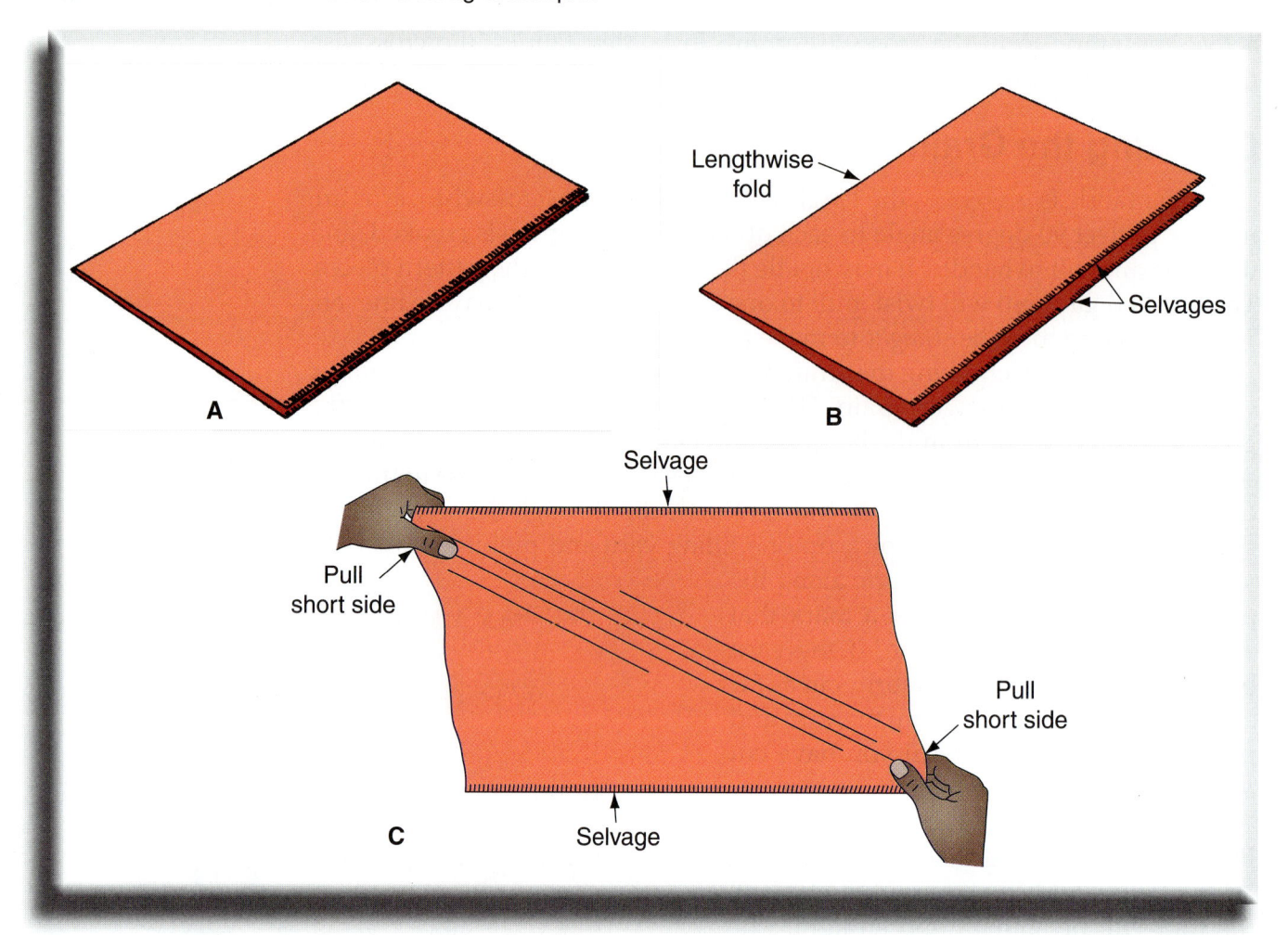

25-4 If the fabric grain is straight, all edges match and the fabric lies flat (A). If the grain is not straight, the selvages and cut edges do not match (B). The grain will need to be straightened (C).
Goodheart-Willcox Publisher

Preparing the Pattern

Remove your pattern pieces from the envelope. Look at the sketches of the pattern pieces on the sewing guide sheet. The guide sheet will state which pattern pieces you need for the garment or view you are making. Many pieces will be printed on one large piece of tissue paper. You will need to cut these apart, but you do not need to cut directly on the cutting line. You will do this later when you cut out your fabric. Return the pattern pieces you are not using to the envelope. If you are working on your pattern in class, write your name on each of the pattern pieces to avoid losing them.

If your pattern pieces are badly wrinkled, press them with a dry, warm iron. Be careful not to press tiny wrinkles into each piece.

When using a multisized pattern, you will notice three or four cutting lines on each pattern piece. Mark your size with a felt-tip pen or highlighter. This will help you follow the correct cutting line when you are ready to cut out your pattern. You can also cut the pattern piece out on the cutting line you intend to use before pinning it to the fabric.

Altering the Pattern

Check your measurements with the chart on the back of your pattern envelope. If they are not the same (allowing for ease), you will have to *adjust* or *alter* your pattern. Altering patterns is better than altering finished garments. It is more accurate and assures better fit. A finished garment might not have enough extra fabric to make the needed changes.

Altering the Length

The most common adjustments are for length. Many pattern pieces are labeled *lengthen or shorten here* in one or two places. This phrase is often found at the bottom cutting edge of a pattern piece.

Altering the bottom edge of pattern pieces does not solve all fitting problems. You may need an adjustment in the middle of pattern pieces instead. Look for two parallel lines that are close together. These are the *adjustment lines*. You may find the phrase *lengthen or shorten here* next to them, but not always.

Look for these markings, and then choose from the following methods:

- *Lengthen at the bottom edge.* In this case, lengthen the piece by taping a piece of paper to the bottom. Measure the length amount you need from the original cutting line. Draw a new line that is parallel to the original, **24-5**.
- *Shorten at the bottom edge.* To shorten the pattern piece at the bottom edge, measure the desired length amount up from the original line. Draw a new cutting line that is parallel to the first. Be sure to lengthen or shorten all pieces the same amount.
- *Lengthen at the adjustment line.* To lengthen the pattern piece, cut between the two lines. Place a piece of paper under the pattern. Spread the pattern the needed distance and tape to the paper. Redraw the cutting lines at the sides to form straight lines, **24-6**.
- *Shorten at the adjustment line.* To shorten the pattern, measure up from the adjustment line the amount to be shortened. Draw a new line. Fold the pattern at the adjustment line and bring the fold to the newly drawn line. Tape in place and redraw the cutting lines, 21-6.

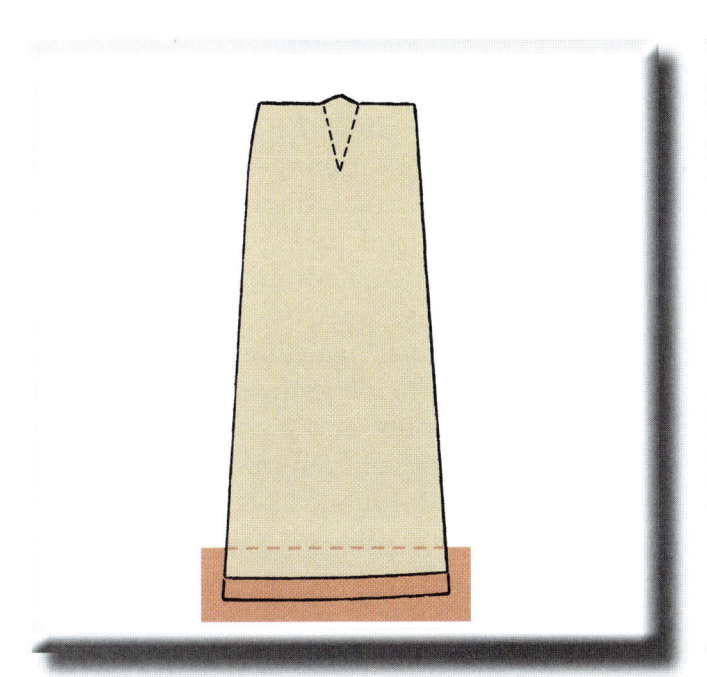

25-5 To lengthen the bottom edge of a pattern, tape extra paper below the cutting line. Draw a new cutting line that is parallel to the original. Fill in the adjacent seam lines and cutting lines. *Goodheart-Willcox Publisher*

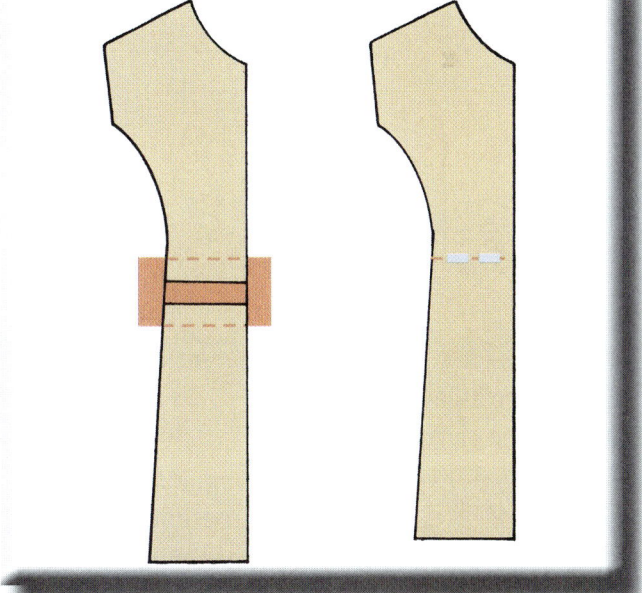

25-6 To lengthen, cut between the adjustment lines and spread the pattern apart. To shorten, fold at the adjustment line and tape. *Goodheart-Willcox Publisher*

Altering the Width

It may be necessary to make adjustments in the width of pattern pieces in the waist, hip, or thigh areas. Make these adjustments in both front and back pattern pieces. If the total amount of the alteration is less than two inches, you can increase or decrease one-fourth the amount you need on each of the side seams. If you require larger adjustments, you may find a different pattern size to be more appropriate. You might also consult with your teacher or an alterations book for additional adjustment techniques.

- *Increase the size of a waistline in pants and skirts.* Tape a strip of paper along the front and back side edges of your pattern pieces from the waist to the hip. Measure out from the cutting line at the waist one-fourth of the total amount you need to add. For instance, if the total alteration is 1 inch, add ¼ inch to the front and back side seams. Redraw the cutting lines, tapering to the hip line, **25-7**. If there is a waistband or waistline facing, make the same amount of adjustment to these pattern pieces. Cut the waistband pattern apart at the side seam markings. Increase each side one-half the amount necessary.

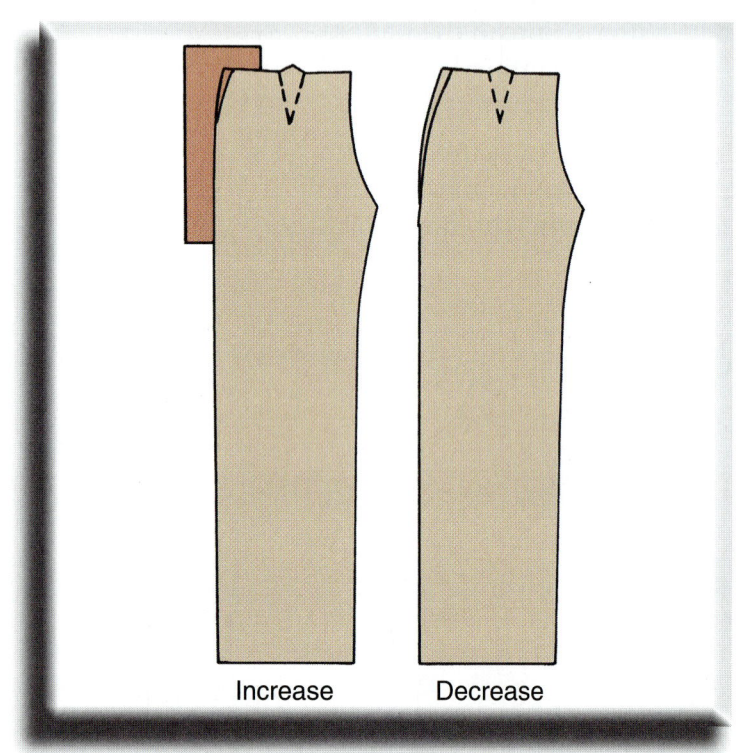

- *Decrease the size of the waistline.* Measure in one-fourth the amount you need at each side seam. Redraw the cutting lines on the pattern pieces, tapering down to the hipline. If there is a waistband, fold out one-half of the alteration amount at the side seam markings and tape in place.

- *Increase the hip and thigh area of straight skirts and pants.* Tape a strip of paper to the pattern from the waist to the hemline. At the side hipline, measure out from the cutting line one-fourth the total amount you need on the front and back pieces and mark with a pencil. Redraw the cutting lines. To do this, taper the lines upward to the original waistline. Measure out from the hemline the same amount as at the hipline and make a mark. Draw a straight line from the hipline mark to the hemline mark, **25-8**.

- *Decrease the hip and thigh area.* Measure in from the cutting line at the hipline one-fourth of the total amount you need. Redraw the lines, tapering to the waistline and drawing straight down to the hemline. For pants, some of the width adjustments should be made on the inner leg seams as well as the outer leg seams. See your teacher for guidance if your pattern requires this adjustment.

25-7 To increase or decrease the width of the waist, measure in or out one-fourth of the needed amount at the wide waistline edge. Redraw the cutting lines, tapering to the hipline. *Goodheart-Willcox Publisher*

The Pattern Layout

The sewing guide sheet from your pattern suggests many layouts, 25-9. The **layout** shows you how to put your pattern pieces on your fabric for cutting. Find the one that matches your pattern size, project or view, and fabric width. You will want to use a *With Nap* layout if your fabric has a nap, pile, or one-way design. Draw a circle around it so you can refer to it easily.

Folding the Fabric

The layout diagram will indicate how to fold your fabric before pinning on the pattern. First, determine which is the right side of your fabric. Some plain weaves are identical on both sides. In that case, you can use either side, but use the same one for all pattern pieces.

Fold most fabrics with the right sides together. The pattern pieces are then placed on the wrong side of the fabric. Sometimes there are advantages to folding the fabric with the wrong sides together. This will make it easier to transfer pattern markings later. Either method will work. Stripes and plaids should be folded with the right side out so it is easier to match the design.

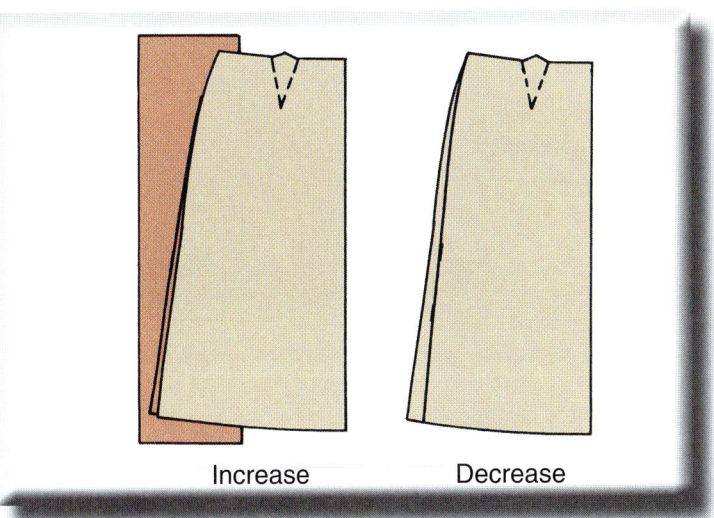

25-8 To increase or decrease the width of the hips, measure in or out one-fourth the needed amount at the side hipline. Redraw the cutting lines, tapering to the waist and extending down to the hemline.
Goodheart-Willcox Publisher

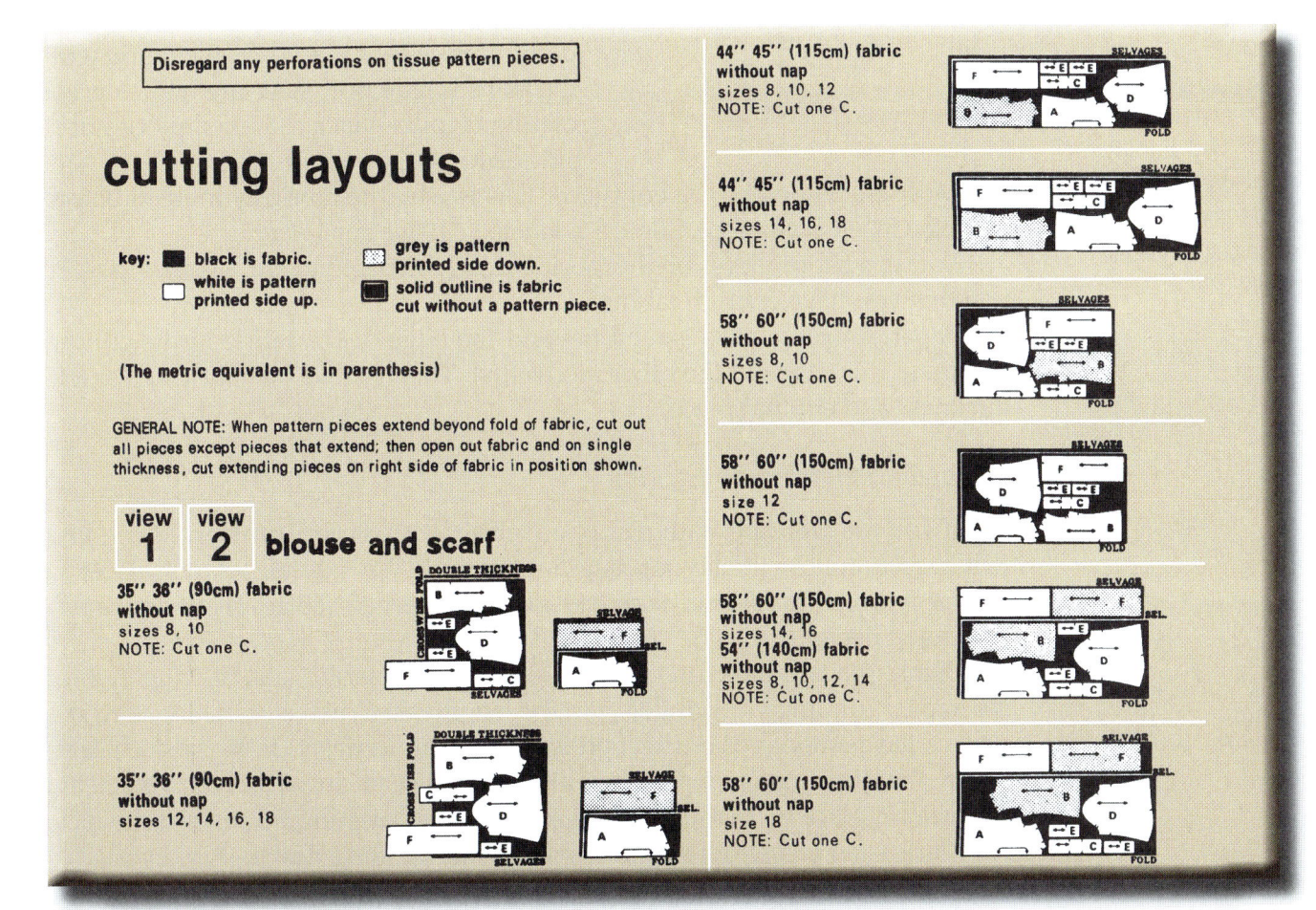

25-9 Many layouts are shown on the guide sheet of a pattern. *The Simplicity Pattern Co, Inc.*

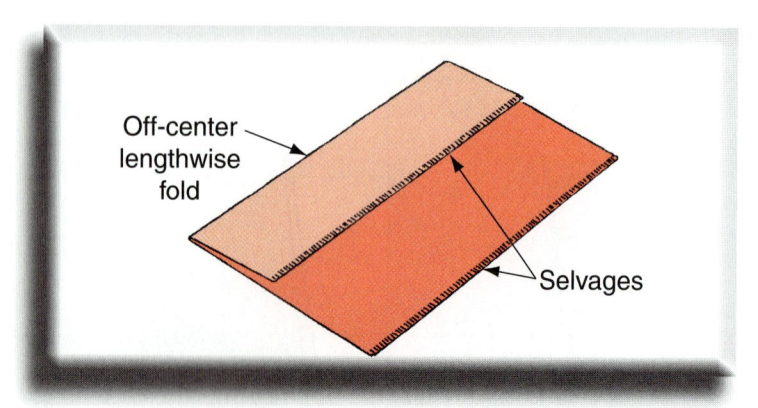

25-10 Some layouts suggest an off-center lengthwise fold.
Goodheart-Willcox Publisher

Your pattern may call for one or more of the following types of folds:

- *Lengthwise fold.* Fold the fabric lengthwise so the two fabric selvages are together.
- *Off-center lengthwise fold.* Fold one selvage toward the other. They should not match, but they should be parallel. One part of the fabric is two thicknesses while the other part is a single thickness, **25-10**.
- *Double fold.* Fold the fabric lengthwise so the selvages meet in the center.
- *Crosswise fold.* Place the cut edges together and match them.
- *Bias fold.* This fold runs diagonally across the fabric. Fold the selvage so it is parallel to the crosswise grain.

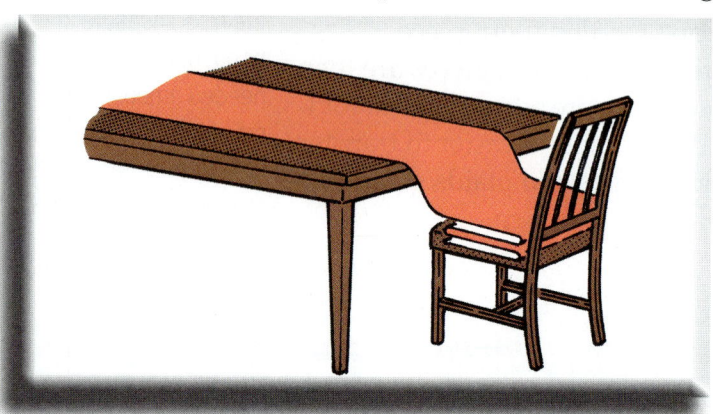

Your fabric may be longer than the table you are using. If so, let one end rest in a chair, **25-11**. This prevents strain on the fabric and keeps it from sliding off the table.

Placing the Pattern Pieces

Lay your pattern pieces on the fabric following the cutting layout diagram. Most pattern pieces are placed on the fabric with the printed side up. These are white on the cutting layouts. Place a shaded piece print-side down.

25-11 Let extra fabric rest on a chair while you work. This reduces the pull on the fabric.
Goodheart-Willcox Publisher

Most pieces need to be cut twice. This is why the fabric is doubled before cutting. Check each piece. Some are labeled *cut one* or *cut four*.

Lay all pattern pieces on the fabric before you begin to cut. This will assure you that you have enough fabric.

A pattern piece may extend beyond the edge of the fabric in the cutting layout. In this case, cut the other pieces first. Then unfold the fabric to a single thickness and cut that piece.

Napped and Patterned Fabrics

If you are working with a napped fabric, such as corduroy or velvet, you will need to follow the layout diagram for *With Nap*. Lay all pattern pieces in the same direction. This is also the case for patterned fabrics that have an up and down design.

Before placing the pattern pieces on a napped fabric, test the direction of the nap by running your finger over the lengthwise surface of the fabric. If the surface feels smooth, the direction is referred to as *down*. If the surface feels rough, the direction is *up*. For the richest color on corduroy, velvet, velveteen, and velour, place the pattern pieces so the nap is running up toward the face. Fur fabrics and terrycloth should have the nap running down.

Plaids may be even or uneven depending on the lines of the plaid. An *even plaid* has a balanced design in both the lengthwise and crosswise directions.

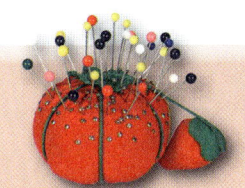

Did You Know?

Sewing for a Cause

You are learning a skill you can put to use in helping others. Perhaps you are a member of an FCCLA chapter looking for a service project. Have you thought about using your sewing skills? Clothes, blankets, layettes, and stuffed toys are needed even in your own community. Several nationwide groups support local efforts to sew such items as the following:

- **Project Linus.** Volunteers create blankets for seriously ill or traumatized children through the organization *Project Linus*. Project Linus has delivered over three million *security* blankets to children around the world. For more information, see the Project Linus website.
- **ABC Quilts.** This group provides quilts for infants and children who are infected with HIV, affected by drugs or alcohol, or abandoned. This is a national project operated by American Mothers, Inc. called *ABC Quilts* (At-Risk-Babies and Children Quilts), completed quilts are distributed to area hospitals and agencies that deal with at-risk babies and children. For more information, see the American Mothers website.
- **Care Wear.** These volunteers make clothes for premature and low-birthweight infants in neonatal units of hospitals. *Care Wear* is a nationwide volunteer group providing handmade baby items to hospitals in their local communities. Patterns for making the items can be found on the Care Wear website.
- **Newborns in Need.** Volunteers gather/make clothes, blankets, and toys for sick and needy newborns in hospitals, especially premature babies who are too tiny to wear regular infant clothing. *Newborns in Need* is a volunteer organization with chapters across the country seeking layette items for needy infants. Go to the Newborns in Need website to find information on how to make and donate these layette items.
- **Sewing for cancer patients.** Chemotherapy turbans and soft hats for cancer patients, wheelchair totes, walker caddies, lap robes, and hospital bed saddlebags are just some of the patterns available at the Home Sewing Association's website. This organization also provides advice on organizing group sewing projects and shares stories from groups doing so across the country.

These are just a few of the many ways you can help others using your sewing skills. Can you think of others?

These are the easiest to sew. Use a *Without Nap* layout for even plaids. To match the design at the seams, place corresponding notches on the same line and color of the plaid.

An *uneven plaid* has an unbalanced design in both the lengthwise and crosswise directions, making it more difficult to sew. Place all pieces in the same lengthwise direction, following the *With Nap* layout diagram. Match the design at the seams and openings, such as a button-front design.

Striped fabrics are also considered even or uneven. For even stripes, use a *Without Nap* layout. Fold the fabric so that the stripes are identical on each side of the fold. For uneven stripes, use the *With Nap* layout.

Pinning the Pattern Pieces

Before you start to pin the pattern to the fabric, check the points in **25-12**. Then begin working with the large pieces at one end of the fabric.

25-12 Check these points before you start to pin pattern to fabric.

Check These Points Before You Pin

- All pattern pieces are assembled that will be needed for the view selected. All other pieces are in the envelope.
- Your name is on the guide sheet, envelope, and each pattern piece.
- Adjustments and alterations, if needed, are made.
- The fold of the fabric is grain perfect. No wrinkles are showing, and all edges match.
- Pattern details have been studied. You know how many pieces to cut. You can identify cutting lines, dots, notches, darts, buttons, and hems.

If you must place a pattern piece on a fold, it will state so on the pattern. Place that edge directly on the fold of the fabric. Pin along that edge first.

If the piece does not need to be along a fold, the grain line is a straight line with an arrow at each end, **25-13**. This line must be parallel to the grain of the fabric. With the pattern and fabric lying flat on the table, push a pin through all layers at the point of each arrow. Then measure from the point of each arrow to the folded edge of the fabric. The two distances should be the same. If they are different, remove one pin and shift the pattern slightly. Insert the pin again and remeasure. Repeat until the grain line arrow is parallel to the fabric grain.

Smooth the pattern pieces from the grain line or fold line toward the edges as you work. Pat, rather than pull, the pattern and fabric.

Insert pins about 6 inches apart **25-14**. On curved edges or slippery fabric, place them closer together. Point pins at right angles (perpendicular) to cutting lines and fold lines. Point them diagonally into corners. Do not put pins across the cutting lines.

When you have finished pinning, compare your pattern layout once more with your layout diagram to be certain you have followed it exactly. Measure again from the grain lines to the edge of your fabric. Obtain final approval from your teacher before you begin cutting.

25-13 A straight line with arrows represents the lengthwise grain line. Measure from the tip of both ends of the arrow to the fabric edge. *Jack Klasey*

Cutting

Bent-handled shears are the best for cutting out a garment. The design allows the blade to lie flat on the table while cutting. Since the fabric is raised only slightly, you can cut exactly along the cutting lines.

Cut with long, smooth strokes. Keep your free hand lightly on the pattern and fabric near the location you are cutting. Cut slowly enough to be aware of notches and any alterations. Do not cut beyond your cutting line. You could damage a section of fabric that you need for another piece.

As you approach a notch on your cutting line, cut to the base with the point of your shears. Cut outward to the tip of the notch. Cut back inward to complete the notch, still using the tip of your shears. This allows you to match up garment sections more easily. Cutting notches outward will give you room to make a smaller seam allowance if you later need it for better fit. Double or triple notches can be cut across the top making one wide notch rather than two or three small ones so close together.

Some patterns show the notches pointing inward only, 25-15. It is still a good idea to cut the notches outward in case you have to adjust the seams later on.

When finished, leave the pattern pieces pinned to the fabric until you are ready to sew them. Save some of the large fabric scraps. You can use them later to test fabric marking products and for practice stitching.

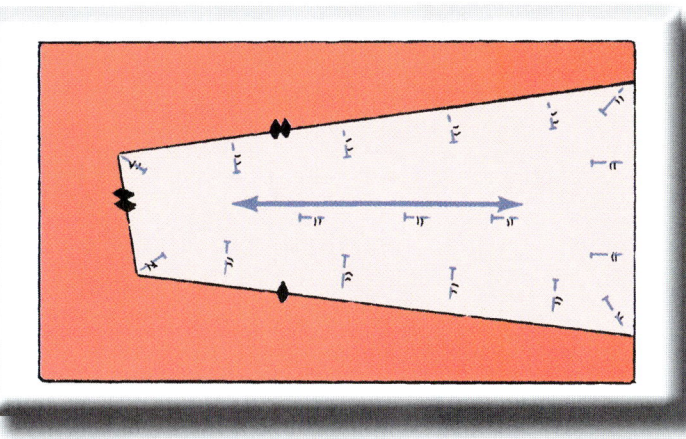

25-14 Notice how the pins are placed in this pattern piece. *Goodheart-Willcox Publisher*

Transferring Pattern Markings

When you have finished cutting your garment, find the pieces with markings that need to be transferred to the fabric. These markings include center front, center back, darts, tucks, pleats, dots, buttons, buttonholes, pockets, and the top of sleeves. They are the markings that help you put the garment together correctly. If your pattern piece shows seam lines, do not mark them. Most sewing machines have a gauge you can follow to sew straight, even seams. Multisized patterns will not have seam line markings.

Remove only the pins that are in the way of markings you need to make. The other pins will hold the pattern in place.

You can use several methods to transfer markings to fabrics. A tracing wheel with dressmaker's tracing paper is one of the most common. Other methods include tailor's chalk, fabric marking pens, and basting.

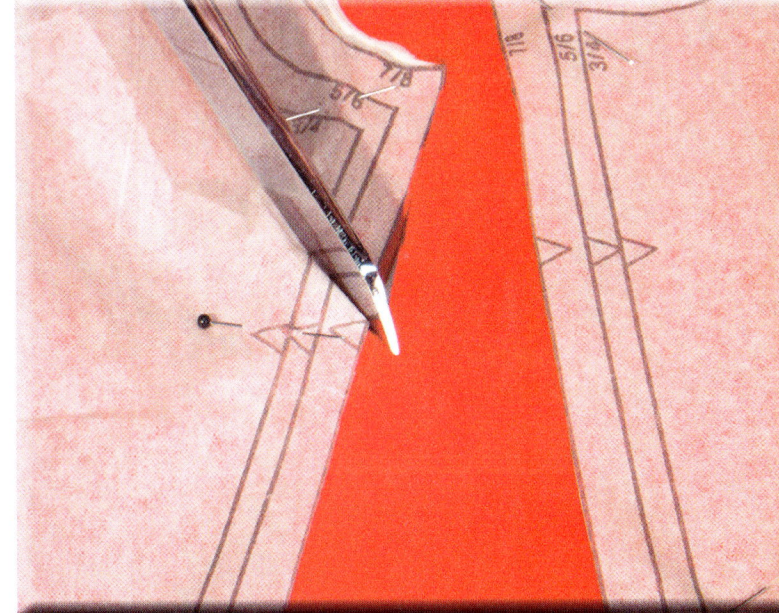

25-15 Cut notches to the outside of the seam allowance. *Jack Klasey*

Dressmaker's Tracing Paper and Tracing Wheel

Dressmaker's tracing paper has a special coating that is transferred to the fabric with a tracing wheel. Use only light-colored tracing paper on light-colored fabrics. Dark colors show on the right side. Use medium- and dark-colored tracing paper for medium- to dark-colored fabrics.

Some tracing paper makes permanent marks, so be careful when using this method of marking. Before you begin, test the paper on a scrap of fabric. Check to see that the markings do not show on the right side. Some newer paper is *disappearing tracing paper.* These markings can typically be washed away with a sponge or soft cloth and clear water. Markings from disappearing tracing paper can disappear after 48 to 72 hours. Use it only on projects you can start and finish in a short amount of time. This type of tracing paper is *not* recommended for use on dry-cleanable fabrics. Just as with permanent tracing paper, test the paper on a scrap of fabric before using it.

There are two types of tracing wheels. A *serrated-edge* tracing wheel leaves a dotted line on the fabric. This type is suitable for firmly woven or knit fabrics of solid colors or subdued prints. A *smooth-edge* tracing wheel leaves a solid line on the fabric and can also be used on these same fabrics. In addition, it can be used for plaids, prints, doubleknits, wool flannel, and delicate fabrics.

To use the tracing paper, place the colored side of the paper next to the wrong side of the fabric. Use a sheet of cardboard to protect the table. Then roll the tracing wheel along the markings you want to transfer. Use a ruler to mark straight lines, **25-16**. Use only enough pressure to make the markings show on the wrong side. Too much pressure will cause the marks to show on the right side.

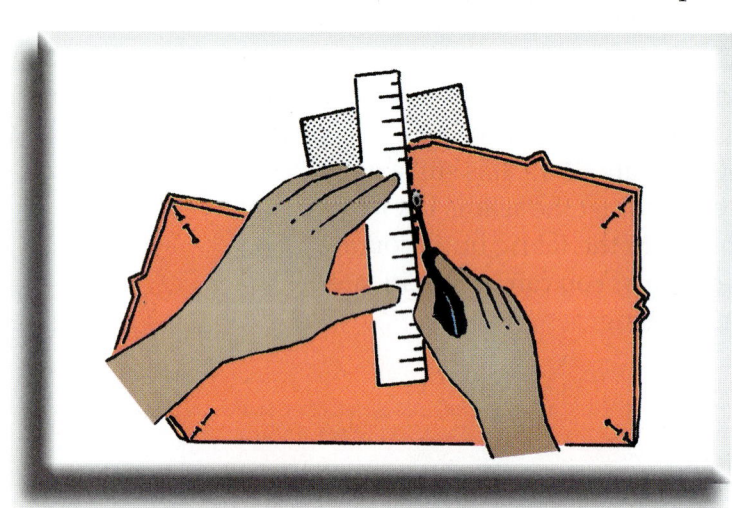

25-16 A tracing wheel and dressmaker's carbon paper are often used for marking. Always mark a fabric scrap as a test before marking the garment.
Goodheart-Willcox Publisher

Tailor's Chalk

Tailor's chalk or a chalk pencil can be used for marking details on most fabrics. Only one layer of fabric is marked at a time. Pins are often used with tailor's chalk for marking.

With the pattern facing upward, push a straight pin through all layers at each point to be marked. Turn the piece upside down. With a ruler as a guide, draw a chalk line between the pins, **25-17**. (Draw on the wrong side of the fabric.) Then with this same side facing upward, push pins down through all layers. Turn the piece upside down again. Carefully remove the pattern, easing the tissue over the pinheads. Be careful not to pull out the pins. Again draw chalk lines between the pins.

Chalk lines tend to rub off, so handle the pieces carefully. The chalk will disappear when you launder or dry-clean the garment.

Fabric Marking Pens

Fabric marking pens are another option for transferring pattern markings. These pens contain disappearing ink. Therefore, you can use the pens to transfer markings to either the right or wrong side of your fabric.

The ink may be water soluble, which means that the ink rinses out of the fabric with water. After constructing your garment, wash it to remove the water-soluble pen marks.

Another type of ink evaporates from the fabric. Place air-evaporating pen marks when you are ready to sew. They contain an ink that evaporates in less than 48 hours.

To use a fabric marking pen, stick pins straight through the pattern tissue and both fabric layers at all the marking points. Starting from the outside edges of the pattern, carefully separate the layers of fabric just enough to place an ink dot where the pin is inserted. Mark both layers of fabric. Then remove the pin. Work your way from the outer cut edges to the center or the centerfold until all pins have been marked.

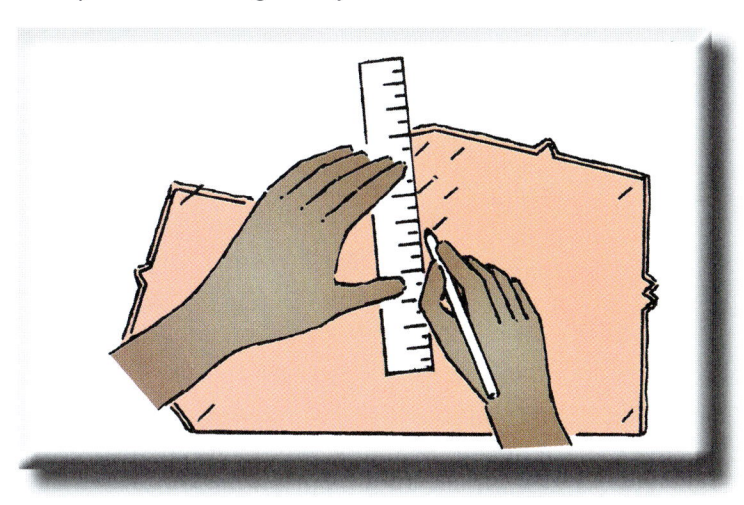

25-17 One way to mark is to insert pins at important construction details. Turn the garment piece over and mark the details with tailor's chalk.
Goodheart-Willcox Publisher

Basting to Transfer Pattern Markings

A good way to mark both the right and wrong sides of a fabric is by basting. To baste, make long, loose stitches by hand or machine. Use a contrasting color of the thread. Basting is sometimes done to transfer other kinds of markings to the right side. These might be used to indicate pockets or buttonholes, *25-18*. Basting takes more time than other marking methods, but it is very accurate. It does not damage the fabric. After using the markings, remove the basting stitches.

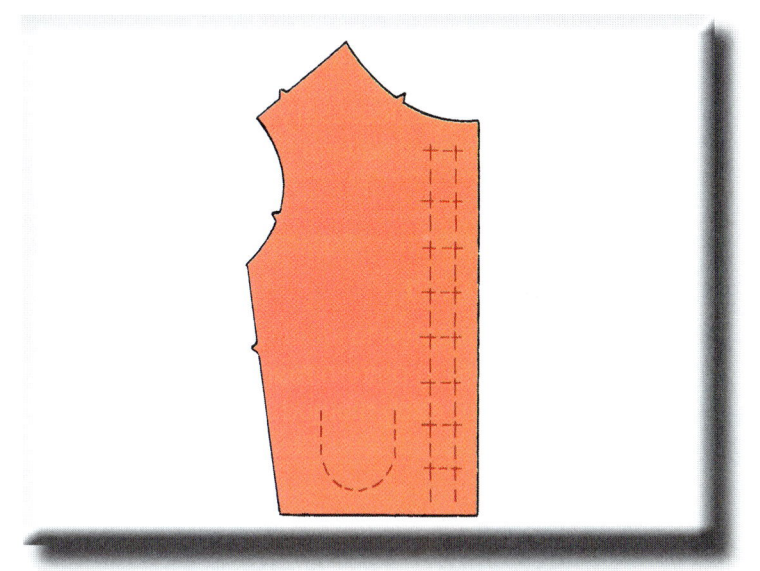

Leave the pattern pieces pinned to the fabric until you are ready to sew them together. This makes the pieces easy to identify.

25-18 Marking garments with basting stitches takes time, but it is neat and accurate.
Goodheart-Willcox Publisher

Summary

- Preshrink the fabric, if necessary, before pinning the pattern to the fabric. You may also need to straighten the grain of the fabric.
- With off-grain fabric, the lengthwise yarns and the crosswise yarns are not at a perfect 90 degree angle to each other. Straighten the fabric by pulling opposite corners.
- Check your measurements with the chart on the pattern envelope. If they are not the same, alter your pattern. Altering patterns is better than altering finished garments.
- The layout shows you how to put your pattern pieces on the fabric for cutting. Find the one that matches your pattern size, project or view, and fabric width.
- Place pins about 6 inches apart. On curved edges or slippery fabric, place them closer together. Pins should not cross cutting lines.
- Cut with long, smooth strokes using bent-handle shears. Cut notches outward to allow for seam adjustments.
- After cutting, transfer necessary markings to the fabric using one of several methods.

Graphic Organizer

Create a fishbone diagram to identify four methods for transferring pattern markings. List two supporting details for each method.

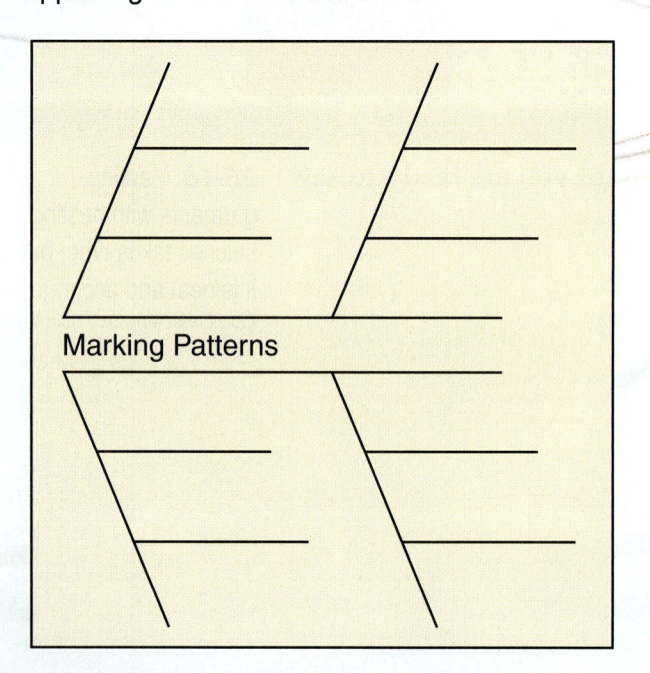

Marking Patterns

Review the Facts

1. How do you decide what method to use to preshrink your fabric?
2. Describe how to find the lengthwise, crosswise, and bias grains of a fabric.
3. Why should the fabric grain be straight before you pin and cut out a garment?
4. Explain one way to identify if the fabric was cut along the crosswise grain.
5. Why should you make alterations to pattern pieces rather than to your garment?
6. Explain how to lengthen a pattern piece in the middle of the pattern.
7. List three fabric folds that pattern layouts sometimes suggest.
8. How should you place the pins when pinning the pattern to the fabric?
9. Summarize how to use dressmaker's tracing paper and a tracing wheel to transfer pattern markings.
10. What is a good way to mark both the right and wrong sides of a garment piece?

Think Critically

11. **Draw conclusions.** What are the advantages of studying the pattern and guide sheet before you begin using them?
12. **Predict consequences.** If you are sewing fabric with nap, predict what might happen if you use a cutting layout for a fabric without nap.
13. **Make inferences.** Determine which marking method you would use for each of the following fabrics: chambray, wool blend, and taffeta. What are the advantages and disadvantages of using each fabric/marking method combination?

Apparel Applications

14. **Determine fabric preparation.** Obtain samples of several types of fabrics and bring them to class. With a classmate, decide whether each requires preshrinking and by which method. Share your ideas with the class.
15. **Grain test.** Pull along the lengthwise, crosswise, and true bias grains of a woven fabric. Notice the lengthwise grain stretches the least. Which stretches the most? Discuss how this knowledge may help you determine which fabric to use.
16. **Alteration practice.** Practice altering the length of patterns. Lengthen one pattern piece at the bottom edge. Shorten a different piece at the adjustment lines. (Undo all practice alterations before using the pattern pieces.)
17. **Guide sheet review.** Study your pattern guide sheet. Make a list of all the types of information provided on the guide sheet. How does this information apply to making your garment?
18. **Fabric-folding demonstration.** On a length of fabric, demonstrate each of the five types of folds described in this chapter.

Academic Connections

19. **Math.** Suppose you need to alter the hip section of a pants pattern to add 2 inches. How much would you need to add to the side seam of the pattern to make this alternation? If you needed to reduce the hip area by 2½ inches, how much would you need to reduce the side seam?
20. **Science.** Test three different ways of marking each of the following types of fabrics: polyester/cotton blend broadcloth, wool suiting, and corduroy. Create a chart to compare the results. Then test wet and dry methods for removing each type of mark. Compare the results and add them to your chart. Share your findings with the class.

Workplace Connections

21. **Layout problem.** Presume you work in a fabric store. Suppose the recommended fabric width for a customer's pattern is 45 inches. Your customer finds a suitable fabric that is 60 inches wide and uses the fabric width conversion chart in the back of the pattern book to determine how much to buy. Your customer asks for your help in determining a layout for this fabric. How would you solve this problem?
22. **Pinning demonstration.** Presume you are working with a 4-H group or scout group on a sewing project. Demonstrate to the group how to accurately pin pattern pieces to fabric following the sewing guide sheet.

Volunteer Sewing

Are there certain organizations in your community that do sewing projects to meet the needs of various target populations—premature infants, cancer patients, or those displaced by natural disasters? If there are, consider using your sewing skills to help meet these needs.

As an individual or team, consider partnering with a community organization to fill clothing needs. Use the FCCLA *Planning Process* to develop a *Community Service* project. See your adviser for information as needed.

Chapter 26

Basic Sewing Skills

Chapter Objectives

After studying this chapter, you will be able to
- **operate** the sewing machine properly.
- **construct** darts and seams.
- **apply** various seam finishes to seams.
- **demonstrate** how to trim, grade, and clip seams.
- **summarize** how to apply facings and interfacings.
- **describe** how to apply various types of fasteners and zippers.
- **demonstrate** how to mark, finish, and secure a hem.
- **demonstrate** pressing techniques.

Key Terms

seam	darts	understitching
seam allowance	seam finish	stitch-in-the-ditch
backstitching	trimming	hem
staystitching	grading	double-fold hem
directional stitching	clipping	bound buttonhole
basting	notching	machine-worked buttonhole
easing	facings	
gathers	clean finish	hand-worked buttonhole

Reading with Purpose

Take time to reread sentences or paragraphs that cause confusion or raise questions. Rereading will clarify content and strengthen your understanding of key concepts.

At this point, you know that a sewing machine is a fine, delicate piece of machinery. You are ready to use it carefully and skillfully.

A quick review of terms will remind you that stitches hold two pieces of fabric together. A row of stitches forms a **seam**. The usual **seam allowance**, or width between the fabric edge and the seam, is ⅝ inch, **26-1**.

26-1 Notice the relationship between a seam and a seam allowance.
Goodheart-Willcox Publisher

Machine Stitching Techniques

Before you start to sew, pull the spool and bobbin threads out about 5 inches behind the presser foot. This prevents the tangling and knotting of thread at the beginning of the seam. Is the take-up lever at its highest point? If not, the thread will pull out of the needle as you start.

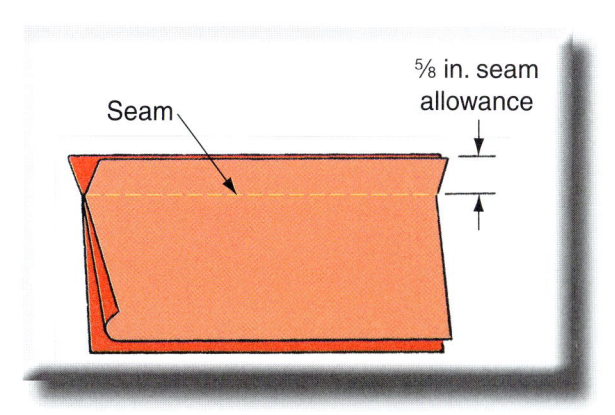

Place the fabric under the presser foot. Keep most of the fabric to the left of the needle so you can see the seam guides on the throat plate. The fabric edges should line up with one of the seam guides. For instance, if you are sewing a ⅝-inch seam, the fabric edges should lie exactly on the ⅝-inch line.

Using your right hand, turn the hand wheel and lower the needle into the starting point. Lower the presser foot with your right hand while holding the fabric with your left hand.

Sew Safely
When using the sewing machine, hold the fabric near the presser foot while keeping your fingers well away from the needle. Use a needle guard on your machine if you have one.

Start to stitch at a slow, constant speed. Keep both hands lightly on the fabric near the presser foot. Do not push or pull the fabric; just guide it. Watch the seam guide, not your line of stitching or the needle, as you sew.

When you stop, move the take-up lever to its highest point by turning the hand wheel if your machine does not do this automatically. Then raise the presser foot and pull the fabric to the back. Cut threads, leaving about 3 inches if you need to tie them to prevent the stitches from coming loose.

As you sew, remove each pin as the presser foot comes to it. If you hit a pin with the machine needle, the needle or pin could bend or break. It is best to remove pins rather than sewing over them if at all possible.

Sometimes you need to turn a corner while stitching, **26-2**. To do this, stitch to within ⅝ inch of the corner. Stop. (Many presser feet are ⅝ inch in length so when the front of the foot reaches the edge of the fabric, it is time to stop and turn.) Be sure the needle is down into the fabric. Lift the presser foot. Turn the fabric. Lower the presser foot, and continue to sew.

Backstitching

Instead of tying threads at the start and end of each seam, you can secure your thread by **backstitching**. Take three or four stitches forward. Then put your machine in reverse and carefully sew backward, directly over the other stitches. Then sew forward again. This locks your stitches so the seam will not pull apart.

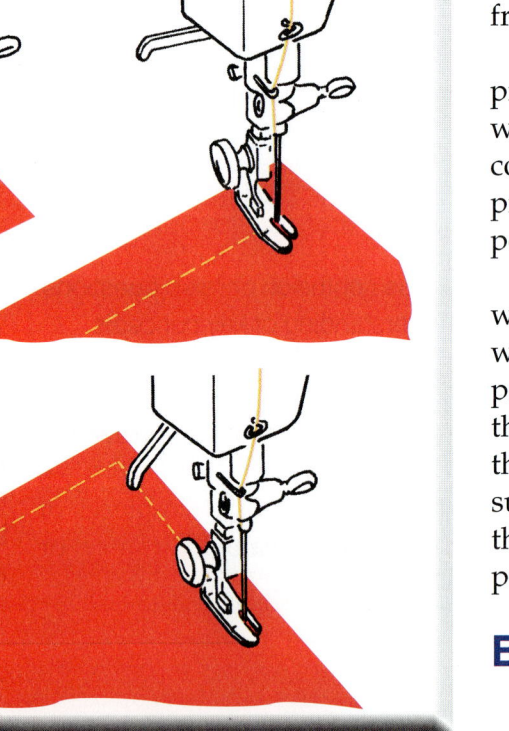

26-2 To turn a corner, insert the needle into the garment. Raise the presser foot, and turn the garment. Lower the foot and sew.
Goodheart-Willcox Publisher

Staystitching

Staystitching is a line of regular machine stitching on a single thickness of fabric that helps stabilize curved or bias fabric edges and prevents them from stretching. It is sewn ⅛ inch or less from the seam line (toward the cut edge). Use the same thread you use to make the garment. Sew around curves and along bias edges.

For many years, staystitching was used on all fabrics. Today, it is used less often. Many modern fabrics do not stretch or fray. The yarns are *locked* into position with finishes. Loosely woven or delicate fabrics still require staystitching.

Directional Stitching

To preserve the position of the fabric grain, use **directional stitching**, or stitching with the grain whenever possible. This helps keep fabrics from stretching out of shape or curling.

To find which direction to sew, you can test each piece yourself. Rub your finger down along a cut edge of a woven fabric. Then rub it up along the same edge. Which way feels smoother? Sew in that direction. As a rule, sew from a wide area to a narrow area, such as a skirt hem edge to the waist, and from the top of a curve to the bottom. Stitch straight edges in either direction. See **26-3** for directional stitching guidelines.

Basting

Basting is a way to temporarily join layers of fabric together until you permanently stitch them on the machine. There are several methods of basting. Using pins is the most common method. Basting can also be done using hand stitching or machine stitching. Use the following guidelines for basting methods:

- *Pin baste.* Place pins perpendicular (pivot at a 90-degree angle) to the seam line when pin basting. Insert the pins at the seam line, but perpendicular to the seam line. The pin heads should be to the right of the presser foot so you can remove them as you stitch.

- *Hand baste.* To hand baste, use a single thread no longer than your arm. Thread the needle with the end that came off the spool of thread first. Your thread will tangle less as you sew. Make a knot in the other end.

- *Machine baste.* Before machine basting, set the stitch length control to 6 or 8 stitches per inch. Sew along the regular seam line. Do not backstitch or knot the thread ends.

26-3 Directional stitching keeps fabrics from stretching out of shape or curling.
Goodheart-Willcox Publisher

To remove the basting stitches without damaging the fabric, clip the top thread every few inches. Then pull the bottom thread. In addition to using basting stitches to transfer pattern markings to garment pieces, it is also helpful to check the fit of a garment. After machine-basting the seams, try on the garment. If it fits, sew over the basting stitches for a permanent seam. If you need to sew a narrower or wider seam, baste again, possibly with another color thread. Remove the first basting stitches, and recheck the fit.

Use hand basting in detail areas where pin basting is not secure enough and machine basting is too difficult to do. It is also best for sheer or slippery fabrics.

Easing

Easing is the process of joining two edges of fabric together when one edge is slightly larger than the other. Easing should not cause visible gathers or pleats to form in the seam line. After stitching, the seam should be smooth. Use easing when making set-in sleeves, joining shoulder seams, and attaching waistbands, **26-4**.

To ease two edges together, follow these steps:

1. Stitch one row of machine basting close to the seam line in the larger piece of fabric.
2. Stitch a second row of stitches ¼ inch away from the first row of stitching in the seam allowance.
3. Pin the ends of the two pieces together with the eased side up. Pull the threads and distribute the fullness evenly. Pin in place.
4. Stitch along the seam line, carefully avoiding the creation of any tucks or folds.

When there is only a small amount of fullness to ease, you may be able to use pins only. To do this, pin the ends of the pieces of fabric and the exact center together. Then pinning as you work, distribute the fullness of the larger piece evenly across the shorter piece.

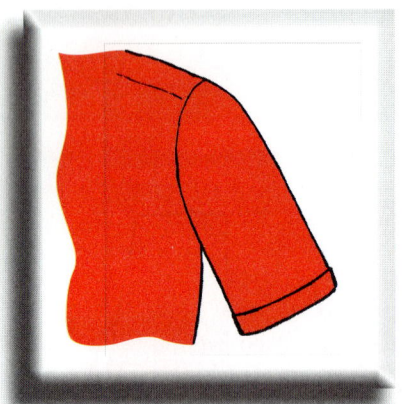

26-4 Set-in sleeves are eased to fit into the armhole of garments.
Goodheart-Willcox Publisher

Gathering

Gathers are tiny, soft folds of fabric that form when you sew a larger piece of fabric to a smaller piece. Puffed sleeves and gathered skirts use gathers, **26-5**. Gathers are fuller than easing.

To gather, follow these steps:

1. Sew one row of machine basting (6 to 8 stitches per inch) next to the regular seam line in the seam allowance.
2. Sew another row of machine basting ¼ inch away from the seam line toward the cut edge. Leave long threads at both ends.
3. With the right sides of the fabric together, pin the edges together matching notches, seams, and other markings.
4. Gently pull both bobbin threads, gathering up the full edge until it lies flat against the shorter edge between the pins. Fasten these threads by wrapping them in a figure eight around the pin at the end, **26-6**.
5. Repeat from the other end of the machine stitching.
6. Arrange the gathers evenly and place additional pins perpendicular to the stitching.
7. Stitch the gathered piece to the matching piece with the gathered side up. Backstitch at the beginning of the seam to secure stitches. Stitch slowly as you hold the gathers to prevent any folds from forming in the seam. Remove pins as you sew.
8. Backstitch to secure the end of the seam.

26-5 The extra fabric in puffed sleeves is gathered to fit into the armhole seam.
Goodheart-Willcox Publisher

Darts

Darts provide shape and fullness to a garment so it fits the curves of the body. Darts should point to the fullest part of body curves. For instance, on slacks and skirts, darts begin at the waistline and taper to the hipline. This allows fullness around the hips. In jackets, blouses, and shirts, darts taper to the fullest part of the bust or chest. Sew darts before sewing other seams in a garment. This is because darts cross other seam lines.

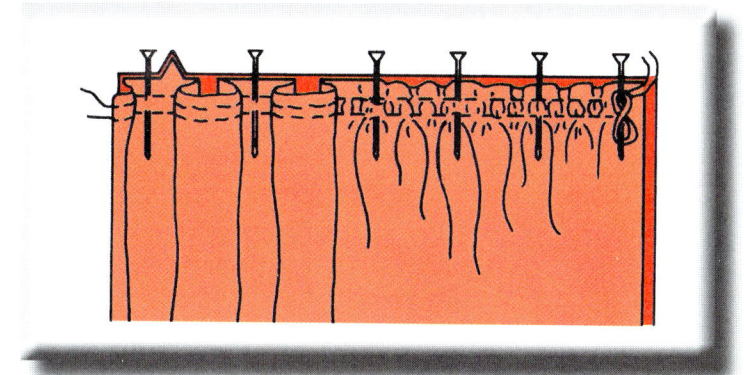

To make a dart, begin at the widest end of the dart and sew to the point. To prevent the point from puckering, the last three stitches should be made on the fold, 26-7. You can backstitch at the wide end of the dart to secure the stitching, however, never backstitch at the point. Instead, tie the threads securely by hand at the point of the dart.

If you are sewing a dart with two points, start stitching at the center of the dart and stitch to the point at one end. Then turn your work over, and place your needle in the spot where you began for the other end of the dart. Stitch to the point at other end. Tie the threads at both points. However, you can backstitch in the center of the dart to secure the threads.

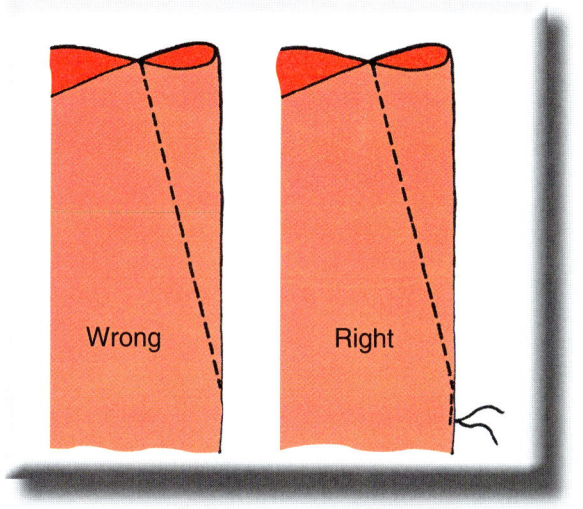

26-6 Secure the threads by wrapping them around a pin. Then pull the other ends to gather. *Goodheart-Willcox Publisher*

Pressing Darts

The next step is to press the darts. Press darts along the stitching line, from the widest end to the point. Use a pressing ham to add shape as you press. Press vertical darts toward the center front or center back. Press horizontal darts downward. If a dart is wide or made of bulky fabric, you can slash it to within 1 inch of the point and press it open.

26-7 To prevent the fabric from puckering at the point of the dart, make the last three stitches of the dart on the fold. *Goodheart-Willcox Publisher*

Seams and Seam Finishes

Most seams in apparel construction are plain seams. These seams may need a seam finish to prevent the edges from raveling. There are other types of seams that you may want to use. These include the topstitched, flat-fell, welt, and French seams.

Plain Seams

The most common seam is the *plain seam*. It is suitable for all areas of a garment and for most fabrics except sheers and laces. The machine stitch length is usually 10 to 12 stitches per inch.

To make a plain seam:

1. Place the right sides together, matching the cut edges and notches. Insert pins at ends and notches. Then insert pins about 5 inches apart along the rest of the seam line. Pins should be perpendicular to the seam line. The heads of the pins should lie within the seam allowance.

2. Sew along the seam line. Secure the threads at both ends by backstitching. Be sure to remove the pins as you sew.

Figure 26-8 shows the three steps in pressing open a plain seam.

1. Press the seam flat with right sides together.
2. Open the two garment pieces. With the wrong side up, press the seam open. For best results, use a seam roll for this step. The seam roll lets the garment fall away from the seam so the edges of the seam will not show through to the right side. Use only the tip of the iron when pressing seams open.
3. Press the seam open with right sides up, using a dry press cloth between the iron and your fabric.

Topstitched Seams

The *topstitched seam* is a plain seam with a row of machine stitching on one or both sides of the seam line. Topstitched seams are often used for a decorative effect on sport clothes. You will find topstitching on pockets and pleats or to emphasize seam lines.

To make a topstitched seam, first stitch a plain seam. For one row of stitching, press the seam allowance to one side. Topstitch the desired distance from the seam on the right side of the fabric through all three thicknesses, 26-9.

For two rows of stitching, press the seam allowance open. Topstitch on both sides of the seam line through both layers of fabric.

When topstitching collars, cuffs, or pockets, stitch carefully and slowly. Use your presser foot as a guide to sew the same distance from the seam line on each piece. A slightly longer stitch helps create more attractive lines of stitching on the outside of the garment.

Flat-fell Seams

Flat-fell seams are decorative, yet strong and functional. Whenever raw edges are not desirable, this seam is ideal. They are often used on shirts, undergarments, sportswear, jeans, pajamas, and other clothing receiving hard wear, 26-10. They are suitable for all fabrics except those that are very heavy. Straight or slightly curved areas are appropriate for this type of seam.

To make a flat-fell seam:

1. Stitch a plain seam with the wrong sides together.
2. Trim the under seam allowance to ⅛ inch.
3. Press the seam to one side with the wider part covering the trimmed seam allowance.
4. Turn under the edge of the top seam allowance and evenly fold it over the trimmed edge.
5. Stitch close to the folded edge through all thicknesses. Keep the right side of the garment up as you sew.

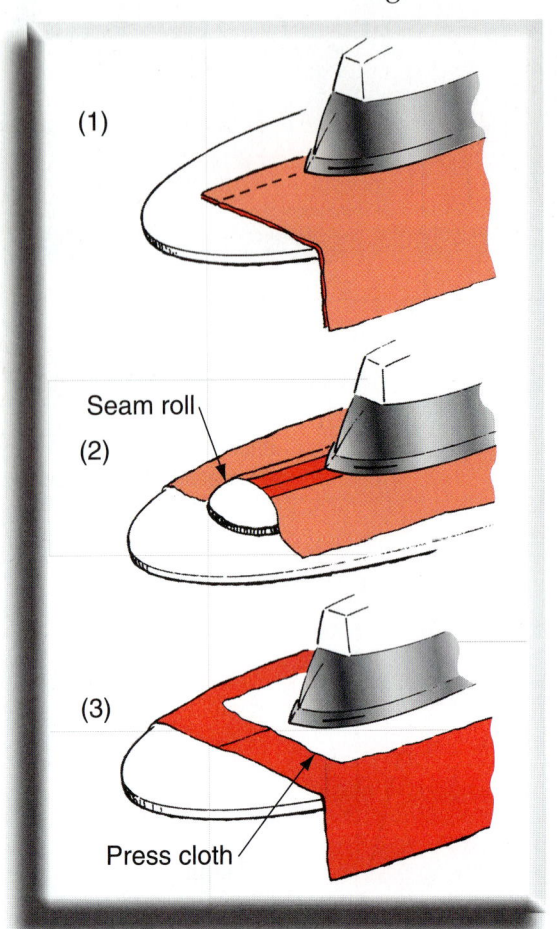

26-8 Follow these steps when pressing a plain seam. (1) Press with right sides together. (2) Press seam open, wrong sides up. (3) Press seam open, right sides up.
Goodheart-Willcox Publisher

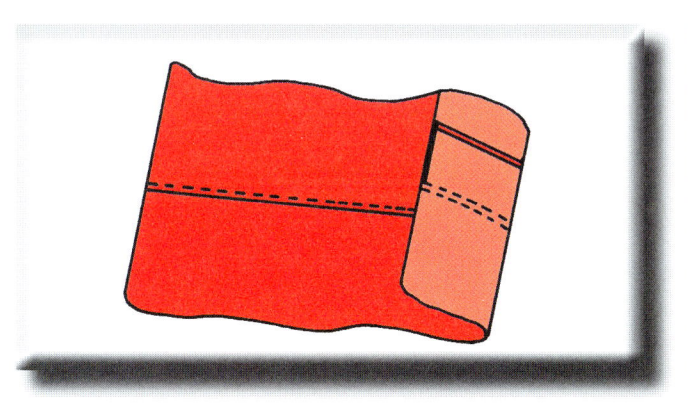

26-9 Topstitched seams create a decorative effect on garments. *Goodheart-Willcox Publisher*

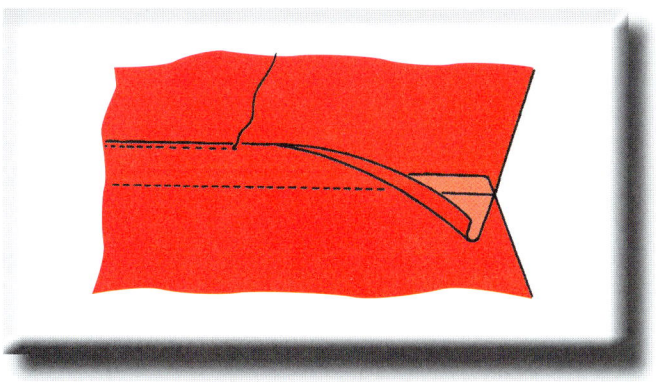

26-10 Flat-fell seams provide sturdy construction on jeans and sportswear. *Goodheart-Willcox Publisher*

Welt Seams

Welt seams are a variation of the flat-fell seam, but are less bulky, **26-11**. For this reason, they are often used on heavy fabrics. They are easier to sew and can be used on straight or slightly curved seams.

To make a welt seam:

1. Sew a plain seam with right sides together.
2. Trim one seam allowance to ¼ inch.
3. Press the other seam allowance over the trimmed edge.
4. With right sides up, stitch through the outer fabric and the wider seam allowance. The distance between the seam line and the second row of stitching can vary, depending on the look you want.
5. For a padded look, press the seam, right side down, over a bath towel.

French Seams

A *French seam* is a narrow seam within a seam, **26-12**, and is useful on fabrics that ravel easily. It is also an ideal seam for sheer fabrics because no raw edges show. Use French seams only for straight seams.

To make a French seam:

1. Place the fabric wrong sides together and pin.
2. Stitch about ¼ inch from the edge.
3. Trim the seam to ⅛ inch.

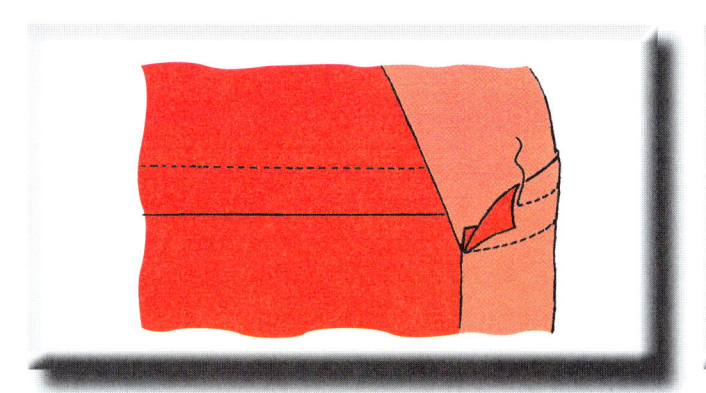

26-11 A welt seam is a good choice for heavy fabrics. *Goodheart-Willcox Publisher*

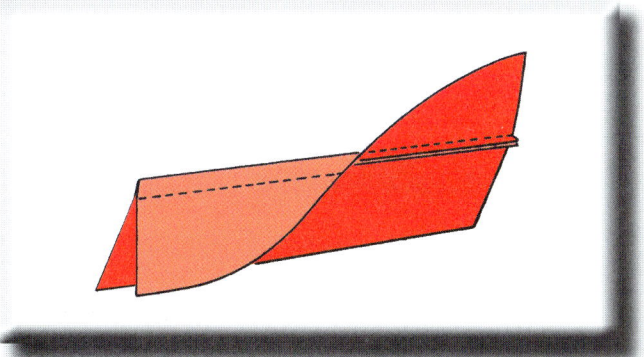

26-12 A French seam provides an attractive finish for sheer fabrics. *Goodheart-Willcox Publisher*

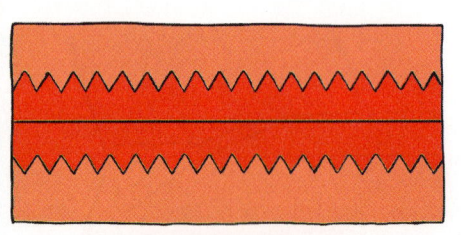

Pinked seams finishes should be used only on fabrics that do not ravel.

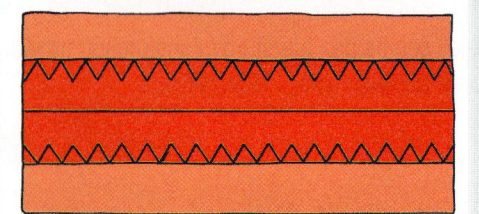

A zigzag finish is easy to do with a zigzag setting on the sewing machine.

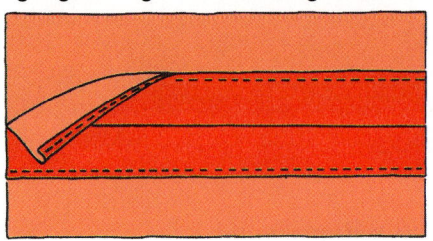

A turned and stitched finish is a good choice for lightweight fabrics.

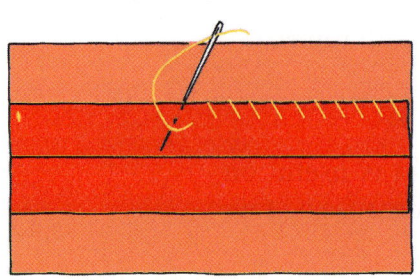

A hand overcast finish prevents raveling on bulky fabrics.

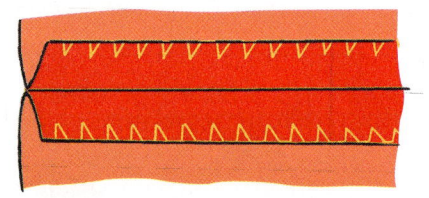

A serger can be used to make a machine overcast finish.

26-13 Choose one of these seam finishes based on the weight of the fabric and if it ravels easily. *Goodheart-Willcox Publisher*

4. Press the seam flat.
5. Fold the right sides together and stitch ¼ inch from edge. This will enclose the first seam in the second seam.
6. Press the seam to one side, working from the inside (wrong side) of the garment.

Seam Finishes

A **seam finish** is a way of treating a seam edge to prevent raveling and to make the seam stronger and longer wearing. Many firmly woven fabrics do not need seam finishes. The yarns are locked together and do not ravel. Most knits and nonwoven fabrics do not need seam finishes. Loosely-woven and sheer fabrics do require seam finishes. There are several ways to finish seams, 26-13.

Pinked Finish

Pinked seam finishes look nice, but they do not prevent raveling. Use them only on fabrics that do not ravel. To improve the durability of this seam finish, machine stitch ¼ inch from the edge of the seam allowance before pinking the edges.

After sewing the seam, press it flat. Pink the edges. Then place the seam on a seam roll and press it open.

Machine Zigzag Finish

Your machine likely has a zigzag setting. A *machine zigzag finish* is quick and easy, and it prevents raveling. It puckers less than a line of straight stitches because it has more *give*. This finish works best on medium and heavyweight fabrics.

Press the seam open. Adjust the stitch width, using a narrower stitch width for lightweight fabrics and a wider one for heavyweight fabrics. Stitch close to the edge of the seam allowance through a single layer of fabric.

Turned and Stitched Finish

A *turned and stitched seam finish* looks neat and prevents raveling. Consider using this finish for unlined jackets of lightweight fabrics, or edges of facings for sheer and lightweight fabrics. It is too bulky for medium and heavyweight fabrics.

After stitching the seam, press it open. Turn the edges under ¼ inch. Stitch close to the fold.

Hand Overcast

Fabrics that are bulky or that ravel easily may require a *hand-overcast finish*. It prevents raveling, and it leaves a flat seam. The disadvantage is that it takes a lot of time.

Press the seam open. Trim all notches and frayed edges. Using a single thread, sew a loose overcast stitch. Do each seam allowance separately.

Machine Overcast

Sergers and some sewing machines can make a *machine-overcast finish*. Firm, medium-weight fabrics are candidates for this type of finish. The stitches are more bulky than hand-overcast stitches.

Press the seam open. Stitch through a single layer of the seam allowance. The needle should move back and forth across the cut edge of the seam allowance. It should reach only slightly outside the cut edge.

Seam Treatments

In some garment areas, a regular seam allowance is too bulky. This is especially so in enclosed areas such as necklines, collars, and cuffs. Curved seams and corners also will be bulky. You can eliminate this bulk by trimming, grading, and clipping seams.

Trimming

Trimming is cutting off part of the seam allowance. To trim a seam, cut away part of the seam allowance, leaving a ⅛- to ¼-inch seam allowance. Curved areas, such as the underarm section of an armhole seam or the center back seam of pants, are usually trimmed to ¼ inch.

Trim corners and points before turning and pressing them. Collars and cuffs, for example, will lie smooth and flat if you trim them before turning. To trim a right-angle corner, cut diagonally across the seam allowance. Cut close to the stitching, but not through it, **26-14**.

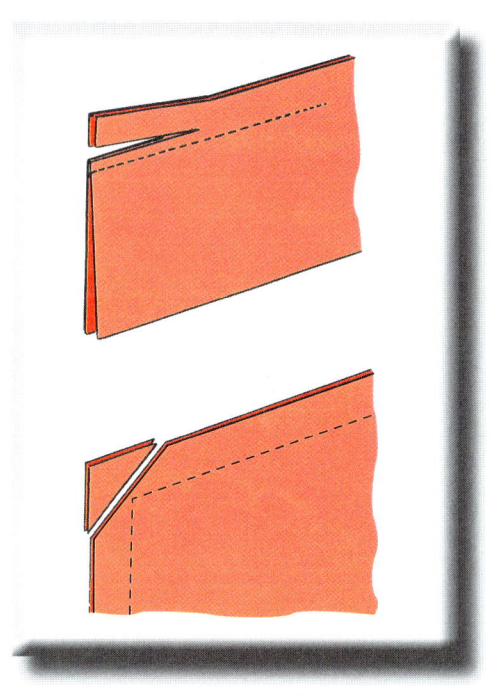

Grading

For heavier fabrics or for places with three layers of fabric, grading is better. **Grading** involves trimming each seam allowance to a different width. This prevents a ridge from showing on the outside of the garment. Enclosed seams—such as collars, cuffs, pockets, and facings—are good candidates for grading.

When grading a seam, make sure the seam allowance closest to the outside of the garment is the widest. This will prevent press marks from showing on the finished side of the garment. Trim this seam allowance to ¼ inch. Trim the other seam allowance to ⅛ inch.

If a corner has a sharper point, as the one in **26-15**, cut diagonally across the seam allowance. Then make another cut on each side of the corner to remove the extra fabric.

26-14 To remove bulk, trim seams to ⅛ inch or ¼ inch. Trim corners at right angles.
Goodheart-Willcox Publisher

Clipping and Notching

Curved seams will not lie flat unless they are clipped. **Clipping** is making straight cuts into the seam allowance. It is done after the seam is trimmed or graded.

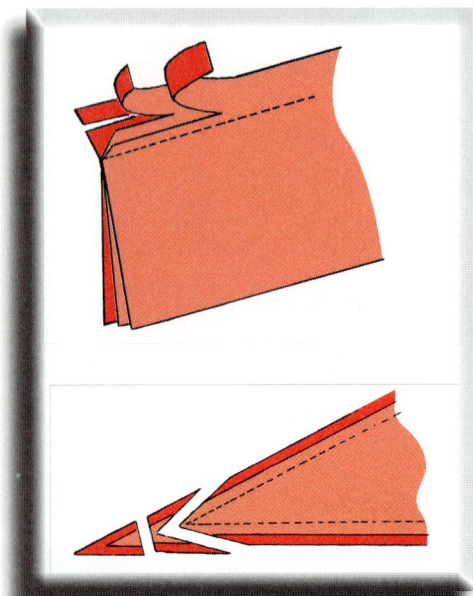

26-15 Grading seams means cutting each seam allowance to a different width. As illustrated, grade and clip sharp.
Goodheart-Willcox Publisher

To clip, use the tips of sharp shears. Cut to within ⅛ inch of the seam line, but not through it. If you have staystitched the seam, clip to the staystitching. Clip every ¼ inch to ½ inch depending on the sharpness of the curve.

When a seam curves inward, use the tips of your shears to clip straight into the seam allowance, allowing the seam to curve without puckering. Necklines, armholes, and waistlines are inward curves. When a seam curves outward, use the **notching** process—with the tips of your shears clip V-shaped sections from the seam allowance without cutting through the stitching. See 26-16. When the seam is turned, the remaining notches will come together to make a flat, even seam. Rounded collars and pockets are outward curves.

Facings

Facings cover the raw edges in a garment such as at the armholes, neckline, or other garment openings. In addition to covering the raw edge, facings add some firmness to the open areas and keep them from stretching out of shape. They do not usually show on the right side of the garment.

There are three main types of facings: extended, fitted, and bias. See 26-17.

- *Extended facing.* An extended facing is cut as part of a garment piece. The facing part is then folded to the inside. Front or back openings often use an extended facing. Your pattern will indicate when a facing is an extended one.

- *Fitted facing.* A fitted facing, or a shaped facing, is cut the same shape as the raw edge of the garment and is a separate pattern piece. Stitch the facing to the matching garment edge and turn it to the inside of the garment.

- *Bias facing.* Another type of facing is a bias facing. This is a narrow strip of bias fabric you stitch to the edge that requires a facing. Necklines, armholes, and other gently curved edges often have bias facings. You can cut bias strips of fabric or purchase ready-made bias tape in a matching color. After attaching the narrow facing to the garment edge, the free edge is hand stitched or topstitched to the garment.

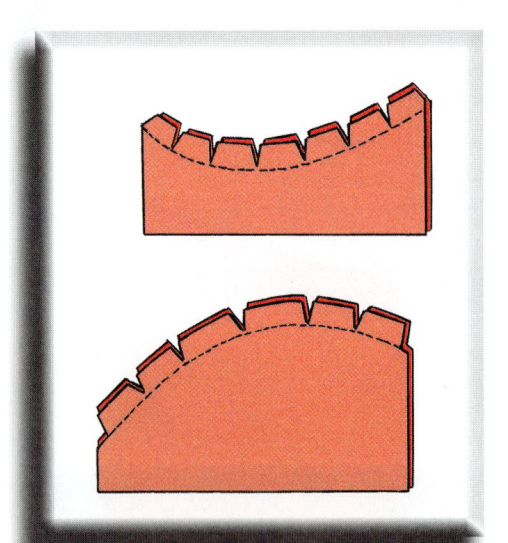

Stitching the Facing

The first step in constructing a fitted facing is to sew the facing pieces together. Then finish the outer free edges to prevent raveling. There are several ways to finish the edges, depending on the weave and weight of the fabric. Use the following guidelines:

- *Clean finish.* Light to medium-weight fabrics can use clean finish. To **clean finish** the facing edge, first staystitch ¼ inch from the raw edge. Then fold the edge of the facing under along the line of stitching. Stitch again close to the folded edge.

26-16 Clip straight into inward curves. Clip V-shaped sections out of outward curves.
Goodheart-Willcox Publisher

- *Pinked finish.* If the fabric does not ravel easily, a pinked edge will offer an attractive finish. Machine stitch the facing edge ¼ inch from the unnotched edge. Trim the edge with pinking shears.
- *Overcast finish.* On heavy fabrics that ravel easily, overcast the raw edge either by hand or by machine.

Attaching the Facing

To attach the facing to the garment, follow these steps:

1. Pin the right sides together matching notches and seams.
2. Stitch the facing to the garment. Backstitch at the beginning and ending of the seam to secure the stitches.
3. Trim, grade, and clip the seam as needed.
4. Press the seam toward the facing.
5. Understitching the seam gives the edge a crisp finish and prevents the facing from rolling to the outside. **Understitching** is a row of stitching you sew close to the seam line through the facing and the seam allowances. When understitching, sew on the right side of the facing, keeping the seam allowances toward the facing. Pull the fabric slightly on either side of the seam line as you sew, **26-18**.
6. Turn the facing to the inside and press.
7. Fasten or tack the free edge of the facing to the seam allowances with hand stitches. A quicker option is to **stitch-in-the-ditch** on the outside of the garment. Using short machine stitches, stitch directly into the *well* of the seam through all layers of fabric.

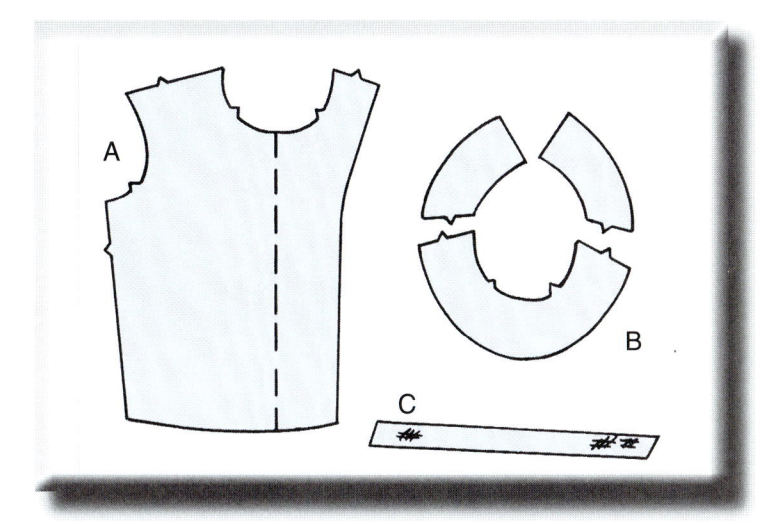

26-17 The three types of facings are (A) extended, (B) fitted, and (C) bias.
Goodheart-Willcox Publisher

26-18 Understitching the facing to the seam allowances helps to hold the facing in place.
Goodheart-Willcox Publisher

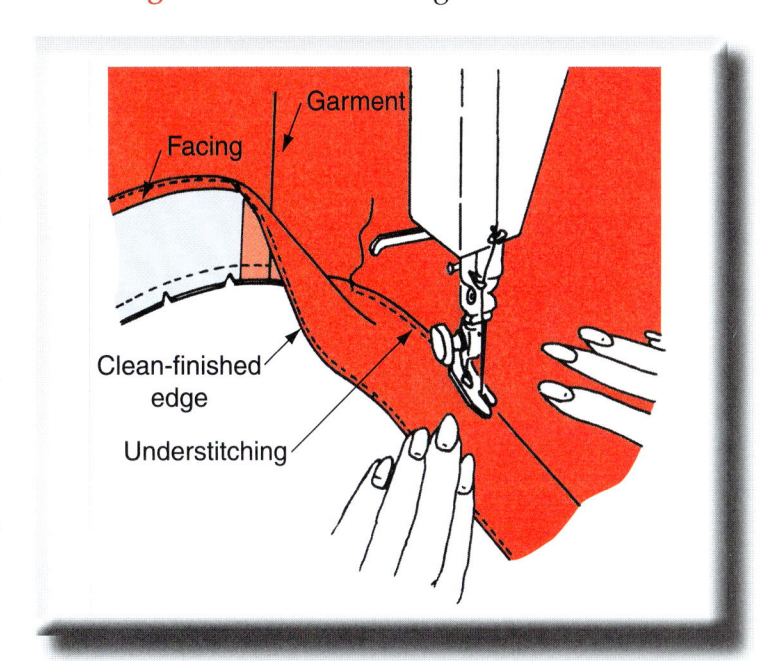

Interfacing

Interfacing is a layer of fabric between the garment and the facing. It adds body and firmness to the outer fabric. It also prevents stretching and provides extra reinforcement. You will use interfacing in collars, cuffs, lapels, facings, and waistbands, and in areas of such stress as under buttons and around buttonholes. See **26-19**. Interfacing gives garments a better appearance and makes them more durable.

A wide variety of interfacing fabrics are available. Consider the look you want to achieve. A heavier-weight interfacing gives a crisp look whereas a lighter weight gives a softer look. As a general rule, choose an interfacing that is a little lighter in weight than your garment fabric.

Read the care requirements carefully before you buy. Make sure the cleaning requirements for the interfacing are the same as the finished garment. For instance, if you plan to wash the garment, you want to use a washable interfacing fabric. Also verify that the interfacing is preshrunk if you are using it in a washable garment.

Types of Interfacing Fabrics

There are three main types of interfacing fabrics: woven, nonwoven, and fusible.

- *Woven interfacings.* Because woven interfacings have grain, you must cut the pattern pieces with the same grain as the facing and outer fabric. Woven interfacings come in a wide range of weights and work best with woven fabrics.

- *Nonwoven interfacings.* Because they have no grain, nonwoven interfacings can be cut in any direction. They do not ravel, are preshrunk, and are washable and dry-cleanable. Nonwoven interfacings are available in various weights. All-bias types stretch in all directions. They can be used on all fabrics. However, use interfacings with no stretch mainly for craft and decorating projects.

- *Fusible interfacings.* These interfacings have a resin on one side of the fabric that melts with heat and moisture and bonds to the fabric pieces. Fusible interfacings may be woven, nonwoven, or knit. Use fusible interfacings with garment fabrics that are firm to avoid having the outline of the interfacing show on the outside. They are also useful in waistbands and for stabilizing buttonholes if the fabric ravels easily.

26-19 Interfacing (white areas) provides a framework within a garment to shape, support, and stabilize.
Pellon, Div. of Freudenberg Nonwovens

Attaching Interfacing Fabrics

You must sew woven and nonwoven interfacings to the garment. Follow these steps:

1. Pin the interfacing to the wrong side of the fabric.
2. Machine baste ½ inch from the fabric edge.
3. Trim the interfacing close to the stitching line.
4. Cut diagonally ¼ inch across any interfacing corners to reduce bulk. Do not cut the garment fabric.

To attach fusible interfacings:

1. Trim away all seam allowances, hem allowances, and corners.
2. Place the adhesive side of the interfacing on the wrong side of your fabric.
3. Fuse following the manufacturer's directions, 26-20.

You can also apply fusible interfacings to the garment facings rather than to the outer garment fabric. This prevents the edge of the interfacing from showing on the outside of the garment.

Zippers

Zippers come in all lengths, weights, styles, and colors. The back of your pattern envelope lists the length and type of zipper you need.

Preshrink zippers that have cotton tape. Polyester tapes do not require preshrinking. Then press the tape to remove any packaging folds. Do not press the coils (teeth) of nylon or polyester zippers. A hot iron will melt them.

Most zippers are sewn into place by machine. To do this, you must change the regular presser foot to a *zipper foot*. See 26-21. You can stitch closer to the zipper coils when using a zipper foot.

There are several methods, or *zipper applications*, for attaching a zipper to the garment. Your pattern guide sheet will recommend which method to use. The two most common methods are centered and lapped. Invisible zipper application is another method.

26-20 For fusible interfacing to fuse properly, you need steam, heat, and pressure. Place a press cloth over the garment part. *Pellon, Div. of Freudenberg Nonwovens*

Centered Zippers

You can use *centered zippers* at center front and center back openings. Center the zipper coils in the seam line. Use two rows of stitching—one on each side of the seam line. The two rows are an equal distance from the seam line, usually ⅜ inch.

Follow these steps for a centered zipper application:

1. Find the two garment pieces that you will join with the zipper. Put the right sides together and pin along the seam line.
2. Measure the zipper length and add 1 inch. From the top of the seam line, measure down this distance. Mark that point with tailor's chalk.
3. Sew a regular seam, beginning at the bottom edge of the garment piece and ending at the chalk mark. Backstitch to secure thread ends. Then move the stitch length control to the longest possible stitch. Baste the rest of the seam on the seam line.
4. Press the seam open.
5. Remove the presser foot, and attach the zipper foot. Adjust the zipper foot so the foot is to the right of the needle.
6. Open the zipper. Keep the zipper pull pointing toward the top of the zipper.

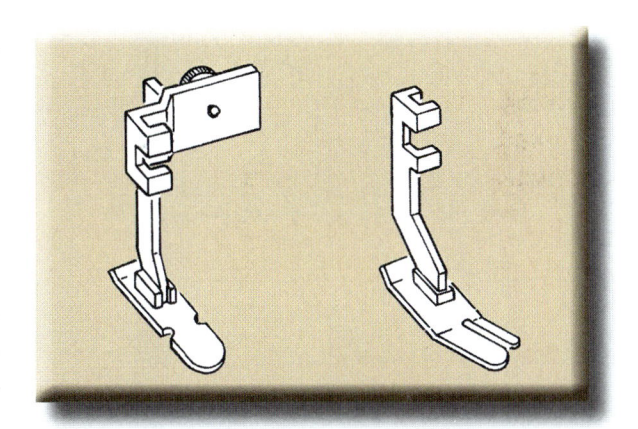

26-21 A zipper foot (left) lets you sew closer to the zipper coils than a regular presser foot (right). *Goodheart-Willcox Publisher*

Place the zipper face down on the seam allowance. Match the bottom stop of the zipper to the start of the basting stitches. One side of the zipper's coil should lie just next to the seam line. Pin in place. See **26-22**.

7. Machine baste from bottom to top, stitching through the zipper tape and the seam allowance only. When you sew next to the pull tab, tilt the tab to make the zipper tape lie flat against the fabric. Remove the pins as you sew.
8. Adjust the zipper foot so it is to the left of the needle. Place the other side of the zipper's coil on the seam line. Pin in place, **26-23**.
9. Baste from bottom to top, stitching through the zipper tape and the other seam allowance, removing the pins as you sew.
10. Close the zipper. Set the stitch control at 10 to 12 stitches per inch. Move the zipper foot to the right side of the needle.
11. Place the garment flat, with the right side up. Position the zipper foot with the needle to the left side to sew the right side of the zipper. Sew the zipper to the garment, stitching through the garment, seam allowance, and zipper tape. Stitch from the seam line ⅜ inch across the bottom of the zipper. Stop with the needle in the fabric and turn the garment 90 degrees (pivot). Continue stitching the length of the zipper ⅜ inch from the seam line to the top of the zipper. Reposition the zipper foot with the needle on the right side. Stitch the left side of the zipper in the same way, **26-24**.

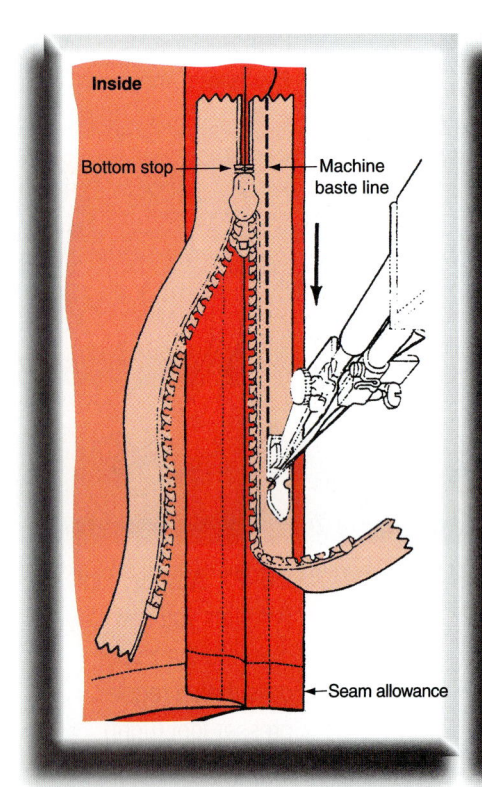

26-22 Machine baste the zipper tape to the seam allowance only. *Talon, Inc.*

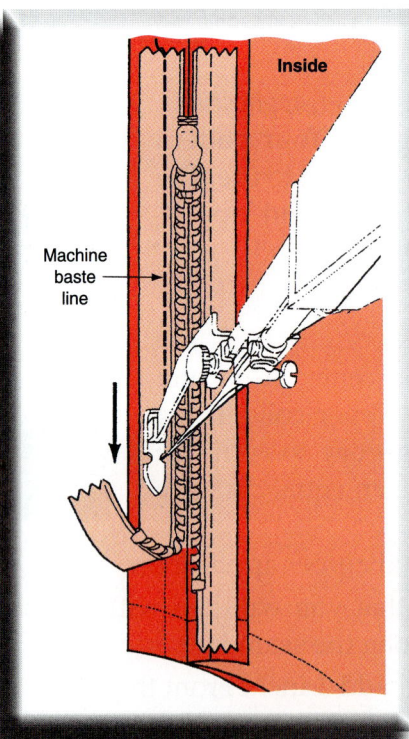

26-23 The second row of stitches attaches the other side of the zipper tape to the seam allowance only. *Talon, Inc.*

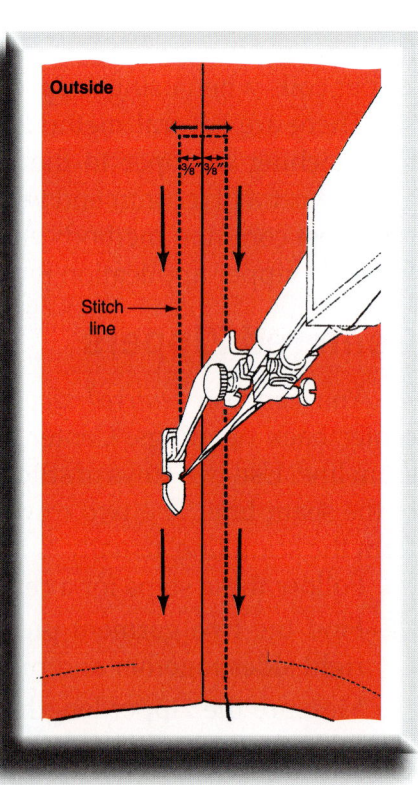

26-24 For the final step, close the zipper and readjust stitch to regular length. Turn the garment right side up. Beginning at the bottom seam line, stitch across the bottom ⅜ inch, pivot, and stitch through the tape, seam allowance, and garment to the top of the zipper. *Talon, Inc.*

12. Remove the basting stitches in the seam line. If the seam puckers, remove the basting stitches in the seam allowances. Press.

Lapped Zippers

In a *lapped zipper application*, one side of the zipper opening forms a lap over the zipper. The zipper coil is less visible in lapped zippers than in centered zippers. Most openings in side seams are closed with lapped zippers because the lap hides the zipper from view. You can also use lapped zippers for other garment openings, such as the center back.

Follow these steps for a lapped zipper application:

1. Sew, baste, and press the zipper seam as for a centered zipper.
2. Attach the zipper foot so it is to the right of the needle. Open the zipper. Place the bottom stop of the zipper on top of the first basting stitch. The coil should lie exactly on the seam line, **26-25**.
3. Machine baste through the zipper tape and the right seam allowance, sewing from bottom to top. Stitch very close to the zipper coil. As you sew next to the pull tab, tilt it so you can keep your stitches straight.
4. Close the zipper. Turn it right side up. This creates a fold along the stitches just sewn.
5. Move the zipper foot to the left of the needle. Readjust stitch to regular length. Stitch very close to the edge of the fold, **26-26**. Sew from bottom to top.

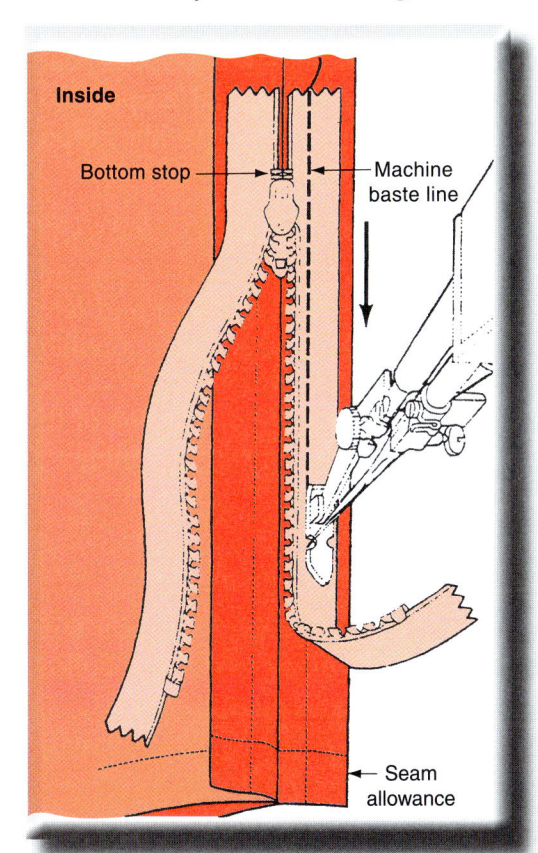

26-25 Machine baste one side of the zipper to the seam allowance only using a zipper foot. *Talon, Inc.*

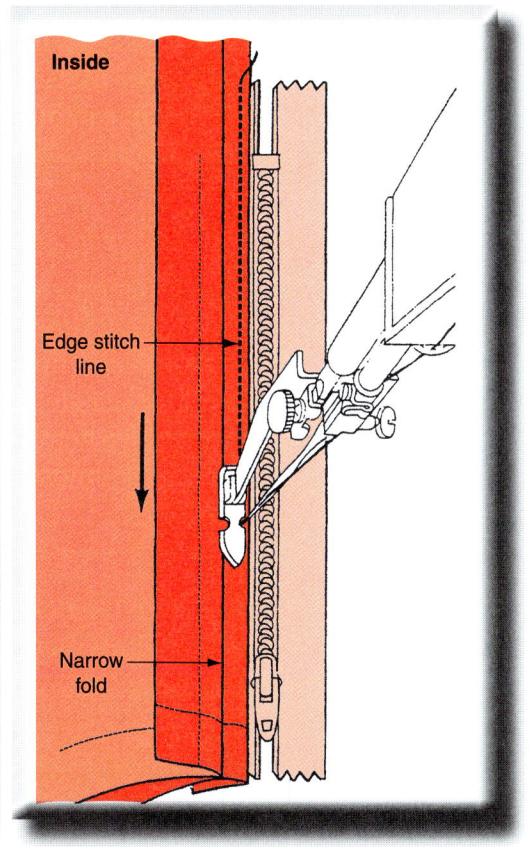

26-26 Readjust stitch to regular length. Close zipper and turn face up. Move the zipper foot to the left of the needle. Edge stitch on the fold. Begin at the bottom of the tape and continuing to the top of the zipper. *Talon, Inc.*

6. With the right side up, sew across the bottom of the zipper from the seam line and out ⅜ inch. Stop and turn the garment 90 degrees and stitch up the side of the zipper ⅜ inch from the seam line to the top of the zipper, 26-27. Stitch through the zipper coil, seam allowance, and garment.
7. Pull the threads at the bottom of the zipper to the wrong side. Tie a knot to secure them.
8. Remove the basting stitches.

The *fly front zipper* is a variation of the lapped zipper. The difference is that the seam allowance is extra wide for the fly front zipper to allow for a larger lap. If your pattern calls for a fly front zipper, the guide sheet will give complete directions.

Invisible Zippers

From the right side of a garment, an *invisible zipper* looks like a regular seam. The pull tab is the only clue to the zipper placement. See 26-28.

Sew invisible zippers in an open seam. Sew the rest of the seam after the zipper is in place. To attach this type of zipper, follow the steps in the zipper package. Invisible zippers require a special zipper foot. You can buy this foot where you purchase the zipper.

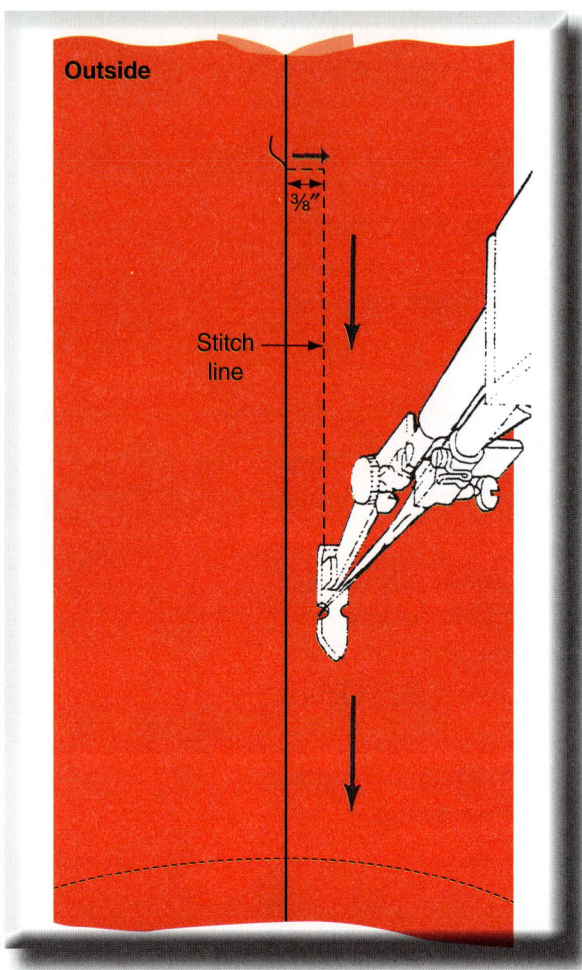

26-27 Spread the garment flat with the right side up and the zipper facing the feed dogs of the machine. Beginning at the seam line at the zipper bottom, stitch ⅜ inch across the bottom, pivot, and up the side of the zipper, stitching through all layers. Bring the thread ends to the underside and tie.
Talon, Inc.

Hems

When all other construction steps are done, press the garment and let it hang for a day. This will give it time to stretch to its final shape. Then it will be ready to hem. A **hem** produces a finished edge on a garment.

Hemming is one of the last steps in sewing a garment, but it is one of the most important. Whether the hemline is above the knee or at the ankles, it should be smooth, even, and almost invisible.

Marking a Hem

Try on the garment with the undergarments and shoes you will wear with it. Also, wear jackets and belts if they will be a part of the finished outfit. Follow these steps to mark the hem:

1. Stand in front of a long mirror, and test several different lengths. When you decide on the length that is best for you, mark it with a pin.
2. Mark the hem location. Use a skirt marker, yardstick, or meterstick. The easiest way to mark an even hem on a dress or skirt is to have someone help you. As you stand still looking straight ahead, the other person can move around you. Measure up from the floor to the desired hemline. Place pins parallel to the floor and about 3 inches apart. For pants, fold under at the top of the shoe in the front. The hem edge should just touch the shoe.

Chapter 26   Basic Sewing Skills   459

In the back, the hemline should be about ½ inch longer than the top of the shoe.

3. Double-check the length by folding the fabric up at the marked line. Turn it inside the garment, and pin it. Is the hem parallel to the floor? Do you like the length?
4. Remove the garment. Move the pins so they are at right angles to the cut edge of the hem. Baste close to the hemline, 26-29. Match the seam lines in the hem to the seam lines in the garment.
5. Decide how wide the hem should be. The pattern pieces suggest a hem width. Use this as a guide. With a ruler or sewing gauge, measure the desired distance up from the hemline, 26-30. Mark the line with tailor's chalk.
6. Cut along the marked line. Be careful to cut only the extra hem allowance; do not cut into the garment.

Removing Extra Fullness in Hems

When a garment is flared, the hem does not lie flat. The extra fabric puckers at the upper edge. This extra fullness must be eased in to fit flat against the garment. To ease:

1. Machine baste ¼ inch from the cut edge of the hem.
2. Turn the hem up. Pin the hem to the garment at each seam line.
3. Pick up the bobbin thread with a pin. Pull up gently to slightly gather the fabric on both sides, 26-31. Repeat this several times, until all extra fullness is gathered and spread evenly around the garment.

The hem will look smoother if you remove some of the gathered fullness by shrinking. Do this with steam. To shrink:

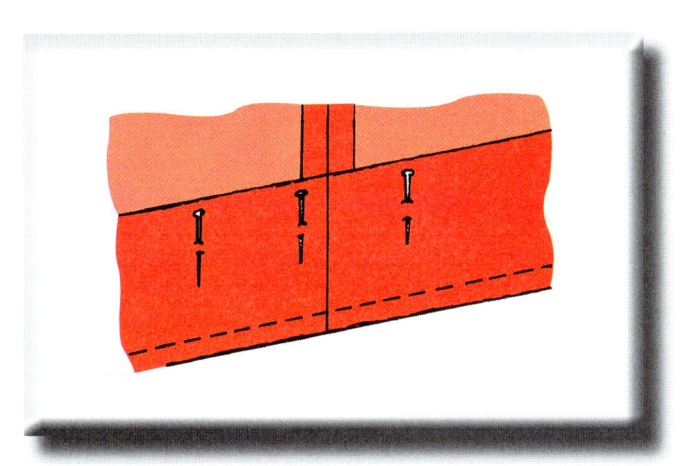

26-28 Only the pull tab of the invisible zipper can be seen on the outside of the garment. No stitches show. *Jack Klasey*

26-29 To hold the hem in place, insert pins at right angles to the cut edge of the hem. Baste close to the hemline. *Goodheart-Willcox Publisher*

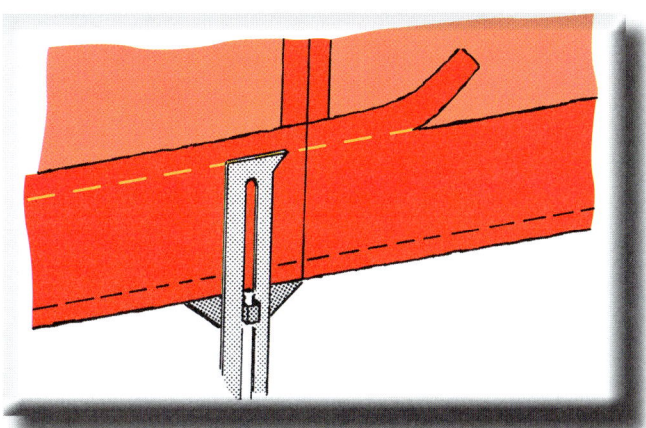

26-30 Mark the width of the hem with tailor's chalk. Cut off the extra fabric. *Goodheart-Willcox Publisher*

1. Place a piece of brown paper between the hem and the garment to prevent press marks.
2. Hold the steam iron slightly above the hem, letting the steam penetrate the fabric.
3. Flatten the gathers with your fingers, keeping your fingers away from the steam.
4. Press the hem.

Some fabrics are difficult to ease and shrink. Remove the extra fullness in these by *tapering* the seam, **26-32**. To taper, use the following steps:

1. Mark the hemline.
2. Insert the sewing machine needle into the seam line slightly above the hemline. Sew along the seam line to the hemline. At the hemline, pivot slightly and angle the seam inward.
3. Remove the original stitches, and trim the seam allowance.
4. Press seams open. Repeat this process on the other seams.

Finishing Hem Edges

Hem finishes are much like seam finishes. The finish you use depends on the garment style and the fabric weight. Choose from these methods, **26-33**:

- *Pinked finish.* To finish fabrics that do not ravel, machine stitch ¼ inch from the cut edge and then pink the edge.
- *Machine zigzag or overcast finish.* For fabrics that ravel, zigzag or overcast the edge above a row of machine stitching. This method gives a very flat hem. It is great for shirts and blouses that will be tucked into other garments.
- *Turned-and-stitched finish.* Fabrics that ravel can also be finished in other ways. They can be turned and stitched. Turn the edges under ¼ inch and stitch close to fold. This method is bulky, so use it on straight hems of medium or lightweight fabrics.
- *Seam binding.* Use seam binding for medium or heavyweight fabrics. It works best on straight hems. With the right side of the fabric up, lap the tape over the hem edge ¼ inch. Stitch close to the lapped edge of the tape.

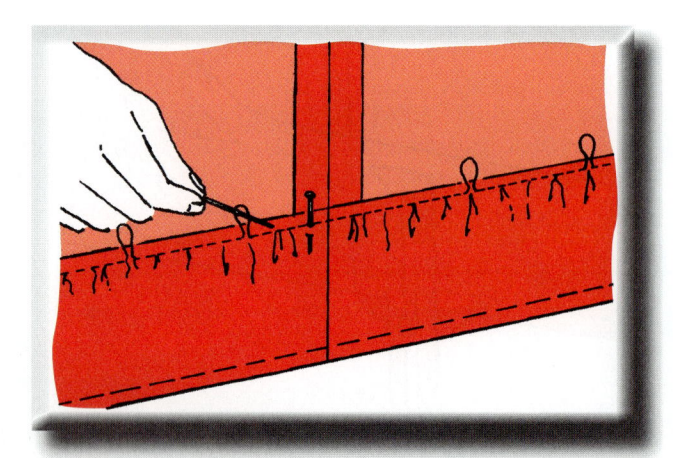

26-31 To ease in extra fullness, pull up gently on the bobbin thread. Repeat several times around hem.
Goodheart-Willcox Publisher

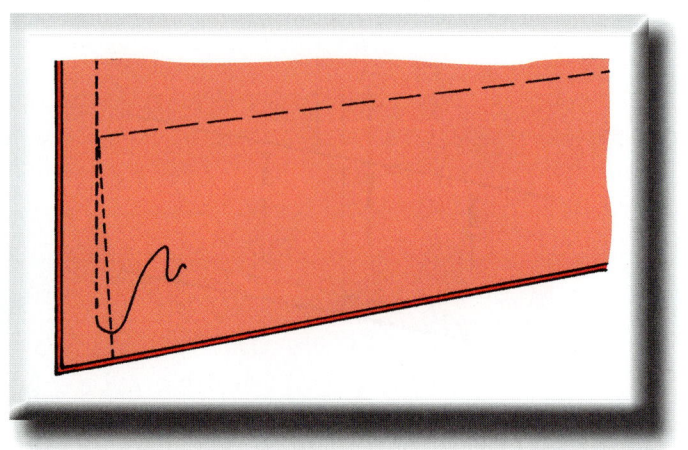

26-32 You can remove extra fullness by tapering seams.
Goodheart-Willcox Publisher

- *Stretch lace.* Use stretch lace for medium and lightweight fabrics and knits. Because it stretches, it works well on curved hems. Lap it over the right side of the fabric ¼ inch and stitch it in place close to the edge of the lapped edge of the lace. Use a straight stitch for woven fabrics and a zigzag stitch for knits.
- *Bias tape.* Use bias tape for fabrics that ravel a great deal. It is also good to use on circular or very full skirts. It is a bulky finish, so use it only on medium and heavyweight fabrics. Open one fold of the tape. With right sides together, sew in the tape crease to join the tape to the hem allowance. Turn the tape up and over the cut edge of the hem.

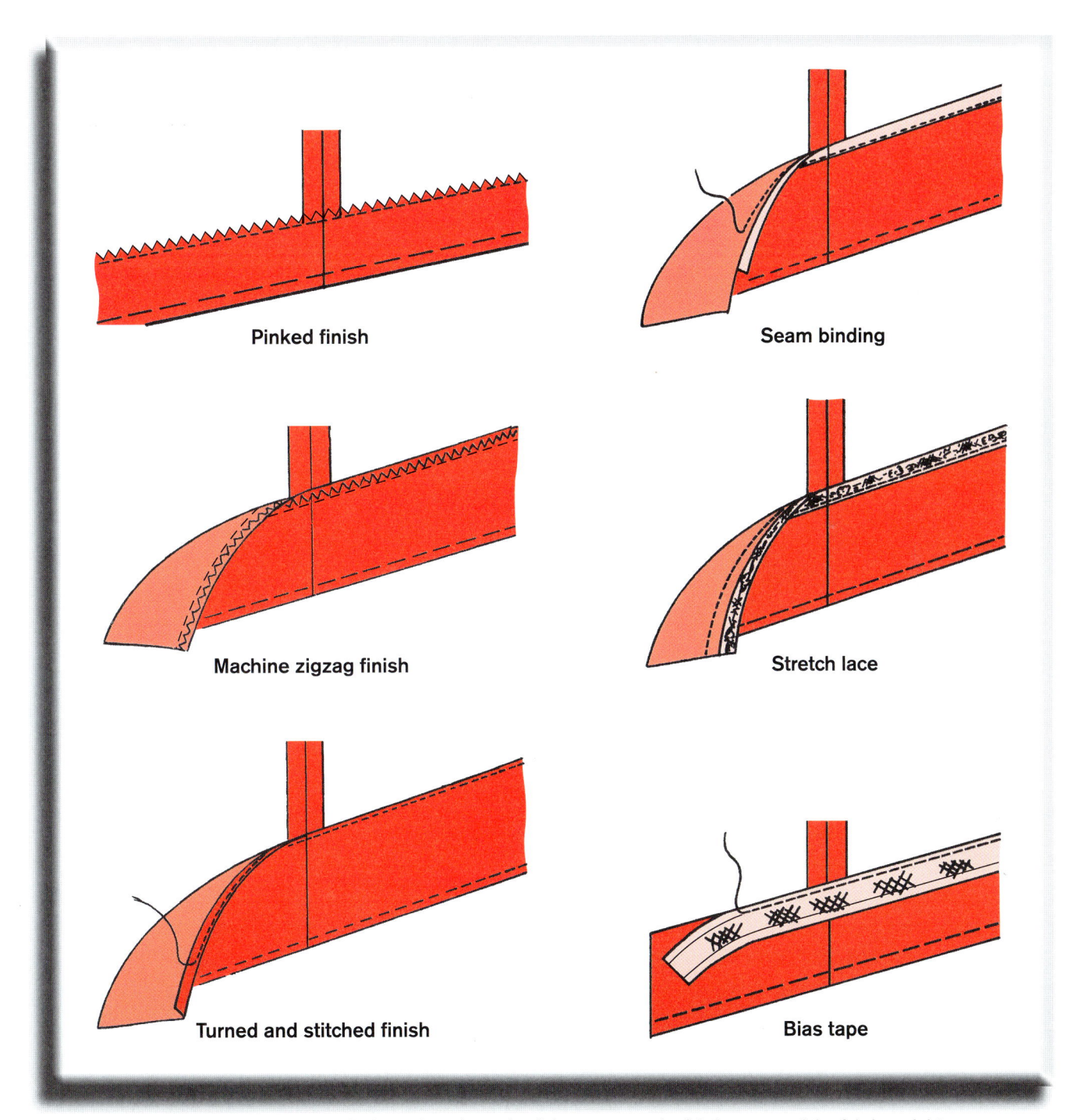

Pinked finish

Seam binding

Machine zigzag finish

Stretch lace

Turned and stitched finish

Bias tape

26-33 The hem finish you choose will depend on the style of the garment, the fabric type, and the fabric weight.
Goodheart-Willcox Publisher

Securing Hems

After finishing the hem edge of the garment, you are ready to secure the hem edge to the garment. You can do this by using hand stitches, machine stitches, or fusing. When sewing hems by hand, no stitches show on the right side of the garment. Machine stitching is fast and easy. Use it for more casual wear, on knits, or when you desire a decorative machine stitch.

Trends Making News

Quilting—an Outlet for Creativity

As people look for ways to creatively fill their leisure time, many have found a renewed interest in quilting. Quilts are most often used as warm covers for beds. Other uses include wall hangings, tote bags, place mats, and vests.

Quilting is the joining together of two layers of fabric and an in-between layer of padding with stitches. The stitching, which is both decorative and functional, can be done by hand or machine.

The top layer of the quilt is often made with *patchwork*—the sewing together of cloth of various colors and shapes to form a quilt top. The top layer can also be made of one piece of fabric with a printed design on it, or a design may be appliquéd to the upper fabric. If a solid color fabric is used, the rows of stitches create a pattern in the quilt. Parallel rows of stitching form a geometric design.

The inner layer, called *batting*, is often polyester fiberfill, down, or cotton. Polyester fleece can also be used. This inner layer gives warmth to the quilt. The bottom layer, called the lining or backing, is usually one piece of firmly woven fabric.

If a quilt is to be sewn by hand, as they were traditionally made, the three layers of the quilt are often stretched on a quilting frame. Quilting begins in the center and proceeds outward. Small stitches are made through all layers. Handmade quilts are treasured more because of the time it takes to make them. They are also more expensive than those made by machine. Antique quilts can be very valuable heirlooms.

Quilting can also be done by machine. Most people who do quilting today sew the quilts by machine. The newest sewing machines offer many features that make the repetitive actions quick and easy to do. Special presser feet help keep the layers of fabric from sliding when stitched.

If you plan to use a pattern for a garment or accessory, quilt the fabric before cutting out the pattern sections. Quilting reduces the size of the fabric.

Follow these steps when machine quilting:
1. Press the top and back fabrics.
2. Layer the fabrics beginning with the backing fabric. Place them on a flat surface right side down. Then place the filler fabric on top. Finally, place the top fabric over the filler with the right side of the fabric facing up.
3. Hand-baste all layers together from the center outward to prevent the layers from shifting. Use long, loose stitches.
4. Set your machine stitch length at 6 to 8 stitches per inch and reduce the pressure on the presser foot. If you have a *walking presser foot*, the layers will be less likely to shift while sewing.
5. If you are following a design, begin sewing in the center of the project and work outward.
6. If you are making parallel rows of stitching, work from one side to the other. Mark one line along the edge of the fabric and stitch on this line. Then—using a *quilting attachment* as a guide—stitch the remaining rows an equal distance apart.

Hand-Stitched Hems

To secure a hem with hand stitches, use a fine needle with a single thread. Hold the garment so the hem is on top and facing you. Stitch from right to left if you are right-handed or left to right if you are left-handed.

Space the stitches evenly for a neat look. Keep the stitches slightly loose so the fabric does not pucker.

You can use several types of hand stitches for securing hems. These include the hemming stitch, slip stitch, blind stitch, and catch stitch. See **26-34** for illustrations of these stitches.

- *Hemming stitch.* The hemming stitch is a strong hand-sewing stitch. You can use it for hems with almost any type of finish.

  Secure the thread in the hem edge with a knot or small backstitch. Pick up a yarn from the garment. Then bring the needle straight up or at an angle through the hem allowance. Move about ¼ inch to the left, and pick up another yarn from the garment. Repeat this process making stitches across the hem edge. When you reach the end of the thread, secure it with a backstitch in the hem edge and begin again.

- *Slip stitch.* The slip stitch hardly shows on either side of the fabric. The thread is hidden under a fold along the edge of the hem allowance. Since a fold is needed, this stitch is used for hems with a turned-and-stitched finish or a bias tape finish.

  Secure the thread in the hem edge. Pick up a yarn from the garment. Bring the needle straight up and into the fold on the hem edge, then across about ¼ inch inside the fold. Next, bring the needle straight down, and pick up another yarn from the garment. Repeat this process around hem.

- *Blind stitch.* The blind stitch shows even less than the slip stitch. The thread is hidden from view because it lies between the hem allowance and the garment. This is an advantage because it prevents the thread from wearing and snagging. The stitches are loose to allow the two layers of fabric to move slightly without pulling.

  Secure the thread in the hem edge. Fold the hem edge up, away from the garment. Pick up a yarn from the garment. Move the needle diagonally up and to the left about ¼ inch. Pick up a yarn from the hem allowance. Move the needle diagonally down and to the left, and pick up a yarn from the garment. Make the stitches loose, repeating them around the hem.

- *Catch stitch.* This stitch is good to use with knits and fabrics that stretch because it *gives*. It can also be used to attach facings at seams.

  Work from left to right with the needle pointing to the left. Take a stitch through the edge of the hem. Take a tiny stitch in the garment ¼ inch to

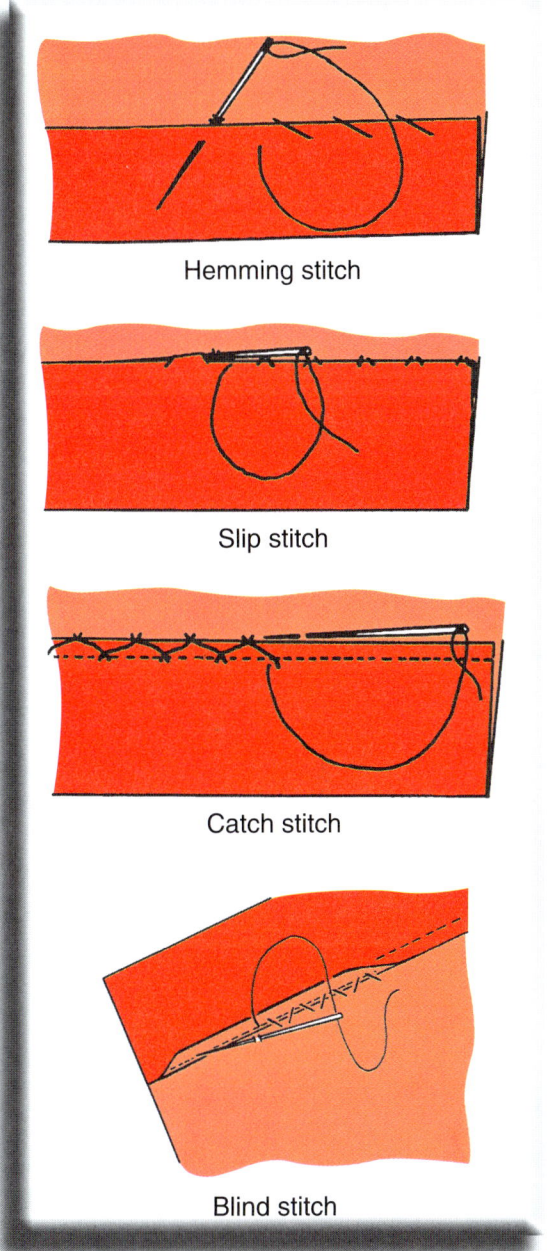

Hemming stitch

Slip stitch

Catch stitch

Blind stitch

26-34 Use one of these stitches to secure the hem.
Goodheart-Willcox Publisher

the right, close to the hem edge. Take the next stitch in the hem so that the stitches form an X. Continue, alternating stitches between the garment and the hem, keeping the stitches fairly loose.

Machine-Stitched Hems

You can secure hems in other ways. Some sewing machines are equipped to sew a blind stitch. Check your machine's manual, and follow its directions.

A **double-fold hem** is a machine-stitched hem made with two folds of fabric of equal depth. The cut edge is in the crease of the outer fold. One or two rows of stitches show on the right side of the garment. It works best on straight edges where there is no excess fullness.

To make a double-fold hem, turn under the hem at the desired length and press. Trim to one inch from the fold. Unfold the edge and turn the raw edge in to meet the pressed fold. Press this fold. Then refold the edge, forming the double-fold hem. Stitch along the inner fold and edge stitch on the outer fold.

Fused Hems

You can also use a fusible material to secure hems. The heat of an iron causes it to melt and bond the hem to the garment. This method is quick and easy, but you need to take some special precautions when using it. Always follow the manufacturer's directions. Read the care label to be sure you can clean it the same way you clean the garment. Check to see that the garment is the right length; this type of hem is permanent.

Test a piece of the fusible material on fabric scraps to avoid any problems later. The material should bond the two fabrics together completely. It should not change the color or texture of the fabrics.

Do not let the iron touch the fusible material. Once it melts onto the iron, it is difficult to remove. When you are ready to bond the hem, use a press cloth to protect the garment from the heat of the iron.

Place fusible web between the hem and the garment about ¼ inch below the top edge of the hem. Pin in place. Press lightly between the pins to hold the layers in place. Remove the pins and cover with a press cloth. Then press a small section at a time until the hem is secure.

Fasteners

A variety of fasteners are useful to close garments, **26-35**. These include buttons, hooks and eyes, snaps, and hook-and-loop tape. Use each alone or in combination with other fasteners. Some are both serviceable and decorative. Your pattern will recommend the type of fastener to use. Many times the choice depends on whether the opening edges are to meet or to overlap.

26-35 The fasteners used on this jacket are both serviceable and decorative.
Butterick Company, Inc.

Buttons and Buttonholes

Buttons and buttonholes have been used to close garments for many centuries. Buttons are not only functional, but decorative as well. They come in a wide variety of materials and colors. You can use buttons and buttonholes when the opening to be secured overlaps.

Before sewing buttons in place, always make the buttonholes. Buttonholes are usually on the right front side for female garments. For male clothing, buttonholes are on the left front side.

There are three types of buttonholes:

- *Bound buttonhole.* In a **bound buttonhole**, the edges are finished with fabric. Bound buttonholes give tailored garments a custom-made appearance. They are made in the garment before the facing is attached.
- *Machine-worked buttonhole.* In a **machine-worked buttonhole**, the edges are worked over with thread using a zigzag stitch machine. They are made after the garment is constructed. Machine-worked buttonholes are used for most items of clothing and are especially durable.
- *Hand-worked buttonhole.* In a **hand-worked buttonhole**, the edges are worked over with thread using a buttonhole stitch. They are used on very loosely woven and lightweight fabrics.

Marking for Buttons and Buttonholes

Transfer the markings for buttonholes from the pattern piece to the outside of the garment. The markings should be accurate and follow the grain of the fabric. Be sure that the marking method that you use does not leave a permanent mark on your garment. Consider using machine basting, hand basting, or tailor's chalk for this task. Mark the location and length of each buttonhole.

The length of the buttonhole depends on the size of your buttons. Measure both the diameter and the thickness of the button. The total of these two measurements is the length you should make your buttonholes.

Once you sew the buttonholes, you can determine the placement of the buttons. Pin the garment closed. For a horizontal buttonhole, push a pin through the buttonhole ⅛ inch from the outer end. For a vertical buttonhole, push a pin through ⅛ inch below the top of the buttonhole. Attach the buttons where the pins enter the fabric.

Machine-Worked Buttonholes

Most buttonholes are made by machine. On some machines, you can make buttonholes by adjusting the zigzag stitch. Other sewing machines have a built-in buttonhole setting and a special buttonhole presser foot. Follow the directions provided with your machine for making buttonholes. Always make a sample buttonhole on a scrap of fabric before making one on your garment. Be sure to use the same number of layers of fabric and interfacing as your garment.

Use small, sharp scissors to slash open the finished buttonholes. Begin in the center and cut toward each corner, carefully using the tip of your scissors. A pin inserted at each end of the buttonhole will keep you from cutting too far.

Attaching Buttons

Attach buttons using a double strand of thread. Sew-through buttons have two to four holes through which you sew. You will need to create a thread shank to allow space for the buttoned garment to lie smoothly. Shank buttons have an attached loop on the back that forms a shank. They need only a small thread shank. Some sewing machines will sew on buttons. Here are some quick guidelines for sewing buttons:

- *Sew-through buttons.* Place your button on the marking and put a pin or toothpick on the top. From the garment underside, bring the needle and thread through the fabric and button, over the pin and back through the fabric. Repeat this action five or six times. Remove the pin or toothpick and pull the button up. Bring the needle up between the garment and the button and wind the thread around the stitches several times to make a shank. Bring the needle and thread through to the garment underside and secure.

- *Shank buttons.* Bring the needle and thread up through the fabric from the underside to the top, through the shank, and back through the fabric loosely. Repeat this action five or six times. Bring the needle up between the garment and the button and wind the thread under the button to form the thread shank. Then bring the needle and thread through to the underside and secure.

Snaps

Use snaps to hold overlapping edges together at locations where there is little strain. Snaps have two sections, the ball half and the socket half. Snaps come in various sizes. Use large, heavy snaps on sportswear, coats, and jackets.

To sew on snaps, follow these steps:

1. Place the ball half of the snap on the underside of the overlapping section.
2. Using the overcast stitch, take three or four small stitches close together through each hole. Make sure stitches do not show on the right side of the garment.
3. Carry the thread under the snap from hole to hole until all ball sections have been attached.
4. Fasten the thread ends securely with a couple of stitches.
5. To mark the position for the socket part of the snap, overlap the edges. Push a pin through the center hole of the ball part.
6. Attach the socket part at this location using the overcast stitch. A pin inserted in the hole in the socket part of the snap will help hold the snap in place as you sew.

Hooks and Eyes

Hooks and eyes are more secure than snaps. Use them on parts of garments where there is extra strain. Use small sizes at neck edges and larger hooks and eyes on waistbands for pants, shorts, and skirts where there is more strain.

The eyes are either round or straight. Use a round eye when the two edges just meet. If the edges overlap, use a straight eye.

To attach hooks and eyes:

1. Place the hook on the inside of the garment just a slight distance from the edge so it does not show.
2. Stitch around each hole using an overcast stitch. Make sure stitches do not go through to the outside of the garment.
3. Place a few stitches at the end of the hook to hold it flat against the fabric.
4. Secure the threads.
5. Place the round eye on the inside of the opposite edge so that the loop extends slightly beyond the edge. The garment edges should just meet when the hook and eye is fastened. The straight eye is sewn to the underlap part of the garment exactly opposite the hook. Sew the eye on as you did the hook.

Trouser hooks and eyes are often used on the waistbands of jeans, pants, shorts, and sportswear, 26-36. They are very durable. They are sewn, clamped, or hammered into the fabric. It is best to use them on firmly woven fabrics as they could damage lightweight fabrics. To attach, follow the manufacturer's directions on the package.

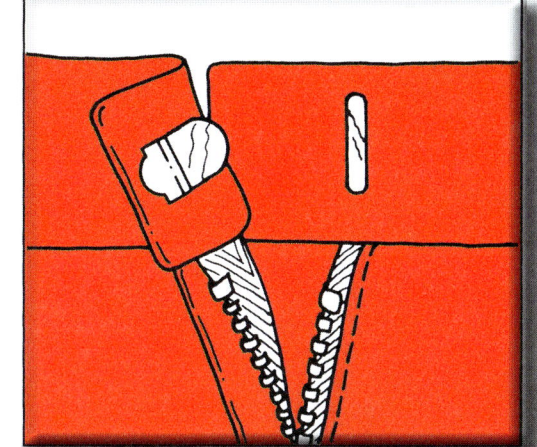

26-36 Trouser hook and eyes are good for use on sportswear and other clothes that take hard wear.
Goodheart-Willcox Publisher

Hook-and-Loop Tape

Hook-and-loop tape is used on edges that overlap. It consists of two strips of nylon fabric. One strip has tiny loops and the other strip is fuzzy. When the two strips are pressed together, they hold fast to one another. To open the garment, pull the two strips apart. The strips of tape can be cut to the desired length, shape, or size. Precut squares and circles can also be purchased. Hook-and-loop tape is often used on jackets, children's clothes, craft items, camping equipment, and household items.

To attach hook-and-loop tape:

1. Cut the tape to the desired size.
2. Place the fuzzy side of the strip on the underside of the overlapping garment edge, 26-37.
3. Stitch around all four edges by hand or machine.
4. Place the looped side of the strip on the underlap so that the garment closes properly.
5. Stitch in place through all fabric thicknesses. Secure the threads.

26-37 Place the fuzzy side of hook-and-loop tape on the underside of the overlap. Place the looped side on the underlap.
Goodheart-Willcox Publisher

Pressing Techniques

Good pressing techniques are as important as good sewing techniques. A carefully constructed garment will look better if you press as you sew. Pressing of the completed garment will take less time and effort. The end result will be a professional-looking garment, 26-38. As you set up your machine to sew, set up your pressing equipment. This includes your iron, ironing board, pressing ham, and press cloth.

Follow these guidelines for pressing as you sew:

- Set the iron at the correct temperature. Determine the temperature setting by the fiber content of the fabric. Press a scrap of your fabric to check the temperature setting before you begin. If the iron temperature is too hot, it will stick to the fabric, cause puckers in the fabric, or melt the fabric.
- Remember that pressing is not ironing. Pressing is lifting the iron and setting it down again on the fabric. The heat, steam, and weight of the iron do the work. The iron is not moved back and forth, as in ironing. Pressing is usually all that is needed during garment construction. Ironing is often done after laundering to remove wrinkles.
- Press all seams and darts before they are crossed with other lines of stitching.
- Press seams flat first, and then press them open.
- Press darts from the widest end to the point. Press vertical darts toward the garment center and horizontal darts downward.

26-38 Pressing as you sew yields professional-looking results. With practice and experience, you can become an expert.
Simplicity Pattern Co.

- Press curved seams and darts over a rounded surface such as a pressing ham. The pressing ham allows curved garment sections to lie smoothly against the firm, rounded surface.
- Press on the wrong side (underside) of the garment whenever possible. This will prevent a shine from appearing on the outside of the garment. Seams and darts can be easily pressed from the wrong side.
- If you must press on the right side, use a press cloth, especially with dark fabrics. A press cloth can be dampened if more steam is needed.

- Press with the fabric grain, in the direction of your stitching.
- Be careful not to stretch edges or curves out of shape.
- Do not press over pins. This may scratch the soleplate of the iron and the pins may leave an impression in the fabric.
- Use care when working with fusible fabrics. If the adhesive comes in contact with the iron, it will melt and stick to it. This can be difficult to remove from the iron. Ironing over a piece of waxed paper will help restore the smooth surface.
- To press gathers, place the garment over the end of the ironing board, wrong side up. Press the gathers below the seam line by sliding the iron point up into the gathers. This will avoid flattening the gathers having a pleated look. Press the seam allowance away from the seam line with the point of the iron. Then press the seam allowances flat to reduce bulk.
- Press sleeves using a sleeve board, 26-39. Use a sleeve board to press sleeves without creases.
- Never press any sharp creases in your garment until the fit has been checked.

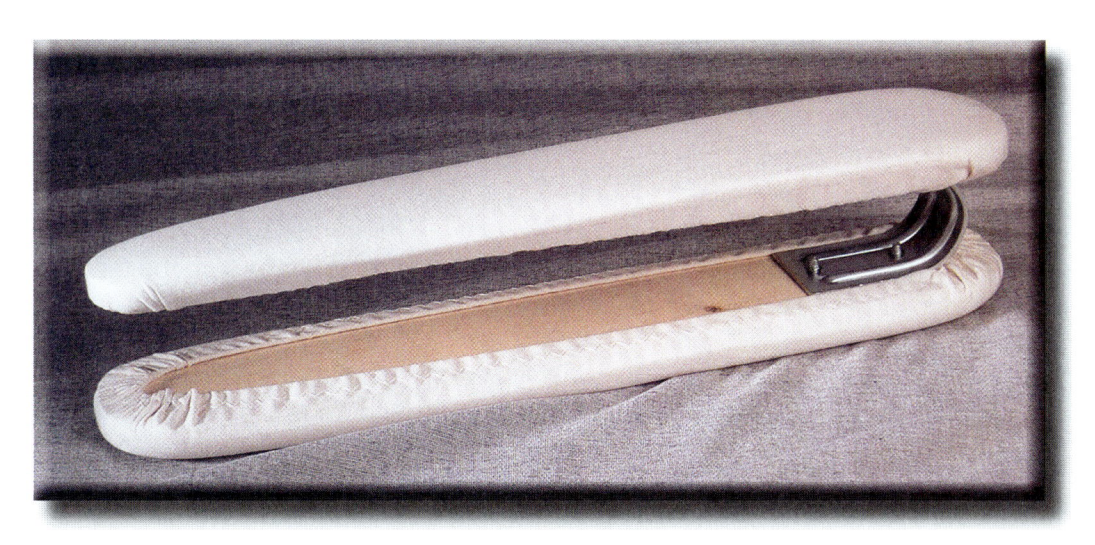

26-39 A sleeve board allows you to press sleeve seams open without forming creases.
June Tailor, Inc.

Summary

- Staystitching and directional stitching help to maintain the shape of the garment.
- Darts provide shape and fullness to a garment so it fits the curves of the body.
- Most seams used in clothing construction are plain seams. These seams may need a seam finish to prevent the edges from raveling. Other types of seams are the topstitched, flat-fell, welt, and French seams.
- In some garment areas, a regular seam allowance is too bulky. Eliminate this bulk by trimming, grading, and clipping seams.
- Facings are used to cover raw edges in a garment such as at the armholes, neckline, or other garment openings. Facings may be extended from the garment piece, separate fitted or shaped pieces, or a strip of bias fabric.
- A wide variety of interfacing fabrics are available. A heavier weight interfacing gives a crisp look whereas a lighter weight gives a softer look.
- Zippers come in all lengths, weights, styles, and colors. Two common methods for attaching zippers are centered and lapped.
- Hemming is one of the last steps in sewing a garment. It should be smooth, even, and almost invisible on the outside of the garment.
- A variety of fasteners are used to close garments. These include buttons, hooks and eyes, snaps, and hook-and-loop tape. Each can be used alone or in combination with other fasteners. Some are both serviceable and decorative.
- Good pressing techniques are as important as good sewing techniques. A carefully constructed garment will look better if you press as you sew.

Graphic Organizer

Create a T-chart. In the left column, list the main headings in the chapter. In the right column, list the supporting details for each heading.

Main Headings	Supporting Details

Review the Facts

1. What should you do to make sure the thread will not be pulled out of the needle when you start to sew?
2. What is backstitching? When would you use it?
3. Why is staystitching done?
4. Explain the difference between the appearance of easing and gathering.
5. How do you prevent a pucker from forming at the end of a dart?
6. Which seam would you use for a sheer fabric that ravels easily?
7. Press seam open. Turn the edges under ¼ inch. Stitch close to fold. These are the directions for the _____ seam finish.
8. Contrast clipping and notching.
9. What is the purpose of understitching?
10. What are three types of interfacing? On what type of fabric would you use each?
11. Name two reasons for using interfacing.
12. Which zipper application, centered or lapped, would you use for a side seam?
13. Which hem finish could you use on a shirt or blouse that will be tucked into another garment?
14. The blind stitch is often used to secure a hem. Explain how it is done.

15. Which type of fastener would you use for an edge that just meets?
16. List two guidelines to follow when pressing during the construction of a garment.

Think Critically

17. **Analyze seams and finishes.** Select ten ready-to-wear items of clothing from your wardrobe. Identify the types of seams and seam finishes used. Analyze why the clothing manufacturer might have used each.
18. **Identify cause and effect.** What will happen to a curved, fitted facing if it is not trimmed, graded, and clipped before it is turned and pressed?
19. **Identify evidence.** Some people do not like to take the time to press as they sew. How would you explain to them the importance of this practice? What evidence can you provide?

Apparel Applications

20. **Demonstrate machine know-how.** Learning to use the sewing machine with precision is essential for successful sewing. Practice using the sewing machine. Learn to start and stop, sew straight, sew around curves, turn corners, and backstitch.
21. **Demonstrate directional stitching.** Practice directional stitching. Cut diagonally across two fabric scraps. Stitch up one of the edges. Stitch down the other edge. Compare.
22. **Practice easing.** Ease one edge of a fabric sample. Gather the edge of another fabric sample. Attach both to a third fabric sample. Practice easing sample without forming any gathers or tucks.
23. **Practice darts.** Cut two pieces of fabric 6 inches by 8 inches. Mark dart lines on each piece. Sew one dart with three stitches taken along the fold at the point. Sew the other dart without taking these stitches. Tie both dart points to secure. Press over a tailor's ham. Which dart puckers and which lies smoothly?
24. **Demonstrate seams and finishes.** Make samples of each type of seam and seam finish using 6-inch by 8-inch fabric swatches. Use two swatches for each sample.
25. **Demonstrate hem proficiency.** Practice securing a hem.
26. **Demonstrate pressing proficiency.** With a classmate, practice using various pressing equipment. Then use a camcorder or digital camera with video-clip capabilities to record your demonstration showing how to use various pieces of pressing equipment. Share your videos with the class.

Academic Connections

27. **Social studies.** Investigate the invention of the zipper. How did the zipper impact the apparel industry? Use presentation software to create an illustrated report of your findings.
28. **Reading.** Obtain an invisible zipper of a short length and the necessary zipper foot. Read through the application directions that come with the package. Practice inserting the invisible zipper. How helpful were the directions? Write a summary about your experience.

Workplace Connections

29. **Demonstrate zipper application.** Presume you are a sewing instructor at a local fabric shop. You will be teaching your beginners class how to apply centered and lapped zippers. Prepare your demonstrations following the chapter guidelines and give your demonstrations to the class.
30. **Portfolio builder.** Suppose you are applying for a job as a tailor for a major department store. The department manager, who is conducting your interview, requested that you bring a portfolio demonstrating your sewing ability. Create and neatly mount examples of all sewing techniques outlined in this chapter. Put your samples in a portfolio binder to take to your interview.

Fashion Construction—Child

Prepare a *Fashion Construction* STAR Event to display your skills in clothing construction. For this event, sew a garment using at least eight sewing-construction techniques for a child's garment. Follow the FCCLA STAR Event guidelines for *Fashion Construction*. See your adviser for information as needed.

Chapter 27

Advanced Sewing Skills

Chapter Objectives

After studying this chapter, you will be able to
- **identify** various types of collars, sleeves, pockets, waistline treatments, and casings.
- **demonstrate** how to construct various types of collars, sleeves, pockets, waistline treatments, and casings.
- **demonstrate** how to attach a collar with or without a facing.
- **describe** how elastic is used when constructing garments.
- **summarize** guidelines for sewing with knits and pile fabrics.

Key Terms

flat collar
rolled collar
standing collar
patch pocket
in-seam pocket
front hip pocket
waistband
waistline facing
casing
self-casing
applied casing

Reading with Purpose

On separate sticky notes, write five reasons why the information in this chapter is important to you. Think about how this information could help you at school, work, or home. As you read the chapter, place the sticky notes on the pages that relate to each reason.

After you have become successful making simple garments, you may be ready to construct something more difficult and detailed. Advanced sewing skills can enable you to make items that feature collars, sleeves, and pockets. Advanced sewing projects may include waistbands, faced waistlines, and casings. Some fabrics are more difficult to sew than others and require special handling techniques. Learning these advanced sewing skills will help you make many styles of shirts, blouses, pants, and jackets.

Collars

All types of shirts, blouses, and jackets use collars. They come in a variety of shapes and sizes. Since collars are close to the face, it is important they be well made and fit properly.

In a well-made collar, both sides of the collar are identical. Curves should be smooth and points precise. The underside of the collar should not show along the edge.

There are three basic types of collars, 27-1:

- *Flat collars.* The **flat collar** lies flat against the garment. It is used on dresses, blouses, and children's clothing. Other names for flat collars include a *Peter Pan collar* or a *shaped collar*. The notched edge of the collar is almost identical to the shape of the neck edge of the garment. This shaping allows the collar to lie flat. The upper and lower collar pieces are cut from the same pattern.

- *Rolled collars.* The **rolled collar** stands up from the neck slightly and forms a roll around the neck. The upper and lower layers of the collar utilize separate pattern pieces. The undercollar is usually cut slightly smaller, in two pieces, and on the bias. This causes the collar to form a roll.

- *Standing collars.* The **standing collar** stands up from the neck edge of the garment. Other names for standing collars include band collar or mandarin collar. It may also fold over for a turtleneck style. The standing collar may be cut from either a shaped or a straight piece of fabric. If the collar is to turn over, it is cut on the bias.

Shirt collars are also a form of standing collar. They consist of two parts: the collar and a neckband. Both are usually interfaced. The collar is first attached to a band, and then the band is attached to the shirt.

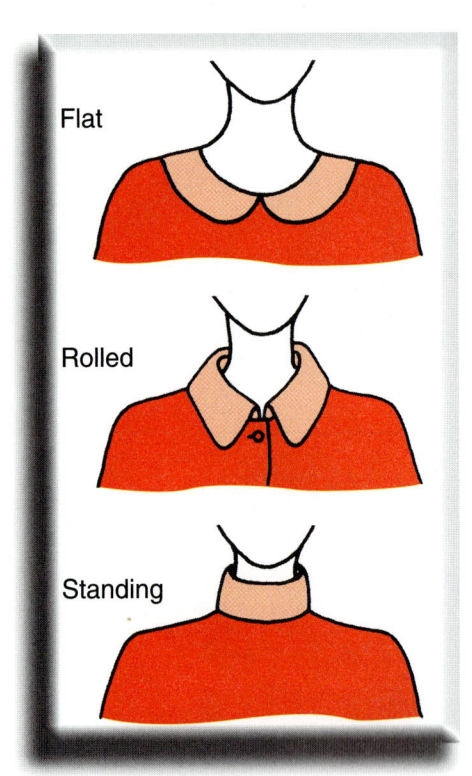

27-1 The three basic styles of collars are flat, rolled, and standing.
Goodheart-Willcox Publisher

Constructing a Collar

Sew most collars together before attaching them to garments. Collars need the support that interfacing provides. Though collar styles vary, most are used in the following steps:

1. Trim corners off the interfacing on pointed collars before attaching. This will reduce bulk in the points.
2. Either stitch or fuse the interfacing to the wrong side of the under collar. If you use fusible interfacing, trim the seam allowances off before fusing the interfacing to the under collar.
3. Trim the interfacing close to the stitching.
4. Pin the right sides of the collar pieces together. Stitch along the unnotched edge. Leave the notched edge open so you can turn the collar right side out.
5. Reinforce corners and curves with shorter stitches. (*Note:* For bulkier fabrics, stop stitching at the corner with the needle in the fabric, pivot and sew one diagonal stitch across the collar point, pivot again, and continue stitching the collar. This diagonal stitch allows more room for the seam allowance when you turn the collar.)
6. Trim and grade the seam allowances. Clip at the curves.
7. Understitch the under collar to the seam allowances. This will prevent the under collar from rolling out at the seam line and showing along the edges.
8. Turn the collar to the right side and press.

Attaching a Collar There are several different methods for attaching the collar to the garment. Most collars require using a full-fitted facing, a partial facing, or no facing at all. Facings hide the neckline seam allowances. When there is no facing, attach the collar so the garment neckline seam allowances are between the layers of the collar. See your pattern guide sheet for specific directions for attaching collars.

Collars with Full-Fitted Facings

When attaching a collar using a full-fitted facing, first finish the unnotched edge with an appropriate edge finish. Then follow these steps:

1. Staystitch and clip the neckline edge of the garment.
2. Pin the collar to the neck edge matching notches and other markings. Machine baste the collar in place stitching just inside the seam line.
3. Pin the facing over the collar with right sides together. Match notches and other markings. Stitch through all thicknesses.
4. Trim, grade, and clip the seam allowances.
5. Understitch the facing to the seam allowances, 27-2.
6. Press the collar and facing. Tack the facing edge to the shoulder seam allowances.

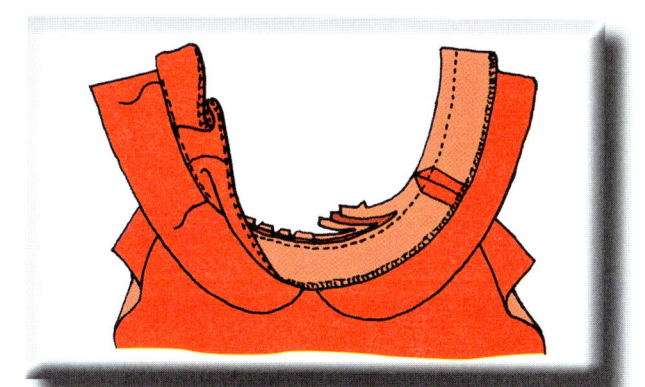

Collars with Partial Facings

Flat and rolled collars are usually attached using a partial facing. Follow these steps:

1. Staystitch the neckline edge of the garment and clip.
2. Pin the collar to the neck edge of the garment matching notches. Machine baste the collar to the neck edge from the front opening to the shoulder markings.
3. Machine baste the under collar only to the back neck edge between the shoulder markings.
4. With right sides together, pin the front facings to the neckline. Clip neck edge at shoulder markings.
5. Stitch entire neck seam, but do not catch the free edge of the collar back in the seam.
6. Trim, grade, and clip the seam allowances.
7. Turn the facing to the inside and press.
8. Understitch the facing to the neckline seam allowance.
9. Turn under the free edge of the collar ⅝ inch and trim to ¼ inch.
10. Use a slip stitch to attach the free edge to the back neck seam.

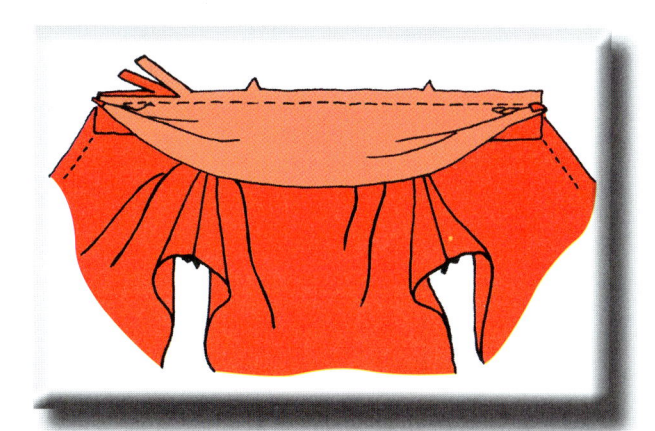

Collars with No Facing

A standing collar is usually attached with no facing. When attaching a collar without a facing, follow these steps:

1. Clip the neck edge of the garment to the staystitching.
2. Pin the right side of the collar to the garment neck edge, leaving the other layer of the collar free. Match notches and other markings.
3. Stitch, grade, and clip the seam, 27-3.

27-2 After stitching the facing to the neckline edge, trim, grade, and clip the seam allowances. Understitch the facing to the seam allowances.
Goodheart-Willcox Publisher

27-3 Be careful not to catch the other layer of the collar in the stitching line.
Goodheart-Willcox Publisher

4. Press the seam allowances toward the collar. Press under the seam allowance on the free layer of the collar and trim to ¼ inch.
5. Pin the folded edge over the neckline seam. Stitch the folded edge in place by hand using a slip stitch.

Sleeves

There are many different styles and lengths of sleeves. The three most common styles are kimono, raglan, and set-in sleeves, 27-4.

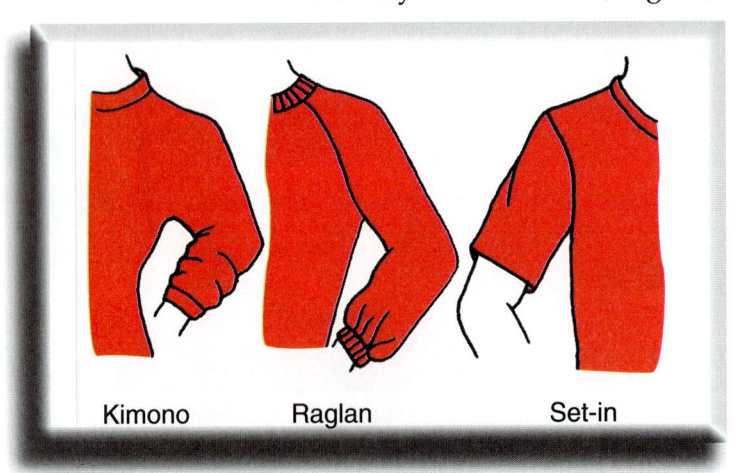

- *Kimono sleeves.* Formed as continuous extensions out from the shoulder area, there is no seam line connecting the garment and kimono sleeve.
- *Raglan sleeves.* Front and back diagonal seams from the underarm to the neckline attach raglan sleeves to the garment. A curved seam or a shaped dart creates shoulder shaping. Raglan sleeves are a good choice for hard-to-fit shoulders. The seams can be adjusted for differences in body shape.
- *Set-in sleeves.* Seams that go around the armhole at the tip of the shoulders are used to attach set-in sleeves to the garment. The area of the sleeve at the end of the shoulders must be shaped and curved to fit smoothly over the arms. The set-in sleeve is larger than the armhole to which it is joined. This allows the arm to move freely. Some set-in sleeves styles have a great deal of fullness that is gathered and then attached to the armhole edge. Other styles require easing the sleeve into the armhole. This creates a smooth appearance with no visible gathers. Set-in sleeves are the most difficult to sew of the three styles.

27-4 Most sleeves are variations of these three basic styles.
Goodheart-Willcox Publisher

Kimono Sleeves

To make a kimono sleeve, follow these steps:

1. Pin the garment front and back together at the underarm and side seams. Match markings and notches.
2. Begin at the lower edge of the garment and stitch the seam line. Try not to stretch the fabric around the curve.
3. Reinforce the underarm seam by stitching again around the curved area just inside the seam line in the seam allowance, 27-5.
4. Clip the seam at the curve and press the seam open.

Your pattern guide sheet may ask you to further reinforce the seam by sewing a strip of seam binding or bias tape into the seam line. Follow the instructions given on your guide sheet.

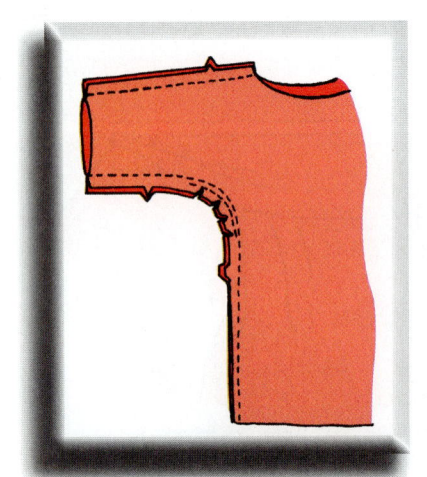

27-5 Kimono sleeves need to be reinforced at the underarm curve.
Goodheart-Willcox Publisher

Raglan Sleeves

Use the following steps to sew a raglan sleeve:

1. Stitch the shoulder dart.

2. Slash the dart and press it open.
3. With right sides together, pin the diagonal seams of the sleeves to the garment, matching notches.
4. Stitch each seam, and then stitch the seam again just inside the first row of stitches in the seam allowance to reinforce the seam.
5. Clip the seam below the notches and press the seam open, 27-6.
6. Stitch the entire underarm and side seam.

27-6 The diagonal seams in the raglan sleeve are clipped and pressed open before the underarm seam is joined. *Goodheart-Willcox Publisher*

Set-In Sleeves

There are two ways to sew set-in sleeves to the garment. You can join them to the garment before sewing the underarm sleeve seams and side seams. This is the *open-sleeve method*. You can also join the sleeves to the garment after sewing these seams. This is the *closed-sleeve method*. Your pattern guide sheet will indicate the best method to use. However, you may find that you prefer one method over the other.

Open-Sleeve Method

Before sewing the side seams and underarm seams, you can join set-in sleeves to the garment. This method is best for sleeves that fit smoothly and have little fullness to ease into the armhole. This method is often used for making shirts.

To attach sleeves before sewing the side seams and underarm seams, follow these steps:

1. Machine baste the sleeve cap area if your pattern guide sheet suggests that you do so, 27-7. Some sleeves can be attached without machine basting.
2. With right sides together, pin the sleeve to the armhole matching notches, dots, and ends. Adjust fullness if necessary.
3. Stitch the seam with the sleeve side up.
4. Press seam allowances toward the sleeve.
5. If your pattern suggests topstitching the seam, press the seam allowances toward the garment. Topstitch close to the seam line.
6. Stitch the entire underarm and side seam.

Closed-Sleeve Method

To set in the sleeves after sewing the seams, first construct the sleeve. Follow these steps:

1. To ease in the excess fullness in the sleeve, machine baste two rows of stitches around the sleeve top between the notches, 27-8. Stitch one row just outside the ⅝-inch seam line. Stitch the other row ⅜ inch from the edge. Leave a couple of inches of thread at the end of each row of stitching. Do not backstitch.
2. Stitch the underarm seam and press open.

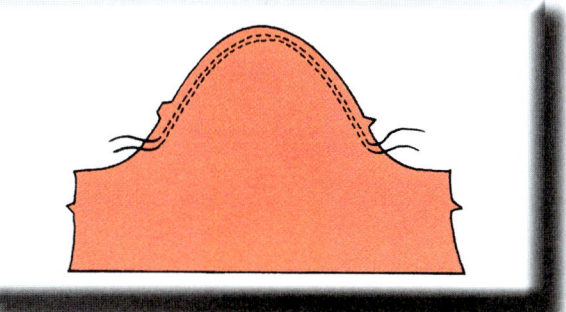

27-7 Machine basting the sleeve cap allows you to ease in the extra fullness. *Goodheart-Willcox Publisher*

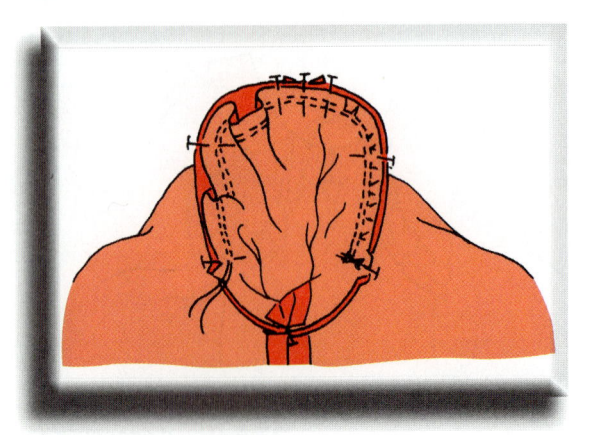

27-8 Pull the basting threads until the sleeve is eased against the armhole edge. *Goodheart-Willcox Publisher*

3. With the garment wrong side out and the sleeve right side out, slip the sleeve into the armhole. Pin right sides together at the markings, notches, and underarm seam.
4. Pull up the basting threads until the sleeve fits the armhole, 27-9. Adjust the fullness evenly between the notches and markings. Pin about every ½ inch.
5. With the sleeve side up, stitch the sleeve to the armhole, 27-10. Stitch carefully to avoid puckers or tucks. Do not sew over pins, remove them as you sew.
6. Make a second row of stitching between the notches in the underarm area to reinforce the seam. Stitch ⅜ inch from the edge.
7. Trim the seam allowances in the underarm area only.
8. Press the seam allowances together and then turn them toward the sleeve. Do not press the sleeve seam along the cap area after the sleeve is set in.

Pockets

Pockets are a very important feature in many garment designs. They are not only decorative, but also functional. Because they may be a prominent design feature, it is important they be constructed well.

There are three main types of pockets:

- **Patch pockets** are made from fabric pieces that are stitched on the outside of a garment. These are often used on shirts, blouses, skirts, pants, and shorts.
- **In-seam pockets** are sewn in the side seam of a garment. If they are made properly, they do not show when the garment is worn.
- **Front hip pockets** are angular pockets often used on the front of pants and skirts. They are a variation of the in-seam pocket.

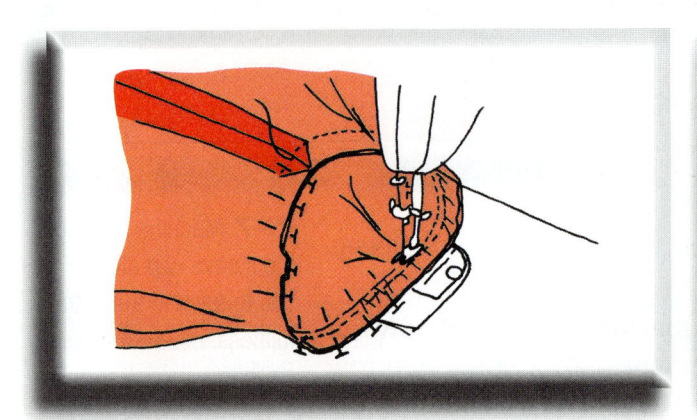

27-9 Carefully stitch the sleeve into the armhole to avoid tucks and puckers. *Goodheart-Willcox Publisher*

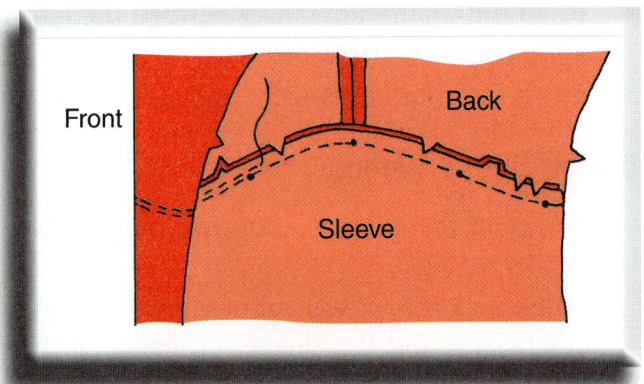

27-10 Set-in sleeves can be attached before underarm seams are sewn. *Goodheart-Willcox Publisher*

Patch Pockets

Patch pockets can be made from the same fabric as the garment or of a contrasting fabric. Most pockets are unlined, but if the fabric is thin and soft, you may want to line the pockets.

To make an unlined patch pocket:

1. Finish the top edge of the pocket.
   - For light- to medium-weight fabrics, turn under ¼ inch along the top and stitch to form a hem.
   - For heavier fabrics, zigzag or serge the hem edge. Turn the hem to the right side along the fold line. Stitch ends on the seam line and trim, **27-11**.
2. If the pocket has rounded edges:
   - Machine baste ⅜ inch from the curved edges, 27-11.
   - Pull up the threads until the seam allowance curves in and lies flat against the pocket.
   - Trim and notch the seam allowance to reduce bulk and avoid puckers.
   - Press the pocket.
3. If the pocket has square corners:
   - Staystitch around the pocket on the seam line. This forms a guide for turning and pressing the edge of the pocket before it is attached to the garment, **27-12**.
   - Press the corners diagonally to the wrong side. Trim the corners.
   - Press all seam allowances under along the staystitching line, mitering the corners to form sharp points.
4. To attach the patch pocket to the garment:
   - Pin the pocket to the outside of the garment on the marking line.
   - Stitch the pocket to the garment close to the edge of the pocket. Backstitch at the upper corners to prevent the pocket from pulling loose. Or, bring the thread ends to the inside of the garment and tie them together.
   - The pocket can also be topstitched to the garment, stitching ¼ inch from the edge, or sewn on with hand stitches.

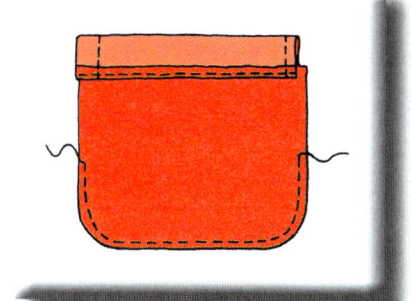

27-11 Trim the seam allowance on the hem of the patch pocket. Machine baste the curved edges.
Goodheart-Willcox Publisher

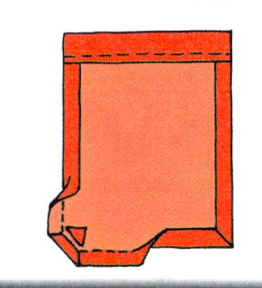

27-12 To form a straight edge on the sides of a square patch pocket, staystitch on the seam line. Press under along the stitching line, trimming and mitering the corners.
Goodheart-Willcox Publisher

In-Seam Pockets

In-seam pockets are the simplest pockets to make. They are either cut from a separate pattern piece or are an extension of the garment front and back. If the pattern pieces are separate, cut these pieces from lining fabric to reduce the bulk and give a flatter look.

To make an in-seam pocket:

1. Stitch the pocket to the front and back if the pockets are separate pieces.
2. Press the seam allowances toward the pockets.
3. Pin the back to the front at sides, matching notches and markings. Pin pocket edges together.

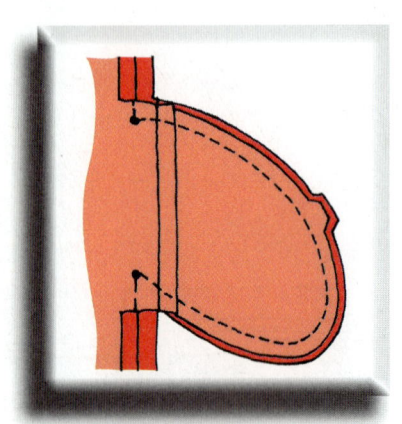

4. Stitch the side seam and around the pocket.
5. Clip the back seam allowance above and below the pocket, 27-13.
6. Press the garment seam allowances open. Press the pocket seam allowances flat. Turn the pocket toward the front and press lightly at the pocket opening.

27-13 Clip only the back seam allowance above and below the pocket so the seam can be pressed open.
Goodheart-Willcox Publisher

Front Hip Pockets

Many jeans, pants, shorts, and skirts have partially hidden hipline pockets sometimes called slant pockets or Western pockets. Front hip pockets include two different pieces. The back portion forms a part of the garment that is attached at the waist and side seams. The other piece is the pocket facing, which finishes the opening edge.

To make the front hip pocket:

1. Stitch a piece of seam binding along the upper side edge of the front. This will prevent the pocket from stretching.
2. Stitch the pocket facing to the upper side edge of the front, right sides together.
3. Trim the seam, being careful not to cut the seam binding.
4. Turn the pocket to the inside and press, 27-14.
5. Topstitch the seam if desired.
6. Stitch the back portion of the pocket to the pocket facing, right sides together. Keep the front free as you stitch.
7. Press the pocket.
8. Baste the upper and side edges of the pocket to the garment along the seam lines.
9. Stitch the front to the back along the side seams.

Waistline Treatments

27-14 To make a front hip pocket, follow these steps.
Goodheart-Willcox Publisher

The waistline edge of pants, shorts, and skirts must be finished in some way. The three most common ways of finishing waistlines are with a waistband, a facing, or a casing.

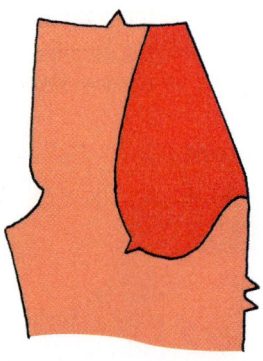

A. Attach the pocket facing at the pocket opening.

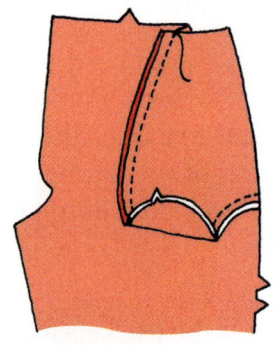

B. Sew the back portion of the pocket to the pocket facing.

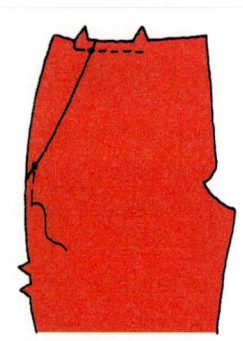

C. Baste the pocket in place along the seam lines and complete the garment.

- A **waistband** is a strip of fabric attached at the waistline edge of the garment. It may be straight or curved and is visible above the waistline.
- A **waistline facing** is a curved piece of fabric attached at the waistline edge and folds to the inside of the garment. It is not visible above the waistline.
- A **casing** is a fabric piece that encloses a drawstring or elastic that draws the garment snugly against the body. Casings will be discussed later in this chapter.

Waistbands

When the garment you are making includes a waistband, be sure to interface it. Interfacing prevents the waistband from stretching and rolling over when the garment is worn. Attach the interfacing to the waistband before sewing the waistband to the garment. Follow these construction steps:

1. Machine baste the interfacing to the waistband as your pattern guide sheet explains. A fusible interfacing can also be used.
2. Press under the seam allowance on the long unnotched edge of the band and trim to ¼ inch.
3. With right sides together, pin the notched edge of the band to the waistline, **27-15**. Match notches, seams, and other markings. Ease to fit if necessary.
4. Stitch, trim, and grade the seam. Clip, too, if the seam is curved.
5. Press the seam allowances toward the waistband.
6. You are now ready to stitch the ends of the band. With right sides together, fold the waistband along the fold line. See **27-16**. Match the folded edge of the band exactly with the seam line. Stitch across the ends.
7. Trim the seams and corners to reduce bulk.
8. Turn the band right side out and press.
9. Pin the free folded edge of the band over the waist seam line.
10. Slip stitch the entire band in place by hand, making sure the stitches do not show on the outside of the garment.

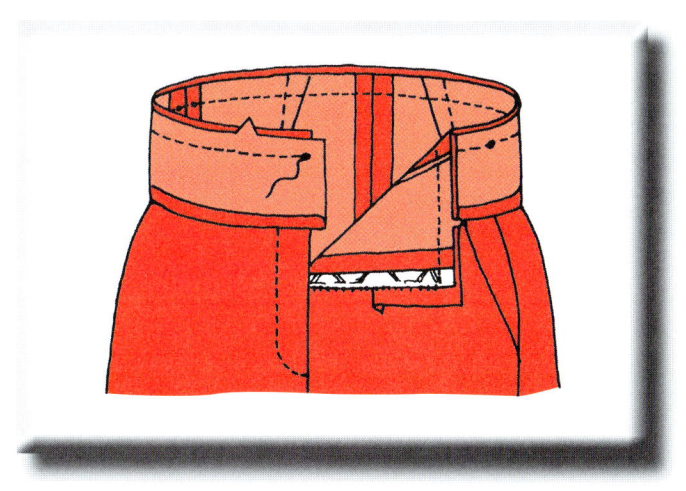

27-15 Baste or fuse interfacing to the waistband. With right sides together, stitch the band to the waist. *Goodheart-Willcox Publisher*

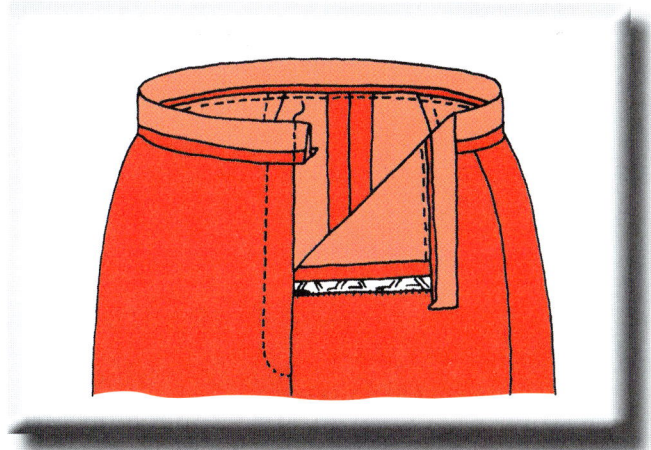

27-16 With right sides together, fold the waistband along the fold line. Stitch the ends and trim. *Goodheart-Willcox Publisher*

Sometimes a pattern will feature a waistband that is topstitched on the outside of the garment. The steps for attaching a waistband in this manner are similar to the previous steps given. However, when you first sew the waistband to the garment, pin the right side of the band to the wrong side of the garment. The long folded edge of the band will later be brought to the right side of the garment. Then, after pinning the folded edge over the seam line, stitch close to the folded edge of the waistband.

Waistline Facings

A facing may be used to finish the waistline edge of a garment. Use interfacing to reinforce the waist area. You can sew it to the facing pieces, or to the waistline edge of the garment. Your pattern may also suggest using seam binding or tape to prevent stretching. Place the seam binding over the seam line on the inside of the garment. Machine baste it in place on the seam line.

To attach a waistline facing, follow these steps:

1. Join the side seams of the facing.
2. Finish the unnotched edge of the facing using a finishing method appropriate for your fabric.
3. Pin the facing to the garment with right sides together. Stitch, easing the garment to fit.
4. Trim, grade, and clip the seam.
5. Press the seam allowances toward the facing.
6. Understitch the seam allowances to the facing.
7. Turn the facing to the inside and press.
8. Tack the facing to the seam allowances (and zipper tape if used) with a few hand stitches. Turn under the ends of the facing and hand stitch in place.

Casings

Casings, fabric pieces that are used to enclose drawstrings or elastic, are often found in sportswear. Shorts, skirts, slacks, sweats, and swim trunks often use casings at the waistlines. Casings are also used at sleeve edges on shirts and dresses and hemlines on sweatpants. Necklines sometimes feature casings. Casings are comfortable to wear because they easily adapt to the shape of the body.

Casings are quick and easy to make. They are generally made one of two ways. A casing that is formed by turning back the edge of the garment piece is called a **self-casing**. When a separate piece of fabric or bias tape is attached to the garment to form the casing, it is called an **applied casing**.

Self-Casings

To make a self-casing, follow these steps:

1. Turn under ¼ inch along the casing edge of the garment and press. (The amount to be turned under may vary. It will be specified on your pattern guide sheet.) If the fabric is bulky, finish the raw edge with a zigzag stitch or overcast using a serger.
2. Turn the casing edge to the inside along the fold line and press again, **27-17**.

3. Stitch close to the inner edge, leaving an opening to insert the drawstring or elastic. Your pattern may suggest that you also stitch close to the upper edge to keep the elastic from rolling.

Applied Casings

To make an applied casing, follow these steps:

1. With right sides together, pin the casing to the garment. Turn in the ends.
2. Stitch a ¼-inch seam.
3. Press the seam allowance toward the casing and understitch through the casing and seam allowance.
4. Fold the casing to the inside. Turn under ¼ inch along the raw edge of the casing, or zigzag or serge the edge.
5. Stitch the edge of the casing to the garment leaving an opening for the elastic. See **27-18**.

Sometimes a pattern may call for a separate band at the waist or sleeve openings. Elastic is inserted into the band. This method is often used with knit fabrics. The serger can be used with this method. First stitch the band into a circle. Then press in half lengthwise, wrong sides together. Divide the band into quarters and mark with pins. Pin the band to the garment, right sides together. Match seams and markings. Serge the band to the garment, leaving an opening to insert the elastic.

A one-piece dress or jacket may call for an applied casing using a strip of bias fabric or bias tape. If you are using a strip of fabric, turn under the long edges of the casing ¼ inch and press. Bias tape is already folded along both sides. Pin the casing in place following the markings on the pattern. Turn in the ends of the casing so the edges just meet. Stitch close to both long edges of the casing, **27-19**. Leave the ends open to insert the elastic or drawstring.

Inserting Elastic in Casings

Once the casing is sewn, elastic is usually inserted. Elastic is available in different types and widths. When selecting elastic for a casing, choose one that is about ¼ inch narrower than the casing width. This allows room to easily insert the elastic. If the elastic is too narrow, it will twist and roll inside the casing. Your pattern envelope will recommend the type and size of elastic to use.

To determine the length of elastic to use, hold a piece of elastic around the body where the casing is to be located. Pull the elastic snugly, but not too tight. Add 1 inch to this length to overlap the ends of the elastic.

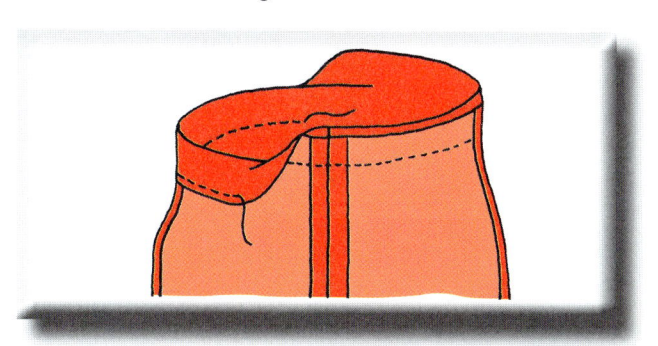

27-17 For a self-casing, turn the casing edge to the inside and stitch close to the edge.
Goodheart-Willcox Publisher

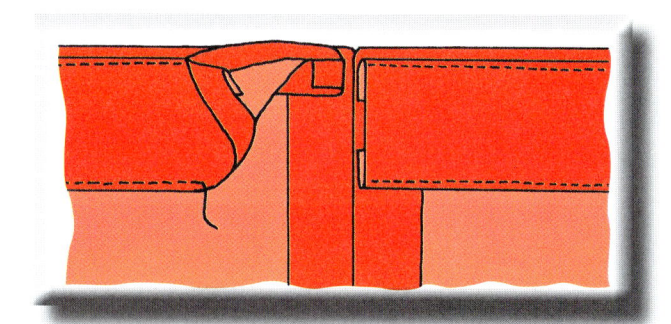

27-18 An applied casing is stitched to the garment edge. It is then folded to the inside and stitched again.
Goodheart-Willcox Publisher

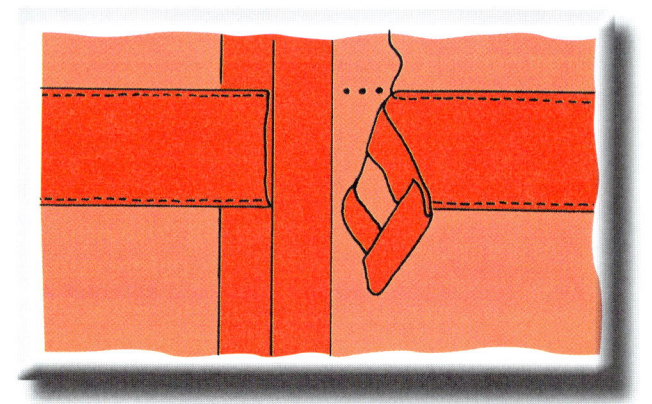

27-19 A bias strip of fabric or bias tape may be sewn on to form a casing on one-piece dresses or jackets.
Goodheart-Willcox Publisher

Follow these steps to insert the elastic through the casing:

1. Fasten a safety pin to one end of the elastic.
2. Insert the pin into the casing opening and work the pin through to the other end. Leave several inches of elastic extending from each end.
3. Overlap the ends ½ inch and pin together with the safety pin.
4. Try on the garment to check the fit and adjust the elastic if needed.
5. Zigzag or straight stitch several times across the overlapping ends of the elastic.
6. Stitch the opening in the casing closed.

Attaching Elastic Directly to Garment

Elastic is sometimes attached directly to a waistline, sleeve, or pant leg edge. The elastic is then folded inside to form a casing. This is a good method to use with knit fabrics. A serger makes the technique especially easy and quick.

To attach elastic directly to a garment, follow these steps:

1. Cut a piece of elastic to the desired length.
2. Overlap the ends of the elastic and stitch securely.
3. Divide the elastic into four sections and mark with pins, 27-20.
4. Divide the garment edge into four sections and mark with pins.
5. Place the elastic on the wrong side of the garment with the edges even. Match the pin markings and pin in place.
6. Serge or zigzag the elastic to the garment. Stretch the elastic to fit the garment as you sew.
7. Turn the elastic and casing to the inside of the garment.
8. Using a straight stitch, sew through the casing, elastic, and garment, stretching the elastic as you sew.

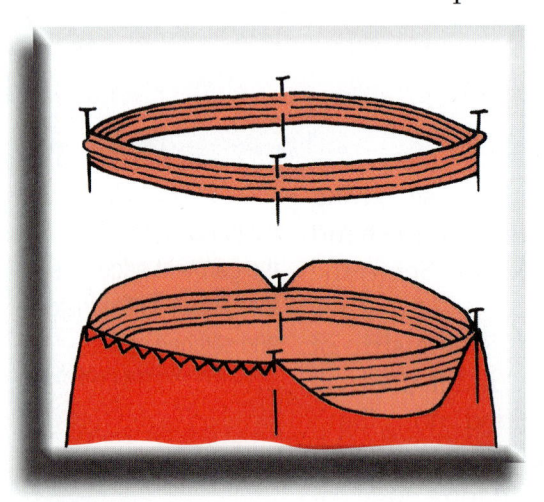

27-20 To attach elastic directly to a garment edge, first divide the elastic into four sections. Divide the garment edge into four sections also. Match the pins and stitch the edges together.
Goodheart-Willcox Publisher

Sewing with Knits

Clothes made of knit fabrics are popular among teens. Knits are comfortable to wear and easy to maintain, 27-21. Because knit fabrics stretch more than woven fabrics, they are ideal for activewear.

Sewing with knits requires some special handling techniques. It is best to wash knits before cutting. Even if the fabric is preshrunk, excess sizing should be removed. Sizing can cause your sewing machine to skip stitches and leave behind a gummy residue on your machine needle. Steam out any fold lines in the fabric.

Pinning and Cutting Knits

When pinning and cutting, lay knits on a large, flat surface. The fabric will stretch if allowed to hang over the edge. Though knits have no grain, locate lengthwise ribs in the fabric. Make certain grain line arrows follow these ribs. Use the *with nap* pattern layout to avoid any color differences in the finished garment.

Use very sharp shears for cutting to avoid snags. Make sure pins are also sharp. When marking, use chalk or a marking pen. Tracing wheels can snag knits or leave permanent markings.

Sewing Knit Fabrics

When sewing with knits, use a ballpoint needle with your sewing machine. Ballpoint needles gently separate the yarns as they enter the fabric. Pointed needles pierce the yarns causing runs and snags.

Select a needle size appropriate for the weight of the fabric. Lightweight knits use lower numbers (size 9 or 11) than heavier knits (size 14 or 16). Be sure to use a new needle when sewing knits to avoid snags, runs, and skipped stitches.

Thread should have some elasticity to prevent the stitches from breaking. Choose all-purpose polyester or cotton-wrapped polyester thread.

Seams in knits should have some stretch to them. This also prevents the stitches from breaking. Use one of the following methods:

- *Method 1.* If you use a straight stitch, stretch the seam slightly as you sew. Stitch on the seam line. Then stitch again ¼ inch from the seam line in the seam allowance. Trim close to the second stitching.
- *Method 2.* Use a narrow zigzag stitch to sew the seam. Trim the seam to ¼ inch and then zigzag or overcast the edge.
- *Method 3.* Use a serger machine to sew the seam. It is ideal to use with knits because it is fast and easy. The machine sews the seam, trims the seam allowance, and overcasts the edge in one motion. The 3-thread or 3/4-thread overlock stitches are best to use.

Some seams, such as at the shoulder or waistline, should not stretch. Stabilize these seams by sewing twill tape or seam binding into the seam. Topstitching also helps stabilize seams.

In the button and buttonhole areas, apply fusible interfacing. This prevents stretching and gives needed stability.

Before hemming your garment, allow it to hang for a day or so. Any stretching will occur before you sew the hem.

There are several ways to hem knits. Choose from the following:

- On sportswear, topstitching or a zigzag stitch give a casual look.
- A serger can be used to create an overcast hem edge.
- If hand sewing is your choice, the catch stitch allows for the greatest give.

27-21 Knits are comfortable to wear and most are easy to sew. *Photo courtesy of McCall Pattern Co.*

Did You Know?

Fleece—A Popular Choice for Cold-Weather Wear

You can sew a warm top quickly by choosing a fleece fabric. Fleece fabrics are knitted then brushed to create a fuzzy, downy surface on both sides of the fabric. They retain very little water, so they are good for outerwear. In addition, they will not run, ravel, or shrink.

When sewing with fleece, it may be hard to tell the right side from the wrong side. To check, stretch the fabric on the crosswise grain. Fleece fabrics generally curl to the wrong side. It is still best to mark the right side when each garment piece is cut out.

Follow these pointers when sewing fleece:

- Use polyester thread and a universal or ballpoint machine needle.
- Choose a needle size based on the weight of the fleece, but use the smallest size possible.
- Set the stitch length at 7 to 9 stitches per inch for most loose-fitting garments and low-stress seams. If seams need to *give*, shorten the stitch length to 12 to 14 stitches per inch. This provides more strength in high-stress seams.
- If using a serger, use a 3/4-thread seam.
- Because fleece does not ravel, you can eliminate bulk on collars, cuffs, and pockets by using the cut edge as the finished edge.

Pressing is not recommended, but if it is necessary during construction, hold the iron above the fabric and steam only. Then press with your fingers so the fleece lies in the desired position. Never place the iron directly on the fleece as this contact may leave a permanent imprint or melt the fabric.

Butterick Co., Inc.

Sewing with Pile Fabrics

If you are sewing a pile fabric, you will need to follow a few guidelines. A pile fabric has ends or loops of yarn extending above the surface of the fabric. Terry cloth is a pile fabric with a looped surface. If the loops are cut, it is called a cut pile fabric. Examples of cut pile fabrics are corduroy, velvet, and velour. Fleece is another popular type of pile fabric. Most fleece fabrics have a knit backing, **27-22**.

A pile creates a nap on the fabric. A nap is a layer of fiber ends above the fabric surface. The nap lies in one direction on a pile fabric. If you run your hand in the direction of the nap, it will feel smooth. If you stroke your hand in the opposite direction, it will feel rough. This texture affects the color of the napped fabric.

When you sew with napped fabrics, it is important that the nap run in the same direction in the entire garment. If a section is cut in the opposite direction, a difference in color or shading will be noticeable.

When sewing with pile fabrics, follow these guidelines:

- Choose a simple design with few seams.
- Follow the cutting layout for *with nap* fabrics. For richer color, the pile should go upward.
- Pretrim the pattern pieces for easier cutting of high-loft fabrics.
- Use long pins to pin pattern to bulky fabrics.
- Mark with pins and chalk.
- Use a size 14 stretch machine needle, which has a longer shaft to prevent skipping of stitches. Set the stitch length for 9 stitches per inch.
- Hand basting may be necessary to prevent slippage, or use a double-sided basting tape.

27-22 Pile knits, such as the fleece fabric in this shirt, are best suited for garments with few seams. *Shutterstock*

Pressing Pile Fabrics

Pressing pile fabrics requires special techniques to prevent the crushing the pile. Always place an extra piece of the pile fabric against the pile of the garment when pressing. When pressing the garment on the wrong side, place the piece of fabric on the ironing board, pile side up. When pressing the garment on the right side, lay the piece of pile fabric against the right side of the garment before pressing. Press lightly with steam. You can also use a needle board or plush pile bath towel for pressing pile fabric. If you use the bath towel, you will need to carefully remove any lint left by the towel.

For high-loft fabrics such as fleece, pressing is not recommended. The iron may leave a permanent imprint on these fabrics. Hold the iron above the fabric and steam. Set the iron down on its heel rest, and finger press to set the fabric in the desired position.

Summary

- There are three types of collars: flat, rolled, and standing. They can be attached with a full fitted facing, a partial facing, or with no facing.
- The three most common styles of sleeves are kimono, raglan, and set-in. The easiest to make is the kimono sleeve. The set-in sleeve is the most difficult to sew. It is attached to the garment with a seam that goes around the armhole.
- Patch pockets, in-seam pockets, and front hip pockets are the most common styles of pockets. Patch pockets can be made from the same fabric or a contrasting fabric.
- The three most common ways of finishing waistlines are with a waistband, a facing, or a casing.
- Casings, fabric pieces that are used to enclose drawstrings or elastic, are often found in sportswear. Shorts, skirts, slacks, sweats, and swim trunks often use casings at the waistline.
- Sewing with knits and pile fabrics require special handling techniques. When you sew with napped fabrics, it is important that the nap run in the same direction in the entire garment. If not, a slight difference in color might be noticed between the parts of the garment.

Graphic Organizer

Create a T-chart on a sheet of paper. In the left column, write the main chapter headings. In the right column, write supporting details for each heading.

Main Headings	Supporting Details

Review the Facts

1. What causes a collar to roll rather than to lie flat?
2. What can you do to keep the under collar from rolling out and showing at the edge of a collar?
3. Which sleeve style has a diagonal seam extending from the underarm to the neckline?
4. Describe how to ease in the fullness in a set-in sleeve.
5. Which type of pocket is not visible when the garment is worn?
6. Describe how to make straight sides and sharp corners on a square pocket.
7. What can be done to stabilize seams and keep them from stretching, such as on a front hip pocket?
8. How does a waistband differ from a waistline facing?
9. List four places where casings might be used on a garment.
10. If a casing is 1 inch wide, what width of elastic should you use?
11. Describe three techniques for sewing with knits discussed in this chapter.
12. What might cause parts of a velvet garment to appear a different color?
13. Identify two clothing construction steps described in this chapter for which using a serger was suggested.
14. Name two reasons why it is more difficult to sew with knit and pile fabrics?

Think Critically

15. **Compare and contrast.** Compare and contrast the advantages and disadvantages of the three styles of sleeves. Consider appearance, wearability, and ease of construction.
16. **Compare and contrast.** Compare and contrast the three waistline treatments described in this chapter. Consider appearance, wearability, and ease of construction.

17. **Draw conclusions.** To make a shirt, you might use several of the sewing techniques described in this chapter, such as collars, set-in sleeves, and patch pockets. Draw conclusions about whether it is more economical to buy a ready-to-wear shirt or sew a similar shirt. Consider dollar costs as well as time involved.

Apparel Applications

18. **Photo essay.** Create a photo essay showing various garments. Identify the types of collars, sleeves, pockets, and waistline treatments each design features. Share your photo essay with the class.
19. **Pocket practice.** Demonstrate your ability to make curved and square patch pockets using the patterns provided by your teacher.
20. **Edge finish comparison.** Compare different methods used to finish fabric edges. Experiment with a zigzag stitch, an overcast stitch on the serger, and a hemmed edge. Use the same methods on both woven fabrics and knit fabrics. Write a paper summarizing your results.
21. **Knit fabric dictionary.** Collect and mount samples of various knit fabrics on index cards. Identify and classify the knits by type. List garment styles appropriate for each type of knit.
22. **Practice pressing.** Press a piece of pile fabric on a flat surface and then against a piece of the same fabric. Compare the results.

Academic Connections

23. **Writing.** Use Internet and print resources to research how to use sewing techniques described in this chapter to restyle garments to accommodate individuals with special needs. Write an illustrated report of your findings to share with the class.
24. **Social studies.** Investigate Internet and print resources for charitable-sewing project ideas for which you can use the sewing techniques in this chapter. Locate a project pattern and sew the project. Organize your classmates to sew for this cause.

Workplace Connections

25. **Technique demonstration.** Prepare a demonstration for the class on one of the construction techniques described in this chapter. Have the class critique your demonstration.
26. **Portfolio builder.** Suppose you run your own sewing business. You have a new client that wants to see samples of your sewing ability. Create a portfolio demonstrating your ability to proficiently use each of the sewing techniques described in this chapter. Neatly mount your samples and save them in a binder.

Fashion Construction—Teen or Adult

Prepare a *Fashion Construction* STAR Event to display your skills in clothing construction. For this event, sew a garment using at least eight sewing-construction techniques for a teen's or adult's garment. Follow the FCCLA STAR Event guidelines for *Fashion Construction*. See your adviser for information as needed.

Chapter 28

Serging Skills

Chapter Objectives

After studying this chapter, you will be able to
- **summarize** how the serger functions.
- **identify** serger machine parts and basic serger stitches.
- **summarize** how to select thread and accessories for the serger.
- **demonstrate** how to thread and operate the serger, adjusting thread tensions and stitches as needed.
- **demonstrate** proper use of a serger to construct a garment.
- **demonstrate** how to serge various types of seams.
- **perform** routine care of the serger.

Key Terms

sergers
cones
loopers
overedge stitch
flatlock stitch
rolled edge stitch
overlock stitch

cover stitch
chain stitch
cone adapter
spool cap
thread net
chaining off
continuous overcasting technique

narrow double-stitched seam
mock flat-felled seam
flat method of construction
stabilizing

Reading with Purpose

Suppose you are a business owner and have several employees working for you. As you read the chapter, think about what you would like your employees to know. When you finish reading, write a memo to your employees and include key information from the chapter.

Sergers, also called *overlock* or *overedge* machines, provide a factorylike finish to home-sewn garments, **28-1**. These machines join two layers of fabric to form a seam, trim away extra seam allowance width, and overcast (finish) the fabric edges all in one step. See **28-2**.

Sergers first became available for home use in the early 1970s. Before that time, their only use was in the garment industry. People did not immediately accept them, however, due to their limitations. It was nearly ten years later before they really began to gain widespread use. Home sewers liked the job sergers did of stitching and finishing seams in one fast and easy step, but sergers could not be used for all sewing tasks.

Recently, improvements in serger machines make them more suitable for more sewing tasks. The newer machines have many new stitches that are similar to regular sewing machine stitches. The only tasks many of today's sergers cannot do is embroidery and making buttonholes.

28-1 This serged child's T-shirt and shorts makes use of the decorative 5-thread reversible cover stitch to create a unique outfit.
BERNINA of America, Inc.

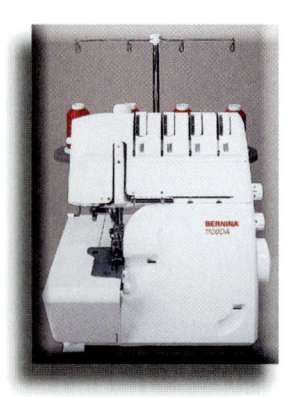

28-2 A serger can give your finished sewing project a professional look.
BERNINA of America, Inc.

In spite of the improvements, most home sewers use the serger to supplement a conventional sewing machine—not replace it. Most sergers stitch on the edge of the fabric only. They are not used for inside areas, such as inserting zippers.

The serger works well on fabrics from lightweight chiffon to heavyweight denim. Most serger stitches are stretchable and are appropriate to use on knit and woven fabrics.

Whether you make an item to wear or an item for your home, serging can enhance its appearance both on the inside and outside. Using a serger gives a professional seam finish to garments such as unlined jackets. Likewise, making hems and ruffles is quick and easy with a serger. You can also give a professional look to items such as curtains and place mats with a serger.

How the Serger Functions

A serger uses two, three, four, or five **cones** (large spools) of thread depending on the model. They use one or two needles, but some models can use three. Sergers do not have bobbins but have loopers, both upper and lower. **Loopers** are the parts of the serger that form the stitch. Unlike a sewing machine—which creates stitches by interlocking bobbin and needle threads—a serger loops thread around the needle thread, encasing the fabric edge. Looper threads do not penetrate the fabric. The needles and loopers form the stitches over the fabric edge as it passes through the machine, **28-3**. During stitching, knife blades trim the seam allowances.

The serger performs many functions at the same time to create the stitches. As you feed the fabric into the machine, it reaches the feed dogs first. As the fabric moves along, the knives trim the edge. Then the loopers and needles form the stitches on the fabric. The fabric then feeds off the stitch finger behind the needle.

Since the serger performs three functions at once and runs much faster than a conventional sewing machine, it can reduce the sewing time of a project by as much as half. Some sergers can stitch at a speed of 1300 to 1500 stitches per minute. The average top speed of a conventional sewing machine is 900 to 1000 stitches per minute.

Serger Machine Parts

Although there are a variety of types and models of sergers, they have many similarities. Following is a list of the names and functions of the basic

28-3 A serger forms a seam, trims away the excess seam allowance, and overcasts the edges to produce a factory like finish. *BERNINA of America, Inc.*

parts you will find on *most* sergers. As you read about each part, locate it on the machine diagram in **28-4**.

- *Thread tension dials (1).* Apply tension to the threads leading to one or two needles and the loopers so they feed at a constant rate.
- *Stitch length dial (2).* Adjusts the number of stitches per inch. Make adjustments by loosening a screw, moving a lever, or turning a dial.
- *Differential feed dial (3).* Adjusts the front and back feed dogs to operate at different speeds. Not all sergers have this control.
- *Handwheel (4).* Turns to raise or lower the needles.
- *Threading diagram (6).* Shows how to thread the upper and lower loopers and the right and left needles.
- *Power switch on/off (7).* Turns on the serger and light.
- *Knives/knife setting (9).* Trim seam allowances as stitches are formed. Sets knife settings. Sergers have upper and lower knives. On some sergers, the knives can be disengaged when trimming is not desired.
- *Feed dogs (11).* Move fabric under the presser foot.
- *Stitch finger (11).* A metal prong around which the stitches form. The stitch finger may be located on the throat plate beside the feed dogs or the presser foot.
- *Presser foot (12).* Holds fabric in place as the serger stitches.
- *Needle threader (13).* A device that helps thread the needles.
- *Presser foot pressure regulator (16).* Adjusts the amount of pressure applied to the presser foot and the fabric.
- *Thread guide support (17).* A knob that supports the thread guides.
- *Spool pins (18).* Hold cones, spools, or tubes of thread.
- *Thread guides (19).* Guide the threads from the cones or spools, through the tension dials, to the needles and loopers.

494   Part 5   Sewing Techniques

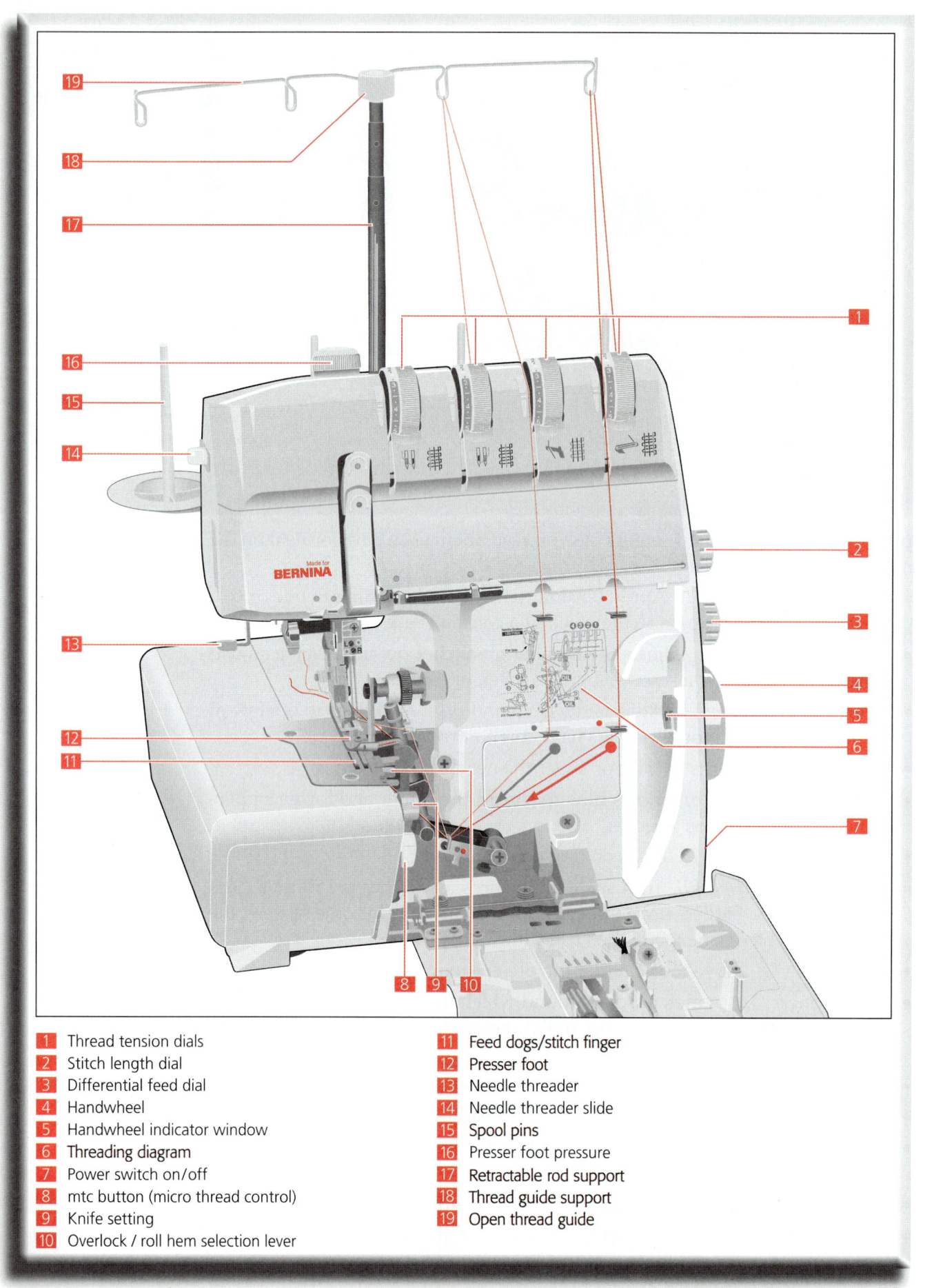

1. Thread tension dials
2. Stitch length dial
3. Differential feed dial
4. Handwheel
5. Handwheel indicator window
6. Threading diagram
7. Power switch on/off
8. mtc button (micro thread control)
9. Knife setting
10. Overlock / roll hem selection lever
11. Feed dogs/stitch finger
12. Presser foot
13. Needle threader
14. Needle threader slide
15. Spool pins
16. Presser foot pressure
17. Retractable rod support
18. Thread guide support
19. Open thread guide

28-4 The diagram shows the major parts of the serger. *Photo courtesy of BERNINA International/BERNINA of America, Inc.*

- *Throat plate.* Covers the area below the needle and presser foot.
- *Stitch width regulator.* Adjusts the position of the knives and stitch finger. Not all sergers have this control.
- *Needle clamp screws.* Hold needles in place.
- *Loopers.* Are necessary in forming stitches, **28-5**. Sergers have one to three loopers. They are referred to as the upper and lower. The two threads that come up from underneath the needle plate are called the lower looper thread and the upper looper thread. Each has its own tension regulator.

Basic Serger Stitches

Serger stitches vary with machine make and model. Knowledge of the various serger stitches will help you select the serger that best suits your needs. The list that follows identifies the most common serger stitches. The serger can also produce decorative stitches to achieve a special effect. Decorative specialty threads can produce an interesting look, adding extra emphasis to the stitches. Refer to the stitch descriptions in **28-6**.

- *Overedge stitch.* The **overedge stitch** is a two-thread stitch used solely as an edge finish on garments. It cannot be used for seaming purposes. It uses one needle and one looper. The overedge stitch gives a quick, durable, and professional seam finish to any fabric you sew on your conventional sewing machine. It is the least bulky stitch and is good for sheer and lightweight fabrics. Unlined jackets, facing edges, hem finishes, and fabrics that require an edge finish to prevent raveling are good choices for the overedge stitch.
- *Flatlock stitch.* The **flatlock stitch** is a two-thread stitch that uses one needle and one looper to join a seam. A three-thread stitch uses two loopers. Sportswear or lingerie elastic application is the primary use for the flatlock. The flatlock stitch generally requires loosening the machine tension; however, follow the guidelines for your specific serger model. Loosening the tension allows you to pull the fabric edges open and flatten them once you stitch the seam. The seam is visible from the right side of the garment, creating a decorative *ladder* effect.

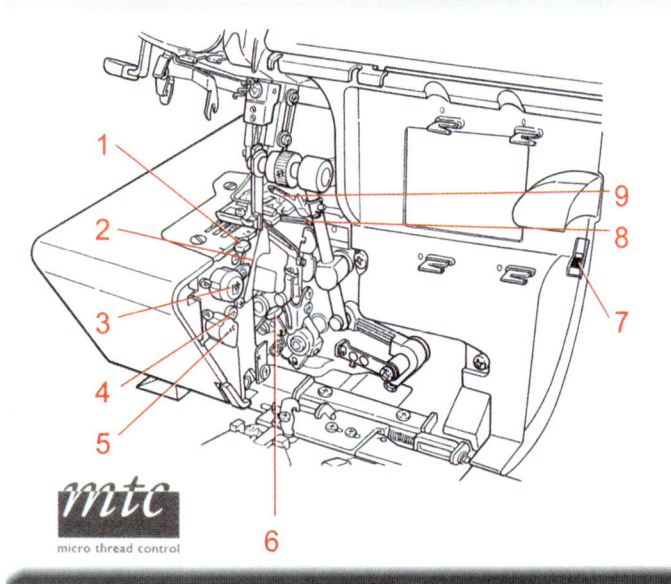

1 Selection lever for overlocking or roll hemming
2 Lower knife
3 Cutting width adjusting dial
4 Lower knife setscrew
5 Micro thread control lever
6 Lower looper auto threader
7 Handwheel indicator window
8 Lower looper
9 Upper looper

28-5 This diagram gives a close-up look at the parts inside the serger cover. *Image courtesy of BERNINA International/BERNINA of America, Inc.*

496   Part 5   Sewing Techniques

Overedge stitch

Overlock stitch

Flatlock stitch

Cover stitch

Rolled edge stitch

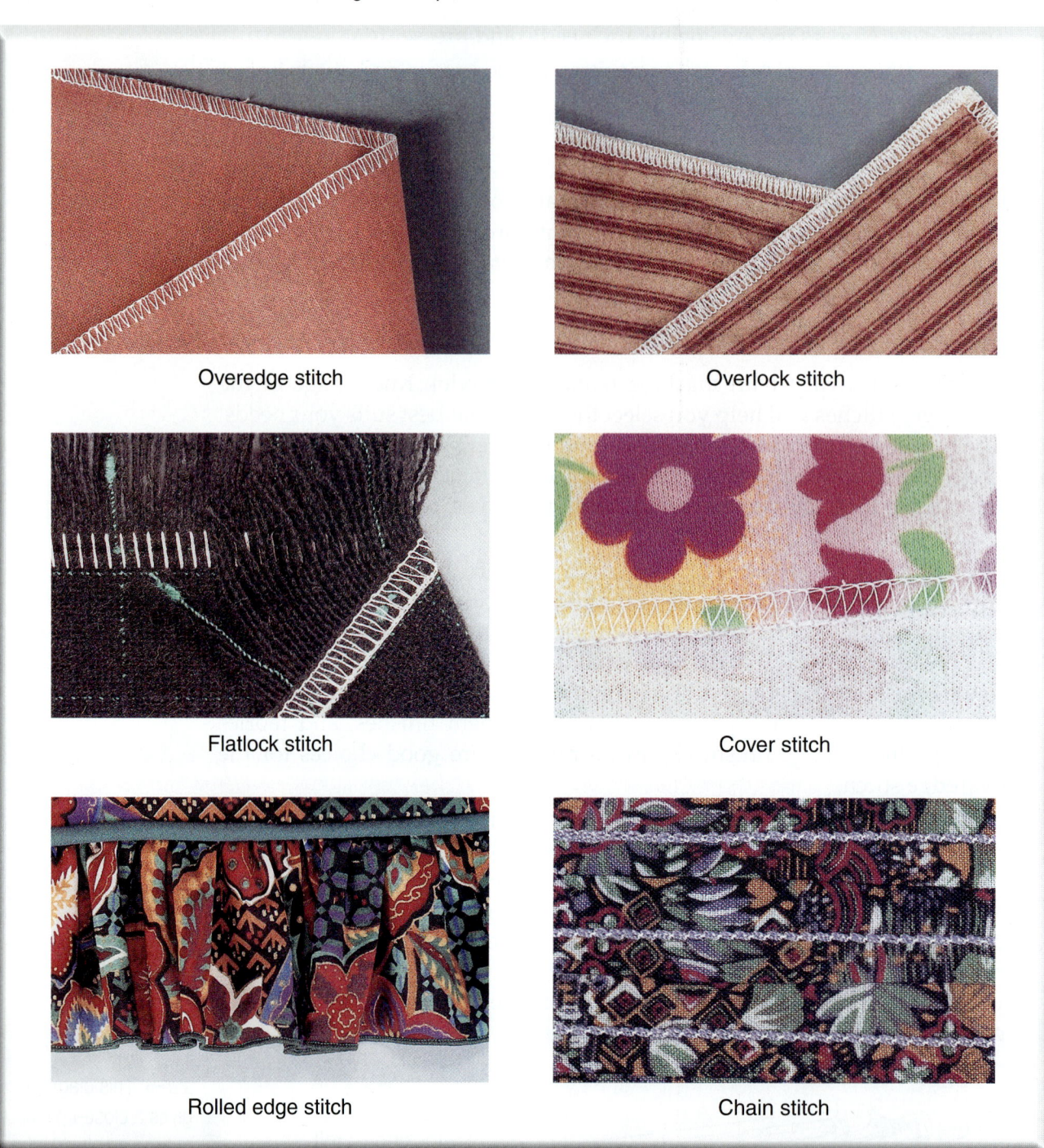

Chain stitch

28-6 These are the six basic stitches created by the serger. They have various uses. *BERNINA of America, Inc.*

- *Rolled edge stitch.* The **rolled edge stitch** is a two- or three-thread stitch. Most three-thread machines will stitch a narrow rolled hem, while only some two-thread machines produce this stitch. A narrow rolled hem uses an unbalanced stitch. This generally requires making adjustments to the machine tension, allowing fabric to roll into a narrow hem (follow the adjustment guidelines for your machine model). This is a timesaving way to finish scarves, napkins, lingerie, ruffles, or anywhere you might use a narrow hem. It is also useful as a seaming technique for sheers, laces, or silk fabrics. The three-thread rolled edge, which uses two loopers, gives a bulkier edge more suited to light- to medium-weight fabrics.

- *Overlock stitch.* The **overlock stitch** is a three-, four-, or five-thread stitch that is useful for seaming purposes. It can stitch, trim, and overedge a seam in one operation similar to the seams found in ready-to-wear. This stitch is the *core* stitch of any serger. Adjusting the stitch width and length can make the stitch suitable for a wide variety of weights and types of fabric.

- *Cover stitch.* The main use for the **cover stitch** is hemming knits. It is one of the newest serger stitches. On the top side, this stretchable stitch resembles two or three parallel rows of topstitching. On the underside, one looper thread interlocks all the needle threads. You do not use the cutting blade when making this stitch. The three-thread cover stitch uses two needles and one looper, creating two rows of topstitching. The four-thread cover stitch uses three needles and one looper, creating three rows of topstitching. Not all machine models have this feature.
- *Chain stitch.* The **chain stitch** does not overlock the edge of the fabric. It can function as a standard straight stitch if the cutting knives are disengaged. The top side looks like a straight stitch, and the underside resembles a chain. The two-thread chain stitch uses one needle and the lower looper on the 4- and 5- thread machines. Another name for the chain stitch is *safety stitch*.

Selecting Thread and Accessories

Although you can use regular sewing thread on your serger, special serger threads offer the following advantages:

- fineness for more delicate finishing and less bulk
- strength
- cross-winding for smooth top feeding during high-speed sewing
- larger quantities
- economy

Because sergers use more thread than conventional sewing machines, serger thread is usually available on cones or tubes. Tubes can have as much as 1,000 yards of thread on them while cones can hold up to 6,000 yards, **28-7**.

Serger threads are generally lighter than regular sewing threads. Because a serger seam requires using more thread, a lighter-weight thread reduces the bulk. The thread must be strong, however, because the serger sews very fast and there is more tension on the thread. It is extremely important to use quality thread to minimize breakage.

The following types of thread are suitable for serging:

- *Cotton-covered polyester or 100 percent polyester serger thread.* This is a finer thread than the thread you use for conventional sewing. The polyester

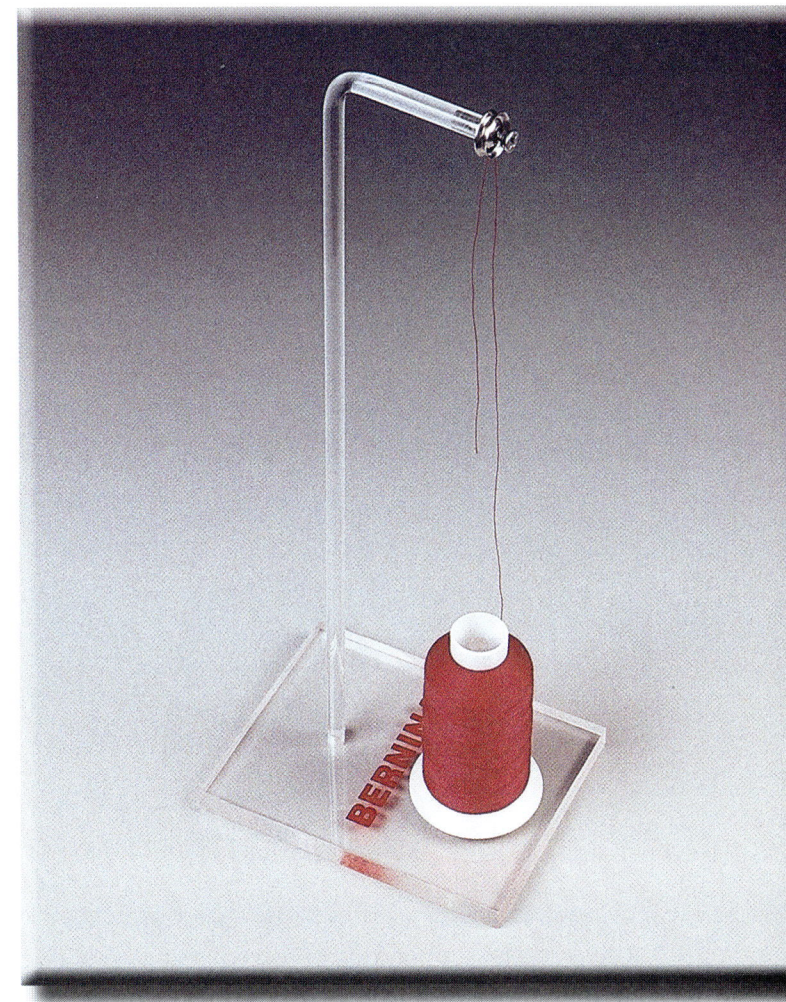

28-7 Buy serger thread on cones or tubes as more thread is used than in conventional sewing.
BERNINA of America, Inc.

makes the thread strong and provides stretch. The cotton wrap provides smoothness and luster.

- *Nylon serger thread.* This is a very strong thread that is recommended for knitted swimwear, lingerie, and active sportswear. It works well for rolled hems.
- *Decorative threads.* Several types of threads are useful for creating decorative effects when serging. These include metallic thread, silk thread, woolly (texturized) nylon, pearl cotton (a crochet thread), machine embroidery thread, lightweight ribbons, and baby yarns.

Because there are color limitations with serger threads, you may not be able to find an exact color match for your fabric. Try selecting a color that blends rather than matches. Also choose a color slightly darker than the fabric. If you have only one thread that matches the fabric, use it for the needle thread, which is more likely to be visible.

A cone adapter and spool cap may come with your serger. The **cone adapter** (sometimes called an *anti-vibration* cone) is used when the thread is on a cone. When using a thread on a tube, remove the adapter. If using thread from a spool, place a **spool cap** (or unreeling disk) over the spool to provide even feeding of thread to the machine. Put the spool of thread on the thread stand with the notch down. Some specialty threads require the use of a **thread net** that helps prevent thread tangling. A thread net is especially helpful when using slippery threads, **28-8**.

Threading the Serger

Follow the directions in the owner's manual provided with your serger to thread the machine. To make threading the machine easier, many manufacturers label the path of the threads with different symbols or colors. Many machines include a color-coded threading guide directly on the machine. The newer machines are easier to thread. Many have a special looper threading aide and a needle threader. Use heavier threads in the loopers, not the needles.

It is essential to thread the loopers and needles in the correct order. Threads may break or stitches may not form properly if the machine is incorrectly threaded. Always thread the loopers before the needles—the upper looper first. The lower looper is the most difficult to thread. You may find that using a tweezers makes this job easier.

Rather than completely rethreading the machine each time you change thread, you can tie the new thread to the old thread. Follow these steps:

1. Clip the current threads below the thread guides located above the spools.
2. Replace the old cones or spools of thread with the new ones.

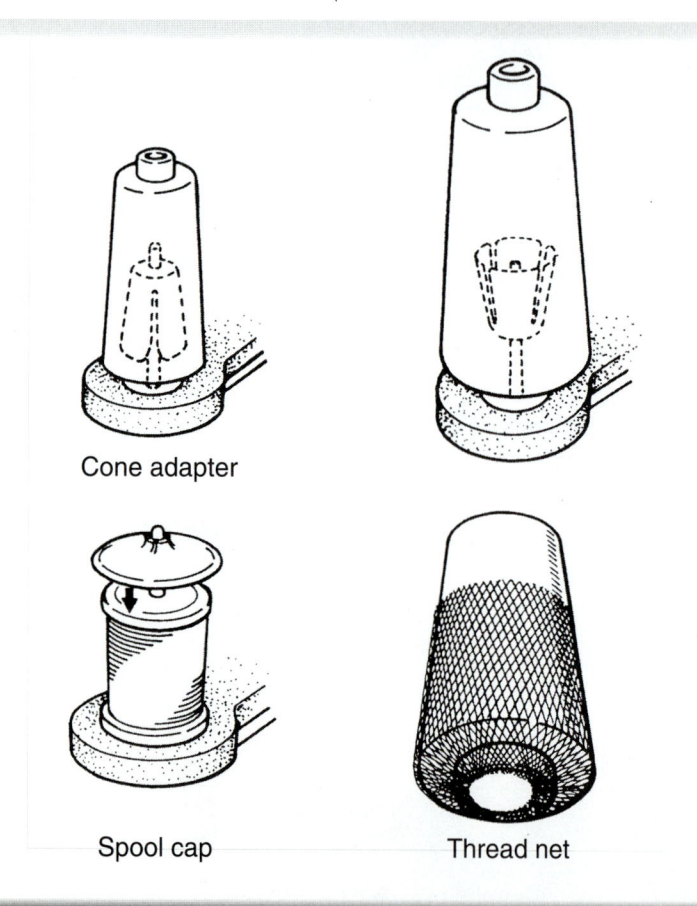

28-8 A cone adapter, spool cap, and thread net are helpful serger accessories. *BERNINA of America, Inc.*

3. Tie the threads from the new spools to the old threads using square knots. Tug on the knots to make sure they are secure, and trim the thread ends one inch from knots, **28-9**.
4. Lift the presser foot and raise the needle. Remove the threads from the tension dials and carefully pull the knots through the guides pulling from behind the presser foot.
5. Do not pull knots through the needles, but clip the knots in front of the needles.
6. Readjust the threads in tension dials and thread the needles.

28-9 Tying threads from new spools to the old threads will save you time in rethreading your serger. *The McCall Pattern Company*

Operating the Serger

After threading the serger, practice using it with fabric scraps. Always use a double layer of fabric in order to check the stitch formation and thread tension. It is also a good idea to use a different color of thread for each looper and needle while you are learning to operate the machine. This will help you learn which thread forms which part of the stitch. Follow these steps:

1. Set all tension dials to 5 (or as directed by the instruction manual).
2. Make sure the upper knife is lowered and in the cutting position.
3. Lower the presser foot. It can remain in this lowered position.
4. Holding the thread chain or tails lightly behind the presser foot, serge a 2- to 3-inch thread chain. This is called **chaining off**.
5. Place the fabric in front of the presser foot where the longer feed dogs will pull the fabric forward. Do not push or pull the fabric. Allow the machine to do the work for you. Watch the stitching guidelines on the machine for the proper seam width.
6. At the end of the seam, continue sewing to form a 3-inch thread chain. Do not raise the presser foot. See *A* in **28-10**.
7. Holding the fabric in one hand, pull the thread chain over the thread cutter on the presser foot shank, *B* in **28-10**.

Check your trial run. See **28-11** and check for the following:

- The upper looper thread (1) lies on the upper side of the fabric and the lower looper thread (2) lies on the underside of the fabric. The loops formed by both threads meet exactly on the edge of the fabric.

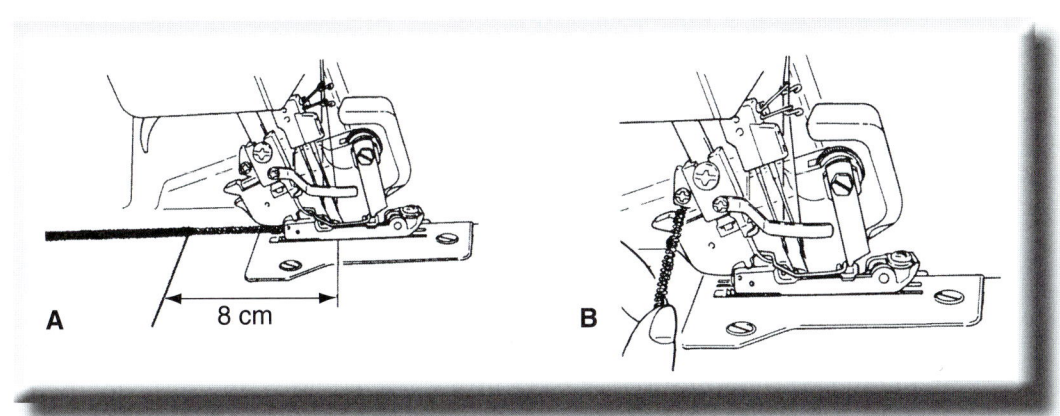

28-10 Be sure to leave a 2- to 3-inch thread chain by continuing to sew off the edge of the fabric (A). Cut the thread chain using the thread cutter (B). *BERNINA of America, Inc.*

- The overlock needle thread (3) anchors both looper threads. It forms a straight stitch on the upper side of the fabric and appears as tiny dots on the underside.
- The double chain looper thread (4) can only be seen on the underside of the fabric and joins the dots together to form a double chain stitch.
- The double chain needle thread (5) forms a separate straight stitch on the upper side of the fabric and appears as tiny dots on the underside.

Now do a trial run using only one color thread and compare the two samples. Check the tension on the same basis as the colored-thread sample and note the differences between the upper and underside of the stitch. Remember, it is not necessary to rethread the machine for this. Cut off the threads above the cones or spools, replace them, and knot this thread onto existing colored thread.

If the stitch formation varies considerably from what it should be, check the following points:

- Is the machine threaded correctly?
- Is the thread lying properly between the tension discs?
- Are all the tension dials set at 5? (Varies by serger model.)
- Is the thread caught?

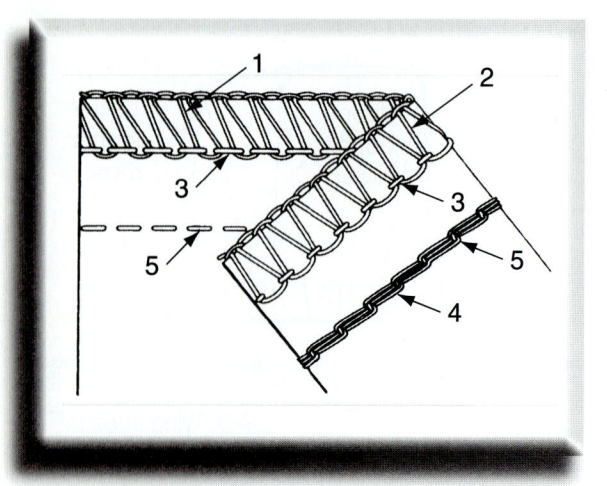

28-11 Check these five points when evaluating your 5-thread overlock chain stitch. *BERNINA of America, Inc.*

Adjusting Thread Tension

When using the serger, you may need to adjust the thread tensions. Changing fabric, thread, or stitch type may require adjustments to the machine. A serger can have as many as five tension regulators—one for each thread. You will need to recognize which thread tension needs adjustment and by how much. With practice, this will become easier.

When tension adjustments are needed, turn the tension dial by only half or one number. Then test sew again and check the results. The following descriptions (may vary slightly by model) and the illustrations in 28-12, will help you recognize thread tension problems:

- If the looper threads meet on the underside of the fabric, tighten the upper looper thread tension or loosen the lower looper thread tension. (A)
- If the looper threads meet on the upper side of the fabric, tighten the lower looper thread tension or loosen the upper looper thread tension. (B)
- If the edge of the fabric curls, the tension of both looper threads is too tight. Loosen upper and lower looper thread tension. (C)
- When the overlock (right-hand) needle thread forms loops on the underside, tighten the overlock needle thread tension. (D)
- The double chain (left-hand) needle thread may form loops on the underside. If so, tighten the double chain needle thread tension. (E)

Other types of problems can occur when sewing with a serger. The chart in 28-13 will help you determine possible solutions to some common problems.

A   B   C

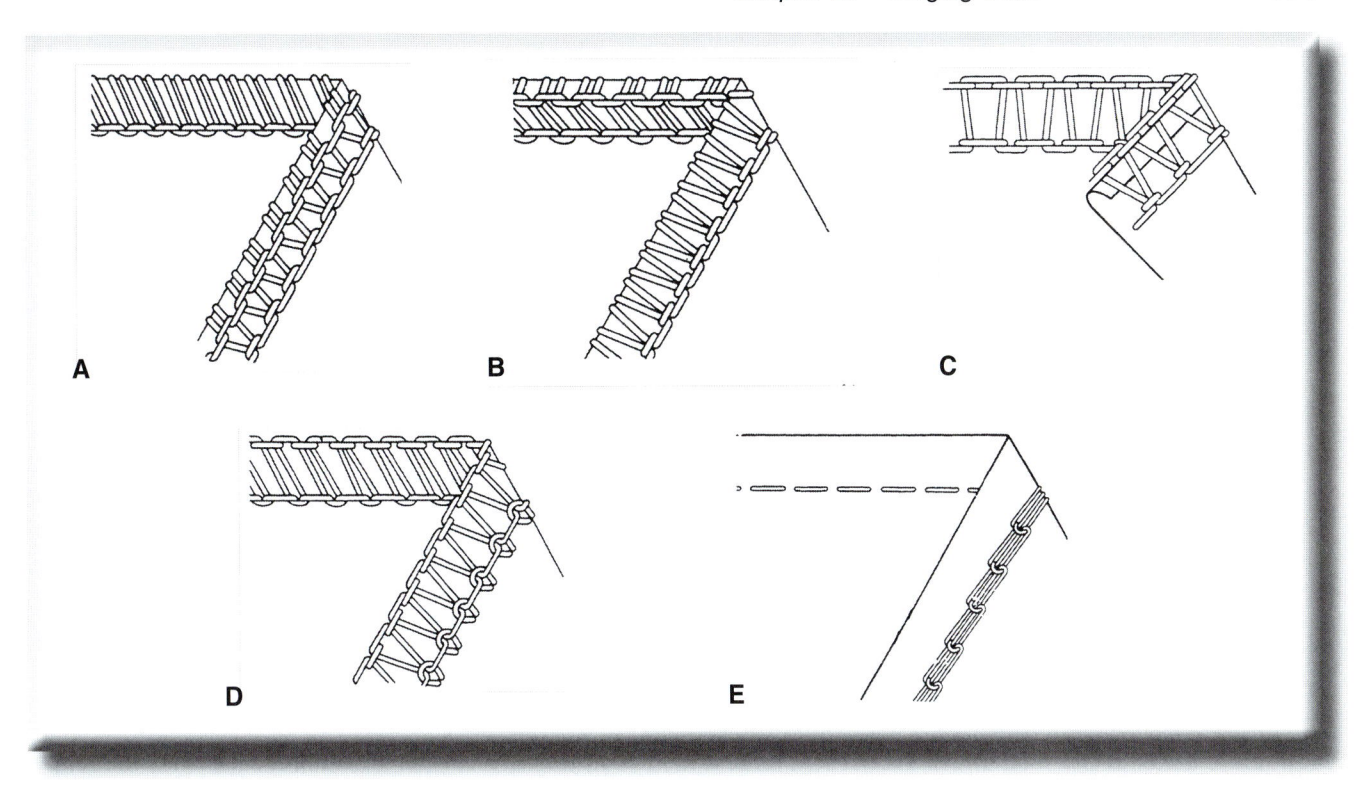

D   E

28-12 The illustrations above will help you learn to adjust the thread tension on your serger. Turn the dial by only half or one number and then test again. *BERNINA of America, Inc.*

Serger Problems and Solutions				
Problem	**Possible Solutions**		**Problem**	**Possible Solutions**
Skipped Stitches	• Check threading: change type of thread; rethread. • Check needle: tighten needle; replace dull or damaged needle; change type or size. • Check tension: loosen slightly.		Needle breaks	• Check for tangled or caught thread. • Check if needle is inserted correctly. • Change to larger needle. • Tighten needle screw.
Thread Breaks	• Check threading: check for tangled or caught thread; check sequence. • Change to higher-quality thread. • Check needle: insert correctly; replace dull or damaged needle. • Check tension: loosen slightly.		Fabric Puckers	• Loosen right- or left-hand needle thread tension. • Check threading; look for tangled or caught thread. • Shorten stitch length. • Hold fabric taut in front of and behind presser foot while sewing. • Adjust differential feed, if available.
Fabric Jams	• Check for tangled or caught thread; chain off after completing stitching. • Lengthen stitch length. • Increase presser foot pressure for heavy fabrics. • Decrease presser foot pressure for light fabrics.				

28-13 If you are having problems with your serging, check this chart for possible solutions.

Adjusting Stitch Length and Width

Whenever you change fabrics, threads, or stitches, you may need to make adjustments in the stitch length and width. As a general rule, you will use shorter, narrower stitches for lightweight fabrics and longer, wider stitches for heavyweight fabrics.

To vary the length of the stitch, use the stitch length adjustment dial. The length of the stitch is the distance in millimeters (mm) between the needle penetrations, **28-14**. The range is generally between 1 mm to 5 mm. If the fabric jams, the stitch length may be too short for the fabric you are using.

The width of the stitch represents the distance in millimeters between the needle thread and the trimmed edge of the fabric. This can range from 1.5 mm to 7.5 mm depending upon the machine you are using. To change the width of the stitch, your serger may have a dial that can be adjusted. Other sergers may require a change in the needle plate. Follow the explanation in your instruction manual for the method your machine uses.

Using a Serger in Clothing Construction

There are three ways you can use the serger in clothing construction. These include the following

- *One-step method.* The first is to use the one-step operation where seams are stitched, trimmed, and overcast all at one time by the serger. For this method, the needle stitches on the seam line. The knives automatically trim the correct amount. If the machine has two needles, the left needle stitches on the seam line. When ⅝-inch seam allowances are used, the left needle is ⅝ inch from the fabric edge, **28-15**.
- *Edge finish method.* The second method involves using the serger only to finish the raw seam edges of the garment. The garment is then stitched together with a sewing machine. This method is recommended for tailored garments sewn from wools, linens, and silk. It is also best to use when fit is uncertain because it allows for letting out seams. If you use this method, the serger knife should just skim the edge of the fabric so nothing is trimmed off the seam allowance.

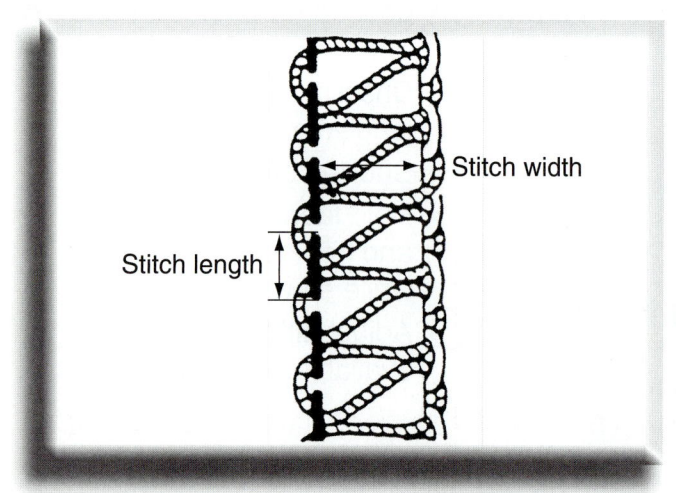

28-14 The length and width of stitches are shown in this diagram. They will need to vary depending on the fabric, thread, and stitch you are using.

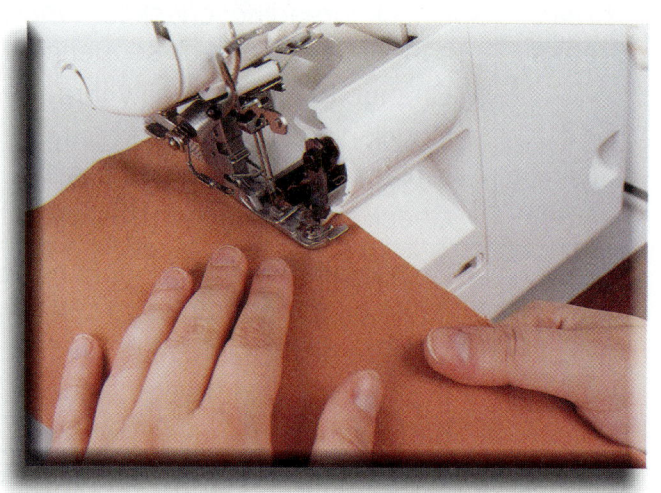

28-15 The left needle is stitching on the ⅝-inch seam line.
BERNINA of America, Inc.

To speed this process up, you can use the **continuous overcasting technique**. Line up the garment sections so the stitching is not broken as you move from the edge of one garment section to the next. Once all of the overcasting is complete, clip the thread chains and separate the garment sections.

- *Narrow double-stitched seam method.* The third method involves first stitching the garment seams together on the sewing machine using the standard ⅝-inch seam. Afterward serge together the two seam allowances as one, placing the needle ⅛ inch from the first line of stitching. This is called a **narrow double-stitched seam**, or a *reinforced seam*. It is often ideal for light- to medium-weight woven fabrics or knit fabrics for which seams need a moderate amount of stretch. You can also use this method to reinforce areas of stress in a garment, such as crotch seams or the underarm area of a set-in sleeve.

The **mock flat-felled seam** is another seam that uses both the conventional sewing machine and the serger. This seam is useful with denim and other heavyweight woven fabrics. To make this seam, you stitch a standard seam with right sides together using the sewing machine. Then with the serger, overlock the seam allowances together, trimming slightly. Press the seam allowances toward one side. Once again with the sewing machine, topstitch from the right side next to the seam line. Then topstitch again, ¼-inch away from the first topstitching line through all layers.

Selecting a Pattern

Many commercial patterns are designed specifically for serger sewing. However, do not limit your pattern selection to those with instructions only for the serger. You can use the serger to sew a garment from any pattern to some degree. Before beginning construction, think through the design, outlining how to make it efficiently with the serger. As you use your serger more, this will quickly become second nature to you. The list in **28-16** suggests the many ways you can use a serger in clothing construction.

Because sergers trim the seam allowances as you sew, they are best to use with garments that do not require precise fitting. Loose, unfitted garments are good choices, or garments made with knits where fit is achieved through the stretch of the fabric.

Using the Serger in Garment Construction

- Seams can be stitched, trimmed, and overcast in one operation.
- Seams stitched using a conventional sewing machine can be overcast to prevent raveling.
- Outer edges of garments can be finished, eliminating the need for facings, ribbings, and bands.
- The inside of unlined garments can have a finished look.
- Narrow or rolled hems can be created quickly on ruffles, flared skirts, or tablecloths and napkins.
- A blind stitch hem can be used instead of hemming garments by hand.
- Lace and elastic can be applied easily.
- Stretch fabrics can be stitched without the worry of broken stitches in the seams when the garment is worn.
- Decorative flatlock stitching using lightweight yarns, metallic threads, and even thin ribbons can be combined to create one-of-a-kind garments and household items.

28-16 The serger can be used in many ways when constructing a garment.

Transferring Pattern Markings

Mark garment pattern pieces with a water-soluble or air-erasable marking pen or tailor's chalk instead of notches. Stitching with a serger removes the notches, making it impossible to locate the markings.

Fit Before You Sew

Be sure to fit before you sew! Once a seam is stitched, the seam allowance is trimmed away, making it virtually impossible to alter seams. Instead, on garment areas where fit is critical, baste seams together with a conventional machine to test for fit. After the garment is correctly fitted, treat the seam allowances as one and serge them together, leaving a ¼-inch to ⅜-inch seam allowance.

Construction Order

The best way to assemble a serged garment is to use the **flat method of construction** whenever possible. With this method, you sew flat pieces rather than pieces *in the round*. For example, you will finish necklines, armholes, sleeves, and hems before serging underarm and side seams. This differs from the usual order for assembling garments. See Figure **28-17** for the construction order for the flat method of serging a T-shirt.

The pattern guide sheet often follows the flat method of construction. Refer to it when deciding construction order.

Serging Seams

Sewing seams with a serger is fast and easy. If you are using the serger to construct a garment, you will need to know the different types of seams you can use. You will also need to know how to serge curves and corners, and how to begin and end a seam. You may need to know how to remove a seam if you make a mistake.

28-17 Construct a basic T-shirt in the order shown here.

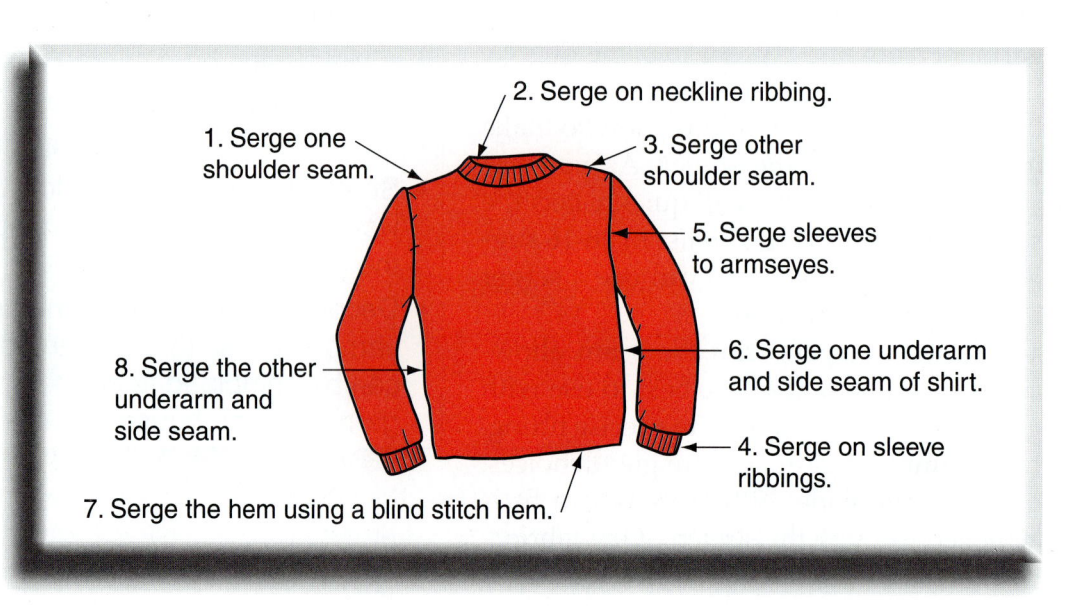

1. Serge one shoulder seam.
2. Serge on neckline ribbing.
3. Serge other shoulder seam.
4. Serge on sleeve ribbings.
5. Serge sleeves to armseyes.
6. Serge one underarm and side seam of shirt.
7. Serge the hem using a blind stitch hem.
8. Serge the other underarm and side seam.

Types of Seams

There are many ways to sew seams using a serger. The type you choose depends on the garment design, type of fabric and durability desired. If you are using a pattern, the guide sheet may suggest the type of seam to use.

The basic types of seams include the following:

- *Overlock seam.* The basic overlock seam can be made using three or four threads. The four-thread seam will be stronger and is useful for a wide variety of garments. It is suitable for woven fabrics, but ideal for use with knits because the seam will stretch. Since the seam allowance is cut off as you sew the seam, you must be sure of the fit before you stitch. To make this seam, place right sides of the fabric together and serge on the ⅝-inch seam line.

- *Serged and topstitched seam.* Another name for this seam is an *exposed* seam because the stitches show on the right side of the garment. Decorative thread can add interest to this type of seam. It is most appropriate to use with light- to medium-weight fabrics. To make this seam, serge with the wrong sides together. To add durability, or to flatten this seam, topstitch the seam allowance to the garment using a conventional sewing machine. First open the fabric and press the seam to one side. Then topstitch the seam to the fabric, 28-18.

- *Lapped seam.* This seam gives a decorative effect on the outside of the garment. It is ideal for reversible garments or for thick, loosely woven fabrics to provide strength. To make this seam, serge to the seam line on one side of the seam. On the other side of the seam, skim the edge of the seam with serging, leaving the seam allowance. Lap the trimmed seam edge over the other, aligning the ⅝-inch seam lines. Use fusible web or fabric glue to hold the layers in place. Using a conventional sewing machine, topstitch the seam together.

- *Flatlocked seam.* This seam offers a decorative effect and typically used on knit sportswear, 28-19. It is suitable for many fabric weights, but do not use it with fabrics that ravel. To make this seam, adjust your serger for flatlocking according to the serger manual. The thread tensions will need to be loosened. Then serge the two layers of fabric together. Pull the two layers apart so the seam allowance lies flat inside the stitching and the cut edges meet.

When serging seams, try to stitch in a continuous manner as described for overcasting seam edges. For example, sew seam after seam without cutting the stitching between the pieces. Leave four inches of serger chain between pieces and cut in the middle when separating pieces.

28-18 A 4-thread overlock stitch was used to give a decorative edge to these patch pockets. They were then stitched to the garment using a conventional sewing machine. BERNINA of America, Inc.

28-19 The 2-thread flatlock seam gives a distinctive look to sportswear. The ladder effect is also used for its decorative look on the outside as well.
BERNINA of America, Inc.

> ### Sew Safely
> When sewing with a serger, use water soluble basting tape, a water soluble glue stick, or pins placed parallel to the left of the seam line to hold seams in place. If using pins, place them about 1 inch from the seam line. Be sure to remove all pins before they reach the cutting area. If a pin should accidentally hit the knives, your serger can be damaged and pieces of pins could fly up in your face. Because of the longer presser foot and feed dog, pins are not as essential with serger sewing. Fabrics shift very little when sewn on a serger.

Serging Curves and Corners

With practice, you will easily master curved edges and corners. To accurately serge inside or outside curves, watch the knife rather than the needle, as you would with a conventional machine. Remember, the serger cuts before it sews. Feed the fabric slowly with your hands at the front of the presser foot.

> ### Sew Safely
> When feeding fabric into the serger, keep your fingers away from the presser foot and knives to avoid injury.

You may want to serge in a circle, beginning and ending at the same place. This is often used on hem edges. When serging in a circle, serge around the circle and overlap the stitching for one inch. Then serge off the edge of the fabric.

If you want a more attractive finish, overlap only a few stitches at the end. Then lift the presser foot and needles and pull the unchained threads from the serger. Tie knots in the threads and trim.

- *Outside corners.* For outside corners, you can stitch along one side of the fabric and off the edge, leaving a chain. Then stitch the next side, crossing and securing the first line of stitching. This also cuts off the chain end of the previous row of stitches. This is the easiest method to use.
- *Inside corners.* Before serging inside corners, mark the stitching line and cutting line in both directions. Clip the corner to within ⅛ inch of the stitching line. With the serger, stitch to the corner, stopping when the blade reaches the corner cut marking. Pull the fabric toward you so the edge is straight, but a pleat forms to the left. Then continue stitching. The fabric will lie flat after serging.

It is not possible to pull threads on a serger once a stitch is formed. A little slack in the stitch is helpful in turning corners or removing a possible thread jam. To achieve the necessary slack, pull to loosen the needle thread between the needle and last thread guide. Gently slide the threads and fabric to the back, off the stitch finger. Continue pulling needle thread and pulling the fabric to the back until you have the needed slack.

Securing Seam Ends

Since backstitching is not possible with a serger, you will need to secure the stitches in some other way. Serger stitches will unravel if they are not secured. If seams are crossed by other stitching, this will secure the ends. If the seams are not crossed, you will need to secure the ends in some manner. There are several ways to do this, including the following:

- *Knot the thread chain.* Place the knot close to the fabric edge.
- *Bury the chain.* After stitching, pull the chain to smooth it out. Thread it through a large-eyed needle or loop turner and run it under 1 to 2 inches of overlocked stitches, **28-20**. Trim the excess thread.
- *Secure the threads while stitching.* At the beginning of a seam, take two stitches. Stop, lift the presser foot, and bring the chain to the front. Place the chain on the seam line, lower the presser foot, and serge over the chain. At the end of the seam, stitch off the fabric one stitch. Lift the presser foot and needle. Slip the chain off the stitch finger. Flip the fabric over and to the front. Lower the presser foot and serge over the last few stitches and off the fabric.
- *Use liquid seam sealant.* Put a dab of sealant on the thread chain and stitches at the end of seam. After it has completely dried, cut the thread tails. Sealant will stiffen and may darken the fabric. This method is best used where it will not show.

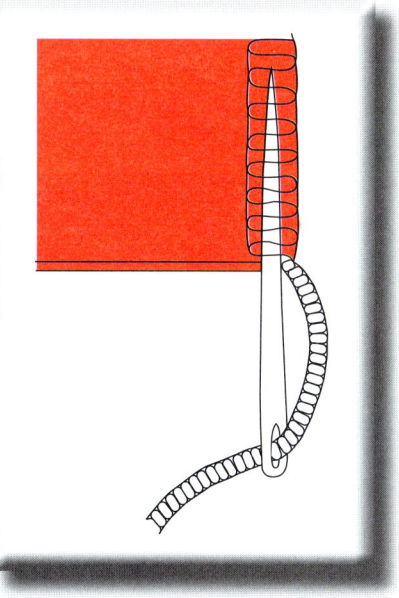

28-20 You can *bury* the thread chain by threading it through a needle and running it under the stitches.

Trends Making News

Sewing—Not Just for Grandma Anymore

What was once thought as a dying art is making a comeback, but for different reasons. Just a few decades ago, people sewed clothes as a way to save money. Today's sewers are more likely to be hobbyists who find a creative outlet in designing and sewing their own clothes or home decor. Many enjoy creating unique, one-of-a-kind quilts. There has been a huge resurgence in quilting over the past decade alone. About 21 million Americans are spending $3.58 billion on quilt fabrics and supplies each year. It is not unusual for a dedicated quilter to spend over $600 a year on supplies.

Though home sewers can save money sewing their own clothes, most sewers do so for pleasure and a sense of accomplishment. A *SewNews* reader survey found 93.5 percent sew because they enjoy it, while 59 percent find sewing relaxing. Another study reported that people sew because it makes them feel energetic, creative, and optimistic. Research also shows sewing reduces stress, with a significant drop in heart rate, blood pressure, and perspiration rate, when compared to other leisure activities.

New and better sewing equipment has also attracted new sewers. Whereas handmade items used to take hours and hours to create, unique and clever items can be quickly embroidered or monogrammed using today's electronic sewing machines. With computerized machines, designs can be scanned from any source and embroidered onto a garment or home accessory. Sergers are also popular today because they can cut garment construction time in half.

Stabilizing Seams

Garment seams stitched with a serger may require stabilization. **Stabilizing** is a way to add extra strength to areas that receive stress while wearing the garment. Shoulder and neckline seams, front areas, and crotch seams are often stabilized. Facings and interfacings will help to stabilize necklines and front opening edges.

One method of stabilizing seams is to use a row of straight stitching along the seam line. Use a conventional sewing machine for this. Then serge the seam, stitching close to the first row of stitching.

You can also serge over twill tape, seam tape, or ribbon. Cut the tape the length of the seam and place it over the seam line. Stitch the seam through the tape, being careful not to cut the tape.

Garments made of knits or loosely woven fabrics generally require more stabilizing. Sew loosely woven fabrics using the serger only as a seam finish. Stitches tend to pull out of a serged seam when the seam is stitched, trimmed, and overcast in one step.

Removing Seams

Serger stitches can be easily ripped out. Use a seam ripper or sharp scissors. To remove seams, use the following methods:

- *Two-thread overlock.* Slide a seam ripper or scissors under the stitches. Pull out the cut threads.
- *Three-thread overlock.* Using sharp scissors cut the loops every three or four stitches. See A in **28-21**. Pull the needle thread and the stitches will come undone. (B)
- *Two-thread double chain stitch.* Cut the needle thread at the end of the seam. (C) Pull the looper thread and the stitches will come undone. (D)

Serger Care

The serger will operate effectively with proper maintenance. Regularly clean and oil it as specified by the manufacturer. Sergers operate at high speeds causing internal parts to rotate more often than conventional sewing machines. Because the fabric is cut as the machine stitches, lint accumulates quickly.

Use a soft brush to remove the lint from the knife area. Also replace needles if stitches are not forming properly. Replace blades when fabric is not cut smoothly. Follow the guidelines in the owner's manual for oiling the machine. Use sewing machine oil—a special type of oil formulated for sewing machines.

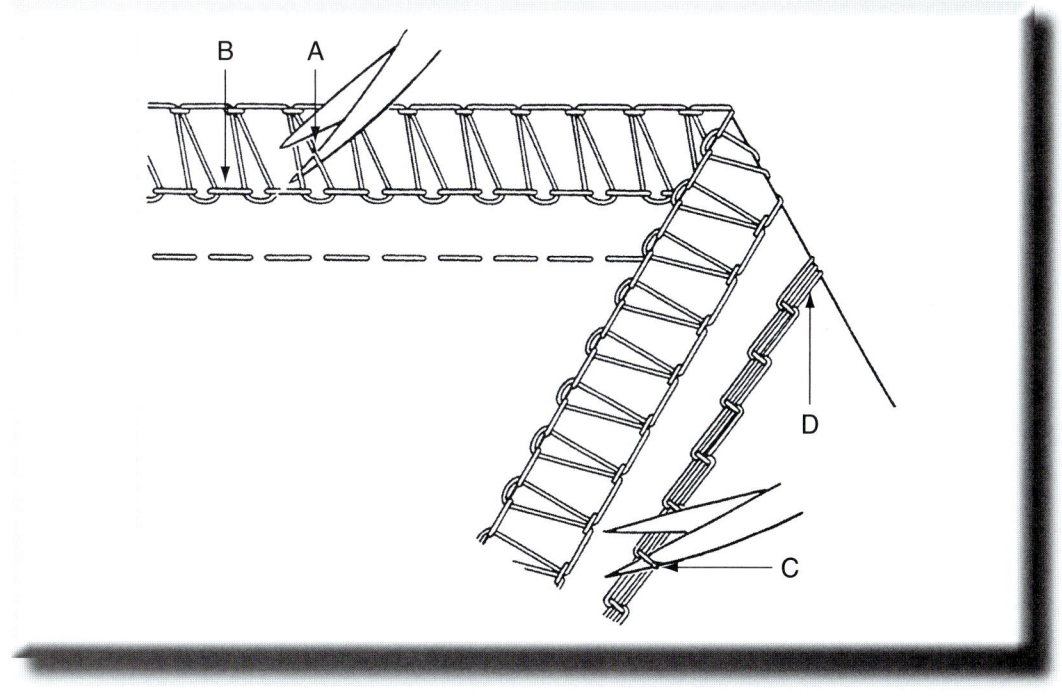

28-21 Follow these steps to remove overlock stitches.
BERNINA of America, Inc.

Summary

- A serger uses two, three, four, or five spools of thread or cones, depending on the model. They use one, two, or three needles. Sergers do not have bobbins but have loopers, both upper and lower.
- Serger stitches vary with machine make and model. The most common stitches include the following: overedge stitch, flatlock stitch, rolled edge stitch, overlock stitch, cover stitch, and chain stitch.
- Special thread designed for serger use offers a number of advantages. Serger thread is generally sold on cones or tubes, which can hold from 1,000 to 6,000 yards of thread.
- Thread tensions and stitch length and width generally need to be adjusted when you change fabrics, threads, or stitches.
- You can use the serger to construct a garment completely or in combination with a conventional sewing machine.
- Use the flat method of construction when serging a garment. With this method, you sew flat pieces rather than pieces in the round.
- There are many ways to sew seams using a serger. The type you choose will depend on the garment design, type of fabric used, and durability desired.
- The serger will operate effectively with proper maintenance. Clean and oil it regularly as specified by the manufacturer.

Graphic Organizer

Create a KWHL chart to identify what you know about serger sewing, what you need to learn, how you are going to learn it, and identify what you have learned.

What I Know	What I Want to Know	How I Will Learn	What I Have Learned

Review the Facts

1. Name the three main functions performed by a serger.
2. What two sewing tasks can a serger not perform?
3. The _____ _____ is a metal prong around which stitches are formed on a serger.
4. The _____ stitch is visible from the face side of the garment and creates a decorative *ladder* effect when the fabric edges are pulled open and flattened.
5. Name two advantages in using thread specifically made for sergers.
6. Explain how to chain off when operating the serger.
7. If the stitch formation is not what it should be, what four things should you check?
8. What is the general rule for selecting stitch length and width?
9. Name the three ways you can use a serger in clothing construction.
10. What methods of transferring pattern markings should not be used when serging seams together?
11. Why is it important to fit before you sew when using the serger?
12. Summarize how to serge an outside corner.
13. Describe one way to secure the end of a seam.
14. Describe one way to stabilize a seam.

Think Critically

15. **Draw conclusions.** Why do you think it took a number of years for sergers to become popular with home sewers? Share your conclusions with the class.
16. **Analyze decisions.** If you could buy only one machine, would you purchase a conventional sewing machine or a serger? Why?
17. **Analyze evidence.** Review reliable consumer product reviews for three serger brands. Choose the same type for each brand (3-thread, 3/4-thread, etc.). What are the pros and cons of each model or brand? How do the features and costs compare? Based on the reviews, which would you purchase if you were buying a serger?

Apparel Applications

18. **Identify serger parts.** Using the instruction manual that came with the serger you will be using, locate and explain the function of each part of the serger. What machine parts does the serger have that the conventional sewing machine does not have?

19. **Demonstrate proficiency.** Practice doing each of the following procedures. For skills that require sample-making, mount samples that show your proficiency and store them in a binder.
    A. Remove and replace the serger needle.
    B. Thread the serger using a different color thread for each spool. Use a cone adapter or spool cap.
    C. Change threads in the serger by tying new threads to old threads.
    D. Demonstrate proficiency in making the various types of stitches your serger can make.
    E. Demonstrate proficiency in making various types of seams with the serger. For each seam, cut two 6- by 2-inch fabric samples to use in creating your samples.
    F. Demonstrate proficiency in sewing inside and outside corners. For each type of corner, cut two 4- by 4-inch fabric samples.

20. **Analyze construction methods.** If you are making a serged garment, outline the steps using the flat method of construction and continuous stitching. If using a conventional sewing machine, how would the order of the steps differ? Write a summary of your analysis.

21. **Solve a serger problem.** If you are having a problem with serging, use the Internet to review websites that can give you help with your serger. Share what you learn online with the class.

22. **Demonstrate machine maintenance.** Follow the guidelines in your serger instruction manual for cleaning and maintaining your serger. Then demonstrate to the class how to clean and maintain the serger.

Academic Connections

23. **Writing.** Select a pattern from an online pattern catalog and print a copy of the pattern envelope. Evaluate the pattern in terms of its suitability for serger construction. How could you use the serger? What would you need to do with a conventional sewing machine? Write a summary of your evaluation.

24. **Reading.** Use the Internet to review the websites for various serger manufacturers. Learn about the models they offer and the newest features. Give an oral report to the class about your findings.

Workplace Connections

25. **Teaching others.** Presume you have several new employees at your small tailoring shop. Using a serger is a key skill. Although your new employees have serger skills, they do not have experience with the flat construction method. Write a summary explaining how to use the flat construction method for your training class. Then give your presentation to the employees (the class).

26. **Demonstrate garment proficiency.** Choose a garment pattern suitable for use with serger sewing. Follow appropriate methods for preparing your fabric and layout and cutting. Sew your garment using the serger or serger and sewing machine as outlined by your pattern guide sheet. After completing each step, take a digital photo of the garment progress and get approval from your teacher. Photograph the completed garment. Use presentation software to create a report on your garment construction. Share your digital report with the class and save a copy in your portfolio.

Take the Lead in Community Service

Are you looking for a way to use your serger skills to help others? Consider making simple flannel or fleece blankets with a serged edge finish. Many local and global nonprofit agencies collect blankets for infants and children. Use the FCCLA *Community Service* project guidelines and your leadership skills in organizing your class to make blankets for children. See your adviser for information and advice as needed.

PART 6

Career Preparation

Chapters

29 Preparing for a Career

30 A Job and a Career

31 Entrepreneurship—
Profiting from Your Skills

Chapter 29

Preparing for a Career

Chapter Objectives

After studying this chapter, you will be able to
- **define** leadership.
- **describe** leadership traits.
- **summarize** the skills involved for effective team membership.
- **identify** student organizations that help prepare students for the world of work.
- **summarize** the order of business during meetings that are conducted according to parliamentary procedure.

Key Terms

leader
leadership
teamwork
interpersonal skills
empathy
communication
verbal communication
nonverbal communication
body language
parliamentary procedure

Reading with Purpose

As you read the chapter, write a letter to yourself. Imagine that you will receive this letter in a few years when you are working at your future job. What would you like to remember from this chapter? In the letter, list key points from the chapter that will be useful in your future career.

Right now, you may not know what career to choose. Depending on your age, you may have some time to think about this decision. You can use this time to learn about the possibilities that are open to you. Meanwhile, work on developing the leadership and teamwork skills that will help you succeed in any career. There are many organizations you can join now that will help you practice these skills.

Leadership

A **leader** is a person who guides a group toward its goals. **Leadership** is the capacity to lead or to direct others on a course or in a direction. Leadership is needed for the successful operation of schools, businesses, cities, and nations.

Why is it important to develop leadership skills? They help you build your *self-confidence* and *self-esteem*. They help you succeed in school and on the job. If you have leadership skills, you can take charge of a project and get it done, **29-1**. Others learn they can rely on you.

Leadership skills are necessary for a class president, football captain, or committee chairperson. They are also important if you work with classmates on a science project. Also consider a job setting. You may be asked to work with two other sales associates to design a window display for a clothing store. Leadership skills will help you accomplish that goal.

Leadership Traits

Leaders are often described in terms of their traits. The following are leadership traits you may want to develop. Leaders

- are self-confident and show a strong sense of responsibility.
- have good communication skills and can express their thoughts clearly and effectively.
- are enthusiastic and can motivate others to do their best.
- stress cooperation and set good examples. They do their share of work just as everyone else does.
- help their teams reach their goals.
- are flexible. They can accept change and can help others accept change, too.
- keep an open mind about decisions and situations and are willing to listen to new ideas.
- are able to delegate responsibilities. They do not do all the work themselves, but assign tasks to those best qualified.
- are good problem-solvers. They can identify a problem and consider all the alternatives and consequences.
- have the confidence to make a decision and carry it out.

29-1 Working on a project and completing it helps you to develop leadership skills.
Shutterstock

Because the traits and skills of a leader are helpful in so many ways, they are worth developing. In school, you have the opportunity to lead in various clubs and organizations. Join one or more groups that interest you and get involved. Volunteer for committee work. Run for an office. The experience and skills you gain will prepare you for leadership roles as an adult.

Effective Team Membership

Emphasis in the workplace today is on sharing responsibility to get a job done. Teamwork is stressed. **Teamwork** means individuals working together to reach a common goal. Using the talents and skills of team members, work is done more efficiently, **26-2**. Productivity is increased.

Team members have a wide variety of personalities and abilities. By recognizing and using the strengths of each member, the goals of the group can be accomplished. For the team to be successful, every member must complete his or her assignments. They must be willing to share ideas, listen to each other, and cooperate to reach group goals.

Interpersonal Skills You Need

To be an effective team member, requires a variety of interpersonal skills. **Interpersonal skills** are the skills you need to get along well with other people and to be an effective team member. When you join a club or organization, you have the opportunity to be with other people who have similar interests as you. You will be able to practice your interpersonal skills. As a future employee, these skills will be of benefit to you.

The following interpersonal skills will help you in organizations that you belong to now. They will also help you be a better employee.

- Develop **empathy**. This is the ability to understand and be sensitive to the feelings, thoughts, and experience of others. With empathy, you are better able to interpret why people think or behave as they do.

- Show respect for other people's feelings and needs. Make requests rather than demands using a pleasant tone of voice and a calm manner. Be courteous to others.

- Be willing to give and take when differences arise. Respect the opinions of others even though they may differ from yours.

- Be able to accept criticism without taking offense. If you must criticize someone else, do so in a tactful manner that does not cause hurt feelings.

- Have a sense of humor. This is especially helpful when tension mounts. It improves relationships and allows communication to flow more easily.

- Keep a positive attitude. If you have a positive attitude, you tend to see the good side of situations and other people. You are optimistic, pleasant, and cheerful. You see life as worthwhile and enjoyable. This makes you pleasant to be around.

- Be honest and trustworthy. Keeping promises and dealing fairly with people are important attributes. Others need to know they can trust you.

- Dependability means people can rely on you. You do what you say you will do. If you say you will be at a meeting, you are there. If you say you will take on a certain responsibility, you can be counted on to complete the task.

29-2 Humansville, Missouri, FCCLA members make a quilt as their annual fundraiser. *Susa Rathbun, Humansville, Missouri*

Communication Skills

For both leaders and team members, communication skills are important. They will help you in your personal relationships and in the groups you join. When you enter the world of work, they will be an important factor in your career success.

Communication is the process of exchanging thoughts, ideas, or information with others. As a worker, you may communicate with supervisors, coworkers, and customers. You may write letters, answer phone calls, or speak to clients. As a member of a student organization, you will communicate with fellow club members, committee members, or officers. You might need to share information on club activities or give a committee report at a club meeting. In either setting, it is important that all messages are understood and interpreted correctly.

There are two ways of communicating. **Verbal communication** involves using words—speaking or writing. **Nonverbal communication** involves sending messages without words. The way a person looks, acts, and reacts all communicate nonverbal messages. Both forms may be used together to communicate a single message.

Verbal Communication

Verbal communication is used to send a message between two or more people. With any form of verbal communication, there is a sender and a receiver. The *sender* begins the process by initiating a conversation, phone call, letter, or e-mail message. The *receiver* is the one who receives the message and interprets it. The communication process is completed when the receiver responds to the message with an accurate interpretation or response, **29-3**.

Most communications involve a speaker and a listener. Both play an important role in making sure the communication process is completed. Speakers must provide clear and accurate messages. Listeners must stay attentive and focused. Remember that listening and hearing are not the same. You hear with your ears, but you have to use your brain in order to listen.

To make sure your verbal messages are received accurately, follow the tips in **29-4**. Likewise, to be a good listener, follow the tips for listeners. Poor listening habits at work can be costly to employers. Mistakes and misunderstandings can lead to lost productivity and dissatisfied customers.

29-3 In the communication process, both sender and receiver must communicate clearly.

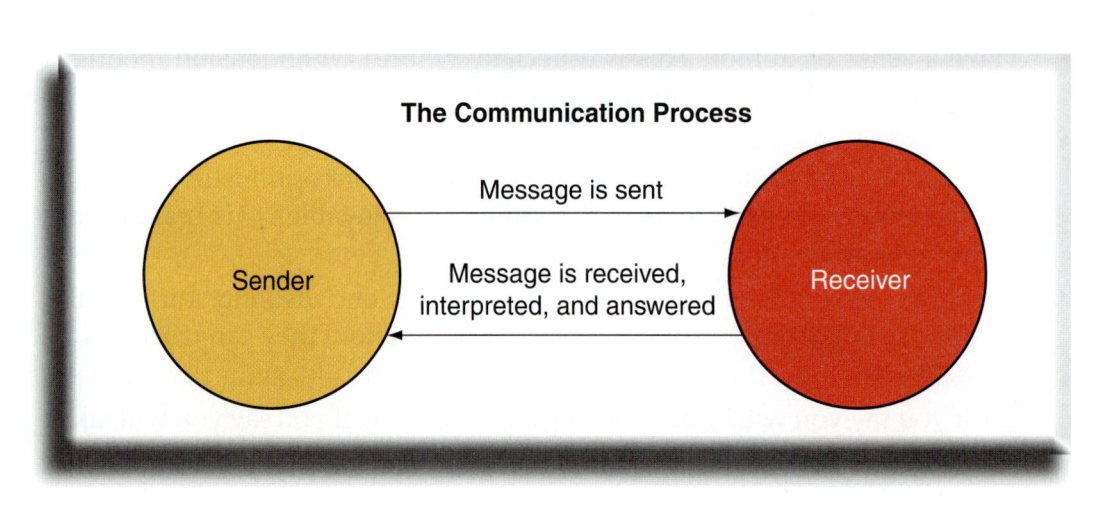

The Communication Process

Sender → Message is sent → Receiver
Sender ← Message is received, interpreted, and answered ← Receiver

Improving Your Communication Skills

Tips for Improving Your Speaking Skills	Tips for Improving Your Listening Skills
• Speak slowly, clearly, and distinctly. Avoid running words together. • Establish eye contact and speak to the listener. • Use a friendly, courteous tone in an upbeat and positive manner. • Be respectful and considerate of listeners' feelings. Avoid hurtful comments or talking down to a person. • Use words with precise, familiar meanings. Avoid the use of slang. • Keep your messages short and to the point. • Make your points in order. • Pause before you begin new thoughts. • Build on your listeners' past knowledge and lead them from there. • Ask questions to be sure your message is being interpreted correctly.	• Pay attention to the speaker. Stop talking, remove any distractions, and stay focused. • Use eye contact and body language to show you are interested. • Empathize with the speaker by trying to understand his or her point of view. • Be patient. Allow the speaker time to make his or her point. • Do not interrupt the speaker. • Do not let your mind race ahead of the speaker. You will lose the speaker's train of thought. • Ask questions that show you are receiving and understanding the message in the two-way communication process. • Reflect back to the speaker what you think was said. This allows the speaker to see if the message was misinterpreted. • Listen to the speaker's tone of voice. Sometimes the way something is said is as important as what is said. • Give nonverbal feedback by nodding and smiling.

29-4 Follow these tips to improve both your speaking and listening skills.

Nonverbal Communication

The nonverbal messages people send are also important to understand. **Body language** is the use of body movements, such as facial expressions and body gestures, to convey messages. Your message is interpreted by what others see. Sometimes you may be aware of the messages you are sending through your body language. You may even send intentional signals. At other times, you may be completely unaware of the messages you are sending. You may even be shocked by the way people react sometimes. Then there are moments when your body reacts spontaneously, such as when you receive good news and jump up and scream.

Everything about you sends signals—the way you sit, the way you stand, the way you hold your arms, and what you do with your hands. Your facial expressions are especially revealing. You can look happy, sad, interested, bored, excited, silly, angry, worried, or confused. Even though your words may be saying one thing, your body language could be sending an entirely different message.

Your overall appearance is another important part of nonverbal communication. Your clothes and your appearance send the first message to people you meet for the first time. Before you say anything, your appearance speaks for you. What is the message you are sending? If you want to make the best possible first impression, such as for a job interview, take a close look at yourself in the mirror. What is the message your appearance is sending? Is it what you want to say? If not, begin making changes in those areas where improvements can be made.

Student Organizations

Many opportunities for leadership and teamwork experience are available in student organizations. Each club needs members who are willing to work for the good of the club. Only a few can be officers, but everyone can take an active role. Everyone can attend meetings, learn parliamentary procedure, and participate in club activities. Everyone should have an opportunity to serve on a committee at least once a year. All members can work toward the development of leadership traits and interpersonal skills.

CTSOs—Purposes and Functions

Although any organization can be beneficial, *career and technical student organizations (CTSOs)* have extra advantages. They help students learn about career opportunities in various fields. They all offer competitive events that allow students to showcase their skills. The following organizations offer opportunities for participation at local, state, and national levels.

- *Family, Career and Community Leaders of America (FCCLA)* is available to students in family and consumer sciences classes. The focus is on the multiple roles of family member, wage earner, and community leader. The organization helps young men and women become leaders and address important personal, family, work, and societal issues through family and consumer sciences education. The purposes of FCCLA are listed in figure **29-5**. Careers related to family and consumer sciences are also explored. Examples of these careers are fashion merchandising, clothing services, food services, and child care services. You can learn more about FCCLA by visiting their website.

- *National FFA Organization (FFA)* is for students interested in the science, business, and technology of agriculture. The organization prepares members for leadership and careers in agricultural science education. It strives to promote leadership, character development, cooperation, service, improved agriculture, and citizenship. See the FFA website for more information.

- *DECA—An Association of Marketing Students* is open to all students in marketing education. Chapter activities help students develop team and leadership skills and learn more about marketing, management, business administration, hospitality, finance, entrepreneurship, and related careers. Learn more about DECA on their website.

Purposes of FCCLA
1. To provide opportunities for personal development and preparation for adult life.
2. To strengthen the function of the family as a basic unit of society.
3. To encourage democracy through cooperative action in the home and community.
4. To encourage individual and group involvement in helping achieve global cooperation and harmony.
5. To promote greater understanding between youth and adults.
6. To provide opportunities for making decisions and for assuming responsibilities.
7. To prepare for the multiple roles of men and women in today's society.
8. To promote family and consumer sciences and related occupations.

29-5 These are the purposes of the student organization, Family, Career and Community Leaders of America. *FCCLA, Inc.*

- *Future Business Leaders of America (FBLA-PBL)* is for students interested in business and business-related careers. Its purpose is to help students choose business occupations and to develop competent, aggressive business leaders. Phil Beta Lambda is for postsecondary students. Learn more about the two strands of this organization on their website.
- *Health Occupations Students of America (HOSA)* is open to students interested in health and health-science related occupations. It helps members develop the traits necessary to become competent leaders and health care workers. You can learn more about HOSA at their website.
- *Future Educators Association (FEA).* This is a student organization for young people interested in education-related careers. It is the newest CTSO, recognized by the U.S. Department of Education in 2010. FEA provides opportunities for personal growth through recognition and leadership activities related to the education profession.
- *SkillsUSA* is for all students in occupational courses preparing for trade, technical, and skilled service occupations, including health occupations. Its motto is "Preparing for leadership in the world of work." SkillsUSA strives to develop students' social and leadership skills as well as their occupational skills, **29-6**. Their mission is to help its members become world-class workers, leaders, and responsible American citizens. Learn more about SkillsUSA by reviewing their website.

Your school may already have a student organization that is related to your career interests. If not, one can be started with your school's approval.

Member Roles and Responsibilities

Your role as a member of an organization carries with it certain responsibility. You may not be an officer or committee chair, but you still have responsibilities. First, you should try to attend all organization meetings. Members need to attend meetings to help plan club activities. Second, you will want to enthusiastically support and participate in club activities. In addition, most activities require special committees to organize the tasks involved in carrying

29-6 These students are participating in a SkillsUSA national meeting. As members of this organization, they are preparing for trade, industrial, technical, and health careers. *Clay Allen for SkillsUSA*

out the activity. Willingly volunteer to serve on committees and help with your share of the work.

You and all members of the organization should do your part. Assess your own skills and decide how best you can help the organization. If asked to take on a leadership role, show your willingness to serve. Consider running for an elected office. Volunteer to chair a committee. By taking a more active role, you will have the opportunity to develop as a person, a leader, and a team member. You will develop skills that will help you throughout life—planning, goal setting, problem solving, decision making, and interpersonal communication.

Conducting Meetings

As you attend meetings of organizations, you will find that they usually follow the same pattern. Most groups conduct their meetings according to **parliamentary procedure**. This is an orderly way of conducting a meeting and discussing group business. Its purpose is to help groups run their meetings fairly and efficiently.

The terms listed in 29-7 are often used during meetings. Once you know these terms, you will understand what happens during meetings. You will be able to participate effectively.

The sequence of events during meetings is called the *order of business*. Most meetings follow the order of business outlined in *Robert's Rules of Order*, a well-known book on parliamentary procedure.

The order of business includes these steps:

1. *Call to order:* A meeting is called to order by the president or presiding officer of the group. He or she may rap a gavel and say, "This meeting will now come to order."

2. *Reading and approving of minutes:* The secretary reads the minutes. The president then says, "Are there any corrections to the minutes?" Any member may point out corrections or additions that should be made to the minutes. At this point, the presiding officer calls for a motion and a second to the motion to approve the minutes. The presiding officer then calls for a vote.

3. *Reports of officers:* The president calls on the officers of the group to give any reports they may have. In most groups, the only officer to give a report at every meeting is the treasurer.

4. *Standing committee reports:* Standing committees are permanent committees of the group as specified in the group's bylaws. Examples include membership, program, and refreshment committees.

Terms Used in Parliamentary Procedure

Adjourn—To end a meeting.

Agenda—A list of things to do and discuss at a meeting.

Amend the motion—To change the wording of a motion that has been made.

Chair—The presiding officer at a meeting, such as the president or chairperson.

Debate—To speak for or against a motion. Every member has a right to debate an issue.

Majority—At least one more than half of the members present at the meeting.

Minutes—A written record of the business covered at a meeting.

Motion—A suggestion by a member that certain action be taken by the group.

Quorum—The number of members who must be present to legally conduct business at a meeting.

Second the motion—The approval of a motion by another member.

Table the question—To delay making a decision on a motion.

The floor—The right to speak in a meeting without interruption from others.

The question—The motion upon which members are called to vote.

29-7 Knowing the terms of parliamentary procedure will help you participate effectively in group meetings.

5. *Special committee reports:* Special committees are those that are set up for a certain purpose only. Once their work is completed, they no longer meet.

6. *Unfinished business:* Unfinished business might include motions that have been tabled from previous meetings.

7. *New business:* During this part of the meeting, ideas for future activities are discussed. Goals may be set, and special committees may be formed.

8. *The program:* This is the heart of the meeting. Programs are usually informative. They may be entertaining as well as educational. Worthwhile programs encourage current members to attend meetings, and they attract new members to the group.

9. *Announcements:* At this time, committees may be thanked for their work, or individuals may be congratulated for special achievements. Members are reminded of upcoming events of interest. The date, time, and place of the next meeting is announced.

10. *Adjournment:* To end the meeting, the president asks for a motion to adjourn, and the motion is voted on.

Summary

- Leadership is the capacity to lead or to direct others on a course or in a direction. Leaders are often described in terms of their traits.
- Teamwork is an important part of today's workplace. Using the talents and skills of team members, work is done more efficiently.
- Interpersonal skills and communication skills are necessary for teams to accomplish their goals.
- Career and technical student organizations offer many opportunities for leadership and teamwork experiences.
- Career and technical student organizations have extra advantages. They help students learn about career opportunities in various fields. They all offer competitive events that allow students to showcase their skills.
- Most groups conduct their meetings according to parliamentary procedure—an orderly way of conducting a meeting and discussing group business.

Graphic Organizer

Create a tree diagram to outline the key points about verbal and nonverbal communication.

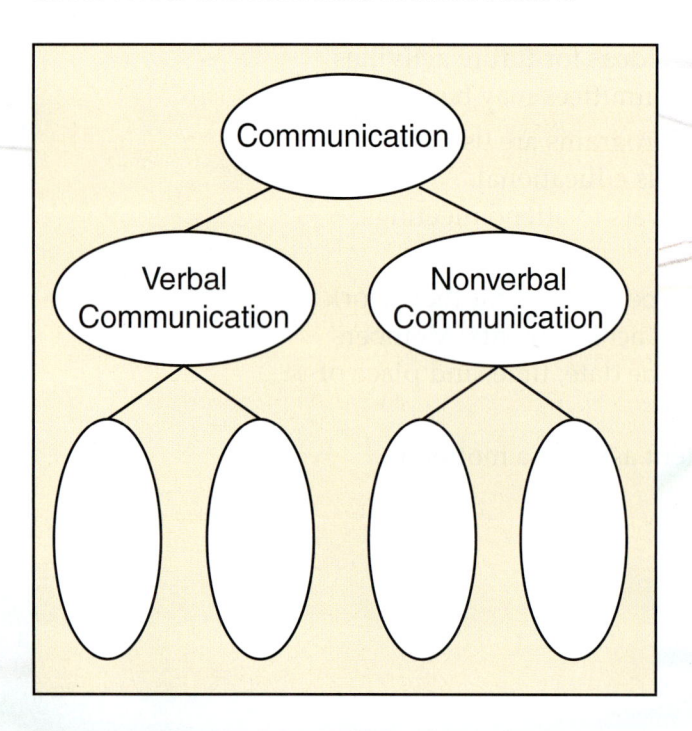

Review the Facts

1. Name five effective leadership traits.
2. What is empathy?
3. Describe three interpersonal skills that will help you be an effective team member.
4. In verbal communication, describe the roles of the sender and the receiver in completing the communication process.
5. What is the difference between listening and hearing?
6. Give two examples of nonverbal communication.
7. List three advantages of membership in career and technical student organizations.
8. Provide three statements that you could use to describe FCCLA to someone who is not familiar with the organization.
9. What is the purpose for using parliamentary procedure?
10. Which comes first, unfinished business or new business, when following *Robert's Rules of Order*?

Think Critically

11. **Analyze decisions.** Make a list of ten characteristics of a good leader. Analyze your list and rank the characteristics in order from the most important to the least important. Be prepared to defend your ranking.
12. **Draw conclusions.** How would you describe a trustworthy person? Draw conclusions about why trust is important for effective teamwork.
13. **Identify relevant information.** How can career and technical student organizations benefit your community? What civic activities can these clubs get involved in? How have these groups helped your community?
14. **Contrast outcomes.** Contrast meetings conducted following the rules of parliamentary procedure with meetings conducted without any organization. What are the pros and cons of each?

Apparel Applications

15. **Role plays.** Work in teams to prepare role plays showing leadership and interpersonal skills in use in school or apparel job settings. Share your team's role play with the class. Have the class critique your team's effective use of leadership and interpersonal skills.
16. **CTSO research.** Use the Internet to explore the websites for the career and technical student organizations described in this chapter. Write a one-page report on the one that most interests you.
17. **CTSO panel.** Invite representatives from each CTSO that is available in your school. Ask each organization representative to tell your class about its group's activities and goals.

Academic Connections

18. **Social studies.** Choose a historical figure who was considered to be a great leader. Research and write a paper describing the traits that made this person a famous leader. Present your findings to the class.
19. **Writing.** Assemble a list of nonschool organizations available to students in your community. Identify the purposes and functions of these groups along with the benefits of membership. Write a summary of your findings.

Workplace Connections

20. **Communication research.** Estimate the amount of time you spend using each of the following forms of communication in an average day: reading, writing, speaking, texting, and listening. Use Internet or print resources to research what studies show to be the average communication usage in the workplace. Compare and contrast your estimates with the research studies. What are the similarities and differences? Write a summary of your conclusions.
21. **Parliamentary procedure practice.** Conduct a meeting according to parliamentary procedure. Plan ahead so you have the necessary officers and committee chairpersons, business to discuss, and a program.
22. **Make motions.** Practice making and seconding motions in a business meeting by role-playing with other class members.

Using Communication Skills

Use the *Leaders at Work Project Sheet* to prepare a speech on the topic of *High Tech Apparel*. Review the guidelines for this topic in the Leaders at Work materials. See your adviser for information as needed. Present your speech to the class and other organizations in your school.

Chapter 30

A Job and a Career

Chapter Objectives

After studying this chapter, you will be able to
- **summarize** the difference between a job and a career.
- **identify** the career clusters and their career pathways.
- **make** career-related decisions based on interests, aptitudes, and abilities.
- **summarize** the process of getting a job, including finding job openings, preparing a résumé, writing a letter of application, filling out job application forms, and interviewing.
- **summarize** what it takes to succeed on the job and the best way to leave a job.
- **identify** examples of how to manage multiple roles.

Key Terms

job	aptitudes	portfolio
career	abilities	letter of application
career clusters	networking	follow-up letter
entry-level job	résumé	mentor
career pathways	chronological résumé	ethical behavior
job shadowing	functional résumé	letter of resignation

Reading with Purpose

Find an article on Google News that relates to the topic covered in this chapter. Print the article and read it before reading the chapter. As you read the chapter, highlight sections of the news article that relates to the text.

When you were a small child, people may have asked you, "What do you want to be when you grow up?" You probably had a ready answer—a nurse, truck driver, doctor, or football player. That decision may have been made because you knew or admired someone in that career. Perhaps a television show or movie influenced you.

At this time in your life, other factors will influence your career decisions. You are likely thinking about how your interests, aptitudes, and skills relate to various careers. You may be investigating how much education you need for a certain career. You might also want to know what the payoffs are through the years in terms of job satisfaction, promotions, salary, and fringe benefits. You may even want to think about how a career choice may influence your lifestyle. For instance, a job may dictate where you live and what hours you work. You may want to look at how you might blend family life with your work.

All of these factors are considerations as you make your first career decisions and enter the world of work. This chapter will help you explore career options. It will also help prepare you for your first job. This might be a part-time job while you are still in high school.

As you read this chapter, you will find the terms *job* and *career* used frequently. What is the difference between these two terms? A **job** refers to a group of tasks performed by a worker, usually to earn money. You might have a job as a sales associate at a fashion boutique or a job on the production line at a clothing manufacturing plant. A person rarely stays at the same job for a lifetime. Instead, a series of increasingly challenging but related jobs leads to a career. A **career** is a succession of related jobs a person has over a span of time that results in professional growth and personal satisfaction.

Exploring the Career Clusters

One of the best ways to learn about all of the different career possibilities you might consider is to look at the career clusters. The **career clusters** are 16 general groupings of occupational and career areas, 30-1. The occupations within these career clusters require a set of common knowledge and skills, or *essential knowledge and skills*. These clusters were designed by educators in partnership with business and industry representatives throughout the country under the direction of the U.S. Department of Education. They encompass over 970 occupations from **entry-level jobs**, those requiring little or no special training through professional-level jobs.

One of the goals of the clusters is to increase learner awareness of career options to make better informed decisions. Surveying the 16 career clusters is a simple way to begin thinking about what might interest you. Read through the descriptions. You might immediately be able to identify several clusters that appeal to you because you know your strengths and weaknesses. You may know where your interests lie and what skills you have. The classes you have taken in school may have revealed to you some of your strengths. Perhaps it is in math, science, or design.

30-1 These 16 career clusters divide 970 occupations into groups that require similar knowledge and skills.

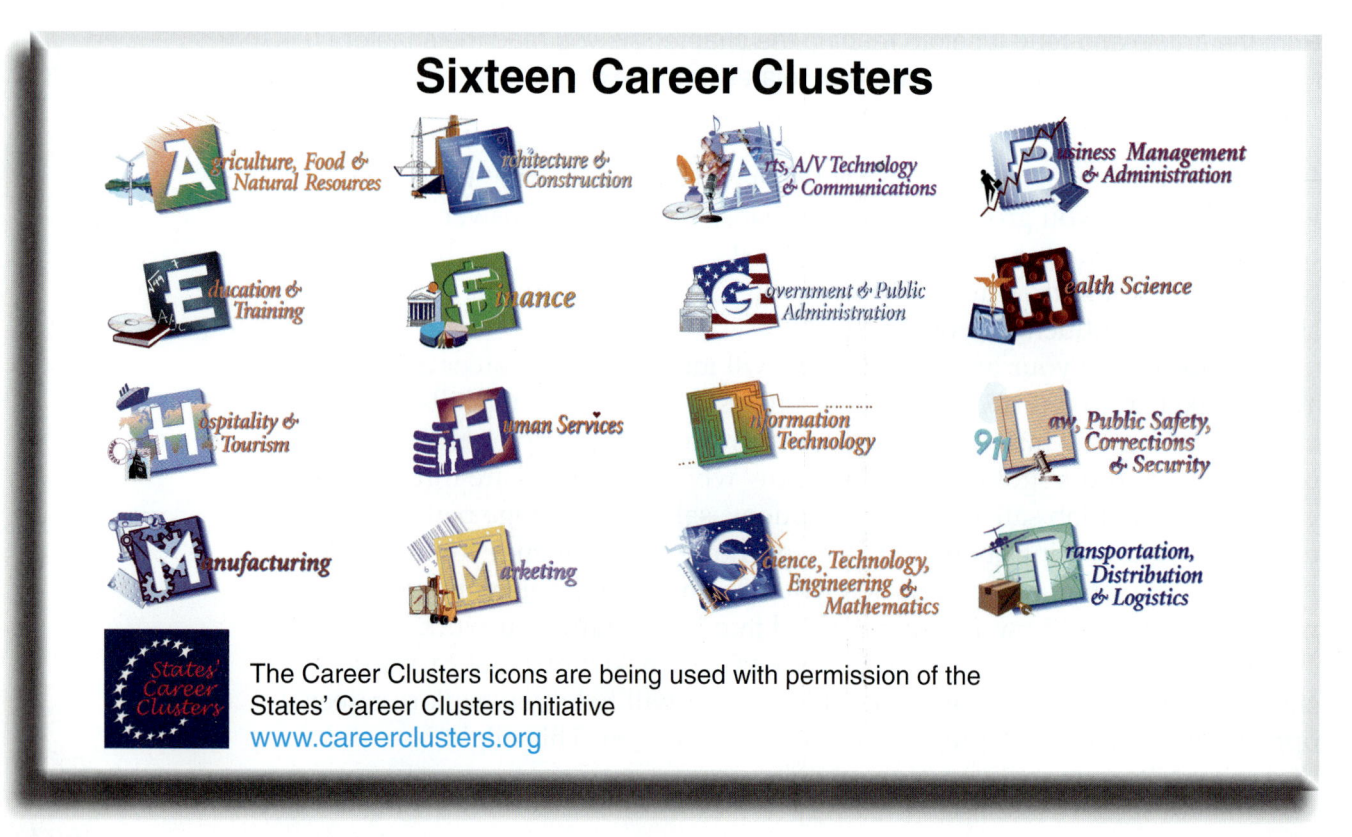

Sixteen Career Clusters

- Agriculture, Food & Natural Resources
- Architecture & Construction
- Arts, A/V Technology & Communications
- Business Management & Administration
- Education & Training
- Finance
- Government & Public Administration
- Health Science
- Hospitality & Tourism
- Human Services
- Information Technology
- Law, Public Safety, Corrections & Security
- Manufacturing
- Marketing
- Science, Technology, Engineering & Mathematics
- Transportation, Distribution & Logistics

The Career Clusters icons are being used with permission of the States' Career Clusters Initiative
www.careerclusters.org

Each cluster is further broken down into career pathways. The **career pathways** are subgroups of the career clusters that often require additional and more specialized knowledge and skills. You can learn these skills in very similar programs of study in school. A *program of study* is the sequence of instruction used to prepare students for occupations in a certain career pathway. When you complete a particular program of study, you will be prepared for several occupations within your area of interest.

Which career cluster is for you? Do you love clothes? Are you always eager to see what the new fashions will be for the next season? If so, a career in the exciting, creative field of fashion design could be for you, 30-2. The career cluster related to fashion design is *Arts, Audio/Video Technology & Communications*. If you are more interested in fashion buying and merchandising, then the cluster for you is *Marketing*. If you see yourself running your own clothing boutique one day, the *Business Management & Administration* cluster will guide your career preparation. Are you fascinated by fibers that can be made into thousands of items from bridal gowns to bulletproof vests? Perhaps you will find your occupation in the *Science, Technology, Engineering & Mathematics* cluster.

Within each of the career clusters and pathways, high schools and post-secondary schools and colleges have designed programs of study. These programs of study include sequential courses based on academic and industry skills standards. You begin a program of study in high school by learning core skills any career requires. You then progress into more technical classes. Many career pathways require a college education. Here you continue to develop your abilities and learn the knowledge and skills necessary for your chosen career pathway.

Job Shadowing

An option that might be available to help you choose a career is job shadowing. **Job shadowing** involves accompanying someone to his or her job to observe what the job entails. With job shadowing, you will see firsthand what this person does on a daily basis. You will view the work environment and observe the tasks the job requires and the skills necessary to carry out the tasks. During your visit, you will be able to ask questions of this person—a wonderful opportunity to get a sense of whether this would be a career of interest to you.

Job shadowing may be arranged by your school as a part of the school curriculum. However, it might be possible for you to arrange a job shadowing

30-2 Fashion design might be the career pathway you will choose. Shutterstock

experience on your own. If you, a family member, or friend knows someone who has a job of interest to you, ask if you can spend some time with this person at work. Many companies also sponsor job-shadowing experiences.

Making Career-Related Decisions

Doing a self-study and exploring the career clusters helps enable you to choose a career that is right for you. Begin by identifying your interests, perhaps even taking an interest survey. Your school's counseling office may offer such surveys. Some are available online. For example, the *CareerOneStop* website has links to skill and interest assessments that are free and you can take online. Identify your **aptitudes**—your natural physical and mental talents. Again, if you are not sure of your aptitudes, tests are available to determine them. For example, if you have an aptitude for math, working in a business field might suit you.

You are born with certain aptitudes, but your abilities are skills you learn. Your **abilities** are the physical and mental skills that develop through learning and practice. Perhaps you are able to play a musical instrument because you took lessons. Maybe your talent lies in designing clothes. Perhaps someone taught you to sew. Sewing is now one of your abilities. An ability assessment is available through *CareerOneStop*. This assessment requires administration by a trained professional, usually a school guidance counselor.

Considering your interests, aptitudes, and abilities makes career decision-making easier. However, selecting one career pathway is still not an easy decision. Deciding on a specific job or occupation may be more challenging. Consider asking yourself the following questions as you look at job possibilities:

- What does this job entail?
- What are the preparation requirements for this job?
- Do I have the personal traits necessary for this job?
- Is this an area I find interesting?
- Do I have the necessary skills and abilities for this job?
- Do I like to work with people or alone?
- Do I like work that is repetitious or work that is continually changing?
- Do I work best in a calm, relaxed atmosphere, or do I work better under pressure?
- Would I like to travel or do I prefer working in the same place every day?
- Am I willing to start at an entry-level position, or would I rather obtain further education and start at a higher level?
- Will this job help me reach my career goals?

A Job for You

Many young people choose to have part-time jobs while still attending school. If you are one of them, you know how difficult it can be to find time for schoolwork, home tasks, and friends, 30-3. Some teens feel they need to work in order to have spending money or to save for college. Others choose jobs to get some experience in a career field that interests them.

There are benefits to having a job. You can meet new people and learn new skills. You may be able to get a job in the field you are considering for your future career. That is the best way of testing your interest and ability.

If you think you might want to get a job, there are some factors to consider. Talk with your parents about how working will fit in with your school and home responsibilities. You will need to consider transportation. Will you be able to walk to work? Is public transportation available? Will you need to drive a car or have someone else drive you to and from work? You will also need to think about what kinds of work you would like to do and what jobs are available in your area.

30-3 When you have a job while you are still in school, you need to learn to manage your time well. *Shutterstock*

Finding Job Openings

When looking for a job, do not be bashful. Talk to people. This is called networking. **Networking** involves exchanging information with others with similar interests. Let people know you want to work. As you talk with people, they will pass the word to others. Friends, neighbors, relatives, religious leaders, teachers, coaches, and counselors may be able to help. They may know of job openings in your community.

Keep your eyes and ears open. Look for *Help wanted* signs in the windows of local businesses. Read job notices on community bulletin boards located in supermarkets, drug stores, and community centers. Listen to classmates as they talk about their jobs. If one has just quit a job, that job may be available. Listening to peers may also give you ideas about where you might want to work. Some jobs are better than others. Consider applying for these jobs even if there are no immediate openings. You could fill out a job application and ask to be called when a job is available.

Many people find jobs using the Internet. If you have access to the Internet, you can search Internet sites providing employment information and job listings. There are various government websites that provide information about the job market. Special job-search sites may list jobs by type, title, and location. These sites may list educational requirements, allow you to post your résumé, and provide direct links to companies with job openings, *30-4*.

The classified ads (want ads) in local newspapers are another source of information about job openings. They give brief descriptions of all kinds of available jobs. Most newspapers now post their classified ads on their websites. If you see an ad that interests you, respond quickly. Job openings listed in classified ads are often filled a day or two after the ads appear.

The federal government has set up *public employment offices* in every state. They help people find jobs in and out of government and do not charge fees for their services. Check the Internet or a telephone book to see if the state employment service has an office near you. If so, you may want to go there to fill out an application and talk with a job counselor. If a job opening matches your interests and skills, an interview will be arranged for you.

Private employment agencies charge fees for their services. Either the employer or the job seeker pays the bill. Many private agencies specialize, dealing only with office workers, salespeople, accountants, or engineers. If a contract is offered to you, be sure to read it carefully. Know exactly what you are agreeing to pay if you accept a job the agency finds for you. Do not sign any contract until you understand all the terms of the agreement.

Preparing a Résumé

Before you actually apply for a job, you will need to prepare a résumé. A **résumé** is a brief account of your career goals, education, work experience, and other employment qualifications. The purpose of a résumé is to promote yourself to potential employers by showing how your experiences and skills match the employer's job requirements.

Your résumé should help you make a good impression on potential employers. It should be neat, well organized, free of errors, and easy to read. A well-written résumé uses descriptive words and phrases that match those used in an employer's job description. You will need to organize this information in a way that captures an employer's attention and highlights your qualifications. Your résumé should be short—just one or two pages. Allow enough white space on the page so your résumé is easy to read. If your résumé is sloppy or confusing, it will not be read, and you will not be hired. If you print your résumé, use a high-quality résumé paper.

30-4 If you have access to a computer, you can locate job openings at various websites. *Shutterstock*

Name and Personal Information

List your name, address, telephone number, and e-mail address on your résumé. If you have a fax number, you can include this, too. You want to be sure the employer can reach you to set up an interview and offer you a job. Think about the layout of your résumé. Place your personal information at the top in a way that balances with the remaining information on your résumé. Figure 30-5 shows several ways to format your personal information.

Summary and Career Objective

A summary and a career objective follow your personal information on your résumé. A summary is optional, but is especially useful for people

Susan L. Wang
624 Pine Street
Irvine, CA 92714
714-555-1234
slwang@e-mail.com

Susan L. Wang
624 Pine Street   714-555-1234
Irvine, CA 92714   slwang@e-mail.com

Susan L. Wang
624 Pine Street
Irvine, CA 92714
714-555-1234
slwang@e-mail.com

30-5 You can present your personal information on your résumé in a variety of ways. No way is right or wrong.

who have much experience and expertise in a specific field. A summary may include skills and accomplishments you acquired through nonwork activities. The summary also relates to your career objective and the job for which you are applying.

A career objective can be your goal or a description of the specific kind of job you want. The following examples show specific and general career objectives:

- *Specific.* "Seeking position as a sewing machine operator in the alterations department of a fashion boutique."
- *General.* "Seeking a challenging position in apparel sales."

A specific job objective is great if it matches the job opening. In contrast, a general job objective shows that you are flexible. This may help an employer consider you for more than just one job opening.

If you are interested in several types of work, you may need to prepare several résumés. Each could have a different career objective. Another option is to not include a career objective. However, most career counselors advise people to include a career objective on every résumé.

Work Experience

Employers are especially interested in the listings under this heading. If you have work experience, the employer knows you can assume responsibility and it shows the employer what you have to offer. The best résumé will describe your job functions in language that showcases your skills and achievements.

Focus on Technology

Posting Your Résumé Online

Many employers have online job boards with varying requirements for posting résumés to their websites. Although this is a convenient way to apply for a job for applicants and employers, there are some details that will help you make the best of posting your résumés online. These include the following:

- Acquire a specific e-mail address to use for your job search and your résumés. Avoid using inappropriate or *cutsey* e-mail names. Doing so may indicate to a potential employer that you are less than serious about employment.

- Alter some of your contact information on your electronic résumé to keep personal information out of the hands of cyber-criminals. Use a post office box and *pay-as-you-go* cellular phone instead of your home address and phone number. Do *not* put your social security number on your résumé (print or electronic).

- Read the privacy policies on online job boards to which you desire to post your résumé. Some reserve the right to sell your personal information, while others promise never to do so.

- Choose only a few online job boards that fit your criteria for meaningful employment and post your résumé to them.

- Remove your résumé from online job boards once you have meaningful employment. Some employers check to see if a person's résumé is still online once they have the job.

List your work experiences in reverse chronological order, with the most recent one first. If you are just entering the job market, consider listing volunteer experiences through which you have acquired job-related skills. If you have gaps in your employment history, you may need to explain them during an interview.

For each employer you list, give a brief description of the work you did on the job. Avoid listing the addresses and phone numbers of your employers. You can provide them to a potential employer when completing a job application. Use such phrases as *responsible for* or *responsibilities included* instead of just focusing on *duties*. Your goal is to show that you have ability to be a responsible, dependable, valuable employee.

When describing your responsibilities, use distinctive words that communicate action or achievement. Verbs that show action—such as *organized, managed,* and *assisted* are good choices. You want a potential employer to view you positively—as an achiever who has something to contribute to the company.

The order of the sections on work experience and education varies. Sometimes work experience is first. Other times education is first. The format you choose for your résumé will dictate the order. Résumé formats will be discussed later in the chapter.

Regardless of order, design your résumé to highlight your strengths. If you feel qualified for a job because of your educational experience, list your educational background first. If you have valuable work experience related to the job you are seeking, list your work experience first.

Education

Under this heading, list all the high schools, vocational schools, colleges, and other schools you have attended. (You do not need to list schools you attended before high school.) List them in reverse chronological order, beginning with the most recent school first.

Give the name and location of each school, dates of attendance, and graduation dates. Describe diplomas, certificates, or degrees you earned and major programs you studied. If you are still in school, list courses you have taken that are most relevant to the job you are seeking. If you received good grades, you may want to mention your grade point average.

Honors, Awards, and Activities

This section allows you to highlight your achievements. List honors, awards, and scholarships you have received. Also list school and community organizations to which you belong. (*Note:* Employers are especially interested in job candidates who show their involvement in activities outside of school or work.) Be sure to mention any leadership positions you have held. If you did not mention volunteer work you have done under *Work experience*, you can list it here.

The name of this section should relate to the items you list in it. You may prefer to call it *Activities, Organizations*, or *Honors and Organizations*. It should point out your accomplishments without exaggeration.

Memberships and Professional Associations

Although this section is optional, include a list of your memberships in school or professional associations if they relate to the job you are seeking. You should list them in order of importance to the position, with the most relevant first. If you have held a leadership position in any of these associations, be sure to mention it here.

Special Skills and Interests

Include this section only if you have skills or hobbies that you think may enhance your job performance. Examples might be computer skills or the ability to speak a second language.

References

Most people do not list references on their résumé. Instead, they write the phrase *References available upon request*. A potential employer can ask the job seeker for his or her references. Most will not do so unless they are seriously interested in you as a job candidate. Then you must be prepared to give them your list of references.

If you include references, give the names, titles (if applicable), and addresses, and phone numbers of three or four people. These should be people who know you well and who could discuss your qualifications, personal qualifications, and your work-related character with employers. Do not use relatives as references. Former employers, club advisors, teachers, and religious leaders are better choices. Before listing someone as a reference, be sure to ask for his or her permission. Failing to do so is rude and can potentially put your reference on the spot if called by an employer. It can hurt your chances of getting a prompt and favorable response to an employer's inquiry.

Personal Information and Questions Employers Cannot Ask

You are not required to give any personal information. By law, employers cannot ask you about some of your personal qualifications. For example, employers cannot ask you specific questions about the following:

- Nationality, color, or race
- Age
- Marital/family status
- Gender
- Religion
- Health/physical abilities or disabilities

If you think some of your personal qualifications might help you get the job, carefully consider including them. In contrast, do not include any personal information that hurt your chances for employment. Think of your résumé as an advertisement. Be truthful and point out your best features.

Before choosing a résumé form, you will want to review the draft of the materials you want to include in your résumé. See Figure 30-6 for a summary of the résumé-writing process.

Choosing a Résumé Format

When choosing your résumé format, you need to think about two things. First, think about how you will present and organize your work history information. Second, analyze how you will visually present your information in terms of layout and formatting to best capture the interest of potential employers.

30-6 Double-check your résumé using these guidelines.

Drafting, Revising, Editing, and Proofreading Your Résumé

- **Draft.** Choose the standard résumé parts or categories of information that best fit your situation. Follow chapter guidelines for writing your descriptions.
- **Revise.** Revise your résumé descriptions to fit the length of your résumé. Use one page if you have a shorter work history and two pages if you have more experience.
- **Edit.** Be sure to include the key words that the employer is looking for. Describe your work responsibilities and accomplishments in language that is currently used in the field. Also, use words or phrases that appear in the job description in case an employer scans your résumé for these words.
- **Format.** Choose a format that best suits your information and the position for which you are applying.
- **Review.** Have someone else review your résumé. Enlist the opinion of someone who has good writing skills and experience with résumé writing.
- **Check spelling/grammar and proofread.** Make sure your résumé is error-free. This is essential if you want to make a good impression with an employer.

There are two basic résumé formats. They are

- *Chronological.* As the most popular résumé format, the **chronological résumé** emphasizes your employers and the work experiences you had with each. Potential employers will expect to see company names, dates of employment, job titles, and a list that describes work responsibilities and accomplishments.
- *Functional.* In contrast to chronological résumé, a **functional résumé** highlights your work experiences by categories of skills and accomplishments. The main advantage of this résumé format is that it showcases your best skills, even though you may not have used some of them in your most recent position. If you have little work experience, this format helps you emphasize skills you used in other capacities, such as with volunteer work.

Whichever format you choose, make sure it is neat and readable. It should highlight your skills and accomplishments in the best possible manner. Figure **30-7 A and B** shows examples of both résumé formats.

Electronic Résumés

Some employers request you to send an electronic résumé via e-mail or posted to the employer's job site. You can also post your electronic résumé to a number of online job-search sites. To create one, save your résumé as *text only* without any formatting. Then review the text only résumé to make sure lines and headers break properly. Save your electronic résumé in a separate file from your formatted résumé. Employers may use electronic résumés to scan for key terms that match their descriptions of ideal job candidates.

Developing a Portfolio

Starting a portfolio while you are in school is a good habit. A **portfolio** is a well-organized collection of materials that shows your abilities and accomplishments. The following list identifies some of the things you can place in your portfolio:

- letter of introduction
- your résumé
- news releases mentioning your name
- samples of articles you write
- examples of your work, such as fashion design or sewing projects, that showcase your ability to use industry tools (include drawings, photos, materials used)
- licenses or certifications you have earned
- references
- recognition, honors, or awards you receive

Organize your portfolio attractively and logically. You may want to organize materials based on their completion dates. Similar items should be grouped together. Place everything in an attractive binder. You might want to make a cover sheet with a table of contents. Some potential employers will want to see your portfolio.

SUSAN L. WANG
624 Pine Street
Irvine, CA 92714
Home: 714-555-1234
Mobile: 714-555-4321
E-mail: slwang@e-mail.com

CAREER OBJECTIVE
Obtain a sales associate position in apparel sales.

EXPERIENCE
March 20XX—present
Sales Associate, Kohl's Department Store, Irvine, CA
Responsibilities:

- Greet, assess, and respond to customer cues about apparel needs; provide assistance with styles, colors, and sizes; communicate effectively with customers, peers, and management
- Serve as point-of-sales and customer service lead
- Assist with replenishing inventory levels, helping to maintain company stock goals
- Assist with markdowns
- Keep fitting rooms and sales floor neat and clean
- Execute department merchandising and operational procedures according to company policy

May 20XX—present
Wardrobe Assistant—Volunteer, Orange County Women's League, Irvine, CA
Responsibilities:

- Organize clothing for fashion shows to ensure quick apparel changes for models
- Assist with choosing models' accessories for the shows
- Assist models with apparel changes

EDUCATION
High School Diploma, June 20XX, Woodbridge Community High School, Irvine, CA
GPA—3.75
Related courses: Fashion merchandising, apparel construction, general business

HONORS AND ACTIVITIES

- First-place award in the *Young Designers Contest* sponsored by the Orange County Women's League
- National Honor Society for 2 years; served as secretary
- FCCLA member for 3 years; served as president and chair of the program committee
- Woodbridge Drama Association for 2 years; served as chair of costume committee

SPECIAL SKILLS AND INTERESTS

- *Computer:* Microsoft Office Suite, CAD—Apparel Design
- *General:* Excellent speaking and written communications; highly organized; ability to prioritize assignments
- *Related apparel interests:* Fashion design and apparel construction; photography

30-7A This résumé is an example of a chronological résumé.

SUSAN L. WANG
624 Pine Street
Irvine, CA 92714
Home: 714-555-1234
Mobile: 714-555-4321
E-mail: slwang@e-mail.com

CAREER OBJECTIVE
Obtain a managerial position in apparel marketing and merchandising.

KEY ACHIEVEMENTS
- Youngest sales associate in the store ever promoted to assistant trainer
- Achieved *Area Sales Associate of the Year* for outstanding customer service and effectively leading and training new sales associates
- Helped to increase department sales 20 percent through effective merchandising sales skills and inventory management
- First-place award in the *Young Designers Contest* sponsored by the Orange County Women's League

SPECIAL SKILLS
- Excellent math, speaking and written communication skills; highly organized; ability to quickly prioritize and implement assignments
- Intuitive fashion sense with ability to promote sales through organization of visual merchandise displays
- Computer: Microsoft Office Suite, CAD—Apparel Design

WORK EXPERIENCE
20XX–present
Kohl's Department Store, Irvine, CA, Sales Associate, Area Supervisor/Apparel and Accessories

EDUCATION
B.A. in Merchandise Marketing in 20XX, Fashion Institute of Design and Merchandising—Orange County, Irvine, CA

High School Diploma, June 20XX, Woodbridge Community High School, Irvine, CA

30-7B A functional résumé shows your work experience according to categories of skills or achievements.

Letter of Application

When you send a résumé to a potential employer, a **letter of application** should accompany it. The purpose of the letter is to get the employer interested enough to arrange an interview with you.

Send a letter of application to the person within a company who has the authority to hire you. In large companies, this is usually the personnel manager or human resources director. In other cases, it may be the head of a department or the president of the company. If you do not know the person to contact, call the company and talk with the receptionist. Ask for the name and title of the person to whom a letter of application should be sent. Ask the receptionist to spell the name so you are sure to get it right.

A letter of application should follow the format of a standard business letter. Print a letter of application on good quality paper. Send the original, not a copy.

A good letter of application is brief and to the point requiring only three paragraphs. The first should explain why you are writing. The second should tell why you think you are right for the job. If you are sending a résumé, mention it here. In the last paragraph, you should request an interview and thank the addressee for considering your application. See Figure **30-8** for a sample letter of application.

Job Application Forms

When you apply for a job, you will probably be asked to fill out a job application form. If so, take this task seriously. Employers often compare the application forms of several job candidates. You will want yours to look neat with accurate information in the correct spaces.

When you fill out a job application form, use your résumé as a guide. It contains most of the information you will need. However, do not expect to be able to substitute your résumé for an application form. Most companies require all job seekers to complete their standard application forms.

Keep the following tips in mind when you fill out application forms.

- Read through the entire application form before you begin writing. Be sure you understand how to respond to all the questions.
- Look for specific directions such as *print* or use *black ink*. Usually these directions are given at the top of an application, but sometimes they are at the end. Follow all directions carefully. Be sure not to write in sections marked *For office use only*. Some employers require you to keyboard your application at a specific computer terminal.
- Bring your résumé, list of references (people whom you have asked in advance), and other important data so you have it at your fingertips. Never write down guesses, only facts.
- Write as neatly as possible.
- Respond to every question. If a question does not apply to you, draw a line through the space or write *Does not apply*. If you simply leave it blank, the employer may think you carelessly skipped over the question.
- Give complete and accurate information, but be concise. Never lie.
- Review the form one last time to make sure you have completed each question and filled in all appropriate spaces, **30-9**.

SUSAN L. WANG
624 Pine Street
Irvine, CA 92714
Home: 714-555-1234
Mobile: 714-555-4321
E-mail: slwang@e-mail.com

July 15, 20XX

Ms. Catherine Griffin, Personnel Director
High-Style Fashions, Inc.
300 N. Main Street
Irvine, CA 92714

Dear Ms. Griffin:

Introduction → The position you advertised in the *Orange County Register* for a full-time sales associate is exactly the kind of job for which I am looking. According to your ad, this position requires excellent communications and customer relations skills. As you can see from my résumé, my educational background and my experience working as a retail sales associate helped prepare me for this position.

Body → For the last two years, I have worked as a part-time sales associate at Kohl's Department Store. While working at this job, I gained experience in greeting and assisting customers with their apparel needs. I had an opportunity to observe full-time staff at work. Through department meetings, I learned how important it is to satisfy customer needs.

As indicated on my enclosed résumé, I graduated from Woodbridge Community High School in June. While in school, I took courses in fashion merchandising, apparel construction, and general business. These courses helped me develop effective communication skills. In addition to my education and work experience, I can offer *High-Style Fashions* a strong work ethic and solid organizational skills.

Conclusion → I am very interested in meeting you and hope that you will contact me for an interview. I am available by phone or e-mail to schedule an interview for this position.

Thank you for your time and consideration of this request. I hope to hear from you soon.

Respectfully,

Susan L. Wang
Susan L. Wang

Enclosure

30-8 A good letter of application should attract attention to your qualifications.

30-9 Complete application forms accurately and neatly. This sample shows the types of information you may need to provide.
Shutterstock

Job Interviews

The goal of your résumé, letter of application, and job application form is to get a job interview. The goal of the job interview is to get a job.

The job interview is the single most important part of the job-seeking process. It gives an employer a chance to ask questions about your qualifications, work habits, and career goals. It gives you an opportunity to learn more about the job and the company.

Preparing for the Interview

Since the job interview is so important, you will want to prepare yourself for it. Good preparation will help you make a positive impression on the employer. It will also help you feel more relaxed and confident.

The first step in preparing for an interview is to research the company. Try to find out the following:

- What is the company's mission or goal statement?
- What products or services does the company offer?
- Who are its customers?
- How large is the company?
- What is its potential for growth?

Some information may be available in libraries. Descriptions of most corporations appear in business and industrial directories. Check with the librarian. People are good sources of information, too. Talk to people who work for the company or to people who know others who work there.

Also check to see if the company has an Internet website. There you will often find information on the company's history, products, and employment needs, **30-10**. Look for Internet addresses in online commercials and magazine ads. You can also do an Internet search to locate their website.

Once your research is complete, start thinking about how you might fit into the company. Prepare yourself for questions the interviewer may ask, such as the following:

- What can you tell me about yourself?
- What kind of work do you want to do?
- Why do you want to work here? What attracted you to this job?
- What accomplishments have you had that show your ability to handle this type of work?
- Why should we hire you?
- What are your career goals?

You should also make a list of questions to ask during the interview. Like good answers, good questions show that you are serious enough about the job to have done some research. Ask questions about the job and the company. The answers you receive may help you decide if you really want to work for a particular employer. You might ask the following:

- How would I be trained for this job?
- What duties would I have, and what tasks would I perform?
- What hours would I work?
- What opportunities are there for advancement?

Avoid asking questions about wages and fringe benefits. Those are topics to discuss after you receive a job offer.

Going to the Interview

First impressions are important in interviews. You will want to look your best. Strive for a clean, neat appearance. Your hair should be clean and neatly styled. Men should be cleanly shaven, and women should be conservative in their use of makeup. Clothes should be clean and pressed. A general rule is to wear clothes that are equal to or a step above what you would wear on the job, **30-11**.

As you go to the interview, take all the items you might need. These include a pen, a pencil, and a copy of your résumé. You may want to take the list of questions you plan to ask. If you are applying for a job as a writer, designer, illustrator, or photographer, you should take samples of your work.

There is one thing you should not take with you—another person. You want to show that you are mature, responsible, and independent.

Finally, be sure you have all the facts. Double-check the date, time, and place of the interview. Know how to get to the location and how long it will take you to get there. Be sure you know the name of the company, the name of the interviewer, and the job title for which you are applying. Allow yourself plenty of time so you arrive a few minutes early. An early arrival will help you begin the interview feeling calm and collected.

30-10 Using the Internet to learn about a company is a good way to prepare for an interview. *Shutterstock*

During the Interview

Begin the interview by greeting the interviewer with a firm handshake. When a seat is offered, sit in a comfortable position, but do not slouch. Try to look and act interested and alert, but relaxed. Do not smoke or chew gum.

Listen carefully to what the interviewer says and the questions he or she asks. Some questions require just a yes or no answer. Others require longer responses. Think before you speak, so your answers are appropriate. Speak slowly and clearly, using good grammar. Do not brag, but do not be bashful

30-11 An interview is your chance to sell yourself to a potential employer. You should look your best.
Shutterstock

about your accomplishments. Be enthusiastic, but not pushy or insincere. Above all, be honest. It is never to your advantage to lie.

Be prepared to answer questions about education, work experiences, interests, skills, and goals. You may be asked about your best and worst subjects in school. You may be asked about your personal strengths and weaknesses. There will be questions about other jobs you have had and which you enjoyed most (or least). Be prepared to explain why you left previous jobs, and if you have ever been fired. Your expectations for the job and your plans for the future may also be questioned. You may be asked what you expect to be paid. A good response is to state a range you feel comfortable with. You may be asked how many hours a week you can work. Many interviewers ask what you plan to be doing 5, 10, or 20 years in the future.

When the interviewer has all the necessary information about you, he or she will probably ask if you have any questions. This is the time for you to ask the questions you have prepared. After finding out more about the job during the interview, you may have some additional questions you would like to ask.

You might be offered the job right then. If so, you need to know your start date, the hours you will work, and how much you will be paid. You also need to know about any fringe benefits, such as health insurance or vacation time. If everything sounds good, you could accept right away. If you want to think about your decision, the interviewer will probably give you a deadline for your decision.

In most interviews, the job applicant does not receive an immediate job offer. Instead, the interviewer usually takes time to consider the applicant's qualifications as well as those of others who apply. The interviewer may tell you that he or she will call you on a certain date, or you may be asked to call the interviewer at a later date. If nothing is said, ask when a decision will be made. You have the right to know what to expect next.

Regardless of what conclusions are reached, end the interview on a positive note and shake the interviewer's hand. Thank him or her for taking the time to talk with you and to consider your qualifications. If you are seriously interested in the job, be sure to say so.

After the Interview

As soon as you have a chance to be alone, go over the interview in your mind. Make notes about the questions you were asked. Were there any that took you by surprise? Think about your answers to all of the questions. Which were your best ones? On which do you need to improve?

Evaluating your interview performance after the interview will help you do even better in your next interview. It will also help you decide what to write in your follow-up letter. The main purpose of the **follow-up letter** is to thank the interviewer for taking the time to talk with you. It also gives you an opportunity to fill in any gaps left open after the interview. If you forgot to mention

Focus on Technology

Technology and the Interview Process Join Forces

It's Monday morning and you're anxious to call about a job opening you saw in Sunday's online newspaper. You call the 800 number given and find yourself talking to a computer! Welcome to one of the latest ways large companies are using technology to reduce the costs of recruiting and interviewing.

As you begin a job search today, you may encounter any of the following interview methods before you even meet someone from the company:

Telephone/computerized interviewing. Applicants call an 800 number and respond to an automated set of questions for the position. Employers then download the responses and sort out those applicants they wish to call for a personal interview.

Computerized interviewing. Companies use a computer to administer a structured interview of all applicants. As a question appears on the screen, the applicant enters his or her response. Printed reports are then generated, and the company selects the applicants to call for personal interviews.

Video interviewing. A video camera tapes the applicant's interview at a prearranged location. The applicant is given a list of questions to answer designed for the specific position. Employers can then view the tape to evaluate the individual.

Videoconferencing. Video equipment is used as an interactive tool between the recruiter and the applicant. A *live* interview takes place, but in separate locations. Interviewees speak to the applicants and maintain visual contact using monitors. The screens may use picture-in-a-picture technology so both parties can see each other. This method allows two-way communication, unlike video interviewing.

High-tech interviewing is here to stay. As you begin preparing for the world of work, also be prepared for these new interviewing methods.

---

an important fact during the interview, you can include it in the follow-up letter. Suppose you think the interviewer still doubts your ability to handle the job. You could explain in your follow-up letter why you believe you have the right qualifications for the job. The follow-up letter gives you another chance to state your case and show your enthusiasm. It keeps your name in front of the interviewer, and it may help you get the job, **30-12**.

If the interviewer promised to call you on a certain date, be sure you are available to receive the call. If you were asked to call the interviewer, be sure to do so. Suppose you were told you would "hear something in about two weeks," but two weeks go by without word. Then you have the right to call or e-mail the interviewer and politely ask if a decision has been made.

Do not be too discouraged if you do not get the job. Few job seekers get a job after just one or two interviews. Try to maintain a positive attitude. Think of each interview as a learning experience. Eventually, you should be able to get a job that is just right for you.

Succeeding on the Job

Getting a job is the end of the job-seeking process, but it is just the start of a new work experience. It is a chance to earn money, but also to learn new skills, gain experience in the world of work, and develop ethical workplace behaviors.

SUSAN L. WANG
624 Pine Street
Irvine, CA 92714
Home: 714-555-1234
Mobile: 714-555-4321
E-mail: slwang@e-mail.com

July 25, 20XX

Ms. Catherine Griffin, Personnel Director
High-Style Fashions, Inc.
300 N. Main Street
Irvine, CA 92714

Dear Ms. Griffin:

Thank you for taking time to meet with me yesterday. I enjoyed the opportunity to learn more about your stores and the expectations for your sales associates.

After meeting with you, I am even more enthusiastic about working for *High-Style Fashions*. I am confident that I have the skills and abilities to be a successful full-time sales associate.

I will look forward to hearing your decision and hope it will be favorable. Thank you for your time.

Respectfully,

Susan L. Wang

Susan L. Wang

30-12 After a job interview, it is a good idea to send a follow-up letter.

Starting a New Job

When you begin a new job, your employer may assign you to a mentor. A **mentor** is an experienced coworker who trains and counsels new employees. Listen carefully to explanations about your duties. Follow directions. Concentrate on your work so you will be able to do it well. Perform your duties to the best of your ability, without complaining. A positive attitude is important when you start a new job.

Once you can handle your job well, watch for opportunities to assume new responsibilities, 30-13. That is how you learn even more skills and advance in the world of work.

Getting along with coworkers is a major factor in succeeding on the job. You will need to use your interpersonal skills. To succeed in the workplace, be sure to:

- Display a pleasant attitude and show courtesy to others.
- Do your share of the work, and respect others for the work that they do.
- Show you are responsible by completing your work assignments. Look for ways to help your coworkers if you have the time.
- Use effective communication skills. Avoid gossip, and learn to control your emotions. If you get angry, find a way to cool down.
- Learn from your mistakes and accept any criticism that might come your way. If you do something wrong, do not try to hide it from your supervisor. Admit your error, and ask how to correct the situation.
- Be enthusiastic and show an interest in your work.
- Cooperate with your coworkers and set a good example.
- Keep an open mind, and listen to new ideas.

Getting along with your coworkers will help you enjoy your work and achieve success.

30-13 This employee knows she can advance to department manager if she does a good job in her present position.
Shutterstock

Ethical Workplace Behavior

Ethical workplace behavior is a standard expectation of any employer for any job. **Ethical behavior** means conforming to accepted standards of fairness and good conduct based on an individual's (or employer's) belief of what is right to do. Your ethical behavior—concepts of fairness, right and wrong, and good and bad—affect your job performance.

Integrity, honesty, and confidentiality are examples of highly important ethical behaviors. For instance, giving an honest day's work for an honest day's pay involves practicing ethical behavior. Adopting this behavior benefits both you and your employer. The employer gets the results of your hard work, done to the best of your ability. You get a paycheck, but also receive personal satisfaction. When you are a conscientious worker, you feel good about the work you do every day. Such pride and personal satisfaction give value to your work and make it enjoyable.

Use Communication Devices Effectively

There are many ways to communicate in today's workplace. You have learned some important tips on speaking and listening. Almost 75 percent of workplace communication takes place through speaking and listening. You have also read in previous sections about how to write letters. Two other methods of workplace communication include using the telephone and e-mail.

Telephone Skills

If you have a job that involves using the telephone, it is important to use good telephone manners. Your telephone manners can help or hurt your employer. Others may judge you and your employer by your promptness in answering the phone, as well as your attitude, 30-14.

The following pointers will help you effectively handle phone calls at work:

- Answer the telephone promptly.
- Greet the caller pleasantly, and identify yourself and the company.
- Speak clearly and naturally using a pleasant tone of voice.
- Do not chew gum, eat, or drink when answering a call.
- Listen carefully.
- Write down the name and telephone number of the caller and a brief message. Indicate the time and date of the call.
- If the call is a complaint, remain calm and poised. Take any needed action, but avoid blaming others.
- End the call pleasantly. If you received the call, thank the person for calling. If you placed the call, thank the person for his or her assistance or cooperation.

E-Mail Skills

In today's workplace, e-mail is an important method of communication. E-mail has replaced most office memos. Even communications between companies

30-14 How you relate to customers over the telephone can impact the success of the company that employs you. *Shutterstock*

often take place via the Internet. An e-mail message may contain a few lines of text or several hundred.

Though e-mail is often a less formal type of communication, when used in business certain guidelines apply. Your employer will expect you to use e-mail professionally, including the use of correct grammar, spelling, and punctuation. Follow the guidelines in Figure 30-15.

Safety on the Job

Remaining safety conscious on the job is the responsibility of all workers. Both employees and employers need to recognize workplace hazards and implement safety procedures to prevent injury. Many workplace accidents happen due to careless behavior and a poor attitude toward safety.

Develop Safety Habits

Practicing good safety habits helps prevent workplace accidents—even those in an office setting. A healthy worker—one who eats nutritious meals, gets proper sleep, and maintains a fitness routine—is more alert and less likely to make safety mistakes while working. Such workers also wear protective clothing and safety equipment as appropriate. They also follow their employer's regulations about safety at work. Examples of such safety regulations include acceptable workplace behaviors, lifting properly, preventing fires, keeping work areas neat and clean, and filing an accident report when an injury occurs. You employer's guidelines will also include emergency evacuation procedures for fire and weather emergencies.

Handling Emergencies

Regardless of how well people follow safety procedures and develop safe habits, accidents and injuries do happen on the job. At such times, it is important to remain calm and follow your employer's guidelines for handling emergencies. If an accident occurs, you should

- *Call for help.* Your employer will tell you who to call depending on the severity of an accident or sudden illness. With serious accidents or illness, call for professional help. In most locations, this means calling 911 or other emergency number.
- *Administer first aid.* First aid involves giving immediate, temporary treatment until medical help arrives, 30-16. Many employers provide training classes in first aid and CPR through such organizations as the Red Cross. You can also get this training on your own by taking appropriate classes.

Using E-Mail at Work

- **Check grammar, spelling, and punctuation.** Your e-mail may be viewed as regular business correspondence, so appearance counts.
- **Be positive.** A positive tone to your messages will make them more understandable and also get better responses from the receivers.
- **Do not yell.** Using all uppercase letters is considered YELLING. Use upper- and lowercase letters, just as you would in business reports or letters.
- **Fill the e-mail window accurately.** Be sure to completely fill in the information for *To*, *Date*, *From*, and *Subject*.
- **Make the subject line informative.** A few carefully chosen words tell receivers what the message is about. The information contained in the subject line may determine whether the e-mail message gets read or is deleted without being opened.
- **Remember e-mail is not private.** Write messages that are appropriate for others in the company to read. Also remember that e-mail is not yet considered a legal document.

30-15 These guidelines should be followed when using e-mail at work.

- *File an accident report.* Always file an accident report when an accident or injury occurs on the job—no matter how minor the accident or injury. Use the appropriate report form as your employer requires.

Follow Emergency Evacuation Procedures

In some instances, you may need to evacuate the workplace or move to another area of the workplace. In the case of fire, evacuation of the building is necessary. In contrast, with severe weather, you may need to move to a safe place within the building. Your employer will have specific guidelines about emergency evacuation procedures. Look for copies posted in the building that show emergency evacuation routes. Many companies conduct emergency drills—participate and take them seriously. Your behavior in an actual emergency could save lives.

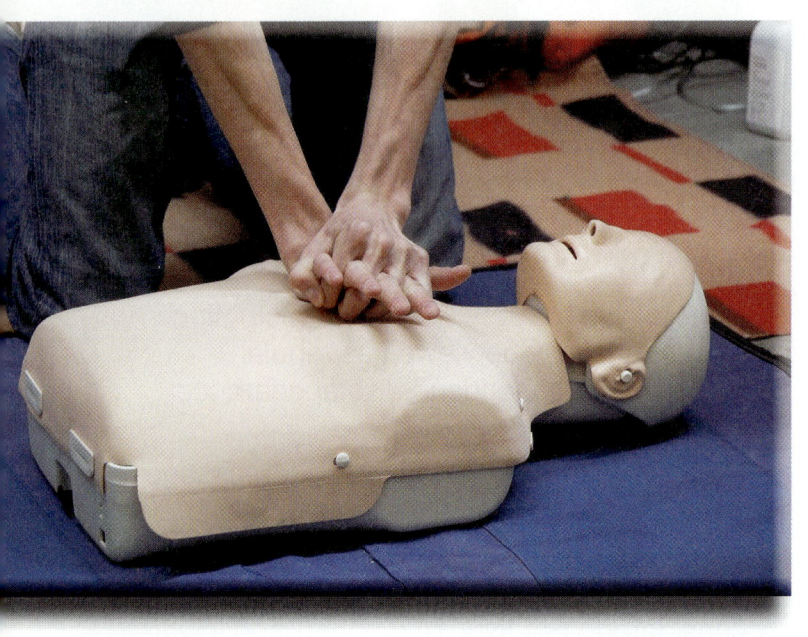

30-16 Many employers offer CPR training to their employees. *Shutterstock*

Leaving a Job

You will have many jobs during the course of your lifetime. Job changes are common today—employee turnover is high for all age groups.

There are many reasons why people leave their jobs. Sometimes they leave for higher pay, more hours, or better working conditions. A change in their personal life can lead to a job change. Marriage, divorce, death, or the birth of children can create new job requirements. Some people change jobs to advance their careers, hoping a new job will lead to new challenges or better use of their skills. Others leave their jobs to further their education.

Before making a job change, it is important to think through your options. Is this the best course of action at this time? Carefully weigh the pros and cons of leaving your current job for another job. If you decide a change is needed, start looking for a new job before leaving your old job, if possible.

There is a right way to leave your job. You want to leave under the best possible circumstances. Inform your employer before you tell your coworkers. Do so at least two weeks prior to leaving your current employer. This allows your employer time to find your replacement.

A **letter of resignation** is appropriate in most businesses. This letter should state when and why you are leaving. It can be brief, but it should be positive. Thank the employer for the opportunity to work there.

During the two weeks before you leave, continue to do your job as you always have. Return any office supplies and organize your workstation. Be pleasant to your coworkers as you may work with them again in a different job. Thank them for their help and friendship.

Managing Multiple Roles

Throughout your life, you will have many roles. Right now you are a student, a son, or a daughter. You may also be a brother or a sister, a friend, a class officer, or an employee. Each role requires that you fulfill certain responsibilities. As you get older, you may take on parenting and career roles. Meeting both family and career responsibilities is challenging. However, balancing multiple roles can also be exciting and rewarding.

Striking a balance among these roles is the key. However, there is no magic way to do this. This is where the following management skills will help:

- *Use the decision-making process when making important personal decisions.* For instance, presume you have a family. You value spending time with your family and want to be a good parent and spouse. Suppose, however, your employer offers you a position as a buyer that requires a great deal of travel. You may enjoy traveling. Taking the position may also help you move ahead in your career, which could help your family financially. How do you decide what to do? One way is to follow the decision-making steps. State the problem, identify goals and resources, and list the alternatives with their advantages and disadvantages. Doing so will help you make the most satisfying decision.

- *Learn to manage your time.* Time must be distributed among several roles, 30-17. For instance, if you are married with children, you will want to spend time with your children and your spouse. How much time will your career require? How much time will you want to retain for yourself? Setting up a weekly schedule may help you manage the hours you have each day. Making lists will keep you organized, too.

- *Develop flexibility.* Flexibility means having the ability to adapt to new situations. For example, suppose you and your spouse are working parents and one of your children becomes ill and is unable to go to school. Can you and your spouse make alternative arrangements at the last minute? Having a plan in place for emergencies such as this allows you to have flexibility.

Whatever career you choose, there will be many challenges and rewards. All careers require hard work and dedication. Enthusiasm and perseverance will help you along the way. The end result will be a lifetime of success and happiness.

30-17 Managing several roles for working parents requires managing your time wisely. *Shutterstock*

Summary

- A career is a succession of related jobs a person has over a span of time that results in professional growth and personal satisfaction.
- The career clusters are 16 general groupings of occupational and career areas. These clusters were designed by educators in partnership with business and industry representatives from throughout the country under the direction of the U.S. Department of Education.
- Career pathways are subcategories of the career clusters. The occupations included in each pathway require a set of common knowledge and skills.
- Selecting one career pathway is not an easy decision. Considering your interests, aptitudes, and abilities will make career decision-making easier.
- Many teens seek part-time jobs while they are still in school. They need to know how to find job openings, prepare a résumé, write a letter of application, fill out a job application form, and interview for a job.
- A positive attitude is important when you start a new job. Listen carefully when your duties are explained to you. Learn to use the telephone and e-mail as your employer recommends.
- The responsibility of all workers is to follow employer safety guidelines. This includes developing safe habits and learning how to handle emergencies.
- There is a right way to leave a job. You want to leave under the best possible circumstances.
- Meeting both family and career responsibilities is challenging. Management skills, such as planning, organizing, decision making, and being flexible, must be used.

Graphic Organizer

Create a fishbone diagram. List the parts of a résumé and two or three supporting details for each.

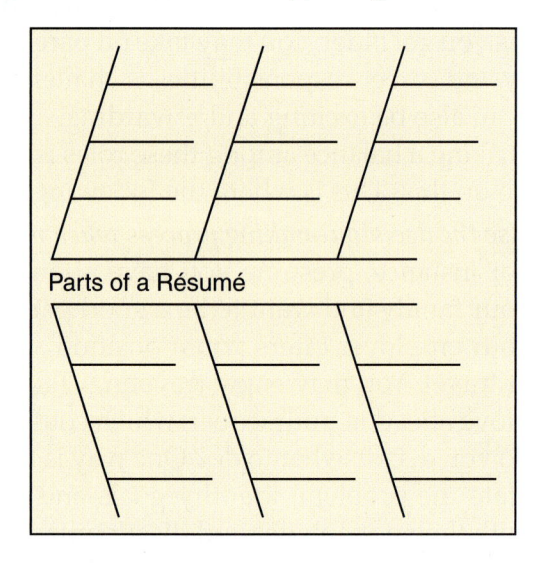

Parts of a Résumé

Review the Facts

1. Explain the difference between a job and a career.
2. What do the occupations in a career pathway have in common?
3. How do aptitudes differ from abilities?
4. Name one advantage and one disadvantage of having a job while going to school.
5. What personal information should you put at the top of your résumé?
6. Contrast a résumé summary and a career objective.
7. When describing your responsibilities on your résumé, why should you use distinctive words that communicate action or achievement?
8. Name three types of information about which employers cannot ask.
9. To whom should you send a letter of application?
10. List three steps in preparing for an interview.
11. What are two purposes of the follow-up letter?
12. What is ethical workplace behavior?
13. True or false. Because e-mail is a less formal type of business communication, the rules of grammar and punctuation are not as important.
14. State two recommended practices for leaving a job.
15. Describe one practice that can help people manage multiple roles.

Think Critically

16. **Make inferences.** Review the list of questions to ask yourself when choosing a career. Infer why is each question is important when making a career decision.
17. **Draw conclusions.** Why do teens you know have part-time jobs today? Do you think these are good reasons for working while still in school? What sacrifices do they make in order to hold jobs? Do the benefits outweigh the sacrifices? Share your conclusions.
18. **Predict consequences.** Why is it important to use proper grammar, spelling, and punctuation when sending e-mail messages? Is it more or less important than when writing letters? Predict the consequences of failing to use effective writing skills.
19. **Recognize values.** How would you advise someone to balance the multiple roles involving a family and a career? What values enter into making decisions that impact both work and family?

Apparel Applications

20. **Career cluster review.** Visit the States' Career Clusters website and investigate two career clusters and their career pathways of interest to you. What information did you learn about these career clusters? Share your findings with the class.
21. **Job shadowing.** Investigate any job-shadowing opportunities available to you through your school, community, family, or friends. Job shadow someone in an apparel career of interest to you. Write a report on your experience.
22. **Assess interests, aptitudes, and abilities.** Take the self-assessments on the *CareerOneStop* website. What information do these self-assessments reveal? What does this tell you about a possible future career? Give an oral report of your findings to the class.

Academic Connections

23. **Reading.** Choose a company for which you might be interested in working. Do an Internet search to find the company website. What information does the company provide on its website? What job openings are listed? Share the job description with the class.
24. **Writing.** Presume you have just had an interview with an apparel manufacturing company. Write a thank-you letter to the person who conducted your interview following chapter guidelines. Have your teacher or other adult critique your letter.

Workplace Connections

25. **Prepare a résumé.** Use Internet or print resources to locate an ad for an apparel job position of interest to you. Prepare a résumé with this job in mind following chapter guidelines. Have your teacher or other adult critique your résumé.
26. **Write a letter.** In conjunction with the résumé you wrote for the previous activity, write a letter of application following chapter guidelines. Have your teacher or other adult critique your letter.
27. **Interview practice.** Prepare for an interview for the job you previously identified by writing your responses to typical interview questions asked by employers. Choose a partner and role-play the job interview. Take turns being the *interviewer* and *interviewee*. Have the class give feedback on the interviews.
28. **Safety savvy.** Presume you work in the visual display department for a department store. You and a coworker are unpacking merchandise for a display when your coworker hurts her back. What immediate action would you take to assist your coworker? What would you do once your coworker received appropriate medical attention? Discuss your answers with the class.

Interview Competition

Participate in the FCCLA competitive *STAR Event* called *Job Interview*. For this event, you will need to use your Family and Consumer Sciences or related occupational skills to develop a portfolio, complete a job application, and participate in an interview. Use the guidelines in the FCCLA *STAR Events Manual* (available online) for this event. See your adviser for information as necessary.

Chapter 31

Entrepreneurship— Profiting from Your Skills

Chapter Objectives

After studying this chapter, you will be able to
- **summarize** the pros and cons of entrepreneurship.
- **analyze** the characteristics of successful entrepreneurs.
- **identify** types of business structures.
- **analyze** entrepreneurial opportunities related to textiles and apparel products and services.
- **summarize** how to prepare for entrepreneurship.
- **analyze** how to choose, price, and market an item to sell.

Key Terms

entrepreneur
entrepreneurship
sole proprietorship
partnership
corporation
franchise
chain
consultant
freelancer
Small Business Administration
business plan

Reading with Purpose

After reading each passage, answer this question: If you explained the information to a friend who is not taking this class, what would you tell him or her?

A growing number of people are choosing to be their own bosses by becoming entrepreneurs. An **entrepreneur** is someone who organizes, manages, and assumes the risks for his or her own business.

The career paths of entrepreneurs are varied, as the following examples show. Sheryl began cutting her neighbor's grass when she was a teen. After graduating from high school, she worked at a local nursery. Sheryl worked hard and learned a lot about lawns, trees, shrubs, and flowers. When she felt ready, she began her own landscaping and yard care business.

Joel grew up in a family with four younger siblings. He enjoyed helping his parents care for them. As a teen, he was a popular neighborhood babysitter. In college, he majored in child development. After working in a few different child care centers, he opened his own.

Rhonda took clothing classes at school and worked in the alternations department of a large clothing store for three years. Later, when she and her husband had their first child, Rhonda decided she wanted to stay at home with the baby. She started an alterations business in her home.

For some people, **entrepreneurship**, the organization and management of a business, is a lifelong career goal. By chance or by plan, they turn a hobby, a special talent, or a part-time job into a full-time career.

For others, entrepreneurship fulfills short-term career goals during a certain stage of the life cycle. Parents who want to spend more time with their children while maintaining a place in the world of work often begin their own businesses, **31-1**. When their children are grown, they may or may not continue those businesses. In other cases, people work as employees until retirement age. Then they begin businesses of their own.

The Pros and Cons of Entrepreneurship

Entrepreneurship has both pros (advantages) and cons (disadvantages). Consider the following factors before making any decision concerning entrepreneurship. The following are some of the advantages cited by entrepreneurs:

- *Freedom.* Entrepreneurs relish the freedom that comes with being their own bosses. They do not have to report to work sites at regular times every day. Instead, they start and end their days when they choose. They enjoy the flexibility of controlling their own time. Entrepreneurs can also control their working conditions. Many work from their homes and do not have to travel to work.
- *Enjoyable work.* Entrepreneurs like getting paid for doing something they enjoy.
- *Financial success.* Entrepreneurs welcome the challenge of developing a new company and seeing how much money they can make. Many entrepreneurs become extremely successful financially.
- *More family time.* Many businesses are started in people's homes because business owners have small children to care for. In this way, parents can stay at home with their children and still earn a living.
- *Sense of contribution to society.* Small businesses create the majority of new jobs in the U.S. economy. Entrepreneurs can take pride in providing employment and job benefits, such as health insurance, to individuals and families. Making these provisions gives the entrepreneur the sense of contributing to the community and economy as a whole.

31-1 Many mothers start their own businesses from their homes so they can be with their children.
Shutterstock

In contrast, there are disadvantages to being an entrepreneur. These include the following:

- *Lost investment.* Starting a small business usually requires an investment of much time and money. The failure rate for small businesses is high. When businesses fail, the money invested in them—as well as other assets—can be lost. Entrepreneurs have sole responsibility for the success or failure of their business. They risk losing not only their own money but also that of investors.
- *Unstable earnings.* An entrepreneur's earnings can rise or fall depending on the success of the business. At times, they may not have enough money to pay themselves.

- *Start-up time.* Beginning entrepreneurs may get frustrated with the length of time it takes to establish their businesses. It may take months or even years before the business becomes profitable, if ever.
- *Long working hours.* Entrepreneurs may have to work extra long hours to get their businesses going. Unexpected problems can also arise that require solutions. It is often difficult to get away on vacations, holidays, or weekends.
- *No paid employee benefits.* Business owners receive no paid benefits except what they provide themselves. This includes insurance, unemployment compensation, retirement benefits, or paid sick leave, vacations, and holidays.
- *Work space challenges.* Getting work done in a home office can be difficult if there are children at home. Parents may need to hire a caregiver. If they cannot work until the children are in bed, parents may not be working during their best time. Also, a home office may not provide the most businesslike atmosphere for clients. It may lack expensive equipment and amenities, such as speedy Internet access. An entrepreneur may have to spend lots of money to acquire the products and services he or she needs to work efficiently.
- *Emotional challenges.* In the beginning, many small businesses are one-person operations. The lack of interaction with other adults can be a negative. It can be lonely in the beginning if you are the only employee. Having a staff also has its drawbacks, especially if a business does poorly and workers must be let go.

Characteristics of Successful Entrepreneurs

After carefully weighing the pros and cons, it is also important to consider personal characteristics. Not everyone has what it takes to become a successful business owner. What does it take to succeed? The following are the characteristics most successful entrepreneurs have in common. Entrepreneurs are

- *highly motivated.* They are deeply committed to achieving success, and will do whatever it takes to succeed, 31-2.
- *well organized and self-disciplined.* They know how to manage their time. They are able to identify the steps needed to complete tasks. They know how to set goals.
- *creative problem-solvers.* They are able to adapt easily to new situations and can act quickly. Decisions may need to be made quickly. They may have to make these decisions on their own in the beginning.

31-2 Entrepreneurs are confident in their ability to succeed.
Shutterstock

- *risk takers.* Starting a business involves many risks, including the risk of losing the money invested. There is also the risk of personal failure in the eyes of family members and friends. Successful entrepreneurs are willing to tolerate these risks.
- *self-confident.* Entrepreneurs are confident in their ability to make decisions and to get the job done. Even if they make the wrong decisions, they have the confidence to bounce back and try again.
- *competitive by nature.* They welcomed challenges throughout their lives and thrive on competition.
- *extremely energetic.* The energy and great physical stamina of most of entrepreneurs helps them to work long hours, if necessary.
- *able to handle stress well.* They also deal with the emotional strain of making difficult decisions.

Do you have these characteristics? Carefully consider your personality type before starting a venture of your own.

Types of Small Businesses

There are three main types of business ownership. The first is a **sole proprietorship**—a business owned by only one person who has full responsibility. He or she makes all the decisions, pays all costs, and receives all the profits.

A **partnership** is a business with two or more owners. This form of business structure offers an owner someone with whom to share responsibilities and costs. Business decisions are made jointly and the partners share the profits. All partners are responsible for one another's actions.

A **corporation** is a legal entity formed to carry out business. The owners of the corporation are *shareholders*—people who have partial ownership as a result of buying company stock. A corporation has a separate identity from the individuals who own or work for this business. This type of business offers some protection to the owners. The shareholders may lose only their initial investment should the corporation fail.

Instead of starting a new business, an entrepreneur may choose to buy into an existing one. Two types of existing businesses include franchises and chains.

- *Franchise.* A **franchise** involves an agreement to sell another company's products or services. The individual who buys a franchise, or *franchisee*, has the exclusive right to sell the product or service in a given area. The franchisee has the right to use the company's name and image, its advertising, and other services. A franchise can make a lot of money for an entrepreneur, but the license to run the franchise can be expensive. The franchisee is also legally bound to follow company rules and guidelines.
- *Chain.* A **chain** is a business that has many locations, but the owner is generally a partnership or corporation. Managers run the businesses, but the owners make all the decisions for all locations in the chain. The Gap, Old Navy, Kohl's, and Talbots are examples of chain businesses.

Entrepreneurial Opportunities

Entrepreneurial opportunities related to fashion, textiles, and apparel vary. They can be either of two types: a product or a service. A *product* is something that exists, such as an item of clothing, which first must be manufactured. It then must be sold to customers. A *service* is work that provides time, skills, or expertise in exchange for money. Examples related to apparel include an alterations business or a tailoring shop.

Creating Products for Sale

New apparel products and new variations of existing apparel products are created every day. For example, fashion designers continually come up with new variations of the clothes you wear. Most designers work for clothing manufacturers, but some would-be fashion designers start out as entrepreneurs. In other words, they create their own designs, beginning with their own sketches. They then produce their designs using their own sewing equipment and find a retailer who will sell their designs.

Other unique products can be created that utilize special skills and talents, such as sewing skills. If you possess any of these skills, these products can form the basis for your own business. Apparel products include clothing and even custom-designed doll clothes. Accessories, such as purses and bags, may be designed and created, forming the basis for a business. If you knit, hand-knitted items such as sweaters, hats, and gloves can be made, 31-3. Some talented knitters create entire garments.

Some people use their skills to create unique home décor items. Handwoven blankets and table accessories can be made. Tablecloths, place mats, table runners, and napkins can be handwoven or sewn. Quilts of all sizes are popular. Quilting is also used to make pillows and other home accessories. Embroidery skills, both hand and machine, can be used to create unique items. Monogramming machines can be used to personalize shirts and jackets. Sports teams, as well as small businesses, might be interested in this product. You can turn your sewing and needlecraft skills into a source of income by selling the items you make.

Selling Products

Not everyone who creates a product for sale wants to do the actual selling. For that reason, there are entrepreneurial opportunities for people who are skilled in selling products. If you are one of these people, you could open a boutique, specializing in teen fashions, bridal wear, children's clothes, or athletic wear. In an accessories store, you could sell hand-knitted ponchos, purses, and sweaters, or embroidered items. A shop featuring unique fabrics or a yarn and needlework shop might interest you, 31-4.

31-3 String ponchos you crochet yourself would be popular with other teens. *Reproduced courtesy of Coats & Clark*

31-4 This young woman has opened a successful children's apparel boutique.
Shutterstock

Opening your own retail store is a major undertaking. It requires a large financial investment and a sound knowledge of business operations. A slightly less-risky venture is to open a *franchise*. Franchised businesses are usually more successful than independent businesses because they are known and trusted by potential customers. As you know, operating a franchise also requires a substantial financial investment. The franchisee must purchase the franchise from the parent company. In addition, a royalty is paid on the products or services sold.

There are other options for selling products other than in a store or shop. It is possible to set up a mail-order business. A *mail-order business* offers products for sale that are then shipped to customers. Products are shown in catalogs, on websites, or advertised in publications read by potential customers. A retail space is not needed to display merchandise, but shipping expenses can add up. Many mail-order businesses start small, even in the entrepreneur's home. As the business grows, additional space can be acquired. If a website is used, a domain name must be selected and registered. There is a fee for this. A website must be designed and a host—a place to store data—must be determined.

Another option for selling products is through a *consignment shop*. You might operate a consignment shop or sell your products in one. Many handcrafted goods from local crafters are sold in consignment shops. The person who creates the product maintains ownership until it is purchased. The store displays the products for sale. When the item sells, a percentage of the retail price is retained by the shop. The remaining amount is paid to the producer of the product. If the item does not sell, it is returned to the producer and the retailer loses no money.

Providing a Service

Providing a service is another entrepreneurial option. It may require the least financial investment, especially if it is an at-home business. Perhaps you have a skill you can offer as a service. For example, maybe you are a skilled sewer. If you have a sewing machine, you can start your own alterations business. Many people have trouble finding clothes that fit. By offering to do alterations for them, you can provide a service and have a nice income. Many people do not know how to make clothing repairs. You could provide this service, as well.

If you are very talented at sewing, you might become a custom *dressmaker* or *tailor*. Dressmakers and tailors can often create custom designs based on photographs or sketches. They take body measurements, recommend fabrics, and construct garments to fit. They often specialize in wedding gowns and special-occasion dresses.

Another service option is a consulting business. A **consultant** is someone who gives advice or ideas to businesses, organizations, or individuals. This person is very knowledgeable in a specialized area. A *wardrobe consultant* helps people plan and build wardrobes to meet their business, social, and leisure needs. A *color analysis consultant* helps clients find their best colors and coordinates the colors in their clothes and cosmetics.

Freelancers work in all areas of the apparel industry. A **freelancer** is someone who provides a specialty service to businesses on an hourly basis or by the job. Business owners hire freelancers when they need to have a job done, but do not have enough work to hire a permanent employee. Fashion photographers and illustrators are often freelancers. They sell their services to newspapers, magazines, catalogs, and Web designers. Other freelancers in the apparel industry include fashion writers and textile sales representatives.

The possibilities for starting your own business are many and varied. That is one of the reasons the idea of entrepreneurship is so intriguing. See the chart in figure **31-5** for a list of entrepreneurial options in the textiles and apparel field.

Preparing for Entrepreneurship

Those thinking about entrepreneurship should work to prepare themselves. They should acquire some knowledge of accounting, business management, and business law. They need to develop skills in communication, decision making, and time management. They also need a thorough understanding of

Entrepreneurial Opportunities Related to Textiles and Apparel

Create Products	Sell Products	Provide a Service
Men's and women's apparel	Retail shop or boutique	Alterations specialist
Children's apparel	Bridal salon	Dressmaker or tailor
Purses and bags	Fabric store	Machine embroidery
Hand-crafted items	Maternity shop	Dry cleaning service
Hand-woven blankets and table accessories	Shoe store	Wardrobe consultant
Doll clothes	Designer boutique	Color analysis consultant
Hand-knitted sweaters, hats, and gloves	Yarn and needlework shop	Freelance photographer or illustrator
Embroidered items	Franchise business	Fashion writer
Monogrammed items	Consignment shop	Personal shopper
Home décor items	Mail-order business	Sewing instructor
Quilts and quilted items	Online business	Textile sales representative

31-5 If your interest is in textiles and apparel, there are many opportunities for entrepreneurship.

the specialty areas of their businesses. They should discuss their ideas with attorneys, financial advisors, and business counselors.

Potential entrepreneurs may want to contact an office of the Small Business Administration (SBA). The **Small Business Administration** was established by the federal government to help people get into business and stay in business. It offers a number of programs that provide financial, technical, and management assistance to new businesses. The SBA can help an entrepreneur develop a **business plan**—a written document that explains how a business runs and operates—that is a requirement of potential lenders. The SBA can help people apply for loans. They also offer workshops, seminars, and courses on running a small business.

Did You Know?

A Business Plan Is Key to Success

Your business plan provides documentation about how you propose to start and operate your business. As you think through your plan, you can address any unanswered questions you have about running your own business.

If you require a bank loan to start your business, having a solid business plan will help you secure the loan. Your plan shows the lender that you have carefully thought through every aspect to help make your business succeed.

A business plan includes the following sections:

- ***Executive summary.*** This is a concise overview of your business plan.
- ***Business description.*** This description offers details on your product or service, your business structure, how you will run your company, and the company's mission or goals.
- ***Industry analysis.*** An overview of the market, this analysis provides information about the current status of the industry and economy in the area in which you want to start your business. It includes detailed information about your competitors and the need for your business.
- ***Target market.*** This section of your business plan identifies who will be buying your product or service, how many customers you may have, and how much they might spend.
- ***Organization/operations.*** The type of business structure and how your business will be run is important to this section of your plan. You will likely identify how many staff members you will have and their positions.
- ***Marketing strategy.*** This section identifies how you plan to sell your product or service. Will you advertise? How much will marketing cost?
- ***Financial plan.*** This includes your startup money, how much of your own money you are investing in the business, who your lender will be, and how you will pay back the lender. Your financial plan includes budgets, cash flow statements, and balance sheets for measuring net worth.

For help in writing a business plan, review the *Small Business Planner* tools on the website for the Small Business Administration (SBA). For additional help and business counseling, locate the SBA district office in your area.

Profiting from Your Skills

If the idea of starting your own business interests you, you can try it out while you are still in school. Taking on a small entrepreneurship project now will help you see the steps that must be followed. You may identify some of the pitfalls to avoid before making a substantial financial investment.

If you decide to proceed, you have some decisions to make. First, you must decide what you will sell or what service you might provide. You must also decide how much to charge for your product or service. If you sell a product, you must decide where to sell it. These are just a few of the many decisions you will need to make as an entrepreneur.

What to Sell

In choosing an item to sell, you need to consider what your customers want to buy. Items you make to sell should be unique and original. Try to find a few things you enjoy making that can be made quickly and inexpensively.

You can get ideas for marketable sewing or needlecraft projects from a number of sources. Start at a fabric store. Pattern catalogs are loaded with fun sewing ideas. Many fabric stores also carry kits, craft supplies, and how-to project books. These can give you ideas for needlecraft projects you might enjoy.

A craft shop is another place to get project ideas. Many craft shops offer classes. You can learn a new handcraft skill and make a project to take home with you. With practice, you can use your new skill to create products to sell, **31-6**.

Craft fairs can also give you ideas for items you might enjoy selling. Seeing products that generate profits for other entrepreneurs may give you some thoughts of your own.

Pricing Your Product

You must consider all of your costs when pricing your product. One of these costs is the cost of materials, including the costs of all the notions. Trims, buttons, thread, and even price tags cost money. Even if scraps are used, they have value that should be included in your sales price.

31-6 A visit to a yarn shop could inspire you to create your own unique accessories.
Shutterstock

Suppose you make stuffed animals to sell. Each animal takes a yard of fabric, two buttons, and a yard of ribbon to make. Your material costs per animal might look like this:

- Fabric $4.00
- Buttons. 3.90
- Ribbon 1.00
- Stuffing 1.90
- Miscellaneous
  (thread, price tags, bags, etc.) 95
- Total $11.75

Also consider your time when pricing your product. Decide how much you want to earn per hour. Carefully figure out how much time it takes you to make each item. To calculate the labor cost per item, multiply your desired wage by the time it takes to make an item. Add this cost to the price of each item. For example, suppose you can cut out and sew a stuffed animal in two hours. If you want to earn $8.00 per hour, you have to include $16.00 in the price of each animal to cover the cost of your labor ($8.00 × 2 = $16.00).

The time you spend selling your products must also be included in the labor costs. Suppose you sell your stuffed animals at a craft fair. If you sell eight animals per hour, it costs you $1.00 in sales time to sell each animal ($8.00 ÷ 8 = $1.00). At a price of $28.75 per toy, you will cover all your expenses ($11.75 + 16.00 + 1.00 = $28.75).

You may find that the prices you must charge is more than most customers are willing to pay. If this happens, look for ways to reduce your costs. Perhaps you can find a less expensive source of materials. Sometimes you can save money by buying large quantities of materials at one time. However, be sure you will use all that you buy before you invest in large amounts of materials. You may decide to lower your labor costs. However, avoid working for less than minimum wage. If you find you are making only $3.00 per hour, for example, you may become frustrated and abandon your business. If you cannot find a way to reduce your product costs, you may have to sell a different product.

Market Your Product

Once you decide what to sell and how much to charge, you must decide where to sell your products. You may have several options. Choose the venue or outlet that may be most enjoyable, as well as profitable, for you.

Schools, places of worship, and shopping malls often hold art fairs and craft shows featuring handmade items, **31-7**. Many community flea markets also include tables of craft items. These events give you the opportunity to sell to a lot of people in a short time. However, there is usually a charge for booth or table space. Remember to figure this cost into the price of your products.

Another option for selling your products may be to market them through gift shops and boutiques. Perhaps shop owners can display your items and take orders for you. There may also be a craft consignment shop in your community. You must share your profits with consignment shop owners.

You can advertise your wares through newspaper ads and posters on community bulletin boards. You can also create your own website. Word of mouth from satisfied customers can become your best advertising.

Some people do not like selling. They feel uncomfortable trying to convince other people to make purchases. However, if you like your products and believe in their quality, they should be easy to sell. In fact, many handmade items are so appealing they practically sell themselves.

31-7 An art fair in your local community may be a good place to sell your products.
Shutterstock

Summary

- A growing number of people choose to be their own bosses and become entrepreneurs. They organize, manage, and assume the risks of their own businesses.
- Entrepreneurship has pros and cons. Consider these factors before making any decision about becoming an entrepreneur.
- Successful entrepreneurs have many personal characteristics in common. Not everyone has what it takes to become a successful business owner.
- Entrepreneurial opportunities can be either of two types: a product or a service. A product is something that exists, such as an item of clothing. It first must be manufactured and then sold to customers. A service is work that provides time, skills, or expertise in exchange for money.
- Those preparing for entrepreneurship should acquire some knowledge of accounting, business management, and business law. They need communication skills, decision-making skills, and time management skills. They also need a thorough understanding of the specialty areas of their businesses.
- When starting a business, you must decide what product you will sell or what service you might provide. You must also decide how much you will charge for your products or services. If you are selling a product, you must decide where you will sell them.

Graphic Organizer

Create a T-chart. In the left column, write the main headings in the chapter. In the right column, write at least three supporting details for each header.

Main Headings	Supporting Details

Review the Facts

1. What are two advantages of entrepreneurship?
2. What are two disadvantages of entrepreneurship?
3. State three personal characteristics successful entrepreneurs often have in common.
4. Entrepreneurial businesses can be divided into three categories. Name these three categories.
5. What are three types of business ownership?
6. Contrast a franchise with a chain.
7. State one advantage and one disadvantage of operating a franchise business.
8. State one advantage and one disadvantage of operating a mail-order business.
9. How does a consultant differ from a freelancer?
10. List three sources of ideas for marketable sewing and needlecraft ideas.
11. Explain how to figure the labor cost that must be added to the price of sewing and needlecraft items sold for profit.
12. What is a disadvantage of selling sewing and needlecraft items at craft shows and flea markets?

Think Critically

13. **Identify evidence.** How important have entrepreneurs been to the success of the U.S. economy? Provide evidence to support your response.
14. **Analyze characteristics.** Review the characteristics of successful entrepreneurs listed in this chapter. Analyze which of these characteristics you have and which you are lacking. Do you think you have what it takes to be a successful entrepreneur?
15. **Analyze pros and cons.** What do you see as the pros and cons of operating a business from home? Share your thoughts with the class.
16. **Make decisions.** If you were to start your own business, what would it be? Explain your decision.

Apparel Applications

17. **Speaker panel.** Invite three entrepreneurs in your community to talk to your class about their experiences in establishing their own businesses.
18. **Identify business types.** Identify at least three businesses in your community that relate to textiles and apparel. Are these businesses sole proprietorships, partnerships, or corporations? Which are franchises and which are chains? Share your findings with the class.
19. **Electronic bulletin board.** Design an electronic bulletin board or blog page on the theme *Entrepreneurial Opportunities Related to Apparel*. Use school-approved Web-based software to create your information and post it to the class Web page. Collaborate with your classmates about your list of opportunities. What can they add?
20. **Crafters review.** Attend a craft show. Give an oral report to the class on what you observed. Describe the types of products sold, the price range of the products, and the location of the show. Also describe the number and types of people who attended the event. If possible, interview one or more of the vendors about the challenges of running their own businesses.

Academic Connections

21. **Writing.** Review the website for the Small Business Administration. Write a report on the business topics this site covers and the services the SBA offers. Share your report with the class.
22. **Reading.** Use Internet or print resources to read about a famous entrepreneur. What were the keys to this person's business success? Use presentation software to prepare a report of your findings to share with the class.
23. **Math.** Record the price of a sewn or handcrafted item you see in a gift shop. Then go to a fabric or craft store and price the materials needed to make a similar item. Compute the cost of making the item yourself. Compare the costs and share your findings in class.

Workplace Connections

24. **Fund-raising project.** If you have embroidery sewing machines, scanners, and a computer program that creates custom embroidery designs in your classroom, offer to embroider logos and designs for clubs and organizations in your school as a fund-raising project. Review the section of the chapter that explains how to charge for your services. Profits can be used to purchase more software and equipment for the classroom.
25. **Write a business plan.** Identify a sewing or needlecraft item that you could make and sell. Write up a business plan that includes an analysis of your costs and what you would charge for your product. Explain where you would sell your product.

Becoming an Entrepreneur

Use the FCCLA *STAR Event* guidelines to prepare for the *Entrepreneurship* competitive event. You can work alone or with a team. For this event you will develop a plan for a small business related to apparel design, textiles, or construction. See your advisor for information as needed.

Appendix A

Metric Conversions for Apparel Construction

Although apparel construction deals mainly with body and fabric measurements, a review of length measurements in the metric system will be helpful in converting U.S. Conventional measurements to the SI Metric system (*SI* stands for International System).

The metric system is simple—it follows the *decimal number system*. That means metric units increase or decrease in size by factors of 10 just like the U.S. monetary system. To increase the amount, you move the decimal point to the right. To decrease the amount, you move the decimal point to the left. For instance, think about how you write one dollar ($1.00). When you move the decimal point one place to the right, you increase the amount 10 times and make it 10 dollars ($10.00). Move the decimal point one more place to the right. You have one hundred dollars ($100.00), which is 10 times more than $10.00. Any metric unit works the same way. In **A-1**, you can see how dollars and meters are similar.

The Meter

The meter is used to measure length or distance. The letter *m* is its symbol. In apparel construction, the meter is used for measuring length. It replaces such U.S. Conventional units as the inch, foot, and yard.

The Prefixes

To understand the SI Metric system, you must know some prefixes. The common metric prefixes are listed in **A-2**, along with the units of measure. *Dice, centi,* and *milli* are added to the unit terms to identify smaller portions. *Deka, hecto,* and *kilo* are added to identify larger portions. Any of the six prefixes can be added to the term *meter*. The most commonly used prefixes in apparel construction are *centi* and *milli*.

When sewing a garment or other project, very short lengths, such as the length you may trim a seam allowance, are measured in *millimeters* and *centimeters*. Body measurements are expressed in *centimeters*.

Ten millimeters equal one centimeter. A meter is slightly longer than a yard, measuring 39.4 inches or 1.1 yard. You can use the multipliers in **A-3** to convert U.S. Conventional measurements to SI Metric and the reverse.

Dollars		Meters
$1000.00	1000	1000 m
$100.00	100	100 m
$10.00	10	10 m
$1.00	1	1. m
$0.10	¹/₁₀	0.1 m
$0.01	¹/₁₀₀	0.01 m
$0.001	¹/₁₀₀₀	0.001 m

A-1 All decimal systems are alike. This chart compares dollars to meters.

Metric Prefixes		
Prefix	Number	Length with Abbreviation
kilo	1000	1 kilometer = 1 km
hecto	100	1 hectometer = 1 hm
deka	10	1 dekameter = 1 dam
	1	1 meter = 1 m
deci	0.1	1 decimeter = 1 dm
centi	0.01	1 centimeter = 1 cm
milli	0.001	1 millimeter = 1 mm

A-2 This table shows the metric prefixes and unit of measure abbreviations in the metric system.

When You Know:	Multiply By:	To Find:
inches	25	millimeters
feet	30	centimeters
yards	0.9	meters
millimeters	0.04	inches
centimeters	0.4	inches
meters	1.1	yards

A-3 This table can help you change from one system of measure to the other. To use it, look up the unit you know in the left column and multiply it by the number in the middle column. Your answer will be approximately the number of units in the right column.

Useful Metrics for Apparel Construction

The following tables contain useful information for converting U.S. Conventional measurements to SI Metrics for apparel construction.

U.S. Conventional to SI Metric Conversions					
U.S Conventional	SI Metric	U.S Conventional	SI Metric	U.S Conventional	SI Metric
⅛ in.	3 mm	3 in.	7.6 cm	6½ in.	16.5 cm
¼ in.	6 mm	3¼ in.	8.2 cm	7 in.	17.8 cm
½ in.	1.3 cm	3½ in.	8.8 cm	7½ in.	19.0 cm
⅝ in.	1.5 cm	3¾ in.	9.5 cm	8 in.	20.3 cm
¾ in.	1.8 cm	4 in.	10.0 cm	8½ in.	21.6 cm
1 in.	2.5 cm	4¼ in.	10.8 cm	9 in.	22.8 cm
1¼ in.	3.2 cm	4½ in.	11.4 cm	9½ in.	24.1 cm
1½ in.	3.8 cm	4¾ in.	12.0 cm	10 in.	25.4 cm
1¾ in.	4.4 cm	5 in.	12.7 cm	10½ in.	26.6 cm
2 in	5.0 cm	5¼ in.	13.3 cm	11 in.	27.9 cm
2¼ in.	5.7 cm	5½ in.	13.9 cm	11½ in.	29.2 cm
2½ in.	6.3 cm	5¾ in.	14.6 cm	12 in.	30.4 cm
2¾ in.	6.9 cm	6 in.	15.2 cm		

Note: Metric conversions have been rounded.

A-4 This table shows U.S. Conventional with SI Metric conversions commonly used in apparel construction.

Fabric Conversion Chart
U.S. Conventional to SI Metric

Yards	⅛	¼	⅜	½	⅝	¾	⅞
Meters	0.15	0.25	0.35	0.50	0.60	0.70	0.80 m
1 Yard	0.95	1.05	1.15	1.30	1.40	1.50	1.60	1.75 m
2 Yards	1.85	1.95	2.10	2.20	2.30	2.40	2.55	2.65 m
3 Yards	2.75	2.90	3.00	3.10	3.20	3.35	3.45	3.55 m
4 Yards	3.70	3.80	3.90	4.00	4.15	4.25	4.35	4.50 m
5 Yards	4.60	4.70	4.80	4.95	5.05	5.15	5.30	5.40 m
6 Yards	5.50	5.60	5.75	5.85	5.95	6.10	6.20	6.30 m

A-5 Use this chart to convert fabric lengths from yards to meters. For instance, to find the metric equivalent of 3¼ yards, find 3 yards in the far left column on the chart. Then move across the chart to the row to the column marked ¼. You will find that 3¼ yards equals 3.0 meters.

Buttons	
⅜ in.	10 mm
7⁄16 in.	11 mm
½ in.	13 mm
9⁄16 in.	14 mm
⅝ in.	16 mm
¾ in.	19 mm
⅞ in.	22 mm
1 in.	25 mm
1⅛ in.	29 mm
1⅜ in.	35 mm

Zippers	
7 in.	20 cm
9 in.	25 cm
12 in.	30 cm
14 in.	35 cm
16 in.	40 cm
18 in.	45 cm
20 in.	50 cm
22 in.	55 cm

Thread	
35 yd.	30 m
100 yd.	90 m
200 yd.	185 m
250 yd.	230 m
300 yd.	275 m
350 yd.	320 m

A-6 The charts for buttons, zippers, and thread are approximate conversions.

Appendix B

Needlecrafts

Needlecrafts can be fun outlets for personal self-expression. You can quilt, embroider, knit, and crochet gifts that are fun to wear and to give. You can also make useful items to sell for profit. Using your creativity to make something offers great personal satisfaction. When others admire your work, you can take even more pride in your skills, B-1.

Perhaps it is sitting at a computer all day long where people can see something on a screen, but you cannot touch it or feel it that is leading to a renewed interest in handcrafts. Handcrafters are people who like to touch things. They enjoy the tactile kinds of crafts for which they can use their hands to create clever or beautiful items.

Doing needlecraft projects can have a number of benefits. They are

- *Enjoyable.* Needle crafts make excellent hobbies because they are so enjoyable to do. According to the *Craft Yarn Council of America*, this is the number one reason people choose to knit or crochet.
- *Relaxing.* Taking a break from daily tasks to do something that you enjoy is relaxing. Forty-two percent of needle-crafters surveyed do so because it is a great stress reliever.
- *Flexible.* Many projects do not require your full concentration. Therefore, they allow flexibility to take part in conversation, listen to music, or watch TV while you do them. Meeting with friends to work on projects together is also fun.
- *Skill-building.* Many people go to yarn shops or coffeehouses to knit and crochet. They join knitting groups to share information and learn new skills with others who enjoy the craft. In yarn shops, they can see the latest yarns and accessories while getting ideas for projects from other customers. Knitting groups, such as the *Knitting Guild Association*, have many chapters in major cities often holding monthly meetings at various locations. Many groups offer classes and seminars with renowned master knitters, B-2.
- *Meaningful.* Handmade items make special gifts. You can give projects to family members and friends as birthday and holiday gifts. A handmade gift means more to the person who receives it. It says you spent time and thought to make something just for that person.
- *Creative.* Another benefit of needlecraft projects is their uniqueness and variety. They provide an avenue for using your creativity and are limited

B-1 Learning a handcraft such as knitting provides enjoyment, relaxation, and personal satisfaction. *Shutterstock*

B-2 Skillful knitters often take courses from master knitters.
Shutterstock

only by a person's imagination. When you are done with your project, you have something that is one-of-a-kind. You may use the same pattern as someone else, but the colors and yarns you select add a personal touch.

People today take great pride in doing things for themselves and having ability to say, "I made it myself." Many have even become home-based entrepreneurs who sell their one-of-a-kind creations. Many young entrepreneurs are crocheting and knitting garments and accessories that appeal to many generations. Dresses, jackets, T-shirt tops, and skirts are popular because of their unique one-of-a-kind appeal.

Embroidery, knitting, and crochet have been favorite needlecrafts for years. These are only a few of the types of needlecrafts available. Counted cross-stitch, shadow stitching, macramé, and soft sculpture are others you could try. Check a local fabric or craft store or online to learn about a new handcraft that interests you.

Embroidery

Embroidery is decorative stitching made by using needle and thread. You can embroider almost any design on almost any item made from fabric. Embroidery can be used to decorate everything from garments to bed linens. Personalized items embroidered with people's names make popular products to sell. Embroidery can be done by hand or machine, **B-3**.

Hand Embroidery

Hand embroidery requires only a few pieces of equipment. The supplies needed for a project can also be bought in kits. A list of supplies includes the following:

- *Floss.* *Embroidery floss* is a six-ply yarn. This means there are six strands of thread lightly twisted together. For a thick, solid look, use all six strands, or separate them to achieve special effects. For instance, the thin stem of a plant could be made using only one or two strands. Experiment with variations to see what effect you like best.

- *Needles.* Special embroidery needles are available, but any needle can be used if its eye is large enough for the thread. Most threads slip through the needle eye easily. If you have one that does not, cutting the floss on a slant may help. Bulky threads can be a problem. Fold these back about an inch at one end. Pinch the fold and squeeze it through the eye of the needle.

- *Scissors.* Although any type of scissors can be used, a small, sharp-pointed pair is best. They will cut deeper into corners and closer to stitches. Always cut with the points. You may cut too far and damage your fabric if you use the back part of the blades.

- *Embroidery hoop.* An *embroidery hoop* is a set of two metal, plastic, or wooden rings. One ring fits inside the other. Fabric is held taut (tightly and smoothly) between the rings to prevent puckering as you embroider. A hoop with an adjustable screw on the outside ring is best. This type of hoop allows you to work with thinner or thicker fabrics.

Hand-Embroidery Techniques

Embroidery thread should be no longer than your arm. Twisting, knotting, and fraying result when you work with longer lengths.

The first step in embroidery is to anchor the thread. This can be done in two ways. You can knot the thread end and insert it into the fabric from the wrong side. You can also make several small stitches and a backstitch close to the starting point. Then bring the needle through to the right side of the fabric.

Most embroidery is done using a few basic stitches. Choose designs within your ability. Once you master the basic stitches, you can vary them for creative effects. As your embroidery skills increase, you may wish to tackle more complex designs.

To end your work, make a tiny backstitch on the wrong side. Then weave the thread through several of the completed stitches. Clip the thread close to the fabric.

Practice basic embroidery stitches until you can comfortably handle the needle, thread, fabric, and hoop. Later, you may want to use some of your samples as decorative patches.

Crewel

Crewel is a type of hand embroidery that is done with a different type of thread. Wool or wool-like yarn is used in crewel. Since yarn is thicker than embroidery floss, the work goes faster. Crewel uses the same equipment and techniques as embroidery.

B-3 The delicate embroidery on the collar and front of this jacket could be done by hand or machine. *The McCall Pattern Company*

Machine Embroidery

Machine embroidery is a quick and easy way to duplicate hand embroidery. Some simple machine embroidery can be done with a basic zigzag sewing machine. However, more sophisticated computerized sewing machines can be programmed to create very complicated embroidery designs, which would take hours of work if done by hand. Designs can be selected from those programmed into the machine, or custom designs can be created by combining different designs and adding lettering. Additional computer software can be purchased to give you more designs from which to choose. Some machines can be connected to your personal computer so you can design your own patterns, or you can use a scanner to copy a design into the computer.

An embroidery hoop must be used with machine embroidery as in hand embroidery. Each machine brand will have its own embroidery hoop accessories.

In addition, a stabilizer fabric should be used. The *stabilizer fabric* is placed under the fabric to be embroidered to support the machine stitches. It prevents puckering and tunneling, resulting in a smooth embroidery design. The stabilizer fabric is removed after the embroidery stitching is completed. There are several types of stabilizer fabrics from which to choose. These include the following:

- *Tear-away stabilizers* are made from a fiber that will tear easily. This type works well with stable woven fabrics. The excess stabilizer is torn away after stitching. Some tear-away stabilizers are available as iron-on fabrics. They are fused to the wrong side of the fabric before it is embroidered.

- *Cut-away stabilizers* must be cut from the outer edges of the embroidery. Some stabilizer fabric remains behind the embroidery. This type is recommended when embroidering ready-to-wear T-shirts.

- *Water soluble stabilizer* looks like a clear plastic sheet but it dissolves in water. After stitching, the excess is torn away. Then the work is placed in water to remove any residues. This type is good to use if all stabilizer fabric needs to be removed after stitching. It is also good to use when transferring designs for free motion embroidery.

Placing the fabric correctly in the hoop is an important element for quality embroidery. See **B-4**. Choose a hoop size large enough to contain the entire design. Loosen the hoop screw enough to get the fabric into the hoop without distorting it. Place the larger outside hoop on a sturdy flat surface. Then place the stabilizer and fabric over it, right side up. Set the smaller inner hoop on top and press down firmly to hoop the fabric. Tighten the hoop screw so the fabric is very taut in the hoop. Once the fabric is in the hoop, do not pull on it. This causes distortion and stretches the fabric, resulting in puckered embroidery.

Use fine or extra fine rayon or cotton embroidery-weight thread for the upper thread. A regular sewing thread can be used for the bobbin. A universal point machine needle is also recommended. Press the finished embroidery on a well padded surface from the wrong side.

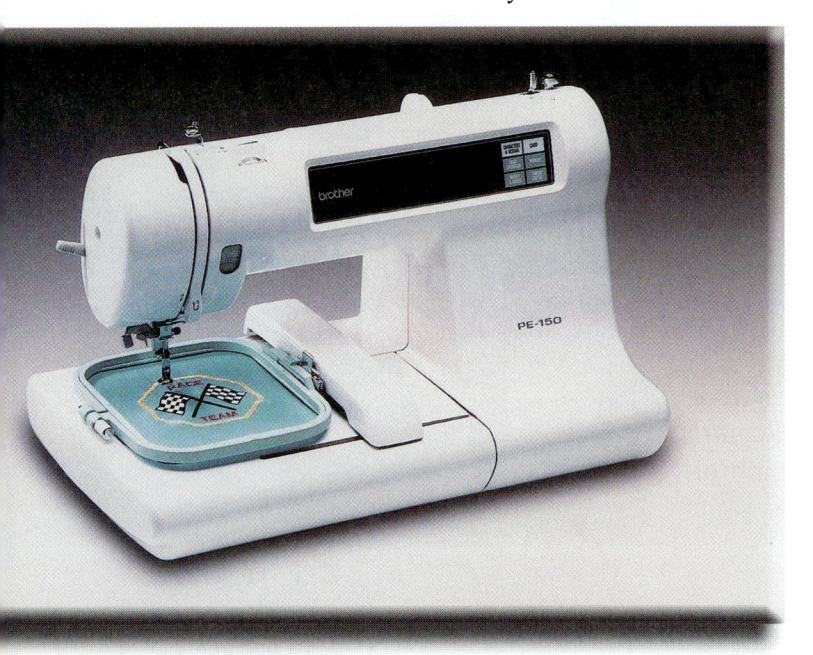

B-4 A hoop that contains the entire design is important for quality results. This computerized machine allows the user to select and view the design on an LCD display before it is created. *Brother International*

Free-motion embroidery can be done with a regular zigzag sewing machine. A design is traced onto the fabric and the fabric is placed in a hoop. Set the stitch width at a wide zigzag setting (4 mm). Lower or cover the feed dogs on the machine. Remove the presser foot and attach a darning foot. Place the hoop under the needle and lower the presser foot lever. Place your hands on the rim of the embroidery hoop—not inside the hoop. Use a fast machine speed as you slowly move the hoop forward, backward, and to the side. Stitches should be close enough so no fabric shows through but the threads do not pile up. Outlining movements and fill-in movements are used to create the design.

Knitting

Knitting is making a garment or article by looping and twisting yarn when using two knitting needles. A single yarn is looped off of one needle and onto the other needle.

Knitting projects make good products to sell because they are unique. Knitting items for yourself or to give as gifts can be fun. Sweaters, scarves, ponchos, and hats are popular knitting projects.

Supplies Needed

Yarn and knitting needles are the main pieces of equipment needed to make most knitted projects. Most knitting yarns are made of either wool or acrylic fibers. Yarn is packaged in skeins that vary in weight from ⅓ to 4 ounces. Two-, three-, or four-ply yarns can be used. (Four-ply yarn is thicker than two-ply yarn.) The directions for your project will tell you what type of yarn and how many skeins to buy.

Be sure to buy all the yarn you need for a project at one time. All yarn that is dyed at the same time is given a certain *dye lot number*, **B-5**. You can be sure skeins with the same dye lot number are exactly the same color. Exact colors are almost impossible to reproduce. If you go back later to buy more yarn, you may have to buy a skein with a different dye lot number. It may be a slightly different color.

Knitting needles may be made of plastic, metal, or bamboo. Because they are less slippery, bamboo needles are ideal for beginners. Sizes range from 00 (small) to 50 (large). They are from 7 to 14 inches long. For easy handling, choose a pair of needles that are size 5 or larger and no longer than 10 inches. When you follow printed directions, the needle size is specified.

Beginners should use single-pointed needles. Experienced knitters can create special effects and patterns by using double-pointed needles. Circular needles are used for making tube-shaped items, such as cuffs, turtleneck collars, and larger circular areas. These articles are seamless.

B-5 Checking the dye lot number on each skein of yarn will ensure that all your yarn is exactly the same color.

Reading Instructions

Read the instructions for any knitting project carefully. Every word is important. If you skip over something, you could ruin your project. Underlining each step as you complete it will help prevent mistakes.

To make directions shorter and simpler, abbreviations are used. All knitters use the same abbreviations. Once you learn them, you will be able to read any knitting directions, **B-6**.

To make sure that a knitted item will be the correct size, a gauge is given. A *gauge* is the number of stitches per inch and the number of rows per inch. If you use the correct size yarn, needles, and knitting tension, a sample of your knitting should match the gauge given in the instructions. If it does not, the item will be either too small or too large.

Standard Knitting Abbreviations

Abbreviation	Term	Abbreviation	Term
k	knit	incl	Including
p	purl	pat	Pattern
st	stitch	sl st	slip stitch
sts	stitches	rnd(s)	round(s)
dec(s)	decrease(s)	sk	skip
inc(s)	increase(s)	rep	repeat
beg	beginning	in.	inch(es)
tog	together	cm	centimeters
sl	slip	mm	millimeters
yo	yarn over	oz.	ounce(s)
psso	pass slip stitch over	g	gram(s)

* An asterisk means to repeat the instructions a certain number of times. For example, "Repeat from * 3 times more" means the instructions will be done a total of four times.

( ) Parentheses also means to repeat instructions. For example, "(k1, p3) 5 times" means the instructions will be done a total of five times.

B-6 Learning the abbreviations used in knitting patterns will help you understand directions finish projects more quickly.

Techniques

Casting on is the first step in knitting. This means putting the first row of stitches on the knitting needle. Your instructions will tell you how many stitches you need.

Knit and *purl stitches* are the basic stitches in knitting. Combinations of these two stitches form many patterns and designs. Other knitting stitches include the *stockinette, garter,* and *ribbing stitches*. To shape items, you need to know how to *increase* and *decrease* stitches.

Try not to put your work down while you are in the middle of a row. If possible, knit to the end of a row. Then push the stitches to the back of the needle so they cannot accidentally slip off the needle. If the needle is full with stitches, wind a small rubber band around the point of the needle or purchase a point protector to keep the stitches from slipping off the needle.

When you are not working on your project, roll your work loosely around the needles. Put it into a bag to keep it from getting soiled.

When you have finished knitting a project, you have to cast off. Stitches are looped together leaving a finished edge. The yarn at the end is knotted to prevent raveling.

As soon as you know how to determine gauge, cast on, knit, purl, and cast off, you can start a project. One of the fun things about knitting is being able to unravel your work and start over if you wish. You will need practice. Most people feel awkward at first. Try to establish good habits. Later, you will be able to relax and work more comfortably with better results.

Crocheting

Crocheting is similar to knitting. However, a single crochet hook is used instead of two knitting needles. The crochet hook is used to pull the thread through a loop or series of loops.

Many articles and garments can be crocheted. Projects made with bulky yarns and bright colors are popular. Scarves, hats, belts, afghans, vests, sweaters, skirts, and shawls are often crocheted, **B-7**. Many instruction booklets are available for making these items.

Supplies Needed

Crochet hooks can be made of steel, aluminum, plastic, or wood. In steel, the sizes range from 14 (small) to 00 (large). In aluminum, plastic, and wood, sizes are designated by either numbers or letters of the alphabet. The smallest is *A* or *zero*. The size of hook you need is determined by what you are making and the weight of your yarn.

Any yarn can be used for crochet, from fine to bulky. Yarn is sold according to weight and ply. A thicker ply results in a heavier yarn. Buy all the yarn you need at one time to be assured it is from the same dye lot. If the dye lot number on all labels match, the colors will be exactly alike.

Techniques

As in knitting, you must control your gauge so your finished project will be the right size. The instructions for any project list a gauge. Learning how to hold the yarn and the hook to get the correct tension will help you get the proper gauge. Measure a 3-inch square practice piece to determine if your gauge is correct. If you have too many stitches, use a larger hook. If you have too few stitches, use a smaller hook.

A *slip knot* is used to start any crochet project. The next step is to form a *starting chain*. A few basic stitches are used to make most crochet projects. These stitches are looped through the chain to form the first row of your project. Rows are looped through rows according to the instructions until the project is completed. By varying, enlarging, or combining basic stitches, you can make all other stitches. Like knitting, crocheting has a set of abbreviations that are commonly used in patterns, **B-8**. Become familiar with these terms to easily understand pattern directions.

B-7 Scarves are quick and easy projects to crochet. *Reproduced courtesy of Coats & Clark*

Standard Crochet Abbreviations

Abbreviation	Term	Abbreviation	Term
st, sts	stitch, stitches	**beg**	beginning
ch	chain	**tog**	together
sc	single crochet	**sk**	skip
dc	double crochet	**sp(s)**	space(s)
hdc	half double crochet	**lp(s)**	loop(s)
tr	triple crochet	**rep**	repeat
rnd(s)	round(s)	**pat**	pattern
sl st	slip stitch	**cm**	centimeters
dec(s)	decrease(s)	**mm**	millimeters
inc(s)	increase(s)	**g**	gram(s)
inc	including	**yo**	yarn over

* An asterisk means to repeat the instructions a certain number of times. For example, "Repeat from * 3 times more" means the instructions will be done a total of four times.

( ) Parentheses also means to repeat instructions. For example, "(sc) 5 times" means the instructions will be done a total of five times.

B-8 As with knitting, learning the abbreviations used in crochet patterns will help you understand directions and finish projects more quickly.

Glossary

A

abilities. The physical and mental skills that develop through learning and practice. (30)

accented neutral color scheme. A color scheme combining a neutral color with a bright color accent. (16)

accessories. Items that accompany the main outfit, such as belts, jewelry, scarves, hats, neckties, handbags, and shoes. (7)

adjustment lines. Two parallel lines that show where to shorten or lengthen a pattern piece. (23)

advertorials. Advertising presented in the form of a newspaper article or magazine story. (10)

agitation. The action that traditional automatic washers use helps to loosen and remove soils from the clothes during the wash cycle. (13)

alterations. Changes made in the size, length, or style of a garment so it will fit properly. (11)

alternatives. Various ways to solve a problem or reach a goal. (8)

analogous color scheme. A color scheme using adjacent colors on the color wheel. (16)

apparel. All men's, women's, and children's clothing. (2)

apparel mart. Buildings where many garment manufacturers have permanent showrooms and sales offices. (4)

applied casing. A casing formed by a separate piece of fabric or bias tape that is attached to the garment. (27)

appliqué. The process of sewing one or more small pieces of contrasting fabric onto a larger piece of fabric or a garment to add a decorative touch. (15)

aptitudes. Natural physical and mental talents. (30)

avant-garde. Fashions that are innovative, extreme, and daring. (2)

B

backstitching. Sewing backward and forward in the same place for a few stitches to secure ends of stitching. (26)

balance. The arrangement of objects in an even, pleasing way with equal visual weight on both sides. (17)

balance of trade. The difference between the values of a country's imports and its exports. (5)

bargain. A sale in which money is saved on items needed. (10)

bartering. Trading one person's skills or goods for another person's skills or goods. (3)

basting. Temporarily joining layers of fabric together until they are permanently stitched on the sewing machine. (26)

bleach. A chemical mixture that removes stains and whitens or brightens fabrics. (13)

blend. Yarn made by spinning different types of staple fibers together into a single yarn. (20)

body language. The use of body movements, such as facial expressions and body gestures, to covey messages. (29)

body measurements. The actual dimensions of the body. (22)

bonding. The process of permanently fastening one fabric to another. (20)

bound buttonhole. A type of buttonhole in which the edges are finished with fabric. (26)

budget. A spending plan that can help people manage money. (8)

business plan. A written document that explains how a business runs and operates. (31)

C

CAD. Software designers use to create textile and garment designs. (5)

café curtains. Curtains hung from clip-on rings that slide along a rod. (23)

CAM. Software workers use to control the steps in producing finished textiles and garments. (5)

career. A succession of related jobs that a person has over a span of time that results in professional growth and personal satisfaction. (30)

career clusters. Groups of occupations or career specialties that are similar to or related to one another by essential knowledge and skills. (30)

career pathways. Subgroups of the career clusters that often require additional and more specialized knowledge and skills. (30)

Care Labeling Rule. Legislation that requires garment manufacturers to provide clear, uniform, and detailed instructions for the care and maintenance of garments. (9)

casing. A fabric piece that encloses a drawstring or elastic that draws the garment snugly against the body. (27)

cellulosic fibers. Fibers made from vegetable (plant) sources. (18)

chain. A business that has many locations, but the owner is generally a partnership or corporation. (31)

chaining off. Serging off the edge of the fabric until a 2- to 3-inch thread chain forms. (28)

chain stitch. A serger stitch that does not overlock the edge of the fabric, but functions as a standard straight stitch when the cutting knives are disengaged. (28)

chain stores. Groups of 12 or more stores owned and managed by a central office. (10)

chronological résumé. A résumé format that emphasizes your employers and the work experiences you had with each, including company names, dates of employment, job titles, and a list that describes work responsibilities and accomplishments. (30)

CIM. Software that connects CAD, CAM, and robotic machine systems. (5)

classic. A style that stays in fashion for a long time. (2)

clean-finish. A method of finishing the raw edge of a facing. Stitch ¼ inch from the edge, turn under on the stitching line, and stitch again close to the edge. (26)

clipping. Making straight cuts into the seam allowance after the seam is trimmed or graded, when working with curved materials. (26)

collection. A group of expensive apparel styles for a season. (6)

colorfast. An item that retains its original color without fading or running. (14)

color scheme. An appealing combination of colors. (16)

color wheel. A chart that shows the relationship among colors or hues. (16)

combination yarn. Yarns made by twisting two or more different yarns into a ply yarn. (20)

command economy. An economy in which the state or some other central authority controls economic activities. Usually found in socialist or communist forms of government. (3)

commission. A percentage of a sales associate's total sales that is paid in addition to his or her salary. (4)

communication. The process of exchanging thoughts, ideas, or information with others. (29)

comparison shopping. Looking at brands of the same or similar products in several stores to compare prices, quality, features, and store services before buying. (10)

complementary colors. Colors located opposite one another on the color wheel. (16)

complementary color scheme. A color scheme using colors opposite each other on the color wheel. (16)

compromise. An agreement where everyone involved agrees to give up a little to reach a mutual agreement. (8)

cone adapter. A device that allows a cone of thread to be used on a spool pin. (28)

cones. Large spools of thread. (28)

conformity. Following or obeying some set standard or authority. (1)

consignment. A form of resale in which a portion of the sale price goes to the shop and the rest goes back to the owner. (10)

consultant. Someone who gives advice or ideas to businesses, organizations, or individuals. (31)

consumer. A person who uses goods and services. (9)

continuous overcasting technique. Lining up several garment sections so the stitching is not broken as you move from the edge of one garment section to the next. (28)

cool color. Blue, green, and purple. (16)

cord yarn. Yarn made by twisting ply yarns together. (20)

corporation. A legal entity formed to carry out a business. The owners of a corporation are shareholders—people who have partial ownership as a result of buying company stock. (31)

costume jewelry. Jewelry that is designed to wear with current fashions and is usually made from inexpensive materials. (11)

cotton. The natural fiber obtained from the cotton plant. (18)

counterfeit goods. Illegal products that may appear identical to legitimate products, but are not made by the original manufacturer. (5)

couture. A French word meaning *sewing* or *dressmaking*, which refers to garments made to fit a particular customer. (6)

cover stitch. A serger stitch used mainly for hemming, producing two or three parallel rows of topstitching on one side. (28)

credit. A promise to pay in the future for what you buy today. (10)

croquis. A body sketch of an idea or concept. (6)

culture. The beliefs and social customs of a particular group of people. (1)

custom-made. Garments that are specially designed for an individual. (4)

customs. Traditions one generation hands down to the next. (3)

cutting and sewing guide sheet. A printed sheet that gives detailed instructions on how to make a garment. (23)

cutting line. A bold line around each pattern piece. (23)

D

darts. A stitched fold that provides shape and fullness to a garment so it fits the curves of the body. (2, 26)

debit card. A card issued by banks that allows the user to deduct money electronically from the user's bank account in payment for goods or services. (10)

decision-making process. A series of steps to go through when making choices. (8)

decorative lines. Lines added to a garment to add interest. (17)

department stores. One-stop shopping that offers a variety of clothing, shoes, and accessories in a wide range of styles, qualities, and prices. (10)

design. An arrangement of elements or details in a product or work of art. (17)

design ease. An extra amount of fullness provided in patterns to give a garment its special look or silhouette. (22)

detergents. A chemical mixture made from petroleum and natural fats and oils used to remove dirt from laundry items. (13)

development. Finding practical ways to use products that researchers create. (4)

diffusion line. A name designer's less-expensive line. (6)

directional stitching. Stitching with the fabric grain to preserve the position of the grain and to keep fabrics from stretching out of shape or curling. (26)

disability. A condition that interferes with a person's ability to perform tasks like walking, lifting, or getting dressed. (12)

discount stores. Stores that have lower prices than department stores. (10)

domestic sourcing. A type of source that occurs in the U.S. (5)

dots. Solid circles on pattern pieces used for matching seams and other construction details. (23)

double-fold hem. A machine-stitched hem made with two folds of fabric of equal depth. (26)

dress codes. A set of rules, usually written, that specifies the required manner of dress. (7)

dry cleaning. The process of cleaning clothes using organic chemical solvents instead of water. (14)

dual-career families. Families in which both parents work outside the home. (8)

dust ruffle. The bed skirt that lies between the mattress and the box spring of a bed. (23)

duvet. A removable cover that fits over a comforter of a bed. (23)

dyes. Coloring agents that are used to add color to fibers, yarns, fabrics, or garments. (21)

E

ease. Extra space in garments to allow for movement and livability. (11)

easing. The process of joining two edges of fabric together when one edge is slightly larger than the other. No visible gathers should form. (26)

e-commerce. Conducting transactions electronically on the Internet. (5)

economics. The way a society chooses to produce, distribute, and consume its goods and services. (3)

elements of design. Color, line, form, and texture. (17)

embroidery. Decorative stitching that creates patterns or designs on fabric. (15)

empathy. The ability to understand and be sensitive to the feelings, thoughts, and experience of others. (29)

emphasis. The center of interest. (17)

entrepreneur. Someone who organizes, manages, and assumes the risks for his or her own business. (31)

entrepreneurship. The organization and management of a business as a lifelong career. (31)

entry-level job. Those jobs requiring little or no special training through those that are professional-level jobs. (30)

enzyme presoak. A laundry product specially formulated to help remove difficult stains before washing. (13)

ethical behavior. Behavior that conforms to accepted standards of fairness and good conduct based on an individual's (or employer's) belief of what is right to do. (30)

ethics. Moral principles that govern the behavior of a group or person. (5)

exports. Goods that are sent out of a country. (5)

F

fabric finish. Any treatment given to fibers, yarns, or fabrics that makes the final product look, feel, or perform differently. (21)

fabrics. Textile product usually made by knitting or weaving yarns together. (18)

fabric softeners. A laundry aid used to make garments soft and fluffy and to reduce wrinkles and static electricity. (13)

facings. Pieces of fabric used to cover raw edges in a garment, such as at the armholes, neckline, or other garment openings. (26)

factory outlet stores. Stores operated by manufacturers that sell only their own merchandise. (10)

fad. Something new in clothing that quickly becomes popular, but only for a short time. (2)

Fair Credit Billing Act. Legislation that protects consumers against unfair billing practices and defective merchandise. (9)

Fair Labor Standards Act. A U.S. law that established a minimum wage, a maximum work-week of 40 hours, and forbade employment of children under 16 in many jobs. (5)

family life cycle. Stages in the life of a family beginning with marriage. (8)

fashion. A particular style of apparel that is popular at a given time. (2)

fashion capitals. Four cities—Paris, New York City, Milan, and London—from where new fashions mostly originate. (6)

fashion center. Cities such as New York, Los Angeles, Dallas, Chicago, Atlanta, and Miami where retail-store buyers come during fashion weeks to view the new collections and make their selections. (4)

fashion cycle. The periodic return of specific styles and general shapes. (2)

fashion merchandising. All phases of planning, buying, and selling apparel. (4)

fashion promotion. Advertising, setting up window and store displays, media publicity, and special events such as fashion shows. (4)

fashion trend. The direction in which a particular change or fashion is moving. (2)

fashion week. A fashion industry event that occurs twice a year and can last up to 10 days. (6)

fasteners. Items that close the opening on garments, such as zippers, buttons, hooks and eyes, snaps, and hook and loop tape. (24)

Federal Hazardous Substances Act. A law that requires some children's clothing pass a use and abuse test for such items as decorative buttons and other attached items. Also covers toys and lead paint. (9)

felt. Fabric made from short wool fibers that interlock to form a solid mass when heat, moisture, and pressure are applied. (20)

fiber dyeing. The process of dyeing fibers before they are spun into yarns. (21)

figure types. Sizing patterns used by pattern companies to group figures according to height, proportion, and body type. (22)

filament. A continuous strand of fiber. (19)

filling yarns. The shorter yarns that run crosswise in woven fabric. (20)

films. Fabrics made of thin sheets of vinyl and urethane. (20)

finance charge. An extra charge you pay for the use of credit. (10)

fine jewelry. Jewelry that is made from gold, silver, or platinum, and may contain precious or semiprecious stones. (11)

flame resistant. A term used in relation to fabrics that are self-extinguishing or easy to extinguish. (12)

Flammable Fabrics Act. A law that states flammability standards for apparel and household textiles. (9)

flat collar. A type of collar that lies flat against the garment, also called a Peter Pan collar or shaped collar. (27)

flatlock stitch. A two-thread stitch that uses one needle and one looper to join a seam. (28)

flat method of construction. Serging flat pieces together rather than *pieces in the round*. (28)

follow-up letter. A letter thanking the interviewer for taking the time to talk with you. It also gives an opportunity to fill in any gaps left open after the interview. (30)

forecasting. Projecting future market trends for the coming months and years. (4)

form. The three-dimensional shape of an object. (17)

franchise. An agreement to sell another company's products or services. (31)

free enterprise system. Another name for a market economy. (3)

freelancer. Someone who provides a specialty service to businesses on an hourly basis or by the job. (31)

front hip pocket. Pocket that is angular and often used on the front of pants and skirts. (27)

functional résumé. A résumé format that highlights your work experiences by categories of skills and accomplishments. (30)

Fur Products Labeling Act. Legislation that requires product labels to include the name of the animal and the country or origin of imported fur products and products made of imported fur. (9)

fusible fabric. A sheer adhesive-coated fabric that joins two other fabrics together when ironed. (15)

G

garment dyeing. The process of dyeing an undyed finished garment after construction. (21)

gathers. Tiny, soft folds of fabric that form when a larger piece of fabric is sewn to a smaller piece. Gathers are fuller than easing. (26)

generic groups. Groups of manufactured fibers that are chemically alike. (9)

globalization. The flow of goods, services, money, labor, and technology across international borders. (5)

global sourcing. A type of sourcing that occurs beyond the U.S. borders. (5)

goals. Something a person wants to accomplish. (8)

grading. Trimming each seam allowance to a different width when working with thicker or layered fabrics. (26)

grain. The direction the lengthwise and crosswise yarns run. (20)

grain line. A line with triangles on both ends used as an aid to place the pattern piece on the straight grain of the fabric. (23)

greige goods. Unfinished fabric ready to be dyed or printed. (21)

H

hand-worked buttonhole. A type of buttonhole in which the edges are worked over with thread using a buttonhole stitch. (26)

hangtags. Heavy paper or cardboard tags also attached to clothing. They are not required by law. (9)

harmony. A sense of unity achieved when the elements of design are used according to the principles of design, creating a pleasing visual image. (17)

haute couture. A French phrase meaning *high fashion* or *high sewing* and is the most exclusive type of couture. (6)

hem. A finished edge on a garment. (26)

heritage. The background and traditions the person acquires from previous generations. (3)

hook-and-loop tape. A fastener that has tiny hooks on one strip and loops on the other that hold together when pressed with the fingers. (12)

hue. The name of a color. (16)

human resources. All resources a person has, such as skills, knowledge, and experience. (8)

I

imports. Goods that come into a country from foreign sources. (5)

impulse buying. Unplanned consumer purchases or *spur of the moment* buying. (10)

individuality. Characteristics that set a person apart from others. (1)

infomercials. Half-hour to an hour television advertisements that promote a product under the guise of a product demonstration by a host or an expert. (10)

in-seam pocket. Pocket that is sewn in the side seam of a garment. (27)

intensity. The brightness or dullness of a color. (16)

interfacing. A fabric used under the outer fabric to prevent stretching and provide shape to a garment. (24)

interpersonal skills. The skills you need to get along well with other people and to be an effective team member. (29)

inventory. An itemized list of goods, possessions, or resources. A wardrobe inventory is an itemized list of clothes and accessories. (7)

ironing. The process of removing wrinkles from damp, washable clothing using heat and pressure in a gliding motion. (14)

irregular. A garment with a slight defect. (10)

J

job. A group of tasks performed by a worker. (30)

job shadowing. Accompanying someone to his or her job to observe what the job entails. (30)

jute. A rough, course natural fiber that has a natural odor and is used for burlap. (18)

K

kimono sleeve. A sleeve that is a seamless extension of the garment's front and back. (2)

knitting. The process of looping yarns together to produce a fabric. (20)

knockoff. Copies of designers' high-priced designs that are sold at lower prices. (6)

L

labels. Small pieces of ribbon or fabric firmly attached or stamped inside in a garment that provide important information required by law. (9)

layaway buying. Buying that allows a store's customers to place small deposits on purchases that the store then holds for them. (10)

layout. Part of the sewing guide sheet that shows how to put pattern pieces on fabric for cutting. (25)

leader. A person who guides a group toward its goals. (29)

leadership. The capacity to lead or to direct others on a course or in a direction. (29)

letter of application. A letter that accompanies a résumé with the purpose of getting the employer interested enough to arrange an interview with the person. (30)

letter of resignation. A letter that states when and why an employee is leaving a company. It can be brief, but it should be positive, thanking the employer for the opportunity to work there. (30)

licensing. An owner who sells the right to use a particular name, image, or design to another party. (6)

line. A group of styles designed for a particular fashion season, such as Spring or Summer. (6) An element of design that gives a sense of movement and direction. (17)

linen. A cloth made from the cellulosic fiber called *flax*. (18)

loopers. The parts of the serger that form the stitch. (28)

M

machine-worked buttonhole. A type of buttonhole in which the edges are worked over with thread using a zigzag stitch machine. (26)

manufactured fibers. Fibers not found in nature. (3)

market economy. A system in which private individuals and businesses respond freely to the needs of the marketplace. (3)

marketing. All of the activities involved in creating and selling profitable products. (4)

market week. Time periods when apparel companies offer the next season's fashion lines. (4)

mass production. The production of many garments at the same time. (3)

media. Various forms of mass communication, such as television, radio, magazines, newspapers, and the Internet. (1)

mentor. An experienced coworker who trains and counsels new employees. (30)

merchandising plan. The producer's plans for creating a line of designs for a given season. (4)

mildew. A discoloration caused by a fungus that grows on some fabrics when they are moist for a period of time. (18)

mix-and-match wardrobe. A wardrobe that includes garments that have been coordinated (put together) to add variety and to create more outfits. (7)

mock flat-felled seam. A seam formed by using both the sewing machine and the serger. Topstitching completes the seam on the outside of the garment. (28)

modesty. Covering the body according to what is considered proper by the society in which you live. (1)

monochromatic color scheme. A color scheme using several values and intensities of one color. (16)

monofilament yarns. Yarns made from a single filament. (20)

multifilament yarns. Yarns made from a group of filaments. (20)

multiple roles. Two or more family roles combined with roles outside the family that are played at the same time. (8)

multisized patterns. Patterns that have several sizes printed on the same pattern tissue. (22)

N

nap. A layer of fiber ends above the fabric surface. (20)

narrow double-stitched seam. After stitching garment seams together on the sewing machine, they are serged together, placing the needle ⅛ inch from the stitching line. (28)

natural fibers. Fibers taken from nature, such as cotton, flax, wool, and silk. (3)

need. Something required for a person's continued survival. (1)

networking. Exchanging information with others who have similar interests. (30)

neutrals. Black, white, and gray are neutrals. White, the absence of color, reflects light. Black absorbs all colors. Gray is a blend of black and white. (16)

nonhuman resources. Material things you have or can use to achieve your goals, including money, tools, time, and community resources. (8)

nonverbal communication. A form of communication that involves sending messages without words. (29)

notches. Diamond-shaped symbols along the cutting line on a pattern piece used to show where pattern pieces should be joined. (23)

notching. Clipping V-shaped sections from the seam allowance on seams that curve outward. (26)

notions. Items other than fabric that become part of a garment, such as thread, fasteners, and interfacing. (23)

O

Occupational Safety and Health Act. A U.S. act that calls for safe and healthful working conditions in the workplace. (5)

off-grain. Fabric grain that is crooked, where the lengthwise yarns and the crosswise yarns are not at a perfect 90-degree angle to each other. (25)

off-price discount stores. Stores that feature brand-name or designer merchandise at below-normal prices. (10)

offshore production. Occurs when a company chooses to produce its products outside the U.S. using their own production guidelines. (5)

optical illusion. A misleading image or visual impression presented to the eyes. (17)

order of priority. Items that are listed from the most important to the least important. (7)

overedge stitch. A two-thread stitch used solely as an edge finish on garments. (28)

overlock stitch. A three-, four-, or five-thread serger stitch that is useful for seaming purposes. (28)

overruns. Items produced by manufacturers, but not ordered by retailers. (10)

P

parliamentary procedure. An orderly way of conducting a meeting and discussing group business. (29)

partnership. A business with two or more owners that share responsibilities and costs. They also make decisions jointly, share profits, and are responsible for one another's actions. (31)

patching. The technique of sewing a small piece of fabric over a hole in a garment. (15)

patch pocket. Type of pocket that is made from fabric pieces that are stitched on the outside of a garment. (27)

patchwork. Small pieces of fabric cut into shapes then sewn together to form a pattern. (15)

pattern. Tissue paper pieces to follow when cutting out fabric for a garment. (23)

pattern grading. The process of adjusting pattern pieces to make garments in a range of sizes, now computerized. (5)

peer pressure. The social pressure a person feels to adopt a type of behavior, dress, or attitude in order to have acceptance in a group. (1)

personality. Everything about a person that makes him or her unique. (1)

piece dyeing. Process of adding dye after the fabric has been made. (21)

piecework. Work done one piece or one step at a time for which payment is made at a set rate per unit. (3)

pile fabric. Yarn ends or loops extending above the surface of a fabric. (20)

pilling. The formation of small balls of fibers on the fabric surface due to wear. (19)

pillow sham. A decorative cover placed over the bed pillow and removed before sleeping. (23)

pinking or scalloping shears. A cutting instrument used to give seam edges a finished look with a zigzag edge. (24)

plain weave. A weave made by passing a filling yarn over one warp yarn and then under one warp yarn. (20)

ply yarn. Yarn made by twisting two or more single yarns together. (20)

portfolio. A well-organized collection of materials that shows your abilities and accomplishments. (30)

preshrinking. Fabrics that were put through a process (washing or dry cleaning) to minimize shrinking when washed or dry cleaned. (25)

press cloth. Cloth used to cover a garment before it is pressed to prevent iron shine. (24)

pressing. The process of removing wrinkles from clothing using steam and a lifting motion. (14)

pressing ham. A firm, round cushion used to help press curved seams and darts. (24)

prestige. Widespread respect and admiration for someone based on his or her achievements. (1)

prêt-a-porter. A French phrase meaning *ready-to-wear*. (6)

prewash soil and stain removers. Products that help remove oily stains and heavy soil. (13)

price points. Categories based on either the wholesale or suggested retail price of the garments. (6)

primary colors. The three colors from which all other colors can be made; red, yellow, and blue. (16)

principles of design. Guidelines for combining and using the elements of design (color, form, line, and texture). (17)

printing. The process of adding color, pattern, or design to fabric surfaces. (21)

priorities. Ranking of the importance of items or options. (8)

proportion. The relationship of one part to another and of all the parts to the whole. (17)

protein fibers. Natural fibers made from animal sources, such as wool and silk. (18)

prototype. A sample design. (6)

Q

quality. The degree to which an item meets certain standards of excellence. (11)

quick response (QR). Various business strategies that reduce the time between fiber production and sales to customers. (5)

quilting. The process of adding a layer of padding between two layers of fabric held together with stitches. (20)

quotas. Limitations on how much of certain goods can be imported. (5)

R

raglan sleeve. A sleeve with diagonal seams in the front and back that extend from the neck to under the arms. (2)

ramie. A strong, lustrous, moisture-absorbent natural fiber found in a shrubby plant that grows often in China and India. (18)

ready-to-wear (RTW). Clothing made in factories in standard sizes and is completely ready for a person to wear. (3)

recycled wool. Fabric made from previously made wool fabrics. (18)

redesigning. Changing a garment's appearance or function. (15)

regular charge account. A charge account that allows a person to charge purchases in exchange for a promise to pay in full within 10 to 30 days after the billing date. (10)

resale shops. Stores that sell clothing that has been owned and worn before. (10)

research. Working to find new products such as fibers, weaves, dyes, and finishing techniques. (4)

resources. Objects or abilities people can use to reach their goals. (8)

restyling. Giving a garment a new and different look. (15)

résumé. A brief account of your career goals, education, work experience, and other employment qualifications. (30)

retail. Selling small quantities of goods to consumers. (4)

retailers. Businesses that buy garments from manufacturers and sell them to customers. (4)

retro. Clothing that resembles styles from at least 20 years ago. (2)

revolving charge account. A charge account that allows a person to make purchases up to a limit set by the creditor when the account was opened. (10)

rhythm. The feeling of movement created by line, shape, or color in a design. (17)

robotic machines. Computer-controlled machines that automatically assemble and package complete garments. (5)

rolled collar. A collar that stands up from the neck slightly and forms a roll around the neck. (27)

rolled edge stitch. A two- or three-thread serger stitch that produces a rolled hem. (28)

rotary cutter. A cutting device with a round blade. (24)

S

satin weave. A weave made by floating a yarn from one direction over four or more yarns from the other direction and then under one yarn. (20)

scissors. Cutting instrument that is usually short with handles that have small, matching holes. (24)

seam. A row of stitches. (26)

seam allowance. Width between the fabric edge and the seam. (26)

seam finish. Treatment of seam edges to prevent raveling and to make the seam stronger and longer wearing. (26)

seam ripper. A small sewing tool with a hooklike blade that is used to remove stitches. (24)

seam roll. A long tubular cushion that allows you to press open seams without leaving marks from the seam allowances. (24)

secondary color. Color made by combining equal amounts of two primary colors; orange, green, and violet. (16)

seconds. Items that are soiled or have flaws. (10)

self-actualization. Needs that relate to a person's success in personal achievements, expressions of personal creativity, and self-fulfillment. (1)

self-adornment. Decorating the body in some manner. (1)

self-casing. A casing formed by turning back the edge of the garment piece. (27)

self-concept. The mental image a person has of himself or herself. (1)

self-esteem. A feeling of personal self-worth. (1)

self-help features. Easy-to-work openings and closures in clothes that make it easier for children to dress themselves. (12)

selvage. Turned filling yarns along each side of the woven fabric, which is very strong and will not ravel. (20)

sergers. Machines that provide a factorylike finish to home-sewn garments. These machines join two layers of fabric to form a seam, trim away extra seam allowance width, and overcast the fabric edges all in one step. Also called *overlock* or *overedge* machines. (28)

set-in sleeve. A sleeve attached to the body of the garment with a seam that circles the armhole near the shoulder. (2)

sewing gauge. A 6-inch ruler with a sliding marker. (24)

shade. Dark value of a color made by adding black to the color. (16)

shape. The outline of an object made up of lines. (17)

shears. Cutting instrument that is usually longer than scissors and the handles are not the same size. (24)

shirred curtains. Curtains with panels gathered onto rods. (23)

silk. A protein fiber that comes from the cocoons of silkworms. (18)

single yarn. The product of the first twisting step. (20)

sizings. A substance used with synthetic fibers to add body and make ironing easier. (13)

skirt marker. A measuring tool used to mark an even hem. (24)

sleeve board. A padded sleeve-shaped board used to help press small details in garments. (24)

Small Business Administration (SBA). An agency established by the federal government to help people get into business and stay in business. It offers programs that provide financial, technical, and management assistance to new businesses. (31)

societies. Groups of people with broad, common interests who live and work together. (3)

sole proprietorship. A business owned by only one person who has full responsibility. (31)

solution dyeing. The process of dyeing manufactured fibers by adding dye to the liquid before the fiber is forced through the spinneret. (21)

solvent. A liquid substance used to dissolve greasy stains. (13)

sorting. Grouping clothes in piles according to how they should be laundered. (14)

source reduction. A decrease in the amount of materials or energy used during the manufacture and distribution of products and packaging. (13)

sourcing. Choosing how, when, and where a company will manufacture its goods or purchase its products. (5)

specialty stores. Stores that sell specific kinds of merchandise. (10)

spinneret. A small nozzle with many tiny holes, through which a thick liquid is extruded to make manufactured fibers. (19)

split-complementary color scheme. A color scheme using one color with the two colors on the sides of its opposite complement. (16)

spool cap. A device placed over the thread spool to provide even feeding of thread to the serger. (28)

spun yarns. Yarn made from short, staple fibers. (20)

stabilizing. Adding extra strength to seams and areas that receive stress during wearing. (28)

stain. A spot or discoloration on apparel caused by various liquids or solid materials. (13)

standards. A set of criteria, established by authorities, used to judge whether or not products meet certain levels of performance and quality. (9)

standard sizes. The set of body measurements used by most pattern companies. (22)

standing collar. A collar that stands up from the neck edge of the garment. (27)

staple fibers. Short strands of fiber. (19)

starch. A laundry aid that produces a crisp, smooth surface on fabrics. (13)

status. A person's position in relation to others. (1)

staystitching. Sewing a line of regular machine stitching on a single thickness of fabric that helps stabilize curved or bias fabric edges and prevent stretching. (26)

stitching line. A broken line just inside the cutting line on single-sized pattern pieces. (23)

stitch-in-the-ditch. Using short machine stitches, stitch directly into the *well* of the seam through all layers of fabric. (26)

stock dyeing. Process of adding dye to loose fibers. (21)

store brand. The name of a retail chain used as the store's exclusive label on their merchandise. (6)

structural lines. Lines formed as the pieces of a garment are sewn together. (17)

style. A particular design, shape, or type of garment or apparel item. (2)

sweatshop. A manufacturing plant that may use child labor, pay lower than minimum wages, not pay overtime, or have unclean or unsafe facilities. (5)

synthetics. Manufactured fibers that are made completely from chemicals. (3)

T

tape measure. A flexible measuring tool used to take body measurements. (24)

tariffs. Taxes a government assess on imports that makes them more costly for consumers. (5)

teamwork. Involves individuals working together to reach a common goal. (29)

technical drawing. Design created using computer technology. (6)

technology. The manner of accomplishing a task using current technical methods or knowledge. (3)

tertiary color. Color made by combining equal amounts of a primary and a secondary hue, resulting in red-violet, blue-violet, blue-green, yellow-green, yellow-orange, and red-orange. (16)

Textile Fiber Products Identification Act (TFPIA). Legislation requiring manufacturers to tell what fibers are in textile products. (9)

texture. How a fabric feels and looks on the surface. (17)

texturing. Fibers that are twisted, crimped, coiled, or looped to vary the appearance and stretch. (19)

thimble. A metal or plastic device that is placed over the middle or ring finger of your sewing hand to help push the needle through the fabric. (24)

thread clipper. A cutting device with a spring action that reopens the blade after each cut. (24)

thread net. A device that helps prevent thread tangling. (28)

thrift shops. Resale shops that are often run by not-for-profit organizations to raise money for charitable causes. (10)

tie-dyeing. A method of dyeing fabric where sections of fabric are tied tightly with string or rubber bands and dyed causing the tied portions to resist the dye, resulting in a design. (15)

tint. Light value of a color made by adding white to the color. (16)

trade associations. Member companies that research, promote, and provide educational services for their industries. (6)

trade deficit. A negative trade balance. (5)

trademark name. An identifying name, symbol, or design that sets a manufacturer's product apart from similar products or competitors. (9)

trade surplus. Occurs when the value of a country's exports exceeds the value of imports. (5)

trendsetter. A person who takes the lead or sets an example. (2)

triadic color scheme. A color scheme using three colors that form an equal-sided triangle on the color wheel. (16)

trimming. Cutting off part of the seam allowance. (26)

true bias. The grain of the fabric that runs at a 45-degree angle. (25)

twill weave. A weave made when the filling yarns float over one and under two or more warp yarns. (20)

U

understitching. A row of stitches on the facing placed close to the seam line through the facing and the seam allowances. This keeps the facing from rolling to the outside of the garment. (26)

unisex. Patterns designed for either males or females. (22)

Universal Product Codes (UPC). Identifying series of barcodes that can be computer-scanned throughout various stages of product production, distribution, and sales. (5)

V

valance. A horizontal fabric treatment across the top of a window. (23)

value. The lightness or darkness of a color. (16)

values. The qualities, standards, principles, and ideals you consider important or desirable. (1)

vanity sizing. Manufactures that use a larger cut of clothing, but the sizes they are labeled are not increased in attempt to appeal to the consumer. (11)

verbal communication. Communication that uses words—speaking and writing. (29)

vertical integration. A company that handles several or all steps in production and/or distribution. (4)

vintage. Second-hand clothing with a sense of history. (2)

virgin wool. Fibers that have never been used before for a fabric or garment. (18)

W

waistband. A strip of fabric attached at the waistline edge of the garment and is visible above the waistline. (2, 27)

waistline facing. A curved piece of fabric attached at the waistline, that folds to the inside of the garment. (27)

wardrobe. A collection of clothes and accessories a person has to wear. (7)

wardrobe plan. A plan that includes the clothes you currently have and which items you will need to add in the future. (7)

warm color. Red, orange, and yellow. (16)

warp knitting. A process of knitting in which loops are made by one or more sets of warp yarns. (20)

warp yarns. The longer yarns that run the length of a fabric. (20)

water hardness. The amount of minerals, usually calcium and magnesium, contained in the water. (13)

water softener. A product or device used to soften the water. (13)

wearing ease. Extra room allowed in patterns for clothes to fit comfortably. (22)

weaving. The process of interlacing yarns at right angles to each other to create a fabric. (20)

weft knitting. Process of knitting in which loops are made as yarn is added in the crosswise direction of the fabric. (20)

wholesale. Selling quantities of goods for resale. (4)

Wool Products Labeling Act. A law that requires any textile product that contains some wool be labeled with the percentage and type of wool present and its country of origin. (9)

wool. A natural protein fiber made from the fleece (hair) of sheep or lambs. (18)

woolen yarns. Wool yarns made from short fibers (less than two inches). (18)

worsted yarns Wool yarns made from combed sliver using longer fibers. (18)

woven fabric. Fabric created by interlacing yarns at right angles to each other. (20)

Y

yarn. A continuous strand made of fibers. (18)

yarn dyeing. A dyeing process in which yarns are first wound onto spools and then placed in a dye bath. (21)

Index

A

AAFA, 135
abilities, 530
accented neutral color scheme, 292
accessories, 147, 216–221
    belts, 221
    buying, 216–221
    definition, 147
    handbags, 218–219
    jewelry, 220–221
        costume, 220
        fine, 220
        precious stones, 220
        semiprecious stones, 220
    neckties, 219–220
    scarves, 219
    shoes, 217–218
    sneakers, 218
acetate, 174–175, 338, 372
acid-wash finish, 372
Acrilan, 175
acrylic, 174–175, 340, 344
adjacent colors, 291
adjustment lines, 399
Adolfo, 124
advance, 290
advertisement, 197
advertorials, 197
aging stage, 160
agitation, 248
A-line dress, 57–58
A-line skirt, 53–54
alterations
    alterations specialist, 99
    considering before purchasing, 214
    definition, 214
    for meeting clothing needs, 165
    length, 272
    measurements in females, 384–385
    measurements in males, 386
    width, 272–273
alternatives, 157
American Apparel and Footwear Association, 135
American Society for Testing and Materials, 179
analogous color scheme, 291
ancient civilizations, 70–71
    Egypt, 70
    Greece, 70–71
    Minoan, 70
    Roman, 71
anidex, 174
Anso, 175
anti-vibration cone, 498
Antron, 175
apparel
    definition, 41
    history, 69–81
        1600s, 72–73
        1700s, 73–75
        1800s, 75–77
        1900 to 1950, 77–79
        1950 to 2000, 79–80
        early wearing, 69–70
        Middle Ages, 71–72
        today, 81
    industry, 89–93, 104–113
apparel decisions
    buying, 214–216
        care requirements, 215
        price versus quality, 215–216
    factors affecting, 158–161
        family life cycle, 158–160
        family values, goals, and priorities, 160–161
        multiple roles of family members, 160
    selecting appropriate clothes, 148–151
        community customs, 151
        school, 149
        special occasions, 149–150
        work clothes, 150–151
apparel industry, 89–93, 104–113
    balance of trade, 104–105
    custom work in production, 93
    design and product development, 90–91
    domestic sourcing, 106
    environmental efforts, 111
    free trade agreements, 106
    global sourcing, 106–107
    history of safe work environments, 107–109
    labor laws, 109–110
    production, 91–93
    research and marketing, 90
    sales and marketing, 93
    structure of, 90
    sweatshops, 107, 109–110
    trade laws and agreements, 105
    U.S. and world economies, 104–113
    World Trade Organization, 106
Apparel Industry Partnership, 110
apparel mart, 93
apparel production, 89
applied casing, 482
appliqués, 165, 273–274
    definition, 274
    for redesign, 165
aptitudes, 530
aramid, 174
Arkwright, Richard, 73–74
Armani, Giorgio, 132
artificial silk, 79
ascot collar, 49–50
ASTM International, 179
asymmetrical design, 57
Australian Wool Innovation Ltd., 328
avant-garde, 44
aviator, 59–60
Azlon®, 174

B

back fullness dress silhouette, 47–48
backpacks, 161
backstitching, 444
bags, 403
balance, 310
balance of trade, 104–105
Balenciaga, Cristobal, 123
ball-headed pins, 413

balloon sleeve, 51
ballpoint pins, 413
bamboo, 337–338
band collar, 50
bar codes, 116
bargain, 197
bartering, 67
basic weaves, 352–354
basket weave, 353
basting, 445
basting thread, 415
bateau neckline, 48–49
batwing sleeve, 52
BBB, 178
Beene, Geoffrey, 124
beginning stage, 158
bell-bottom pant, 46, 55–56
bell dress silhouette, 47–48
bell sleeve, 51
Bell, Thomas, 74
belts, 221
Bemberg, 175
Bermuda shorts, 55
Better Business Bureaus, 178
better price point, 126
bib front, 53
bikini length, 55
bishop sleeve, 51
black tie, 150
Blahnik, Monolo, 132
Blass, Bill, 124
bleach, 246
bleed, 367
blend, 351
bloomers, 78
blouses, 52–53, 212
    points to check for quality, 212
    styles, 52–53
blouson dress, 57–58
boat neckline, 48–49
bobbin cover, 420–421
bobbin winder, 419–420
bobbin winder tension disc, 419–420
body language, 519
body measurements, 381–386
    definition, 381
    females, 382–385
    males, 385–386
body shape, choosing a flattering pattern, 401
bolero, 59–60
boll, 323
bomber jacket, 59–60
bonding fabrics, 359

bound buttonhole, 465
boutique, 188
bow collar, 50
box jacket, 60
box pleat skirt, 54
boyish look, 78, 123
bridge price point, 126
budget, 162
budget price point, 127
Burch, Tory, 132
Burrows, Stephen, 132
business casual, 151
businesses, types of, 558, 560
    chain, 558
    corporation, 558
    franchise, 558
    mail-order, 560
    partnership, 555, 558
    sole proprietorship, 558
business plan, 562
butterfly sleeve, 52
Butterick, Ebenezer, 77
button-down collar, 50
buttonholes, 211, 465–466
    as quality indicator in apparel, 211
    sewing, marking, and attaching, 465–466
buttonhole twist, 415
buttons, 416
    as quality indicator in apparel, 211
    sewing, marking, and attaching, 271, 465–466
    sew-through, 466
    shank, 466
button-tab and epaulet sleeve, 51
buyers, 95

C

CAD, 114–116, 130–131
café curtains, 404
CAFTA-DR, 106
CAM, 114–116
camisole, 53
cape coat, 61
cape sleeve, 52
capri pants, 55
cap sleeve, 52
carded sliver, 323
cardigan jacket, 59–60
cardigan neckline, 48–49
carding, 323
Cardin, Pierre, 124

career
    clusters, 528–530
    decision making, 530
    definition, 528
    education and training, 85–99
    developing a portfolio, 537
    ethical behavior, 547–548
    in apparel, 90–93
    interviews, 542–545
    in textile industry, 87–89
    letter of application, 540–541
    pathways, 529
    preparation, 515–523
    résumé preparation and creation, 532–537
    roles and functions, 85–99
career and technical student organizations, 520
career clusters, 528–530
career pathways, 529
career preparation, 515–523
    communication skills, 518–520
    conducting meetings, 522–523
    effective team membership, 516–520
    leadership, 515–516
    student organizations, 520–522
    workplace traits needed, 516–520
CareerOneStop, 530
Care Labeling Rule, 173, 175–176, 253–255
care labels, 253–256
    symbols, 256
    understanding, 253–255
Cartwright, Edmund, 73–74
Cashin, Bonnie, 124
casings, 481–484
    definition, 481
    sewing, 482–484
        applied, 483
        attaching elastic, 484
        inserting elastic, 483–484
        self-casings, 482–483
Cassini, Oleg, 124
casual dress, 151
Celanese, 175
cellulosic fibers, 322, 335
centered zippers, 455
CFDA, 135
chain, business, 558
chaining off, 499
chain stitch, 497
chain stores, 188
Chanel, Coco, 122–123

Chanel jacket, 59–60
check, payment with, 199–201
Chelsea collar, 50
chemical engineer, 88
chemise dress style, 57–58
chesterfield coat, 61
chief engineer, 92
childbearing stage, 159
children, 225–231
Children's Apparel Manufacturers Association, 135
children's clothing, 226–231
    history of colors, 226
    infants, 227–228
    preschoolers, 228–230
    school-age, 230–231
    selecting, 225–231
    toddlers, 228–229
chiton, 71
Chromspun, 175
chronological résumé, 537
CIM, 116
circular skirt, 54–55
Claiborne, Liz, 124
clam diggers, 55
classic, 43
classic length, 55
Clean Air Act, 111
clean finish, 452
cleaning fluids, 247
Clean Water Act, 111
clipping, 451
closed-sleeve method, 477–478
closures, as quality indicator in apparel, 211
clothes
    as communication, 30–33
        first impressions, 33
        personality, 30–31
        self-concept, 32–33
        values, 31–32
    caring for, 240–249
    daily care, 239–242
    dry cleaning, 264–265
    drying, 262–263
        drip-drying, 263
        flat, 263
        line, 262–263
        machine, 262
    influences on choices, 33–37
        activities, 33–34
        climate, 35
        cost, 36
        family and friends, 36
        flattering garments, 35
        media, 37
    meeting human needs, 25–33
        love and acceptance needs, 27–28
        physical needs, 26
        safety and security needs, 26–27
    repairs of, 269–271
        quick repairs, 271
    selecting for others, 225–235
        children, 225–231
        older adults, 232–233
        other adults, 231–232
        people with disabilities, 233–235
    storage, 242–243
        daily, 242
        seasonal, 242–243
    washing, 259–261
        preparation of, 256–259
clothes swaps, 167
clothing care, 239–249
    equipment, 247–249
        agitation, 248
        dryers, 248–249
        irons and ironing boards, 249
        washers and dryers, 248–249
    products, 243–247
        bleach, 246
        enzyme presoaks, 246
        fabric softeners, 246–247
        laundry detergents, 243–244
        prewash soil and stain removers, 245
        solvents or cleaning fluids, 247
        starch and sizings, 247
        water softener, 245
    stain removal, 240–242
clothing care products, 243–247
coachman coat, 61
coat dress, 58
coat styles, 59, 61
collars, 49–51, 212, 473–476
    as quality indicator in apparel, 212
    definition, 49
    sewing, 473–476
        attaching, 474–476
        constructing, 474
    styles, 49–51
collection, 122
color, 285–299, 365–368
    adding color to a textile, 365–368
        colorfastness, 366–367
        dyeing, 365–366
        environmentally friendly, 373
        printing, 367–368
    and personality, 299
    choosing your best color, 292–299
    cool, 290
    for body type, 296–298
    for hair and eyes, 293–295
    for skin tone, 293, 295
    meaning of and symbolism, 286
    most popular, 298
    seasonal, 294–295
    terms, 286–288
    warm, 290
    wheel, 288–292
color analysis consultant, 561
colorfast,
    definition, 258
    in relation to dyeing, 366–367
colorists, 88
color schemes, 290–292
color sense, 292
color terms, 286–288
color wheel, 288, 290–292
    definition, 288
    schemes, 290–292
    warm and cool colors, 290
combed sliver, 324
combination yarn, 351
combing, 324
command economy, 68
commission, 96
communication, 518–520, 548–549
    e-mail, 548–549
    improving, 519
    nonverbal, 519–520
    skills, 518–520
    telephone, 548
    verbal, 518
community customs, 151
comparison shopping, 195–196
complaint letter, 182–183
complementary color, 289
complementary color scheme, 291
compromise, 161
computer engineer, 88

computer-aided design, 114–116, 130–131
    definition, 114
    in design and manufacturing, 114–116, 130–131
computer-aided manufacturing, 114–116
computer-integrated manufacturing, 116
cone adapter, 498
cones, 492
conformity, 28
consignment, 191
consignment shop, 560
consultant, 560
consumerism
    Consumer Products Safety Act, 173, 176–178
    definition, 171
    federal legislation, 172–175
    handling a complaint, 181–183
        consumer assistance, 182
        contact your credit card company, 182
        return the item, 182
        write a letter, 182
    protection agencies and organizations, 178–179
    responsibilities, 179–183
    rights, 179–180
    tips to consider before purchasing, 181
Consumer Product Safety Commission, 176–178
Consumer Products Safety Act, 173, 176–178
Consumer Products Safety Improvement Act, 173, 176–178
consumer rights, 179–180
continuous overcasting technique, 503
convertible collar, 50
cool color, 290
Coolmax, 175
cord yarn, 350
corporation, 558
costing engineer, 93
costing the fabric, 88
cost-per-wearing, 164
costume jewelry, 220
cotton, 322–324, 330
Council of Fashion Designers of America, Inc., 135
counterfeit goods, 113
Courreges, Andre, 124

couture, 122–125
cover stitch, 497
cowl neckline, 48–49
CPSC, 176–178
credit, 201
credit limit, 202
Creslan, 175
crew neckline, 48–49
Crompton, Samuel, 74
crop pants, 55
croquis, 130
cross-dyeing, 366
crosswise grain, 352, 428
CTSOs, 520
culottes, 56–57
culture, 28–29
    as fashion influence, 65–66
    definition, 29
    self-adornment, 28–29
curved eyes, 416
custom-made, definition, 93
customs, 66, 151
    definition, 66
    in a community, 151
cut-offs, 273
cut pile fabric, 354
cutters, 91
cutting and sewing guide sheet, 397–398
cutting line, 399
cutting tools, 409–410

D

Dacron, 175
darts, 57, 447
    definition, 57
    sewing, 447
debit card, 200
DECA, 520
decision making, 155
decision-making process, 156–158
deck pants, 55
decorative lines, 305
decorator fabrics, 401
de Givenchy, Herbert, 124
de la Renta, Oscar, 132
delicate, 262
department stores, 188
design
    definition, 303
    elements of, 305–309
        form and shape, 308
        line, 305–308
        texture, 309

    principles of, 309–313
        balance, 310
        emphasis, 313
        proportion, 310–312
        rhythm, 312–313
    textile, 87
design assistant, 91
designer
    of fashion, 90–91, 114–115
    of textiles, 87, 114–115
designer price point, 126
detergents, 243
development, 89
dhoti, 66
diffusion line, 126
digital printing, 368
Dior, Christian, 79, 122–123, 135
directional stitching, 445
dirndl skirt, 54–55
disability, 233
disappearing tracing paper, 438
discount stores, 189
display directors, 97
dobby weave, 355
Dolce and Gabana, 132
Dolce, Domenico, 132
dolman sleeve, 52
domestic sourcing, 106
Dominican Republic-Central America-United States Free Trade Agreement, 106
dots, 399
double-breasted, 59–60
double-fold hem, 464
double knit, 357
drawing, cotton production, 323
dress codes, 149
dresses, quality checkpoints, 213
dressing appropriately, 148
dressmaker, 560
dressmaker's pins, 413
dressmaking, couture, 122
dress shirt, 53
dress styles, 57–58
dress up, other uses of clothing, 279
dress up, special occasions, 149
drop-waist dress, 57–58
dry cleaning, 264–265
dry process, 257
dry spinning, 336
dryers, 248–249
drying clothes, 262–263
dual-career families, 160
DuPont Company, 79

Duraspun, 175
dust ruffle, 405
duvet, 404
dyeing, 274–275, 365–366
dyes, 365

E

ease, 208
easing, 446
e-commerce, 117
economics, 67–68
    as fashion influence, 67
    command economy, 68
    definition, 67
    market economy, 67–68
education and training, 88, 89, 91, 92, 94–95, 96, 97, 99
Egypt, ancient, 70
elastic
    attaching to garment, 484
    inserting in casings, 483
elastoester, 174, 341–342, 344
elements of design, 305–309
    definition, 305
    form and shape, 308
    line, 305–308
    texture, 309
Ellis, Perry, 124
embossing, 372
embroidery, 273–274
empathy, 517
emphasis, 313
empire dress, 57–58
engineers, 88, 92–93
    in apparel, 92–93
    in textiles, 88
Enka, 175
entrepreneur, 555
entrepreneurship, 555–565
    characteristics of successful entrepreneurs, 557–558
    definition, 555
    opportunities, 559–561
        creating products for sale, 559
        providing a service, 560–561
        selling products, 559–560
    preparing for, 561–562
    profiting from skills, 563–565
        marketing your product, 564–565
        pricing your product, 563–564
        what to sell, 563
    pros and cons, 556–557
    types of small businesses, 558
entry-level jobs, 528
environmentally friendly fibers, 111–112
enzyme presoak, 246
epaulets, 61
equipment, clothing care, 247–249
essential knowledge and skills, 528
esteem, 28–30
Estron, 175
ethics, 113–114, 547–548
    at the workplaces, 547–548
    definition, 113
    ethical and unethical industry practices, 113–114
    ethical behavior, 547
evaluate, 142
evaporating marking pens, 412
expert, 197
exports, 104
extruded, 336

F

fabric
    as quality indicator in apparel, 211
    choosing, 401–402
    conversion chart for different widths, 397
    definition, 321
    dictionary, 360–361
    finishes, 368–373
    finishing, 87
    grain, 428–429
    knitted, 355–358
    other constructions, 358–361
    painting, 275
    preparation for sewing, 427–429
    production, 87
    woven, 351–355
fabric finishes, 368–373
    affecting performance, 368–371
    affecting appearance and texture, 371–372
    definition, 368
    environmentally friendly, 373
fabric finishing, 87
fabric grain, 428–429
fabric production, 87
fabric softeners, 246–247
face plate, 419–420
facings, 452–453
    attaching, 453
    definition, 452
    stitching, 452–453
factory outlet stores, 190
fad, 44
Fair Credit Billing Act, 182
Fair Labor Standards Act, 109
family, 160–162
    dual-career, 160
    life cycle, 158–160
    multiple roles, 160
    resources, 162
    values, goals, and priorities, 160–161
Family, Career and Community Leaders of America, 39, 63, 83, 101, 119, 137, 153, 169, 185, 205, 223, 237, 251, 267, 279, 301, 317, 333, 347, 363, 375, 391, 407, 425, 435, 441, 471, 489, 511, 520–521, 525, 553, 567
family life cycle, 158–160
fashion
    as a style, 42–43
    associations, 134–135
    capitals, 127–128
    categories, 126
    center, 93
    consultants, 97
    coordinators, 96–97
    cycles, 46–47
    definition, 41
    fabrics, choosing, 401–402
    importance of, 41–42
    influences, 65–69
        cultural, 65–66
        economic, 67
        political, 66–67
        religious, 66
        social, 66
        technology, 68–69
    models, 98–99
    news, 134
    terms, 42–46
    writers, 98
fashion capitals, 127–128
fashion center, 93
fashion consultants, 97
fashion coordinators, 96–97
fashion cycles, 46–47
fashion cycle silhouettes, 48

Index

fashion design, 128–131
    inspiration, 128–130
        arts, 129
        historical and ethnic costume, 129
        nature, 129
        observations, 130
        textiles, 129
    process, 128–131
        creating design ideas, 130
        inspiration, 128–130
        making samples, 131
    publications, 134–135
fashion designers
    definition, 90–91, 114–115
    of today, 131–133
    work locations, 127–128
fashion directors, 97
Fashion Group International, 135
fashion illustrators, 98
fashion merchandising, 94
fashion models, 98–99
fashion promotion, 94
fashion trend, 42
fashion week, 128
fashion writers, 98
fasteners
    buttons and buttonholes, 416, 465–466
    definition, 415
    history of, 415
    hook-and-loop tape, 417, 467
    hooks and eyes, 416, 466–467
    reparation of, 271
    sewing, 464–467
    snaps, 416, 466
    zippers, 211, 416, 455–458
FBLA, 521
FCCLA, 39, 63, 83, 101, 119, 137, 153, 169, 185, 205, 223, 237, 251, 267, 279, 301, 317, 333, 347, 363, 375, 391, 407, 425, 435, 441, 471, 489, 511, 520–521, 525, 553, 567
FEA, 521
Federal Hazardous Substances Act, 173, 177–178
federal legislation
    consumerism, 172–175
    Care Labeling Rule, 173, 175–176
    Fur Products Labeling Act, 173, 175
    National Organic Program Regulations, 173, 176
    Textile Fiber Products Identification Act, 173
    Wool Products Labeling Act, 173, 175–176
Federal Trade Commission, 174, 175, 177–178, 253
feed dog, 419–420
felt, 358
FFA, 369, 520
FGI, 135
fiber
    characteristics of, 321–323
    dyeing, 366
    environmentally friendly, 111–112
    from recycled materials, 112
    from renewable sources, 111
    generic groups, 174
    manufactured, 335–344
    modifications of manufactured fibers, 336–337
    natural, 322–331
    organically grown, 112–113
    production, 86–87
    protein, 322
    Textile Fiber Products Identification Act, 174–175
figure, 304
figure types, 303–304, 379–380
    definition, 379
    determining, 379–380
filament, 336
filling yarns, 351
films, 359
finance
    budget, 162
    cash, 199
    checks, 199–201
    comparing prices, 215–216
    considering costs of clothing care, 163–164
    credit, 201–202
    debit cards, 200
    layaway buying, 203
    making a spending plan or budget, 162–163
    payments, 199–202
    pricing your product, 564
    stretching clothing dollars, 145–147
finance charge, 199
fine jewelry, 220
finishers, 92
finishes, 368–373
    affecting appearance and texture, 371–372
    affecting performance, 368–371
fitted blouse, 53
fitting single-breasted jacket, 60
flame resistant, 227
flame-resistant finish, 369
Flammable Fabrics Act, 173, 177, 369
flared pant, 55–56
flared skirt, 54–55
flat collar, 473
flatlock stitch, 495
flat method of construction, 504
flax, 325–326, 330
fleece, 486
floats, 354
fly front zipper, 458
follow-up letter, definition, 544
forecasting, 89
formal balance, 310
form and shape, 308
Fortrel, 175
Fortuny, Mariano, 123
franchise, 558
free enterprise system, 67
freelancer, 561
free trade, 105
free trade agreements, 106
front hip pocket, 478
FTA, 106
FTC, 174, 175, 177–178, 253
full-gathered skirt, 54–55
functional résumé, 537
funerals, dressing for, 150
Fur Products Labeling Act, 173, 175
fusible backing, 418
fusible fabric, 274
Future Business Leaders of America, 521
Future Educators of America, 521

G

Gabbana, Stefano, 132
garment
    dyeing, 366
    features, 48–52
        collars, 49–51
        necklines, 48–49
        sleeves, 51–52
    styles, 52–61
        blouses and shirts, 52–53
        dress styles, 57–58
        jackets and coats, 59–61
        pants, 55–57
        skirts, 53–55

gathers, 446
gaucho pants, 55
Gaultier, Jean-Paul, 132
generic groups, 174
Gernreich, Rudi, 124
Giannini, Frida, 123
gin, 323
glass, 174
glazing, 372
globalization, 104
global sourcing, 106–107
Glospan, 175
goals, 156, 160–161, 516
    definition, 516
    of families, 160–161
    setting, 156
goods, 171
gored skirt, 54
grading, 451
grain
    checking, 429
    crosswise, 428
    definition, 352
    lengthwise, 428
    pressing, 429
    straightening, 429
    understanding fabric grain, 428–429
grain line, 399
grayed, 287–288
Greece, ancient, 70–71
greige goods, 365
Gruau, Rene, 129
grunge look, 80
Gucci, Guccio, 123
guide sheet, 433

H

Halston, 124
halter neckline, 48–49
handbags, 218–219
hand overcast, 450–451
hand washing, 261
hand wheel, 419–420
hand-worked buttonhole, definition, 465
hangtags and labels, 171–172
    definition, 172
    use of, 171–172
hang to dry, 262
Hargreaves, James, 74
harmony, 309, 313–314
    achieving in elements of design, 313–314

    as goal of design, 309
    definition, 313
haute couture, 122–123
Health Occupations Students of America, 521
heat transfer printing, 367
heavy-duty thread, 415
hems
    as quality indicator in apparel, 211
    definition, 458
    finishing edges, 460–461
    fused, 464
    hand-stitched, 463–464
    history of, 45
    machine-stitched, 464
    marking, 458–459
    removing extra fullness, 459–460
    repairs of, 271
    securing, 462
    sewing, 458–464
hem gauge, definition, 411
Henley neckline, 48–49
Herculon, 175
heritage, 66
Herrera, Caroline, 132
herringbone twill, 354
high fashion, 122
high sewing, 122
Hilfiger, Tommy, 80, 132
himation, 71
hip-hugger pants, 55–56
hippie, 79
hip-stitched box pleat skirt, 54
history of textiles and apparel, 69–80
    1600s, 72–73
    1700s, 73–75
    1800s, 75–77
    1900 to 1950, 77–79
    1950 to 2000, 79–80
    early wearing, 69–70
    Middle Ages, 71–72
home décor items, 403–405
hook-and-loop tape, 233, 417, 467
hooks and eyes, 211, 416, 466–467
    as quality indicator in apparel, 211
    attaching, 466–467
HOSA, 521
Howe, Elias, 76–77, 419
hue, 286
human resources, 156

I

imports, 104
impulse buying, 196
individuality, 30
industrial engineer, 88
Industrial Revolution, 73–75
industry
    apparel, 89–93
    textile, 85–89
infants, 227–228
infomercials, 197
informal balance, 310
in-seam pocket, 478
intensity, 287–288
interfacing
    attaching, 454–455
    definition, 418
    nonwoven fabrics, 358
    quality indicator in apparel, 212
    types of fabrics, 454
interlock knits, 357
intermediate colors, 289
International Ladies' Garment Workers' Union, 109
International Organization for Standardization, 178
interpersonal skills, 517
interviews, 542–545
invention, 125
inventory, 142
invisible zipper, 458
ironing, 249, 263–264
    boards, 249
    definition, 263
    irons, 249
irregular, 190
ISO, 178

J

jabot collar, 49–50
jacket styles, 59–61
Jacobs, Marc, 132
Jacquard, Joseph Marie, 74
Jacquard weave, 355
Jamaica shorts, 55
James, Charles, 123
jeans, 55–56, 213
    as classics, 55–56
    quality checkpoints, 213
Jersey knits, 357
jewel neckline, 48–49
jewelry, 220–221

costume jewelry, 220
fine jewelry, 220
precious stones, 220
semiprecious stones, 220
job, 529–551
    application forms, 540
    definition, 528
    entry-level, 528
    ethical behavior, 547–548
    finding openings, 531–532
    in retail segment, 94–99
    interviews, 542–545
    leaving a job, 550
    letter of application, 540–541
    résumé preparation and creation, 532–537
    starting a new job, 547
    succeeding in the workplace, 545–550
job application forms, 540
job shadowing, 529–530
jogging pants, 56–57
Johnson, Betsey, 132
Josephine, Empress, 75
Juliet sleeve, 51
jute, 326

K

Kamali, Norma, 132, 189
Karan, Donna, 132
Kay, John, 74
Kennedy, John F., 179
kente cloth, 79
keyhole neckline, 49
kimono sleeve, 51–52, 476
    definition, 52
    sewing, 476
kit projects, 387
Klein, Anne, 124
Klein, Calvin, 132
knickers, 56–57
knife-pleated skirt, 54
knitted fabrics, 355–358
    seamless knit garments, 358
    warp, 357–358
    weft, 356–357
knitting, 355
knockoff, 125
Kors, Michael, 132

L

labels and hangtags, 171–172
    definition, 172
    use of, 171–172

laboratory technician, 88
labor laws, 109–110
Lacroix, Christian, 132
ladder effect, 495
Lagerfeld, Karl, 132
lanolin, 327
lantern sleeve, 51
lap, 323
lapel, 50, 212
    as collar, 50
    as quality indicator in apparel, 212
lapped zipper application, 457
lasers, 91
launching stage, 159
laundering, 253, 259–263
    definition, 253
    drying, 262–263
    washing, 259–261
laundry detergents, 243–244
laundry products, 259–260
Lauren, Ralph, 132
Laurent, Yves Saint, 124
layaway buying, 203
layout, 433
leader, 515
leadership, 515–516
    definition, 515
    traits, 516
leg-of-mutton sleeve, 51
lengthwise grain, 352, 428
leno weave, 355
letter of application, 540–541
letter of resignation, 550
licensing, 125
line, as a collection, 122
linen, 325–326, 330
lines, as element of design, 305–308
    curved, 308
    diagonal, 308
    horizontal, 306
    vertical, 305–306
lines, in pattern pieces, 399
lining, as quality indicator in apparel, 211
linters, 79
loom operators, 88
looms, 351
loopers, 492
Lowell System, 107–108
low-rise pants, 55–56
low wide scoop neckline, 49
luster, 328
Lycra, 175
Lyocell, 111, 174–175, 338, 342

M

machine operators, 88
machine overcast, 451
machine-worked buttonhole, 465
machine zigzag finish, 450
mail-order business, 560
mandarin collar, 49–50
manufactured fibers, 79, 321, 335–344
    characteristics of, 337–344
        acetate, 338, 342
        acrylic, 340, 344
        bamboo, 337–338
        elastoester, 341–342, 344
        lyocell, 338, 342
        modacrylic, 340, 344
        nylon, 339, 343
        olefin, 339–340, 343
        polyester, 338, 343
        rayon, 337, 342
        spandex, 340–341, 344
        triacetate, 338, 342
    definition, 79
    history of, 79
    production of, 336
manufacturing, 88
markers, 91
markers, computer-aided, 115
market analysts, 89
market economy, 67–68
marketing, 89
market researchers, 96
market week, 93
marking tools, 411–412
Maslow, Abraham, 25–26, 28–33
Maslow's Theory of Human Needs, 25–33
mass, 308
mass price point, 127
mass production, 75
McCall Pattern Company, 77
McCall, James, 77
McCardell, Claire, 123
McCartney, Stella, 132
McQueen, Alexander, 132
measuring, 382–386, 410–411
    females, 382–385
    males, 385–386
    tools, 410–411
media, 37
melamine, 174
melon sleeve, 51
melt spinning, 336

mentor, 547
mercerization, 414
merchandise managers, 94–95
merchandising plan, 90
metallic, 174
metallic thread, 415
microfiber textiles, 352
Microlux, 175
MicroSafe, 175
Middle Ages, 71–72
middle people, 190
middy collar, 50
mildew, 322
Milhazes, Beatriz, 129
Miller, Nicole, 133
Minoan civilization, 70
Mischka, Badgley, 132
Missoni, Ottavio, 133
Missoni, Rosita, 133
mix-and-match wardrobe, 145
Miyake, Issey, 133
Mizrahi, Isaac, 133, 189
mock flat-felled seam, 503
modacrylic, 174–175, 340, 344
Modal, 175
modeling, 98–99
moderate price point, 127
modesty, 27
moiré fabric, 372
monochromatic color scheme, 291
monofilament yarns, 350
Montana, Claude, 133
multifilament yarns, 350
multiple roles, 160, 551
    family members, 160
    management, 551
multisized patterns, 387

N

NAFTA, 106
nanotechnology, 371
nap, 354
    with nap, 434–435, 484, 487
    without nap, 435
Napoléon, Bonaparte, 75
narrow double-stitched seam, 503
National FFA Organization, 520
National Institute of Standards Technology, 178
National Organic Program Regulations, 173, 176
National Retailers Federation, 135
natural fibers, 69–70, 322–331
    cotton, 322–324, 330

definition, 321
flax, 325–326, 330
from plants, 326
in early wearing, 69–70
silk, 328–329, 331
wool, 326–328, 331
natural look, 308
necklines, 48–49
neckties, 219–220
needle clamp, 420–421
needle plate, 419–420
needles, 412
needs
    and wants, 144–145
    definition, 25
    family clothing, 162–167
    considering costs of clothing care, 163–164
    considering sewing, 164
    identifying resources, 162
    making a spending plan or budget, 162–163
    other options for meeting needs, 165–167
Nehru collar, 49–50
networking, 531
neutrals, 288
new fashions, 130
NIST, 178
nonhuman resources, 157
nonrenewable resources, 111
nonstore shopping, 191–195
    catalog and online, 191–194
    personal selling, 195
    television, 195
nonverbal communication, definition, 518
NOP regulations, 173, 176
Norell, Norman, 123
no-return policies, 191
North American Free Trade Agreement, 106
nostalgia, 46
notched collar, 50
notches, 399
notching, 452
notions, 396, 414–418
    elastics, 417–418
    fasteners, 415–417
    interfacings, 418
    tapes and trims, 417
    thread, 414–415
novelty yarns, 351

NRF, 135
nylon, 174–175, 215, 259, 339, 343
nylon thread, 414
nytril, 174

O

Occupational Safety and Health Act, 109
off-grain, 429
off-price discount stores, 189
offshore production, 107
olefin, 174–175, 339–340, 343
one-shoulder neckline, 49
online shopping, 315
open-sleeve method, 477
optical illusion, 304
order of business, 522
order of priority, 145
organically grown fibers, 112–113
OSHA, 190
overages, 190
overedge machine. *See* sergers
overedge stitch, 495
overlock machine. *See* sergers
overlock stitch, 496
overruns, 190

P

painting, fabric, 275
palazzo pants, 55–56
pant lengths, 55
pant styles, 55–57
parenting stage, 159
parka, 42, 60
parliamentary procedure, 522–523
partnership, 558
patching, 270
patch pocket, 478
patchwork, 277–278, 462
pattern, 393–401, 430–436
    catalogs, 393–394
    choosing a pattern, 399–401
        filling a need, 400
        flattering the body shape, 401
        match your skill level, 399–400
    cutting and sewing guide sheet, 397–398
    definition, 393
    ease, 388–389
    envelope, 395–397
    layout, 433–435

pieces, 399, 434–436
preparing for sewing, 427–439
types, 400
understanding the pattern, 394–399
pattern envelope, 395–397
pattern grader, 91
pattern grading, 115
pattern layout, 433–435
folding, 433–434
placing pattern pieces, 434–435
pattern maker, 91
pattern markings, 437–439
basting to transfer, 439
dressmaker's tracing paper and tracing wheel, 437–438
fabric marking pens, 439
tailor's chalk, 438
pattern pieces, 399, 434–436
pinning, 435–436
placing, 434–435
preparing, 430–432
pattern sizes, 382–389
measurements in females, 383–384
measurements in males, 385–386
selecting one that fits, 386–389
garment type, 387–388
pattern ease, 388–389
pea jacket, 59–60
peasant, 53
pedal pushers, 55
peer pressure, 28
pencil skirt, 53
permanent press, 262
personality, 30
petal sleeve, 51
Peter Pan collar, 50, 474
physique, 304
piece dyeing, 366
piecework, 75
pile fabric, 354, 486–487
definition, 354
pressing, 487
sewing with, 486–487
pile knits, 357
pile weave, 354
pilling, 339
pillow sham, 405
pincushions, 413
pinked finish, 450
pinking or scalloping shears, 410
pins, 412–413

PLA, 174
plain seam, 447
plain weave, 353
plant engineer, 88
plant manager, 92
pleated skirt, 54
plimsolls, 218
ply yarn, 350
pockets
as quality indicator in apparel, 212
sewing, 478–480
front hem, 480
in-seam, 479–480
patch, 479
Poiret, Paul, 123
politics, as fashion influence, 66–67
polo style coat, 61
polyester, 174–175, 338, 343
polymers, 335
poncho, 60
portfolio, 537
portfolio builder, 25, 137, 169, 237, 301, 317, 333, 347, 471, 489
Posen, Zac, 133
power and light switch, 420–421
power suits, 80
Prada, Miuccia, 133
precured, 369
preschoolers, 228–230
preshrinking, 427–428
preshrunk, 370
press cloth, 418
presser foot, 419–420
presser foot lifter, 420–421
presser foot pressure adjustment, 419–420
pressers, 92
pressing, 263–264, 418, 467–469
definition, 263
equipment, 418
techniques, 467–469
pressing ham, 418
prestige, 29
prêt-a-porter, 125
pretreatment, 256–257
prewash soil and stain removers, 245
price points, 126–127
better, 126
bridge, 126
budget, 127
definition, 126
designer, 126
mass, 127
moderate, 127
primary color, 288–290

princess dress style, 57–58
principles of design, 309–313
balance, 310
definition, 309
emphasis, 313
proportion, 310–312
rhythm, 312–313
printing, 367–368
definition, 367
types of, 367–368
priorities, 145, 160–161
definition, 160
of families, 160–161
order of, 145
private employment agencies, 532
private label, 188
production, 85–89
apparel segment, 89–93
fabric, 87
fabric finishing, 87
fiber, 86–87
textile segment, 85–89
yarn, 87
production engineer, 93
production manager, 92
production seasons, 90
program of study, 529
promotion directors, 97
proportion, 310
protectionism, 105
protein fibers, 322
prototype, 131
publications
Elle, 134
Harper's Bazaar, 134
InStyle, 134
New Look, 79
Teen Vogue, 134
Vogue, 134
Women's Wear Daily, 134
public employment offices, 531
Pucci, Emilio, 124
puffed sleeve, 51
punk, 128
Puritan collar, 50
purl knits, 357

Q

QR, 116–117
quality, 207–216
against price, 215–216
definition, 207
general standards, 210–212

judging, 208–214
    levels of, 210
    quality and fit checkpoints, 212–213
quality control engineer, 93
Quant, Mary, 79, 124
Quick Response, 116–117
quilted parka, 60
quilting, 359, 462
quilting thread, 415
quotas, 105

R

R&D, 88–89
raglan sleeve, 51–52
    definition, 52
    sewing, 476–477
ramie, 326
raschel knits, 357
rayon, 112, 174–175, 215, 337, 342
rayon thread, 414–415
ready-to-wear, 77, 122–127
    definition, 77
    price points, 126–127
    versus couture, 122–125
recede, 290
receiver, 518
recycled wool, 328
recycling, 111, 165, 275–279, 325
    to meet clothing needs, 165
    clothes, 275–279
    definition, 111
    jeans, 325
redesigning, 273–275
    appliqués, 165, 273–274
    definition, 273
    dyeing, 274–275
    embroidery, 273–274
    restyling, 273
    tie-dyeing, 275
    to meet clothing needs, 165
    trims, 273–274
Reese, Tracy, 133
regular charge account, 201
Rei Kawakubo, 132
reinforced seam, 503
reinforcements, as quality indicator in apparel, 211
religion, 66, 150
    as fashion influence, 66
    dressing for services, 150
renewable resources, 111
renting, to meet clothing needs, 167

repairing clothes, 269–271
    buttons, 271
    fasteners, 271
    for meeting clothing needs, 167
    hems, 271
    patching, 270
    snags, 271
    stitching, 270–271
repellant, 368
reprocessed wool, 328
resale shops, 191
research, 88
resilient, 327
resistant, 368
resources, 156–157, 162
    definition, 156
    family, 162
    human, 156
    nonhuman, 157
restyling, 273
résumés, 532–537
    choosing a format, 536–537
    chronological, 537
    definition, 532
    electronic, 537
    functional, 537
    posting online, 534
    preparation and creation, 532–536
retail, 93–99
    alterations, 99
    buyers, 95
    definition, 93
    display directors, 97
    fashion illustrator, 98
    fashion merchandising, 94
    fashion models, 98–99
    fashion promotion, 94
    fashion writers, 98
    market researchers, 96
    merchandise managers, 94–95
    sales associates, 95–96
    segment of industry, 94–99
    stock clerk, 96
retailers, 94
retro and vintage, 44, 46, 129
    as fashion term, 44, 46
    as inspiration to a fashion designer, 129
    definition, 44
reused wool, 328
reverse lever, 420–421
revolving charge account, 201
rhythm, 312

rib knits, 357
right to consumer education, 179
right to redress, 179
robotic machines, 116
Rodarte, 133
Rodriguez, Narciso, 129, 133
rolled collar, 474
rolled edge stitch, 496
roller printing, 367
roll-up sleeve, 51
Roman Empire, 71
rotary cutter, 410
rotary screen printing, 367
roving, 324
Rowley, Cynthia, 133
royalty, 125
RTW, 77, 122–127
ruff collar, 49–50
Rykiel, Sonia, 133

S

safari jacket, 59–60
safety
    as a consumer right, 179
    as consideration for children's clothing, 227
    Consumer Products Safety Act, 173, 176–178
    Consumer Products Safety Improvement Act, 173, 176–178
    Federal Hazardous Substances Act, 173
    Flammable Fabrics Act, 173
    history of creating safe work environments, 107–109
    in the work environment, 110
    laundry, 261, 265
    on the job, 549–550
        developing safe habits, 549
        following emergency evacuation procedures, 550
        handling emergencies, 549–550
    responsibilities for employers and employees, 110
    sewing machine, 444
    using products safely, 180
    with sewing, 506
sailor collar, 50
sales associates, 95–96
sales terms, 197–198

sample maker, 91
Sanchez, Angel, 133
Sander, Jil, 133
saran, 174
sari, 66
sarong, 54–55
sateen, 354
satin, 354
satin weave, 354
SBA, 562
scarves, 219
Schiaparelli, Elsa, 123
school-age children, 230–231
schreiner finish, 354
scissors, 409
scoop neckline, 48–49
scoured, 327
screen printing, 367
seam
    allowance, 443
    as quality indicator in apparel, 211
    definition, 443
    finishes, 450–451
    flat-fell, 448
    French, 449
    plain, 447–448
    ripper, 410
    roll, 418
    sewing with a serger, 504–509
    sewing, 447–452
    topstitched, 448
    treatment, 451–452
    welt, 449
seam allowance, 443
seam finishes, 450–451
    definition, 450
    hand overcast, 450–451
    machine overcast, 451
    machine zigzag, 450
    pinked, 450
    turned and stitched, 450
seam ripper, 410
seam roll, 418
seam treatments, 451–452
    clipping and notching, 451–452
    grading, 451
    trimming, 451
secondary color, 289–290
seconds, 190
SEF, 175
self-actualization, 30
self-adornment, 28–29
self-casing, 482

self-concept, 32–33
self-confidence, 515
self-esteem, 28, 515
self-healing mat, 410
self-help features, 229
selvage, 352, 430
sender, 518
sergers, 491–509
    adjusting stitch and length width, 502
    adjusting thread tension, 500–501
    basic stitches, 495–497
    caring for, 509
    definition, 491
    how it functions, 492
    machine parts, 492–495
    operating, 499–500
    problems and solutions, 501
    safety, 506
    selecting thread and accessories, 497–498
    threading, 498–499
    uses, 503
    with clothing construction, 502–504
        fitting, 504
        order, 504
        selecting a pattern, 503
        transferring pattern markings, 504
    with seams, 504–509
        curves and corners, 506–507
        removing, 509
        securing ends, 507
        stabilizing, 508
        types of, 505
serrated-edge, 438
service, 171, 559
set-in sleeve, 51
    definition, 51
    sewing, 477–478
    variations, 51
sewing
    advanced, 473–487
        casings, 482–484
        collars, 473–476
        pockets, 478–480
        sleeves, 476–478
        waistline, 480–482
    bags, 403
    couture, 122
    darts, 447

    equipment, 409–423
    facings, 452–453
    factors to consider, 165
    fasteners, 464–467
        buttons and buttonholes, 465–466
        hook-and-loop tape, 467
        hooks and eyes, 466–467
        snaps, 466
    hems, 458–464
        finishing edges, 460–461
        fused, 464
        hand-stitched, 463–464
        machine-stitched, 464
        marking, 458–459
        removing extra fullness, 459–460
        securing, 462
    home décor items, 403–405
    interfacings, 454–455
    kit projects, 387, 484–485
    machine, 419–423
    machine stitching techniques, 443–446
    preparation of, 427–439
    purpose of, 166
    seams and seam finishes, 447–452
    sergers, 491–509
    sports equipment, 403
    stuffed toys, 403
    with pile fabrics, 486–487
    zippers, 455–458
        centered, 455–457
        invisible, 458
        lapped, 457–458
sewing equipment, 409–423
    cutting tools, 409–410
    machine, 419–423
    marking tools, 411–412
    measuring tools, 410–411
    needles, 412
    notions, 413–414
    pincushions, 413
    pins, 412–413
    pressing equipment, 418
    thimbles, 413
sewing for a cause, 435
sewing gauge, 411
sewing kits, 387, 484–485
    knit fabrics, 485
    learn to sew with, 387
    pinning and cutting, 484–485

sewing machine, 419–423
    caring for, 423
    history of, 76–77
    instruction manual, 421
    minor problems and cures, 422
    parts, 419–421
    stitching techniques, 443–446
    using, 421–422
sewing machine operators, 92
sewing preparation, 427–439
    equipment, 409–423
    pattern layout, 433–435
    pattern pieces, 430–432
    pinning pattern pieces, 435–436
    preparing the fabric, 427–429
    transferring pattern markings, 437–439
shade, 287
shape and form, 308
shaped collar, 474
shareholders, 558
sharing, to meet clothing needs, 167
shawl collar, 51
shears, 409
sheath style, 57–58
shell, 53
shift style, 57–58
shirred curtains, 404
shirt, 52–53, 212
    quality checkpoints, 212
    styles, 52–53
shirt collar, 50, 474
shirtwaist blouse, 77
shirtwaist dress, 57–58
shoes, 217–218
shoplifting, 180
shopping
    catalog and online, 191–194
    chain, 188–189
    comparison, 195
    department, 188
    discount, 189
    factory outlet, 190
    impulse buying, 196
    in stores, 187–191
    nonstore shopping, 191–195
    online, 315
    payment methods
        cash, 199
        checks, 199–201
        credit, 201–202
        debit cards, 200
        layaway buying, 203
    personal selling, 195

resale shops, 191
    specialty, 188
    strategies, 195–199
    television, 195
    window shop, 192
short shorts, 55
shorts length, 55
Si Ling-Shi, 72
silhouette, 305
silhouettes, in the fashion cycle, 47–48
silk, 328–329, 331
    definition, 328
    history of, 72
silk pins, 413
silk thread, 414
Singer, Isaac, 77
single-breasted, 59–60
single knit, 356
single yarn, 350
size
    determining, 380–381
    getting the right fit, 207–208
    categories, 209–210
sizings, 247
sketcher, 91
sketching assistant, 91
SkillsUSA, 521
skimmer shorts, 55
skirt marker, 410
skirts, 53–55, 213
    quality checkpoints, 213
    styles, 53–55
slacks, quality checkpoints, 213
Slater, Samuel, 73
sleeve board, 418
sleeves, 51–52, 476–478
    sewing, 476–478
    types, 51–52
slit neckline, 49
Small Business Administration, 562
Smith, Willi, 124
smooth-edge, 438
snags, repair of, 271
snaps, 211, 246
    as quality indicator in apparel, 211
    sewing, 466
sneakers, 218
society, 65–66
    as fashion influence, 66
    definition, 65
sole proprietorship, 558
solution dyeing, 366

solvent, 247
Sorona®, 111
sorting, 257–259
source reduction, 244
sourcing, 106–107
    definition, 106
    domestic, 106
    global, 106–107
spandex, 174–175, 340–341, 344
special effect yarns, 352
specialty hair fibers, 322
specialty stores, 188
Spectra, 175
speed controller, 420–421
spinneret, 336
spinners, 88
spinning, 336
split-complementary color scheme, 292
spool cap, 498
spool pin, 419–420
sports equipment, sewing, 403
sport shirt, 53
sports jackets, quality checkpoints, 212
spun silk, 329
spun yarns, 350
square neckline, 49
stabilizing, 508
stains,
    definition, 240
    removal, 240–242, 256–257
standards, 178
standard sizes, 380
standing collar, 474
staple fibers, 336
starch, 247
status, 29
staystitching, 445
stitching, 211, 270–271, 443–446
    as quality indicator in apparel, 211
    backstitching, 444
    basting, 445–446
    directional, 445
    easing, 446
    gathering, 446
    repairing clothes, 270–271
    serger types, 495–497
    staystitching, 445
stitching line, 399
stitch-in-the-ditch, 453
stitch length dial, 420–421
stitch selectors, 420–421

Index **605**

stitch width dial, 419–420
stock clerk, 96
stock dyeing, 366
storage, clothes, 242–243
    daily, 242
    seasonal, 242–243
store brand, 126
store credit, 199
store types, 187–191
    boutique, 188
    chain, 188–189
    department, 188
    discount, 189
    factory outlet, 190
    off-price discount, 189
    resale shops, 191
    specialty, 188
straight eyes, 416
straight pants, 55–56
straight skirt, 53–54
straight trouser skirt, 54
strapless dress, 58
strapless neckline, 49
street fashions, 130
stretched, 323
structural lines, 305
student organizations, 520–522
    member roles and responsibilities, 521–522
    purposes and functions, 520–521
stuffed toys, sewing, 403
style, 42
Sui, Anna, 133
suits, quality checkpoints, 212
sumptuary laws, 67
surplice dress style, 57–58
sustainable products, 111
sweatshops, 107, 109–110
sweetheart neckline, 48–49
synthetic fibers, 335
synthetics, 79

T

tailor, 560
tailoring, 93
take-up lever, 419–420
tank top, 53
tape measure, 410
tapered pant, 55–56
tapering, 460
tapes, 417
tariffs, 105

team membership, 516–520
    communication, 518
    effective skills, 517–518
    interpersonal, 517
teamwork, 516
technical drawing, 130
technology
    advances in the apparel industry, 114–117
        CAD/CAM, 114–116
        CIM, 116
        e-commerce and social networking, 117
        Quick Response, 116–117
    as a news source, 134
    as fashion influence, 68–69
    clothes cleaning, 258
    definition, 68
    microfiber textiles, 352
    nanotechnology, 371
    online shopping, 315
    posting a résumé online, 534
Tempest, William, 129
Tencel®, 111, 175, 338
tent style dress, 57–58
tertiary color, 289–290
textile converters, 88
textile designers, 87, 114–115
textile engineers, 88
Textile Fiber Products Identification Act, 173–175
textile industry, 85–89
    converters, 88
    designing, 87
    environmental efforts, 111
    marketing, 89
    research and development, 88–89
    structure of, 86–87
    vertical integration with apparel industry, 99
textile producers, environmental efforts, 111
textiles
    careers, 87–89
    history, 69–80
        1600s, 72–73
        1700s, 73–75
        1800s, 75–77
        1900 to 1950, 77–79
        1950 to 2000, 79–80
        early wearing, 69–70
        inventions, 74
        Middle Ages, 71–72

    industry, 85–89
    today, 81
    uses of, 86
textile sales associate, 89
texture, 309
texturing, 337
TFPIA, 173–175
Thimonnier, Barthélemy, 76
thread, 321
thread clipper, 410
thread cutter, 420–421
thread guides, 419–420
thread net, 498
thread tension dial, 419–420
thrift shops, 191
tie-dyeing, 275, 345
tint, 287
toddlers, 228–229
toga, 71
torch-type fabrics, 177
Toxic Substances Control Act, 111
trade associations, 134–135
trade deficit, 104
trade laws and agreements, 105
trade surplus, 104
trademark name, 174
trading, to meet clothing needs, 167
training and education, 88, 89, 91, 92, 94–95, 96, 97, 99
trench coat, 61
trendsetter, 43, 148
triacetate, 174, 338, 342
triadic color scheme, 292
tricot knits, 357
trimmers, 92
trimming, 451
trims, 273–274, 417
true bias, 428
trumpet sleeve, 51
T-shirt, history of, 34
tubular dress silhouette, 47–48
tunic, 71
turbans, 66
turned and stitched finish, 450
turtle collar, 49–50
twill weave, 353–354
twist, 350

U

U.S. apparel industry and world economies, 104–113
U scoop neckline, 49
U.S. Department of Agriculture, 176, 178

understitching, 453
undertones, 293
Ungaro, Emanuel, 133
union, 110
unisex, 79, 380
Universal Print Codes, 116
UPC, 116
USDA, 176, 178

V

valance, 404
Valentino, 133
value, in colors, 287
values, 31–32, 160–161
    as influence on dress, 32
    definition, 31
    of families, 160–161
vanity sizing, 208
verbal communication, 518
Versace, Gianni, 133
vertical integration, 99
vinal, 174
vintage, 44–46
vinyon, 174
Vionnet, Madeleine, 123
virgin wool, 328
viscose, 175
V-neck neckline, 49
Von Furstenberg, Diane, 133
Vuitton, Louis, 123

W

waistband, 53, 481–482
    definition, 53
    sewing, 481–482
waistline facing, 481
waistline treatments, 480–482
    facing, 482
    sewing, 480–482
wale, 354
Wang, Alexander, 133
Wang, Vera, 125, 133
wants, 144–145
    and needs, 144–145
    definition, 145
wardrobe, 141
wardrobe consultant, 561
wardrobe plan, 141
wardrobe planning, 141–144
    accessories, 147
    adding, 144–145
        needs and wants, 144–145
        prioritizing needs and wants, 145
    benefits of, 141–142
    evaluating, 142–144
    inventory, 142–143
    mixing and matching, 145–147
warm color, 290
warp knitting, 357–358
warp yarns, 351
washers and dryers, 248–249
washing, 259–261
    by hand, 261
    by machine, 259–261
    preparation of, 256–259
        pretreatment, 256–257
        sorting, 257–259
        stain removal, 240–242, 256–257
    wash cycle or agitation speed, 261
    water temperature, 260–261
water hardness, 245
water softener, 245
water-soluble pens, 412
Wear-Dated, 175
wearing ease, 388
weaving, 351–352
weddings, dressing for, 150
weft knitting, 356–357
    definition, 356
    types of, 357
weft yarns, 351
weighted silk, 329
weighting, 372
western shirt, 53
wet process, 257
wet spinning, 336
wetted, 370
Whitney, Eli, 74
wholesale, 93
wipes, 359
wool, 326–328, 331
woolen yarns, 327
Woolmark Brand, 328
Wool Products Labeling Act, 173, 175–176, 327–328
work environments, history of, 107–109
World Trade Organization, 106
worsted yarns, 327
Worth, Charles, 122–123
woven fabrics, 351–355
    basic weaves, 352–354
    definition, 351
    weave variations, 354–355
    weaving, 351–352

wrap coat, 61
wrap skirt, 54–55
writing skills
    complaint letter, 182–183
    e-mail, 548–549
    follow-up letter, 544
    how to write a check, 200
    letter of application, 540
    letter of resignation, 550
    preparing a résumé, 532–536
WTO, 106
WTO Agreement on Textiles and Clothing, 106
Wu, Jason, 129, 133

Y

yarn, 87, 321, 349–351, 366
    blends and combinations, 351
    definition, 321
    dyeing, 366
    production, 87
    single, ply, and cord, 350
    types, 350
    textured, 350
    twist in yarns, 350
yarn dyeing, 366
yarn production, 87

Z

Zantrel, 175
Zeftron, 175
zipper applications, 455
zipper foot, 455
zippers, 416
    as quality indicator in apparel, 211
    centered, 455–456
    invisible, 458
    lapped, 457–458
    sewing, 455–458